Introduction

"You win your pennants in the winter, and try not to lose them over the summer."

"A good trade is one that helps both teams."

"Sometimes the best trades are the ones you don't make."

As most fans know, the pennant isn't always won on the playing field in the heat of July or down the stretch in September. More often than not, the decisive factor is a piece of strategy engineered in the cold of December, when baseball's front office masterminds shuffle the cards in search of a winning hand.

Once it was all so simple: you had extra pitchers but needed an outfielder; your buddy in Cleveland or Chicago or Detroit had outfielders to spare but needed pitching. You called him up, you talked it over, and you made a deal. Simple.

Trades today are not nearly as frequent as they once were. It has become more and more difficult to make any kind of a trade, thanks to long-term contracts, no-trade clauses, free-agent status, and drug rumors. Frustrated general managers no longer ask scouts if the player under discussion can still play; they're forced to ask agents and accountants about his seniority status, when his option year is coming, and who will bear the deferred payments due under his old contract.

"Your key players," explains Harry Dalton, Milwaukee general manager who has played the trade game as well as anyone alive, "are now under long-term contracts and can't be traded easily. Your younger players aren't so well known to teams, and they're more important to you now, because they can't leave you as free agents yet. And the few stars who are available in trades are getting paid so much that you can't move them freely.

"For all those reasons, the talent is finally getting locked in. With more players entering the free-agent auction, the clubs are forced to react instead of acting. They either look for talent in the open market or they don't get much. You do it, or you die. The old-fashioned system of simply trading players is being crowded out."

To the players themselves, the changes are most welcome. For close to a century they had been bound to clubs by a perpetually renewable reserve clause in the standard contract. They could play when and where they were told to, or they could retire. Today they can file for free agency after six years in the major leagues. If they've spent ten years in the majors and the last five with the same team, they can veto a trade. In addition, many players have managed to have clauses inserted into their contracts that can either bar any trade or designate a limited number of teams to which they can be dealt. These clauses have provided players with a financial windfall, with some teams paying bonuses to induce them to accept a trade.

Consequently, it's a whole new ball game in the trade mart. "You used to be able to horse-trade," recalls Gabe Paul. "Once upon a time, you'd have a roster of twenty-five players, and all twenty-five were available to be traded. Today you can maybe trade half of the twenty-five. You can't take two top-quality players of equal ability and make a trade; not if one of them has four years left on his contract and the other only has one year. I was talking to one general manager about a possible trade, and it got so complex that he suddenly just started waving his arms in the air."

If the age of the major trade is over, then a vital and exciting portion of the game has been lost. Trades, whether blockbusters or unnoticed transactions involving unknown ballplayers, can have a major impact on the pennant race, and can sometimes indicate or dictate the direction of a franchise. Without question, the great Baltimore Orioles clubs of the last two decades were turned from contenders to champions by the Frank Robinson trade of December 9, 1965. Robbie not only led the Orioles to a World Series sweep over the Dodgers, but won the American League Triple Crown as well. More innocuous deals can also have long-term effects, as when the Dodgers traded a minor hurler named Bruce Ellingsen to Cleveland for seventeen-year-old third baseman Pedro Guerrero.

But if the simple player trade is increasingly becoming a lost art, a new assortment of arts has sprung up to take its place. The varying options facing a club have led to a wide variety of management styles. Some, like Baltimore, build from within, dipping into the free agent market only for helpful role players, and signing their own best players to long-term contracts that keep them out of the open market. The Angels and Yankees have chosen to spend lavishly, with money as no object, both for players in the free agent draft and for those about to enter it. Calvin Griffith in Minnesota has cashed in players about to become unreasonably expensive by dealing them to richer clubs for outstanding prospects and large amounts of cash. The Mets have come to rely almost entirely on their farm system, with a few key players coming over in trades. And the irrepressible Whitey Herzog in St. Louis continues to wheel and deal as if he'd never heard of those accursed restrictions on player movement.

In one form or other, trades and sales will continue. They keep the players and fans on their toes. They can enliven an otherwise dismal season. With the recent development of the annual off-season free agent sweepstakes, they keep baseball in the public eye and on the top of the sports pages throughout the winter. They're the best, most controversial, and most indispensable part of the game within the game of baseball.

The sections that follow list all the trades, sales, and re-entry free agent signings made by every team from 1900 up to the opening of the 1984 season. Every trade is listed under both teams involved; three-team trades are listed as involving a "swing" team that acts as intermediary between two others, with that fact noted below the trade.

In order to qualify for inclusion in this book, a trade must involve a player who has played, or someday would play, in the major leagues. Selections in the minor league free-agent drafts are not included; neither are the signings of players who have been released by a major league club.

The astute reader will quickly note a paucity of that most frequent inhabitant of the transactions column, the player to be named later. In the vast majority of player to be named later transactions, that player is either named shortly thereafter, or never specified, with the club accepting cash instead. Where there has been a short interval between the deal and the designation of the player, or where the interval has fallen entirely within the off-season, the deal is listed simply as player for player.

The Baseball Trade Register

The Baseball Trade Register

JOSEPH L. REICHLER

COLLIER BOOKS
Macmillan Publishing Company
New York
COLLIER MACMILLAN PUBLISHERS
London

EDITORIAL AND PRODUCTION STAFF

David B. Biesel
Jackie Dickens
Robert Keefe
Casey Kwang-Chong Lee
Jeffrey Neuman
Fred C. Richardson
David Shaw
Bob Talmage

Macmillan Publishing Company
866 Third Avenue, New York, N.Y. 10022
Collier Macmillan Canada, Inc.

Library of Congress Cataloging in Publication Data
Reichler, Joseph L., 1915-
The baseball trade register.
Includes index.
1. Baseball—United States—Records. 2. National League of Professional Baseball Clubs—Statistics.
3. American League of Professional Baseball Clubs—Statistics. I. Title.
GV877.R375 1984 796.357'64 84-12522
ISBN 0-02-603110-8
ISBN 0-02-029670-3 (pbk.)

First Collier Books Edition 1984

10 9 8 7 6 5 4 3 2 1

Printed in the United States of America

The Baseball Trade Register is also available in a hardcover edition published by Macmillan Publishing Company.

Contents

The Baseball Trade Register

Where there has been an extraordinarily long delay in finalizing the deal, the date of transfer of the player to be named is noted below the trade.

Inevitably, in a work of this size and scope, some errors will creep in, and some deals will unfortunately be left out. All corrections and suggestions are heartily welcomed.

Atlanta Braves

The Best Trades

1. Acquired Chris Chambliss and Luis Gomez from the Toronto Blue Jays for Barry Bonnell, Joey McLaughlin, and Pat Rockett, December 5, 1979.
2. Acquired Pat Dobson, Davy Johnson, Roric Harrison, and Johnny Oates from the Baltimore Orioles for Earl Williams and Taylor Duncan, December 30, 1972.
3. Acquired Clete Boyer from the New York Yankees for Bill Robinson and Chi Chi Olivo, November 29, 1966.
4. Acquired Doyle Alexander, Larvell Blanks, and $50,000 from the Texas Rangers for Adrian Devine and Pepe Frias, December 6, 1979.
5. Acquired Carl Morton from the Montreal Expos for Pat Jarvis, February 28, 1973.

The Worst Trades

1. Traded Gary Matthews to the Philadelphia Phillies for Bob Walk, March 25, 1981.
2. Traded Felix Millan and George Stone to the New York Mets for Gary Gentry and Danny Frisella, November 2, 1972.
3. Sold Joe Niekro to the Houston Astros for $35,000, April 6, 1975.
4. Traded Joe Torre to the St. Louis Cardinals for Orlando Cepeda, March 17, 1969.
5. Traded Pat Dobson to the New York Yankees for Frank Tepedino, Wayne Nordhagen, Alan Closter, and Dave Cheadle, June 7, 1973.

Trader: Ted Turner

The Atlanta Braves' media guide describes the club's owner as a "modern day hero among today's masses." While many might quarrel with this description, few would deny the dynamic nature of this tempestuous man. Turner has managed to combine his holdings in television and sports to spread the domain of the Braves beyond Atlanta to the nation as a whole.

Turner purchased the Braves on January 14, 1976. Right from the start he showed his willingness to become involved in all phases of the club's operation, even donning the uniform for a brief stint as manager before being called off by the league president. He has been willing to spend money prodigiously; over the years he has acquired as free agents Andy Messersmith, Gary Matthews, Al Hrabosky, Terry Forster, Claudell Washington, Gaylord Perry, and Pete Falcone at a cost of millions of dollars. In addition, he has added through trades Chris Chambliss, Bob Watson, Len Barker, Jeff Burroughs, and Gene Garber. While many of these acquisitions proved unwise, none can deny that the Braves have gone from being a perennial doormat to a powerful contender under his guidance.

Turner's best deal is the one that brought first baseman Chris Chambliss to the Braves during the winter of 1979. The Braves gave up outfielder Barry Bonnell, reliever Joey McLaughlin, and infielder Pat Rockett for Chambliss and shortstop Luis Gomez. That deal has paid long-term dividends, unlike his trade of five players and a quarter of a million dollars for Jeff Burroughs. Burroughs had one fine season for the Braves, but was unable to repeat, and was eventually traded to Seattle for pitcher Carlos Diaz, who then went to the Mets for Tom Hausman; hardly an adequate return on such a large investment. Similarly, Turner vented his frustration with free agent signee Gary Matthews by sending him to Philadelphia for pitcher Bob Walk.

On the whole, while Turner's free-agent expenditures have brought him headlines, they have had relatively little effect on the team on the field. This is a club largely built from its own farm system, with such key players as Chambliss, Watson, Garber, and Pascual Perez being added through trades.

DATE		ACQUIRED	FROM		IN EXCHANGE FOR
April 4, 1966	OF	Marty Keough	Cincinnati Reds		Cash and minor league player to be named later
April 28, 1966		Cash	Chicago Cubs	OF	Billy Cowan
May 16, 1966	SS	Gil Garrido	San Francisco Giants		Cash
May 28, 1966	P	Ted Abernathy	Chicago Cubs	1B	Lee Thomas
May 29, 1966	OF	John Herrnstein	Chicago Cubs	OF	Marty Keough
June 15, 1966	P	Joey Jay	Cincinnati Reds	P	Hank Fischer
June 15, 1966	P	Don Schwall	Pittsburgh Pirates	P	Billy O'Dell
Oct 13, 1966	OF C	Gene Ratliff John Hoffman minor league IF Ed Pacheco	Houston Astros	P P OF	Tom Dukes Dan Schneider Lee Bales
Nov 29, 1966	3B	Clete Boyer	New York Yankees	OF P	Bill Robinson Chi Chi Olivo
Dec 31, 1966	OF P	Dave Nicholson Bob Bruce	Houston Astros	2B 3B P	Sandy Alomar Eddie Mathews Arnie Umbach
May 31, 1967		Cash	San Francisco Giants	OF	Ty Cline
May 31, 1967	C	Charlie Lau	Baltimore Orioles		Cash
June 6, 1967	C	Bob Uecker	Philadelphia Phillies	C-1B	Gene Oliver
June 12, 1967	OF	Tito Francona	Philadelphia Phillies		Cash
June 15, 1967	P	Claude Raymond	Houston Astros	P	Wade Blasingame
Oct 8, 1967	SS 1B	Sonny Jackson Chuck Harrison	Houston Astros	P IF	Denny Lemaster Denis Menke
Oct 10, 1967	1B	Deron Johnson	Cincinnati Reds	1B OF P	Jim Beauchamp Mack Jones Jay Ritchie
Dec 7, 1967	C P	Bob Tillman Dale Roberts	New York Yankees	3B	Bobby Cox
April 1, 1968	P	Stu Miller	Baltimore Orioles		Cash
June 11, 1968	P P IF	Milt Pappas Ted Davidson Bob Johnson	Cincinnati Reds	SS P P	Woody Woodward Clay Carroll Tony Cloninger
July 29, 1968	IF	Wayne Causey	California Angels		Cash

DATE		ACQUIRED	FROM		IN EXCHANGE FOR
Dec 3, 1968		Cash	Philadelphia Phillies	1B	Deron Johnson
Dec 4, 1968	3B	Bob Aspromonte	Houston Astros	IF	Marty Martinez
March 17, 1969	1B	Orlando Cepeda	St. Louis Cardinals	1B	Joe Torre
March 25, 1969	C	Dave Adlesh	St. Louis Cardinals	IF	Bob Johnson
June 10, 1969		Cash	New York Yankees	P	Ken Johnson
June 12, 1969	OF	Tony Gonzalez	San Diego Padres	IF IF	Walt Hriniak Van Kelly minor league OF Andy Finlay
Aug 19, 1969		Cash	Montreal Expos	P	Claude Raymond
Aug 22, 1969		Cash	Oakland Athletics	OF	Tito Francona
Sept 8, 1969	P	Hoyt Wilhelm	California Angels		Cash
Sept 9, 1969	P	Bob Priddy	California Angels		Cash
Oct 21, 1969	P	Dave Wickersham	Kansas City Royals	OF	Ron Tompkins
Nov 27, 1969		Cash	California Angels	P	Paul Doyle
Dec 2, 1969	P	Larry Jaster	Montreal Expos	P	Jim Britton minor league C Don Johnson
Dec 3, 1969	P	Jim Nash	Oakland Athletics	OF	Felipe Alou
June 23, 1970		Cash	Chicago Cubs	P	Milt Pappas
June 29, 1970	OF	Jimmie Hall	Chicago Cubs		Cash
July 12, 1970	P	Don Cardwell	New York Mets		Cash
Aug 31, 1970		Cash	California Angels	OF	Tony Gonzalez
Sept 21, 1970		Cash	Chicago Cubs	P	Hoyt Wilhelm
Oct 21, 1970	SS	Marty Perez	California Angels		Minor league C John Burns
Nov 30, 1970	P	Hoyt Wilhelm	Chicago Cubs	1B	Hal Breeden
Dec 1, 1970	P	Ron Herbel	New York Mets	3B	Bob Aspromonte
Dec 2, 1970	OF	Hank Allen minor leaguers P Paul Click and IF John Ryan	Milwaukee Brewers	C	Bob Tillman

DATE		ACQUIRED	FROM		IN EXCHANGE FOR
Aug 14, 1971	IF	Tony LaRussa	Oakland Athletics		Cash
Dec 2, 1971	C	Paul Casanova	Texas Rangers	C	Hal King
June 15, 1972	P 1B	Joe Hoerner Andre Thornton	Philadelphia Phillies	P P	Jim Nash Gary Neibauer
June 29, 1972	P	Denny McLain	Oakland Athletics	1B	Orlando Cepeda
Oct 20, 1972	P	Tom Phoebus	Chicago Cubs	IF	Tony LaRussa
Oct 27, 1972	P	Jim Panther	Texas Rangers	OF	Rico Carty
Nov 2, 1972	P P	Gary Gentry Danny Frisella	New York Mets	2B P	Felix Millan George Stone
Dec 30, 1972	P P 2B C	Pat Dobson Roric Harrison Davy Johnson Johnny Oates	Baltimore Orioles	C IF	Earl Williams Taylor Duncan
Feb 28, 1973	P	Carl Morton	Montreal Expos	P	Pat Jarvis
March 27, 1973	C	Dick Dietz	Los Angeles Dodgers		Cash
April 22, 1973	OF	Norm Miller	Houston Astros	P	Cecil Upshaw
May 8, 1973	P	Al Santorini	St. Louis Cardinals	P	Tom Murphy
May 14, 1973	C	Gene Lamont	Detroit Tigers	C	Bob Didier
May 19, 1973	1B	Joe Pepitone	Chicago Cubs	1B	Andre Thornton
May 22, 1973	C	Larry Howard	Houston Astros		Minor league C Tom Helerle
May 24, 1973	2B	Chuck Goggin	Pittsburgh Pirates		Cash
June 7, 1973	1B OF P P	Frank Tepedino Wayne Nordhagen Al Closter Dave Cheadle	New York Yankees	P	Pat Dobson
July 18, 1973		Cash	Kansas City Royals	P	Joe Hoerner
Aug 7, 1973	P	Joe Niekro	Detroit Tigers		Cash
Dec 3, 1973	P SS	Barry Lersch Craig Robinson	Philadelphia Phillies	P	Ron Schueler
Dec 4, 1973	1B	Bob Beall	Philadelphia Phillies	SS	Gil Garrido
March 26, 1974	P	Buzz Capra	New York Mets		Cash
March 26, 1974	C	Vic Correll	Boston Red Sox	2B	Chuck Goggin
April 1, 1974	OF	Ivan Murrell	San Diego Padres		Cash
June 14, 1974		Cash	New York Mets	P	Jack Aker

DATE		ACQUIRED	FROM		IN EXCHANGE FOR
Sept 10, 1974	P	Mike Thompson	St. Louis Cardinals		Cash
Sept 14, 1974		Cash	St. Louis Cardinals	P	Barry Lersch
Nov 2, 1974	OF	Dave May minor league P Roger Alexander	Milwaukee Brewers	OF	Hank Aaron
Nov 8, 1974	OF	Clarence Gaston	San Diego Padres	P	Danny Frisella
Dec 3, 1974	1B	Richie Allen	Chicago White Sox		Player to be named later and cash
		(Chicago received Jim Essian, May 15, 1975.)			
March 29, 1975	1B	Reggie Sanders	Detroit Tigers	1B	Jack Pierce
April 6, 1975		$35,000.	Houston Astros	P	Joe Niekro
April 17, 1975	C	Earl Williams and cash	Baltimore Orioles	P	Jimmy Freeman
May 7, 1975	C OF	Jim Essian Barry Bonnell and cash	Philadelphia Phillies	1B C	Richie Allen Johnny Oates
May 15, 1975		Completion of Richie Allen trade of December 3, 1974.	Chicago White Sox	C	Jim Essian
May 28, 1975	P P	Elias Sosa Ray Sadecki	St. Louis Cardinals	P OF	Ron Reed Wayne Nordhagen
June 7, 1975	P SS	Blue Moon Odom Bob Belloir	Cleveland Indians	P	Roric Harrison
June 11, 1975	1B	Ed Goodson	San Francisco Giants	SS	Craig Robinson
June 30, 1975	P	Bruce Dal Canton	Kansas City Royals	P	Ray Sadecki and cash
		(Two minor league pitchers were assigned to Atlanta farm team on September 4, 1975 to complete the trade.)			
Nov 17, 1975	OF OF OF IF	Jimmy Wynn Tom Paciorek Lee Lacy Jerry Royster	Los Angeles Dodgers	OF 1B	Dusty Baker Ed Goodson
Dec 12, 1975	P	Roger Moret	Boston Red Sox	P	Tom House
Dec 12, 1975	SS	Darrell Chaney	Cincinnati Reds	OF	Mike Lum
Dec 12, 1975	OF P P	Ken Henderson Dick Ruthven Danny Osborn	Chicago White Sox	OF IF	Ralph Garr Larvell Blanks
April 7, 1976	OF	Terry Crowley	Cincinnati Reds	P	Mike Thompson
April 10, 1976	P	Andy Messersmith	Los Angeles Dodgers		No compensation (free agent signing)
June 13, 1976	1B SS IF	Willie Montanez Craig Robinson Mike Eden	San Francisco Giants	3B SS	Darrell Evans Marty Perez
June 15, 1976	C	Pete Varney	Chicago White Sox	P	Blue Moon Odom

DATE		ACQUIRED	FROM		IN EXCHANGE FOR
June 23, 1976	P	Mike Marshall	Los Angeles Dodgers	P OF	Elias Sosa Lee Lacy
July 24, 1976		Cash	Montreal Expos	C	Earl Williams
Nov 17, 1976	OF	Gary Matthews	San Francisco Giants		No compensation (free agent signing)
Nov 29, 1976		Cash	New York Yankees	OF	Jimmy Wynn
Dec 9, 1976	OF	Jeff Burroughs	Texas Rangers	OF OF P P P	Ken Henderson Dave May Carl Morton Roger Moret Adrian Devine and $250,000.
March 29, 1977		Cash	Oakland Athletics	P	Pablo Torrealba
April 30, 1977		Cash	Texas Rangers	P	Mike Marshall
June 15, 1977	P	Steve Hargan	Texas Rangers		Cash
Dec 7, 1977		Cash	New York Yankees	P	Andy Messersmith
Dec 8, 1977	P P OF	Adrian Devine Tommy Boggs Eddie Miller (Part of four-team trade involving Texas, Atlanta, Pittsburgh, and New York Mets.)	Texas Rangers	1B	Willie Montanez
Feb 15, 1978	OF	Mike Lum	Cincinnati Reds		No compensation (free agent signing)
June 15, 1978	P	Gene Garber	Philadelphia Phillies	P	Dick Ruthven
Sept 22, 1978		Cash	Pittsburgh Pirates	OF	Clarence Gaston
Feb 23, 1979		Cash	Seattle Mariners	P	Mike Davey
March 31, 1979	SS	Pepe Frias	Montreal Expos	P	Dave Campbell
May 25, 1979	P	Bo McLaughlin	Houston Astros	P	Frank LaCorte
Oct 19, 1979		Cash	Montreal Expos	P	Jamie Easterly
Nov 20, 1979	P	Al Hrabosky	Kansas City Royals		No compensation (free agent signing)
Dec 3, 1979	C	Bill Nahorodny	Chicago White Sox		Minor league P Rick Wieters
Dec 4, 1979		No compensation (free agent signing)	Montreal Expos	OF	Rowland Office
Dec 5, 1979	1B SS	Chris Chambliss Luis Gomez	Toronto Blue Jays	OF SS P	Barry Bonnell Pat Rockett Joey McLaughlin

DATE		ACQUIRED	FROM		IN EXCHANGE FOR
Dec 6, 1979	P SS	Doyle Alexander Larvell Blanks and $50,000.	Texas Rangers	P SS	Adrian Devine Pepe Frias
Feb 15, 1980		Minor league P Gary Melson	Cleveland Indians	P	Don Collins
March 28, 1980		Minor league P Greg Field	Pittsburgh Pirates	P	Eddie Solomon
Nov 17, 1980	OF	Claudell Washington	New York Mets		No compensation (free agent signing)
Dec 12, 1980	P	John Montefusco minor league OF Craig Landis	San Francisco Giants	P	Doyle Alexander
Jan 12, 1981	P	Gaylord Perry	New York Yankees		No compensation (free agent signing)
March 7, 1981	P	Carlos Diaz	Seattle Mariners	OF	Jeff Burroughs
March 25, 1981	P	Bob Walk	Philadelphia Phillies	OF	Gary Matthews
Feb 1, 1982	P	Donnie Moore	St. Louis Cardinals	P	Dan Morogiello
March 23, 1982	P	Roger Weaver	Detroit Tigers	OF	Eddie Miller
April 6, 1982		No compensation (free agent signing)	San Diego Padres	P	John Montefusco
April 23, 1982	1B	Bob Watson	New York Yankees		Minor league P Scott Patterson
April 28, 1982		Cash	Kansas City Royals	OF	Steve Hammond
June 30, 1982	P	Pascual Perez minor league SS Carlos Rios	Pittsburgh Pirates	P	Larry McWilliams
Sept 10, 1982	P	Tom Hausman	New York Mets	P	Carlos Diaz
Dec 10, 1982	P	Terry Forster	Los Angeles Dodgers		No compensation (free agent signing)
Jan 25, 1983	P	Pete Falcone	New York Mets		No compensation (free agent signing)
June 15, 1983	1B	Mike Jorgensen	New York Mets		$75,000.
Aug 28, 1983	P	Len Barker	Cleveland Indians	P OF 3B	Rick Behenna Brett Butler Brook Jacoby and $150,000.
		(Butler and Jacoby were sent to Cleveland at the end of the season.)			
Jan 6, 1984		No compensation (free agent signing)	New York Yankees	P	Phil Niekro
Feb 14, 1984		Minor league P Ron Meredith	Houston Astros	P	Jose Alvarez

Boston Braves

The Best Trades

1. Acquired Rogers Hornsby from the New York Giants for Shanty Hogan and Jimmy Welsh, January 10, 1928.
2. Acquired Tommy Holmes from the New York Yankees for Buddy Hassett and Gene Moore, February 5, 1942.
3. Acquired Bob Elliott and Hank Camelli from the Pittsburgh Pirates for Billy Herman, Elmer Singleton, Whitey Wietelmann, and Stan Wentzel, September 30, 1946.
4. Acquired Lew Burdette and $50,000 from the New York Yankees for Johnny Sain, August 30, 1951.
5. Acquired Ginger Beaumont, Claude Ritchey, and Patsy Flaherty from the Pittsburgh Pirates for Ed Abbaticchio, December, 1906.

The Worst Trades

1. Traded Vic Willis to the Pittsburgh Pirates for Vive Lindaman, Dave Brain, and Del Howard, December 15, 1905.
2. Traded Rogers Hornsby to the Chicago Cubs for Percy Jones, Socks Seibold, Lou Leggett, Freddie Maguire, Bruce Cunningham, and $200,000, November 7, 1928.
3. Traded Eddie Stanky and Alvin Dark to the New York Giants for Buddy Kerr, Sid Gordon, Willard Marshall, and Red Webb, December 14, 1949.
4. Traded Burleigh Grimes to the St. Louis Cardinals for Fred Frankhouse and Bill Sherdel, June 16, 1930.
5. Traded Larry Benton, Herb Thomas, and Zack Taylor to the New York Giants for Hugh McQuillan, Kent Greenfield, and Doc Farrell, June 12, 1927.

Trades: The Trades That Won Their Pennants

Throughout the history of the Braves franchise, whether in Boston, Milwaukee, or Atlanta, every successful pennant campaign has been directly preceded by a key trade that put them over the top. The Boston Braves won just two pennants in their history, in 1914 and 1948; in each case, trades were the key.

Shortly after George Stallings took over the reins of the club in 1913, he proceeded to change the face of his lethargic crew, bringing in hard-nosed fighters who wouldn't stand for losing. Early in the 1914 season he acquired infielder Red Smith from Brooklyn and outfielders Possum Whitted and Ted Cather from St. Louis. Each would play a role in the Miracle Braves' stretch run, but the most important role would be played by Johnny Evers, picked up before the season from Chicago.

When the Cubs replaced Evers as manager before the '14 season, they realized it would be for the best if they traded him rather than make him play for his successor, Hank O'Day. They sent him to Boston for Bill Sweeney and cash. Evers was among the Braves' batting leaders in 1914, and his leadership and inspirational play won him the Chalmers Cup, awarded to the league's most valuable player at year's end.

The Braves' next title came in 1948, and again trades provided the winning edge. The Braves picked up Eddie Stanky from Brooklyn for Ray Sanders, Bama Rowell, and cash, and added slugger Jeff Heath from the St. Louis Browns, but the deal that won the pennant was the one that sent second baseman Billy Herman, infielder Whitey Wietelmann, pitcher Elmer Singleton, and outfielder Stan Wentzel to Pittsburgh for third baseman Bob Elliott and catcher Hank Camelli. Herman was plagued by a sore arm and played in only fifteen games for the Pirates, while Elliott won the MVP Award in 1947 for Boston and led the pennant-winning '48 club in homers and RBIs. Elliott held down third for the Braves for five solid seasons, making this one of the most one-sided transactions in baseball history.

DATE		ACQUIRED	FROM		IN EXCHANGE FOR
Unknown		Cash	Chicago Cubs	P	Frank Killen
Jan 10, 1900	P 2B P	Kirtly Baker Shad Barry Bill Dinneen	Washington Senators		Cash
Jan 1900	C	Jack Clements	Cleveland Spiders		Cash
Jan 1900	P	Nig Cuppy	St. Louis Cardinals		Cash
Jan 1900		Cash	Pittsburgh Pirates	P	Jouett Meekin
Feb 17, 1900		Cash	New York Giants	3B	Piano Legs Hickman
Feb 17, 1900		Cash	New York Giants	OF	Charlie Frisbee
Feb 1901	2B	Gene DeMontreville	Brooklyn Dodgers		Cash
May 1901	OF	Duff Cooley	Pittsburgh Pirates		Cash
May 1901	OF	Elmer Smith	Pittsburgh Pirates		Cash
June 1901	OF	Jimmy Slagle	Philadelphia Phillies	2B	Shad Barry
July 1901		Cash	New York Giants	OF	Frank Murphy
Feb 1902		Cash	Pittsburgh Pirates	OF	Fred Crolius
April 1902	P	Mal Eason	Chicago Cubs		Cash
July 1902	3B	Charlie Dexter	Chicago Cubs	2B	Bobby Lowe
June 1903	OF	Tom McCreery	Brooklyn Dodgers		Cash
June 1903		Cash	Washington Senators	C	Malachi Kittredge
June 1903	P	Pop Williams	Philadelphia Phillies		Cash
Jan 1904	P	Kaiser Wilhelm	Pittsburgh Pirates		Cash
Aug 7, 1904	C	Doc Marshall	New York Giants		Cash
Sept 11, 1904	OF	George Barclay	St. Louis Cardinals		Cash
Oct 1904		Waiver price	Detroit Tigers	OF	Duff Cooley

DATE		ACQUIRED	FROM		IN EXCHANGE FOR
Dec 20, 1904	P 3B	Chick Fraser Harry Wolverton	Philadelphia Phillies	P	Togie Pittinger
June 6, 1905	C	Gabby Street	Cincinnati Reds		Cash
June 6, 1905	1B	Cozy Dolan	Cincinnati Reds		Cash
July 30, 1905		Cash	Cincinnati Reds	C	Gabby Street
Dec 15, 1905	3B 1B P	Dave Brain Del Howard Vive Lindaman	Pittsburgh Pirates	P	Vic Willis
Dec 1905		Cash	Detroit Tigers	OF	Duff Cooley
Jan 1906	C	Jack O'Neill	Chicago Cubs		Waiver price
Jan 1906	P	Big Jeff Pfeffer	Chicago Cubs		Cash
Feb 1906		Cash	Chicago Cubs	C	Pat Moran
March 1906	SS	Al Bridwell	Cincinnati Reds	3B P	Jim Delahanty Chick Fraser
May 13, 1906	P	Gus Dorner	Cincinnati Reds		Cash
Dec 1906	OF 2B P	Ginger Beaumont Claude Ritchey Patsy Flaherty	Pittsburgh Pirates	2B	Ed Abbaticchio
June 24, 1907	2B OF	Bill Sweeney Newt Randall	Chicago Cubs	OF	Del Howard
Oct 7, 1907	1B C SS OF P	Dan McGann Frank Bowerman Bill Dahlen George Browne George Ferguson	New York Giants	1B SS C	Fred Tenney Al Bridwell Tom Needham
Jan 1908	C	Harry Smith	Pittsburgh Pirates		Cash
Feb 1908		Cash	Cincinnati Reds	3B	Dave Brain
April 1908	IF	Jack Hannifan	New York Giants		Cash
June 1908	P P	Tom McCarthy Harley Young	Pittsburgh Pirates	P	Irv Young
June 1908	OF	Beals Becker	Pittsburgh Pirates		Cash
Aug 1908	OF	Herbie Moran	Philadelphia Athletics		Cash
Sept 1908		Cash	Chicago Cubs	OF	George Browne
Feb 1909	OF	Roy Thomas	Pittsburgh Pirates		Cash
May 1909	C	Chick Autry	Cincinnati Reds	OF	Bill Chappelle

DATE		ACQUIRED	FROM		IN EXCHANGE FOR
July 16, 1909	P P 2B	Buster Brown Lew Richie Dave Shean	Philadelphia Phillies	OF 2B	Johnny Bates Charlie Starr
Sept 1909	2B	Charlie Starr	Pittsburgh Pirates		Cash
Dec 1909	2B	Buck Herzog	New York Giants	OF	Beals Becker
Feb 1910	OF	Fred Liese	Chicago Cubs	OF	Ginger Beaumont
April 1910	OF	Doc Miller	Chicago Cubs	P	Lew Richie
May 1910	2B	Ed Abbaticchio	Pittsburgh Pirates		Cash
June 1, 1910	P	Sam Frock	Pittsburgh Pirates	P	Kirby White
Sept 1910	OF	Art Krueger	Cleveland Indians		Cash
Sept 1910		Cash	Pittsburgh Pirates	1B	Bud Sharpe
Jan 1911	3B P	Scotty Ingerton Big Jeff Pfeffer	Chicago Cubs	2B	Dave Shean
March 1911		Cash	Cincinnati Reds	OF	Fred Beck
March 1911	3B	Harry Steinfeldt	Chicago Cubs		Cash
June 10, 1911	C C P	Johnny Kling Al Kaiser Orlie Weaver	Chicago Cubs	P OF 2B	Cliff Curtis Wilbur Good Bill Collins
June 1911	P	Hank Griffin	Chicago Cubs	C	Jimmy Austin
July 22, 1911	C SS	Hank Gowdy Al Bridwell	New York Giants	2B	Buck Herzog
July 1911	P	Cy Young	Cleveland Indians		Waiver price
Aug 1, 1911	OF	Mike Donlin	New York Giants		Cash
Oct 1911	SS	Dave Shean	Chicago Cubs		Cash
Dec 1911	3B	Art Devlin	New York Giants		Cash
Jan 1912		Cash	Pittsburgh Pirates	2B	Art Butler
Feb 1912	OF	Vin Campbell	Pittsburgh Pirates	OF	Mike Donlin
July 1, 1912	OF	John Titus	Philadelphia Phillies	OF	Doc Miller
Nov 1912		Cash	Chicago Cubs	SS	Al Bridwell
Dec 1912	OF	Bris Lord	Philadelphia Athletics		Cash
Dec 1912	2B	Bill McKechnie	Pittsburgh Pirates		Cash

DATE		ACQUIRED	FROM		IN EXCHANGE FOR
Dec 1912	P OF	George Davis Guy Zinn	New York Yankees		Cash
Feb 1913		Cash	Cincinnati Reds	C	Johnny Kling
April 10, 1913	OF	Joe Connolly	Washington Senators		Cash
April 15, 1913		Waiver price	New York Yankees	3B	Bill McKechnie
June 1913	SS	Tex McDonald	Cincinnati Reds		Cash
June 1913	3B	Charlie Deal	Detroit Tigers		Cash
July 1913	OF	Otis Clymer	Chicago Cubs		Cash
Jan 1914	OF	Herbie Moran	Cincinnati Reds		Cash
Feb 1914	2B	Johnny Evers	Chicago Cubs	2B	Bill Sweeney and cash
June 1914	OF OF	Possum Whitted Ted Cather	St. Louis Cardinals	P	Hub Perdue
June 1914	OF	Josh Devore	Philadelphia Phillies	SS	Jack Martin
July 1914	3B	Red Smith	Brooklyn Dodgers		Cash
Feb 14, 1915	OF	Sherry Magee	Philadelphia Phillies	OF 3B	Possum Whitted Oscar Dugey and cash
April 18, 1915		Cash	New York Yankees	P	Ensign Cottrell
May 1, 1915	SS	Dick Egan	Brooklyn Dodgers		Cash
May 1, 1915	P	Pat Ragan	Brooklyn Dodgers		Cash
Aug 1915	OF	Fred Snodgrass	New York Giants		Cash
Sept 3, 1915	OF	Zip Collins	Pittsburgh Pirates		Cash
Feb 10, 1916	1B P P	Ed Konetchy Frank Allen Elmer Knetzer	Pittsburgh (Federal League)		Cash
April 12, 1916	P	Ed Reulbach	Pittsburgh Pirates		Cash
April 1916		Cash	Cincinnati Reds	P	Elmer Knetzer
May 1916	OF	Larry Chappell	Cleveland Indians		Cash
June 1916		Cash (Pittsburgh returned Compton to Boston ten days later.)	Pittsburgh Pirates	OF	Pete Compton
Jan 1917	OF	Joe Kelly	Chicago Cubs	C	Earl Blackburn

DATE		ACQUIRED	FROM		IN EXCHANGE FOR
May 28, 1917	P	Scott Perry	Cincinnati Reds		Waiver price
July 12, 1917		Waiver price	Philadelphia Phillies	2B	Johnny Evers
July 29, 1917		Waiver price	Pittsburgh Pirates	2B	Joe Wilhoit
Aug 1, 1917		Waiver price	Cincinnati Reds	OF	Sherry Magee
Aug 16, 1917	C	Chief Meyers	Brooklyn Dodgers		Waiver price
Oct 1917	C	Bill Wagner	Pittsburgh Pirates		Cash
Dec 1917	C	John Henry	Washington Senators		Cash
Jan 4, 1918	2B C	Larry Doyle Art Wilson and $15,000.	Chicago Cubs	P	Lefty Tyler
Jan 8, 1918	2B	Buck Herzog	New York Giants	2B P	Larry Doyle Jesse Barnes
April 1918		Cash	Philadelphia Athletics	P	Scott Perry
June 19, 1918		Cash	New York Yankees	OF	Ham Hyatt
Oct 1918	2B	Jimmy Smith	New York Giants		Cash
Jan 1919		Cash	New York Yankees	OF	Al Wickland
Feb 1919	SS	Lena Blackburne	Cincinnati Reds	IF	Wally Rehg
Feb 1919	1B	Walter Holke	New York Giants	IF	Jimmy Smith
Feb 1919	P	Al Demaree	New York Giants		Cash
March 6, 1919	P	Ray Keating	New York Yankees		Cash
April 14, 1919		Cash	Brooklyn Dodgers	1B	Ed Konetchy
May 1919	OF	Jim Thorpe	New York Giants	P	Pat Ragan
May 1919	OF	Walt Cruise	St. Louis Cardinals		Cash
May 1919		Cash	Philadelphia Phillies	SS	Lena Blackburne
May 1919		Cash	Philadelphia Phillies	C	Walt Tragesser
June 12, 1919	3B	Tony Boeckel	Pittsburgh Pirates		Waiver price
June 1919	P	Larry Cheney	Brooklyn Dodgers		Waiver price

DATE		ACQUIRED	FROM		IN EXCHANGE FOR
Aug 15, 1919	P P P C	Joe Oeschger Red Causey Johnny Jones Mickey O'Neil and $55,000.	New York Giants	P	Art Nehf
Aug 1919	OF 3B	Les Mann Charlie Pick	Chicago Cubs	2B	Buck Herzog
Aug 1919		Waiver price	Philadelphia Phillies	P	Larry Cheney
May 1920		Cash	Boston Red Sox	OF	Gene Bailey
June 1920		Cash	Philadelphia Phillies	2B	Johnny Rawlings
Aug 28, 1920		Waiver price	Pittsburgh Pirates	P	Mule Watson
Nov 9, 1920		Cash	St. Louis Cardinals	OF	Les Mann
Feb 23, 1921	OF OF 3B	Billy Southworth Fred Nicholson Walter Barbare and $15,000.	Pittsburgh Pirates	SS	Rabbit Maranville
June 30, 1921	P	Mule Watson	Pittsburgh Pirates		Waiver price
July 1921		Cash	Brooklyn Dodgers	P	Eddie Eayrs
Sept 1921		Cash	Chicago Cubs	OF	John Sullivan
Feb 18, 1922	P	Rube Marquard	Cincinnati Reds	SS P	Larry Kopf Jack Scott
July 30, 1922		$100,000.	New York Giants	P	Hugh McQuillan
Jan 1923	1B	Stuffy McInnis	Cleveland Indians		Waiver price
June 7, 1923	P C	Jesse Barnes Earl Smith	New York Giants	C P	Hank Gowdy Mule Watson
Nov 12, 1923	OF SS OF	Casey Stengel Dave Bancroft Bill Cunningham (Bancroft was named Boston manager.)	New York Giants	OF P	Billy Southworth Joe Oeschger
Dec 15, 1923	SS	Cotton Tierney (Powell announced his intention to retire after the 1924 season. He remained with Boston, and Philadelphia received cash instead.)	Philadelphia Phillies	SS OF	Hod Ford Ray Powell
Jan 1924	SS	John Kelleher	Chicago Cubs		Cash
June 5, 1924	P	Dinty Gearin	New York Giants		Cash
June 17, 1924	P	Lou North	St. Louis Cardinals		Cash
July 6, 1924		Cash	Pittsburgh Pirates	C	Earl Smith
Feb 4, 1925	OF	Bernie Neis	Brooklyn Dodgers	SS	Cotton Tierney

DATE		ACQUIRED	FROM		IN EXCHANGE FOR
April 17, 1925	P	Rosy Ryan	New York Giants	P	Tim McNamara
July 1, 1925	IF	Doc Gautreau	Philadelphia Athletics		Cash
July 25, 1925	2B	Andy High	Brooklyn Dodgers		Waiver price
Oct 7, 1925	C 1B 2B	Zack Taylor Jimmy Johnston Eddie Brown	Brooklyn Dodgers	P C OF	Jesse Barnes Mickey O'Neil Gus Felix
Feb 1926		Cash	Cleveland Indians	3B	Ernie Padgett
April 19, 1926	OF	Jack Smith	St. Louis Cardinals		Cash
April 1926		Cash	Brooklyn Dodgers	3B	Bill Marriott
June 1926	P	George Mogridge	New York Yankees		Waiver price
July 20, 1926	2B	Eddie Moore	Pittsburgh Pirates		Cash
Oct 7, 1926		Waiver price	New York Giants	2B	Jimmy Johnston
Nov 5, 1926	1B	Jack Fournier	Brooklyn Dodgers		Cash
June 12, 1927	P P SS	Hugh McQuillan Kent Greenfield Doc Farrell	New York Giants	C P P	Zack Taylor Larry Benton Herb Thomas
July 18, 1927		Waiver price	New York Giants	OF	Les Mann
Dec 18, 1927	SS	Jimmy Cooney	St. Louis Cardinals		Waiver price
Jan 10, 1928	SS	Rogers Hornsby	New York Giants	C OF	Shanty Hogan Jimmy Welsh
Feb 1928	C	Zack Taylor	New York Giants		Cash
March 25, 1928	3B	Les Bell	St. Louis Cardinals	2B	Andy High and $25,000.
May 27, 1928	1B	George Sisler	Washington Senators		$7,500.
June 15, 1928	P C P P	Ben Cantwell Al Spohrer Bill Clarkson Virgil Barnes	New York Giants	P	Joe Genewich
June 23, 1928	SS	Howard Freigau	Brooklyn Dodgers		Cash
Nov 7, 1928	P P C 2B P	Socks Seibold Percy Jones Lou Legett Freddie Maguire Bruce Cunningham and $200,000.	Chicago Cubs	2B	Rogers Hornsby
Dec 8, 1928	2B	Rabbit Maranville	St. Louis Cardinals		Cash

DATE	ACQUIRED		FROM	IN EXCHANGE FOR	
Dec 8, 1928	OF	George Harper	St. Louis Cardinals		Cash
Dec 13, 1928	C	Pat Collins	New York Yankees		$7,500.
Dec 29, 1928	3B	Joe Dugan	New York Yankees		Waiver price
June 14, 1929	OF	Jimmy Welsh	New York Giants	IF	Doc Farrell
July 4, 1929		Cash	Brooklyn Dodgers	P	Kent Greenfield
July 6, 1929		Waiver price	Chicago Cubs	C	Zack Taylor
July 14, 1929	C	Jack Cummings	New York Giants		Cash
Sept 17, 1929	3B	Gene Robertson	New York Yankees		Cash
Oct 29, 1929		Waiver price	Chicago Cubs	3B	Les Bell
April 9, 1930	P	Burleigh Grimes	Pittsburgh Pirates	P	Percy Jones and cash
May 12, 1930	P	Tom Zachary	New York Yankees		Waiver price
June 16, 1930	P P	Fred Frankhouse Bill Sherdel	St. Louis Cardinals	P	Burleigh Grimes
Oct 14, 1930	P OF	Bill McAfee Wes Schulmerich	Chicago Cubs	P OF	Bob Smith Jimmy Welsh
Jan 1931	C	Al Bool	Pittsburgh Pirates		Waiver price
Jan 1931	P	Hal Haid	St. Louis Cardinals		Waiver price
May 28, 1931	P	Ray Moss	Brooklyn Dodgers		Cash
May 28, 1931	2B	Bill Hunnefield	Cleveland Indians		Waiver price
June 30, 1931		Waiver price	New York Giants	2B	Bill Hunnefield
Dec 17, 1931		Waiver price	Chicago Cubs	OF	Lance Richbourg
Dec 1931	C	Pinky Hargrave	Washington Senators		Waiver price
March 19, 1932	OF	Freddy Leach	New York Giants		$10,000.
May 18, 1932		Waiver price	St. Louis Cardinals	P	Bill Sherdel
Dec 29, 1932	C	Shanty Hogan	New York Giants		$25,000.
June 12, 1933	P	Ray Starr	New York Giants		Cash
June 17, 1933	OF 3B	Hal Lee Pinky Whitney	Philadelphia Phillies	3B OF	Fritz Knothe Wes Schulmerich and cash

DATE		ACQUIRED	FROM		IN EXCHANGE FOR
Aug 2, 1933	P	Bob Smith	Cincinnati Reds		Waiver price
Dec 1933	P	Dick Barrett	Philadelphia Athletics		Cash
May 26, 1934	P	Jumbo Elliott	Philadelphia Phillies		Cash
June 12, 1934		Waiver price	Brooklyn Dodgers	P	Tom Zachary
Sept 11, 1934		Waiver price	St. Louis Cardinals	OF	Red Worthington
June 15, 1935	P	Danny MacFayden	Cincinnati Reds		Waiver price
Dec 12, 1935	2B C P OF	Tony Cuccinello Al Lopez Ray Benge Bobby Reis	Brooklyn Dodgers	P OF	Ed Brandt Randy Moore
Dec 1935		Cash	Washington Senators	C	Shanty Hogan
Jan 29, 1936	IF	Mickey Haslin	Philadelphia Phillies	3B	Pinky Whitney
Feb 6, 1936	P OF	Johnny Babich Gene Moore	Brooklyn Dodgers	P	Fred Frankhouse
May 1936	IF	Mickey Haslin	Philadelphia Phillies		Cash
July 6, 1936	SS	Rabbit Warstler	Philadelphia Athletics		Waiver price
Aug 4, 1936	P	Fabian Kowalik	Philadelphia Phillies	P	Ray Benge
Dec 4, 1936	3B	Eddie Mayo	New York Giants	IF	Mickey Haslin
Jan 6, 1937	SS	Tommy Thevenow	Cincinnati Reds		Cash
Jan 27, 1937		Cash	New York Giants	P	Ben Cantwell
May 12, 1937		Cash	Cincinnati Reds	1B	Buck Jordan
June 15, 1937	P	Frank Gabler and $35,000.	New York Giants	3B	Wally Berger
June 1937	OF	Roy Johnson	New York Yankees		Waiver price
June 1937	3B	Gil English	Detroit Tigers		Cash
Feb 2, 1938		Cash	St. Louis Cardinals	P	Guy Bush
May 2, 1938		Cash	Chicago White Sox	P	Frank Gabler
May 23, 1938	P	Tommy Reis	Philadelphia Phillies		Cash
Aug 1, 1938	3B	Joe Stripp	St. Louis Cardinals		Cash

DATE		ACQUIRED	FROM		IN EXCHANGE FOR
Aug 10, 1938	SS	Eddie Miller	Cincinnati Reds	P P 3B C OF	Tommy Reis Johnny Babich Gil English Johnny Riddle Vince DiMaggio and cash
Dec 13, 1938	OF 1B	Jimmy Outlaw Buddy Hassett	Brooklyn Dodgers	OF P	Gene Moore Ira Hutchinson
Dec 16, 1938	C OF	Al Todd Johnny Dickshot and cash	Pittsburgh Pirates	C	Ray Mueller
Dec 29, 1938	OF	Al Simmons	Washington Senators		Cash
Feb 3, 1939	OF	Gene Moore	Brooklyn Dodgers	P	Fred Frankhouse
March 31, 1939	P	Bill Posedel	Brooklyn Dodgers	C	Al Todd
June 15, 1939	SS	Bill Schuster and cash	Pittsburgh Pirates	1B	Elbie Fletcher
June 15, 1939	P	Bill Kerksieck	Philadelphia Phillies		Cash
Aug 19, 1939		Waiver price	Cincinnati Reds	P	Milt Shoffner
Aug 31, 1939		Cash	Cincinnati Reds	OF	Al Simmons
Dec 6, 1939	1B	Les Scarsella and cash	Cincinnati Reds	P	Jim Turner
Dec 6, 1939	P	Jim Tobin and cash	Pittsburgh Pirates	P	Johnny Lanning
Dec 8, 1939	P	Bill Swift and cash	Pittsburgh Pirates	P	Danny MacFayden
March 3, 1940		Cash	Pittsburgh Pirates	OF	Debs Garms
May 7, 1940	OF	Lloyd Waner	Pittsburgh Pirates	P	Nick Strincevich
May 29, 1940	OF	Gene Moore	Brooklyn Dodgers		Cash
June 14, 1940	C	Ray Berres and $40,000.	Pittsburgh Pirates	C	Al Lopez
June 15, 1940	P 2B	Manny Salvo Al Glossop	New York Giants	3B	Tony Cuccinello
July 24, 1940		Waiver price	Chicago Cubs	SS	Rabbit Warstler
July 1940		Cash	Brooklyn Dodgers	P	Lou Fette
Feb 25, 1941	1B	Babe Dahlgren	New York Yankees		Cash
June 12, 1941	P	Johnny Hutchings	Cincinnati Reds	OF	Lloyd Waner
June 15, 1941		Cash	Chicago Cubs	1B	Babe Dahlgren

DATE		ACQUIRED	FROM		IN EXCHANGE FOR
June 20, 1941		Cash	Pittsburgh Pirates	P	Joe Sullivan
July 21, 1941	OF	Frank Demaree	New York Giants		Waiver price
Feb 5, 1942	OF	Tommy Holmes	New York Yankees	1B OF	Buddy Hassett Gene Moore
Feb 7, 1942	C	Ernie Lombardi	Cincinnati Reds		Cash
March 1942		Cash	New York Giants	C	Ray Berres
April 4, 1942	OF	Frenchy Bordagaray	New York Yankees		Cash
Sept 25, 1942		Cash	New York Yankees	3B	Hank Majeski
Dec 4, 1942	SS P	Eddie Joost Nate Andrews and $25,000.	Cincinnati Reds	SS	Eddie Miller
Jan 1943		Cash	St. Louis Cardinals	OF	Frank Demaree
April 27, 1943	C 2B	Hugh Poland Connie Ryan	New York Giants	C	Ernie Lombardi
May 12, 1943		Cash	Philadelphia Phillies	P	Manny Salvo
Feb 5, 1945	OF	Johnny Hopp	St. Louis Cardinals	SS	Eddie Joost and $40,000.
May 23, 1945	P	Mort Cooper	St. Louis Cardinals	P	Red Barrett and $60,000.
June 16, 1945	OF	Joe Medwick	New York Giants	C P	Clyde Kluttz Ewald Pyle
July 14, 1945	P	Bill Lee	Philadelphia Phillies		Cash
Aug 22, 1945		Cash	Cincinnati Reds	P	Nate Andrews
Aug 1945		Cash	Detroit Tigers	P	Jim Tobin
Feb 5, 1946	OF	Johnny Wyrostek	St. Louis Cardinals		Cash
Feb 5, 1946	OF	Johnny Hopp	St. Louis Cardinals		$40,000.
April 15, 1946	1B P	Ray Sanders Max Surkont	St. Louis Cardinals		$25,000.
April 18, 1946	P	Jim Konstanty and cash	Cincinnati Reds	OF	Max West
April 24, 1946	P	Si Johnson	Philadelphia Phillies		Cash
May 14, 1946	P	Ernie White	St. Louis Cardinals		Cash
June 3, 1946	OF	Mike McCormick	Cincinnati Reds		Cash
June 9, 1946	OF	Danny Litwhiler	St. Louis Cardinals		Cash

DATE	ACQUIRED	FROM	IN EXCHANGE FOR
June 12, 1946	C Don Padgett	Brooklyn Dodgers	Cash
June 12, 1946	OF Johnny Barrett	Pittsburgh Pirates	OF Chuck Workman
June 15, 1946	2B Billy Herman	Brooklyn Dodgers	C Stew Hofferth
July 8, 1946	C Ken O'Dea	St. Louis Cardinals	Cash
Sept 30, 1946	3B Bob Elliott C Hank Camelli	Pittsburgh Pirates	2B Billy Herman P Elmer Singleton OF Stan Wentzel SS Whitey Wietelmann
Dec 9, 1946	P Red Barrett	St. Louis Cardinals	Cash
March 25, 1947	Cash	Pittsburgh Pirates	P Lou Tost
April 18, 1947	P Johnny Beazley	St. Louis Cardinals	Cash
May 27, 1947	P Andy Karl	Philadelphia Phillies	C Don Padgett
June 7, 1947	P Clyde Shoun	Cincinnati Reds	Cash
June 13, 1947	P Bill Voiselle and cash	New York Giants	P Mort Cooper
Nov 18, 1947	OF Jim Russell C Bill Salkeld P Al Lyons	Pittsburgh Pirates	1B Johnny Hopp 2B Danny Murtaugh
Dec 4, 1947	OF Jeff Heath	St. Louis Browns	Cash
March 1, 1948	2B Bobby Sturgeon	Chicago Cubs	3B Dick Culler
March 6, 1948	2B Eddie Stanky	Brooklyn Dodgers	2B Bama Rowell 1B Ray Sanders and $40,000.
April 19, 1948	1B Ray Sanders	Brooklyn Dodgers	$60,000.
May 11, 1948	OF Marv Rickert	Cincinnati Reds	OF Danny Litwhiler
Dec 15, 1948	OF Pete Reiser	Brooklyn Dodgers	OF Mike McCormick
May 11, 1949	Cash	Chicago White Sox	P Clyde Shoun
June 15, 1949	OF Ed Sauer	Pittsburgh Pirates	C Phil Masi
Sept 26, 1949	Cash	Chicago White Sox	C Bill Salkeld
Dec 14, 1949	3B Sid Gordon SS Buddy Kerr OF Willard Marshall P Red Webb	New York Giants	2B Eddie Stanky SS Alvin Dark

DATE		ACQUIRED	FROM		IN EXCHANGE FOR
Dec 14, 1949		Cash	Pittsburgh Pirates	OF	Marv Rickert
Dec 14, 1949	IF	Gene Mauch and cash	Chicago Cubs	P	Bill Voiselle
Dec 24, 1949	OF	Luis Olmo	Brooklyn Dodgers	OF OF	Jim Russell Ed Sauer and cash
April 18, 1950	P	Bob Chipman	Chicago Cubs		Cash
May 10, 1950	C	Walker Cooper	Cincinnati Reds	2B	Connie Ryan
Aug 8, 1950	P	Mickey Haefner	Chicago White Sox		Cash
April 16, 1951	P	Blix Donnelly	Philadelphia Phillies		Waiver price
May 13, 1951	P	Sid Schacht	St. Louis Browns		Waiver price
May 14, 1951		Waiver price	St. Louis Browns	P	Bobby Hogue
Aug 30, 1951	P	Lew Burdette and $50,000.	New York Yankees	P	Johnny Sain
Oct 11, 1951	SS	Jack Cusick	Chicago Cubs	OF	Bob Addis
March 26, 1952		Waiver price	St. Louis Cardinals	IF	Gene Mauch
April 8, 1952	P	Sheldon Jones and $50,000.	New York Giants	OF	Bob Elliott
June 4, 1952		Cash	Cincinnati Reds	OF	Willard Marshall
Dec 20, 1952	P	Monk Dubiel	Chicago Cubs	P	Sheldon Jones

Brooklyn Dodgers

The Best Trades

1. Acquired Preacher Roe, Billy Cox, and Gene Mauch from the Pittsburgh Pirates for Dixie Walker, Vic Lombardi, and Hal Gregg, December 8, 1947.
2. Acquired Dolf Camilli from the Philadelphia Phillies for Eddie Morgan and $45,000, March 6, 1938.
3. Acquired Billy Herman from the Chicago Cubs for Johnny Hudson, Charlie Gilbert, and $65,000, May 6, 1941.
4. Acquired Lefty O'Doul and Fresco Thompson from the Philadelphia Phillies for Clise Dudley, Jumbo Elliott, Hal Lee, and cash, October 14, 1930.
5. Acquired Burleigh Grimes, Al Mamaux, and Chuck Ward from the Pittsburgh Pirates for Casey Stengel and George Cutshaw, January 9, 1918.

The Worst Trades

1. Traded Ernie Lombardi, Babe Herman, and Wally Gilbert to the Cincinnati Reds for Tony Cuccinello, Joe Stripp, and Clyde Sukeforth, March 14, 1932.
2. Traded Al Lopez, Tony Cuccinello, Ray Benge, and Bobby Reis to the Boston Braves for Ed Brandt and Randy Moore, December 12, 1935.
3. Traded Bill Dahlen to the New York Giants for Charlie Babb and John Cronin, December 12, 1903.
4. Traded Burleigh Grimes to the New York Giants in a three-team trade that brought Butch Henline from the Philadelphia Phillies, January 9, 1927.
5. Traded Jeff Pfeffer to the St. Louis Cardinals for Ferdie Schupp and Hal Janvrin, June 18, 1921.

Trader: Larry MacPhail

The Brooklyn Dodgers had their ups and downs during their long history, but few of the "down" periods sank as low as that of the late 1930s. On the field, the Dodgers were being kept out of the cellar only by some truly wretched Philadelphia clubs; off the field, its ownership had collapsed and it was in receivership. But Larry MacPhail was not a man to back off from a challenge.

First, MacPhail somehow wrangled $50,000 out of the banks to purchase Dolf Camilli, who became an immediate longball favorite, tripling the home run total of the previous year's club leader. The success of this purchase persuaded the Brooklyn Trust Bank to let MacPhail write his own ticket; whenever he needed money, he had only to ask. With this infusion of new money and new confidence, MacPhail set about building a winning club that would stay on top for a generation.

Cash figured prominently in most of MacPhail's key transactions. In July of 1939, MacPhail claimed outfielder Dixie Walker from Detroit on waivers; Walker's timely hitting soon had newspapers calling him "The People's Cherce." Young shortstop Pee Wee Reese was purchased from the Boston Red Sox's Louisville farm club. Outfielder Joe Medwick was acquired along with pitcher Curt Davis for $125,000 and four players. Pitcher Kirby Higbe cost another $100,000 when the Dodgers beat out the Giants' efforts to acquire the hard-throwing righthander. And catcher Mickey Owen came over from the Cardinals for $60,000 and two players. These players were the nucleus of the Dodger team that won the pennant in 1941 and just missed in '42 despite winning 104 games.

At this peak of success, MacPhail announced he was leaving baseball to accept a commission on the staff of Major General Brehon Somervell for the duration of World War II. His successor, Branch Rickey, would build on and greatly enhance the team MacPhail had constructed, making the Brooklyn Dodgers the dominant team of the first decade after the war.

DATE		ACQUIRED	FROM	IN EXCHANGE FOR
Jan 1900	OF	Jimmy Sheckard	Baltimore Orioles	Cash
	P	Jerry Nops		
	C	Broadway Aleck Smith		
	P	Frank Kitson		
	P	Harry Howell		
	P	Joe McGinnity		
Jan 1900	2B	Gene DeMontreville	Baltimore Orioles	Cash
Jan 1900	C	Farmer Steelman	Louisville Colonels	Cash

DATE		ACQUIRED	FROM		IN EXCHANGE FOR
Feb 1900		Cash	Philadelphia Phillies	P	Al Maul
May 1900	3B	Lave Cross	St. Louis Cardinals		Cash
June 1900		Cash	Philadelphia Phillies	P	Jack Dunn
July 1900	P	Gus Weyhing	St. Louis Cardinals		Cash
Feb 1901		$3,000.	Philadelphia Phillies	SS	Hughie Jennings
Feb 1901		Cash	Boston Braves	2B	Gene DeMontreville
April 1901		Cash	Philadelphia Athletics	C	Farmer Steelman
May 1901	OF	Tom McCreery	Pittsburgh Pirates	1B	Lefty Davis
June 1901	OF	Cozy Dolan	Chicago Cubs		Cash
July 2, 1901	3B	Charlie Irwin	Cincinnati Reds		Cash
July 1901	P	Doc Newton	Cincinnati Reds		Cash
July 1902	P C	LeRoy Evans Joe Wall	New York Giants		Cash
Jan 30, 1903	1B	Jack Doyle Cash	Brooklyn Dodgers	1B	Jack Doyle Cash
Jan 1903	P	Henry Thielman	Cincinnati Reds		Cash
Feb 1903		Waiver price	Pittsburgh Pirates	P	Lave Winham
Feb 1903	C	Fred Jacklitsch	Philadelphia Phillies		Cash
March 1903	3B	Sammy Strang	Chicago Cubs		Cash
May 1903	OF	John Dobbs	Chicago Cubs		Cash
June 1903	P	Jack Doscher	Chicago Cubs		Cash
June 1903		Cash	Boston Braves	OF	Tom McCreery
July 1903	P	Bill Reidy	St. Louis Browns	P	Clarence Wright
July 1903		Cash	St. Louis Browns	P	LeRoy Evans
Dec 12, 1903	SS	Bill Dahlen	New York Giants	P SS	John Cronin Charlie Babb
Feb 1904	P	Ed Poole	Cincinnati Reds		Cash
Feb 1904	C	Bill Bergen	Cincinnati Reds		Cash

DATE		ACQUIRED	FROM		IN EXCHANGE FOR
April 30, 1904		Cash	Philadelphia Phillies	1B OF	Jack Doyle Deacon Van Buren
Aug 1, 1904	P	Doc Scanlan	Pittsburgh Pirates		Cash
Aug 18, 1904	P	Fred Mitchell	Philadelphia Phillies		Cash
Sept 1904		Waiver price	New York Yankees	P	Ned Garvin
Feb 1905		Cash	New York Giants	3B	Sammy Strang
April 1905	3B	Bob Hall	New York Giants		Cash
Dec 30, 1905	OF OF 3B P	Billy Maloney Jack McCarthy Doc Casey Buttons Briggs and $2,000.	Chicago Cubs	OF	Jimmy Sheckard
May 8, 1906		Cash	Chicago Cubs	OF	Doc Gessler
Aug 1, 1906	P	Chappie McFarland	Pittsburgh Pirates		Waiver price
July 5, 1907	OF	Al Burch	St. Louis Cardinals		Cash
Jan 1908	3B	Tommy Sheehan	Pittsburgh Pirates		Cash
Nov 1908	C	Doc Marshall	Chicago Cubs		Waiver price
Sept 1909		Cash	Washington Senators	OF	Jimmy Sebring
May 1910		Cash	Cincinnati Reds	SS	Tommy McMillan
April 1911	OF	Hub Northen	Cincinnati Reds		Cash
Aug 31, 1911	P	Elmer Steele	Pittsburgh Pirates		Cash
Dec 1911	P	Eddie Stack	Philadelphia Phillies		Cash
April 1912		Cash	St. Louis Cardinals	P	Sandy Burk
May 1912		Cash	Chicago Cubs	2B	Red Downs
May 1912	P	Cliff Curtis	Philadelphia Phillies		Cash
Nov 1912	P	Elmer Brown	St. Louis Browns		Cash
May 1913	C	Mike Hechinger	Chicago Cubs		Waiver price
Aug 14, 1913	P	Ed Reulbach	Chicago Cubs	P	Eddie Stack and cash
Dec 1913	SS	Joe Tinker	Cincinnati Reds	2B	Dick Egan and $6,500.

(Tinker demanded $2,000 of the purchase price; when this was refused, he jumped to the Federal League and the deal was cancelled.)

April 1914	2B	Dick Egan	Cincinnati Reds	OF P	Herbie Moran Earl Yingling
June 1914	P	Casey Hageman	St. Louis Cardinals	OF	Joe Riggert
June 1914		Cash	Cincinnati Reds	C	Tex Erwin
June 1914		Cash	Chicago Cubs	P	Casey Hageman
July 1914	P	Bill Steele	St. Louis Cardinals		Cash
July 1914		Cash	Boston Braves	3B	Red Smith
Feb 22, 1915		Waiver price	Cincinnati Reds	P	Fred Toney
May 1, 1915		Cash	Boston Braves	SS	Dick Egan
May 1, 1915		Cash	Boston Braves	P	Pat Ragan
June 13, 1915	P	Phil Douglas	Cincinnati Reds		Cash
Aug 31, 1915	P	Rube Marquard	New York Giants		Waiver price
Aug 1915	P	Larry Cheney	Chicago Cubs	3B	Joe Schultz and $3,000.
Aug 1915	SS	Ivy Olson	Cincinnati Reds		Waiver price
Sept 8, 1915		Cash	Chicago Cubs	P	Phil Douglas
Feb 10, 1916	OF	Dave Hickman	Baltimore Orioles		Cash
Feb 10, 1916	OF	Mike Mowrey	Pittsburgh (Federal League)		Cash
Feb 10, 1916	C	Chief Meyers	New York Giants		Waiver price
Aug 20, 1916	1B	Fred Merkle	New York Giants	C	Lew McCarty
May 1917	C	Ernie Krueger	New York Giants		Waiver price
Aug 16, 1917		$3,500.	Chicago Cubs	1B	Fred Merkle
Aug 16, 1917		Waiver price	Boston Braves	C	Chief Meyers
Jan 9, 1918	SS P P	Chuck Ward Burleigh Grimes Al Mamaux	Pittsburgh Pirates	OF 2B	Casey Stengel George Cutshaw
Feb 1918	P	Clarence Mitchell	Cincinnati Reds		Cash
July 15, 1918	P	George Smith	New York Giants		Cash
July 1918	C	Jimmy Archer	Pittsburgh Pirates		Cash

DATE		ACQUIRED	FROM		IN EXCHANGE FOR
Sept 1918		Cash	Cincinnati Reds	C	Jimmy Archer
Oct 1918		Cash	New York Giants	P	George Smith
Feb 1, 1919	OF	Tommy Griffith	Cincinnati Reds	1B	Jake Daubert
April 14, 1919	1B	Ed Konetchy	Boston Braves		Cash
June 2, 1919	2B	Pete Kilduff	Chicago Cubs	IF	Lee Magee
June 1919		Waiver price	Boston Braves	P	Larry Cheney
July 1919	UT	Lee Magee	Cincinnati Reds		Cash
Aug 1919	3B	Doug Baird	St. Louis Cardinals		Cash
Oct 1919		Cash	Philadelphia Phillies	C	Mack Wheat
Jan 1920		Cash	Washington Senators	SS	Frank O'Rourke
March 1920	OF	Bill Lamar	Boston Red Sox		Cash
May 1920		Cash	New York Giants	3B	Doug Baird
May 1920	SS	Bill McCabe	Chicago Cubs		Cash
July 1920		Cash	Pittsburgh Pirates	OF	Wally Hood
Dec 15, 1920	P	Dutch Ruether	Cincinnati Reds	P	Rube Marquard
May 1921	P	Sweetbreads Bailey	Chicago Cubs		Cash
June 18, 1921	P IF	Ferdie Schupp Hal Janvrin	St. Louis Cardinals	P	Jeff Pfeffer
July 4, 1921		Waiver price	Philadelphia Phillies	1B	Ed Konetchy
July 1921	P	Eddie Eayrs	Boston Braves		Cash
Dec 1921		Cash	Chicago White Sox	P	Ferdie Schupp
Jan 24, 1922	SS	Sam Crane	Cincinnati Reds		Cash
Feb 17, 1922		Cash	Cincinnati Reds	C	Ernie Krueger
March 14, 1922	OF	Possum Whitted	Pittsburgh Pirates		Cash
Sept 18, 1922		Waiver price	Cleveland Indians	P	Sherry Smith
Jan 2, 1923	OF	Turner Barber	Chicago Cubs		Cash

DATE		ACQUIRED	FROM		IN EXCHANGE FOR
Feb 11, 1923	P	George Smith	Philadelphia Phillies	P	Clarence Mitchell
Feb 15, 1923	1B	Jack Fournier	St. Louis Cardinals	OF 1B	Hy Myers Ray Schmandt
May 1923		Cash	St. Louis Browns	1B	Dutch Schliebner
July 6, 1923		Waiver price	Chicago White Sox	P	Leon Cadore
Nov 1923	SS	Johnny Mitchell	Boston Red Sox		Cash
Dec 1923	P	Bonnie Hollingsworth	Washington Senators	OF	Bert Griffith
April 27, 1924	2B	Milt Stock	St. Louis Cardinals	C	Mike Gonzalez
May 16, 1924	P	Tiny Osborne	Chicago Cubs		Cash
June 13, 1924	P	Bill Doak	St. Louis Cardinals	P	Leo Dickerman
Dec 17, 1924		Cash	Washington Senators	P	Dutch Ruether
Feb 4, 1925	SS	Cotton Tierney	Boston Braves	OF	Bernie Neis
April 20, 1925	P	Joe Oeschger	Philadelphia Phillies		Waiver price
May 1, 1925	P	Bill Hubbell	Philadelphia Phillies	P	Art Decatur
May 10, 1925	3B	Bob Barrett	Chicago Cubs	OF	Tommy Griffith
May 16, 1925	SS	Hod Ford	Philadelphia Phillies		Waiver price
July 25, 1925		Waiver price	Boston Braves	2B	Andy High
Aug 1925		Cash	Chicago White Sox	SS	Moe Berg
Oct 7, 1925	P C OF	Jesse Barnes Mickey O'Neil Gus Felix	Boston Braves	C 1B 2B	Zack Taylor Jimmy Johnston Eddie Brown
Nov 9, 1925	SS	Rabbit Maranville	Chicago Cubs		Waiver price
Jan 1926	2B	Chick Fewster	Cleveland Indians		Cash
April 1926	3B	Bill Marriott	Boston Braves		Cash
June 15, 1926	2B	Sammy Bohne	Cincinnati Reds		Cash
Aug 13, 1926	OF	Max Carey	Pittsburgh Pirates		Waiver price
Nov 5, 1926		Cash	Boston Braves	1B	Jack Fournier

DATE		ACQUIRED	FROM		IN EXCHANGE FOR
Dec 1926		Cash	Washington Senators	C	Mickey O'Neil
Jan 9, 1927	C	Butch Henline	New York Giants	P	Burleigh Grimes
		(Part of three-team trade involving Brooklyn, New York, and Philadelphia.)			
Feb 28, 1927	2B	Jake Flowers	St. Louis Cardinals	P	Bob McGraw
Dec 1927	SS	Howard Freigau	Chicago Cubs	3B	Johnny Butler
March 13, 1928	OF	Rube Bressler	Cincinnati Reds		Waiver price
June 8, 1928	1B C	Joe Harris Johnny Gooch	Pittsburgh Pirates	C	Charlie Hargreaves
June 23, 1928		Cash	Boston Braves	SS	Howard Freigau
Dec 9, 1928	P	Vic Aldridge	New York Giants		Waiver price
		(Aldridge refused to report and retired.)			
Dec 11, 1928	SS	Glenn Wright	Pittsburgh Pirates	P 2B	Jesse Petty Harry Riconda
April 18, 1929	C	Val Picinich	Cincinnati Reds	C P	Johnny Gooch Rube Ehrhardt
May 14, 1929	P	Alex Ferguson	Philadelphia Phillies		Cash
July 4, 1929	P	Kent Greenfield	Boston Braves		Cash
July 24, 1929	P	Luther Roy	Philadelphia Phillies	P	Lou Koupal
Feb 1930	P	Dolf Luque	Cincinnati Reds	P	Doug McWeeny
Oct 14, 1930	OF 2B	Lefty O'Doul Fresco Thompson	Philadelphia Phillies	P P OF	Clise Dudley Jumbo Elliott Hal Lee and cash
May 7, 1931	1B	Mickey Heath	Cincinnati Reds	OF	Harvey Hendrick
May 28, 1931		Cash	Boston Braves	P	Ray Moss
June 15, 1931		Waiver price	St. Louis Cardinals	2B	Jake Flowers
Jan 23, 1932	OF	Hack Wilson	St. Louis Cardinals		Minor league P Bob Parham and $45,000.
March 14, 1932	2B 3B C	Tony Cuccinello Joe Stripp Clyde Sukeforth	Cincinnati Reds	OF 3B C	Babe Herman Wally Gilbert Ernie Lombardi
May 7, 1932	OF	Danny Taylor	Chicago Cubs		Cash
Dec 15, 1932	P	Ray Benge and $15,000.	Philadelphia Phillies	P 2B 3B	Cy Moore Mickey Finn Jack Warner

DATE		ACQUIRED	FROM		IN EXCHANGE FOR
Dec 1932		Waiver price	New York Giants	C	Paul Richards
Feb 1933	2B P	Jake Flowers Ownie Carroll	St. Louis Cardinals	P SS	Dazzy Vance Gordon Slade
June 16, 1933	1B	Sam Leslie	New York Giants	OF P	Lefty O'Doul Watty Clark
June 23, 1933		Cash	Pittsburgh Pirates	C	Val Picinich
Dec 1933	P	Art Herring	Detroit Tigers		Cash
Dec 1933		Cash	Cincinnati Reds	P	Joe Shaute
May 16, 1934	P	George Earnshaw	Chicago White Sox		Cash
May 30, 1934	P	Harry Smythe	New York Yankees		Waiver price
June 12, 1934	P	Tom Zachary	Boston Braves		Waiver price
Dec 31, 1934	C	Babe Phelps	Chicago Cubs		Waiver price
Dec 12, 1935	P OF	Ed Brandt Randy Moore	Boston Braves	2B C P OF	Tony Cuccinello Al Lopez Ray Benge Bobby Reis
Jan 1936		$40,000.	New York Giants	1B	Johnny McCarthy
Jan 1936	1B	Buddy Hassett	New York Yankees		Cash
Feb 6, 1936	P	Fred Frankhouse	Boston Braves	P OF	Johnny Babich Gene Moore
Feb 20, 1936		Cash	New York Giants	1B	Sam Leslie
May 1936	OF	George Watkins	Philadelphia Phillies		Cash
July 1936		Cash	St. Louis Cardinals	P	George Earnshaw
Dec 3, 1936	OF	Tom Winsett	St. Louis Cardinals	OF	Frenchy Bordagaray
Dec 4, 1936	3B P	Cookie Lavagetto Ralph Birkofer	Pittsburgh Pirates	P	Ed Brandt
Dec 5, 1936	P SS	Roy Henshaw Woody English	Chicago Cubs	2B	Lonny Frey
June 11, 1937	P	Freddie Fitzsimmons	New York Giants	P	Tom Baker
July 1937		Cash	St. Louis Cardinals	OF	Randy Moore
Aug 9, 1937	P	Ben Cantwell	New York Giants		Cash
Oct 4, 1937	SS	Leo Durocher	St. Louis Cardinals	OF 2B 3B P	Johnny Cooney Jim Bucher Joe Stripp Roy Henshaw

DATE		ACQUIRED	FROM		IN EXCHANGE FOR
March 6, 1938	1B	Dolf Camilli	Philadelphia Phillies	1B	Eddie Morgan and $45,000.
April 15, 1938	OF	Ernie Koy	New York Yankees		Cash
May 1938		Waiver price	Pittsburgh Pirates	OF	Heinie Manush
May 1938	P	Vito Tamulis	St. Louis Browns		Waiver price
July 8, 1938		Cash	Cincinnati Reds	SS	Woody English
July 11, 1938	OF	Tuck Stainback	Philadelphia Phillies	OF	Gib Brack
Aug 8, 1938	P	Wayne LaMaster	Philadelphia Phillies	P	Max Butcher
Sept 14, 1938	C	Ray Hayworth	Detroit Tigers		Waiver price
Sept 14, 1938	3B	Don Ross	Detroit Tigers		Cash
Dec 13, 1938	OF	Jimmy Outlaw	Cincinnati Reds		Cash
Dec 13, 1938	OF P	Gene Moore Ira Hutchinson	Boston Braves	OF 1B	Jimmy Outlaw Buddy Hassett
Dec 19, 1938	C	Luke Sewell	Chicago White Sox		Cash
Jan 1939	P	Boots Poffenberger	Detroit Tigers		Waiver price
Feb 3, 1939	P	Fred Frankhouse	Boston Braves	OF	Gene Moore
March 31, 1939	C	Al Todd	Boston Braves	P	Bill Posedel
March 1939	P	Jim Winford	St. Louis Cardinals		Waiver price
May 3, 1939	SS	Lyn Lary	Cleveland Indians		Cash
May 5, 1939	P	Gene Schott	Cincinnati Reds		Cash
June 15, 1939	OF	Mel Almada	St. Louis Browns		$25,000.
July 24, 1939	OF	Dixie Walker	Detroit Tigers		Waiver price
Aug 12, 1939	P	Al Hollingsworth	New York Yankees		Cash
Aug 14, 1939		Waiver price	St. Louis Cardinals	SS	Lyn Lary
Aug 23, 1939	OF	Jimmy Ripple	New York Giants	C	Ray Hayworth
Dec 8, 1939	C	Gus Mancuso	Chicago Cubs	C	Al Todd
Dec 26, 1939	2B	Boze Berger	Boston Red Sox		Waiver price

DATE		ACQUIRED	FROM		IN EXCHANGE FOR
Feb 6, 1940	C	Herman Franks	St. Louis Cardinals		Cash
Feb 12, 1940	OF	Joe Vosmik	Boston Red Sox		$25,000.
April 15, 1940		Cash (Sale was cancelled by Commissioner Landis.)	St. Louis Cardinals	P	Newt Kimball
May 15, 1940	P	Lee Grissom	New York Yankees		Waiver price
May 25, 1940	1B	Jimmy Wasdell	Washington Senators		Cash
May 27, 1940	OF	Joe Gallagher	St. Louis Browns	OF	Roy Cullenbine
May 29, 1940		Cash	Boston Braves	OF	Gene Moore
June 12, 1940	OF P	Joe Medwick Curt Davis	St. Louis Cardinals	OF P P 1B	Ernie Koy Carl Doyle Sam Nahem Bert Haas and $125,000.
June 13, 1940		Cash	St. Louis Cardinals	P	Ira Hutchinson
July 1940	P	Lou Fette	Boston Braves		Cash
Aug 23, 1940		Waiver price	Cincinnati Reds	OF	Jimmy Ripple
Nov 11, 1940	P	Kirby Higbe	Philadelphia Phillies	P P C	Vito Tamulis Bill Crouch Mickey Livingston and $100,000.
Nov 19, 1940		Cash	St. Louis Cardinals	P	Tot Pressnell
Dec 4, 1940	C	Mickey Owen	St. Louis Cardinals	C	Gus Mancuso Minor league P John Pintar and $65,000.
Dec 9, 1940	3B	Lew Riggs	Cincinnati Reds	2B	Pep Young
Feb 5, 1941	P	Lefty Mills	St. Louis Browns		Cash
April 22, 1941	P	Mace Brown	Pittsburgh Pirates		Cash
May 6, 1941	P	Vito Tamulis	Philadelphia Phillies	P	Lee Grissom
May 6, 1941	3B	Billy Herman	Chicago Cubs	2B OF	Johnny Hudson Charlie Gilbert and $65,000.
Aug 20, 1941	P	Larry French	Chicago Cubs		Waiver price
Dec 10, 1941	OF	Don Padgett	St. Louis Cardinals		$30,000.
Dec 10, 1941		Cash	Boston Red Sox	P	Mace Brown

DATE		ACQUIRED	FROM		IN EXCHANGE FOR
Dec 10, 1941	OF	Johnny Rizzo	Philadelphia Phillies		Cash
Dec 12, 1941	3B	Arky Vaughan	Pittsburgh Pirates	2B P C 1B	Pete Coscarart Luke Hamlin Babe Phelps Jimmy Wasdell
Feb 24, 1942	OF	Gene Moore	New York Yankees		Cash
March 13, 1942	C	Billy Sullivan	Detroit Tigers		Cash
April 30, 1942	P	Schoolboy Rowe	Detroit Tigers		Cash
May 19, 1942	1B	Babe Dahlgren	Chicago Cubs		Cash
Aug 30, 1942	P	Bobo Newsom	Washington Senators		$25,000.
Aug 31, 1942		Cash	Washington Senators	OF	Gene Moore
Dec 12, 1942	P	Rube Melton	Philadelphia Phillies	P	Johnny Allen and $30,000.
Feb 1, 1943	2B	Steve Mesner	Cincinnati Reds		Waiver price
		(Landis voided the sale because Mesner had already been drafted at the time of the deal.)			
March 8, 1943	OF	Roberto Ortiz	Philadelphia Phillies		Cash
March 9, 1943	OF 2B	Lloyd Waner Al Glossop	Philadelphia Phillies	1B	Babe Dahlgren
March 24, 1943		Cash	Philadelphia Phillies	P	Schoolboy Rowe
March 24, 1943	C	Bobby Bragan	Philadelphia Phillies	P	Tex Kraus and cash
April 22, 1943	P P	Johnny Allen George Washburn	Philadelphia Phillies		Cash
May 15, 1943		Cash	Chicago Cubs	OF	Hal Peck
May 20, 1943		Cash	Washington Senators	3B	Alex Kampouris
May 20, 1943		Cash	Philadelphia Phillies	P	Newt Kimball
July 6, 1943		Cash	New York Giants	OF	Joe Medwick
July 15, 1943	P P	Fritz Ostermueller Archie McKain	St. Louis Browns	P	Bobo Newsom
July 31, 1943	P P IF	Bill Lohrman Bill Sayles Joe Orengo	New York Giants	1B P	Dolf Camilli Johnny Allen
		(Camilli refused to report to New York and retired.)			
Sept 28, 1943		Cash	Chicago Cubs	2B	Al Glossop
June 6, 1944	2B	Eddie Stanky	Chicago Cubs	P	Bob Chipman

DATE		ACQUIRED	FROM		IN EXCHANGE FOR
March 28, 1945		$20,000.	Philadelphia Phillies	P	Whit Wyatt
June 15, 1945	C	Johnny Peacock	Philadelphia Phillies	OF	Ben Chapman
March 18, 1946		Cash	Cincinnati Reds	SS	Claude Corbitt
April 27, 1946		Cash	New York Giants	OF	Goody Rosen
May 1946		Cash	New York Giants	OF	Jack Graham
June 12, 1946		Cash	Boston Braves	C	Don Padgett
June 15, 1946	C	Stew Hofferth	Boston Braves	2B	Billy Herman
Oct 19, 1946		Cash	Pittsburgh Pirates	P	Art Herring
Dec 4, 1946	P	Ed Heusser	Cincinnati Reds	OF	Augie Galan
Dec 5, 1946	P	Al Gerheauser	Pittsburgh Pirates	SS	Eddie Basinski
Jan 30, 1947	OF	Walter Sessi	St. Louis Cardinals		Cash
May 3, 1947	OF	Al Gionfriddo and $100,000.	Pittsburgh Pirates	P P P IF C	Kirby Higbe Hank Behrman Cal McLish Gene Mauch Dixie Howell
May 10, 1947		Cash	Philadelphia Phillies	1B	Howie Schultz
May 13, 1947		Cash	Cincinnati Reds	OF	Tommy Tatum
June 14, 1947	P	Hank Behrman	Pittsburgh Pirates		Cash
Nov 14, 1947		Cash	Pittsburgh Pirates	1B	Ed Stevens
Nov 14, 1947		Cash	Pittsburgh Pirates	SS	Stan Rojek
Dec 8, 1947	P 3B SS	Preacher Roe Billy Cox Gene Mauch	Pittsburgh Pirates	OF P P	Dixie Walker Hal Gregg Vic Lombardi
March 6, 1948	2B 1B	Bama Rowell Ray Sanders and $40,000.	Boston Braves	2B	Eddie Stanky
April 15, 1948		Waiver price	Philadelphia Phillies	2B	Bama Rowell
April 19, 1948		$60,000.	Boston Braves	1B	Ray Sanders
June 17, 1948		Waiver price	Chicago Cubs	SS	Gene Mauch
June 28, 1948		Waiver price	St. Louis Browns	OF	Don Lund

DATE		ACQUIRED	FROM		IN EXCHANGE FOR
Dec 15, 1948	OF	Mike McCormick	Boston Braves	OF	Pete Reiser
May 16, 1949	2B	Hank Schenz	Chicago Cubs	3B	Bob Ramazzotti
May 18, 1949	OF	Johnny Hopp and $25,000. (Trade was cancelled on June 7, 1949.)	Pittsburgh Pirates	OF	Marv Rackley
Sept 14, 1949		Cash	Philadelphia Phillies	OF	Dick Whitman
Oct 14, 1949		$100,000.	Chicago Cubs	P 1B	Paul Minner Preston Ward
Nov 4, 1949		Cash	Pittsburgh Pirates	2B	Hank Schenz
Dec 24, 1949	OF OF	Jim Russell Ed Sauer and cash	Boston Braves	OF	Luis Olmo
May 10, 1950		Cash	Cincinnati Reds	P	Willie Ramsdell
Oct 10, 1950	OF	Hank Edwards and cash	Chicago Cubs	1B 1B	Chuck Connors Dee Fondy
June 8, 1951	OF	Dick Whitman and cash	Philadelphia Phillies	OF	Tommy Brown
June 15, 1951	P C OF 3B	Johnny Schmitz Rube Walker Andy Pafko Wayne Terwilliger	Chicago Cubs	C P 2B OF	Bruce Edwards Joe Hatten Eddie Miksis Gene Hermanski
July 21, 1951		Waiver price	Cincinnati Reds	OF	Hank Edwards
May 25, 1952		Waiver price	Cincinnati Reds	P	Phil Haugstad
June 9, 1952	SS	Rudy Rufer and cash	Cincinnati Reds	OF	Cal Abrams
June 15, 1952	P	Bud Byerly and cash	Cincinnati Reds	P	Bud Podbielan
Aug 1, 1952		Waiver price	New York Yankees	P	Johnny Schmitz
Sept 23, 1952		Waiver price	Washington Senators	3B	Wayne Terwilliger
Oct 10, 1952		Cash	Cincinnati Reds	P	Clyde King
Oct 14, 1952	P SS OF	Bob Mahoney Stan Rojek Ray Coleman and $90,000.	St. Louis Browns	SS	Billy Hunter
Jan 17, 1953	2B	Roy Hartsfield and $50,000.	Milwaukee Braves	OF	Andy Pafko
Feb 16, 1953	P	Russ Meyer (Part of four-team trade involving Milwaukee, Philadelphia Phillies, Brooklyn, and Cincinnati.)	Milwaukee Braves	IF OF	Rocky Bridges Jim Pendleton
May 26, 1953		Waiver price	Washington Senators	OF	Carmen Mauro

DATE		ACQUIRED	FROM		IN EXCHANGE FOR
July 10, 1953		Waiver price	Detroit Tigers	P	Ralph Branca
March 28, 1954	2B	Dick Young and $50,000.	Philadelphia Phillies	IF	Bobby Morgan
June 9, 1954	1B C P	Charlie Kress Johnny Bucha Ernie Nevel and cash	Detroit Tigers	1B	Wayne Belardi
Aug 8, 1954		Waiver price	St. Louis Cardinals	P	Ben Wade
Dec 13, 1954		Minor leaguers John Jancse and Harry Schwegeman and $50,000.	Baltimore Orioles	3B P	Billy Cox Preacher Roe
March 17, 1955	1B	Frank Kellert and cash	Baltimore Orioles	P	Erv Palica
June 9, 1955	OF	Bob Borkowski and cash	Cincinnati Reds	P	Joe Black
Sept 12, 1955		Waiver price	Kansas City Athletics	P	Glenn Cox
Oct 11, 1955		Waiver price	Chicago Cubs	1B	Frank Kellert
Dec 9, 1955	3B P	Randy Jackson Don Elston	Chicago Cubs	3B P OF	Don Hoak Russ Meyer Walt Moryn
April 16, 1956	P OF	Lee Wheat Tom Saffell and cash	Kansas City Athletics	C	Tim Thompson
May 14, 1956		$20,000.	Baltimore Orioles	P	Billy Loes
May 15, 1956	P	Sal Maglie	Cleveland Indians		Cash
May 15, 1956		Cash	Chicago Cubs	P	Jim Hughes
June 25, 1956		Waiver price	Baltimore Orioles	OF	Dick Williams
July 29, 1956	OF	Dale Mitchell	Cleveland Indians		Cash
July 30, 1956		Waiver price	St. Louis Cardinals	1B	Rocky Nelson
Dec 13, 1956	P	Dick Littlefield and $30,000. (Trade was cancelled when Robinson retired.)	New York Giants	2B	Jackie Robinson
April 5, 1957	P 1B OF	Ron Negray Tim Harkness Elmer Valo minor league SS Mel Geho and $75,000.	Philadelphia Phillies	SS	Chico Fernandez
May 20, 1957	3B	Bob Kennedy	Chicago White Sox		Cash
May 23, 1957	P	Don Elston	Chicago Cubs	P P	Jackie Collum Vito Valentinetti

DATE	ACQUIRED	FROM		IN EXCHANGE FOR
June 4, 1957	$30,000.	Baltimore Orioles	P	Ken Lehman
Sept 1, 1957	Waiver price	New York Yankees	P	Sal Maglie

Chicago Cubs

The Best Trades

1. Acquired Three Finger Brown and Jack O'Neill from the St. Louis Cardinals for Jack Taylor and Larry McLean, November 12, 1903.
2. Acquired Grover Alexander and Bill Killefer from the Philadelphia Phillies for Mike Prendergast, Pickles Dillhoefer, and $55,000, December 11, 1917.
3. Acquired Randy Hundley and Bill Hands from the San Francisco Giants for Lindy McDaniel, Don Landrum, and Jim Rittwage, December 2, 1965.
4. Acquired Ferguson Jenkins, Adolfo Phillips, and John Herrnstein from the Philadelphia Phillies for Larry Jackson and Bob Buhl, April 21, 1966.
5. Acquired Kiki Cuyler from the Pittsburgh Pirates for Sparky Adams and Pete Scott, November 28, 1927.

The Worst Trades

1. Traded Lou Brock, Paul Toth, and Jack Spring to the St. Louis Cardinals for Ernie Broglio, Bobby Shantz, and Doug Clemens, June 15, 1964.
2. Traded Ron Davis to the New York Yankees for Ken Holtzman, June 10, 1978.
3. Traded Dolf Camilli to the Philadelphia Phillies for Don Hurst, June 11, 1934.
4. Traded Ron Perranoski, Lee Handley, John Goryl, and $25,000 to the Los Angeles Dodgers for Don Zimmer, April 8, 1960.
5. Traded two players to be named later (Bill Caudill, April 1, 1982, and Jay Howell, August 2, 1982) to the New York Yankees for Pat Tabler, August 19, 1981.

Trades: Disasters, Fiascos, and Assorted Imbroglios

During the winter of 1935, the Cubs' management was approached by Charles Graham, owner of the San Francisco Seals of the Pacific Coast League. Graham had a young centerfielder he was trying to peddle for $25,000. William Wrigley, the Cubs' owner, was aware that the youngster had sustained a knee injury that limited his playing time in '34, and wondered whether the injury would have a long-term affect on his ability to play every day.

"Take him on trial," suggested Graham. "Give us a couple of players and a down payment. Keep him until July and give him a thorough looking-over. If you're not satisfied then, the deal's off."

But Wrigley's misgivings prevailed. Even with a money-back guarantee, the Cubs weren't willing to take a chance. The outfielder, Joe DiMaggio, went on to a moderately successful career elsewhere.

By comparison, then, the infamous Lou Brock deal doesn't look all that bad. True, a pitcher who would go on to a 7–19 record in his three years with the Cubs isn't much return for a sure Hall of Famer at age twenty-five, but at least the Cubs were willing to look at Brock before giving him away.

Not all of the Cubs' deals have been disastrous. The cornerstones of their pennant-contending team of the late 1960s came over in two very shrewd trades: Bill Hands and Randy Hundley were acquired from the Giants for Lindy McDaniel and Don Landrum, and Ferguson Jenkins and Adolfo Phillips came from the Phillies for Larry Jackson and Bob Buhl. When Jenkins asked to be traded eight years later, the Cubs received in return a group of players including Bill Madlock. When the time came to deal Rick Monday, they received Bill Buckner and Ivan DeJesus from the Dodgers. In each of these deals, the Cubs traded a player of known but limited value for good young players with the chance to become great ones. The trade of Bruce Sutter for Leon Durham, Ken Reitz and Ty Waller was another deal of this type.

But taken as a whole, the accumulation of deals has kept the club down. Brock for Ernie Broglio. Ron Perranoski for Don Zimmer. Tony Taylor for Ed Bouchee. Ray Culp for Bill Schlesinger. Ken Holtzman for Rick Monday. Ron Davis for an over-the-hill Ken Holtzman. Bill North for Bob Locker. Bill Madlock for Bobby Murcer. Burt Hooton for Eddie Solomon and Geoff Zahn. The good deals they have made have been more than offset by the bad ones, and that fact, as much as any fatiguing effect of playing all their home games in the heat of the afternoon, has kept the Cubs out of the World Series since 1945.

DATE		ACQUIRED	FROM		IN EXCHANGE FOR
Unknown	P	Frank Killen	Boston Braves		Cash
Jan 1900	P	Bert Cunningham	Pittsburgh Pirates		Cash
Jan 1900	2B	Cupid Childs	St. Louis Cardinals		Cash
Jan 1900	OF	Charlie Dexter	Louisville Colonels		Cash
Jan 1900	SS	Billy Clingman	Washington Senators		Cash
Feb 10, 1900	OF	Jack McCarthy	Pittsburgh Pirates		$2,000.
April 28, 1900		Cash	Philadelphia Phillies	3B	Harry Wolverton
Feb 1901		Cash	New York Giants	1B	John Ganzel
Feb 1901	1B	Jack Doyle	New York Giants	3B	Sammy Strang
April 1901	OF C	Topsy Hartsel Mike Kahoe	Cincinnati Reds		Cash
May 1901	P	Rube Waddell	Pittsburgh Pirates		Cash
June 1901		Cash	Brooklyn Dodgers	OF	Cozy Dolan
Feb 1902		Cash	New York Giants	1B OF	Jack Doyle Jim Delahanty
April 1902		Cash	Boston Braves	P	Mal Eason
July 1902	OF	Jack Hendricks	New York Giants	C	Hal O'Hagan

DATE		ACQUIRED	FROM		IN EXCHANGE FOR
July 1902	2B	Bobby Lowe	Boston Braves	3B	Charlie Dexter
July 1902	OF	John Dobbs	Cincinnati Reds		Cash
March 1903		Cash	Brooklyn Dodgers	3B	Sammy Strang
April 1903	P	Bob Wicker	St. Louis Cardinals	P	Bob Rhoads
April 1903		Cash	Philadelphia Phillies	P	Pop Williams
May 1903		Cash	Brooklyn Dodgers	OF	John Dobbs
June 1903		Cash	Brooklyn Dodgers	P	Jack Doscher
July 1903	SS	Otto Williams	St. Louis Cardinals		Cash
July 1903	P	Clarence Currie	St. Louis Cardinals		Cash
Dec 12, 1903	P C	Three Finger Brown Jack O'Neill	St. Louis Cardinals	P C	Jack Taylor Larry McLean
Jan 1904	OF	Solly Hofman	Pittsburgh Pirates		Cash
April 20, 1904		Cash	Pittsburgh Pirates	2B	Bobby Lowe
July 20, 1904	2B	Shad Barry	Philadelphia Phillies	P P	Frank Corridon Jack Sutthoff
May 20, 1905		Cash	Cincinnati Reds	2B	Shad Barry
Dec 30, 1905	OF	Jimmy Sheckard	Brooklyn Dodgers	OF OF 3B P	Billy Maloney Jack McCarthy Doc Casey Buttons Briggs and $2,000.
Jan 1906		Waiver price	Boston Braves	C	Jack O'Neill
Jan 1906		Cash	Boston Braves	P	Big Jeff Pfeffer
Feb 1906	C	Pat Moran	Boston Braves		Cash
March 1906	3B	Harry Steinfeldt	Cincinnati Reds	3B P	Hans Lobert Jake Weimer
May 8, 1906	OF	Doc Gessler	Brooklyn Dodgers		Cash
June 2, 1906	P	Orval Overall	Cincinnati Reds	P	Bob Wicker and $2,000.
July 1, 1906	P	Jack Taylor	St. Louis Cardinals	P C	Fred Beebe Pete Noonan and cash
Oct 1906	P	Jack Harper	Cincinnati Reds	P	Chick Fraser

DATE		ACQUIRED	FROM		IN EXCHANGE FOR
June 24, 1907	OF	Del Howard	Boston Braves	2B OF	Bill Sweeney Newt Randall
June 27, 1907		Cash	Washington Senators	C	Mike Kahoe
June 1908	C	Doc Marshall	St. Louis Cardinals		Cash
Sept 1908	P	Andy Coakley	Cincinnati Reds		Cash
Sept 1908	OF	George Browne	Boston Braves		Cash
Oct 1908	OF	John Kane	Cincinnati Reds		Cash
Nov 1908		Waiver price	Brooklyn Dodgers	C	Doc Marshall
Dec 1908	C	Tom Needham	New York Giants		Cash
May 20, 1909	P	Pat Ragan	Cincinnati Reds		Cash
May 21, 1909		Waiver price	Washington Senators	OF	George Browne
Jan 1910		Cash	Pittsburgh Pirates	OF	Vin Campbell
Feb 1910	OF	Ginger Beaumont	Boston Braves	OF	Fred Liese
April 1910	P	Lew Richie	Boston Braves	OF	Doc Miller
July 1910	P	Bill Foxen	Philadelphia Phillies	1B	Fred Luderus
Jan 1911	2B	Dave Shean	Boston Braves	3B P	Scotty Ingerton Big Jeff Pfeffer
March 1911		Cash	Boston Braves	3B	Harry Steinfeldt
April 1911	P	Charlie Smith	Boston Red Sox		Cash
May 1911	P	Lefty Leifield	Pittsburgh Pirates		Cash
June 10, 1911	P OF 2B	Cliff Curtis Wilbur Good Bill Collins	Boston Braves	C C P	Johnny Kling Al Kaiser Orlie Weaver
June 1911	C	Jimmy Austin	Boston Braves	P	Hank Griffin
Aug 9, 1911	1B	Kitty Bransfield	Philadelphia Phillies		Cash
Aug 1911	P	Jack Rowan	Philadelphia Phillies	P	Cliff Curtis
Oct 1911		Cash	Boston Braves	SS	Dave Shean
Oct 1911	C	Dick Cotter	Philadelphia Phillies	C	Peaches Graham
Jan 1912	P	Ensign Cottrell	Pittsburgh Pirates		Cash

DATE		ACQUIRED	FROM		IN EXCHANGE FOR
May 1912	2B	Red Downs	Brooklyn Dodgers		Cash
June 22, 1912	OF P	Tommy Leach Lefty Leifield	Pittsburgh Pirates	P OF	King Cole Solly Hofman
Aug 1912	3B	Tom Downey	Philadelphia Phillies		Cash
Nov 1912	SS	Al Bridwell	Boston Braves		Cash
Dec 15, 1912	P IF OF 3B OF	Bert Humphries Red Corriden Pete Knisely Art Phelan Mike Mitchell	Cincinnati Reds	SS P C	Joe Tinker Grover Lowdermilk Harry Chapman
April 1913		Cash	St. Louis Cardinals	OF	Jimmy Sheckard
May 1913		Waiver price	Brooklyn Dodgers	C	Mike Hechinger
June 8, 1913	C	Roger Bresnahan	St. Louis Cardinals		Cash
July 29, 1913		Waiver price	Pittsburgh Pirates	OF	Mike Mitchell
July 1913		Cash	Boston Braves	OF	Otis Clymer
July 1913	P	Earl Moore	Philadelphia Phillies		Cash
Aug 14, 1913	P	Eddie Stack and cash	Brooklyn Dodgers	P	Ed Reulbach
Sept 23, 1913	P	George McConnell	New York Yankees		Cash
Feb 1914	2B	Bill Sweeney and cash	Boston Braves	2B	Johnny Evers
June 1914	P	Casey Hageman	Brooklyn Dodgers		Cash
July 20, 1914	SS	Claud Derrick	Cincinnati Reds	1B	Fritz Mollwitz
Aug 1914	OF	Johnny Bates	Cincinnati Reds	P	Elmer Koestner
July 1915	SS	Alex McCarthy	Pittsburgh Pirates		Cash
Aug 8, 1915		Cash	Philadelphia Phillies	P	Bert Humphries
Aug 1915	3B	Joe Schultz and $3,000.	Brooklyn Dodgers	P	Larry Cheney
Sept 8, 1915	P	Phil Douglas	Brooklyn Dodgers		Cash
Jan 1916		Cash	Cincinnati Reds	SS	Bob Fisher

DATE		ACQUIRED	FROM		IN EXCHANGE FOR
Jan 1916		Cash	Pittsburgh Pirates	OF	Joe Schultz
Feb 3, 1916		Cash	Philadelphia Phillies	OF	Wilbur Good
Feb 10, 1916	C	Nick Allen	Buffalo (Federal League)		Cash
Feb 10, 1916	P C SS C OF P OF P SS UT P	Three Finger Brown Clem Clemens Mickey Doolan Bill Fischer Max Flack Claude Hendrix Les Mann Dykes Potter Joe Tinker Rollie Zeider George McConnell	Chicago (Federal League)		Cash
Feb 10, 1916	P	Tom Seaton	Newark (Federal League)		Cash
Feb 10, 1916	2B	Steve Yerkes	Pittsburgh (Federal League)		Cash
Feb 10, 1916	P SS	Gene Packard Charlie Pechous	Kansas City Athletics		Cash
June 2, 1916	3B	Charlie Deal	St. Louis Browns		Cash
July 22, 1916	1B	Fritz Mollwitz	Cincinnati Reds		Cash
July 29, 1916	C 2B	Art Wilson Otto Knabe	Pittsburgh Pirates	OF C	Wildfire Schulte Bill Fischer
July 1916		Cash	Pittsburgh Pirates	IF	Alex McCarthy
Aug 28, 1916	2B OF OF	Larry Doyle Herb Hunter Merwin Jacobson	New York Giants	3B SS	Heinie Zimmerman Mickey Doolan
Jan 1917	C	Earl Blackburn	Boston Braves	OF	Joe Kelly
Feb 4, 1917		Cash	Pittsburgh Pirates	1B	Fritz Mollwitz
April 2, 1917	P	Al Demaree	Philadelphia Phillies	P	Jimmy Lavender and $5,000.
April 26, 1917		Waiver price	Cincinnati Reds	P	Scott Perry
April 1917		Cash	St. Louis Cardinals	P	Gene Packard
July 17, 1917		Waiver price	Cincinnati Reds	P	Dutch Ruether
Aug 15, 1917	2B	Pete Kilduff	New York Giants	P	Al Demaree
Aug 16, 1917	1B	Fred Merkle	Brooklyn Dodgers		$3,500.
Aug 1917		Cash	Pittsburgh Pirates	OF	Harry Wolfe

DATE		ACQUIRED	FROM		IN EXCHANGE FOR
Dec 11, 1917	P C	Grover Alexander Bill Killefer	Philadelphia Phillies	P C	Mike Prendergast Pickles Dillhoefer and $55,000.
Dec 26, 1917	OF	Dode Paskert	Philadelphia Phillies	OF	Cy Williams
Dec 1917		Cash	Pittsburgh Pirates	C	Jimmy Archer
Jan 4, 1918	P	Lefty Tyler	Boston Braves	2B C	Larry Doyle Art Wilson and $15,000.
June 2, 1919	IF	Lee Magee	Brooklyn Dodgers	2B	Pete Kilduff
July 25, 1919	OF	Dave Robertson	New York Giants	P	Phil Douglas
Aug 1919	2B	Buck Herzog	Boston Braves	OF 3B	Les Mann Charlie Pick
Jan 1920	2B	Zeb Terry	Pittsburgh Pirates		Cash
Feb 1920		Cash	New York Giants	3B	Fred Lear
May 1920		Cash	Brooklyn Dodgers	SS	Bill McCabe
Dec 1920		Waiver price	Cincinnati Reds	OF	Dode Paskert
May 1921		Cash	Brooklyn Dodgers	P	Sweetbreads Bailey
July 1, 1921	P	Elmer Ponder	Pittsburgh Pirates	OF	Dave Robertson
Sept 1921	OF	John Sullivan	Boston Braves		Cash
May 30, 1922	OF	Cliff Heathcote	St. Louis Cardinals	OF	Max Flack
Jan 2, 1923		Cash	Brooklyn Dodgers	OF	Turner Barber
Jan 1924		Cash	Boston Braves	SS	John Kelleher
May 16, 1924		Cash	Brooklyn Dodgers	P	Tiny Osborne
Oct 27, 1924	1B 2B P	Charlie Grimm Rabbit Maranville Wilbur Cooper	Pittsburgh Pirates	P 2B 1B	Vic Aldridge George Grantham Al Niehaus
May 10, 1925	OF	Tommy Griffith	Brooklyn Dodgers	3B	Bob Barrett
May 23, 1925	C OF	Mike Gonzalez Howard Freigau	St. Louis Cardinals	C	Bob O'Farrell
June 15, 1925		Waiver price	Philadelphia Phillies	SS	Barney Friberg
Nov 9, 1925		Waiver price	Brooklyn Dodgers	SS	Rabbit Maranville

DATE		ACQUIRED	FROM		IN EXCHANGE FOR
Dec 11, 1925	SS	Jimmy Cooney	St. Louis Cardinals	P	Vic Keen
June 7, 1927	P	Hal Carlson	Philadelphia Phillies	P SS	Tony Kaufmann Jimmy Cooney
June 7, 1926		Waiver price	Detroit Tigers	P	Wilbur Cooper
June 21, 1926	P	Walter Huntzinger	St. Louis Cardinals		Waiver price
June 22, 1926		Waiver price	St. Louis Cardinals	P	Grover Alexander
June 14, 1927	P	Wayland Dean	Philadelphia Phillies		Cash
July 12, 1927	3B	Fred Haney	Boston Red Sox		Cash
Sept 4, 1927	P	Art Nehf	Cincinnati Reds		Cash
Nov 28, 1927	OF	Kiki Cuyler	Pittsburgh Pirates	3B OF	Sparky Adams Pete Scott
Dec 1927	P	Mike Cvengros	Pittsburgh Pirates	P	Fred Fussell
Dec 1927	3B	Johnny Butler	Brooklyn Dodgers	SS	Howard Freigau
Nov 7, 1928	2B	Rogers Hornsby	Boston Braves	P P C 2B P	Socks Seibold Percy Jones Lou Legett Freddie Maguire Bruce Cunningham and $200,000.
Feb 1929	C	Johnny Schulte	Philadelphia Phillies		Cash
July 6, 1929	C	Zack Taylor	Boston Braves		Waiver price
Oct 29, 1929	3B	Les Bell	Boston Braves		Waiver price
June 29, 1930	IF	Doc Farrell	St. Louis Cardinals		Waiver price
Aug 24, 1930	P	Jesse Petty	Pittsburgh Pirates		Cash
Oct 13, 1930	P	Les Sweetland	Philadelphia Phillies		Cash
Oct 14, 1930	P OF	Bob Smith Jimmy Welsh	Boston Braves	P OF	Bill McAfee Wes Schulmerich
Oct 14, 1930	P	Jakie May	Cincinnati Reds		Cash
Jan 1931		Waiver price	Cincinnati Reds	3B	Clyde Beck
Jan 1931		Cash	Pittsburgh Pirates	P	Bob Osborn
April 1, 1931		Waiver price	Cincinnati Reds	OF	Cliff Heathcote
June 13, 1931	C	Rollie Hemsley	Pittsburgh Pirates	C	Earl Grace

DATE	ACQUIRED		FROM	IN EXCHANGE FOR	
July 27, 1931		Waiver price	Philadelphia Phillies	P	Sheriff Blake
Dec 17, 1931	OF	Lance Richbourg	Boston Braves		Waiver price
Dec 1931	P	Burleigh Grimes	St. Louis Cardinals	P OF	Bud Teachout Hack Wilson
May 7, 1932		Cash	Brooklyn Dodgers	OF	Danny Taylor
Nov 30, 1932	OF	Babe Herman	Cincinnati Reds	P C OF OF	Bob Smith Rollie Hemsley Johnny Moore Lance Richbourg
April 29, 1933	OF	Taylor Douthit	Cincinnati Reds		Waiver price
Aug 4, 1933		Waiver price	St. Louis Cardinals	P	Burleigh Grimes
Nov 21, 1933	OF	Chuck Klein	Philadelphia Phillies	P SS OF	Ted Kleinhans Chief Hogsett Harvey Hendrick and $65,000.
May 15, 1934	P	Jim Weaver	St. Louis Browns		Waiver price
June 11, 1934	1B	Don Hurst	Philadelphia Phillies	1B	Dolf Camilli
Oct 26, 1934	C	Ken O'Dea	St. Louis Cardinals	P	Pat Malone
Nov 21, 1934	P	Tex Carleton	St. Louis Cardinals	P P	Bud Tinning Dick Ward and cash
Nov 22, 1934	P OF	Larry French Freddie Lindstrom	Pittsburgh Pirates	P P OF	Guy Bush Jim Weaver Babe Herman
Dec 31, 1934		Waiver price	Brooklyn Dodgers	C	Babe Phelps
May 21, 1936	OF P	Ethan Allen Curt Davis	Philadelphia Phillies	OF P	Chuck Klein Fabian Kowalik
Oct 8, 1936	1B P	Ripper Collins Roy Parmelee	St. Louis Cardinals	P	Lon Warneke
Dec 2, 1936		Cash	St. Louis Browns	OF	Ethan Allen
Dec 5, 1936	2B	Lonny Frey	Brooklyn Dodgers	P SS	Roy Henshaw Woody English
Feb 4, 1938		Cash	Cincinnati Reds	2B	Lonny Frey
April 16, 1938	P	Dizzy Dean	St. Louis Cardinals	P P OF	Curt Davis Clyde Shoun Tuck Stainback and $185,000.
Dec 6, 1938	SS OF C	Dick Bartell Hank Leiber Gus Mancuso	New York Giants	OF SS C	Frank Demaree Bill Jurges Ken O'Dea

DATE	ACQUIRED	FROM	IN EXCHANGE FOR
Dec 8, 1938	P Ray Harrell	St. Louis Cardinals	Cash
Jan 24, 1939	OF Jim Gleeson	New York Yankees	$25,000.
May 29, 1939	P Claude Passeau	Philadelphia Phillies	OF Joe Marty P Ray Harrell P Kirby Higbe
Dec 6, 1939	SS Billy Rogell	Detroit Tigers	SS Dick Bartell
Dec 8, 1939	C Al Todd	Brooklyn Dodgers	C Gus Mancuso
Dec 27, 1939	P Ken Raffensberger	St. Louis Cardinals	2B Steve Mesner SS Gene Lillard and cash
July 22, 1940	1B Zeke Bonura	Washington Senators	Cash
July 24, 1940	SS Rabbit Warstler	Boston Braves	Waiver price
Dec 4, 1940	SS Billy Myers	Cincinnati Reds	OF Jim Gleeson SS Bobby Mattick
Feb 4, 1941	P Tot Pressnell	Cincinnati Reds	Cash
May 6, 1941	2B Johnny Hudson OF Charlie Gilbert and $65,000.	Brooklyn Dodgers	3B Billy Herman
June 15, 1941	1B Babe Dahlgren	Boston Braves	Cash
Aug 20, 1941	Waiver price	Brooklyn Dodgers	P Larry French
Sept 2, 1941	P Hank Gornicki	St. Louis Cardinals	Cash
Dec 1, 1941	Waiver price	Pittsburgh Pirates	P Hank Gornicki
Dec 4, 1941	P Bob Bowman	New York Giants	OF Hank Leiber
May 13, 1942	Cash	St. Louis Browns	1B Babe Dahlgren
	(Ten-day conditional sale; Dahlgren was returned to the Cubs on May 19, 1940.)		
May 19, 1942	Cash	Brooklyn Dodgers	1B Babe Dahlgren
June 1, 1942	1B Jimmie Foxx	Boston Red Sox	Waiver price
July 8, 1942	P Lon Warneke	St. Louis Cardinals	$75,000.
Nov 14, 1942	OF Ival Goodman	Cincinnati Reds	Cash
Nov 17, 1942	C Bennie Warren	Pittsburgh Pirates	Cash
Jan 27, 1943	P Paul Derringer	Cincinnati Reds	Cash
April 16, 1943	Cash	Philadelphia Phillies	P George Washburn

DATE		ACQUIRED	FROM		IN EXCHANGE FOR
May 15, 1943	OF	Hal Peck	Brooklyn Dodgers		Cash
July 1943		Cash	Philadelphia Phillies	P	Dick Barrett
Aug 5, 1943	C	Mickey Livingston	Philadelphia Phillies	P	Bill Lee
Sept 28, 1943	2B	Al Glossop	Brooklyn Dodgers		Cash
June 6, 1944	P	Bob Chipman	Brooklyn Dodgers	2B	Eddie Stanky
Dec 1944		Cash	Boston Red Sox	C	Billy Holm
June 23, 1945	P	Ray Starr	Pittsburgh Pirates		Waiver price
July 27, 1945	P	Hank Borowy	New York Yankees		$97,000.
Jan 21, 1946		Cash	Philadelphia Phillies	SS	Roy Hughes
April 4, 1946		Waiver price	New York Giants	C	Bennie Warren
May 1946	1B	Mickey Rocco	Cleveland Indians	1B	Heinz Becker
June 15, 1946		Cash	Philadelphia Phillies	OF	Charlie Gilbert
Jan 25, 1947		Cash	Pittsburgh Pirates	P	Hi Bithorn
April 16, 1947	2B	Lonny Frey	Cincinnati Reds		Cash
June 25, 1947		Cash	New York Yankees	2B	Lonny Frey
July 7, 1947		Waiver price	New York Giants	C	Mickey Livingston
Oct 8, 1947		Cash	Cincinnati Reds	OF	Marv Rickert
March 1, 1948	3B	Dick Culler	Boston Braves	2B	Bobby Sturgeon
May 2, 1948	3B	Jeff Cross	St. Louis Cardinals		Cash
May 20, 1948		Waiver price	Philadelphia Phillies	P	Paul Erickson
June 17, 1948	SS	Gene Mauch	Brooklyn Dodgers		Waiver price
Aug 3, 1948	SS	Emil Verban	Philadelphia Phillies		Waiver price
Oct 4, 1948	OF	Harry Walker	Philadelphia Phillies	OF	Bill Nicholson
Oct 11, 1948		Cash	Philadelphia Phillies	P	Russ Meyer
Dec 8, 1948	P 3B	Cal McLish Frankie Gustine	Pittsburgh Pirates	C P	Clyde McCullough Cliff Chambers

DATE		ACQUIRED	FROM		IN EXCHANGE FOR
Dec 14, 1948	P P	Monk Dubiel Dutch Leonard	Philadelphia Phillies	P 1B	Hank Borowy Eddie Waitkus
May 16, 1949	3B	Bob Ramazzotti	Brooklyn Dodgers	2B	Hank Schenz
June 6, 1949	P	Bob Muncrief	Pittsburgh Pirates		Waiver price
June 15, 1949	OF OF	Frankie Baumholtz Hank Sauer	Cincinnati Reds	OF OF	Harry Walker Peanuts Lowrey
Sept 14, 1949		Waiver price	Philadelphia Athletics	3B	Frankie Gustine
Oct 14, 1949	P 1B	Paul Minner Preston Ward	Brooklyn Dodgers		$100,000.
Dec 14, 1949	P	Bill Voiselle	Boston Braves	IF	Gene Mauch and cash
April 18, 1950		Cash	Boston Braves	P	Bob Chipman
June 7, 1950	OF	Ron Northey	Cincinnati Reds	C	Bob Scheffing
Oct 10, 1950	1B 1B	Chuck Connors Dee Fondy	Brooklyn Dodgers	OF	Hank Edwards and cash
June 15, 1951	C P 2B OF	Bruce Edwards Joe Hatten Eddie Miksis Gene Hermanski	Brooklyn Dodgers	P C OF 3B	Johnny Schmitz Rube Walker Andy Pafko Wayne Terwilliger
Oct 4, 1951	C OF	Johnny Pramesa Bob Usher	Cincinnati Reds	OF C	Bob Borkowski Smoky Burgess
Oct 11, 1951	OF	Bob Addis	Boston Braves	SS	Jack Cusick
Jan 3, 1952	P	Willie Ramsdell	Cincinnati Reds	P	Frank Hiller
June 15, 1952	OF	Tommy Brown	Philadelphia Phillies		Cash
Dec 3, 1952	C	Clyde McCullough	Pittsburgh Pirates	P	Dick Manville and $25,000.
Dec 20, 1952	P	Sheldon Jones	Boston Braves	P	Monk Dubiel
June 4, 1953	OF C P OF	Ralph Kiner Joe Garagiola Howie Pollet Catfish Metkovich	Pittsburgh Pirates	C P 1B 3B OF OF	Toby Atwell Bob Schultz Preston Ward George Freese Bob Addis Gene Hermanski $150,000.
June 12, 1953	P	Bubba Church	Cincinnati Reds	P P	Fred Baczewski Bob Kelly
Nov 30, 1953		Waiver price	Chicago White Sox	C	Carl Sawatski
Dec 7, 1953		Cash	Milwaukee Braves	OF	Catfish Metkovich
March 20, 1954	P	Dave Cole and cash	Milwaukee Braves	SS	Roy Smalley

DATE		ACQUIRED	FROM		IN EXCHANGE FOR
April 30, 1954	1B	Steve Bilko	St. Louis Cardinals		$12,500.
May 19, 1954	C	Walker Cooper	Pittsburgh Pirates		Waiver price
June 14, 1954	OF	Hal Rice	Pittsburgh Pirates	OF	Luis Marquez
Sept 8, 1954		Waiver price	New York Giants	C	Joe Garagiola
Sept 30, 1954		Waiver price	Chicago White Sox	3B	Bill Serena
Oct 1, 1954	OF	Ted Tappe	Cincinnati Reds	P	Johnny Klippstein
	P	Harry Perkowski		P	Jim Willis
	OF	Jim Bolger			
Nov 16, 1954	P	Sam Jones	Cleveland Indians	OF	Ralph Kiner
	OF	Gale Wade and $60,000.			
March 19, 1955		Cash	Philadelphia Phillies	P	Dave Cole
Oct 11, 1955	1B	Frank Kellert	Brooklyn Dodgers		Waiver price
Nov 28, 1955	C	Hobie Landrith	Cincinnati Reds	P	Hal Jeffcoat
Dec 9, 1955		Cash	Philadelphia Phillies	OF	Frankie Baumholtz
Dec 9, 1955	3B	Don Hoak	Brooklyn Dodgers	3B	Randy Jackson
	P	Russ Meyer		P	Don Elston
	OF	Walt Moryn			
March 30, 1956	OF	Pete Whisenant	St. Louis Cardinals	OF	Hank Sauer
May 15, 1956	P	Jim Hughes	Brooklyn Dodgers		Cash
Sept 1, 1956		Waiver price	Cincinnati Reds	P	Russ Meyer
Nov 13, 1956	P	Elmer Singleton	Cincinnati Reds	3B	Don Hoak
	3B	Ray Jablonski		P	Warren Hacker
				OF	Pete Whisenant
Dec 11, 1956	P	Tom Poholsky	St. Louis Cardinals	C	Hobie Landrith
	P	Jackie Collum		P	Jim Davis
	C	Ray Katt		P	Sam Jones
		minor league P Wally Lammers		3B	Eddie Miksis
Dec 11, 1956	C	Charlie Silvera	New York Yankees		Cash
April 16, 1957	P	Dick Littlefield	New York Giants	3B	Ray Jablonski
	OF	Bob Lennon		C	Ray Katt
April 20, 1957	P	Ed Mayer	St. Louis Cardinals	OF	Jim King
	OF	Bobby Del Greco			
May 1, 1957	1B	Dale Long	Pittsburgh Pirates	3B	Gene Baker
	OF	Lee Walls		1B	Dee Fondy
May 13, 1957	3B	Bobby Morgan	Philadelphia Phillies		Cash

DATE		ACQUIRED	FROM		IN EXCHANGE FOR
May 23, 1957	P P	Jackie Collum Vito Valentinetti	Brooklyn Dodgers	P	Don Elston
June 8, 1957	OF	Chuck Tanner	Milwaukee Braves		Waiver price
Aug 24, 1957		Cash	Cleveland Indians	P	Vito Valentinetti
Sept 10, 1957		Cash	New York Yankees	OF	Bobby Del Greco
Nov 10, 1957	P OF	Ben Johnson Charlie King and cash	Milwaukee Braves	2B	Casey Wise
Dec 5, 1957	P C	Taylor Phillips Sammy Taylor	Milwaukee Braves	OF P P	Eddie Haas Don Kaiser Bob Rush
Dec 10, 1957	P	Freddy Rodriguez	New York Giants	P	Tom Poholsky
March 30, 1958		Cash	Milwaukee Braves	P	Dick Littlefield
April 3, 1958	OF	Bobby Thomson	San Francisco Giants	OF	Bob Speake and cash
May 6, 1958	OF	Paul Smith	Pittsburgh Pirates		Cash
May 8, 1958	P	Hersh Freeman	Cincinnati Reds	P	Turk Lown
May 20, 1958	3B	Alvin Dark	St. Louis Cardinals	P	Jim Brosnan
Aug 23, 1958	1B	Jim Marshall	Baltimore Orioles		Waiver price
Jan 23, 1959	C	Earl Averill	Cleveland Indians	P OF	Johnny Briggs Jim Bolger
March 9, 1959	P	Riverboat Smith	Boston Red Sox	OF	Chuck Tanner
May 4, 1959	3B	Randy Jackson	Cleveland Indians	P	Riverboat Smith
May 12, 1959	P	Seth Morehead	Philadelphia Phillies	P	Taylor Phillips
May 19, 1959	OF	Irv Noren	St. Louis Cardinals	OF	Charlie King
Nov 21, 1959	1B	Dick Gernert	Boston Red Sox	P 1B	Dave Hillman Jim Marshall
Dec 6, 1959	OF	Frank Thomas	Cincinnati Reds	P OF OF	Bill Henry Lou Jackson Lee Walls
Jan 11, 1960	OF	Richie Ashburn	Philadelphia Phillies	P 3B OF	John Buzhardt Alvin Dark Jim Woods
April 5, 1960		Cash	San Francisco Giants	1B	Dale Long

DATE		ACQUIRED	FROM		IN EXCHANGE FOR
April 8, 1960	3B	Don Zimmer	Los Angeles Dodgers	P 3B	Ron Perranoski John Goryl minor league OF Lee Handley and $25,000.
May 13, 1960	1B P	Ed Bouchee Don Cardwell	Philadelphia Phillies	2B C	Tony Taylor Cal Neeman
May 19, 1960	P	Mark Freeman	New York Yankees	P	Art Ceccarelli
June 15, 1960	OF	Jim McKnight	St. Louis Cardinals	OF	Walt Moryn
Aug 13, 1960		Minor league C Don Prohovich and cash	Chicago White Sox	C	Earl Averill
Aug 31, 1960		Cash	Detroit Tigers	1B	Dick Gernert
March 31, 1961	IF IF	Andre Rodgers Daryl Robertson	Milwaukee Braves	P P	Moe Drabowsky Seth Morehead
April 1, 1961	OF	Jim McAnany	Los Angeles Angels	OF	Lou Johnson
May 9, 1961	UT	Mel Roach	Milwaukee Braves	OF	Frank Thomas
July 7, 1961		Cash	Cleveland Indians	P	Joe Schaffernoth
April 26, 1962	OF	Bobby Gene Smith	New York Mets	C	Sammy Taylor
April 30, 1962	P	Bob Buhl	Milwaukee Braves	P	Jack Curtis
June 5, 1962	OF SS	Don Landrum Alex Grammas	St. Louis Cardinals	OF P	Bobby Gene Smith Daryl Robertson
Sept 1, 1962	P	Paul Toth	St. Louis Cardinals	P	Harvey Branch
Oct 17, 1962	P C P	Larry Jackson Jimmie Schaffer Lindy McDaniel	St. Louis Cardinals	OF P C	George Altman Don Cardwell Moe Thacker
Nov 28, 1962	1B	Steve Boros	Detroit Tigers	P	Bob Anderson
Dec 3, 1962	3B	Ken Aspromonte	Milwaukee Braves	3B	Jim McKnight
March 28, 1963	C P P	Merritt Ranew Hal Haydel Dick LeMay	Houston Astros	P P-OF	Jug Gerard Danny Murphy
June 24, 1963	IF	Leo Burke	St. Louis Cardinals	P	Barney Schultz
Dec 13, 1963	P	Dick Scott	Los Angeles Dodgers	P C	Jim Brewer Cuno Barragan
Dec 15, 1963	P	Fred Norman	Kansas City Athletics	OF	Nelson Mathews
May 15, 1964	P	Jack Spring	Los Angeles Angels		Cash
June 2, 1964	P	Lew Burdette	St. Louis Cardinals	P	Glen Hobbie

DATE		ACQUIRED	FROM		IN EXCHANGE FOR
June 3, 1964	OF	Len Gabrielson	Milwaukee Braves	C	Merritt Ranew and $40,000.
June 15, 1964	P P OF	Ernie Broglio Bobby Shantz Doug Clemens	St. Louis Cardinals	OF P P	Lou Brock Jack Spring Paul Toth
Aug 15, 1964		Cash	Philadelphia Phillies	P	Bobby Shantz
Dec 1, 1964	P	Frank Baumann	Chicago White Sox	C	Jimmie Schaffer
Dec 9, 1964	SS	Roberto Pena and cash	Pittsburgh Pirates	SS	Andre Rodgers
Jan 15, 1965	OF	George Altman	New York Mets	OF	Billy Cowan
March 27, 1965	P	Bill Faul	Detroit Tigers		Cash
April 10, 1965	P	Bob Humphreys	St. Louis Cardinals	2B	Bobby Pfeil minor league P Hal Gibson
April 14, 1965	P	Ted Abernathy	Cleveland Indians		Cash
May 11, 1965	P	Dave Dowling	St. Louis Cardinals		Waiver price
May 29, 1965	OF C P	Harvey Kuenn Ed Bailey Bob Hendley	San Francisco Giants	C OF	Dick Bertell Len Gabrielson
May 30, 1965		Cash	Philadelphia Phillies	P	Lew Burdette
Dec 2, 1965	C P	Randy Hundley Bill Hands	San Francisco Giants	P OF P	Lindy McDaniel Don Landrum Jim Rittwage
Jan 10, 1966	OF	Wes Covington	Philadelphia Phillies	OF	Doug Clemens
Feb 15, 1966		Cash	California Angels	C	Ed Bailey
March 30, 1966	OF	Carl Warwick	Baltimore Orioles	C	Vic Roznovsky
April 2, 1966	OF	Ken Hunt	Washington Senators	P	Bob Humphreys
April 21, 1966	OF OF P	Adolfo Phillips John Herrnstein Ferguson Jenkins	Philadelphia Phillies	P P	Larry Jackson Bob Buhl
April 23, 1966		Cash	Philadelphia Phillies	OF	Harvey Kuenn
April 28, 1966	OF	Billy Cowan	Atlanta Braves		Cash
May 28, 1966	1B	Lee Thomas	Atlanta Braves	P	Ted Abernathy
May 29, 1966	OF	Marty Keough	Atlanta Braves	OF	John Herrnstein
June 22, 1966	P	Curt Simmons	St. Louis Cardinals		Cash

DATE		ACQUIRED	FROM		IN EXCHANGE FOR
Dec 7, 1966	P	Ray Culp and cash	Philadelphia Phillies	P	Dick Ellsworth
April 3, 1967		Cash	San Francisco Giants	C	Don Bryant
April 25, 1967	P	Dick Radatz	Cleveland Indians	OF	Bob Raudman and cash
May 14, 1967	OF	Ted Savage	St. Louis Cardinals		Cash
May 14, 1967		Cash	St. Louis Cardinals	OF	Don Young
May 22, 1967		Cash	Chicago White Sox	IF	Jimmy Stewart
June 12, 1967	C P	Johnny Stephenson Rob Gardner	New York Mets	P	Bob Hendley
July 24, 1967	P	Bob Shaw	New York Mets		Cash
Aug 1, 1967	OF	Don Young	St. Louis Cardinals		Cash
Aug 2, 1967		Cash	New York Mets	P	Cal Koonce
Aug 2, 1967		Cash	California Angels	P	Curt Simmons
Aug 4, 1967	P	Pete Mikkelsen	Pittsburgh Pirates		Waiver price
Aug 20, 1967		Cash	New York Mets	P	Bill Connors
Oct 13, 1967		Cash	St. Louis Cardinals	OF	Jim Hicks
Nov 30, 1967	OF	Lou Johnson	Los Angeles Dodgers	2B	Paul Popovich
Nov 30, 1967		Minor league OF Bill Schlessinger and cash	Boston Red Sox	P	Ray Culp
March 30, 1968	P	Bobby Tiefenauer	Cleveland Indians	P	Rob Gardner
April 3, 1968	1B	Dick Nen	Washington Senators		Cash
April 22, 1968	P P	Jack Lamabe Ron Piche	St. Louis Cardinals	P P	Pete Mikkelsen Dave Dowling
April 23, 1968	OF P	Jim Hickman Phil Regan	Los Angeles Dodgers	OF P	Ted Savage Jim Ellis
May 4, 1968	OF	Aaron Pointer	Houston Astros	OF	Byron Browne
June 27, 1968	C	Gene Oliver	Boston Red Sox		Cash
June 28, 1968	OF	Willie Smith	Cleveland Indians	OF	Lou Johnson
Oct 1, 1968		Cash	Washington Senators	1B	Dick Nen

DATE		ACQUIRED	FROM		IN EXCHANGE FOR
Jan 9, 1969	P	Ted Abernathy	Cincinnati Reds	C OF	Bill Plummer Clarence Jones minor league P Ken Myette
Jan 15, 1969	OF	Manny Jimenez	Pittsburgh Pirates	IF P	Ron Campbell Chuck Hartenstein
March 28, 1969	IF	Charley Smith	San Francisco Giants		Cash
April 19, 1969	IF	Nate Oliver	New York Yankees	IF	Lee Elia
April 25, 1969	P	Dick Selma	San Diego Padres	P P IF	Joe Niekro Gary Ross Francisco Libran
April 27, 1969	P	Don Nottebart	Cincinnati Reds		Minor league IF Jim Armstrong and cash
June 11, 1969	IF	Paul Popovich	Montreal Expos	OF P	Adolfo Phillips Jack Lamabe
Aug 11, 1969	P	Ken Johnson	New York Yankees		Cash
Sept 11, 1969	OF	Jimmie Hall	New York Yankees		Minor league P Terry Bongiovanni and cash
Nov 17, 1969	OF	Johnny Callison	Philadelphia Phillies	P OF	Dick Selma Oscar Gamble
Dec 4, 1969	OF	Boots Day	St. Louis Cardinals	P	Rich Nye
March 29, 1970	C	J. C. Martin	New York Mets	C	Randy Bobb
April 22, 1970		Cash	Montreal Expos	OF	Jim Qualls
May 12, 1970	C	Jack Hiatt	Montreal Expos	OF	Boots Day
May 29, 1970	IF	Phil Gagliano	St. Louis Cardinals	P	Ted Abernathy
June 23, 1970	P	Roberto Rodriguez	San Diego Padres		Cash
June 23, 1970	P	Milt Pappas	Atlanta Braves		Cash
June 29, 1970		Cash	Atlanta Braves	OF	Jimmie Hall
July 9, 1970	P	Juan Pizarro	California Angels	P	Archie Reynolds
July 29, 1970	1B	Joe Pepitone	Houston Astros		Cash
Sept 1, 1970		Cash	Chicago White Sox	P	Bob Miller
Sept 16, 1970	OF	Tommy Davis	Oakland Athletics		Cash
Sept 21, 1970	P	Hoyt Wilhelm	Atlanta Braves		Cash

DATE		ACQUIRED	FROM		IN EXCHANGE FOR
Oct 12, 1970	SS	Hector Torres	Houston Astros	SS	Roger Metzger
Nov 30, 1970	1B	Hal Breeden	Atlanta Braves	P	Hoyt Wilhelm
Nov 30, 1970	C	Danny Breeden	Cincinnati Reds	OF-1B	Willie Smith
Nov 30, 1970	OF 1B	Jose Ortiz Ossie Blanco	Chicago White Sox	P P 1B	Pat Jacquez Dave Lemonds Roe Skidmore
Dec 1, 1970		Cash	Houston Astros	C	Jack Hiatt
Dec 3, 1970	3B	Carmen Fanzone	Boston Red Sox	IF	Phil Gagliano
May 19, 1971	C	Chris Cannizzaro	San Diego Padres	IF	Garry Jestadt
June 17, 1971	1B	Ramon Webster	Oakland Athletics		Cash
Aug 31, 1971	C OF	Frank Fernandez Bill McNulty	Oakland Athletics	OF	Adrian Garrett
Nov 29, 1971	OF	Rick Monday	Oakland Athletics	P	Ken Holtzman
Dec 3, 1971	OF	Jose Cardenal	Milwaukee Brewers	OF P P	Brock Davis Jim Colborn Earl Stephenson
Dec 17, 1971		Cash	Los Angeles Dodgers	C	Chris Cannizzaro
Jan 20, 1972	P	Jack Aker	New York Yankees	OF	Johnny Callison
April 7, 1972	P	Dan McGinn	Montreal Expos	SS 1B	Hector Torres Hal Breeden
April 20, 1972	P	Tom Phoebus	San Diego Padres		Cash
June 2, 1972		Cash	Chicago White Sox	P	Phil Regan
June 28, 1972		Cash	Oakland Athletics	OF	Art Shamsky
Aug 18, 1972	C	Ellie Hendricks	Baltimore Orioles	1B	Tommy Davis
Oct 20, 1972	IF	Tony LaRussa	Atlanta Braves	P	Tom Phoebus
Oct 27, 1972	C	Francisco Estrada	Baltimore Orioles	C	Ellie Hendricks
Nov 21, 1972	P	Bob Locker	Oakland Athletics	OF	Billy North
Nov 30, 1972	P	Dave LaRoche	Minnesota Twins	P P	Bill Hands Joe Decker minor league P Bob Maneely
May 19, 1973	1B	Andre Thornton	Atlanta Braves	1B	Joe Pepitone
Aug 13, 1973	OF	Rico Carty	Texas Rangers		Cash

DATE		ACQUIRED	FROM		IN EXCHANGE FOR
Aug 29, 1973	1B	Gonzalo Marquez	Oakland Athletics	1B	Pat Bourque
Aug 31, 1973	P	Mike Paul	Texas Rangers	P	Larry Gura
Sept 11, 1973		Cash	Oakland Athletics	OF	Rico Carty
Oct 25, 1973	3B 2B	Bill Madlock Vic Harris	Texas Rangers	P	Ferguson Jenkins
Nov 3, 1973	P	Horacio Pina	Oakland Athletics	P	Bob Locker
Nov 7, 1973	OF	Jerry Morales	San Diego Padres	2B IF	Glenn Beckert Bobby Fenwick
Dec 6, 1973	C	George Mitterwald	Minnesota Twins	C	Randy Hundley
Dec 11, 1973	P P C P	Steve Stone Ken Frailing Steve Swisher Jim Kremmel	Chicago White Sox	3B	Ron Santo
March 19, 1974	P	Willie Prall	San Francisco Giants	C	Ken Rudolph
March 23, 1974	P	Scipio Spinks	St. Louis Cardinals	OF	Jim Hickman
April 1, 1974	P	Tom Dettore and cash	Pittsburgh Pirates	IF	Paul Popovich
July 10, 1974	2B	Billy Grabarkewitz	Philadelphia Phillies		Cash
July 28, 1974	C	Rick Stelmaszek	California Angels	P	Horacio Pina
Oct 23, 1974	P P 2B	Darold Knowles Bob Locker Manny Trillo	Oakland Athletics	OF	Billy Williams
April 6, 1975	OF	Champ Summers and cash	Oakland Athletics	P	Jim Todd
April 28, 1975		Minor league P Howell Copeland	Oakland Athletics	OF	Matt Alexander
May 2, 1975	P P	Geoff Zahn Eddie Solomon	Los Angeles Dodgers	P	Burt Hooton
July 31, 1975		Cash	California Angels	OF-1B	Adrian Garrett
Oct 28, 1975	P	Mike Garman minor league IF Bobby Hrapmann	St. Louis Cardinals	SS	Don Kessinger
Dec 22, 1975	SS	Mick Kelleher	St. Louis Cardinals	2B	Vic Harris
April 13, 1976	C	Randy Hundley	San Diego Padres		Cash
April 19, 1976		Cash	Oakland Athletics	C	Tim Hosley
May 17, 1976	P 1B-OF	Steve Renko Larry Biittner	Montreal Expos	1B	Andre Thornton
June 8, 1976	P	Joe Coleman	Detroit Tigers		Cash

DATE		ACQUIRED	FROM		IN EXCHANGE FOR
Sept 8, 1976	P	Ramon Hernandez	Pittsburgh Pirates		Cash
Nov 24, 1976		No compensation (free agent signing)	Chicago White Sox	P	Steve Stone
Dec 8, 1976	OF	Sheldon Mallory	Kansas City Royals	1B	Pete LaCock
		(Part of three-team trade involving Kansas City, Chicago Cubs, and New York Mets.)			
Dec 8, 1976	OF	Jim Dwyer	New York Mets	OF	Sheldon Mallory
		(Part of three-team trade involving Chicago Cubs, New York Mets, and Kansas City.)			
Dec 8, 1976	OF	Greg Gross	Houston Astros	IF	Julio Gonzalez
Jan 11, 1977	1B SS	Bill Buckner Ivan DeJesus minor league P Jeff Albert	Los Angeles Dodgers	OF P	Rick Monday Mike Garman
Feb 5, 1977	OF	Gene Clines and cash	Texas Rangers	P	Darold Knowles
Feb 11, 1977	OF 3B	Bobby Murcer Steve Ontiveros minor league P Andy Muhlstock	San Francisco Giants	3B 2B	Bill Madlock Rob Sperring
Feb 16, 1977	OF	Dave Schneck	Cincinnati Reds	OF	Champ Summers
Feb 28, 1977		Minor league P Mark Covert	St. Louis Cardinals	P	Buddy Schultz
March 15, 1977		Cash	Oakland Athletics	IF	Jerry Tabb
March 15, 1977	P	Jim Todd	Oakland Athletics	P	Joe Coleman
April 20, 1977	P	Pete Broberg	Seattle Mariners	P	Jim Todd
May 28, 1977	OF	Bobby Darwin	Boston Red Sox	P	Ramon Hernandez
July 30, 1977	P	Dave Roberts	Detroit Tigers		Cash
Aug 5, 1977		Cash	Oakland Athletics	P	Dave Giusti
Aug 18, 1977	P	Larry Anderson and cash	Chicago White Sox	P	Steve Renko
Oct 25, 1977		Minor league P Manny Seaone	Philadelphia Phillies	OF	Jose Cardenal
Oct 25, 1977	C	Larry Cox	Seattle Mariners		Minor league P Steve Hamrick
Oct 31, 1977	P P	Woodie Fryman Bill Caudill	Cincinnati Reds	P	Bill Bonham
Nov 30, 1977	OF	Dave Kingman	New York Yankees		No compensation (free agent signing)
Dec 5, 1977		Minor leaguers P Norm Churchill and OF Bruce Compton	Cleveland Indians	IF	Dave Rosello

DATE		ACQUIRED	FROM		IN EXCHANGE FOR
Dec 8, 1977	C OF	Dave Rader Hector Cruz	St. Louis Cardinals	OF C	Jerry Morales Steve Swisher and cash
March 29, 1978	2B	Rodney Scott and cash	Oakland Athletics	P	Pete Broberg
April 1, 1978		Cash	Oakland Athletics	3B	Mike Adams
June 9, 1978	OF	Jerry White	Montreal Expos	P	Woodie Fryman
June 10, 1978	P	Ken Holtzman	New York Yankees	P	Ron Davis
June 15, 1978	P	Lynn McGlothen	San Francisco Giants	OF	Hector Cruz
June 15, 1978	OF	Mike Vail	Cleveland Indians	OF	Joe Wallis
June 26, 1978	P	Denny DeBarr	Cleveland Indians	P	Paul Reuschel
Aug 6, 1978	2B	Davy Johnson	Philadelphia Phillies	P	Larry Anderson
Dec 14, 1978	OF	Sam Mejias	Montreal Expos	2B OF	Rodney Scott Jerry White
Feb 23, 1979	C 2B OF P	Barry Foote Ted Sizemore Jerry Martin Dick Botelho minor league P Henry Mack	Philadelphia Phillies	2B C OF	Manny Trillo Dave Rader Greg Gross
March 20, 1979	OF	Luis Delgado	Seattle Mariners	C	Larry Cox
March 20, 1979	2B	Steve Dillard	Detroit Tigers	IF	Ed Putman
May 3, 1979	P	Doug Capilla	Cincinnati Reds		Minor league P Mark Gilbert
May 23, 1979	P	Dick Tidrow	New York Yankees	P	Ray Burris
June 26, 1979		Minor league P Pete Semall	New York Yankees	OF	Bobby Murcer
June 28, 1979	OF	Ken Henderson	Cincinnati Reds		Cash
July 4, 1979	OF	Miguel Dilone	Oakland Athletics		Cash
July 4, 1979		Cash	Cincinnati Reds	OF	Sam Mejias
Aug 17, 1979	C	Mike O'Berry and cash	Boston Red Sox	2B	Ted Sizemore
Aug 30, 1979	C	Bruce Kimm	Detroit Tigers		Cash
Oct 17, 1979	2B	Mike Tyson	St. Louis Cardinals	P	Donnie Moore
April 2, 1980	3B	Lenny Randle	Seattle Mariners		Cash

DATE		ACQUIRED	FROM		IN EXCHANGE FOR
April 7, 1980	P	Mark Lemongello	Toronto Blue Jays		Cash
May 7, 1980		Cash	Cleveland Indians	OF	Miguel Dilone
June 23, 1980	C	Cliff Johnson	Cleveland Indians	OF	Karl Pagel and cash
Oct 17, 1980	P	Jay Howell	Cincinnati Reds	C	Mike O'Berry
Dec 9, 1980	OF 3B IF	Leon Durham Ken Reitz Ty Waller	St. Louis Cardinals	P	Bruce Sutter
Dec 11, 1980		Minor league P Mike King	Oakland Athletics	C-1B IF	Cliff Johnson Keith Drumright
Dec 12, 1980	2B P	Joe Strain Phil Nastu	San Francisco Giants	OF OF	Jerry Martin Jesus Figueroa minor league IF Mike Turgeon
Dec 12, 1980	OF	Hector Cruz	Cincinnati Reds	OF	Mike Vail
Jan 8, 1981		No compensation (free agent signing)	Cincinnati Reds	1B	Larry Biittner
Feb 28, 1981	OF	Steve Henderson and cash	New York Mets	OF-1B	Dave Kingman
March 28, 1981	P	Ken Kravec	Chicago White Sox	P	Dennis Lamp
April 1, 1981		Cash	Detroit Tigers	IF	Mick Kelleher
April 6, 1981	C	Butch Benton	New York Mets		Cash
April 27, 1981	P	Tom Filer and cash	New York Yankees	C	Barry Foote
June 4, 1981	OF	Bobby Bonds	Texas Rangers		Cash
June 12, 1981	P P	Doug Bird Mike Griffin and $400,000.	New York Yankees	P P	Rick Reuschel Jay Howell
Aug 15, 1981	UT	Bob Molinaro	Chicago White Sox	P	Lynn McGlothen
		(Cubs received Molinaro on March 29, 1982.)			
Aug 19, 1981	3B	Pat Tabler	New York Yankees		Player to be named later
		(Yankees received Bill Caudill, April 1, 1982, and Jay Howell, August 20, 1982.)			
Oct 23, 1981	2B	Junior Kennedy	Cincinnati Reds		$50,000.
Dec 7, 1981	P	Allen Ripley	San Francisco Giants	P	Doug Capilla
Dec 8, 1981	P	Ferguson Jenkins	Texas Rangers		No compensation (free agent signing)
Dec 8, 1981	P	Bill Campbell	Boston Red Sox		No compensation (free agent signing)
Dec 9, 1981	OF	Gary Woods	Houston Astros	OF	Jim Tracy

DATE		ACQUIRED	FROM		IN EXCHANGE FOR
Dec 28, 1981	P	Paul Mirabella	Toronto Blue Jays	P	Dave Geisel
Jan 14, 1982		No compensation (free agent signing)	Montreal Expos	C	Tim Blackwell
Jan 27, 1982	SS 3B	Larry Bowa Ryne Sandberg	Philadelphia Phillies	SS	Ivan DeJesus
Jan 30, 1982		No compensation (free agent signing)	Detroit Tigers	OF	Jerry Turner
March 16, 1982	OF-1B	Dan Briggs	Montreal Expos	P	Mike Griffin
March 26, 1982	2B	Bump Wills	Texas Rangers	P	Paul Mirabella minor league P Paul Semall and cash
April 1, 1982		Continuation of Pat Tabler trade of August 18, 1981.	New York Yankees	P	Bill Caudill
Aug 2, 1982		Completes Pat Tabler trade of August 18, 1981.	New York Yankees	P	Jay Howell
Sept 1, 1982		Cash	Philadelphia Phillies	OF	Bob Molinaro
Oct 15, 1982	P	Alan Hargesheimer	San Francisco Giants	P	Herman Segelke
Nov 29, 1982	2B	Jay Loviglio	Chicago White Sox		Cash
Dec 9, 1982	P	Rich Bordi	Seattle Mariners	OF	Steve Henderson
Dec 10, 1982	P	Chuck Rainey	Boston Red Sox	P	Doug Bird
Dec 10, 1982	P	Reggie Patterson	Chicago White Sox	OF	Ty Waller
Dec 10, 1982	OF	Wayne Nordhagen	Toronto Blue Jays		No compensation (free agent signing)
Jan 20, 1983	3B	Ron Cey	Los Angeles Dodgers		Minor league P Vance Lovelace minor league OF Dan Cataline
Jan 25, 1983	P P	Steve Trout Warren Brusstar	Chicago White Sox	SS 3B P P	Scott Fletcher Pat Tabler Randy Martz Dick Tidrow
April 1, 1983	C	Steve Lake	Milwaukee Brewers		Minor league P Rich Buonotony and cash
April 2, 1983	SS	Tom Veryzer	New York Mets		Minor league Ps Craig Weissman and Bob Schilling
May 22, 1983	P P	Dick Ruthven Bill Johnson	Philadelphia Phillies	P	Willie Hernandez
July 16, 1983	OF	Thad Bosley	Chicago White Sox		Cash

DATE		ACQUIRED	FROM		IN EXCHANGE FOR
Sept 30, 1983	P	Mike Chris	San Francisco Giants		Cash
Dec 7, 1983	P	Scott Sanderson	San Diego Padres	1B P 3B	Carmelo Martinez Craig Lefferts Allan Ramirez
		(Part of three-team trade involving Chicago Cubs, San Diego, and Montreal.)			
Jan 5, 1984	IF	Richie Hebner	Pittsburgh Pirates		No compensation (free agent signing)
March 26, 1984	P	Tim Stoddard	Oakland Athletics		Minor leaguers P Stan Kyles and OF Stan Boderick
March 26, 1984	OF OF P	Gary Matthews Bob Dernier Porfirio Altamirano	Philadelphia Phillies	P C	Bill Campbell Mike Diaz
March 30, 1984	C P	Don Werner Dick Botelho	Kansas City Royals	P	Alan Hargesheimer and a player to be named later

Cincinnati Reds

The Best Trades

1. Acquired George Foster from the San Francisco Giants for Frank Duffy and Vern Geishert, May 29, 1971.
2. Acquired Joe Morgan, Jack Billingham, Denis Menke, Cesar Geronimo, and Ed Armbrister from the Houston Astros for Lee May, Tommy Helms, and Jimmy Stewart, November 29, 1971.
3. Acquired Edd Roush, Christy Mathewson, and Bill McKechnie from the New York Giants for Buck Herzog and Red Killefer, July 20, 1916.
4. Acquired Bucky Walters from the Philadelphia Phillies for Spud Davis, Al Hollingsworth, and $50,000, June 13, 1938.
5. Acquired Tom Seaver from the New York Mets for Steve Henderson, Dan Norman, Doug Flynn, and Pat Zachry, June 15, 1977.

The Worst Trades

1. Traded Christy Mathewson to the New York Giants for Amos Rusie, December 15, 1900.
2. Traded Frank Robinson to the Baltimore Orioles for Milt Pappas, Jack Baldschun, and Dick Simpson, December 9, 1965.
3. Traded Curt Flood and Joe Taylor to the St. Louis Cardinals for Marty Kutyna and Ted Wieand, December 5, 1957.
4. Traded Orval Overall to the Chicago Cubs for Bob Wicker and $2,000, June 2, 1906.
5. Traded Hal McRae and Wayne Simpson to the Kansas City Royals for Richie Scheinblum and Roger Nelson, November 30, 1972.

Trader: Bob Howsam

In January of 1967, Bob Howsam joined the Cincinnati Reds as general manager. The Reds were a seventh-place club that had just suffered its first sub-.500 season since 1960. Worse, the Reds had, just one year earlier, perpetrated one of the greatest misjudgments in baseball history, trading away Frank Robinson because they believed him to be "an old thirty," with decline just a few years away. Robinson declined as far as the American League Triple Crown in '66 while leading Baltimore to a world championship. Howsam's task was to reverse this slide into mediocrity.

To say that he succeeded would be a severe understatement. Howsam took the talent on hand, added several strong prospects from the minor leagues, and traded shrewdly to create The Big Red Machine, the dominant team in the National League through the 1970s. It never hurts to inherit a Pete Rose and a Tony Perez, or to have a Johnny Bench and a Dave Concepcion making their way through the minors to the parent club. But having and developing talent isn't enough — just ask fans in Boston or San Francisco. Building a winning team takes good judgment about who can do the jobs best, not just today but in the years to come.

Cincinnati won 102 games in 1970 with a powerful team loaded with home-grown talent, augmented by the acquisitions of Jim Merritt, Bobby Tolan, Wayne Granger, Clay Carroll, and Woody Woodward. But they fell eleven games off the pace in '71, and Howsam took decisive action. He traded Lee May, who had averaged 37 homers and 100 RBIs in the previous three seasons, Tommy Helms, starting second baseman for the past six years, and Jimmy Stewart to Houston for Joe Morgan, Jack Billingham, Denis Menke, Cesar Geronimo, and Ed Armbrister. All Morgan did was to win two Most Valuable Player Awards, while Billingham won fifteen games a year and Geronimo played outstanding center field. Thanks largely to this deal, as well as another swindle in which Howsam picked up George Foster from the Giants for a song, the Reds won the NL pennant in '72, divisional titles in '73 and '79, and back-to-back World Series in '75 and '76. Howsam's Reds stood up to the true test of champions: to win, and win consistently, over a long period of time. And his '75 and '76 Series winners, despite their perennial pitching problems, stand among the ranks of baseball's greatest teams.

DATE		ACQUIRED	FROM		IN EXCHANGE FOR
Unknown		Cash	St. Louis Cardinals	OF	Dusty Miller
Feb 27, 1900		Cash	New York Giants	P	Pink Hawley
Feb 29, 1900		Cash	New York Giants	OF	Kip Selbach
April 1900	OF	Dick Harley	Cleveland Spiders		Cash
May 1900	2B	Joe Quinn	St. Louis Cardinals		Cash
Aug 8, 1900		Cash	New York Giants	OF	Elmer Smith
Dec 15, 1900	P	Amos Rusie	New York Giants	P	Christy Mathewson
April 1901		Cash	Chicago Cubs	OF C	Topsy Hartsel Mike Kahoe
May 30, 1901		Cash	New York Giants	OF	Algie McBride
July 2, 1901		Cash	Brooklyn Dodgers	3B	Charlie Irwin

DATE		ACQUIRED	FROM		IN EXCHANGE FOR
July 1901		Cash	Brooklyn Dodgers	P	Doc Newton
April 1902	P	Ed Poole	Pittsburgh Pirates		Cash
July 1902		Cash	Chicago Cubs	OF	John Dobbs
Aug 1902		Cash	St. Louis Cardinals	P	Clarence Currie
Jan 1903		Cash	Brooklyn Dodgers	P	Henry Thielman
May 1903	OF	Cozy Dolan	Chicago White Sox		Cash
June 1903	2B	Tom Daly	Chicago White Sox		Cash
Oct 1903	C	Lee Fohl	Pittsburgh Pirates		Waiver price
Feb 1904		Cash	St. Louis Cardinals	1B	Jake Beckley
Feb 1904		Cash	Brooklyn Dodgers	P	Ed Poole
Feb 1904		Cash	Brooklyn Dodgers	C	Bill Bergen
July 3, 1904		Cash	New York Giants	OF	Mike Donlin
Aug 11, 1904	OF	Jimmy Sebring	Pittsburgh Pirates		Cash
Aug 1904		Cash	New York Giants	P	Claude Elliott
Feb 1905		Cash	St. Louis Cardinals	P	Win Kellum
May 20, 1905	2B	Shad Barry	Chicago Cubs		Cash
June 6, 1905		Cash	Boston Braves	C	Gabby Street
June 6, 1905		Cash	Boston Braves	1B	Cozy Dolan
July 30, 1905	C	Gabby Street	Boston Braves		Cash
Dec 1905	C	Ed Phelps	Pittsburgh Pirates	C	Heinie Peitz
Feb 1906	OF	Jimmy Barrett	Detroit Tigers		Waiver price
Feb 1906	1B	Charlie Carr	Cleveland Indians		Cash
March 1906	3B P	Jim Delahanty Chick Fraser	Boston Braves	SS	Al Bridwell
March 1906	3B P	Hans Lobert Jake Weimer	Chicago Cubs	3B	Harry Steinfeldt
April 1906		Waiver price	New York Yankees	P	Noodles Hahn

DATE		ACQUIRED	FROM		IN EXCHANGE FOR
May 13, 1906		Cash	Boston Braves	P	Gus Dorner
May 17, 1906	1B	Oscar Stanage	St. Louis Cardinals		Cash
May 20, 1906		Cash	Pittsburgh Pirates	C	Ed Phelps
June 2, 1906	P	Bob Wicker and $2,000.	Chicago Cubs	P	Orval Overall
July 14, 1906		$12,000.	New York Giants	OF	Cy Seymour
July 25, 1906	OF	Homer Smoot	St. Louis Cardinals	P 1B	Carl Druhot Shad Barry
Oct 1906	P	Chick Fraser	Chicago Cubs	P	Jack Harper
June 17, 1907		Cash	Pittsburgh Pirates	OF	Harry Wolter
Sept 1907		Cash	St. Louis Browns	2B	Jim Delahanty
Jan 1908		Cash	Pittsburgh Pirates	P	Tom McCarthy
Feb 1908	3B	Dave Brain	Boston Braves		Cash
May 1908		Waiver price	St. Louis Cardinals	P	Charlie Rhodes
July 1908		Cash	New York Giants	3B	Dave Brain
Sept 1908		Cash	Chicago Cubs	P	Andy Coakley
Oct 1908	OF	Mike Mowrey	Philadelphia Phillies		Cash
Oct 1908		Cash	Chicago Cubs	OF	John Kane
Dec 12, 1908	P P	Ed Karger Art Fromme	St. Louis Cardinals	C	Admiral Schlei
Dec 1908		Cash	St. Louis Cardinals	SS	Rudy Hulswitt
May 20, 1909		Cash	Chicago Cubs	P	Pat Ragan
May 1909	OF	Ward Miller and cash	Pittsburgh Pirates	OF	Kid Durbin
May 1909	OF	Bill Chappelle	Boston Braves	C	Chick Autry
June 1909		Waiver price	Boston Red Sox	P	Ed Karger
Aug 22, 1909	2B	Chappy Charles	St. Louis Cardinals	3B	Mike Mowrey
Jan 20, 1910	P	Harry Coveleski	Philadelphia Phillies	P	Ad Brennan
Jan 1910		Cash	Philadelphia Phillies	P	Bob Ewing

DATE		ACQUIRED	FROM		IN EXCHANGE FOR
Feb 1910	P 3B	Fred Beebe Alan Storke	St. Louis Cardinals	2B OF P	Miller Huggins Rebel Oakes Frank Corridon
April 1910	P	Bill Burns	Chicago White Sox		Cash
April 1910		Cash	St. Louis Browns	P	Bob Spade
May 1910	SS	Tommy McMillan	Brooklyn Dodgers		Cash
May 1910	P	Slow Joe Doyle	New York Yankees		Cash
Feb 1911	OF 3B P	Johnny Bates Eddie Grant George McQuillan	Philadelphia Phillies	P P OF 3B	Fred Beebe Jack Rowan Dode Paskert Hans Lobert
March 1911	OF	Fred Beck	Boston Braves		Cash
April 1911		Cash	Brooklyn Dodgers	OF	Hub Northen
May 11, 1911	P	Frank Smith	Boston Red Sox		Cash
July 15, 1911	P	Bert Humphries	Philadelphia Phillies	OF P	Fred Beck Bill Burns
Jan 1912	P	John Frill	St. Louis Browns		Waiver price
June 1912	C	Earl Blackburn	Pittsburgh Pirates		Cash
Aug 1912	P	Ralph Works	Detroit Tigers		Cash
Nov 16, 1912	IF	Red Corriden	Detroit Tigers		Cash
Dec 15, 1912	SS P C	Joe Tinker Grover Lowdermilk Harry Chapman	Chicago Cubs	P IF OF 3B OF	Bert Humphries Red Corriden Pete Knisely Art Phelan Mike Mitchell
Feb 1913	C	Johnny Kling	Boston Braves		Cash
May 22, 1913	P 3B OF	Red Ames Heinie Groh Josh Devore and $20,000.	New York Giants	P 3B	Art Fromme Eddie Grant
June 5, 1913	3B P	John Dodge Red Nelson	Philadelphia Phillies	OF OF	Josh Devore Beals Becker
June 1913		Cash	New York Giants	3B	Eddie Grant
June 1913		Cash	Boston Braves	SS	Tex McDonald
July 1913	OF	Jimmy Sheckard	St. Louis Cardinals		Waiver price

DATE		ACQUIRED	FROM		IN EXCHANGE FOR
Oct 1913	OF	Bert Daniels	New York Yankees		Cash
Dec 12, 1913	2B C	Buck Herzog Grover Hartley	New York Giants	OF	Bob Bescher
		(Hartley jumped to the Federal League and Herzog was made Cincinnati manager.)			
Dec 1913	OF	Doc Miller	Philadelphia Phillies		Cash
Dec 1913	2B	Dick Egan and $6,500.	Brooklyn Dodgers	SS	Joe Tinker
		(Tinker demanded $2,000 of the purchase price; when this was refused, he jumped to the Federal League and the deal was cancelled.)			
Jan 1914		Cash	Boston Braves	OF	Herbie Moran
April 1914	OF P	Herbie Moran Earl Yingling	Brooklyn Dodgers	2B	Dick Egan
June 1914	C	Tex Erwin	Brooklyn Dodgers		Cash
July 16, 1914		Waiver price	Boston Red Sox	1B	Dick Hoblitzell
July 20, 1914	1B	Fritz Mollwitz	Chicago Cubs	SS	Claud Derrick
Aug 1914	P	Elmer Koestner	Chicago Cubs	OF	Johnny Bates
Aug 1914	OF	Bill Holden	New York Yankees		Waiver price
Nov 1914	C	Red Dooin	Philadelphia Phillies	2B	Bert Niehoff
Dec 14, 1914	SS	Ivy Olson	Cleveland Indians		Cash
Feb 22, 1915	P	Fred Toney	Brooklyn Dodgers		Waiver price
April 8, 1915	C	Ivy Wingo	St. Louis Cardinals	OF C	Mike Gonzalez Bob Bescher
June 13, 1915		Cash	Brooklyn Dodgers	P	Phil Douglas
June 1915	2B	Bill Rodgers	Boston Red Sox		Cash
July 6, 1915		Waiver price	New York Giants	C	Red Dooin
July 24, 1915		Cash	St. Louis Cardinals	P	Red Ames
Aug 19, 1915		$3,000.	New York Giants	P	Rube Benton
Aug 1915		Waiver price	Brooklyn Dodgers	SS	Ivy Olson
Dec 23, 1915	P	Earl Moseley	Newark (Federal League)		$5,000.
Dec 23, 1915	2B	Baldy Louden	Buffalo (Federal League)		Cash
Dec 1915	SS	Larry Kopf	Philadelphia Athletics		Cash

DATE		ACQUIRED	FROM		IN EXCHANGE FOR
Jan 1916	SS	Bob Fisher	Chicago Cubs		Cash
Feb 10, 1916	P	Jim Bluejacket	Brooklyn (Federal League)		Cash
Feb 10, 1916	P	Al Schulz	Buffalo (Federal League)		Cash
Feb 10, 1916	C	Emil Huhn	Newark (Federal League)		Cash
April 1916	P	Elmer Knetzer	Boston Braves		Cash
July 20, 1916	P OF 3B	Christy Mathewson Edd Roush Bill McKechnie	New York Giants	2B OF	Buck Herzog Red Killefer
July 22, 1916		Cash	Chicago Cubs	1B	Fritz Mollwitz
April 24, 1917	OF	Jim Thorpe	New York Giants		Cash
		(Thorpe was returned to the Giants on August 1, 1917.)			
April 26, 1917	P	Scott Perry	Chicago Cubs		Waiver price
May 28, 1917		Waiver price	Boston Braves	P	Scott Perry
July 17, 1917	P	Dutch Ruether	Chicago Cubs		Waiver price
Aug 1, 1917	OF	Sherry Magee	Boston Braves		Waiver price
Feb 1918		Cash	Brooklyn Dodgers	P	Clarence Mitchell
March 1918		$20,000.	Pittsburgh Pirates	3B	Bill McKechnie
April 28, 1918	2B	Lee Magee	New York Yankees	C	Tommy Clarke
April 1918	P	Rube Foster	Boston Red Sox	2B	Dave Shean
		(Foster refused to report to Cincinnati; Cincinnati received cash instead.)			
April 1918	P	Roy Mitchell	Chicago White Sox		Cash
June 20, 1918		Cash	New York Giants	P	George Smith
July 25, 1918		Cash	New York Giants	P	Fred Toney
Sept 1918	C	Jimmy Archer	Brooklyn Dodgers		Cash
Dec 9, 1918		Cash	New York Yankees	P	Pete Schneider
Feb 1, 1919	1B	Jake Daubert	Brooklyn Dodgers	OF	Tommy Griffith
Feb 2, 1919	C	Bill Rariden	New York Giants	1B	Hal Chase
Feb 1919	IF	Wally Rehg	Boston Braves	SS	Lena Blackburne

DATE		ACQUIRED	FROM		IN EXCHANGE FOR
Feb 1919	IF	Jimmy Smith	New York Giants		Cash
March 8, 1919	P	Slim Sallee	New York Giants		Waiver price
March 15, 1919	P	Ray Fisher	New York Yankees		Waiver price
June 1919	OF	Billy Zitzmann	Pittsburgh Pirates		Cash
July 1919		Cash	Brooklyn Dodgers	UT	Lee Magee
July 1920	2B	Eddie Sicking	New York Giants		Cash
Sept 5, 1920		Waiver price	New York Giants	P	Slim Sallee
Nov 22, 1920	P	Eppa Rixey	Philadelphia Phillies	P OF	Jimmy Ring Greasy Neale
Dec 15, 1920	P	Rube Marquard	Brooklyn Dodgers	P	Dutch Ruether
Dec 1920	OF	Dode Paskert	Chicago Cubs		Waiver price
June 2, 1921	OF	Greasy Neale	Philadelphia Phillies		Waiver price
June 28, 1921		Cash	Philadelphia Phillies	IF	Jimmy Smith
Dec 6, 1921	C OF	Mike Gonzalez George Burns and $150,000.	New York Giants	3B	Heinie Groh
Jan 24, 1922		Cash	Brooklyn Dodgers	SS	Sam Crane
Feb 17, 1922	C	Ernie Krueger	Brooklyn Dodgers		Cash
Feb 18, 1922	SS P	Larry Kopf Jack Scott	Boston Braves	P	Rube Marquard
July 30, 1922	P	Rube Benton	New York Giants		Cash
Aug 2, 1923		Waiver price	Philadelphia Phillies	P	Johnny Couch
Dec 11, 1923	P	Carl Mays	New York Yankees		Cash
May 30, 1924	OF	Curt Walker	Philadelphia Phillies	OF	George Harper
June 20, 1924	OF	Cliff Lee	Philadelphia Phillies		Cash
Oct 1924		Waiver price	Washington Senators	OF	Pat Duncan
March 30, 1925		Cash	Philadelphia Phillies	1B	Lew Fonseca
April 2, 1925		Waiver price	Philadelphia Phillies	OF	George Burns
April 22, 1925	OF	Hy Myers	St. Louis Cardinals		Cash

DATE	ACQUIRED	FROM	IN EXCHANGE FOR
May 4, 1925	Cash	St. Louis Cardinals	OF Hy Myers
May 20, 1925	OF Al Niehaus	Pittsburgh Pirates	P Tom Sheehan
June 23, 1925	OF Joe Schultz	Philadelphia Phillies	Cash
July 9, 1925	1B Walter Holke	Philadelphia Phillies	Waiver price
Feb 1, 1926	1B Wally Pipp	New York Yankees	$7,500.
Feb 10, 1926	C Val Picinich	Boston Red Sox	$7,500.
May 11, 1926	P Art Nehf	New York Giants	Cash
June 15, 1926	Cash	Brooklyn Dodgers	2B Sammy Bohne
July 6, 1926	SS Everett Scott	Chicago White Sox	Waiver price
Feb 9, 1927	1B George Kelly and cash	New York Giants	OF Edd Roush
Sept 4, 1927	Cash	Chicago Cubs	P Art Nehf
March 13, 1928	Waiver price	Brooklyn Dodgers	OF Rube Bressler
April 18, 1929	C Johnny Gooch P Rube Ehrhardt	Brooklyn Dodgers	C Val Picinich
Oct 14, 1929	OF Harry Heilmann	Detroit Tigers	Cash
Oct 16, 1929	OF Bob Meusel	New York Yankees	Waiver price
Feb 2, 1930	SS Leo Durocher	New York Yankees	Waiver price
Feb 1930	P Doug McWeeny	Brooklyn Dodgers	P Dolf Luque
April 4, 1930	Waiver price	Washington Senators	OF Earl Webb
May 21, 1930	P Larry Benton	New York Giants	2B Hughie Critz
May 27, 1930	OF Pat Crawford	New York Giants	OF Ethan Allen P Pete Donohue
Sept 13, 1930	P Ownie Carroll	New York Yankees	Cash
Oct 14, 1930	Cash	Chicago Cubs	P Jakie May
Oct 29, 1930	OF Wally Roettger	New York Giants	Cash
Jan 1931	3B Clyde Beck	Chicago Cubs	Waiver price
April 1, 1931	OF Cliff Heathcote	Chicago Cubs	Waiver price

DATE		ACQUIRED	FROM		IN EXCHANGE FOR
May 7, 1931	OF	Harvey Hendrick	Brooklyn Dodgers	1B	Mickey Heath
June 15, 1931	OF	Taylor Douthit	St. Louis Cardinals	OF	Wally Roettger
Dec 2, 1931	2B	Andy High	St. Louis Cardinals	OF	Nick Cullop and cash
Dec 1931	OF	Wally Roettger	St. Louis Cardinals		Cash
Jan 26, 1932		Cash	St. Louis Cardinals	SS	Hod Ford
Feb 4, 1932	2B	George Grantham	Pittsburgh Pirates		Cash
March 14, 1932	OF 3B C	Babe Herman Wally Gilbert Ernie Lombardi	Brooklyn Dodgers	2B 3B C	Tony Cuccinello Joe Stripp Clyde Sukeforth
April 11, 1932	OF	Chick Hafey	St. Louis Cardinals	OF P	Harvey Hendrick Benny Frey and cash
May 10, 1932	P	Benny Frey	St. Louis Cardinals		Cash
June 5, 1932	OF	Harvey Hendrick	St. Louis Cardinals		Cash
June 25, 1932		Waiver price	Philadelphia Phillies	OF	Cliff Heathcote
Nov 30, 1932	P C OF OF	Bob Smith Rollie Hemsley Johnny Moore Lance Richbourg	Chicago Cubs	OF	Babe Herman
Dec 17, 1932	1B	Jim Bottomley	St. Louis Cardinals	OF P	Estel Crabtree Ownie Carroll
April 29, 1933		Waiver price	Chicago Cubs	OF	Taylor Douthit
May 7, 1933	P 2B P	Paul Derringer Sparky Adams Allyn Stout	St. Louis Cardinals	SS P P	Leo Durocher Butch Henline Jack Ogden
Aug 2, 1933		Waiver price	Boston Braves	P	Bob Smith
Aug 3, 1933		Waiver price	St. Louis Browns	C	Rollie Hemsley
Sept 1, 1933	C	Jack Crouch	St. Louis Browns		Waiver price
Oct 17, 1933	OF 2B	Adam Comorosky Tony Piet	Pittsburgh Pirates	P OF	Red Lucas Wally Roettger
Nov 15, 1933	P	Glenn Spencer	New York Giants	2B	George Grantham
Nov 1933	C	Harry McCurdy	Philadelphia Phillies		Cash
Dec 20, 1933	SS	Mark Koenig	Philadelphia Phillies	3B SS	Otto Bluege Irv Jeffries
Dec 1933	SS	Gordon Slade	St. Louis Cardinals		Waiver price

DATE		ACQUIRED	FROM		IN EXCHANGE FOR
Dec 1933	P	Tony Freitas	Philadelphia Athletics		Cash
Dec 1933	P	Joe Shaute	Brooklyn Dodgers		Cash
Jan 11, 1934	C P	Bob O'Farrell Syl Johnson (O'Farrell was named Cincinnati manager.)	St. Louis Cardinals	P	Glenn Spencer
May 8, 1934	P OF OF	Ted Kleinhans Wes Schulmerich Art Ruble	Philadelphia Phillies	P OF	Syl Johnson Johnny Moore
June 25, 1934	P	Dazzy Vance	St. Louis Cardinals		Waiver price
Nov 3, 1934	OF	Ival Goodman	St. Louis Cardinals		$25,000.
Nov 3, 1934	3B	Lew Riggs	St. Louis Cardinals		$30,000.
Nov 13, 1934	P	Danny MacFayden	New York Yankees		Cash
Dec 13, 1934	1B	Johnny Mize (Mize was returned to St. Louis because of a bad knee.)	St. Louis Cardinals		Cash
Dec 14, 1934	SS	Billy Myers and cash	New York Giants	SS P	Mark Koenig Allyn Stout
Dec 19, 1934	OF	Sammy Byrd	New York Yankees		Cash
June 4, 1935		Cash	Chicago White Sox	2B	Tony Piet
June 15, 1935		Waiver price	Boston Braves	P	Danny MacFayden
June 21, 1935	OF	Babe Herman	Pittsburgh Pirates		Cash
Dec 12, 1935	SS	Tommy Thevenow	Pittsburgh Pirates		Cash
Jan 29, 1936		Cash	Cleveland Indians	C	Billy Sullivan
March 21, 1936	2B	Johnny Burnett	St. Louis Browns	1B	Jim Bottomley
May 31, 1936	P	Bill Hallahan	St. Louis Cardinals		Cash
Aug 6, 1936	P	Bill Walker	St. Louis Cardinals	P	Si Johnson
Dec 2, 1936	C	Spud Davis	St. Louis Cardinals		Cash
Dec 2, 1936	SS	Charley Gelbert	St. Louis Cardinals		Cash
Jan 6, 1937		Cash	Boston Braves	SS	Tommy Thevenow
April 1, 1937		Cash	Detroit Tigers	OF	Babe Herman
May 12, 1937	1B	Buck Jordan	Boston Braves		Cash

DATE		ACQUIRED	FROM		IN EXCHANGE FOR
June 1937		Cash	New York Giants	P	Jumbo Brown
July 3, 1937	P	Joe Cascarella	Washington Senators		Cash
July 9, 1937		Waiver price	Detroit Tigers	SS	Charley Gelbert
Aug 4, 1937	OF	Kiddo Davis	New York Giants		Cash
Feb 4, 1938	2B	Lonny Frey	Chicago Cubs		Cash
April 25, 1938	P	Jim Weaver	St. Louis Browns		Cash
June 6, 1938	OF	Wally Berger	New York Giants	2B	Alex Kampouris
June 10, 1938	P	Justin Stein	Philadelphia Phillies	2B	Buck Jordan
June 13, 1938	P	Bucky Walters	Philadelphia Phillies	C P	Spud Davis Al Hollingsworth and $50,000.
July 8, 1938	SS	Woody English	Brooklyn Dodgers		Cash
Aug 10, 1938	P P 3B C OF	Tommy Reis Johnny Babich Gil English Johnny Riddle Vince DiMaggio and cash	Boston Braves	SS	Eddie Miller
Dec 8, 1938	OF	Frenchy Bordagaray	St. Louis Cardinals	OF	Dusty Cooke
Dec 13, 1938		Cash	Brooklyn Dodgers	OF	Jimmy Outlaw
March 16, 1939	3B	Bill Werber	Philadelphia Athletics		Cash
May 5, 1939		Cash	Brooklyn Dodgers	P	Gene Schott
Aug 5, 1939		Cash	Philadelphia Phillies	OF	Bud Hafey
Aug 19, 1939	P	Milt Shoffner	Boston Braves		Waiver price
Aug 19, 1939		Cash	Philadelphia Phillies	P	Peaches Davis
Aug 31, 1939	OF	Al Simmons	Boston Braves		Cash
Dec 6, 1939	P	Jim Turner	Boston Braves	1B	Les Scarsella and cash
Jan 4, 1940	P	Joe Beggs	New York Yankees	P	Lee Grissom
Jan 4, 1940		Waiver price	St. Louis Browns	P	Johnny Niggeling
May 8, 1940	OF	Johnny Rizzo	Pittsburgh Pirates	OF	Vince DiMaggio

DATE		ACQUIRED	FROM		IN EXCHANGE FOR
June 15, 1940	OF	Morrie Arnovich	Philadelphia Phillies	OF	Johnny Rizzo
Aug 23, 1940	OF	Jimmy Ripple	Brooklyn Dodgers		Waiver price
Aug 1940		Cash	Pittsburgh Pirates	P	Dutch Dietz
Dec 4, 1940	OF SS	Jim Gleeson Bobby Mattick	Chicago Cubs	SS	Billy Myers
Dec 9, 1940	2B	Pep Young	Brooklyn Dodgers	3B	Lew Riggs
Dec 10, 1940		Cash	New York Giants	OF	Morrie Arnovich
Dec 16, 1940	P	Tot Pressnell	St. Louis Cardinals		Cash
Dec 30, 1940	P	Monte Pearson	New York Yankees	3B	Don Lang and $20,000.
Feb 4, 1941		Cash	Chicago Cubs	P	Tot Pressnell
May 12, 1941		Cash	Pittsburgh Pirates	C	Bill Baker
May 14, 1941	OF	Ernie Koy	St. Louis Cardinals		Cash
June 12, 1941	OF	Lloyd Waner	Boston Braves	P	Johnny Hutchings
Dec 4, 1941	C	Rollie Hemsley	Cleveland Indians		Cash
Dec 9, 1941		Cash	New York Giants	3B	Bill Werber
Feb 7, 1942		Cash	Boston Braves	C	Ernie Lombardi
March 26, 1942	OF	Gee Walker	Cleveland Indians		Cash
May 2, 1942		Cash	Philadelphia Phillies	OF	Ernie Koy
May 6, 1942	P	Clyde Shoun	St. Louis Cardinals		Cash
July 16, 1942	OF	Frankie Kelleher	New York Yankees	P	Jim Turner
Nov 14, 1942		Cash	Chicago Cubs	OF	Ival Goodman
Dec 4, 1942	SS	Eddie Miller	Boston Braves	SS P	Eddie Joost Nate Andrews and $25,000.
Jan 27, 1943		Cash	Chicago Cubs	P	Paul Derringer
Feb 1, 1943		Waiver price (Landis voided the sale because Mesner had already been drafted at the time of the deal.)	Brooklyn Dodgers	2B	Steve Mesner
April 2, 1943		Cash	Philadelphia Phillies	SS	Garton Del Savio

DATE		ACQUIRED	FROM		IN EXCHANGE FOR
May 27, 1944		Cash	Pittsburgh Pirates	P	Ray Starr
June 15, 1944	P	Harry Gumbert	St. Louis Cardinals		Cash
Aug 19, 1944	OF	Jo-Jo White	Philadelphia Athletics		Cash
Aug 22, 1945	P	Nate Andrews	Boston Braves		Cash
March 18, 1946	SS	Claude Corbitt	Brooklyn Dodgers		Cash
April 18, 1946	OF	Max West	Boston Braves	P	Jim Konstanty and cash
June 3, 1946		Cash	Boston Braves	OF	Mike McCormick
Dec 4, 1946	OF	Augie Galan	Brooklyn Dodgers	P	Ed Heusser
April 16, 1947		Cash	Chicago Cubs	2B	Lonny Frey
April 28, 1947		Waiver price	Pittsburgh Pirates	P	Bob Malloy
May 13, 1947	OF	Tommy Tatum	Brooklyn Dodgers		Cash
June 7, 1947	1B	Babe Young	New York Giants	P	Joe Beggs
June 7, 1947		Cash	Boston Braves	P	Clyde Shoun
June 14, 1947	P C	Ken Raffensberger Hugh Poland	Philadelphia Phillies	C	Al Lakeman
Oct 8, 1947	OF	Marv Rickert	Chicago Cubs		Cash
Dec 10, 1947		Cash	Pittsburgh Pirates	P	Elmer Riddle
Dec 11, 1947	P	Tommy Hughes	Philadelphia Phillies	1B	Bert Haas
Feb 7, 1948	OF	Johnny Wyrostek and cash	Philadelphia Phillies	SS	Eddie Miller
May 11, 1948	OF	Danny Litwhiler	Boston Braves	OF	Marv Rickert
Nov 8, 1948	P	Ken Burkhart	St. Louis Cardinals	1B	Babe Young
June 8, 1949		Cash	Chicago White Sox	1B	Charlie Kress
June 13, 1949	C	Walker Cooper	New York Giants	C	Ray Mueller
June 15, 1949	OF OF	Harry Walker Peanuts Lowrey	Chicago Cubs	OF OF	Frankie Baumholtz Hank Sauer
July 27, 1949		Waiver price	Pittsburgh Pirates	P	Harry Gumbert
Dec 14, 1949	2B OF	Lou Klein Ron Northey	St. Louis Cardinals	OF	Harry Walker

DATE		ACQUIRED	FROM		IN EXCHANGE FOR
May 10, 1950		Cash	Philadelphia Phillies	2B	Jimmy Bloodworth
May 10, 1950	P	Willie Ramsdell	Brooklyn Dodgers		Cash
May 10, 1950	2B	Connie Ryan	Boston Braves	C	Walker Cooper
June 7, 1950	C	Bob Scheffing	Chicago Cubs	OF	Ron Northey
Sept 7, 1950		Cash	St. Louis Cardinals	OF	Peanuts Lowrey
July 21, 1951	OF	Hank Edwards	Brooklyn Dodgers		Waiver price
July 21, 1951		Waiver price	Cleveland Indians	OF	Barney McCosky
Aug 1, 1951		Waiver price	St. Louis Cardinals	C	Bob Scheffing
Oct 4, 1951	OF C	Bob Borkowski Smoky Burgess	Chicago Cubs	C OF	Johnny Pramesa Bob Usher
Dec 10, 1951	C IF 1B P	Andy Seminick Eddie Pellagrini Dick Sisler Niles Jordan	Philadelphia Phillies	C P 2B	Smoky Burgess Howie Fox Connie Ryan
Jan 3, 1952	P	Frank Hiller	Chicago Cubs	P	Willie Ramsdell
April 9, 1952		Cash	Pittsburgh Pirates	P	Hooks Iott
May 13, 1952	3B OF	Eddie Kazak Wally Westlake	St. Louis Cardinals	1B SS	Dick Sisler Virgil Stallcup
May 23, 1952	P	Bubba Church	Philadelphia Phillies	OF P	Johnny Wyrostek Kent Peterson
May 25, 1952	P	Phil Haugstad	Brooklyn Dodgers		Waiver price
June 4, 1952	OF	Willard Marshall	Boston Braves		Cash
June 9, 1952	OF	Cal Abrams	Brooklyn Dodgers	SS	Rudy Rufer and cash
June 15, 1952	P	Bud Podbielan	Brooklyn Dodgers	P	Bud Byerly and cash
Aug 7, 1952		Cash	Cleveland Indians	OF	Wally Westlake
Aug 28, 1952	OF P P OF	Jim Greengrass Johnny Schmitz Ernie Nevel Bob Marquis and $35,000.	New York Yankees	P	Ewell Blackwell
Sept 1, 1952	P	Howie Judson	Chicago White Sox	OF	Hank Edwards
Oct 10, 1952	P	Clyde King	Brooklyn Dodgers		Cash
Oct 14, 1952	OF	Gus Bell	Pittsburgh Pirates	OF C OF	Cal Abrams Joe Rossi Gail Henley

DATE		ACQUIRED	FROM		IN EXCHANGE FOR
Feb 16, 1953	2B	Rocky Bridges and cash	Milwaukee Braves	1B	Joe Adcock
		(Part of four-team trade involving Milwaukee Braves, Philadelphia Phillies, Brooklyn, and Cincinnati.)			
Feb 17, 1953		Cash	New York Yankees	P	Johnny Schmitz
April 17, 1953		Waiver price	Pittsburgh Pirates	2B	Eddie Pellagrini
May 3, 1953		Cash	Cleveland Indians	C	Hank Foiles
May 23, 1953	P	Jackie Collum	St. Louis Cardinals	P	Eddie Erautt
June 12, 1953	P P	Fred Baczewski Bob Kelly	Chicago Cubs	P	Bubba Church
Dec 2, 1953	P	Jack Crimian and $100,000.	St. Louis Cardinals	SS	Alex Grammas
Dec 10, 1953	P 2B 3B	Saul Rogovin Connie Ryan Rocky Krsnich	Chicago White Sox	OF	Willard Marshall
April 18, 1954	SS	Johnny Lipon	Chicago White Sox	3B	Grady Hatton
June 12, 1954		Cash	Philadelphia Phillies	P	Herm Wehmeier
June 15, 1954	P	Karl Drews	Philadelphia Phillies		Cash
Oct 1, 1954	P P	Johnny Klippstein Jim Willis	Chicago Cubs	OF P OF	Ted Tappe Harry Perkowski Jim Bolger
Dec 8, 1954	3B P	Ray Jablonski Gerry Staley	St. Louis Cardinals	P	Frank Smith
Feb 10, 1955		Cash	Chicago White Sox	OF	Lloyd Merriman
April 13, 1955	P	Bob Hooper	Cleveland Indians		Cash
April 30, 1955	C P OF	Smoky Burgess Steve Ridzik Stan Palys	Philadelphia Phillies	C OF OF	Andy Seminick Glen Gorbous Jim Greengrass
May 10, 1955	P	Hersh Freeman	Boston Red Sox		Cash
June 9, 1955	P	Joe Black	Brooklyn Dodgers	OF	Bob Borkowski and cash
June 23, 1955	OF	Sam Mele	Boston Red Sox		Cash
July 26, 1955		Cash	Chicago White Sox	2B	Bobby Adams
Sept 11, 1955		Waiver price	New York Yankees	P	Gerry Staley
Nov 28, 1955	P	Hal Jeffcoat	Chicago Cubs	C	Hobie Landrith
Jan 31, 1956	P IF	Brooks Lawrence Sonny Senerchia	St. Louis Cardinals	P	Jackie Collum

DATE		ACQUIRED	FROM		IN EXCHANGE FOR
April 9, 1956	1B	George Crowe	Milwaukee Braves	OF P	Bob Hazle Corky Valentine
April 10, 1956	P	Frank Smith	St. Louis Cardinals		Waiver price
May 1, 1956	P	Paul LaPalme	St. Louis Cardinals	3B	Milt Smith
May 11, 1956	OF	Jim Dyck	Baltimore Orioles		$25,000.
May 16, 1956	OF SS	Joe Frazier Alex Grammas	St. Louis Cardinals	OF	Chuck Harmon
June 22, 1956		Waiver price	Chicago White Sox	P	Paul LaPalme
Sept 1, 1956	P	Russ Meyer	Chicago Cubs		Waiver price
Nov 13, 1956	3B P OF	Don Hoak Warren Hacker Pete Whisenant	Chicago Cubs	P 3B	Elmer Singleton Ray Jablonski
April 13, 1957		Waiver price	Boston Red Sox	P	Russ Meyer
May 20, 1957		Waiver price	Washington Senators	SS	Rocky Bridges
June 12, 1957		Cash	Washington Senators	OF	Art Schult
June 26, 1957		Waiver price	Philadelphia Phillies	P	Warren Hacker
Dec 4, 1957	P	Bill Wight	Baltimore Orioles		Waiver price
Dec 5, 1957	P P	Marty Kutyna Ted Wieand	St. Louis Cardinals	OF OF	Curt Flood Joe Taylor
Dec 9, 1957	P	Bob Purkey	Pittsburgh Pirates	P	Don Gross
Dec 16, 1957	P	Harvey Haddix	Philadelphia Phillies	OF	Wally Post
Dec 28, 1957	1B	Dee Fondy	Pittsburgh Pirates	1B	Ted Kluszewski
April 3, 1958		Waiver price	Detroit Tigers	OF	Stan Palys
April 23, 1958	3B	Fred Hatfield	Cleveland Indians	P	Bob Kelly
May 8, 1958	P	Turk Lown	Chicago Cubs	P	Hersh Freeman
June 15, 1958	P	Don Newcombe	Los Angeles Dodgers	1B P	Steve Bilko Johnny Klippstein
June 23, 1958	P	Alex Kellner	Kansas City Athletics		Waiver price
June 23, 1958		Waiver price	Chicago White Sox	P	Turk Lown
June 24, 1958	1B	Walt Dropo	Chicago White Sox		Waiver price
Oct 3, 1958	P 3B OF	Bob Mabe Eddie Kasko Del Ennis	St. Louis Cardinals	1B P SS	George Crowe Alex Kellner Alex Grammas

DATE	ACQUIRED	FROM	IN EXCHANGE FOR
Jan 30, 1959	P Whammy Douglas OF Jim Pendleton OF Frank Thomas OF Johnny Powers	Pittsburgh Pirates	C Smoky Burgess P Harvey Haddix 3B Don Hoak
May 1, 1959	P Don Rudolph OF Lou Skizas	Chicago White Sox	OF Del Ennis
June 6, 1959	OF Jim Bolger and cash	Cleveland Indians	3B Willie Jones
June 8, 1959	P Jim Brosnan	St. Louis Cardinals	P Hal Jeffcoat
June 23, 1959	1B Whitey Lockman	Baltimore Orioles	1B Walt Dropo
July 1, 1959	3B Willie Jones	Cleveland Indians	Cash
Nov 21, 1959	C Frank House	Kansas City Athletics	P Tom Acker
Dec 6, 1959	P Bill Henry OF Lou Jackson OF Lee Walls	Chicago Cubs	OF Frank Thomas
Dec 15, 1959	Cash	Baltimore Orioles	OF Johnny Powers
April 29, 1960	Cash	Cleveland Indians	OF Pete Whisenant
May 18, 1960	P Bob Grim	Cleveland Indians	Cash
June 15, 1960	OF Harry Anderson OF Wally Post	Philadelphia Phillies	OF Tony Gonzalez OF Lee Walls
July 29, 1960	Cash	St. Louis Cardinals	P Bob Grim
July 29, 1960	Cash	Cleveland Indians	P Don Newcombe
Aug 2, 1960	P Marshall Bridges	St. Louis Cardinals	Waiver price
Oct 15, 1960	C Danny Kravitz	Kansas City Athletics	C Dutch Dotterer
Dec 3, 1960	Cash	Milwaukee Braves	2B Billy Martin
Dec 15, 1960	P Joey Jay P Juan Pizarro	Milwaukee Braves	SS Roy McMillan
Dec 15, 1960	3B Gene Freese	Chicago White Sox	P Juan Pizarro P Cal McLish
April 27, 1961	C Bob Schmidt 2B Don Blasingame P Sherman Jones	San Francisco Giants	C Ed Bailey
July 21, 1961	P Ken Johnson	Kansas City Athletics	Cash
Aug 14, 1961	C Darrell Johnson	Philadelphia Phillies	Cash
Sept 16, 1961	P Dave Sisler and cash	Washington Senators	P Claude Osteen
Dec 15, 1961	P Johnny Klippstein OF Marty Keough	Washington Senators	P Dave Stenhouse C Bob Schmidt

DATE		ACQUIRED	FROM		IN EXCHANGE FOR
Dec 21, 1961		Cash	New York Mets	P	Howie Nunn
Jan 30, 1962	OF	Dan Dobbek	Minnesota Twins	C	Jerry Zimmerman
April 20, 1962	C	Hank Foiles	Baltimore Orioles		Cash
May 7, 1962	3B	Don Zimmer	New York Mets	P 3B	Bob Miller Cliff Cook
May 8, 1962	P	Ted Wills	Boston Red Sox		Cash
Aug 13, 1962		Cash	Kansas City Athletics	P	Moe Drabowsky
Nov 24, 1962	3B	Harry Bright	Washington Senators	1B	Rogelio Alvarez
Nov 27, 1962	P	Jim Owens	Philadelphia Phillies	2B	Cookie Rojas
Dec 15, 1962	P	Dick Luebke minor league IF Willard Oplinger	Baltimore Orioles	OF	Joe Gaines
Jan 24, 1963		Minor league P Scott Breeden	Los Angeles Dodgers	3B	Don Zimmer
March 25, 1963		Cash	Philadelphia Phillies	P	Johnny Klippstein
April 21, 1963		Cash	New York Yankees	1B	Harry Bright
May 5, 1963	P	Dom Zanni	Chicago White Sox	P	Jim Brosnan
May 16, 1963		Cash	Minnesota Twins	OF	Wally Post
May 23, 1963	OF	Bob Skinner	Pittsburgh Pirates	OF	Jerry Lynch
July 1, 1963	2B C	Charlie Neal Sammy Taylor	New York Mets	C	Jesse Gonder
July 1, 1963		Cash	Washington Senators	2B	Don Blasingame
Aug 1, 1963	OF	Gene Green	Cleveland Indians	C	Sammy Taylor
Oct 9, 1963	C	Jim Campbell	Houston Astros		Cash
Nov 26, 1963		Cash	Pittsburgh Pirates	3B	Gene Freese
Jan 20, 1964	OF P	Jim Dickson Wally Wolf and cash	Houston Astros	SS	Eddie Kasko
May 13, 1964	P	Ryne Duren	Philadelphia Phillies		Cash
June 13, 1964		Minor league P Jim Saul and cash	St. Louis Cardinals	OF	Bob Skinner
July 19, 1964		Cash	New York Mets	2B	Bobby Klaus

DATE	ACQUIRED	FROM	IN EXCHANGE FOR
Dec 4, 1964	P Jerry Arrigo	Minnesota Twins	OF Cesar Tovar
Dec 14, 1964	OF Charlie James P Roger Craig	St. Louis Cardinals	P Bob Purkey
May 4, 1965	P Jim Duffalo	San Francisco Giants	P Bill Henry
July 28, 1965	P Larry Locke	California Angels	Cash
Dec 9, 1965	P Milt Pappas P Jack Baldschun OF Dick Simpson	Baltimore Orioles	OF Frank Robinson
April 4, 1966	Cash and minor league player to be named later	Atlanta Braves	OF Marty Keough
May 20, 1966	Cash	New York Mets	P Jerry Arrigo
June 3, 1966	Cash	California Angels	P Larry Locke
June 15, 1966	P Hank Fischer	Atlanta Braves	P Joey Jay
Aug 15, 1966	P Dick Stigman P Bill Stafford (Cincinnati received Stigman and Stafford on December 15, 1966.)	Boston Red Sox	P Hank Fischer
Aug 16, 1966	P Jerry Arrigo	New York Mets	Cash
Sept 27, 1966	P Aurelio Monteagudo	Houston Astros	Cash
Dec 15, 1966	OF Floyd Robinson	Chicago White Sox	P Jim O'Toole
May 31, 1967	P Bob Lee	Los Angeles Dodgers	Cash
June 23, 1967	2B Jake Wood	Detroit Tigers	Cash
Sept 18, 1967	P Bill Henry	New York Yankees	2B Len Boehmer
Oct 10, 1967	1B Jim Beauchamp OF Mack Jones P Jay Ritchie	Atlanta Braves	1B Deron Johnson
Oct 20, 1967	P Ron Tompkins	Kansas City Athletics	OF Floyd Robinson P Darrell Osteen
Nov 8, 1967	IF Bob Johnson	New York Mets	1B-OF Art Shamsky
Nov 21, 1967	P George Culver 1B Fred Whitfield	Cleveland Indians	OF Tommy Harper
Nov 29, 1967	P Bill Kelso P Jorge Rubio	California Angels	P Sammy Ellis
Jan 11, 1968	OF Alex Johnson	St. Louis Cardinals	OF Dick Simpson
Feb 8, 1968	C Pat Corrales minor league IF Jimmy Williams	St. Louis Cardinals	C Johnny Edwards

DATE		ACQUIRED	FROM		IN EXCHANGE FOR
June 11, 1968	SS P P	Woody Woodward Clay Carroll Tony Cloninger	Atlanta Braves	P P IF	Milt Pappas Ted Davidson Bob Johnson
Oct 11, 1968	P OF	Wayne Granger Bobby Tolan	St. Louis Cardinals	OF	Vada Pinson
Nov 21, 1968	P	Jim Merritt	Minnesota Twins	SS	Leo Cardenas
Dec 5, 1968	OF	Leon Wagner	Chicago White Sox		Cash
Dec 5, 1968	P	Jack Fisher	Chicago White Sox	C P	Don Pavletich Don Secrist
Jan 9, 1969	C OF	Bill Plummer Clarence Jones minor league P Ken Myette	Chicago Cubs	P	Ted Abernathy
March 18, 1969		Cash (Kelso was returned to Cincinnati on March 29.)	Baltimore Orioles	P	Bill Kelso
March 30, 1969	OF	Ted Savage	Los Angeles Dodgers	C	Jimmie Schaffer
April 27, 1969		Minor league IF Jim Armstrong and cash	Chicago Cubs	P	Don Nottebart
June 13, 1969	P	Al Jackson	New York Mets		Cash
June 30, 1969	C	Danny Breeden	San Diego Padres		Cash
July 7, 1969	P	Camilo Pascual	Washington Senators		Cash
Oct 24, 1969		Cash	California Angels	P	Mel Queen
Nov 5, 1969	P	Ray Washburn	St. Louis Cardinals	P	George Culver
Nov 25, 1969	P P P	Pedro Borbon Jim McGlothlin Vern Geishert	California Angels	OF IF	Alex Johnson Chico Ruiz
Dec 15, 1969	OF	Angel Bravo	Chicago White Sox	P	Jerry Arrigo
Jan 14, 1970	P	Bill Harrelson minor league IF Dan Loomer	California Angels	P	Jack Fisher
April 5, 1970		Cash	Milwaukee Brewers	OF	Ted Savage
June 15, 1970	OF	Ty Cline	Montreal Expos	OF	Clyde Mashore
Oct 20, 1970	P	Ed Sprague	Oakland Athletics		Cash
Nov 30, 1970	OF-1B	Willie Smith	Chicago Cubs	C	Danny Breeden
Dec 15, 1970	P	Greg Garrett	California Angels	P	Jim Maloney

DATE	ACQUIRED	FROM	IN EXCHANGE FOR
May 8, 1971	OF Buddy Bradford	Cleveland Indians	IF Kurt Bevacqua
May 13, 1971	OF Al Ferrara	San Diego Padres	OF Angel Bravo
May 29, 1971	OF George Foster	San Francisco Giants	SS Frank Duffy P Vern Geishert
Nov 29, 1971	2B Joe Morgan 3B Denis Menke P Jack Billingham OF Ed Armbrister OF Cesar Geronimo	Houston Astros	1B Lee May 2B Tommy Helms OF Jimmy Stewart
Dec 3, 1971	P Tom Hall	Minnesota Twins	P Wayne Granger
Dec 6, 1971	OF Ted Uhlaender	Cleveland Indians	P Milt Wilcox
March 24, 1972	2B Julian Javier	St. Louis Cardinals	P Tony Cloninger
May 19, 1972	1B Joe Hague	St. Louis Cardinals	OF Bernie Carbo
June 11, 1972	C Bob Barton	San Diego Padres	C Pat Corrales
Sept 16, 1972	Cash	New York Yankees	P Steve Blateric
Nov 28, 1972	OF Bill Voss	St. Louis Cardinals	P Pat Jacquez
Nov 30, 1972	P Roger Nelson OF Richie Scheinblum	Kansas City Royals	OF Hal McRae P Wayne Simpson
Nov 30, 1972	OF Larry Stahl	San Diego Padres	Cash
March 27, 1973	IF Phil Gagliano OF Andy Kosco	Boston Red Sox	P Mel Behney
June 12, 1973	P Fred Norman	San Diego Padres	OF Gene Locklear P Mike Johnson and cash
June 15, 1973	P Terry Wilshusen minor league P Thor Skogan	California Angels	OF Richie Scheinblum
July 27, 1973	IF Ed Crosby minor league C Gene Dusen	St. Louis Cardinals	P Ed Sprague 2B Roe Skidmore
Aug 29, 1973	P Steve Kealey	Chicago White Sox	P Jim McGlothlin
Nov 9, 1973	P Clay Kirby	San Diego Padres	OF Bobby Tolan P Dave Tomlin
Dec 4, 1973	OF Merv Rettenmund SS Junior Kennedy and minor league C Bill Wood	Baltimore Orioles	P Ross Grimsley and minor league C Wally Williams
Feb 18, 1974	P Pat Darcy and cash	Houston Astros	IF Denis Menke
March 19, 1974	OF-1B Terry Crowley	Texas Rangers	Cash

DATE		ACQUIRED	FROM		IN EXCHANGE FOR
Oct 22, 1974	IF	John Vukovich	Milwaukee Brewers	P	Pat Osborn
Oct 25, 1974		Cash	Chicago White Sox	P	Roger Nelson
April 15, 1975	P	Mac Scarce	New York Mets	P	Tom Hall
Oct 24, 1975	P	Luis Sanchez minor league P Carlos Alfonso	Houston Astros	P	Joaquin Andujar
Dec 12, 1975	3B	Bob Bailey	Montreal Expos	P	Clay Kirby
Dec 12, 1975	OF	Mike Lum	Atlanta Braves	SS	Darrell Chaney
Dec 12, 1975	P	Rich Hinton minor league OF Jeff Sovern	Chicago White Sox	P	Clay Carroll
April 5, 1976	SS	Rudi Meoli	San Diego Padres	OF	Merv Rettenmund
April 7, 1976	P	Mike Thompson	Atlanta Braves	OF	Terry Crowley
Nov 6, 1976	IF	Hugh Yancy	Chicago White Sox	OF	Tom Spencer
Nov 6, 1976	P	Jim Sadowski	Pittsburgh Pirates	P	Tom Carroll
Nov 8, 1976		Minor league P Art DeFilippis	Texas Rangers	P	Mike Thompson
Nov 18, 1976		No compensation (free agent signing)	New York Yankees	P	Don Gullett
Dec 16, 1976	P P	Woodie Fryman Dale Murray	Montreal Expos	1B P	Tony Perez Will McEnaney
Feb 16, 1977	OF	Champ Summers	Chicago Cubs	OF	Dave Schneck
March 28, 1977	P	Bill Caudill	St. Louis Cardinals	OF	Joel Youngblood
March 29, 1977	P	Mike Caldwell	St. Louis Cardinals	P	Pat Darcy
May 21, 1977	P SS	Shane Rawley Angel Torres	Montreal Expos	P	Santo Alcala
June 15, 1977	P	Tom Seaver	New York Mets	P IF OF OF	Pat Zachry Doug Flynn Steve Henderson Dan Norman
June 15, 1977		Minor league IF Craig Henderson	California Angels	P	Gary Nolan
June 15, 1977	P	Doug Capilla	St. Louis Cardinals	P	Rawley Eastwick
June 15, 1977		Minor leaguers P Dick O'Keefe and IF Garry Pyka	Milwaukee Brewers	P	Mike Caldwell

DATE		ACQUIRED	FROM		IN EXCHANGE FOR
June 15, 1977	SS	Rick Auerbach	Texas Rangers		Cash
Sept 19, 1977		Minor league P Frank Newcomer and cash	Boston Red Sox	3B	Bob Bailey
Oct 31, 1977	P	Bill Bonham	Chicago Cubs	P P	Woodie Fryman Bill Caudill
Oct 31, 1977		Cash	Toronto Blue Jays	P	Joe Henderson
Dec 9, 1977	OF-1B	Dave Collins	Seattle Mariners	P	Shane Rawley
Feb 15, 1978		No compensation (free agent signing)	Atlanta Braves	OF	Mike Lum
Feb 25, 1978	P	Doug Bair	Oakland Athletics	1B	Dave Revering and cash
March 6, 1978	P	George Cappuzzello minor league OF John Valle	Detroit Tigers	P	Jack Billingham
March 28, 1978	P	Dave Tomlin	Texas Rangers		Cash
May 19, 1978	OF	Ken Henderson	New York Mets	P	Dale Murray
Dec 5, 1978		No compensation (free agent signing)	Philadelphia Phillies	1B	Pete Rose
May 3, 1979		Minor league P Mark Gilbert	Chicago Cubs	P	Doug Capilla
May 25, 1979	P	Sheldon Burnside	Detroit Tigers	OF	Champ Summers
June 28, 1979		Cash	Chicago Cubs	OF	Ken Henderson
June 28, 1979	OF	Hector Cruz	San Francisco Giants	P	Pedro Borbon
July 4, 1979	OF	Sam Mejias	Chicago Cubs		Cash
Oct 17, 1980	C	Mike O'Berry	Chicago Cubs	P	Jay Howell
Dec 12, 1980	OF	Mike Vail	Chicago Cubs	OF	Hector Cruz
Jan 8, 1981	1B	Larry Biittner	Chicago Cubs		No compensation (free agent signing)
Jan 21, 1981	IF	German Barranca	Kansas City Royals	OF	Cesar Geronimo
June 8, 1981	SS	Rafael Landestoy	Houston Astros	1B	Harry Spilman
Sept 19, 1981	2B P	Neil Fiala Joe Edelen	St. Louis Cardinals	P	Doug Bair
Oct 23, 1981		$50,000.	Chicago Cubs	2B	Junior Kennedy
Nov 4, 1981		Minor league Ps Bryan Ryder and Freddie Tolliver	New York Yankees	OF	Ken Griffey

DATE		ACQUIRED	FROM		IN EXCHANGE FOR
Dec 11, 1981	OF	Clint Hurdle	Kansas City Royals	P	Scott Brown
Dec 18, 1981	OF-1B	Cesar Cedeno	Houston Astros	3B	Ray Knight
Dec 23, 1981		No compensation (free agent signing)	New York Yankees	OF	Dave Collins
Feb 9, 1982	3B	Wayne Krenchicki	Baltimore Orioles	P	Paul Moskau
Feb 10, 1982	C P P	Alex Trevino Jim Kern Greg Harris	New York Mets	OF	George Foster
March 26, 1982	OF	Dallas Williams minor league P Brooks Carey	Baltimore Orioles	C	Joe Nolan
April 1, 1982	P	Bob Shirley	St. Louis Cardinals	 P	Minor league P Jose Brito Jeff Lahti
April 6, 1982		Cash	Houston Astros	P	Mike LaCoss
Aug 23, 1982		Minor leaguers 3B Wade Rowdon and OF Leo Garcia	Chicago White Sox	P	Jim Kern
Sept 7, 1982		Cash	Detroit Tigers	2B	German Barranca
Sept 8, 1982		Cash	Montreal Expos	P	Dave Tomlin
Oct 15, 1982	P	Ted Power	Los Angeles Dodgers		Cash
Dec 15, 1982		No compensation (free agent signing)	New York Yankees	P	Bob Shirley
Dec 16, 1982	P	Charlie Puleo minor leaguers C Lloyd McClendon and OF Jason Felice	New York Mets	P	Tom Seaver
Jan 5, 1983	P	Rich Gale	San Francisco Giants	OF	Mike Vail
Jan 10, 1983	1B	John Harris	California Angels	C	Mike O'Berry
March 31, 1983	IF	Kelly Paris	St. Louis Cardinals		Minor league P Jim Strichek
March 31, 1983	C	Alan Knicely	Houston Astros	P	Bill Dawley minor league OF Tony Walker
May 9, 1983		Minor league P Brett Wise and John Franco	Los Angeles Dodgers	IF	Rafael Landestoy
June 30, 1983	P	Pat Underwood	Detroit Tigers	IF	Wayne Krenchicki
Sept 27, 1983		Cash	Montreal Expos	P	Greg Harris
Nov 12, 1983	P	Bob Owchinko	Pittsburgh Pirates		Cash

DATE		ACQUIRED	FROM		IN EXCHANGE FOR
Nov 21, 1983	3B	Fran Mullins	Chicago White Sox	C	Steve Christmas
Nov 21, 1983	IF	Wayne Krenchicki	Detroit Tigers		Cash
Nov 28, 1983		Cash	Chicago White Sox	IF	Kelly Paris
Dec 6, 1983	1B	Tony Perez	Philadelphia Phillies		Player to be named later
Dec 7, 1983	OF	Dave Parker	Pittsburgh Pirates		No compensation (free agent signing)
March 30, 1984		Minor league P Charlie Nail	Detroit Tigers	OF	Dallas Williams

Houston Astros

The Best Trades

1. Acquired Jerry Reuss from the St. Louis Cardinals for Scipio Spinks and Lance Clemons, April 15, 1972.
2. Acquired Dickie Thon from the California Angels for Ken Forsch, April 1, 1981.
3. Acquired Mike Cuellar and Ron Taylor from the St. Louis Cardinals for Hal Woodeshick and Chuck Taylor, June 15, 1965.
4. Acquired Joaquin Andujar from the Cincinnati Reds for Luis Sanchez and Carlos Alfonso, October 24, 1975.
5. Acquired Alan Ashby from the Toronto Blue Jays for Joe Cannon, Pedro Hernandez, and Mark Lemongello, November 27, 1978.

The Worst Trades

1. Traded Joe Morgan, Denis Menke, Jack Billingham, Cesar Geronimo, and Ed Armbrister to the Cincinnati Reds for Lee May, Tommy Helms, and Jimmy Stewart, November 29, 1971.
2. Traded Mike Cuellar, Enzo Hernandez, and Elijah Johnson to the Baltimore Orioles for Curt Blefary and John Mason, December 4, 1968.
3. Traded Manny Mota to the Pittsburgh Pirates for Howie Goss and cash, April 4, 1963.
4. Traded Joaquin Andujar to the St. Louis Cardinals for Tony Scott, June 7, 1981.
5. Traded John Mayberry and Dave Grangaard to the Kansas City Royals for Lance Clemons and Jim York, December 2, 1971.

Trader: Spec Richardson

In the twenty-three seasons since the Astros have joined the National League, they have won only one half-pennant, their divisional title in 1980. They've finished above .500 just six times in their history. At least part of this woeful story lies in their abysmal record in the trading market. Nearly every major deal they've made, particularly those engineered by general manager Spec Richardson, has blown up in their faces.

Under the Richardson regime the Astros dispatched Joe Morgan, Rusty Staub, Mike Cuellar, Jim Wynn, John Mayberry, Jack Billingham, Mike Marshall, Dave Giusti, and many others only slightly less prominent to teams all around both leagues, usually receiving players of marginal value in return. "Most of the guys we traded didn't play for the Astros like they played for their new clubs," Richardson says. "And some of the players we received were disappointments." True enough, but one of the clearest effects of playing in the Astrodome is how it hurts hitters, and any hitter is going to perform substantially better elsewhere, while power hitters the Astros might pick up are going to look awful.

The most obvious example of this effect is in the Astros' infamous Joe Morgan trade. Morgan was a perfect player for the Dome: he got on base often, could take an extra base on a hit or steal, and could hit with enough power to be effective on the road as well. May, on the other hand, was a pure slugger whose statistics were certain to suffer from playing in the Dome. Another classic was the trade of Mike Cuellar for lead-footed Curt Blefary. Still other trades resulting from their inability to recognize the Dome's effect on offensive performance include Rusty Staub for Donn Clendenon and Jesus Alou (with Jack Billingham and Skip Guinn replacing Clendenon when he refused to report), Jim Wynn for Claude Osteen, and John Mayberry for Jim York and Lance Clemons.

Richardson did make some good trades, picking up Denis Menke and Denny Lemaster from Atlanta for Sonny Jackson and Chuck Harrison; Fred Gladding from Detroit for an aging Eddie Mathews; and Roger Metzger from the Cubs for Joe Pepitone. But his long series of misjudgments put the Astros in a deep hole out of which they have only recently dug themselves.

DATE		ACQUIRED	FROM		IN EXCHANGE FOR
Oct 13, 1961	P	Al Cicotte	St. Louis Cardinals		Cash
Dec 1, 1961	P P	Bob Bruce Manny Montejo	Detroit Tigers	P	Sam Jones
March 24, 1962	P	Tom Borland	Boston Red Sox	OF	Dave Philley
May 7, 1962	OF P	Carl Warwick John Anderson	St. Louis Cardinals	P	Bobby Shantz
May 9, 1962	P	Don McMahon	Milwaukee Braves		Cash
June 22, 1962	P	Russ Kemmerer	Chicago White Sox	P	Dean Stone
July 20, 1962		Cash	Detroit Tigers	3B	Don Buddin
Aug 11, 1962	2B	Johnny Temple	Baltimore Orioles		Cash
Oct 12, 1962	OF	Dick Williams	Baltimore Orioles		Cash
Nov 26, 1962	1B	Pete Runnels	Boston Red Sox	OF	Roman Mejias
Nov 30, 1962	P P OF	Connie Grob Don Nottebart Jim Bolger	Milwaukee Braves	1B	Norm Larker
Nov 30, 1962	P OF	Dick LeMay Manny Mota	San Francisco Giants	2B	Joey Amalfitano
Dec 10, 1962	OF	Carroll Hardy	Boston Red Sox	OF	Dick Williams
March 28, 1963	P P-OF	Jug Gerard Danny Murphy	Chicago Cubs	C P P	Merritt Ranew Hal Haydel Dick LeMay
April 2, 1963		Cash	Cleveland Indians	OF	Ellis Burton

DATE		ACQUIRED	FROM		IN EXCHANGE FOR
April 4, 1963	OF	Howie Goss and cash	Pittsburgh Pirates	OF	Manny Mota
April 21, 1963	P	Hal Brown	New York Yankees		Cash
July 14, 1963		Cash	Baltimore Orioles	P	George Brunet
Sept 30, 1963		Cash	Cleveland Indians	P	Don McMahon
Oct 9, 1963		Cash	Cincinnati Reds	C	Jim Campbell
Oct 10, 1963	P	Claude Raymond	Milwaukee Braves		$30,000.
Dec 10, 1963	2B	Nellie Fox	Chicago White Sox	P P-OF	Jim Golden Danny Murphy and cash
Jan 20, 1964	SS	Eddie Kasko	Cincinnati Reds	OF P	Jim Dickson Wally Wolf and cash
Feb 17, 1964	OF P	Jim Beauchamp Chuck Taylor	St. Louis Cardinals	OF	Carl Warwick
May 12, 1964	P	George Brunet	Baltimore Orioles		Cash
May 20, 1964	P	Don Larsen	San Francisco Giants		Cash
June 15, 1964	OF	Joe Gaines	Baltimore Orioles	OF	Johnny Weekly and cash
Aug 18, 1964		Cash	Los Angeles Angels	P	George Brunet
April 4, 1965		Minor league IF Mickey Sinnerud	Milwaukee Braves	OF	Frank Thomas
April 24, 1965	IF	Bob Saverine and cash	Baltimore Orioles	P	Don Larsen
May 13, 1965	OF	Lee Maye	Milwaukee Braves	P 1B	Ken Johnson Jim Beauchamp
June 4, 1965	1B	Jim Gentile (Kansas City received Fazio on October 15.)	Kansas City Athletics	P 2B	Jess Hickman Ernie Fazio
June 14, 1965	C	Gus Triandos	Philadelphia Phillies		Cash
June 15, 1965	P P	Mike Cuellar Ron Taylor	St. Louis Cardinals	P P	Hal Woodeshick Chuck Taylor
July 6, 1965	P	Don Lee	California Angels	OF	Al Spangler
July 10, 1965	OF	Frank Thomas	Philadelphia Phillies		Cash
Sept 14, 1965	P	Jack Lamabe	Boston Red Sox	P	Darrell Brandon
Oct 19, 1965	P	Tom Parsons and cash	New York Mets	C	Jerry Grote

DATE		ACQUIRED	FROM		IN EXCHANGE FOR
Dec 1, 1965	OF C	Dave Nicholson Bill Heath	Chicago White Sox	P	Jack Lamabe minor league P Ray Cordeiro and cash
Dec 15, 1965	P	Barry Latman	California Angels		Minor league C Ed Pacheco and cash
Jan 6, 1966	P	Gary Kroll	New York Mets	OF	Johnny Weekly and cash
April 3, 1966	2B	Felix Mantilla	Boston Red Sox	SS	Eddie Kasko
May 17, 1966	P	Aurelio Monteagudo	Kansas City Athletics		Cash
July 19, 1966	OF	Tony Curry	Cleveland Indians	1B	Jim Gentile
July 20, 1966	3B	Gene Freese	Chicago White Sox	SS	Jim Mahoney and cash
Sept 27, 1966		Cash	Cincinnati Reds	P	Aurelio Monteagudo
Oct 13, 1966	P P OF	Tom Dukes Dan Schneider Lee Bales	Atlanta Braves	OF C	Gene Ratliff John Hoffman minor league IF Ed Pacheco
Dec 31, 1966	2B 3B P	Sandy Alomar Eddie Mathews Arnie Umbach	Atlanta Braves	OF P	Dave Nicholson Bob Bruce
Jan 4, 1967	OF P C	Jim Landis Jim Weaver Doc Edwards	Cleveland Indians	OF C	Lee Maye Ken Retzer
Feb 10, 1967		Cash	New York Mets	P	Ron Taylor
March 24, 1967	IF	Derrell Griffith	New York Mets	2B	Sandy Alomar
May 8, 1967		Cash	Philadelphia Phillies	P	Dick Farrell
June 3, 1967	OF	Jackie Brandt	Philadelphia Phillies		Cash
June 15, 1967	P	Wade Blasingame	Atlanta Braves	P	Claude Raymond
June 29, 1967	P	Larry Sherry	Detroit Tigers	OF	Jim Landis
July 20, 1967		Cash	Cleveland Indians	P	Gary Kroll
Aug 7, 1967	SS	Hector Torres	California Angels	P	Jim Weaver
Aug 17, 1967	P	Fred Gladding	Detroit Tigers	3B	Eddie Mathews
Sept 23, 1967	P	John Buzhardt	Baltimore Orioles		Cash
Oct 8, 1967	P IF	Denny Lemaster Denis Menke	Atlanta Braves	SS 1B	Sonny Jackson Chuck Harrison

DATE		ACQUIRED	FROM		IN EXCHANGE FOR
Feb 9, 1968	OF	Lee Thomas	Chicago White Sox		Minor league OFs Tom Murray and Levi Brown
May 4, 1968	OF	Byron Browne	Chicago Cubs	OF	Aaron Pointer
June 15, 1968	OF P	Dick Simpson Hal Gilson	St. Louis Cardinals	OF	Ron Davis
Oct 11, 1968	C	Johnny Edwards minor league C Tommy Smith	St. Louis Cardinals	P C	Dave Giusti Dave Adlesh
Oct 17, 1968		Cash	Kansas City Royals	1B	Chuck Harrison
Dec 4, 1968	P	Dooley Womack	New York Yankees	OF	Dick Simpson
Dec 4, 1968	IF	Marty Martinez	Atlanta Braves	3B	Bob Aspromonte
Dec 4, 1968	OF-1B	Curt Blefary and minor leaguer John Mason	Baltimore Orioles	P SS	Mike Cuellar Enzo Hernandez and minor league IF Elijah Johnson
Dec 16, 1968		Minor league C John Jones	Kansas City Royals	C C	Buck Martinez Tommy Smith and minor league IF Mickey Sinnerud
Dec 21, 1968	P	Bill Monbouquette	San Francisco Giants		Cash
Jan 22, 1969	OF 1B P P	Jesus Alou Donn Clendenon Jack Billingham Skip Guinn and $100,000. (Clendenon refused to report, and Houston sent Billingham, Guinn, and cash on April 8, 1969.)	Montreal Expos	1B	Rusty Staub
April 3, 1969		Cash	Montreal Expos	P	Steve Shea
April 3, 1969		Cash	Montreal Expos	P	Howie Reed
Aug 8, 1969	P	Ron Willis	St. Louis Cardinals		Cash
Aug 24, 1969	P	Jim Bouton	Seattle Pilots	P P	Dooley Womack Roric Harrison
Aug 30, 1969	OF	Tommy Davis	Seattle Pilots	OF OF	Danny Walton Sandy Valdespino
Oct 22, 1969		Cash	San Diego Padres	P	Danny Coombs
Nov 21, 1969		Cash	Seattle Pilots	P	Wayne Twitchell
Dec 4, 1969	1B	Joe Pepitone	New York Yankees	1B-OF	Curt Blefary
June 13, 1970	P	George Culver	St. Louis Cardinals	1B SS	Jim Beauchamp Leon McFadden
June 22, 1970		Cash	Oakland Athletics	OF	Tommy Davis

DATE		ACQUIRED	FROM		IN EXCHANGE FOR
July 29, 1970		Cash	Chicago Cubs	1B	Joe Pepitone
Oct 12, 1970	SS	Roger Metzger	Chicago Cubs	SS	Hector Torres
Dec 1, 1970	C	Jack Hiatt	Chicago Cubs		Cash
Oct 14, 1971		Cash	Montreal Expos	P	Denny Lemaster
Nov 3, 1971	C	Bob Stinson	St. Louis Cardinals	IF	Marty Martinez
Nov 29, 1971	1B 2B OF	Lee May Tommy Helms Jimmy Stewart	Cincinnati Reds	2B 3B P OF OF	Joe Morgan Denis Menke Jack Billingham Ed Armbrister Cesar Geronimo
Dec 2, 1971	P P	Jim York Lance Clemons	Kansas City Royals	1B	John Mayberry minor league IF Dave Grangaard
Dec 3, 1971	P	Dave Roberts	San Diego Padres	IF P P	Derrel Thomas Bill Greif Mark Schaeffer
April 15, 1972	P	Jerry Reuss	St. Louis Cardinals	P P	Scipio Spinks Lance Clemons
June 6, 1972		Cash	New York Yankees	P	Wade Blasingame
July 29, 1972		Cash	California Angels	C	Jack Hiatt
Nov 27, 1972	OF	Tommie Agee	New York Mets	OF P	Rich Chiles Buddy Harris
Nov 28, 1972	C IF	Skip Jutze Milt Ramirez	St. Louis Cardinals	SS IF	Ray Busse Bobby Fenwick
March 26, 1973		Cash	Los Angeles Dodgers	P	George Culver
March 28, 1973		Cash	Montreal Expos	C	Bob Stinson
April 4, 1973	SS	Hector Torres	Montreal Expos		Cash
April 22, 1973	P	Cecil Upshaw	Atlanta Braves	OF	Norm Miller
May 22, 1973		Minor league C Tom Helerle	Atlanta Braves	C	Larry Howard
June 8, 1973	SS	Ray Busse	St. Louis Cardinals	2B	Stan Papi
July 31, 1973		Cash	Oakland Athletics	OF	Jesus Alou
Aug 18, 1973	2B	Dave Campbell and cash	St. Louis Cardinals	OF	Tommie Agee
Oct 23, 1973	SS	Mick Kelleher	St. Louis Cardinals		Cash
Oct 23, 1973	P	Dan Neumeier	Chicago White Sox	IF	Hector Torres

DATE		ACQUIRED	FROM		IN EXCHANGE FOR
Oct 31, 1973	C	Milt May	Pittsburgh Pirates	P	Jerry Reuss
Nov 3, 1973	P	Jerry Johnson	Cleveland Indians	P	Cecil Upshaw
Nov 3, 1973	P	Fred Scherman and cash	Detroit Tigers	P	Jim Ray and minor league SS Gary Strickland
Dec 6, 1973	P	Claude Osteen minor league P Dave Culpepper	Los Angeles Dodgers	OF	Jimmy Wynn
Feb 18, 1974	IF	Denis Menke	Cincinnati Reds	P	Pat Darcy and cash
March 28, 1974	OF	Ollie Brown	California Angels		Cash
June 24, 1974		Cash	Philadelphia Phillies	OF	Ollie Brown
Aug 15, 1974		Minor league P Ron Selak	St. Louis Cardinals	P	Claude Osteen
	P	Dan Larson			
Oct 24, 1974	OF	Jose Cruz	St. Louis Cardinals		Cash
Oct 29, 1974	IF	Ken Boswell	New York Mets	OF	Bob Gallagher
Dec 3, 1974	1B	Enos Cabell	Baltimore Orioles	1B	Lee May
	IF	Rob Andrews		OF	Jay Schleuter
Dec 13, 1974		Cash	St. Louis Cardinals	SS	Mick Kelleher
April 6, 1975	P	Joe Niekro	Atlanta Braves		$35,000.
June 8, 1975		Cash	Montreal Expos	P	Fred Scherman
Sept 30, 1975	P	Mike Barlow	St. Louis Cardinals	OF	Mike Easler
Oct 24, 1975	P	Joaquin Andujar	Cincinnati Reds	P	Luis Sanchez minor league P Carlos Alfonso
Dec 6, 1975	OF	Leon Roberts	Detroit Tigers	C	Milt May
	C	Terry Humphrey		P	Dave Roberts
	P	Gene Pentz		P	Jim Crawford
	P	Mark Lemongello			
Dec 11, 1975	P	Joe McIntosh	San Diego Padres	3B	Doug Rader
	P	Larry Hardy			
Dec 12, 1975	3B	Art Howe	Pittsburgh Pirates	2B	Tommy Helms
Jan 8, 1976		Cash	New York Yankees	P	Jim York
June 6, 1976	C	Ed Herrmann	California Angels	C	Terry Humphrey
				P	Mike Barlow
Aug 3, 1976		Cash	San Diego Padres	P	Tom Griffin
Dec 8, 1976	IF	Julio Gonzalez	Chicago Cubs	OF	Greg Gross

DATE		ACQUIRED	FROM		IN EXCHANGE FOR
Jan 12, 1977		Minor league P Alan Griffin and cash	Seattle Mariners	C	Skip Jutze
March 30, 1977	P	Roy Thomas	Seattle Mariners	IF	Larry Milbourne
June 15, 1977	P SS OF	Randy Niemann Mike Fischlin Dave Bergman (Houston received Bergman on November 23.)	New York Yankees	OF	Cliff Johnson
June 15, 1977	OF	Dennis Walling and cash	Oakland Athletics	OF	Willie Crawford
Dec 5, 1977	IF	Jimmy Sexton	Seattle Mariners	OF	Leon Roberts
Dec 9, 1977	P	Randy Wiles	St. Louis Cardinals		Minor league P Ron Selak
March 29, 1978		Cash	Toronto Blue Jays	P	Mike Stanton
June 8, 1978	P	Frank Riccelli	St. Louis Cardinals	OF	Bob Coluccio
June 9, 1978		Cash	Montreal Expos	C	Ed Herrmann
June 15, 1978		Cash	San Francisco Giants	SS	Roger Metzger
June 23, 1978		Cash	St. Louis Cardinals	P	Roy Thomas
July 1, 1978	SS OF	Rafael Landestoy Jeff Leonard	Los Angeles Dodgers	OF	Joe Ferguson and cash
Sept 11, 1978	IF	Mike Buskey	Philadelphia Phillies		Cash
Nov 27, 1978	C	Alan Ashby	Toronto Blue Jays	OF SS P	Joe Cannon Pedro Hernandez Mark Lemongello
Dec 4, 1978	OF	Gary Woods	Toronto Blue Jays		Minor league P Don Pisker
Dec 8, 1978	SS	Craig Reynolds	Seattle Mariners	P	Floyd Bannister
April 27, 1979	P	George Throop	Kansas City Royals	2B	Keith Drumright
May 25, 1979	P	Frank LaCorte	Atlanta Braves	P	Bo McLaughlin
June 13, 1979	P P	Pete Ladd Bobby Sprowl and cash	Boston Red Sox	1B	Bob Watson
Nov 19, 1979	P	Nolan Ryan	California Angels		No compensation (free agent signing)
Feb 20, 1980		Minor league OF Keith Bodie	New York Mets	C	Reggie Baldwin
Dec 4, 1980	P	Don Sutton	Los Angeles Dodgers		No compensation (free agent signing)
Feb 10, 1981	P	Rick Lysander	Oakland Athletics	IF	Jimmy Sexton

DATE		ACQUIRED	FROM		IN EXCHANGE FOR
Feb 11, 1981		Minor leaguers C Stan Hough and IF Randy Rogers	New York Mets	C	Bruce Bochy
April 1, 1981	2B	Dickie Thon	California Angels	P	Ken Forsch
April 1, 1981	SS	Kiko Garcia	Baltimore Orioles	OF	Chris Bourjos and cash
April 3, 1981	OF	Jim Lentine and cash	Cleveland Indians	SS	Mike Fischlin
April 3, 1981		Minor league OF John Csefalvay	New York Mets	OF	Gary Rajsich
April 20, 1981	1B	Mike Ivie	San Francisco Giants	1B OF	Dave Bergman Jeff Leonard
June 7, 1981	OF	Tony Scott	St. Louis Cardinals	P	Joaquin Andujar
June 8, 1981	1B	Harry Spilman	Cincinnati Reds	SS	Rafael Landestoy
Aug 31, 1981	2B	Phil Garner	Pittsburgh Pirates	2B P	Johnny Ray minor league OF Kevin Houston Randy Niemann
Oct 23, 1981	P	Rickey Keeton	Milwaukee Brewers	P	Pete Ladd
Dec 9, 1981	OF	Jim Tracy	Chicago Cubs	OF	Gary Woods
Dec 18, 1981	3B	Ray Knight	Cincinnati Reds	OF-1B	Cesar Cedeno
March 28, 1982		Minor league P Steve Dunnegan	Philadelphia Phillies	UT	Dave Roberts
April 6, 1982	P	Mike LaCoss	Cincinnati Reds		Cash
June 8, 1982	P	Dan Boone	San Diego Padres	3B	Joe Pittman
Aug 30, 1982	OF P P	Kevin Bass Frank DiPino Mike Madden and cash	Milwaukee Brewers	P	Don Sutton
Dec 10, 1982	P	Mike Scott	New York Mets	OF	Danny Heep
Dec 10, 1982	OF	Omar Moreno	Pittsburgh Pirates		No compensation (free agent signing)
Jan 12, 1983	P	Bob Veselic	Minnesota Twins	P	Rick Lysander
Feb 25, 1983		No compensation (free agent signing)	Toronto Blue Jays	P	Randy Moffitt
March 16, 1983	C	George Bjorkman	St. Louis Cardinals		Minor league P Jeff Meadows
March 31, 1983	P	Bill Dawley minor league OF Tony Walker	Cincinnati Reds	C	Alan Knicely
Aug 10, 1983	OF	Jerry Mumphrey	New York Yankees	OF	Omar Moreno

DATE		ACQUIRED	FROM		IN EXCHANGE FOR
Dec 8, 1983		No compensation (free agent signing)	California Angels	P	Frank LaCorte
Dec 21, 1983	P	Craig Minetto	Baltimore Orioles	P	Bobby Sprowl
Feb 14, 1984	1B	Enos Cabell	Detroit Tigers		No compensation (free agent signing)
Feb 14, 1984	P	Jose Alvarez	Atlanta Braves		Minor league P Ron Meredith
Feb 22, 1984		No compensation (free agent signing)	St. Louis Cardinals	3B	Art Howe
Feb 24, 1984	C	Tom Wieghaus	Montreal Expos		Player to be named later
March 25, 1984	OF	Alan Bannister	Cleveland Indians		Cash

Los Angeles Dodgers

The Best Trades

1. Acquired Pedro Guerrero from the Cleveland Indians for Bruce Ellingsen, April 3, 1974.
2. Acquired Ron Perranoski, Lee Handley, John Goryl, and $25,000 from the Chicago Cubs for Don Zimmer, April 8, 1960.
3. Acquired Burt Hooton from the Chicago Cubs for Geoff Zahn and Eddie Solomon, May 2, 1975.
4. Acquired Phil Regan from the Detroit Tigers for Dick Tracewski, December 15, 1965.
5. Acquired Jimmy Wynn from the Houston Astros for Claude Osteen and Dave Culpepper, December 6, 1973.

The Worst Trades

1. Traded Ron Cey to the Chicago Cubs for Vance Lovelace and Dan Cataline, January 20, 1983.
2. Traded John Roseboro, Ron Perranoski, and Bob Miller to the Minnesota Twins for Mudcat Grant and Zoilo Versalles, November 28, 1967.
3. Traded Rudy Law to the Chicago White Sox for Bert Geiger and Cecil Espy, March 30, 1982.
4. Traded Davey Lopes to the Oakland A's for Lance Hudson, February 8, 1982.
5. Traded Bill Buckner, Ivan DeJesus, and Jeff Albert to the Chicago Cubs for Rick Monday and Mike Garman, January 11, 1977.

Builder: Al Campanis

The Los Angeles Dodgers are probably the most efficiently run organization in baseball. Relying primarily on their productive farm system, they've been one of the most consistently successful teams in baseball in the last ten years. Faith in the Dodgers' judgment runs so strong that when they traded twenty-one-year-old minor league strikeout phenom Sid Fernandez to the Mets in 1983, most baseball insiders immediately concluded that Fernandez wasn't all he'd been cracked up to be.

The Dodgers employ the largest scouting staff in baseball, with twenty-four full-time and twenty-two part-time scouts scouring the United States and Latin America. The effort costs close to one million dollars per major leaguer produced, but can pay long-term dividends: the Dodgers kept the same starting infield going for nine years, and all four (Steve Garvey, Davey Lopes, Bill Russell, and Ron Cey) were products of their farm system.

This doesn't mean they never make mistakes. Their efforts in the free agent market have been disastrous, paying a total of over five million dollars for Don Stanhouse and Dave Goltz. But unlike many teams, they recognized their mistakes, cut the players, and accepted the losses. The club exudes stability, and is as far from George Steinbrenner's approach to running a team as Los Angeles is from New York. (Interestingly enough, it is also a far cry from the methods of Dodger icon Branch Rickey, who was a firm believer in trading a player a year too soon rather than a year too late. Rickey would never have allowed that infield to stay together for so long. And when he did deal them, he would have gotten more than the handful of minor leaguers they received for Lopes and Cey.)

Probably the greatest of all recent Dodger deals was the acquisition of Pedro Guerrero from the Indians for Bruce Ellingsen. But Al Campanis has not been loath to make trades; among the other players acquired in trade by the Dodgers in recent years are Dick Allen, Frank Robinson, Tommy John, Andy Messersmith, pitcher Mike Marshall, Jim Wynn, Dusty Baker, Burt Hooton, Reggie Smith, Rick Monday, and Jerry Reuss. The magic of the Dodger name has led to a great overrating of many of their supposed prospects, and has led to some trades that in retrospect look horribly one-sided. Only time will tell if the Sid Fernandez for Bob Bailor and Carlos Diaz trade will be another L.A. heist.

DATE		ACQUIRED	FROM		IN EXCHANGE FOR
June 15, 1958	1B P	Steve Bilko Johnny Klippstein	Cincinnati Reds	P	Don Newcombe
Aug 4, 1958		Cash	Cleveland Indians	3B	Randy Jackson
Dec 4, 1958	OF P	Wally Moon Phil Paine	St. Louis Cardinals	OF	Gino Cimoli
Dec 23, 1958	OF P P	Rip Repulski Jim Golden Gene Snyder	Philadelphia Phillies	2B	Sparky Anderson
June 9, 1959		Waiver price	Philadelphia Phillies	IF	Solly Drake
June 15, 1959	OF P	Chuck Essegian Lloyd Merritt	St. Louis Cardinals	3B	Dick Gray
April 5, 1960	OF	Gordie Windhorn minor league 1B Dick Sanders	New York Yankees	P	Fred Kipp
April 8, 1960	P 3B	Ron Perranoski John Goryl minor league OF Lee Handley and $25,000.	Chicago Cubs	3B	Don Zimmer
April 11, 1960		$25,000.	Cleveland Indians	P	Johnny Klippstein
May 6, 1960	P	Nels Chittum	Boston Red Sox	OF	Rip Repulski
May 7, 1960	1B	Gail Harris	Detroit Tigers	OF	Sandy Amoros
June 15, 1960	P	Jim Donohue	St. Louis Cardinals	OF	John Glenn

DATE		ACQUIRED	FROM		IN EXCHANGE FOR
June 15, 1960	P	Ray Semproch and cash	Detroit Tigers	P	Clem Labine
Dec 15, 1960		Cash	Baltimore Orioles	OF	Earl Robinson
Dec 16, 1960		Cash	New York Yankees	P	Danny McDevitt
Jan 31, 1961		Cash	Kansas City Athletics	C	Joe Pignatano
March 30, 1961	P	Howie Reed and cash	Kansas City Athletics	P	Ed Rakow
May 4, 1961	P SS	Dick Farrell Joe Koppe	Philadelphia Phillies	OF 3B	Don Demeter Charley Smith
May 30, 1961	SS	Daryl Spencer	St. Louis Cardinals	SS OF	Bob Lillis Carl Warwick
Dec 15, 1961	OF	Lee Walls and $100,000.	New York Mets	2B	Charlie Neal
March 24, 1962	3B	Andy Carey	Chicago White Sox		Minor leaguers IF Ramon Conde and 1B Jim Koranda
Oct 11, 1962		Cash	New York Mets	C	Norm Sherry
Oct 11, 1962		Cash	New York Mets	OF	Dick Smith
Nov 26, 1962	1B	Bill Skowron	New York Yankees	P	Stan Williams
Nov 30, 1962	P	Bob Miller	New York Mets	1B 2B	Tim Harkness Larry Burright
Jan 24, 1963	3B	Don Zimmer	Cincinnati Reds		Minor league P Scott Breeden
April 1, 1963		Cash	New York Mets	OF	Duke Snider
June 24, 1963		Cash	Washington Senators	3B	Don Zimmer
July 20, 1963	2B	Marv Breeding	Washington Senators	P	Ed Roebuck
Oct 14, 1963		Cash	Washington Senators	C	Mike Brumley
Dec 6, 1963		Cash	Washington Senators	1B	Bill Skowron
Dec 13, 1963	P C	Jim Brewer Cuno Barragan	Chicago Cubs	P	Dick Scott
April 9, 1964	OF	Lou Johnson and $10,000.	Detroit Tigers	P	Larry Sherry
Sept 10, 1964		Cash	Baltimore Orioles	P	Ken Rowe
Oct 15, 1964		Cash	Washington Senators	P	Nick Willhite
Oct 15, 1964	OF	Dick Smith	New York Mets	P	Larry Miller
Nov 30, 1964		Cash	Washington Senators	C	Doug Camilli

DATE	ACQUIRED	FROM	IN EXCHANGE FOR
Dec 4, 1964	P Claude Osteen SS John Kennedy and $100,000.	Washington Senators	OF Frank Howard P Phil Ortega P Pete Richert 1B Dick Nen
May 11, 1965	P Nick Willhite	Washington Senators	Cash
Dec 15, 1965	P Phil Regan	Detroit Tigers	SS Dick Tracewski
May 10, 1966	Cash	Detroit Tigers	P Johnny Podres
May 27, 1966	P Dick Egan	California Angels	P Howie Reed
Sept 10, 1966	SS Dick Schofield	New York Yankees	P Thad Tillotson and cash
Nov 29, 1966	2B Ron Hunt OF Jim Hickman	New York Mets	OF Tommy Davis IF Derrell Griffith
Dec 1, 1966	3B-OF Bob Bailey SS Gene Michael	Pittsburgh Pirates	SS Maury Wills
Dec 15, 1966	P Bob Lee	California Angels	P Nick Willhite
April 3, 1967	P Jack Cullen OF John Miller and $25,000.	New York Yankees	3B John Kennedy
May 10, 1967	1B Len Gabrielson	California Angels	IF Johnny Werhas
May 31, 1967	Cash	Cincinnati Reds	P Bob Lee
Nov 28, 1967	P Mudcat Grant SS Zoilo Versalles	Minnesota Twins	C Johnny Roseboro P Ron Perranoski P Bob Miller
Nov 30, 1967	Cash	New York Yankees	SS Gene Michael
Nov 30, 1967	2B Paul Popovich	Chicago Cubs	OF Lou Johnson
Feb 13, 1968	C Tom Haller minor league P Frank Kasmeta	San Francisco Giants	2B Ron Hunt 2B Nate Oliver
March 26, 1968	OF Rocky Colavito	Chicago White Sox	Cash
April 3, 1968	P Hank Aguirre	Detroit Tigers	Cash
April 23, 1968	OF Ted Savage P Jim Ellis	Chicago Cubs	OF Jim Hickman P Phil Regan
Oct 21, 1968	Cash	Montreal Expos	3B Bob Bailey
Oct 21, 1968	P Pete Mikkelsen	St. Louis Cardinals	Cash
Dec 4, 1968	OF Andy Kosco	New York Yankees	P Mike Kekich
Dec 5, 1968	Two minor leaguers	Kansas City Royals	C Jim Campanis

DATE		ACQUIRED	FROM		IN EXCHANGE FOR
March 30, 1969	C	Jimmie Schaffer	Cincinnati Reds	OF	Ted Savage
April 17, 1969	P	Al McBean	San Diego Padres	SS P	Tommy Dean Leon Everitt
June 11, 1969	SS OF	Maury Wills Manny Mota	Montreal Expos	OF-1B IF	Ron Fairly Paul Popovich
Aug 15, 1969	P	Jim Bunning	Pittsburgh Pirates		Minor leaguers OF Ron Mitchell and IF Chuck Coggin and cash
Sept 1, 1969	P	Jack Jenkins	Washington Senators		Cash
Sept 28, 1970		Cash	St. Louis Cardinals	P	Fred Norman
Oct 5, 1970	1B	Richie Allen	St. Louis Cardinals	2B C	Ted Sizemore Bob Stinson
Dec 11, 1970	C	Duke Sims	Cleveland Indians	P P	Alan Foster Ray Lamb
Feb 10, 1971	P	Al Downing	Milwaukee Brewers	OF	Andy Kosco
March 13, 1971		Cash	California Angels	C	Jeff Torborg
Oct 21, 1971	OF	Larry Hisle	Philadelphia Phillies	1B	Tom Hutton
Oct 22, 1971	OF	Paul Powell	Minnesota Twins	OF	Bobby Darwin
Dec 2, 1971	OF P	Frank Robinson Pete Richert	Baltimore Orioles	P P C 1B	Doyle Alexander Bob O'Brien Sergio Robles Royle Stillman
Dec 2, 1971	P IF	Tommy John Steve Huntz	Chicago White Sox	1B	Richie Allen
Dec 2, 1971		Minor league P Bernie Beckman and cash	Detroit Tigers	C	Tom Haller
Dec 17, 1971	C	Chris Cannizzaro	Chicago Cubs		Cash
March 27, 1972		Cash	New York Mets	3B	Bill Sudakis
April 14, 1972	C	Dick Dietz	San Francisco Giants		Cash
Oct 26, 1972	P	Rudy Arroyo minor league P Greg Milliken	St. Louis Cardinals	OF	Larry Hisle
Nov 28, 1972	P 3B	Andy Messersmith Ken McMullen	California Angels	OF P P IF OF	Frank Robinson Bill Singer Mike Strahler Billy Grabarkewitz Bobby Valentine
March 26, 1973	P	George Culver	Houston Astros		Cash
March 27, 1973		Cash	Atlanta Braves	C	Dick Dietz

DATE	ACQUIRED	FROM	IN EXCHANGE FOR
April 24, 1973	Cash	Milwaukee Brewers	SS Tim Johnson
Aug 10, 1973	Cash	Philadelphia Phillies	P George Culver
Oct 27, 1973	SS Rick Auerbach	Milwaukee Brewers	Cash
Dec 5, 1973	P Mike Marshall	Montreal Expos	OF Willie Davis
Dec 5, 1973	OF Tommie Agee	St. Louis Cardinals	P Pete Richert
Dec 6, 1973	OF Jimmy Wynn	Houston Astros	P Claude Osteen minor league P Dave Culpepper
April 3, 1974	IF Pedro Guerrero	Cleveland Indians	P Bruce Ellingsen
July 11, 1974	1B Gail Hopkins	San Diego Padres	Cash
Jan 29, 1975	Cash	San Francisco Giants	OF Von Joshua
May 2, 1975	P Burt Hooton	Chicago Cubs	P Geoff Zahn P Eddie Solomon
July 15, 1975	Cash	California Angels	P Jim Brewer
Nov 17, 1975	OF Dusty Baker 1B Ed Goodson	Atlanta Braves	OF Jimmy Wynn OF Tom Paciorek OF Lee Lacy IF Jerry Royster
March 2, 1976	2B Ted Sizemore	St. Louis Cardinals	OF Willie Crawford
March 31, 1976	C Elly Rodriguez	California Angels	OF Jesus Alvarez and cash
April 10, 1976	No compensation (free agent signing)	Atlanta Braves	P Andy Messersmith
June 15, 1976	OF Reggie Smith	St. Louis Cardinals	C Joe Ferguson OF Bob Detherage minor league IF Fred Tisdale
June 23, 1976	P Elias Sosa OF Lee Lacy	Atlanta Braves	P Mike Marshall
Dec 20, 1976	C Johnny Oates minor league P Quincy Hill	Philadelphia Phillies	IF Ted Sizemore
Jan 11, 1977	OF Rick Monday P Mike Garman	Chicago Cubs	1B Bill Buckner SS Ivan DeJesus minor league P Jeff Albert
Feb 7, 1977	P Hank Webb minor league P Dick Sanders	New York Mets	SS Rick Auerbach
Sept 2, 1977	Cash	Toronto Blue Jays	OF John Hale
Sept 2, 1977	Cash	Chicago White Sox	OF Henry Cruz

DATE		ACQUIRED	FROM		IN EXCHANGE FOR
Sept 8, 1977		Cash	Seattle Mariners	C	Kevin Pasley
Nov 22, 1977	P	Terry Forster	Pittsburgh Pirates		No compensation (free agent signing)
Nov 23, 1977		Cash	Minnesota Twins	P	Dennis Lewallyn
		(Lewallyn was returned to the Dodgers on April 15, 1978.)			
Jan 31, 1978		Cash	Pittsburgh Pirates	P	Elias Sosa
May 17, 1978	OF	Billy North	Oakland Athletics	OF	Glenn Burke
May 20, 1978	P P	Larry Landreth Gerry Hannahs	Montreal Expos	P	Mike Garman
July 1, 1978	OF	Joe Ferguson and cash	Houston Astros	SS OF	Rafael Landestoy Jeff Leonard
Nov 14, 1978	IF	Derrel Thomas	San Diego Padres		No compensation (free agent signing)
Nov 21, 1978		No compensation (free agent signing)	New York Yankees	P	Tommy John
Jan 18, 1979		No compensation (free agent signing)	Pittsburgh Pirates	OF	Lee Lacy
Feb 15, 1979	OF	Gary Thomasson	New York Yankees	C	Brad Gulden
April 7, 1979	P	Jerry Reuss	Pittsburgh Pirates	P	Rick Rhoden
May 11, 1979		Cash	Milwaukee Brewers	P	Lance Rautzhan
May 11, 1979	P	Lerrin LaGrow	Chicago White Sox		Cash
Nov 15, 1979	P	Dave Goltz	Minnesota Twins		No compensation (free agent signing)
Nov 17, 1979	P	Don Stanhouse	Baltimore Orioles		No compensation (free agent signing)
Dec 3, 1979		Cash	San Diego Padres	OF	Von Joshua
Dec 4, 1979	OF	Jay Johnstone	New York Yankees		No compensation (free agent signing)
July 11, 1980		Cash	Texas Rangers	P	Charlie Hough
Sept 13, 1980	P	Dennis Lewallyn	Texas Rangers	SS	Pepe Frias
Dec 4, 1980		No compensation (free agent signing)	Houston Astros	P	Don Sutton
Feb 5, 1981		No compensation (free agent signing)	Kansas City Royals	C	Jerry Grote
March 30, 1981	OF	Ken Landreaux	Minnesota Twins	OF	Mickey Hatcher minor league P Matt Reeves
Dec 9, 1981	OF P C	Jorge Orta Larry White Jack Fimple	Cleveland Indians	P 2B	Rick Sutcliffe Jack Perconte
Dec 11, 1981	SS	Mark Belanger	Baltimore Orioles		No compensation (free agent signing)

DATE		ACQUIRED	FROM		IN EXCHANGE FOR
Jan 6, 1982		Minor leaguers P Paul Voigt and C Scotti Madison	Minnesota Twins	P OF	Bobby Castillo Bobby Mitchell
Feb 8, 1982		Minor league 2B Lance Hudson	Oakland Athletics	2B	Davey Lopes
March 30, 1982	 OF	Minor league P Bert Geiger Cecil Espy	Chicago White Sox	OF	Rudy Law
April 5, 1982		No compensation (free agent signing)	San Francisco Giants	1B	Reggie Smith
April 28, 1982	C	Jose Morales	Baltimore Orioles	3B	Leo Hernandez
Oct 15, 1982		Cash	Cincinnati Reds	P	Ted Power
Dec 10, 1982		No compensation (free agent signing)	Atlanta Braves	P	Terry Forster
Dec 21, 1982		No compensation (free agent signing)	San Diego Padres	1B	Steve Garvey
Dec 28, 1982	P	Pat Zachry	New York Mets	OF	Jorge Orta
Jan 20, 1983		Minor league P Vance Lovelace minor league OF Dan Cataline	Chicago Cubs	3B	Ron Cey
March 28, 1983		Minor league SS Ivan Mesa	Minnesota Twins	OF	Tack Wilson
March 29, 1983		Minor league Ps Steve Walker Jody Johnston and cash	New York Mets	OF	Mark Bradley
May 9, 1983	IF	Rafael Landestoy	Cincinnati Reds		Minor league P Brett Wise and John Franco
Aug 19, 1983	P	Rick Honeycutt	Texas Rangers	P P	Dave Stewart Ricky Wright and $200,000.
Dec 7, 1983		Minor leaguers C Joe Szeneley P Jose Torres and P John Serritella	Kansas City Royals	P	Joe Beckwith
Dec 8, 1983	P UT	Carlos Diaz Bob Bailor	New York Mets	P	Sid Fernandez
Feb 7, 1984		No compensation (free agent signing)	Montreal Expos	UT	Derrel Thomas

Milwaukee Braves

The Best Trades

1. Acquired Joe Adcock from the Cincinnati Reds for Rocky Bridges and cash, February 16, 1953.
2. Acquired Red Schoendienst from the New York Giants for Danny O'Connell, Bobby Thomson, and Ray Crone, June 15, 1957.
3. Acquired Felipe Alou, Billy Hoeft, Ed Bailey, and Ernie Bowman from the San Francisco Giants for Del Crandall, Bob Shaw, and Bob Hendley, December 3, 1963.

The Worst Trades

1. Traded Johnny Antonelli, Don Liddle, Ebba St. Claire, Billy Klaus, and $50,000 to the New York Giants for Bobby Thomson and Sammy Calderone, February 1, 1954.
2. Traded Sid Gordon, Sam Jethroe, Max Surkont, Curt Raydon, Fred Walters, Larry Lasalle, and $100,000 to the Pittsburgh Pirates for Danny O'Connell, December 26, 1953.
3. Traded Roy McMillan to the New York Mets for Jay Hook and Adrian Garrett, May 8, 1964.

Trader: John Quinn

When the Braves moved from Boston to Milwaukee in the spring of 1953, they brought with them a young, strong, farm-built team that had few weaknesses. They spent the next several years trying to plug those few remaining holes, with only moderate success. As a result, this good-hit, good-pitch team never quite jelled into the club it could have been.

The biggest hole was at second base, which had been a problem ever since the club dealt away Eddie Stanky in 1949. Quinn tried to fill the second base hole by trading a package including outfielders Sid Gordon and Sam Jethroe, along with pitcher Max Surkont, three farm hands, and $75,000 for Pirate Danny O'Connell. O'Connell's glove was sound, but his bat was a liability, and he was eventually dealt to New York, along with Bobby Thomson and Ray Crone, for Red Schoendienst. Schoendienst was exactly the catalyst the club needed, batting .310 for the Braves as they won the first of two successive National League titles. But Schoendienst developed tuberculosis in 1959 and the Braves were forced again to trade for a second baseman. This time outfielder Billy Bruton was shipped to the Tigers for Frank Bolling.

The Braves got outstanding frontline pitching throughout the 1950s from Warren Spahn and Lew Burdette, but failed to fill in the staff around them. Their first major trade after coming to Milwaukee was probably their worst deal: they sent Johnny Antonelli along with three other players to the Giants for Bobby Thomson and Sam Calderone. The promising young lefthander had been signed for a $50,000 bonus out of high school, but had failed to impress the Braves in his early outings spread over four seasons. But Antonelli was just twenty-four when they traded him away, and he bloomed immediately upon reaching New York, going 21–7 while leading the league in winning percentage, earned run average, and shutouts. The holes in the staff grew larger as John McHale, who had succeeded Quinn as general manager in 1959, traded Joey Jay and Juan Pizarro to Cincinnati for Roy McMillan. McMillan was a fine defensive shortstop but, like O'Connell before him, couldn't hit well enough to make his glove worthwhile. Jay made the deal look foolish right away by winning twenty-one in each of his first two seasons with the Reds; Pizarro averaged fifteen wins a year for the next four, and was still pitching effectively twelve years after the trade was made. Because of deals like this, a strong ballclub with such great stars as Hank Aaron, Eddie

Mathews, Spahn, and Burdette, along with such useful ballplayers as Del Crandall, Wes Covington, and Joe Adcock, managed just two pennants in a decade and a half in contention.

DATE		ACQUIRED	FROM		IN EXCHANGE FOR
Jan 17, 1953	OF	Andy Pafko	Brooklyn Dodgers	2B	Roy Hartsfield and $50,000.
Feb 16, 1953	P	Russ Meyer and cash	Philadelphia Phillies	1B	Earl Torgeson
		(Part of four-team trade involving Milwaukee Braves, Philadelphia Phillies, Brooklyn, and Cincinnati.)			
Feb 16, 1953	IF OF	Rocky Bridges Jim Pendleton	Brooklyn Dodgers	P	Russ Meyer
		(Part of four-team trade involving Milwaukee, Philadelphia Phillies, Brooklyn, and Cincinnati.)			
Feb 16, 1953	1B	Joe Adcock	Cincinnati Reds	2B	Rocky Bridges and cash
		(Part of four-team trade involving Milwaukee Braves, Philadelphia Phillies, Brooklyn, and Cincinnati.)			
Dec 7, 1953	OF	Catfish Metkovich	Chicago Cubs		Cash
Dec 26, 1953	2B	Danny O'Connell	Pittsburgh Pirates	OF P OF P P	Sid Gordon Max Surkont Sam Jethroe Curt Raydon Fred Walters minor league P Larry Lasalle and $100,000.
Feb 1, 1954	OF C	Bobby Thomson Sammy Calderone	New York Giants	P P C IF	Johnny Antonelli Don Liddle Ebba St. Claire Billy Klaus and $50,000.
Feb 10, 1954	C	Charlie White and $10,000.	Baltimore Orioles	P	Vern Bickford
March 20, 1954	SS	Roy Smalley	Chicago Cubs	P	Dave Cole and cash
April 13, 1955		Cash	Baltimore Orioles	P	Jim Wilson
April 30, 1955		Cash	Philadelphia Phillies	SS	Roy Smalley
June 3, 1955	C	Del Rice	St. Louis Cardinals	OF	Pete Whisenant
April 9, 1956	OF P	Bob Hazle Corky Valentine	Cincinnati Reds	1B	George Crowe
Feb 12, 1957	OF	Charlie King Cash	Detroit Tigers	2B	Jack Dittmer
April 3, 1957	3B	Dick Cole	Pittsburgh Pirates	OF	Jim Pendleton
June 8, 1957		Waiver price	Chicago Cubs	OF	Chuck Tanner
June 15, 1957	2B	Red Schoendienst	New York Giants	2B P OF	Danny O'Connell Ray Crone Bobby Thomson

DATE		ACQUIRED	FROM		IN EXCHANGE FOR
Oct 15, 1957		Waiver price	New York Giants	P	Dave Jolly
Nov 10, 1957	2B	Casey Wise	Chicago Cubs	P OF	Ben Johnson Charlie King and cash
Dec 5, 1957	OF P P	Eddie Haas Don Kaiser Bob Rush	Chicago Cubs	P C	Taylor Phillips Sammy Taylor
March 30, 1958	P	Dick Littlefield	Chicago Cubs		Cash
April 19, 1958		Waiver price	St. Louis Cardinals	P	Phil Paine
May 24, 1958		Cash	Detroit Tigers	OF	Bob Hazle
June 13, 1958	C	Joe Lonnett	Philadelphia Phillies	C	Carl Sawatski
March 31, 1959	C SS 2B	Stan Lopata Ted Kazanski Johnny O'Brien	Philadelphia Phillies	P SS 2B	Gene Conley Joe Koppe Harry Hanebrink
April 11, 1959	1B	Mickey Vernon	Cleveland Indians	P	Humberto Robinson
July 21, 1959	2B	Bobby Avila	Boston Red Sox		Waiver price
Aug 20, 1959	1B	Ray Boone	Kansas City Athletics		Waiver price
Sept 12, 1959	OF	Enos Slaughter	New York Yankees		Waiver price
Oct 12, 1959		Cash	Kansas City Athletics	P	Bob Trowbridge
Oct 15, 1959	C P	Charlie Lau Don Lee	Detroit Tigers	P C 2B	Don Kaiser Mike Roarke Casey Wise
May 11, 1960	P	George Brunet	Kansas City Athletics	P	Bob Giggie
May 17, 1960	1B	Ron Jackson	Boston Red Sox	1B	Ray Boone
June 11, 1960		Cash	Chicago White Sox	P	Bob Rush
June 23, 1960	3B	Alvin Dark	Philadelphia Phillies	3B	Joe Morgan
Oct 31, 1960	IF	Andre Rodgers	San Francisco Giants	3B	Alvin Dark
Nov 28, 1960	C	Dick Brown	Chicago White Sox		Cash
Dec 3, 1960	2B	Billy Martin	Cincinnati Reds		Cash

DATE		ACQUIRED	FROM		IN EXCHANGE FOR
Dec 7, 1960	2B OF	Frank Bolling Neil Chrisley	Detroit Tigers	OF P C 2B	Bill Bruton Terry Fox Dick Brown Chuck Cottier
Dec 15, 1960	SS	Roy McMillan	Cincinnati Reds	P P	Joey Jay Juan Pizarro
March 31, 1961	P P	Moe Drabowsky Seth Morehead	Chicago Cubs	IF IF	Andre Rodgers Daryl Robertson
May 9, 1961	OF	Frank Thomas	Chicago Cubs	UT	Mel Roach
May 10, 1961		Waiver price	Chicago White Sox	OF	Wes Covington
June 1, 1961	IF	Billy Consolo	Minnesota Twins	2B	Billy Martin
June 10, 1961	1B	Bob Boyd	Kansas City Athletics		Cash
June 15, 1961	C	Sammy White	Boston Red Sox		Cash
July 4, 1961	P	Johnny Antonelli	Cleveland Indians		Cash
Oct 11, 1961		Cash	New York Mets	P P	Ken MacKenzie Johnny Antonelli
Oct 16, 1961		Cash	New York Mets	OF	Neil Chrisley
Nov 28, 1961		Cash	New York Mets	OF	Frank Thomas
April 30, 1962	P	Jack Curtis	Chicago Cubs	P	Bob Buhl
May 9, 1962		Cash	Houston Astros	P	Don McMahon
June 24, 1962	2B	Ken Aspromonte and cash	Cleveland Indians	P	Bob Hartman
Nov 27, 1962	OF OF P	Ty Cline Don Dillard Frank Funk	Cleveland Indians	1B P	Joe Adcock Jack Curtis
Nov 30, 1962	1B	Norm Larker	Houston Astros	P P OF	Connie Grob Don Nottebart Jim Bolger
Dec 3, 1962	3B	Jim McKnight	Chicago Cubs	3B	Ken Aspromonte
March 23, 1963		Cash	New York Mets	P	Carl Willey
May 4, 1963	OF	Bubba Morton	Detroit Tigers		Cash
May 8, 1963	SS	Chico Fernandez	Detroit Tigers	OF	Lou Johnson and cash
May 8, 1963	P	Larry Foss	New York Mets	SS	Chico Fernandez
June 15, 1963	1B P	Gene Oliver Bob Sadowski	St. Louis Cardinals	P	Lew Burdette

DATE	ACQUIRED		FROM	IN EXCHANGE FOR	
Aug 8, 1963		Cash	San Francisco Giants	1B	Norm Larker
Oct 10, 1963		$30,000.	Houston Astros	P	Claude Raymond
Oct 15, 1963		Cash	New York Mets	SS	Amado Samuel
Dec 2, 1963		Cash	New York Mets	OF	Hawk Taylor
Dec 3, 1963	OF P C SS	Felipe Alou Billy Hoeft Ed Bailey Ernie Bowman	San Francisco Giants	C P P	Del Crandall Bob Shaw Bob Hendley
April 1, 1964	3B	Mike de la Hoz	Cleveland Indians	OF	Chico Salmon
April 9, 1964	C OF	Jimmie Coker Gary Kolb	St. Louis Cardinals	C	Bob Uecker
May 8, 1964	P OF	Jay Hook Adrian Garrett	New York Mets	SS	Roy McMillan
June 3, 1964	C	Merritt Ranew and $40,000.	Chicago Cubs	OF	Len Gabrielson
Aug 8, 1964	P	Frank Lary	New York Mets	P	Dennis Ribant and cash
Oct 14, 1964	P	Dan Osinski	Los Angeles Angels	C P	Phil Roof Ron Piche
Nov 23, 1964		Cash	New York Mets	P	Warren Spahn
Feb 1, 1965	P	Billy O'Dell	San Francisco Giants	C	Ed Bailey
March 20, 1965		Cash	New York Mets	P	Frank Lary
April 4, 1965	OF	Frank Thomas	Houston Astros		Minor league IF Mickey Sinnerud
May 13, 1965	P 1B	Ken Johnson Jim Beauchamp	Houston Astros	OF	Lee Maye
July 21, 1965	C	Jesse Gonder	New York Mets	OF	Gary Kolb
Aug 18, 1965		Cash	New York Mets	P	Dave Eilers
Sept 9, 1965	C	Johnny Blanchard	Kansas City Athletics		Cash
Dec 15, 1965	OF P P	Lee Thomas Arnie Earley Jay Ritchie	Boston Red Sox	P P	Bob Sadowski Dan Osinski

Montreal Expos

The Best Trades

1. Acquired Mike Torrez from the St. Louis Cardinals for Bob Reynolds, June 15, 1971.
2. Acquired Ron Hunt from the San Francisco Giants for Dave McDonald, December 30, 1970.
3. Acquired Al Oliver from the Texas Rangers for Larry Parrish and Dave Hostetler, March 31, 1982.
4. Acquired Tony Perez and Will McEnaney from the Cincinnati Reds for Woodie Fryman and Dale Murray, December 16, 1976.
5. Acquired Bill Lee from the Boston Red Sox for Stan Papi, December 7, 1978.

The Worst Trades

1. Traded Ken Singleton and Mike Torrez to the Baltimore Orioles for Dave McNally, Rich Coggins, and Bill Kirkpatrick, December 4, 1974.
2. Traded Andre Thornton to the Cleveland Indians for Jackie Brown, December 10, 1976.
3. Traded Don Stanhouse, Gary Roenicke, and Joe Kerrigan to the Baltimore Orioles for Rudy May, Randy Miller, and Bryn Smith, December 7, 1977.
4. Traded Mike Marshall to the Los Angeles Dodgers for Willie Davis, December 5, 1973.
5. Traded Don Carter and $300,000 to the Cleveland Indians for Manny Trillo, August 17, 1983.

Trader: John McHale

If the Expos could have restricted their dealings to making trades with Spec Richardson of the Astros, they would have compiled an awfully impressive record.

Their first deal with Houston came during their first season, when they traded Jesus Alou and Donn Clendenon for Rusty Staub. The deal, which would have been favorable enough, became even better when Clendenon refused to go, announcing his retirement, which was promptly unannounced when Commissioner Bowie Kuhn persuaded Houston to accept Jack Billingham and Skip Guinn instead. The second deal, one year later, brought troublesome reliever Mike Marshall to Montreal for outfielder Don Bosch. Staub became a Montreal favorite, dubbed "Le Grand Orange" by Expos fans. Marshall became one of the best relievers in the game, known for his remarkable durability as well as his effectiveness.

But the Expos have displayed a lack of patience, negating their best deals just a few years later. Staub was sent to the Mets in 1972 for Mike Jorgensen, Ken Singleton, and Tim Foli. Singleton, in turn, was traded to Baltimore with Mike Torrez for Dave McNally, Bill Kirkpatrick, and Rich Coggins before the 1975 season; McNally lasted two months with the Expos, and Kirkpatrick and Coggins even less. Marshall, meanwhile, went to the Dodgers after three years in Montreal in exchange for Willie Davis. While Marshall was winning a Cy Young Award and leading the league with an all-time record 106 appearances, Davis was only leading the league in unpaid bills and salary advances. (To complete the chain, Davis was sent to Texas for Don Stanhouse, and Stanhouse went with Gary Roenicke and Joe Kerrigan to Baltimore for Rudy May, Randy Miller, and Bryn Smith.) At no time in this remarkable series of transactions did the Expos get equal value for what they gave up.

John McHale has been able to exploit some opponents' blind spots: when the Red Sox were looking to unload Bill Lee, the Expos took him off their hands for Stan Papi. When the Mets found themselves with two top short relievers, the Expos were only too happy to give them

Ellis Valentine for Jeff Reardon. But too many of their deals have sought to plug one hole by opening up another, particularly in the middle of the infield. Of all the trades they've made, perhaps the most crucial was when they sent second baseman Tony Bernazard to Chicago for Rich Wortham, creating a hole at second they are still trying desperately to fill. The front office has done a spectacular job of finding and developing great talents like Andre Dawson, Gary Carter, and Steve Rogers. But it must bear the responsibility for not finding the useful role-players they need to win a pennant.

DATE	ACQUIRED	FROM	IN EXCHANGE FOR
Oct 16, 1968	OF Don Bosch	New York Mets	Cash
Oct 21, 1968	3B Bob Bailey	Los Angeles Dodgers	Cash
Jan 22, 1969	1B Rusty Staub	Houston Astros	OF Jesus Alou 1B Donn Clendenon P Jack Billingham P Skip Guinn and $100,000.
	(Clendenon refused to report, and Houston sent Billingham, Guinn, and cash on April 8, 1969.)		
March 25, 1969	Cash	Kansas City Royals	2B Juan Rios
March 25, 1969	1B Don Pepper	Detroit Tigers	Cash
April 3, 1969	P Steve Shea	Houston Astros	Cash
April 3, 1969	P Howie Reed	Houston Astros	Cash
June 3, 1969	P Gary Waslewski	St. Louis Cardinals	P Mudcat Grant
June 11, 1969	OF-1B Ron Fairly IF Paul Popovich	Los Angeles Dodgers	SS Maury Wills OF Manny Mota
June 11, 1969	OF Adolfo Phillips P Jack Lamabe	Chicago Cubs	IF Paul Popovich
June 15, 1969	P Dick Radatz	Detroit Tigers	Cash
June 15, 1969	P Steve Renko 3B Kevin Collins minor league Ps Bill Cardon and Dave Colon	New York Mets	1B Donn Clendenon
Aug 19, 1969	P Claude Raymond	Atlanta Braves	Cash
Sept 13, 1969	IF Marv Staehle	Seattle Pilots	Cash
Dec 2, 1969	P Jim Britton minor league C Don Johnson	Atlanta Braves	P Larry Jaster
Dec 3, 1969	P Joe Sparma	Detroit Tigers	P Jerry Robertson
April 6, 1970	C Jack Hiatt	San Francisco Giants	Cash

DATE	ACQUIRED		FROM	IN EXCHANGE FOR	
April 20, 1970	OF	Jim Gosger	San Francisco Giants		Cash
April 22, 1970	OF	Jim Qualls	Chicago Cubs		Cash
May 12, 1970	OF	Boots Day	Chicago Cubs	C	Jack Hiatt
May 15, 1970	1B	Dave McDonald	New York Yankees	P	Gary Waslewski
May 15, 1970	P	Rich Nye	St. Louis Cardinals		Cash
June 15, 1970	P	John O'Donoghue	Milwaukee Brewers		Cash
June 15, 1970	OF	Clyde Mashore	Cincinnati Reds	OF	Ty Cline
Dec 30, 1970	2B	Ron Hunt	San Francisco Giants	3B	Dave McDonald
March 31, 1971	OF SS	Ron Swoboda Rich Hacker	New York Mets	OF	Don Hahn
June 15, 1971	P	Mike Torrez	St. Louis Cardinals	P	Bob Reynolds
Oct 14, 1971	P	Denny Lemaster	Houston Astros		Cash
Oct 20, 1971	P	Ron Taylor	New York Mets		Cash
March 24, 1972	SS	Cesar Gutierrez	Detroit Tigers		Cash
April 5, 1972	SS OF 1B	Tim Foli Ken Singleton Mike Jorgensen	New York Mets	OF	Rusty Staub
April 7, 1972	SS 1B	Hector Torres Hal Breeden	Chicago Cubs	P	Dan McGinn
June 14, 1972	C	Tim McCarver	Philadelphia Phillies	C	John Bateman
Nov 6, 1972	OF	Jorge Roque	St. Louis Cardinals	C	Tim McCarver
Feb 28, 1973	P	Pat Jarvis	Atlanta Braves	P	Carl Morton
March 28, 1973	C	Bob Stinson	Houston Astros		Cash
April 4, 1973		Cash	Houston Astros	SS	Hector Torres
May 22, 1973	P	Mickey Scott	Baltimore Orioles		Cash
July 10, 1973	OF	Jim Lyttle	Kansas City Royals		Cash
July 16, 1973		Cash	New York Mets	P	John Strohmayer
Aug 13, 1973	2B	Bernie Allen	New York Yankees		Cash

DATE	ACQUIRED	FROM	IN EXCHANGE FOR
Sept 6, 1973	1B-OF Felipe Alou	New York Yankees	Cash
Sept 18, 1973	OF Jose Morales	Oakland Athletics	Cash
Dec 5, 1973	OF Willie Davis	Los Angeles Dodgers	P Mike Marshall
Dec 7, 1973	Cash	Milwaukee Brewers	OF Felipe Alou
Dec 20, 1973	1B Larry Biittner	Texas Rangers	P Pat Jarvis
April 1, 1974	P Don Carrithers	San Francisco Giants	C John Boccabella
April 4, 1974	Cash	California Angels	P Bill Stoneman
Aug 7, 1974	OF Jim Northrup	Detroit Tigers	Cash
Sept 5, 1974	Cash	St. Louis Cardinals	2B Ron Hunt
Sept 16, 1974	Cash	Baltimore Orioles	OF Jim Northrup
Dec 4, 1974	P Woodie Fryman	Detroit Tigers	P Tom Walker C Terry Humphrey
Dec 4, 1974	P Dave McNally OF Rich Coggins minor league P Bill Kirkpatrick	Baltimore Orioles	OF Ken Singleton P Mike Torrez
Dec 5, 1974	P Don Stanhouse SS Pete Mackanin	Texas Rangers	OF Willie Davis
Dec 6, 1974	Minor leaguers IF Rudy Kinard and 1B Ed Kurpiel	St. Louis Cardinals	1B-OF Ron Fairly
March 26, 1975	Cash	Oakland Athletics	OF Don Hopkins
March 31, 1975	Cash	Kansas City Royals	C Bob Stinson
June 8, 1975	P Fred Scherman	Houston Astros	Cash
June 15, 1975	1B Nate Colbert	Detroit Tigers	Cash
June 20, 1975	Cash	New York Yankees	OF Rich Coggins
July 18, 1975	OF Jim Lyttle	Chicago White Sox	Cash
July 25, 1975	OF Jim Dwyer	St. Louis Cardinals	SS Larry Lintz
Sept 2, 1975	Cash	Philadelphia Phillies	P John Montague
Dec 12, 1975	P Clay Kirby	Cincinnati Reds	3B Bob Bailey
Dec 12, 1975	2B Rodney Scott	Kansas City Royals	Cash
May 17, 1976	1B Andre Thornton	Chicago Cubs	P Steve Renko 1B-OF Larry Biittner

DATE		ACQUIRED	FROM		IN EXCHANGE FOR
July 21, 1976	OF IF	Del Unser Wayne Garrett	New York Mets	OF OF	Jim Dwyer Pepe Mangual
July 24, 1976	C	Earl Williams	Atlanta Braves		Cash
Nov 6, 1976	P P OF	Bill Greif Angel Torres Sam Mejias	St. Louis Cardinals	P IF OF	Steve Dunning Pat Scanlon Tony Scott
Nov 17, 1976	2B	Dave Cash	Philadelphia Phillies		No compensation (free agent signing)
Nov 23, 1976	C OF	Joe Ferguson Bob Detherage	St. Louis Cardinals	P IF	Larry Dierker Jerry Davanon
Dec 10, 1976	P	Jackie Brown	Cleveland Indians	1B	Andre Thornton
Dec 16, 1976	1B P	Tony Perez Will McEnaney	Cincinnati Reds	P P	Woodie Fryman Dale Murray
March 15, 1977	P	Jeff Terpko	Texas Rangers	IF	Rodney Scott
April 6, 1977		Cash	Minnesota Twins	P	Don Carrithers
April 27, 1977	SS	Chris Speier	San Francisco Giants	SS	Tim Foli
May 21, 1977	P	Santo Alcala	Cincinnati Reds	P SS	Shane Rawley Angel Torres
May 22, 1977	P	Stan Bahnsen	Oakland Athletics	1B	Mike Jorgensen
June 15, 1977	P C	Wayne Twitchell Tim Blackwell	Philadelphia Phillies	C P	Barry Foote Dan Warthen
July 13, 1977		Cash	California Angels	P	Tom Walker
July 14, 1977	P	Fred Holdsworth	Baltimore Orioles	P	Dennis Blair
Sept 29, 1977	P	Rick Sawyer	San Diego Padres		Cash
Nov 10, 1977	P	Darold Knowles	Texas Rangers		Cash
Dec 7, 1977	P P P	Rudy May Randy Miller Bryn Smith	Baltimore Orioles	P P OF	Don Stanhouse Joe Kerrigan Gary Roenicke
Dec 21, 1977	P	Ross Grimsley	Baltimore Orioles		No compensation (free agent signing)
Jan 30, 1978	2B	Tito Fuentes	Detroit Tigers		Cash
Feb 15, 1978		Cash	Chicago White Sox	1B	Frank Ortenzio
		(Ortenzio was returned to Montreal on April 4, 1978.)			
March 23, 1978		Cash	Seattle Mariners	P	Santo Alcala
		(Alcala was returned to Montreal before the start of the 1979 season.)			
March 29, 1978	P	Tim Jones	Pittsburgh Pirates	P	Will McEnaney
March 29, 1978		Cash	Minnesota Twins	UT	Jose Morales

DATE		ACQUIRED	FROM		IN EXCHANGE FOR
May 20, 1978	P	Mike Garman	Los Angeles Dodgers	P P	Larry Landreth Gerry Hannahs
June 9, 1978	P	Woodie Fryman	Chicago Cubs	OF	Jerry White
June 9, 1978	C	Ed Herrmann	Houston Astros		Cash
July 20, 1978	1B	Tom Hutton	Toronto Blue Jays		Cash
July 21, 1978		Cash	St. Louis Cardinals	3B	Wayne Garrett
Sept 5, 1978		Cash	Philadelphia Phillies	IF	Pete Mackanin
Dec 5, 1978	1B	Tony Solaita	California Angels		Cash
Dec 7, 1978	P	Bill Lee	Boston Red Sox	IF	Stan Papi
Dec 8, 1978	SS	Jim Mason	Texas Rangers	OF	Mike Hart
Dec 14, 1978	2B OF	Rodney Scott Jerry White	Chicago Cubs	OF	Sam Mejias
Jan 9, 1979	P	Elias Sosa	Oakland Athletics		No compensation (free agent signing)
March 31, 1979	P	Dave Campbell	Atlanta Braves	SS	Pepe Frias
June 13, 1979	C	John Tamargo	San Francisco Giants	SS	Joe Pettini and cash
July 20, 1979	DH	Rusty Staub	Detroit Tigers		Minor league C Randy Schafer and cash
July 30, 1979	P	Dyar Miller	Toronto Blue Jays	1B	Tony Solaita
Aug 30, 1979	P	Dale Murray	New York Mets		Cash
Oct 19, 1979	P	Jamie Easterly	Atlanta Braves		Cash
Nov 8, 1979		No compensation (free agent signing)	New York Yankees	P	Rudy May
Nov 20, 1979		No compensation (free agent signing)	Boston Red Sox	1B	Tony Perez
Nov 27, 1979	SS 1B-OF	Bill Almon Dan Briggs	San Diego Padres	2B	Dave Cash
Dec 4, 1979	OF	Rowland Office	Atlanta Braves		No compensation (free agent signing)
Dec 7, 1979	OF	Ron LeFlore	Detroit Tigers	P	Dan Schatzeder
Dec 12, 1979		Cash	Chicago White Sox	P	Bill Atkinson
March 15, 1980	IF	Jerry Manuel	Detroit Tigers	C	Duffy Dyer
March 31, 1980	SS 3B	LaRue Washington Chris Smith	Texas Rangers	1B	Rusty Staub

DATE	ACQUIRED	FROM	IN EXCHANGE FOR
July 11, 1980	IF Dave Oliver	Cleveland Indians	P Ross Grimsley
Aug 11, 1980	P John D'Acquisto and cash	San Diego Padres	OF Randy Bass
Aug 31, 1980	1B Willie Montanez	San Diego Padres	IF Tony Phillips
Sept 22, 1980	Cash	Milwaukee Brewers	P Jamie Easterly
Nov 3, 1980	No compensation (free agent signing)	California Angels	P John D'Acquisto
Dec 6, 1980	No compensation (free agent signing)	Chicago White Sox	OF Ron LeFlore
Dec 12, 1980	P Rich Wortham	Chicago White Sox	2B Tony Bernazard
Jan 15, 1981	Cash	Toronto Blue Jays	3B Ken Macha
Feb 18, 1981	P Ray Burris	New York Mets	No compensation (free agent signing)
May 10, 1981	IF Mike Phillips	San Diego Padres	Cash
May 29, 1981	P Jeff Reardon OF Dan Norman	New York Mets	OF Ellis Valentine
Aug 20, 1981	1B John Milner	Pittsburgh Pirates	1B Willie Montanez
Sept 1, 1981	P Grant Jackson	Pittsburgh Pirates	$50,000.
Dec 11, 1981	SS Frank Taveras	New York Mets	P Steve Ratzer and cash
Jan 14, 1982	C Tim Blackwell	Chicago Cubs	No compensation (free agent signing)
Jan 14, 1982	1B Ken Phelps	Kansas City Royals	P Grant Jackson
March 16, 1982	P Mike Griffin	Chicago Cubs	OF-1B Dan Briggs
March 30, 1982	Cash	Detroit Tigers	P Elias Sosa
March 31, 1982	1B Al Oliver	Texas Rangers	3B-OF Larry Parrish 1B Dave Hostetler
April 5, 1982	C Brad Gulden	New York Yankees	C Bobby Ramos
May 22, 1982	P Kim Seaman	San Diego Padres	2B Jerry Manuel
June 8, 1982	2B Jerry Manuel	San Diego Padres	P Mike Griffin
June 15, 1982	P Dan Schatzeder	San Francisco Giants	Cash
Aug 2, 1982	2B Doug Flynn	Texas Rangers	Cash
Aug 4, 1982	OF Joel Youngblood	New York Mets	P Tom Gorman

DATE		ACQUIRED	FROM		IN EXCHANGE FOR
Aug 14, 1982	P	Randy Lerch	Milwaukee Brewers		Cash
Sept 8, 1982	P	Dave Tomlin	Cincinnati Reds		Cash
Oct 7, 1982	1B	Rick Lancellotti	San Diego Padres		Cash
Oct 26, 1982		Cash	New York Yankees	C	Brad Gulden
Nov 3, 1982	C	Bobby Ramos	New York Yankees		Cash
Feb 2, 1983	OF	Jim Wohlford	San Francisco Giants	SS	Chris Smith
Feb 7, 1983		No compensation (free agent signing)	San Francisco Giants	2B	Joel Youngblood
March 31, 1983		Cash	Seattle Mariners	1B	Ken Phelps
May 4, 1983	P	Chris Welsh	San Diego Padres		Cash
May 4, 1983	P	Bob James	Detroit Tigers		Cash
May 25, 1983	OF	Mike Vail	San Francisco Giants	IF	Wallace Johnson
Aug 2, 1983		Cash	Pittsburgh Pirates	P	Dave Tomlin
Aug 17, 1983	2B	Manny Trillo	Cleveland Indians		Minor league OF Don Carter and $300,000.
Sept 16, 1983	OF	Gene Roof	St. Louis Cardinals		Cash
Sept 27, 1983	P	Greg Harris	Cincinnati Reds		Cash
Dec 7, 1983	P	Gary Lucas	San Diego Padres	P	Scott Sanderson
Dec 7, 1983	OF	Rusty McNealy and cash	Oakland Athletics	P	Ray Burris
Dec 20, 1983		Minor league P Tim Burke	New York Yankees	OF	Pat Rooney
Dec 21, 1983		No compensation (free agent signing)	San Francisco Giants	2B	Manny Trillo
Jan 19, 1984	OF	Miguel Dilone	Pittsburgh Pirates		No compensation (free agent signing)
Jan 20, 1984	OF	Pete Rose	Philadelphia Phillies		No compensation (free agent signing)
Feb 7, 1984	UT	Derrel Thomas	Los Angeles Dodgers		No compensation (free agent signing)
Feb 24, 1984		Player to be named later	Houston Astros	C	Tom Wieghaus
Feb 27, 1984	P OF P	Fred Breining Max Venable Andy McGaffigan	San Francisco Giants	1B	Al Oliver

(San Francisco sent McGaffigan to Montreal on April 1, 1984, after Breining reported to the Expos with a sore arm.)

New York Giants

The Best Trades

1. Acquired Christy Mathewson from the Cincinnati Reds for Amos Rusie, December 15, 1900.
2. Acquired Eddie Stanky and Alvin Dark from the Boston Braves for Sid Gordon, Buddy Kerr, Willard Marshall, and Red Webb, December 14, 1949.
3. Acquired Johnny Antonelli, Don Liddle, Billy Klaus, Ebba St. Claire, and $50,000 from the Milwaukee Braves for Bobby Thomson and Sammy Calderone, February 1, 1954.
4. Acquired Johnny Mize from the St. Louis Cardinals for Ken O'Dea, Bill Lohrman, Johnny McCarthy, and $50,000, December 11, 1941.
5. Acquired Larry Benton, Herb Thomas, and Zack Taylor from the Boston Braves for Hugh McQuillan, Kent Greenfield, and Doc Farrell, June 12, 1927.

The Worst Trades

1. Traded Burleigh Grimes to the Pittsburgh Pirates for Vic Aldridge, February 11, 1928.
2. Traded Lefty O'Doul and cash to the Philadelphia Phillies for Freddy Leach, October 29, 1928.
3. Traded Rogers Hornsby to the Boston Braves for Shanty Hogan and Jimmy Welsh, January 10, 1928.
4. Traded Edd Roush, Christy Mathewson, and Bill McKechnie to the Cincinnati Reds for Buck Herzog and Red Killefer, July 20, 1916.
5. Traded Billy Southworth to the St. Louis Cardinals for Heinie Mueller, June 14, 1926.

Trader: John McGraw

John Joseph McGraw, the legendary "Little Napoleon," ruled the Giants with an iron hand, maintaining control both on and off the field. In three different eras he developed championship teams that each reflected his own fighting spirit. In all he won ten pennants, second only to Casey Stengel, and three world championships.

McGraw viewed the job of managing a ballclub as consisting of three parts: game strategy, handling players, and constructing the team. He bought, sold, and traded more players than any other manager. His unerring judgment enabled him to spot an opponent's potential or his own player's weakness. He was famous for acquiring and reacquiring veteran players considered washed up by their own clubs and coaxing two or three more good years out of them. Jack Scott, Buck Herzog, Bill Dahlen and Heinie Zimmerman all gave the Giants productive seasons late in their careers.

The Giants' greatest trade was their acquisition of Christy Mathewson, a deal that proved to be the most one-sided transaction of all time. Matty was originally picked up by the Giants from a Norfolk, Virginia, team on a conditional basis for $1,500 during the 1900 season. The nineteen-year-old Mathewson reported to the club in June, but was quickly returned to Norfolk after picking up three defeats without a victory for New York. Cincinnati bought Mathewson from Norfolk for the $100 draft price then in effect. Within days of that acquisition, the Reds' owner John T. Brush, who would subsequently purchase a controlling interest in the Giants, sent him to New York for Amos Rusie, a once-great pitcher in the twilight of his career. Rusie was 0–1 in his three appearances with the Reds, while Matty went on to win 373 games en route to immortality.

Oddly enough, Mathewson ended his career in a Cincinnati uniform; he was traded to the Reds in 1916 to become their manager. Matty was just one of three future Hall of Famers acquired by the Reds in the deal: Edd Roush and Bill McKechnie went along as well. He was just about through as a pitcher, and was a wise enough manager to keep himself off the mound. But on September 4, 1916, he made his final major league appearance in a sentimental duel against his old arch-rival, Mordecai "Three Finger" Brown. It was the last game for both, and Matty staggered through to a 10–8 victory.

DATE	ACQUIRED	FROM	IN EXCHANGE FOR
Feb 9, 1900	P Win Mercer	Washington Senators	Cash
Feb 17, 1900	3B Piano Legs Hickman	Boston Braves	Cash
Feb 17, 1900	OF Charlie Frisbee	Boston Braves	Cash
Feb 27, 1900	P Pink Hawley	Cincinnati Reds	Cash
Feb 29, 1900	OF Kip Selbach	Cincinnati Reds	Cash
Feb 1900	C Frank Bowerman	Pittsburgh Pirates	Cash
Feb 1900	Cash	Pittsburgh Pirates	OF Tom O'Brien
Aug 8, 1900	OF Elmer Smith	Cincinnati Reds	Cash
Dec 15, 1900	P Christy Mathewson	Cincinnati Reds	P Amos Rusie
Jan 1901	Cash	Pittsburgh Pirates	OF Elmer Smith
Feb 1901	1B John Ganzel	Chicago Cubs	Cash
Feb 1901	3B Sammy Strang	Chicago Cubs	1B Jack Doyle
May 30, 1901	OF Algie McBride	Cincinnati Reds	Cash
May 1901	P Bill Magee	St. Louis Cardinals	P Chauncey Fisher
June 1901	2B Heinie Smith	Pittsburgh Pirates	P Ed Doheny
July 1901	OF Frank Murphy	Boston Braves	Cash
Feb 1902	1B Jack Doyle OF Jim Delahanty	Chicago Cubs	Cash
May 1902	Cash	Philadelphia Phillies	P Bill Magee
July 1902	C Hal O'Hagan	Chicago Cubs	OF Jack Hendricks
July 1902	OF George Browne	Philadelphia Phillies	Cash

DATE		ACQUIRED	FROM		IN EXCHANGE FOR
July 1902		Cash	Brooklyn Dodgers	P C	LeRoy Evans Joe Wall
Jan 1903		Cash	Pittsburgh Pirates	P	Brickyard Kennedy
July 1903	OF	Moose McCormick	Philadelphia Phillies		Cash
Dec 12, 1903	P SS	John Cronin Charlie Babb	Brooklyn Dodgers	SS	Bill Dahlen
Feb 1904		Cash	Pittsburgh Pirates	P	Roscoe Miller
May 1904	C	Doc Marshall	Philadelphia Phillies		Cash
July 3, 1904	OF	Mike Donlin	Cincinnati Reds		Cash
Aug 7, 1904		Cash	Boston Braves	C	Doc Marshall
Aug 9, 1904		Cash	Pittsburgh Pirates	OF	Moose McCormick
Aug 1904	P	Claude Elliott	Cincinnati Reds		Cash
Jan 1905		Cash	St. Louis Cardinals	C	John Warner
Feb 1905	3B	Sammy Strang	Brooklyn Dodgers		Cash
April 1905		Cash	Brooklyn Dodgers	3B	Bob Hall
June 1906	SS	Jack Hannifan	Philadelphia Athletics		Waiver price
July 13, 1906	OF	Spike Shannon	St. Louis Cardinals	OF C	Sam Mertes Doc Marshall
July 14, 1906	OF	Cy Seymour	Cincinnati Reds		$12,000.
Oct 7, 1907	1B SS C	Fred Tenney Al Bridwell Tom Needham	Boston Braves	1B C SS OF P	Dan McGann Frank Bowerman Bill Dahlen George Browne George Ferguson
April 1908		Cash	Boston Braves	IF	Jack Hannifan
May 1908	OF	Moose McCormick	Philadelphia Phillies		Cash
July 1908	2B	Shad Barry	St. Louis Cardinals		Cash
July 1908		Cash	Pittsburgh Pirates	OF	Spike Shannon
July 1908	3B	Dave Brain	Cincinnati Reds		Cash
Dec 12, 1908	C P OF	Admiral Schlei Bugs Raymond Red Murray	St. Louis Cardinals	C	Roger Bresnahan
Dec 1908		Cash	Chicago Cubs	C	Tom Needham

DATE		ACQUIRED	FROM		IN EXCHANGE FOR
Dec 1909	OF	Beals Becker	Boston Braves	2B	Buck Herzog
May 1910		Cash	St. Louis Cardinals	OF	Elmer Zacher
July 22, 1911	2B	Buck Herzog	Boston Braves	C SS	Hank Gowdy Al Bridwell
Aug 1, 1911		Cash	Boston Braves	OF	Mike Donlin
Dec 1911		Cash	Boston Braves	3B	Art Devlin
May 22, 1913	P 3B	Art Fromme Eddie Grant	Cincinnati Reds	P 3B OF	Red Ames Heinie Groh Josh Devore and $20,000.
June 1913	3B	Eddie Grant	Cincinnati Reds		Cash
July 1913	C	Larry McLean	St. Louis Cardinals	P	Doc Crandall
July 1913	P	Doc Crandall	St. Louis Cardinals		Cash
Dec 12, 1913	OF	Bob Bescher	Cincinnati Reds	2B C	Buck Herzog Grover Hartley
		(Hartley jumped to the Federal League and Herzog was made Cincinnati manager.)			
Aug 14, 1914	P	Marty O'Toole	Pittsburgh Pirates		Cash
Jan 1915	3B	Hans Lobert	Philadelphia Phillies	P 2B C	Al Demaree Milt Stock Bert Adams
Feb 18, 1915	P	Pol Perritt	St. Louis Cardinals		Cash
June 1915	C	Bobby Schang	Pittsburgh Pirates		Cash
July 6, 1915	C	Red Dooin	Cincinnati Reds		Waiver price
July 1915	3B	Howard Baker	Chicago White Sox		Cash
Aug 19, 1915	P	Rube Benton	Cincinnati Reds		$3,000.
Aug 31, 1915		Waiver price	Brooklyn Dodgers	P	Rube Marquard
Aug 1915		Cash	Boston Braves	OF	Fred Snodgrass
Dec 23, 1915	OF	Benny Kauff	Brooklyn (Federal League)		$35,000.
Dec 23, 1915	OF	Edd Roush	Newark (Federal League)		$7,500.
Dec 23, 1915	3B C	Bill McKechnie Bill Rariden	Newark (Federal League)		Cash
Feb 10, 1916		Waiver price	Brooklyn Dodgers	C	Chief Meyers
Feb 10, 1916	P	Fred Anderson	Buffalo (Federal League)		Cash

DATE		ACQUIRED	FROM		IN EXCHANGE FOR
July 20, 1916	2B OF	Buck Herzog Red Killefer	Cincinnati Reds	P OF 3B	Christy Mathewson Edd Roush Bill McKechnie
July 23, 1916	P	Slim Sallee	St. Louis Cardinals		$10,000.
Aug 5, 1916	C	George Gibson	Pittsburgh Pirates		Waiver price
Aug 20, 1916	C	Lew McCarty	Brooklyn Dodgers	1B	Fred Merkle
Aug 28, 1916	3B SS	Heinie Zimmerman Mickey Doolan	Chicago Cubs	2B OF OF	Larry Doyle Herb Hunter Merwin Jacobson
Jan 1917	C	George Gibson	Pittsburgh Pirates		Waiver price
Jan 1917	IF	Jimmy Smith	Pittsburgh Pirates		Waiver price
Jan 1917		Waiver price	Philadelphia Athletics	P	Rube Schauer
April 24, 1917		Cash	Cincinnati Reds	OF	Jim Thorpe
		(Thorpe was returned to the Giants on August 1, 1917.)			
May 1917		Waiver price	Brooklyn Dodgers	C	Ernie Krueger
July 25, 1917		Waiver price	Pittsburgh Pirates	1B	George Kelly
Aug 4, 1917	1B	George Kelly	Pittsburgh Pirates		Waiver price
Aug 5, 1917	2B	Joe Wilhoit	Pittsburgh Pirates		Waiver price
Aug 15, 1917	P	Al Demaree	Chicago Cubs	2B	Pete Kilduff
Jan 8, 1918	2B P	Larry Doyle Jesse Barnes	Boston Braves	2B	Buck Herzog
May 18, 1918	2B	Bert Niehoff	St. Louis Cardinals		Waiver price
June 20, 1918	P	George Smith	Cincinnati Reds		Cash
June 1918	P	Bob Steele	Pittsburgh Pirates		Cash
July 15, 1918		Cash	Brooklyn Dodgers	P	George Smith
July 25, 1918	P	Fred Toney	Cincinnati Reds		Cash
Oct 1918	P	George Smith	Brooklyn Dodgers		Cash
Oct 1918		Cash	Boston Braves	2B	Jimmy Smith
Jan 1919	OF	Lee King	Pittsburgh Pirates		Cash
Feb 2, 1919	1B	Hal Chase	Cincinnati Reds	C	Bill Rariden

DATE		ACQUIRED	FROM		IN EXCHANGE FOR
Feb 1919	IF	Jimmy Smith	Boston Braves	1B	Walter Holke
Feb 1919		Cash	Cincinnati Reds	IF	Jimmy Smith
Feb 1919		Cash	Boston Braves	P	Al Demaree
March 8, 1919		Waiver price	Cincinnati Reds	P	Slim Sallee
May 27, 1919	P	Joe Oeschger	Philadelphia Phillies	P 2B	George Smith Eddie Sicking
May 1919	P	Pat Ragan	Boston Braves	OF	Jim Thorpe
May 1919	C	Mike Gonzalez	St. Louis Cardinals		Waiver price
July 25, 1919	P	Phil Douglas	Chicago Cubs	OF	Dave Robertson
July 1919	C	Frank Snyder	St. Louis Cardinals	P	Ferdie Schupp
Aug 15, 1919	P	Art Nehf	Boston Braves	P P P C	Joe Oeschger Red Causey Johnny Jones Mickey O'Neil and $55,000.
Sept 1919		Waiver price	Chicago White Sox	P	Pat Ragan
Feb 1920	3B	Fred Lear	Chicago Cubs		Cash
May 1920	3B	Doug Baird	Brooklyn Dodgers		Cash
June 8, 1920	SS	Dave Bancroft	Philadelphia Phillies	SS P	Art Fletcher Bill Hubbell and cash
July 1920		Cash	Cincinnati Reds	2B	Eddie Sicking
July 1920		Cash	Boston Red Sox	OF	Jigger Statz
Aug 1920		Cash	St. Louis Cardinals	C	Lew McCarty
Sept 5, 1920	P	Slim Sallee	Cincinnati Reds		Waiver price
June 1921		Cash	Philadelphia Phillies	2B	John Monroe
June 1921		Cash	Detroit Tigers	P	Pol Perritt
July 1, 1921	OF 2B P	Casey Stengel Johnny Rawlings Red Causey	Philadelphia Phillies	OF OF OF	Goldie Rapp Lee King Lance Richbourg
July 25, 1921	OF	Irish Meusel	Philadelphia Phillies	OF C P	Curt Walker Butch Henline Jesse Winters and $30,000.

DATE		ACQUIRED	FROM		IN EXCHANGE FOR
July 1921		Waiver price	Philadelphia Phillies	OF	Lee King
Dec 6, 1921	3B	Heinie Groh	Cincinnati Reds	C OF	Mike Gonzalez George Burns and $150,000.
Dec 1921	OF	Dave Robertson	Pittsburgh Pirates		Cash
July 30, 1922	P	Hugh McQuillan	Boston Braves		$100,000.
July 30, 1922		Cash	Cincinnati Reds	P	Rube Benton
Oct 1922		Waiver price	St. Louis Cardinals	P	Fred Toney
April 1923		Waiver price	Philadelphia Athletics	P	Rube Walberg
May 11, 1923		Waiver price	Philadelphia Phillies	2B	Johnny Rawlings
June 7, 1923	C P	Hank Gowdy Mule Watson	Boston Braves	P C	Jesse Barnes Earl Smith
Nov 12, 1923	OF P	Billy Southworth Joe Oeschger	Boston Braves	OF SS OF	Casey Stengel Dave Bancroft Bill Cunningham
		(Bancroft was named Boston manager.)			
June 5, 1924		Cash	Boston Braves	P	Dinty Gearin
July 1, 1924		Waiver price	Philadelphia Phillies	P	Joe Oeschger
April 17, 1925	P	Tim McNamara	Boston Braves	P	Rosy Ryan
Dec 30, 1925	P	Jimmy Ring	Philadelphia Phillies	P P	Jack Bentley Wayland Dean
May 11, 1926		Cash	Cincinnati Reds	P	Art Nehf
June 14, 1926	OF	Heinie Mueller	St. Louis Cardinals	OF	Billy Southworth
Sept 15, 1926	P	Jack Bentley	Philadelphia Phillies		Waiver price
Oct 7, 1926	2B	Jimmy Johnston	Boston Braves		Waiver price
Dec 20, 1926	2B	Rogers Hornsby	St. Louis Cardinals	2B P	Frankie Frisch Jimmy Ring
Jan 9, 1927	OF C	George Harper Butch Henline	Philadelphia Phillies	P 2B	Jack Scott Fresco Thompson
		(Part of three-team trade involving Philadelphia, New York, and Brooklyn.)			
Jan 9, 1927	P	Burleigh Grimes	Brooklyn Dodgers	C	Butch Henline
		(Part of three-team trade involving Brooklyn, New York, and Philadelphia.)			
Feb 9, 1927	OF	Edd Roush	Cincinnati Reds	1B	George Kelly and cash
May 9, 1927	P	Don Songer	Pittsburgh Pirates		Cash

DATE		ACQUIRED	FROM		IN EXCHANGE FOR
May 25, 1927	C	Mickey O'Neil	Washington Senators		Cash
June 12, 1927	C P P	Zack Taylor Larry Benton Herb Thomas	Boston Braves	P P SS	Hugh McQuillan Kent Greenfield Doc Farrell
June 28, 1927	P	Joe Bush	Pittsburgh Pirates		Waiver price
July 18, 1927	OF	Les Mann	Boston Braves		Waiver price
Jan 10, 1928	C OF	Shanty Hogan Jimmy Welsh	Boston Braves	SS	Rogers Hornsby
Feb 11, 1928	P	Vic Aldridge	Pittsburgh Pirates	P	Burleigh Grimes
Feb 1928		Cash	Boston Braves	C	Zack Taylor
May 1, 1928	C	Bob O'Farrell	St. Louis Cardinals	OF	George Harper
May 29, 1928	1B	Russ Wrightstone	Philadelphia Phillies	OF	Art Jahn
June 15, 1928	P	Joe Genewich	Boston Braves	P C P P	Ben Cantwell Al Spohrer Bill Clarkson Virgil Barnes
July 7, 1928	P	Garland Buckeye	Cleveland Indians		Waiver price
Oct 29, 1928	OF	Freddy Leach	Philadelphia Phillies	OF	Lefty O'Doul and cash
Dec 9, 1928		Waiver price (Aldridge refused to report and retired.)	Brooklyn Dodgers	P	Vic Aldridge
June 14, 1929	IF	Doc Farrell	Boston Braves	OF	Jimmy Welsh
July 14, 1929		Cash	Boston Braves	C	Jack Cummings
Sept 27, 1929		Waiver price	Chicago White Sox	P	Dutch Henry
April 10, 1930	OF	Wally Roettger	St. Louis Cardinals	OF IF	Showboat Fisher Doc Farrell
May 15, 1930	P	Clarence Mitchell	St. Louis Cardinals	P	Ralph Judd
May 21, 1930	2B	Hughie Critz	Cincinnati Reds	P	Larry Benton
May 27, 1930	OF P	Ethan Allen Pete Donohue	Cincinnati Reds	OF	Pat Crawford
Oct 29, 1930		Cash	Cincinnati Reds	OF	Wally Roettger
June 30, 1931	2B	Bill Hunnefield	Boston Braves		Waiver price
March 19, 1932		$10,000.	Boston Braves	OF	Freddy Leach

DATE		ACQUIRED	FROM		IN EXCHANGE FOR
Oct 10, 1932	C P	Gus Mancuso Ray Starr	St. Louis Cardinals	OF C P P	Ethan Allen Bob O'Farrell Bill Walker Jim Mooney
Nov 1932		Waiver price	Pittsburgh Pirates	P	Waite Hoyt
Dec 12, 1932	P OF	Glenn Spencer Gus Dugas	Pittsburgh Pirates	3B	Freddie Lindstrom
		(Part of three-team trade involving New York, Philadelphia, and Pittsburgh.)			
Dec 12, 1932	OF	Kiddo Davis	Philadelphia Phillies	OF OF	Gus Dugas Chick Fullis
		(Part of three-team trade involving New York, Philadelphia, and Pittsburgh.)			
Dec 29, 1932		$25,000.	Boston Braves	C	Shanty Hogan
Dec 1932	C	Paul Richards	Brooklyn Dodgers		Waiver price
April 21, 1933	P	George Uhle	Detroit Tigers		$20,000.
June 12, 1933		Cash	Boston Braves	P	Ray Starr
June 16, 1933	OF P	Lefty O'Doul Watty Clark	Brooklyn Dodgers	1B	Sam Leslie
Nov 15, 1933	2B	George Grantham	Cincinnati Reds	P	Glenn Spencer
Feb 1934	OF	George Watkins	St. Louis Cardinals	OF	Kiddo Davis
Nov 1, 1934	SS	Dick Bartell	Philadelphia Phillies	P SS 3B OF	Pretzels Pezzullo Blondy Ryan Johnny Vergez George Watkins and cash
Dec 11, 1934		Waiver price	Pittsburgh Pirates	P	Jack Salveson
Dec 13, 1934	OF	Kiddo Davis	Philadelphia Phillies	P	Joe Bowman
Dec 14, 1934	SS P	Mark Koenig Allyn Stout	Cincinnati Reds	SS	Billy Myers and cash
Dec 1934	P	Leon Chagnon	Pittsburgh Pirates		Cash
May 25, 1935		Cash	Philadelphia Athletics	C	Paul Richards
Aug 2, 1935	P	Euel Moore	Philadelphia Phillies		Cash
Sept 24, 1935	P	Dick Coffman	St. Louis Browns		Cash
Dec 9, 1935	2B	Burgess Whitehead	St. Louis Cardinals	P 1B	Roy Parmelee Phil Weintraub and cash
Jan 1936	1B	Johnny McCarthy	Brooklyn Dodgers		$40,000.
Feb 20, 1936	1B	Sam Leslie	Brooklyn Dodgers		Cash

DATE		ACQUIRED	FROM		IN EXCHANGE FOR
Dec 4, 1936	IF	Mickey Haslin	Boston Braves	3B	Eddie Mayo
Dec 8, 1936	3B	Lou Chiozza	Philadelphia Phillies	IF	George Scharein and cash
Jan 27, 1937	P	Ben Cantwell	Boston Braves		Cash
June 11, 1937	P	Tom Baker	Brooklyn Dodgers	P	Freddie Fitzsimmons
June 15, 1937	3B	Wally Berger	Boston Braves	P	Frank Gabler and $35,000.
June 1937	P	Jumbo Brown	Cincinnati Reds		Cash
Aug 4, 1937		Cash	Cincinnati Reds	OF	Kiddo Davis
Aug 9, 1937		Cash	Brooklyn Dodgers	P	Ben Cantwell
Dec 20, 1937		Cash	St. Louis Cardinals	P	Al Smith
March 1938	2B	Bill Cissell	Philadelphia Athletics		Cash
June 6, 1938	2B	Alex Kampouris	Cincinnati Reds	OF	Wally Berger
Dec 6, 1938	OF SS C	Frank Demaree Bill Jurges Ken O'Dea	Chicago Cubs	SS OF C	Dick Bartell Hank Leiber Gus Mancuso
Dec 11, 1938	1B	Zeke Bonura	Washington Senators	IF P	Jim Carlin Tom Baker and $20,000.
May 9, 1939	P	Red Lynn	Detroit Tigers		Cash
Aug 23, 1939	C	Ray Hayworth	Brooklyn Dodgers	OF	Jimmy Ripple
April 26, 1940		$20,000.	Washington Senators	1B	Zeke Bonura
May 14, 1940	P	Bill McGee	St. Louis Cardinals	P P	Harry Gumbert Paul Dean and cash
June 15, 1940	3B	Tony Cuccinello	Boston Braves	P 2B	Manny Salvo Al Glossop
Nov 25, 1940	IF	Joe Orengo	St. Louis Cardinals		Cash
Dec 5, 1940	P	Bob Bowman	St. Louis Cardinals		Cash
Dec 10, 1940	OF	Morrie Arnovich	Cincinnati Reds		Cash
Jan 2, 1941	P	Bump Hadley	New York Yankees		Cash
April 30, 1941		Cash	Philadelphia Athletics	P	Bump Hadley
June 19, 1941	2B	Odell Hale	Boston Red Sox		Waiver price

DATE	ACQUIRED	FROM	IN EXCHANGE FOR
July 21, 1941	Waiver price	Boston Braves	OF Frank Demaree
Dec 4, 1941	OF Hank Leiber	Chicago Cubs	P Bob Bowman
Dec 9, 1941	3B Bill Werber	Cincinnati Reds	Cash
Dec 11, 1941	1B Johnny Mize	St. Louis Cardinals	C Ken O'Dea P Bill Lohrman 1B Johnny McCarthy and $50,000.
March 1942	C Ray Berres	Boston Braves	Cash
May 5, 1942	C Gus Mancuso	St. Louis Cardinals	Cash
May 5, 1942	P Bill Lohrman	St. Louis Cardinals	Cash
April 27, 1943	C Ernie Lombardi	Boston Braves	C Hugh Poland 2B Connie Ryan
July 6, 1943	OF Joe Medwick	Brooklyn Dodgers	Cash
July 31, 1943	1B Dolf Camilli P Johnny Allen	Brooklyn Dodgers	P Bill Lohrman P Bill Sayles IF Joe Orengo
	(Camilli refused to report to New York and retired.)		
June 12, 1944	P Johnny Gee	Pittsburgh Pirates	Cash
June 16, 1945	C Clyde Kluttz P Ewald Pyle	Boston Braves	OF Joe Medwick
Jan 5, 1946	C Walker Cooper	St. Louis Cardinals	$175,000.
April 4, 1946	C Bennie Warren	Chicago Cubs	Waiver price
April 27, 1946	OF Goody Rosen	Brooklyn Dodgers	Cash
May 1, 1946	OF Vince DiMaggio	Philadelphia Phillies	C Clyde Klutz
May 1946	OF Jack Graham	Brooklyn Dodgers	Cash
June 7, 1947	P Joe Beggs	Cincinnati Reds	1B Babe Young
June 13, 1947	P Mort Cooper	Boston Braves	P Bill Voiselle and cash
July 7, 1947	C Mickey Livingston	Chicago Cubs	Waiver price
Jan 16, 1948	IF Jack Conway	Cleveland Indians	Cash
July 1, 1948	P Paul Erickson	Philadelphia Phillies	Waiver price
July 30, 1948	Cash	Pittsburgh Pirates	P Paul Erickson
Dec 14, 1948	Cash	Philadelphia Phillies	P Ken Trinkle

DATE		ACQUIRED	FROM		IN EXCHANGE FOR
June 6, 1949	P	Kirby Higbe	Pittsburgh Pirates	P IF	Ray Poat Bobby Rhawn
June 13, 1949	C	Ray Mueller	Cincinnati Reds	C	Walker Cooper
Aug 22, 1949		$40,000.	New York Yankees	1B	Johnny Mize
Dec 14, 1949	2B SS	Eddie Stanky Alvin Dark	Boston Braves	3B SS OF P	Sid Gordon Buddy Kerr Willard Marshall Red Webb
March 26, 1950	P	Jack Kramer	Boston Red Sox		Cash
May 17, 1950		Cash	Pittsburgh Pirates	C	Ray Mueller
May 1950	P	Jim Hearn	St. Louis Cardinals		Cash
June 5, 1951		Waiver price	Pittsburgh Pirates	OF	Jack Maguire
July 10, 1951	IF	Hank Schenz	Pittsburgh Pirates		Waiver price
July 16, 1951		Waiver price	St. Louis Browns	IF	Bill Jennings
Sept 1, 1951		Waiver price	St. Louis Browns	OF	Earl Rapp
Dec 11, 1951	OF P	Chuck Diering Max Lanier (Stanky was named St. Louis manager.)	St. Louis Cardinals	2B	Eddie Stanky
Dec 13, 1951		Minor league C Jake Schmitt	Philadelphia Phillies	3B	Lucky Lohrke
April 8, 1952	OF	Bob Elliott	Boston Braves	P	Sheldon Jones and $50,000.
May 7, 1952	OF	Bill Howerton	Pittsburgh Pirates		Waiver price
May 8, 1952	OF	Ted Wilson $75,000.	New York Giants	OF	Ted Wilson $75,000.
May 12, 1953		Waiver price	Pittsburgh Pirates	P	Roger Bowman
June 15, 1953		$12,500.	St. Louis Cardinals	C	Sal Yvars
July 1, 1953	P	Marv Grissom	Boston Red Sox		Waiver price
Feb 1, 1954	P P C IF	Johnny Antonelli Don Liddle Ebba St. Claire Billy Klaus and $50,000.	Milwaukee Braves	OF C	Bobby Thomson Sammy Calderone
April 8, 1954		Cash	Baltimore Orioles	P	Dave Koslo
May 18, 1954	OF	Hoot Evers	Boston Red Sox		Waiver price
July 29, 1954		Waiver price	Detroit Tigers	OF	Hoot Evers

DATE		ACQUIRED	FROM		IN EXCHANGE FOR
Sept 8, 1954	C	Joe Garagiola	Chicago Cubs		Waiver price
Dec 14, 1954	C	Del Wilber	Boston Red Sox	SS	Billy Klaus
April 8, 1955		Waiver price	Detroit Tigers	SS	Ron Samford
May 23, 1955	OF	Sid Gordon	Pittsburgh Pirates		Cash
July 31, 1955		Waiver price	Cleveland Indians	P	Sal Maglie
Aug 26, 1955	OF	Gil Coan	Chicago White Sox		Waiver price
March 5, 1956	C	Jim Mangan	Pittsburgh Pirates		Cash
April 21, 1956		$20,000.	Baltimore Orioles	2B	Billy Gardner
June 14, 1956	OF 2B P P C	Jackie Brandt Red Schoendienst Gordon Jones Dick Littlefield Bill Sarni	St. Louis Cardinals	3B C P 1B	Alvin Dark Ray Katt Don Liddle Whitey Lockman
Aug 22, 1956		Waiver price	New York Yankees	OF	Ted Wilson
Oct 1, 1956	P	Gordon Jones	St. Louis Cardinals		Cash
Oct 11, 1956	P	Stu Miller	Philadelphia Phillies	P	Jim Hearn
Dec 13, 1956	2B	Jackie Robinson (Trade was cancelled when Robinson retired.)	Brooklyn Dodgers	P	Dick Littlefield and $30,000.
Feb 26, 1957	1B	Whitey Lockman	St. Louis Cardinals	P	Hoyt Wilhelm
April 16, 1957	3B C	Ray Jablonski Ray Katt	Chicago Cubs	P OF	Dick Littlefield Bob Lennon
May 14, 1957	P	Sandy Consuegra	Baltimore Orioles		Waiver price
June 4, 1957	P	Jim Davis	St. Louis Cardinals		Waiver price
June 15, 1957	2B P OF	Danny O'Connell Ray Crone Bobby Thomson	Milwaukee Braves	2B	Red Schoendienst
Oct 15, 1957	P	Dave Jolly	Milwaukee Braves		Waiver price
Dec 10, 1957	P	Tom Poholsky	Chicago Cubs	P	Freddy Rodriguez
June 14, 1958	P	Joe McClain	St. Louis Cardinals	P	Sal Maglie

New York Mets

The Best Trades

1. Acquired Felix Millan and George Stone from the Atlanta Braves for Gary Gentry and Danny Frisella, November 2, 1972.
2. Acquired Keith Hernandez from the St. Louis Cardinals for Neil Allen and Rick Ownbey, June 15, 1983.
3. Acquired Donn Clendenon from the Montreal Expos for Steve Renko, Kevin Collins, Bill Cardon, and Dave Colon, June 15, 1969.
4. Acquired Tommie Agee and Al Weis from the Chicago White Sox for Tommy Davis, Jack Fisher, Billy Wynne, and Dick Booker, December 15, 1967.
5. Acquired George Foster from the Cincinnati Reds for Alex Trevino, Jim Kern, and Greg Harris, February 10, 1982.

The Worst Trades

1. Traded Nolan Ryan, Leroy Stanton, Don Rose, and Francisco Estrada to the California Angels for Jim Fregosi, December 10, 1971.
2. Traded Amos Otis and Bob Johnson to the Kansas City Royals for Joe Foy, December 3, 1969.
3. Traded Rusty Staub and Bill Laxton to the Detroit Tigers for Mickey Lolich and Bobby Baldwin, December 12, 1975.
4. Traded Tom Seaver to the Cincinnati Reds for Steve Henderson, Dan Norman, Doug Flynn, and Pat Zachry, June 15, 1977.
5. Traded Dave Kingman to the San Diego Padres for Bobby Valentine and Paul Siebert, June 15, 1977.

Trades: The Great Giveaways

Whenever Nolan Ryan pitches a no-hitter or a shutout, or even just another of his routine ten-strikeout games, Met fans shudder. In December 1971, in one of the worst trades of all time, the Mets traded Ryan for Jim Fregosi. And the Mets felt obliged to throw in Don Rose, Leroy Stanton and Francisco Estrada, too. They felt the deal would wrap up a pennant for them. Instead, it turned into one they will never live down, as Ryan went on to fame in Anaheim and fortune in Houston.

Years later, general manager Bob Scheffing gave his explanation of the deal to Jack Lang of the New York *Daily News.* "Ryan was a country boy from Texas, and he and his wife were frightened by the big city. Ryan told me after the 1971 season that he didn't want to spend another year in New York and hoped I would trade him. I don't think he would have walked away from baseball but I couldn't take that chance.

"We really thought we had a chance to win the pennant if we could get a third baseman. Fregosi had been one of the outstanding offensive shortstops in the American League for years. We didn't think he would have any trouble shifting to third."

Fregosi had no trouble shifting to third, but had considerable trouble at the plate, hitting .233 in his season and a half with the Mets. Fregosi was only the most prominent example of the Mets' obsession with their third base problem. Another frustrating case was the trade of Amos Otis to Kansas City for Joe Foy.

Like Fregosi, Foy was to be the answer to their third base woes. Foy batted .236 for the Mets and was gone in a year, while Otis set virtually all the Royals' career batting marks during his fourteen years with the club. Johnny Murphy, the Mets' general manager who made the deal, was looking to give up veteran Tommie Agee, but the Royals held out for Otis. The Royals also wanted a pitcher, and so the Mets included a young hard-thrower named Bob Johnson. Murphy didn't mind giving away Otis, but balked at trading Johnson. The Royals insisted there was no deal without Johnson, and the Mets finally agreed.

An all-star team of former Mets traded away before reaching or while still in their prime would place Rusty Staub at first, Ron Hunt at second, Tim Foli at short, and Dave Kingman at third (stretching a point, but Kingman did play third for San Francisco, and the Mets' problem hasn't been the third basemen they traded away, just the ones they traded *for*). Amos Otis would be in left, Paul Blair in center, and Ken Singleton in right, with Jody Davis behind the plate, and a pitching staff that includes Tom Seaver, Jerry Koosman, Nolan Ryan, Jon Matlack, Jim Bibby, Tug McGraw, and Jeff Reardon.

DATE		ACQUIRED	FROM		IN EXCHANGE FOR
Oct 11, 1961	P P	Ken MacKenzie Johnny Antonelli	Milwaukee Braves		Cash
Oct 13, 1961	1B	Jim Marshall	San Francisco Giants		Cash
Oct 16, 1961	OF	Neil Chrisley	Milwaukee Braves		Cash
Oct 16, 1961	P	Billy Loes	San Francisco Giants		Cash
Nov 28, 1961	OF	Frank Thomas	Milwaukee Braves		Cash
Dec 15, 1961	2B	Charlie Neal	Los Angeles Dodgers	OF	Lee Walls and $100,000.
Dec 21, 1961	P	Howie Nunn	Cincinnati Reds		Cash
April 26, 1962	C	Harry Chiti	Cleveland Indians		Cash
April 26, 1962	C	Sammy Taylor	Chicago Cubs	OF	Bobby Gene Smith
May 7, 1962	P 3B	Bob Miller Cliff Cook	Cincinnati Reds	3B	Don Zimmer
May 7, 1962	P	Vinegar Bend Mizell	Pittsburgh Pirates	1B	Jim Marshall
May 9, 1962	1B	Marv Throneberry	Baltimore Orioles	C	Hobie Landrith and cash
June 15, 1962	OF	Gene Woodling	Washington Senators		Cash
July 13, 1962	C	Joe Pignatano	San Francisco Giants		Cash
Sept 6, 1962	P	Larry Foss	Pittsburgh Pirates		Waiver price
Sept 7, 1962	P	Galen Cisco	Boston Red Sox		Waiver price
Oct 11, 1962	C	Norm Sherry	Los Angeles Dodgers		Cash
Oct 11, 1962	OF	Dick Smith	Los Angeles Dodgers		Cash
Nov 27, 1962	P	Wynn Hawkins	Cleveland Indians		Cash

DATE		ACQUIRED	FROM		IN EXCHANGE FOR
Nov 30, 1962	1B 2B	Tim Harkness Larry Burright	Los Angeles Dodgers	P	Bob Miller
Dec 11, 1962	P 2B SS	Tracy Stallard Pumpsie Green Al Moran	Boston Red Sox	3B	Felix Mantilla
March 23, 1963	P	Carl Willey	Milwaukee Braves		Cash
April 1, 1963	OF	Duke Snider	Los Angeles Dodgers		Cash
May 8, 1963	SS	Chico Fernandez	Milwaukee Braves	P	Larry Foss
May 23, 1963	OF	Jimmy Piersall (Hodges was named Washington manager.)	Washington Senators	1B	Gil Hodges
July 1, 1963	C	Jesse Gonder	Cincinnati Reds	2B C	Charlie Neal Sammy Taylor
July 29, 1963	OF	Duke Carmel	St. Louis Cardinals	OF	Jacke Davis and cash
Aug 5, 1963	P	Ed Bauta	St. Louis Cardinals	P	Ken MacKenzie
Oct 10, 1963	P	Jack Fisher	San Francisco Giants		$30,000.
Oct 15, 1963	SS	Amado Samuel	Milwaukee Braves		Cash
Nov 4, 1963	OF P	George Altman Bill Wakefield	St. Louis Cardinals	P	Roger Craig
Dec 2, 1963	OF	Hawk Taylor	Milwaukee Braves		Cash
March 31, 1964	P	Mike Joyce	Chicago White Sox		Cash
April 14, 1964		Cash	San Francisco Giants	OF	Duke Snider
April 23, 1964	3B	Charley Smith	Chicago White Sox	SS	Chico Fernandez minor league C Bobby Caton and cash
May 8, 1964	SS	Roy McMillan	Milwaukee Braves	P OF	Jay Hook Adrian Garrett
May 30, 1964	P	Frank Lary	Detroit Tigers		Cash
July 19, 1964	2B	Bobby Klaus	Cincinnati Reds		Cash
Aug 8, 1964	P	Dennis Ribant and cash	Milwaukee Braves	P	Frank Lary
Oct 15, 1964	P	Larry Miller	Los Angeles Dodgers	OF	Dick Smith
Nov 23, 1964	P	Warren Spahn	Milwaukee Braves		Cash
Dec 7, 1964	OF P	Johnny Lewis Gordie Richardson	St. Louis Cardinals	P 2B	Tracy Stallard Elio Chacon
Jan 15, 1965	OF	Billy Cowan	Chicago Cubs	OF	George Altman

DATE		ACQUIRED	FROM		IN EXCHANGE FOR
March 20, 1965	P	Frank Lary	Milwaukee Braves		Cash
May 12, 1965	2B	Chuck Hiller	San Francisco Giants		Cash
July 8, 1965	C	Jimmie Schaffer	Chicago White Sox	P	Frank Lary
July 21, 1965	OF	Gary Kolb	Milwaukee Braves	C	Jesse Gonder
Aug 18, 1965	P	Dave Eilers	Milwaukee Braves		Cash
Oct 14, 1965	P	Jack Hamilton	Detroit Tigers		Cash
Oct 19, 1965	C	Jerry Grote	Houston Astros	P	Tom Parsons and cash
Oct 20, 1965	3B	Ken Boyer	St. Louis Cardinals	3B P	Charley Smith Al Jackson
Nov 29, 1965	OF	Al Luplow	Cleveland Indians		Cash
Nov 30, 1965	SS	Ed Bressoud	Boston Red Sox	OF	Joe Christopher
Jan 6, 1966	OF	Johnny Weekly and cash	Houston Astros	P	Gary Kroll
Feb 22, 1966	1B	Dick Stuart	Philadelphia Phillies	C IF IF	Jimmie Schaffer Bobby Klaus Wayne Graham
May 20, 1966	P	Jerry Arrigo	Cincinnati Reds		Cash
June 10, 1966	P	Bob Shaw	San Francisco Giants		Cash
June 15, 1966	P	Bob Friend	New York Yankees		Cash
Aug 6, 1966	P	Ralph Terry	Kansas City Athletics		Cash
Aug 16, 1966		Cash	Cincinnati Reds	P	Jerry Arrigo
Oct 14, 1966	OF	Larry Stahl	Kansas City Athletics		Waiver price
Nov 29, 1966	OF IF	Tommy Davis Derrell Griffith	Los Angeles Dodgers	2B OF	Ron Hunt Jim Hickman
Dec 6, 1966	OF P	Don Bosch Don Cardwell	Pittsburgh Pirates	P OF	Dennis Ribant Gary Kolb
Dec 19, 1966		Cash	Detroit Tigers	C	Chris Cannizzaro
Feb 10, 1967	P	Ron Taylor	Houston Astros		Cash
March 24, 1967	2B	Sandy Alomar	Houston Astros	IF	Derrell Griffith
April 1, 1967	IF P IF	Jerry Buchek Art Mahaffey Tony Martinez	St. Louis Cardinals	SS OF	Ed Bressoud Danny Napoleon and cash
April 26, 1967	P	Jack Lamabe	Chicago White Sox		Cash

DATE		ACQUIRED	FROM		IN EXCHANGE FOR
May 10, 1967	IF	Bob Johnson	Baltimore Orioles		Cash
May 10, 1967	P	John Miller	Baltimore Orioles		Cash
May 10, 1967	3B	Ed Charles	Kansas City Athletics	OF	Larry Elliot and $50,000.
June 10, 1967	P	Nick Willhite	California Angels	P	Jack Hamilton
June 12, 1967	P	Bob Hendley	Chicago Cubs	C P	Johnny Stephenson Rob Gardner
June 24, 1967	P	Dennis Bennett	Boston Red Sox	OF	Al Yates and cash
June 29, 1967	P	Hal Reniff	New York Yankees		Cash
July 11, 1967	2B	Phil Linz	Philadelphia Phillies	2B	Chuck Hiller
July 16, 1967	P	Al Jackson	St. Louis Cardinals	P	Jack Lamabe
July 22, 1967	C	J. C. Martin	Chicago White Sox	3B	Ken Boyer
July 24, 1967	2B	Don Wallace and cash	California Angels	C-1B	Hawk Taylor
July 24, 1967		Cash	Chicago Cubs	P	Bob Shaw
Aug 2, 1967	P	Cal Koonce	Chicago Cubs		Cash
Aug 14, 1967	P	Joe Grzenda	Kansas City Athletics		Cash
Aug 15, 1967		Cash	Chicago White Sox	2B	Sandy Alomar
Aug 20, 1967	P	Bill Connors	Chicago Cubs		Cash
Nov 8, 1967	1B-OF	Art Shamsky	Cincinnati Reds	IF	Bob Johnson
Nov 27, 1967	MGR	Gil Hodges (Hodges was named New York manager.)	Washington Senators	P	Bill Denehy and $100,000.
Nov 29, 1967		Cash	Minnesota Twins	P	Joe Grzenda
Nov 29, 1967	P	Bill Short	Pittsburgh Pirates		Cash
Dec 15, 1967	OF 2B	Tommie Agee Al Weis	Chicago White Sox	OF P P	Tommy Davis Jack Fisher Billy Wynne minor league C Dick Booker
Oct 16, 1968		Cash	Montreal Expos	OF	Don Bosch
June 13, 1969		Cash	Cincinnati Reds	P	Al Jackson

DATE		ACQUIRED	FROM		IN EXCHANGE FOR
June 15, 1969	1B	Donn Clendenon	Montreal Expos	P 3B	Steve Renko Kevin Collins minor league Ps Bill Cardon and Dave Colon
Dec 3, 1969	3B	Joe Foy	Kansas City Royals	3B P	Amos Otis Bob Johnson
Dec 12, 1969	P OF	Ray Sadecki Dave Marshall	San Francisco Giants	IF OF	Bob Heise Jim Gosger
March 29, 1970	C	Randy Bobb	Chicago Cubs	C	J. C. Martin
June 8, 1970		Cash	Boston Red Sox	P	Cal Koonce
July 12, 1970		Cash	Atlanta Braves	P	Don Cardwell
Sept 1, 1970	P	Ron Herbel (San Diego received Gaspar on October 20.)	San Diego Padres	OF	Rod Gaspar
Sept 18, 1970	P	Dean Chance	Cleveland Indians		Cash
Dec 1, 1970	3B	Bob Aspromonte	Atlanta Braves	P	Ron Herbel
March 15, 1971	OF	George Spriggs	Kansas City Royals		Cash
March 30, 1971	P	Jerry Robertson	Detroit Tigers	P P	Dean Chance Bill Denehy
March 31, 1971	OF	Don Hahn	Montreal Expos	OF SS	Ron Swoboda Rich Hacker
Oct 18, 1971	1B P P 2B	Jim Beauchamp Chuck Taylor Harry Parker Tom Coulter	St. Louis Cardinals	OF-1B P P P	Art Shamsky Jim Bibby Rich Folkers Charles Hudson
Oct 20, 1971		Cash	Montreal Expos	P	Ron Taylor
Dec 10, 1971	SS	Jim Fregosi	California Angels	P P OF C	Nolan Ryan Don Rose Leroy Stanton Francisco Estrada
March 27, 1972	3B	Bill Sudakis	Los Angeles Dodgers		Cash
April 5, 1972	OF	Rusty Staub	Montreal Expos	SS OF 1B	Tim Foli Ken Singleton Mike Jorgensen
May 11, 1972	OF	Willie Mays	San Francisco Giants	P	Charlie Williams and $50,000.
Sept 13, 1972		Cash	Milwaukee Brewers	P	Chuck Taylor
Nov 2, 1972	2B P	Felix Millan George Stone	Atlanta Braves	P P	Gary Gentry Danny Frisella
Nov 27, 1972	P	Phil Hennigan	Cleveland Indians	P P	Brent Strom Bob Rauch
Nov 27, 1972	OF P	Rich Chiles Buddy Harris	Houston Astros	OF	Tommie Agee

DATE		ACQUIRED	FROM		IN EXCHANGE FOR
Nov 30, 1972	P	Al Severinsen	San Diego Padres	OF	Dave Marshall
March 28, 1973	OF	Bill McNulty	Texas Rangers	3B	Bill Sudakis
May 14, 1973	C	Jerry May	Kansas City Royals		Cash
July 11, 1973		Cash	Texas Rangers	3B	Jim Fregosi
July 16, 1973	P	John Strohmayer	Montreal Expos		Cash
Sept 23, 1973	P	Bob Miller	Detroit Tigers		Cash
Dec 20, 1973	P	Steve Simpson	San Diego Padres	P	Jim McAndrew
March 26, 1974		Cash	Atlanta Braves	P	Buzz Capra
June 14, 1974	P	Jack Aker	Atlanta Braves		Cash
Oct 13, 1974	1B-3B	Joe Torre	St. Louis Cardinals	P P	Ray Sadecki Tommy Moore
Oct 22, 1974	OF	Gene Clines	Pittsburgh Pirates	C	Duffy Dyer
Oct 29, 1974	OF	Bob Gallagher	Houston Astros	IF	Ken Boswell
Dec 3, 1974	P	Skip Lockwood	California Angels	IF	Bill Sudakis
Dec 3, 1974	OF C P	Del Unser John Stearns Mac Scarce	Philadelphia Phillies	P OF OF	Tug McGraw Don Hahn Dave Schneck
Dec 11, 1974	IF OF	Jack Heidemann Mike Vail	St. Louis Cardinals	IF	Teddy Martinez
Jan 30, 1975	C	Gerry Moses	Detroit Tigers		Cash
Feb 28, 1975	OF	Dave Kingman	San Francisco Giants		$150,000.
March 22, 1975	P	Ken Sanders	California Angels	C	Ike Hampton
April 15, 1975	P	Tom Hall	Cincinnati Reds	P	Mac Scarce
May 3, 1975	SS	Mike Phillips	San Francisco Giants		Cash
Aug 4, 1975		Cash	St. Louis Cardinals	P	Harry Parker
Dec 12, 1975	OF	Joe Lovitto	Texas Rangers	OF	Gene Clines
Dec 12, 1975	P OF	Mickey Lolich Bobby Baldwin	Detroit Tigers	1B P	Rusty Staub Bill Laxton
Feb 24, 1976	P	Bill Hands	Texas Rangers	P	George Stone

DATE		ACQUIRED	FROM		IN EXCHANGE FOR
May 7, 1976		Minor league IF Bryan Jones and cash	Kansas City Royals	P	Tom Hall
June 22, 1976		Minor league P Tom Deidel	Milwaukee Brewers	IF	Jack Heidemann
July 21, 1976	OF OF	Jim Dwyer Pepe Mangual	Montreal Expos	OF IF	Del Unser Wayne Garrett
Sept 17, 1976		Cash	Kansas City Royals	P	Ken Sanders
Dec 8, 1976	OF	Sheldon Mallory	Chicago Cubs	OF	Jim Dwyer
		(Part of three-team trade involving Chicago Cubs, New York Mets, and Kansas City.)			
Dec 9, 1976		Minor league 1B Ed Kurpiel	St. Louis Cardinals	1B OF	Brock Pemberton Leon Brown
Feb 7, 1977	SS	Rick Auerbach	Los Angeles Dodgers	P	Hank Webb minor league P Dick Sanders
Feb 25, 1977	IF	Luis Alvarado	Detroit Tigers		Cash
		(Alvarado was returned to Detroit on April 27, 1977.)			
March 30, 1977	IF	Doug Clarey	St. Louis Cardinals	OF	Benny Ayala
April 26, 1977	IF	Lenny Randle	Texas Rangers	SS	Rick Auerbach and cash
June 15, 1977	P IF OF OF	Pat Zachry Doug Flynn Steve Henderson Dan Norman	Cincinnati Reds	P	Tom Seaver
June 15, 1977	IF P	Bobby Valentine Paul Siebert	San Diego Padres	1B	Dave Kingman
June 15, 1977	3B	Joel Youngblood	St. Louis Cardinals	SS	Mike Phillips
Sept 26, 1977	P	Doc Medich	Seattle Mariners		Cash
Nov 11, 1977		No compensation (free agent signing)	Texas Rangers	P	Doc Medich
Nov 21, 1977	P	Tom Hausman	Milwaukee Brewers		No compensation (free agent signing)
Dec 7, 1977	SS	Tim Foli	San Francisco Giants		Cash
Dec 8, 1977	1B OF OF	Willie Montanez Ken Henderson Tom Grieve	Texas Rangers	P 1B	Jon Matlack John Milner
		(Part of four-team trade involving Texas, New York Mets, Pittsburgh, and Atlanta.)			
Dec 9, 1977	SS	Sergio Ferrer	New York Yankees	3B	Roy Staiger
March 24, 1978	2B	Fred Andrews and cash	Philadelphia Phillies	SS	Bud Harrelson

DATE	ACQUIRED	FROM	IN EXCHANGE FOR
March 26, 1978	Cash	Cleveland Indians	OF Mike Vail
March 27, 1978	Minor league C Ed Cuervo	Philadelphia Phillies	P Jackson Todd
March 29, 1978	P Jim Burton	Boston Red Sox	IF Len Foster
April 5, 1978	P Clarence Metzger	St. Louis Cardinals	Cash
May 19, 1978	P Dale Murray	Cincinnati Reds	OF Ken Henderson
July 4, 1978	Cash	Philadelphia Phillies	P Clarence Metzger
July 28, 1978	OF Gil Flores	California Angels	Cash
Oct 2, 1978	OF Bob Coluccio	St. Louis Cardinals	P Paul Siebert
Dec 5, 1978	P Pete Falcone	St. Louis Cardinals	OF Tom Grieve P Kim Seaman
Dec 8, 1978	P Jesse Orosco minor league P Greg Field	Minnesota Twins	P Jerry Koosman
March 13, 1979	P Ed Glynn	Detroit Tigers	P Mardie Cornejo
March 25, 1979	Cash	Toronto Blue Jays	OF Bobby Brown
March 27, 1979	1B-3B Richie Hebner 2B Jose Moreno	Philadelphia Phillies	P Nino Espinosa
April 19, 1979	SS Frank Taveras	Pittsburgh Pirates	SS Tim Foli minor league P Greg Field
May 25, 1979	No compensation (free agent signing)	Philadelphia Phillies	SS Bud Harrelson
June 15, 1979	P Andy Hassler	Boston Red Sox	Cash
June 15, 1979	P Dock Ellis	Texas Rangers	P Bob Myrick P Mike Bruhert
Aug 2, 1979	OF Jose Cardenal	Philadelphia Phillies	Cash
Aug 12, 1979	P Ed Lynch 1B Mike Jorgensen	Texas Rangers	1B Willie Montanez
Aug 19, 1979	Cash	Seattle Mariners	P Wayne Twitchell
Aug 20, 1979	P Ray Burris	New York Yankees	Cash
Aug 30, 1979	Cash	Montreal Expos	P Dale Murray
Sept 21, 1979	Cash	Pittsburgh Pirates	P Dock Ellis
Oct 26, 1979	P Mark Bomback	Milwaukee Brewers	P Dwight Bernard
Oct 31, 1979	OF Jerry Morales 3B Phil Mankowski	Detroit Tigers	1B Richie Hebner

DATE		ACQUIRED	FROM		IN EXCHANGE FOR
Nov 19, 1979		No compensation (free agent signing)	Pittsburgh Pirates	P	Andy Hassler
Nov 27, 1979		No compensation (free agent signing)	Boston Red Sox	P	Skip Lockwood
Feb 20, 1980	C	Reggie Baldwin	Houston Astros		Minor league OF Keith Bodie
March 8, 1980		No compensation (free agent signing)	Seattle Mariners	3B	Lenny Randle
April 1, 1980		Cash	New York Yankees	1B	Marshall Brant
June 7, 1980	OF	Claudell Washington	Chicago White Sox		Minor league OF Jesse Anderson
June 17, 1980	P	Randy McGilberry	Kansas City Royals	P	Kevin Kobel
July 11, 1980	SS	Bill Almon	Milwaukee Brewers		No compensation (free agent signing)
Nov 17, 1980		No compensation (free agent signing)	Atlanta Braves	OF	Claudell Washington
Dec 12, 1980	UT	Bob Bailor	Toronto Blue Jays	P	Roy Lee Jackson
Dec 15, 1980	P	Randy Jones	San Diego Padres	P IF	John Pacella Jose Moreno
Dec 16, 1980	1B	Rusty Staub	Texas Rangers		No compensation (free agent signing)
Dec 19, 1980	3B	Mike Cubbage	Minnesota Twins		No compensation (free agent signing)
Feb 4, 1981		No compensation (free agent signing)	Chicago White Sox	SS	Bill Almon
Feb 11, 1981	C	Bruce Bochy	Houston Astros		Minor leaguers C Stan Hough and IF Randy Rogers
Feb 18, 1981		No compensation (free agent signing)	Montreal Expos	P	Ray Burris
Feb 28, 1981	OF-1B	Dave Kingman	Chicago Cubs	OF	Steve Henderson and cash
March 31, 1981	OF	Marvell Wynne minor league P John Skinner	Kansas City Royals	P	Juan Berenguer
April 3, 1981	OF	Gary Rajsich	Houston Astros		Minor league OF John Csefalvay
April 5, 1981	P	Danny Boitano	Minnesota Twins		Cash
April 6, 1981		Cash	Chicago Cubs	C	Butch Benton
April 6, 1981		Minor league P Dominick Bullinger	Cleveland Indians	P	Ed Glynn
April 6, 1981	P	Charlie Puleo and cash	Toronto Blue Jays	P	Mark Bomback
May 29, 1981	OF	Ellis Valentine	Montreal Expos	P OF	Jeff Reardon Dan Norman
Dec 11, 1981	P	Steve Ratzer and cash	Montreal Expos	SS	Frank Taveras

DATE		ACQUIRED	FROM		IN EXCHANGE FOR
Dec 11, 1981	P	Jim Kern	Texas Rangers	2B P	Doug Flynn Danny Boitano
Jan 8, 1982	SS	Tom Veryzer	Cleveland Indians	P	Ray Searage
Feb 10, 1982	OF	George Foster	Cincinnati Reds	C P P	Alex Trevino Jim Kern Greg Harris
April 1, 1982	P P	Ron Darling Walt Terrell	Texas Rangers	OF	Lee Mazzilli
May 21, 1982		Cash	Seattle Mariners	C	Rick Sweet
Aug 4, 1982	P	Tom Gorman	Montreal Expos	OF	Joel Youngblood
Sept 10, 1982	P	Carlos Diaz	Atlanta Braves	P	Tom Hausman
Dec 10, 1982	OF	Danny Heep	Houston Astros	P	Mike Scott
Dec 16, 1982	P	Tom Seaver	Cincinnati Reds	P	Charlie Puleo minor leaguers C Lloyd McClendon and OF Jason Felice
Dec 28, 1982	OF	Jorge Orta	Los Angeles Dodgers	P	Pat Zachry
Jan 14, 1983	P	Mike Torrez	Boston Red Sox		Minor league 3B Mike Davis
Jan 24, 1983		No compensation (free agent signing)	California Angels	OF	Ellis Valentine
Jan 25, 1983		No compensation (free agent signing)	Atlanta Braves	P	Pete Falcone
Feb 4, 1983	P	Steve Senteney	Toronto Blue Jays	OF	Jorge Orta
March 29, 1983	OF	Mark Bradley	Los Angeles Dodgers		Minor league Ps Steve Walker Jody Johnston and cash
April 2, 1983		Minor league Ps Craig Weissman and Bob Schilling	Chicago Cubs	SS	Tom Veryzer
April 18, 1983	3B	Tucker Ashford	New York Yankees		Minor leaguers P Steve Ray and IF Felix Perdomo
June 14, 1983	C	Junior Ortiz Minor league P Arthur Ray	Pittsburgh Pirates	OF P	Marvell Wynne Steve Senteney
June 15, 1983	1B	Keith Hernandez	St. Louis Cardinals	P P	Neil Allen Rick Ownbey
June 15, 1983		$75,000.	Atlanta Braves	1B	Mike Jorgensen
Dec 8, 1983	P	Sid Fernandez	Los Angeles Dodgers	P UT	Carlos Diaz Bob Bailor
Jan 15, 1984	1B	Jim Maler	Seattle Mariners		Minor league P John Semprini

DATE		ACQUIRED	FROM		IN EXCHANGE FOR
Jan 20, 1984			Chicago White Sox	P	Tom Seaver
		(Claimed in compensation draft after Chicago lost free agent P Dennis Lamp to Toronto.)			
Jan 27, 1984	P	Dick Tidrow	Chicago White Sox		No compensation (free agent signing)
Feb 19, 1984		Minor league IF Billy Max	Milwaukee Brewers	1B	Kelvin Moore
April 1, 1984		Minor league P Tom Edens	Kansas City Royals	3B	Tucker Ashford

Philadelphia Phillies

The Best Trades

1. Acquired Steve Carlton from the St. Louis Cardinals for Rick Wise, February 25, 1972.
2. Acquired Lefty O'Doul and cash from the New York Giants for Freddy Leach, October 29, 1928.
3. Acquired Jim Bunning and Gus Triandos from the Detroit Tigers for Don Demeter and Jack Hamilton, December 4, 1963.
4. Acquired Cy Williams from the Chicago Cubs for Dode Paskert, December 26, 1917.
5. Acquired Gary Matthews from the Atlanta Braves for Bob Walk, March 25, 1981.

The Worst Trades

1. Traded Grover Alexander and Bill Killefer to the Chicago Cubs for Mike Prendergast, Pickles Dillhoefer, and $55,000, December 11, 1917.
2. Traded Eppa Rixey to the Cincinnati Reds for Jimmy Ring and Greasy Neale, November 22, 1920.
3. Traded Bucky Walters to the Cincinnati Reds for Spud Davis, Al Hollingsworth, and $50,000, June 13, 1938.
4. Traded Ferguson Jenkins, Adolfo Phillips, and John Herrnstein to the Chicago Cubs for Larry Jackson and Bob Buhl, April 21, 1966.
5. Traded Jack Sanford to the San Francisco Giants for Ruben Gomez and Valmy Thomas, December 3, 1958.

Trades: Life on a Shoestring

The Phillies have in recent years been one of the most successful franchises in baseball in trading. Working from a relatively limited nucleus of talent, the Phils have added such stars as Steve Carlton, Garry Maddox, Gary Matthews, Joe Morgan, Al Holland, John Denny, Manny Trillo, and Tug McGraw at minimal expense. It can be argued that they have made only one bad deal in the past ten years, but that one was a doozy: Trillo, Julio Franco, catcher Jerry Willard, George Vukovich, and Jay Baller for Von Hayes. While Hayes may yet become an outstanding player, it is unlikely he will be able to compensate for the long-term loss of Franco and Willard at short and catcher.

The record wasn't always so good. In the first few decades of the twentieth century, the Phillies' policy was constant turnover in search of profits. Their deals rank with Connie

Mack's "fire sales" and Harry Frazee's Rape of the Red Sox in terms of callous unconcern for the team's fans and the notion of winning ball games. No one was immune; future Hall of Famers like Grover Cleveland Alexander and Chuck Klein were casually sold off, as were everyday stars like Dave Bancroft, Irish Meusel, and Lefty O'Doul.

Alexander was the first, sent along with his catcher Bill Killefer to Chicago for $60,000 and two bodies. In 1920, William Baker, the club's owner, sent Bancroft, the club's greatest shortstop ever, to the Giants for Artie Fletcher and $100,000, and a year later shipped Meusel over for another thirty-five grand. Meusel and Bancroft played important roles on the pennant-winning New York clubs of the next four years, as did Casey Stengel, acquired by the Phils from Pittsburgh in 1919 and sent off to the Giants in '21.

Lefty O'Doul was traded with Fresco Thompson to Brooklyn for three players and $100,000. This one was particularly outrageous, since O'Doul was coming off seasons in which he had batted .398 and .383, with his .398 season including a National League record 254 hits. Baker died shortly after this deal, but the policies continued under the new leader, Gerry Nugent, who ascended to the head of the club on the strength of stock owned by his wife, Baker's secretary. Nugent set a new low by selling Chuck Klein, the Phils' most popular star and winner of the National League Triple Crown in 1933, to the Cubs before the '34 season for three players and $65,000. Two years later, Nugent got the now-faded Klein back along with $50,000 for pitcher Curt Davis. Among Nugent's other deals were Dolf Camilli to the Dodgers for $50,000; Bucky Walters to Cincinnati for another $50,000; Claude Passeau for yet another fifty grand from Chicago; Kirby Higbe to Brooklyn for $100,000. The bleeding of the Phillies continued until the sale of the club to Robert M. Carpenter in 1943. Carpenter's family would retain the club for close to forty years, and while the results were often less than satisfactory, none could doubt that at least they were trying to put a winning team on the field.

DATE		ACQUIRED	FROM		IN EXCHANGE FOR
Jan 1900	OF	Jimmy Slagle	Washington Senators		Cash
Feb 1900	P 2B	Tully Sparks Heinie Reitz	Pittsburgh Pirates	OF	Duff Cooley
Feb 1900	P	Al Maul	Brooklyn Dodgers		Cash
April 28, 1900	3B	Harry Wolverton	Chicago Cubs		Cash
June 1900	P	Jack Dunn	Brooklyn Dodgers		Cash
Feb 1901	SS	Hughie Jennings	Brooklyn Dodgers		$3,000.
May 1901		Cash	Philadelphia Athletics	SS	Joe Dolan
June 1901	2B	Shad Barry	Boston Braves	OF	Jimmy Slagle
May 1902	P	Bill Magee	New York Giants		Cash
July 1902		Cash	New York Giants	OF	George Browne
Jan 1903	C	Chief Zimmer	Pittsburgh Pirates		Waiver price
Feb 1903		Cash	Brooklyn Dodgers	C	Fred Jacklitsch
March 1903	P	Warren McLaughlin	Pittsburgh Pirates		Waiver price

DATE		ACQUIRED	FROM		IN EXCHANGE FOR
April 1903	P	Pop Williams	Chicago Cubs		Cash
June 1903		Cash	Boston Braves	P	Pop Williams
July 1903		Cash	New York Giants	OF	Moose McCormick
April 30, 1904	1B OF	Jack Doyle Deacon Van Buren	Brooklyn Dodgers		Cash
July 20, 1904	P P	Frank Corridon Jack Sutthoff	Chicago Cubs	2B	Shad Barry
Aug 18, 1904		Cash	Brooklyn Dodgers	P	Fred Mitchell
Dec 20, 1904	P	Togie Pittinger	Boston Braves	P 3B	Chick Fraser Harry Wolverton
Dec 20, 1904	1B IF OF	Kitty Bransfield Otto Krueger Moose McCormick	Pittsburgh Pirates	1B	Del Howard
Jan 1905	SS	Otto Krueger	Pittsburgh Pirates		Waiver price
March 1905	C	Mike Kahoe	St. Louis Browns		Cash
July 16, 1905	P	Kid Nichols	St. Louis Cardinals		Waiver price
Oct 1906		Cash	Pittsburgh Pirates	P	Charlie Brady
June 10, 1907	P	Charlie Brown	St. Louis Cardinals	P	Johnny Lush
July 15, 1907		Cash	Pittsburgh Pirates	P	Bill Duggleby
Oct 1907	P	Earl Moore	New York Yankees		Waiver price
April 1908		Cash	Pittsburgh Pirates	OF	Roy Thomas
May 1908		Cash	New York Giants	OF	Moose McCormick
Oct 1908		Cash	Cincinnati Reds	OF	Mike Mowrey
March 1909		Cash	New York Yankees	2B	Joe Ward
		(Ward was returned to Philadelphia on May 20, 1909.)			
July 16, 1909	OF 2B	Johnny Bates Charlie Starr	Boston Braves	P P 2B	Buster Brown Lew Richie Dave Shean
Jan 20, 1910	P	Ad Brennan	Cincinnati Reds	P	Harry Coveleski
Jan 1910	P	Bob Ewing	Cincinnati Reds		Cash
July 1910	1B	Fred Luderus	Chicago Cubs	P	Bill Foxen

DATE	ACQUIRED	FROM	IN EXCHANGE FOR
Feb 1911	P Fred Beebe P Jack Rowan OF Dode Paskert 3B Hans Lobert	Cincinnati Reds	OF Johnny Bates 3B Eddie Grant P George McQuillan
May 1911	C Tom Madden	Boston Red Sox	Waiver price
June 1911	C Red Kleinow	Boston Red Sox	Waiver price
July 15, 1911	OF Fred Beck P Bill Burns	Cincinnati Reds	P Bert Humphries
Aug 9, 1911	Cash	Chicago Cubs	1B Kitty Bransfield
Aug 1911	P Cliff Curtis	Chicago Cubs	P Jack Rowan
Oct 1911	C Peaches Graham	Chicago Cubs	C Dick Cotter
Dec 1911	Cash	Brooklyn Dodgers	P Eddie Stack
May 1912	Cash	Brooklyn Dodgers	P Cliff Curtis
May 1912	OF Cozy Dolan	New York Yankees	Cash
July 1, 1912	OF Doc Miller	Boston Braves	OF John Titus
Aug 1912	Cash	Chicago Cubs	3B Tom Downey
Aug 1912	P Red Nelson	St. Louis Browns	Cash
Dec 1912	OF Mike Donlin	Pittsburgh Pirates	Waiver price
	(Donlin refused to report and announced his retirement.)		
Jan 1913	OF Ralph Capron	Pittsburgh Pirates	Cash
June 5, 1913	OF Josh Devore OF Beals Becker	Cincinnati Reds	3B John Dodge P Red Nelson
July 1913	Cash	Chicago Cubs	P Earl Moore
Aug 20, 1913	3B Bobby Byrne P Howie Camnitz	Pittsburgh Pirates	OF Cozy Dolan and cash
Dec 1913	Cash	Cincinnati Reds	OF Doc Miller
June 1914	SS Jack Martin	Boston Braves	OF Josh Devore
Nov 1914	2B Bert Niehoff	Cincinnati Reds	C Red Dooin
Jan 1915	P Al Demaree 2B Milt Stock C Bert Adams	New York Giants	3B Hans Lobert
Feb 14, 1915	P George McQuillan	Pittsburgh Pirates	Waiver price

DATE		ACQUIRED	FROM		IN EXCHANGE FOR
Feb 14, 1915	OF 3B	Possum Whitted Oscar Dugey and cash	Boston Braves	OF	Sherry Magee
Aug 8, 1915	P	Bert Humphries	Chicago Cubs		Cash
Dec 1915		Cash	Pittsburgh Pirates	P	Elmer Jacobs
Feb 3, 1916	OF	Wilbur Good	Chicago Cubs		Cash
Feb 10, 1916	P	Claude Cooper	Brooklyn (Federal League)		Cash
Feb 10, 1916	P	Chief Bender	Baltimore Orioles		Cash
Sept 2, 1916	P	Erv Kantlehner	Pittsburgh Pirates		Cash
April 2, 1917	P	Jimmy Lavender and $5,000.	Chicago Cubs	P	Al Demaree
June 14, 1917	OF	Wildfire Schulte	Pittsburgh Pirates		Waiver price
July 12, 1917	2B	Johnny Evers	Boston Braves		Waiver price
Sept 1917		Waiver price	Chicago White Sox	3B	Bobby Byrne
Dec 11, 1917	P C	Mike Prendergast Pickles Dillhoefer and $55,000.	Chicago Cubs	P C	Grover Alexander Bill Killefer
Dec 26, 1917	OF	Cy Williams	Chicago Cubs	OF	Dode Paskert
Dec 1917		Cash	Washington Senators	OF	Wildfire Schulte
April 4, 1918	P	Milt Watson	St. Louis Cardinals	2B	Bert Niehoff and $500.
July 1, 1918	P	Elmer Jacobs	Pittsburgh Pirates	P	Erskine Mayer
Jan 21, 1919	3B IF P	Doug Baird Stuffy Stewart Gene Packard	St. Louis Cardinals	3B C P	Milt Stock Pickles Dillhoefer Dixie Davis
May 27, 1919	P 2B	George Smith Eddie Sicking	New York Giants	P	Joe Oeschger
May 1919	SS	Lena Blackburne	Boston Braves		Cash
May 1919	C	Walt Tragesser	Boston Braves		Cash
July 14, 1919	P 2B	Lee Meadows Gene Paulette	St. Louis Cardinals	P P 3B	Elmer Jacobs Frank Woodward Doug Baird
Aug 1919	OF	Casey Stengel	Pittsburgh Pirates	OF	Possum Whitted

DATE		ACQUIRED	FROM		IN EXCHANGE FOR
Aug 1919	P	Larry Cheney	Boston Braves		Waiver price
Sept 5, 1919	P	Red Ames (Ames was returned to St. Louis in October.)	St. Louis Cardinals		Cash
Oct 1919	C	Mack Wheat	Brooklyn Dodgers		Cash
Nov 1919		Waiver price	Pittsburgh Pirates	C	Nig Clarke
Dec 1919	P	Johnny Enzmann	Cleveland Indians		Cash
Jan 1920	2B	Dots Miller	St. Louis Cardinals		Cash
April 1920	P	Bert Gallia	St. Louis Browns		Cash
June 8, 1920	SS P	Art Fletcher Bill Hubbell and cash	New York Giants	SS	Dave Bancroft
June 1920	2B	Johnny Rawlings	Boston Braves		Cash
Nov 22, 1920	P OF	Jimmy Ring Greasy Neale	Cincinnati Reds	P	Eppa Rixey
May 1921	OF	Cliff Lee	Pittsburgh Pirates		Waiver price
June 2, 1921		Waiver price	Cincinnati Reds	OF	Greasy Neale
June 28, 1921	IF	Jimmy Smith	Cincinnati Reds		Cash
June 1921	2B	John Monroe	New York Giants		Cash
July 1, 1921	OF OF OF	Goldie Rapp Lee King Lance Richbourg	New York Giants	OF 2B P	Casey Stengel Johnny Rawlings Red Causey
July 4, 1921	1B	Ed Konetchy	Brooklyn Dodgers		Waiver price
July 25, 1921	OF C P	Curt Walker Butch Henline Jesse Winters and $30,000.	New York Giants	OF	Irish Meusel
July 1921	OF	Lee King	New York Giants		Waiver price
Dec 1921		Cash	Philadelphia Athletics	C	Frank Bruggy
July 14, 1922	OF	Johnny Mokan	Pittsburgh Pirates		Cash
Feb 8, 1923		Cash	Philadelphia Athletics	OF	Bevo LeBourveau
Feb 11, 1923	P	Clarence Mitchell	Brooklyn Dodgers	P	George Smith
May 11, 1923	2B	Johnny Rawlings	New York Giants		Waiver price

DATE		ACQUIRED	FROM		IN EXCHANGE FOR
May 22, 1923	P SS	Whitey Glazner Cotton Tierney and $50,000.	Pittsburgh Pirates	P 2B	Lee Meadows Johnny Rawlings
Aug 2, 1923	P	Johnny Couch	Cincinnati Reds		Waiver price
Dec 15, 1923	SS OF	Hod Ford Ray Powell (Powell announced his intention to retire after the 1924 season. He remained with Boston, and Philadelphia received cash instead.)	Boston Braves	SS	Cotton Tierney
Dec 1923	P	Earl Hamilton	Pittsburgh Pirates		Waiver price
May 25, 1924	P	Ray Steineder	Pittsburgh Pirates		Cash
May 30, 1924	OF	George Harper	Cincinnati Reds	OF	Curt Walker
June 6, 1924	OF	Joe Schultz	St. Louis Cardinals		Cash
June 20, 1924		Cash	Cincinnati Reds	OF	Cliff Lee
July 1, 1924	P	Joe Oeschger	New York Giants		Waiver price
March 30, 1925	1B	Lew Fonseca	Cincinnati Reds		Cash
April 2, 1925	OF	George Burns	Cincinnati Reds		Waiver price
April 20, 1925		Waiver price	Brooklyn Dodgers	P	Joe Oeschger
May 1, 1925	P	Art Decatur	Brooklyn Dodgers	P	Bill Hubbell
May 16, 1925		Waiver price	Brooklyn Dodgers	SS	Hod Ford
June 15, 1925	SS	Barney Friberg	Chicago Cubs		Waiver price
June 23, 1925		Cash	Cincinnati Reds	OF	Joe Schultz
July 9, 1925		Waiver price	Cincinnati Reds	1B	Walter Holke
Dec 30, 1925	P P	Jack Bentley Wayland Dean	New York Giants	P	Jimmy Ring
Sept 15, 1926		Waiver price	New York Giants	P	Jack Bentley
Oct 1926	P	Alex Ferguson	Washington Senators		Cash
Jan 9, 1927	P 2B	Jack Scott Fresco Thompson (Part of three-team trade involving Philadelphia, New York, and Brooklyn.)	New York Giants	OF C	George Harper Butch Henline
June 7, 1927	SS P	Jimmy Cooney Tony Kaufmann	Chicago Cubs	P	Hal Carlson
June 14, 1927		Cash	Chicago Cubs	P	Wayland Dean

DATE		ACQUIRED	FROM		IN EXCHANGE FOR
Sept 10, 1927		Cash	St. Louis Cardinals	P	Tony Kaufmann
Dec 13, 1927	OF P	Johnny Schulte Jimmy Ring	St. Louis Cardinals	OF SS C	Johnny Mokan Jimmy Cooney Bubber Jonnard
Dec 1927	P	Bob McGraw	St. Louis Cardinals		Cash
May 11, 1928	C OF	Spud Davis Homer Peel	St. Louis Cardinals	C	Jimmie Wilson
May 29, 1928	OF	Art Jahn	New York Giants	1B	Russ Wrightstone
Oct 29, 1928	OF	Lefty O'Doul and cash	New York Giants	OF	Freddy Leach
Dec 13, 1928	SS	Tommy Thevenow	St. Louis Cardinals	SS	Heinie Sand and $10,000.
Feb 1929		Cash	Chicago Cubs	C	Johnny Schulte
May 14, 1929		Cash	Brooklyn Dodgers	P	Alex Ferguson
July 24, 1929	P	Lou Koupal	Brooklyn Dodgers	P	Luther Roy
Dec 11, 1929	P C	Grover Alexander Harry McCurdy	St. Louis Cardinals	OF P	Homer Peel Bob McGraw
June 1930	C	Tony Rensa	Detroit Tigers		Waiver price
Aug 7, 1930	OF	Fred Brickell	Pittsburgh Pirates	OF	Denny Sothern
Oct 13, 1930		Cash	Chicago Cubs	P	Les Sweetland
Oct 14, 1930	P P OF	Clise Dudley Jumbo Elliott Hal Lee and cash	Brooklyn Dodgers	OF 2B	Lefty O'Doul Fresco Thompson
Nov 6, 1930	SS	Dick Bartell	Pittsburgh Pirates	SS P	Tommy Thevenow Claude Willoughby
Jan 1931		Cash	Pittsburgh Pirates	1B	Eddie Phillips
July 27, 1931	P	Sheriff Blake	Chicago Cubs		Waiver price
Jan 7, 1932		Waiver price	Boston Red Sox	SS	Barney Friberg
May 30, 1932	P SS	Flint Rhem Eddie Delker	St. Louis Cardinals		Cash
June 25, 1932	OF	Cliff Heathcote	Cincinnati Reds		Waiver price
June 28, 1932		Waiver price	St. Louis Cardinals	OF	Rube Bressler
Dec 12, 1932	OF OF	Gus Dugas Chick Fullis	New York Giants	OF	Kiddo Davis

(Part of three-team trade involving New York, Philadelphia, and Pittsburgh.)

DATE		ACQUIRED	FROM		IN EXCHANGE FOR
Dec 15, 1932	P 2B 3B	Cy Moore Mickey Finn Jack Warner	Brooklyn Dodgers	P	Ray Benge and $15,000.
Jan 7, 1933		Waiver price	Boston Red Sox	SS	Barney Friberg
June 17, 1933	3B OF	Fritz Knothe Wes Schulmerich and cash	Boston Braves	OF 3B	Hal Lee Pinky Whitney
Nov 15, 1933	C	Jimmie Wilson	St. Louis Cardinals	C IF	Spud Davis Eddie Delker
		(Wilson was named manager of the Phillies.)			
Nov 21, 1933	P SS OF	Ted Kleinhans Chief Hogsett Harvey Hendrick and $65,000.	Chicago Cubs	OF	Chuck Klein
Nov 1933		Cash	Cincinnati Reds	C	Harry McCurdy
Dec 20, 1933	3B SS	Otto Bluege Irv Jeffries	Cincinnati Reds	SS	Mark Koenig
Jan 1934	OF	Ethan Allen	St. Louis Cardinals		Cash
Feb 11, 1934		Cash	St. Louis Cardinals	P	Flint Rhem
May 8, 1934	P OF	Syl Johnson Johnny Moore	Cincinnati Reds	P OF OF	Ted Kleinhans Wes Schulmerich Art Ruble
May 18, 1934		Cash	St. Louis Cardinals	P	Phil Collins
May 26, 1934		Cash	Boston Braves	P	Jumbo Elliott
June 10, 1934		Cash	Pittsburgh Pirates	P	Ed Holley
June 11, 1934	1B	Dolf Camilli	Chicago Cubs	1B	Don Hurst
June 14, 1934	3B	Bucky Walters	Boston Red Sox		Cash
June 15, 1934	OF	Kiddo Davis	St. Louis Cardinals	OF	Chick Fullis
June 27, 1934		Waiver price	Chicago White Sox	3B	Marty Hopkins
Nov 1, 1934	P SS 3B OF	Pretzels Pezzullo Blondy Ryan Johnny Vergez George Watkins and cash	New York Giants	SS	Dick Bartell
Dec 13, 1934	P	Joe Bowman	New York Giants	OF	Kiddo Davis
May 20, 1935	P	Tommy Thomas	Washington Senators		Waiver price
June 22, 1935		Cash	St. Louis Browns	P	Ron Hansen
Aug 2, 1935		Cash	New York Giants	P	Euel Moore

DATE		ACQUIRED	FROM		IN EXCHANGE FOR
Aug 6, 1935		Cash	New York Yankees	SS	Blondy Ryan
Nov 21, 1935	P C	Claude Passeau Earl Grace	Pittsburgh Pirates	C	Al Todd
Jan 29, 1936	3B	Pinky Whitney	Boston Braves	IF	Mickey Haslin
Jan 1936		Cash	St. Louis Browns	P	Tommy Thomas
May 21, 1936	OF P	Chuck Klein Fabian Kowalik	Chicago Cubs	OF P	Ethan Allen Curt Davis
May 1936		Cash	Boston Braves	IF	Mickey Haslin
May 1936		Cash	Brooklyn Dodgers	OF	George Watkins
July 1936		Cash	St. Louis Cardinals	3B	Johnny Vergez
Aug 4, 1936	P	Ray Benge	Boston Braves	P	Fabian Kowalik
Dec 8, 1936	IF	George Scharein and cash	New York Giants	3B	Lou Chiozza
April 16, 1937	1B	Earl Browne	Pittsburgh Pirates	P	Joe Bowman
Dec 8, 1937	OF	Cap Clark	St. Louis Browns	C	Earl Grace
Dec 29, 1937	P	Al Smith	St. Louis Cardinals		Waiver price
March 6, 1938	1B	Eddie Morgan and $45,000.	Brooklyn Dodgers	1B	Dolf Camilli
May 23, 1938		Cash	Boston Braves	P	Tommy Reis
June 10, 1938	2B	Buck Jordan	Cincinnati Reds	P	Justin Stein
June 13, 1938	C P	Spud Davis Al Hollingsworth and $50,000.	Cincinnati Reds	P	Bucky Walters
June 1938	OF	Tuck Stainback	St. Louis Cardinals		Waiver price
July 11, 1938	OF	Gib Brack	Brooklyn Dodgers	OF	Tuck Stainback
Aug 8, 1938	P	Max Butcher	Brooklyn Dodgers	P	Wayne LaMaster
May 29, 1939	OF P P	Joe Marty Ray Harrell Kirby Higbe	Chicago Cubs	P	Claude Passeau
June 15, 1939		Cash	Boston Braves	P	Bill Kerksieck
July 13, 1939	2B	Roy Hughes	New York Yankees	P	Al Hollingsworth
July 28, 1939	1B	Gus Suhr	Pittsburgh Pirates	P	Max Butcher
Aug 5, 1939	OF	Bud Hafey	Cincinnati Reds		Cash

DATE		ACQUIRED	FROM		IN EXCHANGE FOR
Aug 19, 1939	P	Peaches Davis	Cincinnati Reds		Cash
Oct 27, 1939		Cash	Pittsburgh Pirates	C	Spud Davis
Jan 22, 1940		Waiver price	Pittsburgh Pirates	P	Ray Harrell
June 15, 1940	OF	Johnny Rizzo	Cincinnati Reds	OF	Morrie Arnovich
Nov 11, 1940	P P C	Vito Tamulis Bill Crouch Mickey Livingston and $100,000.	Brooklyn Dodgers	P	Kirby Higbe
March 21, 1941	3B	Bill Nagel	Philadelphia Athletics		Cash
May 6, 1941	P	Lee Grissom	Brooklyn Dodgers	P	Vito Tamulis
Dec 10, 1941		Cash	Brooklyn Dodgers	OF	Johnny Rizzo
May 2, 1942	OF	Ernie Koy	Cincinnati Reds		Cash
Sept 9, 1942		Waiver price (Deal was cancelled by Commissioner Landis.)	Pittsburgh Pirates	C	Bennie Warren
Dec 12, 1942	P	Johnny Allen and $30,000.	Brooklyn Dodgers	P	Rube Melton
Jan 22, 1943	C P	Tom Padden Al Gerheauser and $10,000.	New York Yankees	1B	Nick Etten
March 8, 1943		Cash	Brooklyn Dodgers	OF	Roberto Ortiz
March 9, 1943	1B	Babe Dahlgren	Brooklyn Dodgers	OF 2B	Lloyd Waner Al Glossop
March 24, 1943	P	Schoolboy Rowe	Brooklyn Dodgers		Cash
March 24, 1943	P	Tex Kraus and cash	Brooklyn Dodgers	C	Bobby Bragan
April 2, 1943	SS	Garton Del Savio	Cincinnati Reds		Cash
April 16, 1943	P	George Washburn	Chicago Cubs		Cash
April 22, 1943		Cash	Brooklyn Dodgers	P P	Johnny Allen George Washburn
April 30, 1943	1B	Jimmy Wasdell	Pittsburgh Pirates		Cash
May 12, 1943	P	Manny Salvo	Boston Braves		Cash
May 20, 1943	P	Newt Kimball	Brooklyn Dodgers		Cash
June 1, 1943	OF OF OF	Buster Adams Coaker Triplett Dain Clay	St. Louis Cardinals	OF OF	Danny Litwhiler Earl Naylor

DATE		ACQUIRED	FROM		IN EXCHANGE FOR
June 15, 1943	P	Dutch Dietz	Pittsburgh Pirates	P	Johnny Podgajny
July 1943	P	Dick Barrett	Chicago Cubs		Cash
Aug 5, 1943	P	Bill Lee	Chicago Cubs	C	Mickey Livingston
Dec 30, 1943	C	Babe Phelps and cash	Pittsburgh Pirates	1B	Babe Dahlgren
April 13, 1944	1B	Tony Lupien	Boston Red Sox		Waiver price
June 11, 1944	C	Johnny Peacock	Boston Red Sox		Cash
July 27, 1944	P	Harry Shuman	Pittsburgh Pirates		Waiver price
July 28, 1944	P	Vern Kennedy	Cleveland Indians		Cash
March 28, 1945	P	Whit Wyatt	Brooklyn Dodgers		$20,000.
March 31, 1945	OF	Vince DiMaggio	Pittsburgh Pirates	P	Al Gerheauser
May 8, 1945	3B OF	John Antonelli Glenn Crawford	St. Louis Cardinals	OF	Buster Adams
May 31, 1945	P	Oscar Judd	Boston Red Sox		Waiver price
June 15, 1945	OF	Ben Chapman	Brooklyn Dodgers	C	Johnny Peacock
July 14, 1945		Cash	Boston Braves	P	Bill Lee
Dec 12, 1945	SS	Skeeter Newsome	Boston Red Sox		Cash
Jan 21, 1946	SS	Roy Hughes	Chicago Cubs		Cash
Jan 22, 1946	3B	Jim Tabor	Boston Red Sox		Cash
Feb 5, 1946	P	Al Jurisich	St. Louis Cardinals		Cash
March 25, 1946	C	Rollie Hemsley	New York Yankees		Cash
April 24, 1946		Cash	Boston Braves	P	Si Johnson
May 1, 1946	C	Clyde Kluttz	New York Giants	OF	Vince DiMaggio
May 2, 1946	SS	Emil Verban	St. Louis Cardinals	C	Clyde Kluttz
May 1946	P	Charley Stanceu	New York Yankees		Waiver price
June 15, 1946	OF	Charlie Gilbert	Chicago Cubs		Cash
July 6, 1946	P	Blix Donnelly	St. Louis Cardinals		Cash

DATE		ACQUIRED	FROM		IN EXCHANGE FOR
Dec 9, 1946	P	Dutch Leonard	Washington Senators		Cash
Jan 1947		Cash	Pittsburgh Pirates	P	Hugh Mulcahy
March 21, 1947	OF	Buster Adams	St. Louis Cardinals		Cash
May 3, 1947	OF P	Harry Walker Freddy Schmidt	St. Louis Cardinals	OF	Ron Northey
May 9, 1947	P	Ken Heintzelman	Pittsburgh Pirates		Cash
May 10, 1947	1B	Howie Schultz	Brooklyn Dodgers		Cash
May 27, 1947	C	Don Padgett	Boston Braves	P	Andy Karl
June 14, 1947	C	Al Lakeman	Cincinnati Reds	P C	Ken Raffensberger Hugh Poland
Dec 11, 1947	1B	Bert Haas	Cincinnati Reds	P	Tommy Hughes
Feb 7, 1948	SS	Eddie Miller	Cincinnati Reds	OF	Johnny Wyrostek and cash
April 5, 1948		Cash	Pittsburgh Pirates	SS	Grady Wilson
April 7, 1948	1B	Dick Sisler	St. Louis Cardinals	IF	Ralph LaPointe and $30,000.
April 15, 1948	2B	Bama Rowell	Brooklyn Dodgers		Waiver price
May 15, 1948	P	Nick Strincevich	Pittsburgh Pirates		Cash
May 20, 1948	P	Paul Erickson	Chicago Cubs		Waiver price
July 1, 1948		Waiver price	New York Giants	P	Paul Erickson
Aug 3, 1948		Waiver price	Chicago Cubs	SS	Emil Verban
Sept 13, 1948	C	Hal Wagner	Detroit Tigers		Waiver price
Oct 4, 1948	OF	Bill Nicholson	Chicago Cubs	OF	Harry Walker
Oct 11, 1948	P	Russ Meyer	Chicago Cubs		Cash
Dec 14, 1948	P	Ken Trinkle	New York Giants		Cash
Dec 14, 1948	P 1B	Hank Borowy Eddie Waitkus	Chicago Cubs	P P	Monk Dubiel Dutch Leonard
Sept 14, 1949	OF	Dick Whitman	Brooklyn Dodgers		Cash
April 27, 1950	P	Ken Johnson	St. Louis Cardinals	OF	Johnny Blatnik
May 3, 1950		Waiver price	St. Louis Cardinals	SS	Eddie Miller

DATE		ACQUIRED	FROM		IN EXCHANGE FOR
May 10, 1950	2B	Jimmy Bloodworth	Cincinnati Reds		Cash
June 12, 1950		$10,000.	Pittsburgh Pirates	P	Hank Borowy
April 16, 1951		Waiver price	Boston Braves	P	Blix Donnelly
April 27, 1951	P	Ken Johnson	St. Louis Cardinals	OF	Johnny Blatnik
June 8, 1951	OF	Tommy Brown	Brooklyn Dodgers	OF	Dick Whitman and cash
Dec 10, 1951	C P 2B	Smoky Burgess Howie Fox Connie Ryan	Cincinnati Reds	C IF 1B P	Andy Seminick Eddie Pellagrini Dick Sisler Niles Jordan
Dec 13, 1951	3B	Lucky Lohrke	New York Giants		Minor league C Jake Schmitt
March 21, 1952		Waiver price	Detroit Tigers	P	Ken Johnson
May 12, 1952		Cash	Boston Red Sox	C	Del Wilber
May 23, 1952	OF P	Johnny Wyrostek Kent Peterson	Cincinnati Reds	P	Bubba Church
June 15, 1952		Cash	Chicago Cubs	OF	Tommy Brown
Sept 30, 1952	3B	Tommy Glaviano	St. Louis Cardinals		Waiver price
Feb 16, 1953	1B	Earl Torgeson	Milwaukee Braves	P	Russ Meyer and cash
		(Part of four-team trade involving Milwaukee Braves, Philadelphia Phillies, Brooklyn, and Cincinnati.)			
Aug 25, 1953		Waiver price	Chicago White Sox	IF	Connie Ryan
Aug 31, 1953	OF	Johnny Lindell	Pittsburgh Pirates		Cash
Dec 19, 1953	C	Mike Sandlock	Pittsburgh Pirates		Cash
Jan 13, 1954	P	Murry Dickson	Pittsburgh Pirates	P 3B	Andy Hansen Lucky Lohrke and $70,000.
March 16, 1954		$40,000.	Baltimore Orioles	1B	Eddie Waitkus
March 28, 1954	IF	Bobby Morgan	Brooklyn Dodgers	2B	Dick Young and $50,000.
May 10, 1954		Waiver price	Chicago White Sox	OF	Stan Jok
June 12, 1954	P	Herm Wehmeier	Cincinnati Reds		Cash
June 15, 1954		Cash	Cincinnati Reds	P	Karl Drews
July 18, 1954	3B	Floyd Baker	Boston Red Sox		Cash

DATE		ACQUIRED	FROM		IN EXCHANGE FOR
Aug 22, 1954		Cash	New York Yankees	P	Jim Konstanty
March 19, 1955	P	Dave Cole	Chicago Cubs		Cash
April 30, 1955	SS	Roy Smalley	Milwaukee Braves		Cash
April 30, 1955	C OF OF	Andy Seminick Glen Gorbous Jim Greengrass	Cincinnati Reds	C P OF	Smoky Burgess Steve Ridzik Stan Palys
May 23, 1955	P	Bob Kuzava	Baltimore Orioles		Waiver price
June 15, 1955		Cash	Detroit Tigers	1B	Earl Torgeson
Dec 9, 1955	OF	Frankie Baumholtz	Chicago Cubs		Cash
May 11, 1956	P P P	Harvey Haddix Ben Flowers Stu Miller	St. Louis Cardinals	P P	Murry Dickson Herm Wehmeier
May 14, 1956	2B	Solly Hemus	St. Louis Cardinals	3B	Bobby Morgan
Oct 11, 1956	P	Jim Hearn	New York Giants	P	Stu Miller
Oct 15, 1956		Waiver price	Kansas City Athletics	P	Ben Flowers
Nov 19, 1956	3B OF	Bobby Morgan Rip Repulski	St. Louis Cardinals	OF	Del Ennis
April 5, 1957	SS	Chico Fernandez	Brooklyn Dodgers	P 1B OF	Ron Negray Tim Harkness Elmer Valo minor league SS Mel Geho and $75,000.
May 10, 1957	OF	Chuck Harmon	St. Louis Cardinals	OF	Glen Gorbous
May 13, 1957		Cash	Chicago Cubs	3B	Bobby Morgan
June 26, 1957	P	Warren Hacker	Cincinnati Reds		Waiver price
Dec 11, 1957	OF	Dave Philley	Detroit Tigers		Cash
Dec 16, 1957	OF	Wally Post	Cincinnati Reds	P	Harvey Haddix
March 20, 1958	1B	Joe Collins (Collins refused to report and retired.)	New York Yankees		Cash
April 30, 1958		Cash	Chicago White Sox	P	Tom Qualters
June 13, 1958	C	Carl Sawatski	Milwaukee Braves	C	Joe Lonnett
July 27, 1958	C	Jim Hegan	Detroit Tigers		Minor league OF John Turk and cash
Sept 29, 1958	3B	Gene Freese	St. Louis Cardinals	2B	Solly Hemus

DATE		ACQUIRED	FROM		IN EXCHANGE FOR
Oct 2, 1958	P	Ken Lehman	Baltimore Orioles		Waiver price
Dec 3, 1958	SS	Ruben Amaro	St. Louis Cardinals	OF	Chuck Essegian
Dec 3, 1958	C P	Valmy Thomas Ruben Gomez	San Francisco Giants	P	Jack Sanford
Dec 23, 1958	2B	Sparky Anderson	Los Angeles Dodgers	OF P P	Rip Repulski Jim Golden Gene Snyder
March 31, 1959	P SS 2B	Gene Conley Joe Koppe Harry Hanebrink	Milwaukee Braves	C SS 2B	Stan Lopata Ted Kazanski Johnny O'Brien
May 12, 1959	P	Taylor Phillips	Chicago Cubs	P	Seth Morehead
May 16, 1959	P	Humberto Robinson	Cleveland Indians	P	Granny Hamner
June 9, 1959	IF	Solly Drake	Los Angeles Dodgers		Waiver price
June 14, 1959		Cash	San Francisco Giants	C	Jim Hegan
Dec 4, 1959	OF	Bobby Gene Smith	St. Louis Cardinals	C	Carl Sawatski
Dec 5, 1959	OF 2B	Ken Walters Ted Lepcio minor league P Alex Cosmidis	Detroit Tigers	SS P	Chico Fernandez Ray Semproch
Dec 9, 1959	OF	Johnny Callison	Chicago White Sox	3B	Gene Freese
Jan 11, 1960	P 3B OF	John Buzhardt Alvin Dark Jim Woods	Chicago Cubs	OF	Richie Ashburn
May 12, 1960		Cash	San Francisco Giants	OF	Dave Philley
May 13, 1960	2B C	Tony Taylor Cal Neeman	Chicago Cubs	1B P	Ed Bouchee Don Cardwell
June 15, 1960	OF OF	Tony Gonzalez Lee Walls	Cincinnati Reds	OF OF	Harry Anderson Wally Post
June 23, 1960	3B	Joe Morgan	Milwaukee Braves	3B	Alvin Dark
Aug 9, 1960		Cash	Cleveland Indians	3B	Joe Morgan
Dec 15, 1960	P	Frank Sullivan	Boston Red Sox	P	Gene Conley
April 3, 1961		Cash	Chicago White Sox	2B	Ted Lepcio
May 4, 1961	OF 3B	Don Demeter Charley Smith	Los Angeles Dodgers	P SS	Dick Farrell Joe Koppe
July 2, 1961	OF	Wes Covington	Kansas City Athletics	OF	Bobby Del Greco
Aug 14, 1961		Cash	Cincinnati Reds	C	Darrell Johnson

DATE		ACQUIRED	FROM		IN EXCHANGE FOR
Oct 13, 1961	C	Bob Oldis	Pittsburgh Pirates		Cash
Oct 16, 1961		Cash	Baltimore Orioles	P	Robin Roberts
Nov 28, 1961	OF	Roy Sievers	Chicago White Sox	P 3B	John Buzhardt Charley Smith
Dec 15, 1961	P 3B P	Frank Barnes Andy Carey Cal McLish	Chicago White Sox	3B-OF P	Bob Sadowski Taylor Phillips minor league IF Lou Vassie
		(Carey refused to report, and the Phillies received McLish in exchange for Vassie to complete the trade on March 24, 1962.)			
March 20, 1962	OF	Mel Roach	Cleveland Indians	P OF	Ken Lehman Tony Curry
April 5, 1962	3B	Billy Klaus	Washington Senators		Cash
April 28, 1962	P	Larry Locke and cash	St. Louis Cardinals	P	Don Ferrarese
May 8, 1962		Cash	Los Angeles Angels	IF	Billy Consolo
Nov 21, 1962		Cash	Baltimore Orioles	C	Jimmie Coker
Nov 27, 1962	2B	Cookie Rojas	Cincinnati Reds	P	Jim Owens
Dec 11, 1962	C	Earl Averill	Los Angeles Angels	OF	Jacke Davis
March 14, 1963	P	Ryne Duren	Los Angeles Angels		Cash
March 25, 1963	P	Johnny Klippstein	Cincinnati Reds		Cash
May 4, 1963	OF	Jim Lemon	Minnesota Twins		Cash
June 28, 1963		Cash	Chicago White Sox	OF	Jim Lemon
Nov 28, 1963	3B	Don Hoak	Pittsburgh Pirates	1B OF	Pancho Herrera Ted Savage
Dec 4, 1963	P C	Jim Bunning Gus Triandos	Detroit Tigers	OF P	Don Demeter Jack Hamilton
April 21, 1964	P	Ed Roebuck	Washington Senators		Cash
May 13, 1964		Cash	Cincinnati Reds	P	Ryne Duren
June 29, 1964		Cash	Minnesota Twins	P	Johnny Klippstein
July 16, 1964		Cash	Washington Senators	OF	Roy Sievers
Aug 7, 1964	3B OF	Wayne Graham Frank Thomas	Minnesota Twins	P	Gary Kroll
Aug 15, 1964	P	Bobby Shantz	Chicago Cubs		Cash
Sept 9, 1964	1B	Vic Power	Los Angeles Angels	P	Marcelino Lopez and cash

DATE	ACQUIRED		FROM	IN EXCHANGE FOR	
Oct 15, 1964		Cash	Los Angeles Angels	P	Larry Locke
Oct 15, 1964	P	Rudy May	Chicago White Sox	C	Bill Heath minor league P Joel Gibson
Nov 29, 1964	1B	Dick Stuart	Boston Red Sox	P	Dennis Bennett
Nov 30, 1964		Cash	Los Angeles Angels	1B	Vic Power
Dec 1, 1964	P	Ray Herbert	Chicago White Sox	OF	Danny Cater
Dec 3, 1964	P	Bo Belinsky	Los Angeles Angels	1B P	Costen Shockley Rudy May
April 11, 1965		Cash	Washington Senators	P	Dallas Green
May 30, 1965	P	Lew Burdette	Chicago Cubs		Cash
June 14, 1965		Cash	Houston Astros	C	Gus Triandos
July 10, 1965		Cash	Houston Astros	OF	Frank Thomas
Oct 27, 1965	1B SS C	Bill White Dick Groat Bob Uecker	St. Louis Cardinals	C P OF	Pat Corrales Art Mahaffey Alex Johnson
Nov 29, 1965	2B	Phil Linz	New York Yankees	SS	Ruben Amaro
Dec 6, 1965	OF P	Jackie Brandt Darold Knowles	Baltimore Orioles	P	Jack Baldschun
Jan 10, 1966	OF	Doug Clemens	Chicago Cubs	OF	Wes Covington
Feb 22, 1966	C IF IF	Jimmie Schaffer Bobby Klaus Wayne Graham	New York Mets	1B	Dick Stuart
April 13, 1966	P	Steve Ridzik	Washington Senators		Cash
April 21, 1966	P P	Larry Jackson Bob Buhl	Chicago Cubs	OF OF P	Adolfo Phillips John Herrnstein Ferguson Jenkins
April 23, 1966	OF	Harvey Kuenn	Chicago Cubs		Cash
May 10, 1966	P	Terry Fox	Detroit Tigers		Cash
Nov 30, 1966	OF	Don Lock	Washington Senators	P	Darold Knowles and cash
Dec 7, 1966	P	Dick Ellsworth	Chicago Cubs	P	Ray Culp and cash
Dec 14, 1966	P	Pedro Ramos	New York Yankees	P	Joe Verbanic and cash
Dec 15, 1966	P	Dick Hall	Baltimore Orioles	P	John Morris
April 10, 1967	OF	Tito Francona	St. Louis Cardinals		Cash

DATE		ACQUIRED	FROM		IN EXCHANGE FOR
May 8, 1967	P	Dick Farrell	Houston Astros		Cash
June 3, 1967		Cash	Houston Astros	OF	Jackie Brandt
June 6, 1967	C-1B	Gene Oliver	Atlanta Braves	C	Bob Uecker
June 12, 1967		Cash	Atlanta Braves	OF	Tito Francona
June 22, 1967		Cash	San Francisco Giants	SS	Dick Groat
July 11, 1967	2B	Chuck Hiller	New York Mets	2B	Phil Linz
Dec 15, 1967	C	Mike Ryan and cash	Boston Red Sox	P OF	Dick Ellsworth Gene Oliver
Dec 15, 1967	3B P P	Don Money Woodie Fryman Bill Laxton minor league P Hal Clem	Pittsburgh Pirates	P	Jim Bunning
Dec 3, 1968	1B	Deron Johnson	Atlanta Braves		Cash
Jan 20, 1969	OF	Ron Stone	Baltimore Orioles	C	Clay Dalrymple
April 3, 1969	1B IF	Jim Hutto Jerry Buchek	St. Louis Cardinals	1B	Bill White
May 5, 1969	OF	Rudy Schlesinger	Boston Red Sox	OF	Don Lock
Sept 6, 1969	P	Mike Jackson	Boston Red Sox	P	Gary Wagner
Oct 7, 1969	OF C P OF	Curt Flood Tim McCarver Joe Hoerner Byron Browne	St. Louis Cardinals	1B 2B P	Richie Allen Cookie Rojas Jerry Johnson
		(Flood refused to report to the Philadelphia Phillies and the St. Louis Cardinals sent Willie Montanez and Bob Browning on April 8, 1970 to complete the trade.)			
Nov 17, 1969	P OF	Dick Selma Oscar Gamble	Chicago Cubs	OF	Johnny Callison
Nov 25, 1969	P	Fred Wenz	Boston Red Sox		Cash
April 8, 1970	1B	Willie Montanez minor league P Bob Browning	St. Louis Cardinals		Completion of Curt Flood trade of October 7, 1969
Nov 3, 1970	C P 1B	Greg Goossen Jeff Terpko Gene Martin	Washington Senators	OF	Curt Flood
Dec 16, 1970	OF	Roger Freed	Baltimore Orioles	P 1B OF	Grant Jackson Jim Hutto Sam Parrilla
April 22, 1971	P OF	Ray Peters Pete Koegel	Milwaukee Brewers	OF	John Briggs
June 12, 1971		Minor league Ps Mike Fremuth and Carl Cavanaugh	Detroit Tigers	2B	Tony Taylor

DATE		ACQUIRED	FROM		IN EXCHANGE FOR
Oct 21, 1971	1B	Tom Hutton	Los Angeles Dodgers	OF	Larry Hisle
Feb 8, 1972		Minor league 3B Chico Vaughns	Milwaukee Brewers	IF	Bobby Pfeil
Feb 25, 1972	P	Steve Carlton	St. Louis Cardinals	P	Rick Wise
June 14, 1972	C	John Bateman	Montreal Expos	C	Tim McCarver
June 15, 1972	P P	Jim Nash Gary Neibauer	Atlanta Braves	P 1B	Joe Hoerner Andre Thornton
Aug 2, 1972		Cash	Detroit Tigers	P	Woodie Fryman
Oct 25, 1972	C P	Tom Haller Don Leshnock	Detroit Tigers		Cash
Oct 31, 1972	P P P P	Jim Lonborg Ken Sanders Ken Brett Earl Stephenson	Milwaukee Brewers	3B IF P	Don Money John Vukovich Billy Champion
Nov 30, 1972	OF	Cesar Tovar	Minnesota Twins	P P OF	Ken Sanders Ken Reynolds Joe Lis
Nov 30, 1972	OF	Del Unser minor league IF Terry Wedgewood	Cleveland Indians	OF OF	Oscar Gamble Roger Freed
Jan 29, 1973	P	Rickey Clark	California Angels		Cash
May 2, 1973		Minor league UT Jack Bastable	Oakland Athletics	1B	Deron Johnson
Aug 10, 1973	P	George Culver	Los Angeles Dodgers		Cash
Aug 14, 1973	2B	Billy Grabarkewitz	California Angels	2B P OF	Denny Doyle Aurelio Monteagudo Chris Coletta
Oct 18, 1973	2B	Dave Cash	Pittsburgh Pirates	P	Ken Brett
Nov 7, 1973	P	Frank Linzy	Milwaukee Brewers	P	Bill Wilson
Dec 3, 1973	P	Ron Schueler	Atlanta Braves	P SS	Barry Lersch Craig Robinson
Dec 4, 1973	SS	Gil Garrido	Atlanta Braves	1B	Bob Beall
Dec 7, 1973		Cash	Texas Rangers	OF	Cesar Tovar
Dec 7, 1973	P	Eddie Watt	Baltimore Orioles		Cash
Jan 9, 1974	OF	Jay Johnstone	Oakland Athletics		Cash
Jan 31, 1974	SS	Jackie Hernandez	Pittsburgh Pirates	C	Mike Ryan
March 21, 1974	P	Ed Farmer	New York Yankees		Cash

DATE		ACQUIRED	FROM		IN EXCHANGE FOR
March 29, 1974		Cash	St. Louis Cardinals	IF	Ed Crosby
May 3, 1974	P	Ken Wright	New York Yankees	P	Mike Wallace
June 21, 1974	P	Pete Richert	St. Louis Cardinals		Cash
June 24, 1974	OF	Ollie Brown	Houston Astros		Cash
July 10, 1974		Cash	Chicago Cubs	2B	Billy Grabarkewitz
Dec 3, 1974	P OF OF	Tug McGraw Don Hahn Dave Schneck	New York Mets	OF C P	Del Unser John Stearns Mac Scarce
March 6, 1975	P	Tom Hilgendorf	Cleveland Indians		Minor league OF Nelson Garcia
March 17, 1975	P	Cecilio Acosta	Chicago White Sox		Cash
April 5, 1975	P	Wayne Simpson	Pittsburgh Pirates	OF	Bill Robinson
May 4, 1975	OF	Garry Maddox	San Francisco Giants	1B	Willie Montanez
May 7, 1975	1B C	Richie Allen Johnny Oates	Atlanta Braves	C OF	Jim Essian Barry Bonnell and cash
Sept 2, 1975	P	John Montague	Montreal Expos		Cash
Oct 24, 1975	SS	Sergio Ferrer	Minnesota Twins	C	Larry Cox
Dec 9, 1975	P	Ron Reed	St. Louis Cardinals	OF	Mike Anderson
Dec 10, 1975	P SS	Jim Kaat Mike Buskey	Chicago White Sox	P P OF	Dick Ruthven Roy Thomas Alan Bannister
April 8, 1976		Cash	California Angels	P	Wayne Simpson
April 19, 1976	C	Tim Blackwell	Boston Red Sox		Cash
July 14, 1976	OF	Rich Coggins	Chicago White Sox	OF	Wayne Nordhagen
Nov 17, 1976		No compensation (free agent signing)	Montreal Expos	2B	Dave Cash
Dec 15, 1976	3B	Richie Hebner	Pittsburgh Pirates		No compensation (free agent signing)
Dec 20, 1976	IF	Ted Sizemore	Los Angeles Dodgers	C	Johnny Oates minor league P Quincy Hill
March 15, 1977		No compensation (free agent signing)	Oakland Athletics	1B	Richie Allen
March 26, 1977	OF	Kerry Dineen	New York Yankees	SS	Sergio Ferrer
March 31, 1977		Cash	Minnesota Twins	P	Ron Schueler

DATE		ACQUIRED	FROM		IN EXCHANGE FOR
June 15, 1977	OF P	Bake McBride Steve Waterbury	St. Louis Cardinals	P 3B OF	Tom Underwood Dane Iorg Rick Bosetti
June 15, 1977	C P	Barry Foote Dan Warthen	Montreal Expos	P C	Wayne Twitchell Tim Blackwell
Sept 8, 1977		Cash	Chicago White Sox	C	Bill Nahorodny
Oct 25, 1977	OF	Jose Cardenal	Chicago Cubs		Minor league P Manny Seaone
Dec 8, 1977		Cash	Toronto Blue Jays	1B	Tom Hutton
March 24, 1978	SS	Bud Harrelson	New York Mets	2B	Fred Andrews and cash
March 27, 1978	P	Jackson Todd	New York Mets		Minor league C Ed Cuervo
April 5, 1978	IF	Ramon Aviles	Boston Red Sox		Cash
June 10, 1978	P	Rawley Eastwick	New York Yankees	OF OF	Jay Johnstone Bobby Brown
June 15, 1978	P	Dick Ruthven	Atlanta Braves	P	Gene Garber
July 4, 1978	P	Clarence Metzger	New York Mets		Cash
Aug 6, 1978	P	Larry Anderson	Chicago Cubs	2B	Davy Johnson
Sept 5, 1978	IF	Pete Mackanin	Montreal Expos		Cash
Sept 11, 1978		Cash	Houston Astros	IF	Mike Buskey
Dec 5, 1978	1B	Pete Rose	Cincinnati Reds		No compensation (free agent signing)
Feb 23, 1979	2B C OF	Manny Trillo Dave Rader Greg Gross	Chicago Cubs	C 2B OF P	Barry Foote Ted Sizemore Jerry Martin Dick Botelho minor league P Henry Mack
March 27, 1979	P	Nino Espinosa	New York Mets	1B-3B 2B	Richie Hebner Jose Moreno
March 28, 1979	P	Gary Beare	Milwaukee Brewers	P	Danny Boitano
April 3, 1979	P	Doug Bird	Kansas City Royals	SS	Todd Cruz
April 13, 1979	P	Jack Kucek	Chicago White Sox	3B	Jim Morrison
May 11, 1979		Cash	New York Yankees	P	Jim Kaat
May 25, 1979	SS	Bud Harrelson	New York Mets		No compensation (free agent signing)
Aug 2, 1979		Cash	New York Mets	OF	Jose Cardenal

DATE		ACQUIRED	FROM		IN EXCHANGE FOR
Dec 7, 1979	P	Paul Thormodsgard	Minnesota Twins	IF	Pete Mackanin
March 30, 1980	2B	Stan Papi and cash	Boston Red Sox	C	Dave Rader
May 29, 1980		Cash	Detroit Tigers	2B	Stan Papi
July 25, 1980		Cash	Oakland Athletics	1B	Orlando Gonzalez
Sept 1, 1980		Cash	Milwaukee Brewers	OF	John Poff
Sept 13, 1980	P	Sparky Lyle	Texas Rangers	P	Kevin Saucier
March 1, 1981	OF	Dick Davis	Milwaukee Brewers	P	Randy Lerch
March 25, 1981	OF	Gary Matthews	Atlanta Braves	P	Bob Walk
March 30, 1981		Cash	Chicago White Sox	OF	Greg Luzinski
April 1, 1981	P	Mike Proly	Chicago White Sox	2B	Jay Loviglio
Oct 20, 1981	P	Dave Rajsich	Texas Rangers	IF	Ramon Aviles
Oct 30, 1981	P 1B	Dewey Robinson Gary Holle	Chicago White Sox		Minor league IF Jose Castillo
Nov 20, 1981	C	Bo Diaz	Cleveland Indians	OF P	Lonnie Smith Scott Munninghoff
		(Part of three-team trade involving Cleveland, Philadelphia, and St. Louis.)			
Dec 6, 1981		Cash	California Angels	C	Bob Boone
Jan 27, 1982	SS	Ivan DeJesus	Chicago Cubs	SS 3B	Larry Bowa Ryne Sandberg
Jan 28, 1982	P	Ed Farmer	Chicago White Sox		Free agent signing
		(Chicago selected Joel Skinner of Pittsburgh from the compensation pool.)			
Feb 16, 1982	P	Sid Monge	Cleveland Indians	OF	Bake McBride
March 28, 1982	UT	Dave Roberts	Houston Astros		Minor league P Steve Dunnegan
June 15, 1982	OF	Wayne Nordhagen	Toronto Blue Jays	OF	Dick Davis
June 15, 1982	OF	Bill Robinson	Pittsburgh Pirates	OF	Wayne Nordhagen
Aug 21, 1982		Cash	Chicago White Sox	P	Sparky Lyle
Aug 30, 1982		Cash	Chicago White Sox	P	Warren Brusstar
Sept 1, 1982	OF	Bob Molinaro	Chicago Cubs		Cash
Sept 12, 1982	P	John Denny	Cleveland Indians	OF P	Wil Culmer Jerry Reed minor league P Roy Smith

DATE		ACQUIRED	FROM		IN EXCHANGE FOR
Dec 9, 1982	OF	Von Hayes	Cleveland Indians	2B OF P SS	Manny Trillo George Vukovich Jay Baller Julio Franco minor league C Jerry Willard
Dec 9, 1982	SS	Larry Milbourne	Cleveland Indians		Player to be named later
Dec 14, 1982	2B P	Joe Morgan Al Holland	San Francisco Giants	P P	Mike Krukow Mark Davis minor league OF Charles Penigar
May 2, 1983	OF	Joe Lefebvre	San Diego Padres	P	Sid Monge
May 22, 1983	P	Willie Hernandez	Chicago Cubs	P P	Dick Ruthven Bill Johnson
July 16, 1983		Cash	New York Yankees	2B	Larry Milbourne
July 29, 1983	P	Larry Andersen	Seattle Mariners		Cash
Aug 31, 1983	OF P	Sixto Lezcano Steve Fireovid	San Diego Padres	P	Marty Decker minor league Ps Ed Wojna Darren Burroughs and Lance McCullers
Dec 5, 1983	P	Jerry Koosman	Chicago White Sox	P	Ron Reed
Dec 6, 1983		Player to be named later	Cincinnati Reds	1B	Tony Perez
Dec 28, 1983		No compensation (free agent signing)	Oakland Athletics	2B	Joe Morgan
Jan 20, 1984		No compensation (free agent signing)	Montreal Expos	OF	Pete Rose
March 24, 1984	1B	Dave Bergman	San Francisco Giants	OF	Alejandro Sanchez
March 24, 1984	C OF	John Wockenfuss Glenn Wilson	Detroit Tigers	P 1B	Willie Hernandez Dave Bergman
March 26, 1984	P C	Bill Campbell Mike Diaz	Chicago Cubs	OF OF P	Gary Matthews Bob Dernier Porfirio Altamirano

Pittsburgh Pirates

The Best Trades

1. Acquired Burleigh Grimes from the New York Giants for Vic Aldridge, February 11, 1928.
2. Acquired Bill Virdon from the St. Louis Cardinals for Bobby Del Greco and Dick Littlefield, May 17, 1956.

3. Acquired Manny Mota from the Houston Colt .45s for Howie Goss and cash, April 4, 1963.
4. Acquired Goose Gossage and Terry Forster from the Chicago White Sox for Richie Zisk and Silvio Martinez, December 10, 1976.
5. Acquired Bill Madlock, Lenny Randle, and Dave Roberts from the San Francisco Giants for Ed Whitson, Fred Breining, and Al Holland, June 28, 1979.

The Worst Trades

1. Traded Preacher Roe, Billy Cox, and Gene Mauch to the Brooklyn Dodgers for Dixie Walker, Vic Lombardi, and Hal Gregg, December 8, 1947.
2. Traded Willie Randolph, Doc Ellis, and Ken Brett to the New York Yankees for Doc Medich, December 11, 1975.
3. Traded Bob Elliott and Hank Camelli to the Boston Braves for Billy Herman, Elmer Singleton, Stan Wentzel, and Whitey Wietelmann, September 30, 1946.
4. Traded Gus Bell to the Cincinnati Reds for Cal Abrams, Gail Henley, and Joe Rossi, October 14, 1952.
5. Traded Freddie Patek, Bruce Dal Canton, and Jerry May to the Kansas City Royals for Jackie Hernandez, Bob Johnson, and Jim Campanis, December 2, 1970.

Owner: Barney Dreyfuss

Barney Dreyfuss was one of the true pioneers of the game. Owner of the Pirates at the turn of the century, Dreyfuss built the first steel-structured stadium, won the first National League pennant of the twentieth century, and was the father of the World Series when he boldly challenged the American League champion Boston Red Sox to a post-season playoff to determine the best team in the land in 1903.

An intensely proud man, it galled Dreyfuss to see his Pirates beaten by John McGraw's New York Giants for the pennant in '04 and '05. Dreyfuss vowed not to be beaten again in 1906, and decided that the man he needed was pitcher Vic Willis of Boston. While a shrewd trader, Dreyfuss was known to be extremely fair in offering value in return. He sent third baseman Dave Brain, first baseman Del Howard, and pitcher Vive Lindaman to Boston for Willis. Pirate fans were outraged, since Willis had lost 54 games in the two previous seasons, but Dreyfuss and manager Fred Clarke knew that he had suffered from poor support, both at bat and in the field. Willis justified the owner's faith by leading all pitchers in wins with 22, but the improvement wasn't enough to stop a Chicago juggernaut that won a record 116 games. Willis kept at it, winning 21, 24, and 23 in the subsequent seasons, and the Pirates finally reclaimed the crown in 1909.

The history of baseball might have been different if Dreyfuss had been willing to fork over the price of a train ticket for a hot prospect in 1907. Some of his salesman friends sent him glowing reports of a semipro pitcher in Weiser, Idaho, who was averaging twenty strikeouts a game, and rarely allowing more than a hit or two to the area's best batsmen. He could have been Pittsburgh's for the cost of transportation, but Dreyfuss had heard these stories before, and refused to even take a look at the youngster named Walter Johnson.

For the first two decades of the century, first base bedeviled the Pirates in much the way third base does the Mets, and center field the Dodgers. Dreyfuss made several foolish trades trying to plug this hole. It all started when incumbent Kitty Bransfield ran into some personal problems in 1904 that resulted in a .233 batting average, by far the lowest of his career. Dreyfuss decided the time had come to get rid of him. The replacement he coveted was a highly touted minor leaguer owned by the Phillies, Del Howard. In addition to Bransfield, Pittsburgh sent Moose McCormick and Otto Krueger to the Phils for Howard. Howard never lived up to his notices, and a year later was included in the deal for Willis.

Several years later, Dreyfuss's eye was caught by St. Louis first baseman Ed Konetchy. Konetchy was the Cardinals' cleanup hitter and one of the league's best first sackers. Before the start of the 1914 season, Dreyfuss agreed to give up five players for Konetchy, pitcher Bob Harmon, and third baseman Mike Mowrey. It looked like a terrific deal for the Pirates, but the first base jinx held firm: Konetchy batted just .219 in '14, Harmon lost more than he won, and the duo added insult to injury by jumping to the Federal League the following year. The jinx wasn't broken until the Pirates signed Charlie Grimm from the Little Rock club in 1919, becoming the last of the eighteen men to be tried at the position in just fifteen years.

DATE	ACQUIRED	FROM	IN EXCHANGE FOR
Jan 1900	P Patsy Flaherty P Deacon Phillippe P Walt Woods P Rube Waddell P Icebox Chamberlain C Chief Zimmer C Tacks Latimer SS Honus Wagner 2B Claude Ritchey OF Fred Clarke OF Tommy Leach OF Mike Kelly OF Conny Doyle OF Tom Massitt (Sale of the chief assets of the Louisville franchise to Pittsburgh after Louisville was dropped by the National League.)	Louisville Colonels	P Jack Chesbro 2B Paddy Fox 2B John O'Brien IF Art Madison and $25,000.
Jan 1900	$1,000.	St. Louis Cardinals	OF Patsy Donovan
Jan 1900	Cash	Chicago Cubs	P Bert Cunningham
Jan 1900	P Jouett Meekin	Boston Braves	Cash
Feb 10, 1900	$2,000.	Chicago Cubs	OF Jack McCarthy
Feb 1900	Cash	New York Giants	C Frank Bowerman
Feb 1900	OF Tom O'Brien	New York Giants	Cash
Feb 1900	OF Duff Cooley	Philadelphia Phillies	P Tully Sparks 2B Heinie Reitz
May 10, 1900	C Jack O'Connor	St. Louis Cardinals	Cash
Unknown	Cash	St. Louis Cardinals	C Pop Schriver
Jan 1901	OF Elmer Smith	New York Giants	Cash
Jan 1901	Cash	Detroit Tigers	1B Pop Dillon
Jan 1901	Cash	Cleveland Indians	P Bill Hoffer
April 1901	Cash	Milwaukee Brewers	C Jiggs Donahue

DATE		ACQUIRED	FROM		IN EXCHANGE FOR
May 1901	1B	Lefty Davis	Brooklyn Dodgers	OF	Tom McCreery
May 1901		Cash	Boston Braves	OF	Duff Cooley
May 1901		Cash	Chicago Cubs	P	Rube Waddell
May 1901		Cash	Boston Braves	OF	Elmer Smith
June 1901	P	Ed Doheny	New York Giants	2B	Heinie Smith
July 1901		Cash	Philadelphia Athletics	P	Snake Wiltse
Sept 1901	3B	Jimmy Burke	Chicago White Sox		Cash
Feb 1902	OF	Fred Crolius	Boston Braves		Cash
April 1902		Cash	Cincinnati Reds	P	Ed Poole
Jan 1903	IF	Otto Krueger	St. Louis Cardinals	3B	Jimmy Burke
Jan 1903	P	Brickyard Kennedy	New York Giants		Cash
Jan 1903		Waiver price	Philadelphia Phillies	C	Chief Zimmer
Feb 1903	P	Lave Winham	Brooklyn Dodgers		Waiver price
March 1903		Waiver price	Philadelphia Phillies	P	Warren McLaughlin
June 1903	C	Art Weaver	St. Louis Cardinals		Cash
Oct 1903		Waiver price	Cincinnati Reds	C	Lee Fohl
Jan 1904		Cash	Chicago Cubs	OF	Solly Hofman
Jan 1904		Cash	Boston Braves	P	Kaiser Wilhelm
Feb 1904	P	Roscoe Miller	New York Giants		Cash
April 20, 1904	2B	Bobby Lowe	Chicago Cubs		Cash
April 30, 1904		Cash	Detroit Tigers	2B	Bobby Lowe
Aug 1, 1904		Cash	Brooklyn Dodgers	P	Doc Scanlan
Aug 9, 1904	OF	Moose McCormick	New York Giants		Cash
Aug 11, 1904		Cash	Cincinnati Reds	OF	Jimmy Sebring
Dec 20, 1904	1B	Del Howard	Philadelphia Phillies	1B IF OF	Kitty Bransfield Otto Krueger Moose McCormick

DATE	ACQUIRED		FROM	IN EXCHANGE FOR	
Jan 1905		Waiver price	Philadelphia Phillies	SS	Otto Krueger
March 1905		Waiver price	Washington Senators	OF	Harry Cassady
July 4, 1905	3B	Dave Brain	St. Louis Cardinals	SS	George McBride
Dec 15, 1905	P	Vic Willis	Boston Braves	3B 1B P	Dave Brain Del Howard Vive Lindaman
Dec 1905	C	Heinie Peitz	Cincinnati Reds	C	Ed Phelps
May 20, 1906	C	Ed Phelps	Cincinnati Reds		Cash
June 3, 1906	P	Chappie McFarland	St. Louis Cardinals		Cash
June 3, 1906		Cash	St. Louis Cardinals	P	Ed Karger
Aug 1, 1906		Waiver price	Brooklyn Dodgers	P	Chappie McFarland
Oct 1906	P	Charlie Brady	Philadelphia Phillies		Cash
Dec 1906	2B	Ed Abbaticchio	Boston Braves	OF 2B P	Ginger Beaumont Claude Ritchey Patsy Flaherty
Feb 1907		Cash	Washington Senators	OF	Bob Ganley
June 17, 1907	OF	Harry Wolter	Cincinnati Reds		Cash
June 26, 1907		Cash	Washington Senators	OF	Otis Clymer
July 4, 1907		Cash	St. Louis Cardinals	OF	Harry Wolter
July 15, 1907	P	Bill Duggleby	Philadelphia Phillies		Cash
Oct 1907	P	Babe Adams	St. Louis Cardinals		Cash
Jan 1908	P	Tom McCarthy	Cincinnati Reds		Cash
Jan 1908		Cash	Boston Braves	C	Harry Smith
Jan 1908		Cash	Brooklyn Dodgers	3B	Tommy Sheehan
April 1908	OF	Roy Thomas	Philadelphia Phillies		Cash
June 1908	P	Irv Young	Boston Braves	P P	Tom McCarthy Harley Young
June 1908		Cash	Boston Braves	OF	Beals Becker
July 1908	OF	Spike Shannon	New York Giants		Cash
Feb 1909		Cash	Boston Braves	OF	Roy Thomas

DATE	ACQUIRED	FROM	IN EXCHANGE FOR
May 1909	OF Kid Durbin	Cincinnati Reds	OF Ward Miller and cash
Aug 19, 1909	3B Bobby Byrne	St. Louis Cardinals	3B Jap Barbeau OF Alan Storke
Sept 1909	Cash	Boston Braves	2B Charlie Starr
Jan 1910	Cash	St. Louis Cardinals	P Vic Willis
Jan 1910	OF Vin Campbell	Chicago Cubs	Cash
Jan 1910	Cash	St. Louis Browns	1B Bill Abstein
Feb 1910	P Elmer Steele	Boston Red Sox	Waiver price
May 1910	Cash	Boston Braves	2B Ed Abbaticchio
June 1, 1910	P Kirby White	Boston Braves	P Sam Frock
Sept 1910	1B Bud Sharpe	Boston Braves	Cash
Jan 1911	C Bill Kelly	St. Louis Cardinals	Cash
May 1911	Cash	Chicago Cubs	P Lefty Leifield
July 1911	Cash	Boston Red Sox	P Judge Nagle
Aug 31, 1911	Cash	Brooklyn Dodgers	P Elmer Steele
Jan 1912	Cash	Chicago Cubs	P Ensign Cottrell
Jan 1912	2B Art Butler	Boston Braves	Cash
Feb 1912	OF Mike Donlin	Boston Braves	OF Vin Campbell
Feb 1912	Waiver price	Washington Senators	1B John Flynn
June 22, 1912	P King Cole OF Solly Hofman	Chicago Cubs	OF Tommy Leach P Lefty Leifield
June 1912	Cash	Cincinnati Reds	C Earl Blackburn
Dec 1912	Waiver price	Philadelphia Phillies	OF Mike Donlin
	(Donlin refused to report and announced his retirement.)		
Dec 1912	Cash	Boston Braves	2B Bill McKechnie
Jan 1913	Waiver price	Boston Red Sox	OF Wally Rehg
Jan 1913	Cash	Philadelphia Phillies	OF Ralph Capron
March 1913	Waiver price	St. Louis Browns	SS Rivington Bisland

DATE	ACQUIRED		FROM	IN EXCHANGE FOR	
July 29, 1913	OF	Mike Mitchell	Chicago Cubs		Waiver price
Aug 20, 1913	OF	Cozy Dolan and cash	Philadelphia Phillies	3B P	Bobby Byrne Howie Camnitz
Dec 12, 1913	1B 3B P	Ed Konetchy Mike Mowrey Bob Harmon	St. Louis Cardinals	3B 1B OF OF P	Art Butler Dots Miller Cozy Dolan Owen Wilson Hank Robinson
Jan 1914	P	Pat Bohen	Philadelphia Athletics		Waiver price
Jan 1914	P	Dan Costello	New York Yankees		Waiver price
Jan 1914		Cash	Cleveland Indians	OF	Roy Wood
July 20, 1914		Waiver price	Washington Senators	OF	Mike Mitchell
Aug 14, 1914		Cash	New York Giants	P	Marty O'Toole
Feb 14, 1915		Waiver price	Philadelphia Phillies	P	George McQuillan
Feb 28, 1915		Waiver price	St. Louis Cardinals	OF	Ham Hyatt
Feb 1915	2B	Doc Johnston	Cleveland Indians		$7,500.
March 1915		Cash	New York Yankees	P	Dazzy Vance
June 1915		Cash	New York Giants	C	Bobby Schang
July 1915		Cash	Chicago Cubs	SS	Alex McCarthy
Aug 19, 1915	OF	Ed Barney	New York Yankees		Waiver price
Sept 3, 1915		Cash	Boston Braves	OF	Zip Collins
Dec 1915	P	Elmer Jacobs	Philadelphia Phillies		Cash
Jan 1916	OF	Joe Schultz	Chicago Cubs		Cash
Feb 10, 1916	2B SS	Otto Knabe Jimmy Smith	Baltimore Orioles		Cash
Feb 10, 1916	C	Art Wilson	Chicago White Sox		Cash
April 12, 1916		Cash	Boston Braves	P	Ed Reulbach
June 1916	OF	Pete Compton	Boston Braves		Cash
		(Pittsburgh returned Compton to Boston ten days later.)			
July 29, 1916	OF C	Wildfire Schulte Bill Fischer	Chicago Cubs	C 2B	Art Wilson Otto Knabe
July 1916	IF	Alex McCarthy	Chicago Cubs		Cash

DATE		ACQUIRED	FROM		IN EXCHANGE FOR
Aug 5, 1916		Waiver price	New York Giants	C	George Gibson
Sept 2, 1916		Cash	Philadelphia Phillies	P	Erv Kantlehner
Jan 1917		Waiver price	New York Giants	C	George Gibson
Jan 1917		Waiver price	New York Giants	IF	Jimmy Smith
Feb 4, 1917	1B	Fritz Mollwitz	Chicago Cubs		Cash
May 24, 1917		Waiver price	St. Louis Cardinals	SS	Ike McAuley
June 14, 1917		Waiver price	Philadelphia Phillies	OF	Wildfire Schulte
June 14, 1917	P	Bob Steele	St. Louis Cardinals	3B	Doug Baird
July 25, 1917	1B	George Kelly	New York Giants		Waiver price
July 29, 1917	2B	Joe Wilhoit	Boston Braves		Waiver price
Aug 4, 1917		Waiver price	New York Giants	1B	George Kelly
Aug 5, 1917		Waiver price	New York Giants	2B	Joe Wilhoit
Aug 1917	OF	Harry Wolfe	Chicago Cubs		Cash
Oct 1917		Cash	Boston Braves	C	Bill Wagner
Dec 1917	C	Jimmy Archer	Chicago Cubs		Cash
Unknown	P	Earl Hamilton	St. Louis Browns		Cash
Jan 9, 1918	OF 2B	Casey Stengel George Cutshaw	Brooklyn Dodgers	SS P P	Chuck Ward Burleigh Grimes Al Mamaux
March 1918	3B	Bill McKechnie	Cincinnati Reds		$20,000.
June 1918		Cash	New York Giants	P	Bob Steele
June 1918	3B	Gus Getz	Cleveland Indians		Waiver price
July 1, 1918	P	Erskine Mayer	Philadelphia Phillies	P	Elmer Jacobs
July 1918		Cash	Brooklyn Dodgers	C	Jimmy Archer
Jan 1919	3B	Walter Barbare	Boston Red Sox		Cash
Jan 1919		Cash	New York Giants	OF	Lee King
June 12, 1919		Waiver price	Boston Braves	3B	Tony Boeckel

DATE		ACQUIRED	FROM		IN EXCHANGE FOR
June 1919		Cash	Cincinnati Reds	OF	Billy Zitzmann
July 1919	OF	Fred Nicholson	Detroit Tigers		Waiver price
Aug 1919	OF	Possum Whitted	Philadelphia Phillies	OF	Casey Stengel
Aug 1919		Waiver price	Chicago White Sox	P	Erskine Mayer
Aug 1919		Cash	St. Louis Cardinals	1B	Fritz Mollwitz
Oct 1919		Cash	Washington Senators	P	Frank Miller
Nov 1919	C	Nig Clarke	Philadelphia Phillies		Waiver price
Jan 1920		Cash	Chicago Cubs	2B	Zeb Terry
July 1920	OF	Wally Hood	Brooklyn Dodgers		Cash
Aug 28, 1920	P	Mule Watson	Boston Braves		Waiver price
Feb 23, 1921	SS	Rabbit Maranville	Boston Braves	OF OF 3B	Billy Southworth Fred Nicholson Walter Barbare and $15,000.
May 1921		Waiver price	Philadelphia Phillies	OF	Cliff Lee
June 30, 1921		Waiver price	Boston Braves	P	Mule Watson
July 1, 1921	OF	Dave Robertson	Chicago Cubs	P	Elmer Ponder
July 1921	C	Tony Brottem	Washington Senators		Cash
Dec 29, 1921		Waiver price	Detroit Tigers	2B	George Cutshaw
Dec 1921		Cash	New York Giants	OF	Dave Robertson
March 14, 1922		Cash	Brooklyn Dodgers	OF	Possum Whitted
April 1922	2B	Jack Hammond	Cleveland Indians		Cash
July 14, 1922		Cash	Philadelphia Phillies	OF	Johnny Mokan
Nov 5, 1922	P	Jim Bagby	Cleveland Indians		Waiver price
May 22, 1923	P 2B	Lee Meadows Johnny Rawlings	Philadelphia Phillies	P SS	Whitey Glazner Cotton Tierney and $50,000.
Dec 1923		Waiver price	Philadelphia Phillies	P	Earl Hamilton
May 25, 1924		Cash	Philadelphia Phillies	P	Ray Steineder

DATE		ACQUIRED	FROM		IN EXCHANGE FOR
July 6, 1924	C	Earl Smith	Boston Braves		Cash
July 11, 1924	P	Jeff Pfeffer	St. Louis Cardinals		Waiver price
Oct 27, 1924	P 2B 1B	Vic Aldridge George Grantham Al Niehaus	Chicago Cubs	1B 2B P	Charlie Grimm Rabbit Maranville Wilbur Cooper
May 20, 1925	P	Tom Sheehan	Cincinnati Reds	OF	Al Niehaus
July 1, 1926	P	Joe Bush	Washington Senators		Cash
July 20, 1926		Cash	Boston Braves	2B	Eddie Moore
Aug 13, 1926		Waiver price	Brooklyn Dodgers	OF	Max Carey
Feb 4, 1927	1B	Joe Harris	Washington Senators		Waiver price
May 9, 1927		Cash	New York Giants	P	Don Songer
June 28, 1927		Waiver price	New York Giants	P	Joe Bush
Nov 28, 1927	3B OF	Sparky Adams Pete Scott	Chicago Cubs	OF	Kiki Cuyler
Dec 1927	P	Fred Fussell	Chicago Cubs	P	Mike Cvengros
Feb 11, 1928	P	Burleigh Grimes	New York Giants	P	Vic Aldridge
June 8, 1928	C	Charlie Hargreaves	Brooklyn Dodgers	1B C	Joe Harris Johnny Gooch
July 10, 1928		Cash	St. Louis Cardinals	C	Earl Smith
July 10, 1928		Waiver price	Cleveland Indians	P	Johnny Miljus
Dec 11, 1928	P 2B	Jesse Petty Harry Riconda	Brooklyn Dodgers	SS	Glenn Wright
July 12, 1929	OF	Ira Flagstead	Washington Senators		Waiver price
Aug 28, 1929		Waiver price	St. Louis Cardinals	P	Carmen Hill
Nov 1929		Cash	St. Louis Cardinals	3B	Sparky Adams
April 9, 1930	P	Percy Jones and cash	Boston Braves	P	Burleigh Grimes
Aug 7, 1930	OF	Denny Sothern	Philadelphia Phillies	OF	Fred Brickell
Aug 24, 1930		Cash	Chicago Cubs	P	Jesse Petty
Nov 6, 1930	SS P	Tommy Thevenow Claude Willoughby	Philadelphia Phillies	SS	Dick Bartell

DATE		ACQUIRED	FROM		IN EXCHANGE FOR
Jan 1931	1B	Eddie Phillips	Philadelphia Phillies		Cash
Jan 1931		Waiver price	Boston Braves	C	Al Bool
Jan 1931	2B	Bill Regan	Boston Red Sox		Waiver price
Jan 1931	P	Bob Osborn	Chicago Cubs		Cash
June 13, 1931	C	Earl Grace	Chicago Cubs	C	Rollie Hemsley
Feb 4, 1932		Cash	Cincinnati Reds	2B	George Grantham
Nov 1932	P	Waite Hoyt	New York Giants		Waiver price
Dec 12, 1932	3B	Freddie Lindstrom	New York Giants	P OF	Glenn Spencer Gus Dugas
		(Part of three-team trade involving New York, Philadelphia, and Pittsburgh.)			
June 23, 1933	C	Val Picinich	Brooklyn Dodgers		Cash
Oct 17, 1933	P OF	Red Lucas Wally Roettger	Cincinnati Reds	OF 2B	Adam Comorosky Tony Piet
May 1934	P	Burleigh Grimes	St. Louis Cardinals		Waiver price
May 26, 1934		Cash	New York Yankees	P	Burleigh Grimes
June 10, 1934	P	Ed Holley	Philadelphia Phillies		Cash
Nov 22, 1934	P P OF	Guy Bush Jim Weaver Babe Herman	Chicago Cubs	P OF	Larry French Freddie Lindstrom
Dec 11, 1934	P	Jack Salveson	New York Giants		Waiver price
Dec 1934		Cash	New York Giants	P	Leon Chagnon
June 16, 1935		Cash	Chicago White Sox	P	Jack Salveson
June 21, 1935		Cash	Cincinnati Reds	OF	Babe Herman
Nov 21, 1935	C	Al Todd	Philadelphia Phillies	P C	Claude Passeau Earl Grace
Dec 12, 1935		Cash	Cincinnati Reds	SS	Tommy Thevenow
Jan 30, 1936	OF	Fred Schulte	Washington Senators		Waiver price
July 1936	P	Johnny Welch	Boston Red Sox		Waiver price
Dec 4, 1936	P	Ed Brandt	Brooklyn Dodgers	3B P	Cookie Lavagetto Ralph Birkofer
April 16, 1937	P	Joe Bowman	Philadelphia Phillies	1B	Earl Browne

DATE	ACQUIRED		FROM	IN EXCHANGE FOR	
Oct 1937		Cash	St. Louis Cardinals	C	Tom Padden
Jan 1938		Cash	St. Louis Browns	P	Jim Weaver
May 1938	OF	Heinie Manush	Brooklyn Dodgers		Waiver price
Dec 16, 1938	C	Ray Mueller	Boston Braves	C OF	Al Todd Johnny Dickshot and cash
June 15, 1939	1B	Elbie Fletcher	Boston Braves	SS	Bill Schuster and cash
July 28, 1939	P	Max Butcher	Philadelphia Phillies	1B	Gus Suhr
Oct 27, 1939	C	Spud Davis	Philadelphia Phillies		Cash
Dec 6, 1939	P	Johnny Lanning	Boston Braves	P	Jim Tobin and cash
Dec 8, 1939	P	Danny MacFayden	Boston Braves	P	Bill Swift and cash
Jan 22, 1940	P	Ray Harrell	Philadelphia Phillies		Waiver price
March 3, 1940	OF	Debs Garms	Boston Braves		Cash
April 1940	IF	Ed Leip	Washington Senators		Cash
May 7, 1940	P	Nick Strincevich	Boston Braves	OF	Lloyd Waner
May 8, 1940	OF	Vince DiMaggio	Cincinnati Reds	OF	Johnny Rizzo
June 14, 1940	C	Al Lopez	Boston Braves	C	Ray Berres and $40,000.
Aug 1940	P	Dutch Dietz	Cincinnati Reds		Cash
Dec 2, 1940	2B	Stu Martin	St. Louis Cardinals		Cash
April 22, 1941		Cash	Brooklyn Dodgers	P	Mace Brown
May 12, 1941	C	Bill Baker	Cincinnati Reds		Cash
June 20, 1941	P	Joe Sullivan	Boston Braves		Cash
Dec 1, 1941	P	Hank Gornicki	Chicago Cubs		Waiver price
Dec 12, 1941	2B P C 1B	Pete Coscarart Luke Hamlin Babe Phelps Jimmy Wasdell	Brooklyn Dodgers	3B	Arky Vaughan
Sept 9, 1942	C	Bennie Warren (Deal was cancelled by Commissioner Landis.)	Philadelphia Phillies		Waiver price
Nov 17, 1942		Cash	Chicago Cubs	C	Bennie Warren

DATE		ACQUIRED	FROM		IN EXCHANGE FOR
April 30, 1943		Cash	Philadelphia Phillies	1B	Jimmy Wasdell
June 15, 1943	P	Johnny Podgajny	Philadelphia Phillies	P	Dutch Dietz
Dec 30, 1943	1B	Babe Dahlgren	Philadelphia Phillies	C	Babe Phelps and cash
May 27, 1944	P	Ray Starr	Cincinnati Reds		Cash
June 12, 1944		Cash	New York Giants	P	Johnny Gee
July 27, 1944		Waiver price	Philadelphia Phillies	P	Harry Shuman
March 31, 1945	P	Al Gerheauser	Philadelphia Phillies	OF	Vince DiMaggio
June 23, 1945		Waiver price	Chicago Cubs	P	Ray Starr
Jan 5, 1946	2B	Jimmy Brown	St. Louis Cardinals		$30,000.
April 23, 1946		Cash	St. Louis Browns	1B	Babe Dahlgren
June 12, 1946	OF	Chuck Workman	Boston Braves	OF	Johnny Barrett
Sept 30, 1946	2B P OF SS	Billy Herman Elmer Singleton Stan Wentzel Whitey Wietelmann	Boston Braves	3B C	Bob Elliott Hank Camelli
Oct 19, 1946	P	Art Herring	Brooklyn Dodgers		Cash
Oct 21, 1946	P	Ernie Bonham	New York Yankees	P	Cookie Cuccurullo
Dec 5, 1946	SS	Eddie Basinski	Brooklyn Dodgers	P	Al Gerheauser
Dec 7, 1946	OF	Gene Woodling	Cleveland Indians	C	Al Lopez
Dec 12, 1946	2B	Jimmy Bloodworth	Detroit Tigers		Cash
Dec 26, 1946	C	Clyde Kluttz	St. Louis Cardinals		Cash
Jan 18, 1947	1B	Hank Greenberg	Detroit Tigers		$75,000.
Jan 25, 1947	P	Hi Bithorn	Chicago Cubs		Cash
Jan 1947	P	Hugh Mulcahy	Philadelphia Phillies		Cash
Feb 10, 1947	P	Jim Bagby	Boston Red Sox		Cash
March 22, 1947		Waiver price	Chicago White Sox	P	Hi Bithorn
March 25, 1947	P	Lou Tost	Boston Braves		Cash
April 28, 1947	P	Bob Malloy	Cincinnati Reds		Waiver price

DATE		ACQUIRED	FROM		IN EXCHANGE FOR
May 3, 1947	P P P IF C	Kirby Higbe Hank Behrman Cal McLish Gene Mauch Dixie Howell	Brooklyn Dodgers	OF	Al Gionfriddo and $100,000.
May 9, 1947		Cash	Philadelphia Phillies	P	Ken Heintzelman
June 14, 1947	P	Roger Wolff	Cleveland Indians		Cash
June 14, 1947		Cash	Brooklyn Dodgers	P	Hank Behrman
July 11, 1947	P	Mel Queen	New York Yankees		Cash
Aug 4, 1947	P	Al Lyons	New York Yankees		Cash
Nov 14, 1947	1B	Ed Stevens	Brooklyn Dodgers		Cash
Nov 14, 1947	SS	Stan Rojek	Brooklyn Dodgers		Cash
Nov 18, 1947	1B 2B	Johnny Hopp Danny Murtaugh	Boston Braves	OF C P	Jim Russell Bill Salkeld Al Lyons
Dec 4, 1947	1B	Les Fleming	Cleveland Indians	1B	Elbie Fletcher
Dec 8, 1947	OF P P	Dixie Walker Hal Gregg Vic Lombardi	Brooklyn Dodgers	P 3B SS	Preacher Roe Billy Cox Gene Mauch
Dec 10, 1947	P	Elmer Riddle	Cincinnati Reds		Cash
Dec 1947	OF	Joe Grace	Washington Senators		Cash
Jan 16, 1948	3B	Eddie Bockman	Cleveland Indians		Cash
March 26, 1948	SS	Don Gutteridge	Boston Red Sox		Cash
April 5, 1948	SS	Grady Wilson	Philadelphia Phillies		Cash
May 15, 1948		Cash	Philadelphia Phillies	P	Nick Strincevich
July 30, 1948	P	Paul Erickson	New York Giants		Cash
Nov 20, 1948	P	Bob Muncrief	Cleveland Indians		$20,000.
Dec 8, 1948	C P	Clyde McCullough Cliff Chambers	Chicago Cubs	P 3B	Cal McLish Frankie Gustine
Jan 29, 1949	P	Murry Dickson	St. Louis Cardinals		$125,000.
Feb 9, 1949	OF	Walt Judnich	Cleveland Indians		Waiver price

DATE	ACQUIRED		FROM	IN EXCHANGE FOR	
May 18, 1949	OF	Marv Rackley	Brooklyn Dodgers	OF	Johnny Hopp and $25,000.
		(Trade was cancelled on June 7, 1949.)			
June 6, 1949	P IF	Ray Poat Bobby Rhawn	New York Giants	P	Kirby Higbe
June 6, 1949		Waiver price	Chicago Cubs	P	Bob Muncrief
June 15, 1949	OF	Ed Sauer	St. Louis Cardinals		Cash
June 15, 1949	C	Phil Masi	Boston Braves	OF	Ed Sauer
July 27, 1949	P	Harry Gumbert	Cincinnati Reds		Waiver price
Aug 6, 1949	1B	Jack Phillips	New York Yankees		Cash
Nov 4, 1949	2B	Hank Schenz	Brooklyn Dodgers		Cash
Dec 14, 1949	P	Frank Papish	Cleveland Indians		Cash
Dec 14, 1949	OF	Marv Rickert	Boston Braves		Cash
Feb 2, 1950		Cash	Chicago White Sox	C	Phil Masi
May 17, 1950	C	Ray Mueller	New York Giants		Cash
May 29, 1950		Cash	Chicago White Sox	OF	Marv Rickert
June 12, 1950	P	Hank Borowy	Philadelphia Phillies		$10,000.
July 20, 1950	2B	Bob Dillinger	Philadelphia Athletics		$35,000.
Aug 3, 1950		$15,000.	Detroit Tigers	P	Hank Borowy
Sept 5, 1950		Cash	New York Yankees	1B	Johnny Hopp
May 16, 1951		Cash	Chicago White Sox	2B	Bob Dillinger
May 17, 1951	OF 1B	Erv Dusak Rocky Nelson	St. Louis Cardinals	SS	Stan Rojek
June 1, 1951		Waiver price	St. Louis Browns	1B	Dale Long
June 5, 1951	OF	Jack Maguire	New York Giants		Waiver price
June 15, 1951	OF P P C 3B	Bill Howerton Howie Pollet Ted Wilks Joe Garagiola Dick Cole	St. Louis Cardinals	P OF	Cliff Chambers Wally Westlake
July 10, 1951		Waiver price	New York Giants	IF	Hank Schenz
July 16, 1951		Waiver price	St. Louis Browns	OF	Jack Maguire
Sept 12, 1951		Waiver price	St. Louis Browns	2B	Mike Goliat

DATE		ACQUIRED	FROM		IN EXCHANGE FOR
Sept 19, 1951		Waiver price	Washington Senators	OF	Dino Restelli
Sept 20, 1951		Waiver price	Chicago White Sox	1B	Rocky Nelson
March 4, 1952	P	Jim Suchecki	St. Louis Browns		Cash
April 9, 1952	P	Hooks Iott	Cincinnati Reds		Cash
May 3, 1952	P	George Munger	St. Louis Cardinals	P	Bill Werle
May 5, 1952		Waiver price	Chicago White Sox	P	Jim Suchecki
May 7, 1952		Waiver price	New York Giants	OF	Bill Howerton
Aug 18, 1952	2B P	Johnny Berardino Charlie Ripple and $50,000.	Cleveland Indians	SS P	George Strickland Ted Wilks
Oct 14, 1952	OF C OF	Cal Abrams Joe Rossi Gail Henley	Cincinnati Reds	OF	Gus Bell
Dec 3, 1952	P	Dick Manville and $25,000.	Chicago Cubs	C	Clyde McCullough
April 17, 1953	2B	Eddie Pellagrini	Cincinnati Reds		Waiver price
May 12, 1953	P	Roger Bowman	New York Giants		Waiver price
May 13, 1953		Cash	Washington Senators	C	Ed Fitz Gerald
June 4, 1953	C P 1B 3B OF OF	Toby Atwell Bob Schultz Preston Ward George Freese Bob Addis Gene Hermanski $150,000.	Chicago Cubs	OF C P OF	Ralph Kiner Joe Garagiola Howie Pollet Catfish Metkovich
June 14, 1953	OF	Hal Rice and cash	St. Louis Cardinals	3B	Pete Castiglione
Aug 31, 1953		Cash	Philadelphia Phillies	OF	Johnny Lindell
Dec 19, 1953		Cash	Philadelphia Phillies	C	Mike Sandlock
Dec 26, 1953	OF P OF P P	Sid Gordon Max Surkont Sam Jethroe Curt Raydon Fred Walters minor league P Larry Lasalle and $100,000.	Milwaukee Braves	2B	Danny O'Connell

DATE		ACQUIRED	FROM		IN EXCHANGE FOR
Jan 13, 1954	P 3B	Andy Hansen Lucky Lohrke and $70,000.	Philadelphia Phillies	P	Murry Dickson
May 19, 1954		Waiver price	Chicago Cubs	C	Walker Cooper
May 25, 1954	P	Dick Littlefield	Baltimore Orioles	OF	Cal Abrams
June 14, 1954	OF	Luis Marquez	Chicago Cubs	OF	Hal Rice
Dec 29, 1954		Cash	Detroit Tigers	P	Bob Schultz
Jan 11, 1955	P	Ben Wade and cash	St. Louis Cardinals	P	Paul LaPalme
May 23, 1955		Cash	New York Giants	OF	Sid Gordon
Sept 14, 1955		Waiver price	Kansas City Athletics	OF	Tom Saffell
March 5, 1956		Cash	New York Giants	C	Jim Mangan
April 16, 1956	P	Howie Pollet	Chicago White Sox		Cash
May 5, 1956	P	Luis Arroyo	St. Louis Cardinals	P	Max Surkont
May 15, 1956	C	Hank Foiles	Cleveland Indians	1B	Preston Ward
May 17, 1956	OF	Bill Virdon	St. Louis Cardinals	P OF	Dick Littlefield Bobby Del Greco
June 23, 1956	2B	Spook Jacobs	Kansas City Athletics	P	Jack McMahan
April 3, 1957	OF	Jim Pendleton	Milwaukee Braves	3B	Dick Cole
May 1, 1957	3B 1B	Gene Baker Dee Fondy	Chicago Cubs	1B OF	Dale Long Lee Walls
May 14, 1957	P	Bob Smith	St. Louis Cardinals		Cash
Dec 9, 1957	P	Don Gross	Cincinnati Reds	P	Bob Purkey
Dec 28, 1957	1B	Ted Kluszewski	Cincinnati Reds	1B	Dee Fondy
May 6, 1958		Cash	Chicago Cubs	OF	Paul Smith
May 7, 1958	P	Bob Porterfield	Boston Red Sox		Cash
June 15, 1958	SS	Dick Schofield and cash	St. Louis Cardinals	3B SS	Gene Freese Johnny O'Brien
Jan 30, 1959	C P 3B	Smoky Burgess Harvey Haddix Don Hoak	Cincinnati Reds	P OF OF OF	Whammy Douglas Jim Pendleton Frank Thomas Johnny Powers
April 13, 1959	P	Paul Giel	San Francisco Giants		Waiver price

DATE		ACQUIRED	FROM		IN EXCHANGE FOR
June 13, 1959		Waiver price	Detroit Tigers	P	Bob Smith
Aug 25, 1959	OF	Harry Simpson minor league IF Bob Sagers	Chicago White Sox	1B	Ted Kluszewski
Dec 15, 1959		Cash	Kansas City Athletics	C	Hank Foiles
Dec 15, 1959	C	Hal Smith	Kansas City Athletics	2B P	Ken Hamlin Dick Hall
Dec 21, 1959	OF P	Gino Cimoli Tom Cheney	St. Louis Cardinals	P	Ron Kline
May 28, 1960	P 3B	Vinegar Bend Mizell Dick Gray	St. Louis Cardinals	2B P	Julian Javier Ed Bauta
June 1, 1960	C	Hank Foiles Cash	Kansas City Athletics	C	Danny Kravitz
June 2, 1960	OF	Johnny Powers	Cleveland Indians	C	Hank Foiles
Dec 16, 1960	P	Bobby Shantz	Washington Senators	P 3B 1B	Bennie Daniels Harry Bright R C Stevens
June 15, 1961	OF	Walt Moryn	St. Louis Cardinals		Cash
June 29, 1961	P	Tom Sturdivant	Washington Senators	P	Tom Cheney
Sept 25, 1961		Waiver price	Washington Senators	P	Freddie Green
Oct 10, 1961		Cash	Los Angeles Angels	P	George Witt
Oct 13, 1961		Cash	Philadelphia Phillies	C	Bob Oldis
Dec 21, 1961	SS	Coot Veal	Washington Senators		Cash
May 7, 1962	1B	Jim Marshall	New York Mets	P	Vinegar Bend Mizell
Sept 6, 1962		Waiver price	New York Mets	P	Larry Foss
Nov 19, 1962	SS P	Julio Gotay Don Cardwell	St. Louis Cardinals	SS P	Dick Groat Diomedes Olivo
Nov 20, 1962	C P	Jim Pagliaroni Don Schwall	Boston Red Sox	P 1B	Jack Lamabe Dick Stuart
Dec 15, 1962		Minor league P Ron Honeycutt and cash	Washington Senators	C	Don Leppert
April 4, 1963	OF	Manny Mota	Houston Astros	OF	Howie Goss and cash
May 4, 1963		Cash	Detroit Tigers	P	Tom Sturdivant
May 23, 1963	OF	Jerry Lynch	Cincinnati Reds	OF	Bob Skinner
Nov 26, 1963	3B	Gene Freese	Cincinnati Reds		Cash

DATE		ACQUIRED	FROM		IN EXCHANGE FOR
Nov 28, 1963	1B OF	Pancho Herrera Ted Savage	Philadelphia Phillies	3B	Don Hoak
Dec 14, 1963		Minor league SS Dick Yencha and cash	Baltimore Orioles	P	Harvey Haddix
Dec 14, 1963	P	Bob Allen	Cleveland Indians		Cash
Sept 12, 1964		Waiver price	Chicago White Sox	C	Smoky Burgess
Dec 9, 1964	SS	Andre Rodgers	Chicago Cubs	SS	Roberto Pena and cash
Feb 11, 1965	C	Del Crandall	San Francisco Giants	P OF	Bob Priddy Bob Burda
May 22, 1965	SS	Jose Pagan	San Francisco Giants	SS	Dick Schofield
Aug 25, 1965		Cash	Chicago White Sox	3B	Gene Freese
Oct 1, 1965	OF	Matty Alou	San Francisco Giants	P 3B	Joe Gibbon Ozzie Virgil
Dec 10, 1965	P	Pete Mikkelsen and cash	New York Yankees	P	Bob Friend
April 7, 1966	P	Bob Purkey	St. Louis Cardinals		Cash
June 15, 1966	P	Billy O'Dell	Atlanta Braves	P	Don Schwall
Sept 12, 1966		Cash	Baltimore Orioles	1B-OF	Dave Roberts
Oct 12, 1966	P	Juan Pizarro	Chicago White Sox	P	Wilbur Wood
Oct 17, 1966	P	Bill Short	Boston Red Sox		Cash
Dec 1, 1966	SS	Maury Wills	Los Angeles Dodgers	3B-OF SS	Bob Bailey Gene Michael
Dec 6, 1966	P OF	Dennis Ribant Gary Kolb	New York Mets	OF P	Don Bosch Don Cardwell
April 7, 1967		Cash	Detroit Tigers	C	Jim Price
Aug 4, 1967		Waiver price	Chicago Cubs	P	Pete Mikkelsen
Nov 28, 1967	P	Dave Wickersham	Detroit Tigers	P	Dennis Ribant
Nov 29, 1967	C	Chris Cannizzaro	Detroit Tigers		Cash
Nov 29, 1967		Cash	New York Mets	P	Bill Short
Dec 2, 1967	P	Ron Kline	Minnesota Twins	1B	Bob Oliver
Dec 3, 1967		Cash	Oakland Athletics	C	Jim Pagliaroni

DATE		ACQUIRED	FROM		IN EXCHANGE FOR
Dec 15, 1967	P	Jim Bunning	Philadelphia Phillies	3B P P	Don Money Woodie Fryman Bill Laxton minor league P Hal Clem
June 27, 1968		Cash	Boston Red Sox	P	Juan Pizarro
June 27, 1968	P	Bill Henry	San Francisco Giants		Cash
Aug 31, 1968		Cash	Detroit Tigers	P	Roy Face
Oct 18, 1968		Cash	Kansas City Royals	P	John Gelnar
Oct 21, 1968		Cash	Kansas City Royals	P	Dave Wickersham
Jan 15, 1969	IF P	Ron Campbell Chuck Hartenstein	Chicago Cubs	OF	Manny Jimenez
March 28, 1969	OF IF	Ron Davis Bobby Klaus	San Diego Padres	C P	Chris Cannizzaro Tommie Sisk
May 17, 1969	P	Frank Kreutzer	Washington Senators	P	Jim Shellenback
June 10, 1969	P	Joe Gibbon	San Francisco Giants	P	Ron Kline
Aug 15, 1969		Minor leaguers OF Ron Mitchell and IF Chuck Coggin and cash	Los Angeles Dodgers	P	Jim Bunning
Oct 21, 1969	P C	Dave Giusti Dave Ricketts	St. Louis Cardinals	C	Carl Taylor minor league OF Frank Vanzin
June 22, 1970		Cash	St. Louis Cardinals	P	Chuck Hartenstein
Aug 31, 1970	P	George Brunet	Washington Senators	P	Denny Riddleberger and cash
Sept 14, 1970	P	Mudcat Grant (Oakland received Mangual on October 20.)	Oakland Athletics	OF	Angel Mangual
Dec 2, 1970	P SS C	Bob Johnson Jackie Hernandez Jim Campanis	Kansas City Royals	SS P C	Freddie Patek Bruce Dal Canton Jerry May
Jan 29, 1971	P OF	Nellie Briles Vic Davalillo	St. Louis Cardinals	OF P	Matty Alou George Brunet
Aug 10, 1971	P	Bob Miller	San Diego Padres	OF P	John Jeter Ed Acosta
Aug 10, 1971		Cash	Oakland Athletics	P	Mudcat Grant
Sept 3, 1971	OF	Carl Taylor	Kansas City Royals		Cash
Sept 2, 1972		Cash	Boston Red Sox	P	Bob Veale
Oct 25, 1972	P	Jim Rooker	Kansas City Royals	P	Gene Garber

DATE		ACQUIRED	FROM		IN EXCHANGE FOR
Nov 30, 1972	P P	Jim Foor Norm McRae	Detroit Tigers	OF	Dick Sharon
April 2, 1973	P	Chris Zachary	Detroit Tigers	C	Charlie Sands
May 4, 1973	C	Jerry McNertney	Oakland Athletics		Cash
May 24, 1973		Cash	Atlanta Braves	2B	Chuck Goggin
July 7, 1973	SS	Dal Maxvill	Oakland Athletics		Cash
Aug 1, 1973		Cash	Oakland Athletics	OF	Vic Davalillo
Oct 18, 1973	P	Ken Brett	Philadelphia Phillies	2B	Dave Cash
Oct 31, 1973	P	Jerry Reuss	Houston Astros	C	Milt May
Dec 4, 1973	C IF	Ed Kirkpatrick Kurt Bevacqua minor league 1B Winston Cole	Kansas City Royals	P IF	Nellie Briles Fernando Gonzalez
Dec 5, 1973		Cash	Detroit Tigers	P	Luke Walker
Dec 7, 1973		Minor league OF Burnel Flowers	Cleveland Indians	P	Bob Johnson
Jan 31, 1974	C	Mike Ryan	Philadelphia Phillies	SS	Jackie Hernandez
March 28, 1974	P	Wayne Simpson	Kansas City Royals	P	Jim Foor
April 1, 1974	IF	Paul Popovich	Chicago Cubs	P	Tom Dettore and cash
July 8, 1974		Minor league IF Cal Meier and cash	Kansas City Royals	IF	Kurt Bevacqua
July 11, 1974	C	Chuck Brinkman	Chicago White Sox		Cash
Oct 22, 1974	C	Duffy Dyer	New York Mets	OF	Gene Clines
Dec 6, 1974	P	Jim Ray	Detroit Tigers		Cash
April 5, 1975	OF	Bill Robinson	Philadelphia Phillies	P	Wayne Simpson
Dec 11, 1975	P	Doc Medich	New York Yankees	2B P P	Willie Randolph Ken Brett Dock Ellis
Dec 12, 1975	2B	Tommy Helms	Houston Astros	3B	Art Howe
Sept 8, 1976		Cash	Chicago Cubs	P	Ramon Hernandez
Oct 15, 1976		Cash	Seattle Mariners	P	Jim Minshall
Nov 5, 1976	MGR	Chuck Tanner	Oakland Athletics	C	Manny Sanguillen and $100,000.
Nov 5, 1976		Cash	Oakland Athletics	2B	Tommy Helms

DATE		ACQUIRED	FROM		IN EXCHANGE FOR
Nov 6, 1976	P	Tom Carroll	Cincinnati Reds	P	Jim Sadowski
Dec 7, 1976	P	Grant Jackson	Seattle Mariners	IF IF	Craig Reynolds Jimmy Sexton
Dec 10, 1976	P P	Terry Forster Goose Gossage	Chicago White Sox	OF P	Richie Zisk Silvio Martinez
Dec 15, 1976		No compensation (free agent signing)	Philadelphia Phillies	3B	Richie Hebner
March 15, 1977	2B 3B P	Phil Garner Tommy Helms Chris Batton	Oakland Athletics	P P P P OF OF	Dave Giusti Doc Medich Doug Bair Rick Langford Tony Armas Mitchell Page
April 4, 1977	OF	Mike Easler	California Angels		Minor league P Randy Sealy
June 13, 1977	OF	Jerry Hairston	Chicago White Sox		Cash
June 15, 1977	1B	Jim Fregosi	Texas Rangers	1B	Ed Kirkpatrick
July 27, 1977	P	Dave Pagan	Seattle Mariners	P	Rick Honeycutt
Nov 22, 1977		No compensation (free agent signing)	Los Angeles Dodgers	P	Terry Forster
Nov 23, 1977		No compensation (free agent signing)	New York Yankees	P	Goose Gossage
Dec 8, 1977	P OF	Bert Blyleven John Milner (Part of four-team trade involving Texas, New York Mets, Pittsburgh, and Atlanta.)	Texas Rangers	OF	Al Oliver
Jan 31, 1978	P	Elias Sosa	Los Angeles Dodgers		Cash
March 15, 1978	P	Jim Bibby	Cleveland Indians		No compensation (free agent signing)
March 27, 1978		Cash	Toronto Blue Jays	P	Larry Demery
March 29, 1978	P	Will McEnaney	Montreal Expos	P	Tim Jones
April 4, 1978	C	Manny Sanguillen	Oakland Athletics	OF P 2B	Miguel Dilone Elias Sosa Mike Edwards
May 28, 1978	P	Dave Hamilton	St. Louis Cardinals		Cash
June 5, 1978		Cash	San Diego Padres	IF	Fernando Gonzalez
Sept 13, 1978	OF	Dave May	Milwaukee Brewers		Cash
Sept 22, 1978	OF	Clarence Gaston	Atlanta Braves		Cash

DATE		ACQUIRED	FROM		IN EXCHANGE FOR
Oct 27, 1978		Cash	Boston Red Sox	OF	Mike Easler
Dec 5, 1978	P P SS	Enrique Romo Rick Jones Tommy McMillan	Seattle Mariners	P P SS	Odell Jones Rafael Vasquez Mario Mendoza
Jan 18, 1979	OF	Lee Lacy	Los Angeles Dodgers		No compensation (free agent signing)
March 15, 1979	OF	Mike Easler	Boston Red Sox		Minor league OF George Hill and P Martin Rivas and cash
April 7, 1979	P	Rick Rhoden	Los Angeles Dodgers	P	Jerry Reuss
April 19, 1979	SS	Tim Foli minor league P Greg Field	New York Mets	SS	Frank Taveras
June 28, 1979	3B 3B P	Bill Madlock Lenny Randle Dave Roberts	San Francisco Giants	P P P	Ed Whitson Fred Breining Al Holland
Aug 2, 1979		Cash	New York Yankees	3B	Lenny Randle
Sept 21, 1979	P	Dock Ellis	New York Mets		Cash
Nov 16, 1979		No compensation (free agent signing)	California Angels	P	Bruce Kison
Nov 19, 1979	P	Andy Hassler	New York Mets		No compensation (free agent signing)
Nov 29, 1979		No compensation (free agent signing)	San Francisco Giants	2B	Rennie Stennett
Dec 21, 1979	P	Larry Andersen	Cleveland Indians	OF	Larry Littleton and minor league P John Burden
March 28, 1980	P	Eddie Solomon	Atlanta Braves		Minor league P Greg Field
April 1, 1980	P	Odell Jones	Seattle Mariners	P	Larry Andersen and cash
April 24, 1980		Cash	Seattle Mariners	P	Dave Roberts
June 10, 1980		Cash	California Angels	P	Andy Hassler
Aug 5, 1980	3B P	Kurt Bevacqua Mark Lee	San Diego Padres	OF 3B	Rick Lancellotti Luis Salazar
Sept 11, 1980	P	Jesse Jefferson	Toronto Blue Jays		Cash
Dec 9, 1980	C P P P	Gary Alexander Victor Cruz Rafael Vasquez Bob Owchinko	Cleveland Indians	P C	Bert Blyleven Manny Sanguillen
April 1, 1981	1B	Jason Thompson	California Angels	C P	Ed Ott Mickey Mahler
April 6, 1981	P	Ernie Camacho and cash	Oakland Athletics	P	Bob Owchinko

DATE		ACQUIRED	FROM		IN EXCHANGE FOR
Aug 20, 1981	1B	Willie Montanez	Montreal Expos	1B	John Milner
Aug 31, 1981	2B P	Johnny Ray minor league OF Kevin Houston Randy Niemann	Houston Astros	2B	Phil Garner
Sept 1, 1981		$50,000.	Montreal Expos	P	Grant Jackson
Oct 23, 1981	P	Manny Sarmiento	Boston Red Sox		Cash
Dec 11, 1981	C-OF	Brian Harper	California Angels	SS	Tim Foli
Dec 11, 1981	P	Tom Griffin	San Francisco Giants	1B	Dorian Boyland
Dec 17, 1981		Cash	California Angels	1B	Craig Cacek
Feb 2, 1982			Chicago White Sox	C	Joel Skinner
		(Claimed in compensation draft after Chicago lost free agent P Ed Farmer to Philadelphia.)			
March 21, 1982	P P	Ross Baumgarten Butch Edge	Chicago White Sox	IF P	Vance Law Ernie Camacho
April 3, 1982	P	Paul Moskau	Baltimore Orioles		Cash
April 9, 1982	OF	Reggie Walton	Seattle Mariners		Cash
June 14, 1982	3B	Jim Morrison	Chicago White Sox	P	Eddie Solomon
June 15, 1982	OF	Wayne Nordhagen	Philadelphia Phillies	OF	Bill Robinson
June 30, 1982	P	Larry McWilliams	Atlanta Braves	P	Pascual Perez minor league SS Carlos Rios
Aug 16, 1982	1B-OF	Richie Hebner	Detroit Tigers		Cash
Dec 1, 1982	C	Gene Tenace	St. Louis Cardinals		No compensation (free agent signing)
Dec 10, 1982		No compensation (free agent signing)	Houston Astros	OF	Omar Moreno
Dec 22, 1982	1B-OF	Lee Mazzilli	New York Yankees		Four minor leaguers: P John holland P Tim Burke 1B Jose Rivera OF Don Aubin
June 14, 1983	OF P	Marvell Wynne Steve Senteney	New York Mets	C	Junior Ortiz Minor league P Arthur Ray
Aug 2, 1983	P	Dave Tomlin	Montreal Expos		Cash
Aug 19, 1983	C	Milt May and cash	San Francisco Giants	C	Steve Nicosia

DATE		ACQUIRED	FROM		IN EXCHANGE FOR
Sept 7, 1983	OF	Miguel Dilone minor league P Mike Maitland	Chicago White Sox	P	Randy Niemann
Nov 12, 1983		Waiver price	Cincinnati Reds	P	Bob Owchinko
Dec 6, 1983	P	John Tudor	Boston Red Sox	OF	Mike Easler
Dec 7, 1983		No compensation (free agent signing)	Cincinnati Reds	OF	Dave Parker
Dec 19, 1983	OF	Amos Otis	Kansas City Royals		No compensation (free agent signing)
Jan 5, 1984		No compensation (free agent signing)	Chicago Cubs	IF	Richie Hebner
Jan 19, 1984		No compensation (free agent signing)	Montreal Expos	OF	Miguel Dilone
Feb 7, 1984		No compensation (free agent signing)	Texas Rangers	P	Jim Bibby

St. Louis Cardinals

The Best Trades

1. Acquired Lou Brock, Jack Spring, and Paul Toth from the Chicago Cubs for Ernie Broglio, Bobby Shantz, and Doug Clemens, June 15, 1964.
2. Acquired Orlando Cepeda from the San Francisco Giants for Ray Sadecki, May 8, 1966.
3. Acquired George Hendrick from the San Diego Padres for Eric Rasmussen, May 26, 1978.
4. Acquired Curt Flood and Joe Taylor from the Cincinnati Reds for Marty Kutyna and Ted Wieand, December 5, 1957.
5. Acquired Billy Southworth from the New York Giants for Heinie Mueller, June 14, 1926.

The Worst Trades

1. Traded Three Finger Brown and Jack O'Neill to the Chicago Cubs for Jack Taylor and Larry McLean, November 12, 1903.
2. Traded Steve Carlton to the Philadelphia Phillies for Rick Wise, February 25, 1972.
3. Traded Larry Hisle and John Cumberland to the Minnesota Twins for Wayne Granger, November 29, 1972.
4. Traded Bill Virdon to the Pittsburgh Pirates for Bobby Del Greco and Dick Littlefield, May 17, 1956.
5. Traded Dick Allen to the Los Angeles Dodgers for Ted Sizemore and Bob Stinson, October 5, 1970.

Trader: Branch Rickey

Who's the worst player in baseball's Hall of Fame? Chances are it's this man, who is also undoubtedly the game's outstanding executive genius. His keen insight, outstanding eye for talent, and indefatigable energy left a more emphatic mark on the game than any other individual with the possible exception of Babe Ruth.

As early as 1919, just two years into his twenty-five-year tenure as Cardinals president and manager, Rickey devised his plan for a farm system that would allow the have-not Cardinals to compete on a more equal basis with wealthier clubs. Rickey's system was designed for the Cards to develop their own players rather than buying them from the independent minor league clubs seeking the highest bidder. The first wave of farm-bred players to reach the parent club included Jim Bottomley, Chick Hafey, Tommy Thevenow, Lester Bell, Willie Sherdel, Taylor Douthit, and Flint Rhem. Each was eventually traded or sold to make room for the great players who followed: Pepper Martin, Bill Hallahan, Joe Medwick, Dizzy and Paul Dean, Rip Collins, and Terry Moore. They would in turn be dealt away to make room for Johnny Mize, Enos Slaughter, Mort and Walker Cooper, Stan Musial, Marty Marion, Harry Brecheen, and others. The parent club couldn't absorb all the talent being produced, and so they were sold for king's ransoms, with Rickey pocketing a percentage on every cash transaction.

Rickey firmly believed that it was better to unload a player a year too early than a year too late. He received maximum return for his ballplayers, most of whom declined after leaving St. Louis. Not only did this keep his club young and hungry, but it kept his payroll low by lopping off the more expensive later years of an established star's career. The trade that may best illustrate Rickey's application of these principles was his trade of Rogers Hornsby to the Giants for Frankie Frisch and Jimmy Ring in the winter of 1926.

Hornsby was not only the club's most popular player, but had just managed the team to its first world championship that season. While it was true his own production had slipped a bit, he nonetheless did hit .317, and was just breaking a string of six successive batting titles. But there had been bad blood between Hornsby and Rickey dating back to Rickey's own days as Cardinal manager, and Hornsby aggravated matters by getting into a protracted contract dispute with owner Sam Breadon. Breadon and Rickey approached New York Giants president Charles Stoneham and John McGraw, telling them, "You've wanted Hornsby for a long time. Well, you can have him now if you let us have Frisch and a pitcher." The deal was quickly finalized, and all hell broke loose in St. Louis.

Outraged citizens howled for Rickey's scalp. Rickey and Breadon were hanged in effigy. Newspaper editorials denounced the trade, and fans of long standing vowed they would never attend another Cardinals game. Hornsby didn't help matters by rebounding to have an excellent season, but Frisch himself hit .337, led the league in steals, and kept the Cards in the pennant race to the end. The long-term results vindicated Rickey: Hornsby had just four full seasons left in him, while Frisch gave the Cards ten solid years at second base.

Trader: Whitey Herzog

In five whirlwind days in December 1980, Whitey Herzog turned the Cardinals from a talented enigma into world champions. All of this came despite the fact that the players he dealt away included Ted Simmons, an All-Star catcher who was the club's most popular player; Rollie Fingers and Pete Vuckovich, pitchers who would immediately win back-to-back Cy Young Awards for their new club; and Terry Kennedy and Leon Durham, two of the most talented young players in the game.

The first deal would have been enough for most general managers: he sent Kennedy, the highly prized young catcher, and six other players to San Diego for Fingers, Gene Tenace and Bob Shirley. Not content to own one of the two best relievers in the National League, Herzog went out the next day and got the other one, Bruce Sutter, from the Cubs for three players, most prominently Leon Durham. He rested for two days, then pulled off the blockbuster deal of the decade: Fingers (expendable because of the acquisition of Sutter), Vuckovich, and Simmons (not needed because they had signed free agent Darrell Porter; not wanted because he was unwilling to shift to first base) to Milwaukee for Sixto Lezcano, David Green, Lary Sorenson, and Dave LaPoint. Green, regarded by many to be the top minor league prospect in the game, was the key to the deal; "We wouldn't have made it without him," Herzog maintained.

Herzog's Cards had the best record in the East in strike-riddled 1981, but he wasn't through. Tony Scott went to Houston for Joaquin Andujar; Sorenson and Silvio Martinez went off in a three-team trade that brought in Lonnie Smith; Lezcano, Luis DeLeon, and Garry Templeton, the erratic but awesomely talented shortstop who had worn out his welcome, went to San Diego for Ozzie Smith, Steve Mura, and Alan Olmsted; and in an unnoticed minor league transaction, pitcher Bob Sykes went to the Yankees for Willie McGee. The deals brought the Cards the 1982 World Series title.

So Whitey rested? No, on the June 15th trading deadline he dealt first baseman Keith Hernandez, perennial Gold Glove and former NL MVP and batting champ to the New York Mets for a pair of young pitchers, Neil Allen and Rick Ownbey. Irate fans denounced the trade and demanded Herzog's scalp. But Whitey has heard those screams before, and waits calmly for the passage of time to pass judgment on the deals.

DATE		ACQUIRED	FROM		IN EXCHANGE FOR
Unknown	OF	Dusty Miller	Cincinnati Reds		Cash
Jan 17, 1900	1B	Dan McGann	Washington Senators		Cash
	P	Gus Weyhing			
Jan 1900	OF	Patsy Donovan	Pittsburgh Pirates		$1,000.
Jan 1900		Cash	Chicago Cubs	2B	Cupid Childs
Jan 1900		Cash	Boston Braves	P	Nig Cuppy
Jan 1900	P	Jack Harper	Cleveland Spiders		Cash
	3B	Otto Krueger			
	2B	Joe Quinn			
	P	Jim Hughey			
Feb 11, 1900	3B	John McGraw	Baltimore Orioles		Cash
	2B	Bill Keister			
	C	Wilbert Robinson			
May 10, 1900		Cash	Pittsburgh Pirates	C	Jack O'Connor
May 1900		Cash	Brooklyn Dodgers	3B	Lave Cross
May 1900		Cash	Cincinnati Reds	2B	Joe Quinn
July 1900		Cash	Brooklyn Dodgers	P	Gus Weyhing
Unknown	C	Pop Schriver	Pittsburgh Pirates		Cash
May 1901	P	Chauncey Fisher	New York Giants	P	Bill Magee
Aug 1902	P	Clarence Currie	Cincinnati Reds		Cash
Jan 1903	3B	Jimmy Burke	Pittsburgh Pirates	IF	Otto Krueger
April 1903	P	Bob Rhoads	Chicago Cubs	P	Bob Wicker

DATE		ACQUIRED	FROM		IN EXCHANGE FOR
June 1903		Cash	Pittsburgh Pirates	C	Art Weaver
July 1903		Cash	Chicago Cubs	SS	Otto Williams
July 1903		Cash	Chicago Cubs	P	Clarence Currie
Dec 12, 1903	P C	Jack Taylor Larry McLean	Chicago Cubs	P C	Three Finger Brown Jack O'Neill
Feb 1904	1B	Jake Beckley	Cincinnati Reds		Cash
Sept 11, 1904		Cash	Boston Braves	OF	George Barclay
Jan 1905	C	John Warner	New York Giants		Cash
Feb 1905	P	Win Kellum	Cincinnati Reds		Cash
July 4, 1905	SS	George McBride	Pittsburgh Pirates	3B	Dave Brain
July 16, 1905		Waiver price	Philadelphia Phillies	P	Kid Nichols
Aug 10, 1905		Cash	Detroit Tigers	C	John Warner
May 17, 1906		Cash	Cincinnati Reds	1B	Oscar Stanage
June 3, 1906		Cash	Pittsburgh Pirates	P	Chappie McFarland
June 3, 1906	P	Ed Karger	Pittsburgh Pirates		Cash
July 1, 1906	P C	Fred Beebe Pete Noonan and cash	Chicago Cubs	P	Jack Taylor
July 13, 1906	OF C	Sam Mertes Doc Marshall	New York Giants	OF	Spike Shannon
July 25, 1906	P 1B	Carl Druhot Shad Barry	Cincinnati Reds	OF	Homer Smoot
June 10, 1907	P	Johnny Lush	Philadelphia Phillies	P	Charlie Brown
July 4, 1907	OF	Harry Wolter	Pittsburgh Pirates		Cash
July 5, 1907		Cash	Brooklyn Dodgers	OF	Al Burch
Oct 1907		Cash	Pittsburgh Pirates	P	Babe Adams
May 1908	P	Charlie Rhodes	Cincinnati Reds		Waiver price
June 1908		Cash	Chicago Cubs	C	Doc Marshall
July 1908		Cash	New York Giants	2B	Shad Barry

DATE		ACQUIRED	FROM		IN EXCHANGE FOR
Dec 12, 1908	C	Admiral Schlei	Cincinnati Reds	P P	Ed Karger Art Fromme
Dec 12, 1908	C	Roger Bresnahan	New York Giants	C P OF	Admiral Schlei Bugs Raymond Red Murray
Dec 1908	SS	Rudy Hulswitt	Cincinnati Reds		Cash
Aug 19, 1909	3B OF	Jap Barbeau Alan Storke	Pittsburgh Pirates	3B	Bobby Byrne
Aug 22, 1909	3B	Mike Mowrey	Cincinnati Reds	2B	Chappy Charles
Jan 1910	P	Vic Willis	Pittsburgh Pirates		Cash
Feb 1910	2B OF P	Miller Huggins Rebel Oakes Frank Corridon	Cincinnati Reds	P 3B	Fred Beebe Alan Storke
May 1910	OF	Elmer Zacher	New York Giants		Cash
Jan 1911		Cash	Pittsburgh Pirates	C	Bill Kelly
April 1911	P	Joe Willis	St. Louis Browns		Cash
April 1912	P	Sandy Burk	Brooklyn Dodgers		Cash
April 1913	OF	Jimmy Sheckard	Chicago Cubs		Cash
June 8, 1913		Cash	Chicago Cubs	C	Roger Bresnahan
July 1913		Waiver price	Cincinnati Reds	OF	Jimmy Sheckard
July 1913	P	Doc Crandall	New York Giants	C	Larry McLean
July 1913		Cash	New York Giants	P	Doc Crandall
Aug 25, 1913		Cash	New York Yankees	OF	Frank Gilhooley
Dec 12, 1913	3B 1B OF OF P	Art Butler Dots Miller Cozy Dolan Owen Wilson Hank Robinson	Pittsburgh Pirates	1B 3B P	Ed Konetchy Mike Mowrey Bob Harmon
June 1914	P	Hub Perdue	Boston Braves	OF OF	Possum Whitted Ted Cather
June 1914	OF	Joe Riggert	Brooklyn Dodgers	P	Casey Hageman
July 1914		Cash	Brooklyn Dodgers	P	Bill Steele
Feb 18, 1915		Cash	New York Giants	P	Pol Perritt
Feb 28, 1915	OF	Ham Hyatt	Pittsburgh Pirates		Waiver price

DATE		ACQUIRED	FROM		IN EXCHANGE FOR
April 8, 1915	OF C	Mike Gonzalez Bob Bescher	Cincinnati Reds	C	Ivy Wingo
July 23, 1915		Cash	New York Yankees	OF	Elmer Miller
July 24, 1915	P	Red Ames	Cincinnati Reds		Cash
July 23, 1916		$10,000.	New York Giants	P	Slim Sallee
April 1917	P	Gene Packard	Chicago Cubs		Cash
May 24, 1917	SS	Ike McAuley	Pittsburgh Pirates		Waiver price
May 1917	2B	Gene Paulette	St. Louis Browns		Waiver price
June 14, 1917	3B	Doug Baird	Pittsburgh Pirates	P	Bob Steele
Sept 1917		Waiver price	Detroit Tigers	SS	Tony DeFate
April 4, 1918	2B	Bert Niehoff and $500.	Philadelphia Phillies	P	Milt Watson
May 18, 1918		Waiver price	New York Giants	2B	Bert Niehoff
June 20, 1918		Cash	New York Yankees	P	Hank Robinson
June 1918	OF	Marty Kavanagh	Cleveland Indians		Cash
Aug 1918		Cash	Detroit Tigers	OF	Marty Kavanagh
Jan 21, 1919	3B C P	Milt Stock Pickles Dillhoefer Dixie Davis	Philadelphia Phillies	3B IF P	Doug Baird Stuffy Stewart Gene Packard
Jan 1919	SS	Doc Lavan	Washington Senators		Cash
Feb 1, 1919	OF	Burt Shotton	Washington Senators		Waiver price
May 1919		Waiver price	New York Giants	C	Mike Gonzalez
May 1919		Cash	Boston Braves	OF	Walt Cruise
July 14, 1919	P P 3B	Elmer Jacobs Frank Woodward Doug Baird	Philadelphia Phillies	P 2B	Lee Meadows Gene Paulette
July 1919	P	Ferdie Schupp	New York Giants	C	Frank Snyder
Aug 1919		Cash	Brooklyn Dodgers	3B	Doug Baird
Aug 1919	1B	Fritz Mollwitz	Pittsburgh Pirates		Cash
Sept 5, 1919		Cash	Philadelphia Phillies	P	Red Ames

(Ames was returned to St. Louis in October.)

DATE		ACQUIRED	FROM		IN EXCHANGE FOR
Sept 10, 1919	2B	Hal Janvrin	Washington Senators		Waiver price
Jan 1920		Cash	Philadelphia Phillies	2B	Dots Miller
Aug 1920	C	Lew McCarty	New York Giants		Cash
Nov 9, 1920	OF	Les Mann	Boston Braves		Cash
June 18, 1921	P	Jeff Pfeffer	Brooklyn Dodgers	P IF	Ferdie Schupp Hal Janvrin
May 30, 1922	OF	Max Flack	Chicago Cubs	OF	Cliff Heathcote
Oct 1922	P	Fred Toney	New York Giants		Waiver price
Feb 15, 1923	OF 1B	Hy Myers Ray Schmandt	Brooklyn Dodgers	1B	Jack Fournier
April 27, 1924	C	Mike Gonzalez	Brooklyn Dodgers	2B	Milt Stock
June 6, 1924		Cash	Philadelphia Phillies	OF	Joe Schultz
June 13, 1924	P	Leo Dickerman	Brooklyn Dodgers	P	Bill Doak
June 17, 1924		Cash	Boston Braves	P	Lou North
July 11, 1924		Waiver price	Pittsburgh Pirates	P	Jeff Pfeffer
April 22, 1925		Cash	Cincinnati Reds	OF	Hy Myers
May 4, 1925	OF	Hy Myers	Cincinnati Reds		Cash
May 23, 1925	C	Bob O'Farrell	Chicago Cubs	C OF	Mike Gonzalez Howard Freigau
Dec 11, 1925	P	Vic Keen	Chicago Cubs	SS	Jimmy Cooney
April 19, 1926		Cash	Boston Braves	OF	Jack Smith
June 14, 1926	OF	Billy Southworth	New York Giants	OF	Heinie Mueller
June 21, 1926		Waiver price	Chicago Cubs	P	Walter Huntzinger
June 22, 1926	P	Grover Alexander	Chicago Cubs		Waiver price
Dec 20, 1926	2B P	Frankie Frisch Jimmy Ring	New York Giants	2B	Rogers Hornsby
Feb 28, 1927	P	Bob McGraw	Brooklyn Dodgers	2B	Jake Flowers
Sept 10, 1927	P	Tony Kaufmann	Philadelphia Phillies		Cash
Dec 13, 1927	OF SS C	Johnny Mokan Jimmy Cooney Bubber Jonnard	Philadelphia Phillies	OF P	Johnny Schulte Jimmy Ring

DATE		ACQUIRED	FROM		IN EXCHANGE FOR
Dec 18, 1927		Waiver price	Boston Braves	SS	Jimmy Cooney
Dec 1927		Cash	Philadelphia Phillies	P	Bob McGraw
March 25, 1928	2B	Andy High and $25,000.	Boston Braves	3B	Les Bell
May 1, 1928	OF	George Harper	New York Giants	C	Bob O'Farrell
May 11, 1928	C	Jimmie Wilson	Philadelphia Phillies	C OF	Spud Davis Homer Peel
July 10, 1928	C	Earl Smith	Pittsburgh Pirates		Cash
Dec 8, 1928		Cash	Boston Braves	2B	Rabbit Maranville
Dec 8, 1928		Cash	Boston Braves	OF	George Harper
Dec 13, 1928	SS	Heinie Sand and $10,000.	Philadelphia Phillies	SS	Tommy Thevenow
Aug 28, 1929	P	Carmen Hill	Pittsburgh Pirates		Waiver price
Nov 1929	3B	Sparky Adams	Pittsburgh Pirates		Cash
Dec 11, 1929	OF P	Homer Peel Bob McGraw	Philadelphia Phillies	P C	Grover Alexander Harry McCurdy
April 10, 1930	OF IF	Showboat Fisher Doc Farrell	New York Giants	OF	Wally Roettger
May 15, 1930	P	Ralph Judd	New York Giants	P	Clarence Mitchell
June 16, 1930	P	Burleigh Grimes	Boston Braves	P P	Fred Frankhouse Bill Sherdel
June 29, 1930		Waiver price	Chicago Cubs	IF	Doc Farrell
Jan 1931		Waiver price	Boston Braves	P	Hal Haid
June 15, 1931	2B	Jake Flowers	Brooklyn Dodgers		Waiver price
June 15, 1931	OF	Wally Roettger	Cincinnati Reds	OF	Taylor Douthit
Dec 2, 1931	OF	Nick Cullop and cash	Cincinnati Reds	2B	Andy High
Dec 1931	P OF	Bud Teachout Hack Wilson	Chicago Cubs	P	Burleigh Grimes
Dec 1931		Cash	Cincinnati Reds	OF	Wally Roettger
Jan 23, 1932		Minor league P Bob Parham and $45,000.	Brooklyn Dodgers	OF	Hack Wilson
Jan 26, 1932	SS	Hod Ford	Cincinnati Reds		Cash
Jan 1932	SS	Jimmy Reese	New York Yankees		Waiver price

DATE		ACQUIRED	FROM		IN EXCHANGE FOR
April 11, 1932	OF P	Harvey Hendrick Benny Frey and cash	Cincinnati Reds	OF	Chick Hafey
May 10, 1932		Cash	Cincinnati Reds	P	Benny Frey
May 18, 1932	P	Bill Sherdel	Boston Braves		Waiver price
May 30, 1932		Cash	Philadelphia Phillies	P SS	Flint Rhem Eddie Delker
June 5, 1932		Cash	Cincinnati Reds	OF	Harvey Hendrick
June 28, 1932	OF	Rube Bressler	Philadelphia Phillies		Waiver price
Oct 10, 1932	OF C P P	Ethan Allen Bob O'Farrell Bill Walker Jim Mooney	New York Giants	C P	Gus Mancuso Ray Starr
Dec 17, 1932	OF P	Estel Crabtree Ownie Carroll	Cincinnati Reds	1B	Jim Bottomley
Feb 1933	P SS	Dazzy Vance Gordon Slade	Brooklyn Dodgers	2B P	Jake Flowers Ownie Carroll
May 7, 1933	SS P P	Leo Durocher Butch Henline Jack Ogden	Cincinnati Reds	P 2B P	Paul Derringer Sparky Adams Allyn Stout
Aug 4, 1933	P	Burleigh Grimes	Chicago Cubs		Waiver price
Nov 15, 1933	C IF	Spud Davis Eddie Delker (Wilson was named manager of the Phillies.)	Philadelphia Phillies	C	Jimmie Wilson
Dec 1933		Waiver price	Cincinnati Reds	SS	Gordon Slade
Jan 11, 1934	P	Glenn Spencer (O'Farrell was named Cincinnati manager.)	Cincinnati Reds	C P	Bob O'Farrell Syl Johnson
Jan 1934		Cash	Philadelphia Phillies	OF	Ethan Allen
Feb 11, 1934	P	Flint Rhem	Philadelphia Phillies		Cash
Feb 1934	OF	Kiddo Davis	New York Giants	OF	George Watkins
May 18, 1934	P	Phil Collins	Philadelphia Phillies		Cash
May 1934		Waiver price	Pittsburgh Pirates	P	Burleigh Grimes
June 15, 1934	OF	Chick Fullis	Philadelphia Phillies	OF	Kiddo Davis
June 23, 1934		Cash	Boston Red Sox	P	Flint Rhem
June 25, 1934		Waiver price	Cincinnati Reds	P	Dazzy Vance
Sept 11, 1934	OF	Red Worthington	Boston Braves		Waiver price

DATE		ACQUIRED	FROM		IN EXCHANGE FOR
Oct 26, 1934	P	Pat Malone	Chicago Cubs	C	Ken O'Dea
Nov 3, 1934		$25,000.	Cincinnati Reds	OF	Ival Goodman
Nov 3, 1934		$30,000.	Cincinnati Reds	3B	Lew Riggs
Nov 21, 1934	P P	Bud Tinning Dick Ward and cash	Chicago Cubs	P	Tex Carleton
Dec 13, 1934		Cash	Cincinnati Reds	1B	Johnny Mize
		(Mize was returned to St. Louis because of a bad knee.)			
March 26, 1935		$15,000.	New York Yankees	P	Pat Malone
Dec 9, 1935	P 1B	Roy Parmelee Phil Weintraub and cash	New York Giants	2B	Burgess Whitehead
May 31, 1936		Cash	Cincinnati Reds	P	Bill Hallahan
July 1936	P	George Earnshaw	Brooklyn Dodgers		Cash
July 1936	3B	Johnny Vergez	Philadelphia Phillies		Cash
Aug 6, 1936	P	Si Johnson	Cincinnati Reds	P	Bill Walker
Oct 8, 1936	P	Lon Warneke	Chicago Cubs	1B P	Ripper Collins Roy Parmelee
Dec 2, 1936		Cash	Cincinnati Reds	C	Spud Davis
Dec 2, 1936		Cash	Cincinnati Reds	SS	Charley Gelbert
Dec 3, 1936	OF	Frenchy Bordagaray	Brooklyn Dodgers	OF	Tom Winsett
July 1937	OF	Randy Moore	Brooklyn Dodgers		Cash
Oct 4, 1937	OF 2B 3B P	Johnny Cooney Jim Bucher Joe Stripp Roy Henshaw	Brooklyn Dodgers	SS	Leo Durocher
Oct 1937	C	Tom Padden	Pittsburgh Pirates		Cash
Dec 20, 1937	P	Al Smith	New York Giants		Cash
Dec 29, 1937		Waiver price	Philadelphia Phillies	P	Al Smith
Feb 2, 1938	P	Guy Bush	Boston Braves		Cash
April 16, 1938	P P OF	Curt Davis Clyde Shoun Tuck Stainback and $185,000.	Chicago Cubs	P	Dizzy Dean

DATE		ACQUIRED	FROM		IN EXCHANGE FOR
June 1938		Waiver price	Philadelphia Phillies	OF	Tuck Stainback
Aug 1, 1938		Cash	Boston Braves	3B	Joe Stripp
Dec 8, 1938		Cash	Chicago Cubs	P	Ray Harrell
Dec 8, 1938	OF	Dusty Cooke	Cincinnati Reds	OF	Frenchy Bordagaray
March 1939		Waiver price	Brooklyn Dodgers	P	Jim Winford
Aug 14, 1939	SS	Lyn Lary	Brooklyn Dodgers		Waiver price
Sept 25, 1939		Cash	Cleveland Indians	P	Nate Andrews
Dec 27, 1939	2B SS	Steve Mesner Gene Lillard and cash	Chicago Cubs	P	Ken Raffensberger
Feb 6, 1940		Cash	Brooklyn Dodgers	C	Herman Franks
April 15, 1940	P	Newt Kimball	Brooklyn Dodgers		Cash
		(Sale was cancelled by Commissioner Landis.)			
May 14, 1940	P P	Harry Gumbert Paul Dean and cash	New York Giants	P	Bill McGee
June 12, 1940	OF P P 1B	Ernie Koy Carl Doyle Sam Nahem Bert Haas and $125,000.	Brooklyn Dodgers	OF P	Joe Medwick Curt Davis
June 13, 1940	P	Ira Hutchinson	Brooklyn Dodgers		Cash
Nov 19, 1940	P	Tot Pressnell	Brooklyn Dodgers		Cash
Nov 25, 1940		Cash	New York Giants	IF	Joe Orengo
Dec 2, 1940		Cash	Pittsburgh Pirates	2B	Stu Martin
Dec 4, 1940	C	Gus Mancuso Minor league P John Pintar and $65,000.	Brooklyn Dodgers	C	Mickey Owen
Dec 5, 1940		Cash	New York Giants	P	Bob Bowman
Dec 16, 1940		Cash	Cincinnati Reds	P	Tot Pressnell
May 14, 1941		Cash	Cincinnati Reds	OF	Ernie Koy
Sept 2, 1941		Cash	Chicago Cubs	P	Hank Gornicki
Dec 10, 1941		$30,000.	Brooklyn Dodgers	OF	Don Padgett

DATE		ACQUIRED	FROM		IN EXCHANGE FOR
Dec 11, 1941	C P 1B	Ken O'Dea Bill Lohrman Johnny McCarthy and $50,000.	New York Giants	1B	Johnny Mize
May 5, 1942		Cash	New York Giants	C	Gus Mancuso
May 5, 1942		Cash	New York Giants	P	Bill Lohrman
May 6, 1942		Cash	Cincinnati Reds	P	Clyde Shoun
July 8, 1942		$75,000.	Chicago Cubs	P	Lon Warneke
Jan 1943	OF	Frank Demaree	Boston Braves		Cash
June 1, 1943	OF OF	Danny Litwhiler Earl Naylor	Philadelphia Phillies	OF OF OF	Buster Adams Coaker Triplett Dain Clay
June 15, 1944		Cash	Cincinnati Reds	P	Harry Gumbert
Feb 5, 1945	SS	Eddie Joost and $40,000.	Boston Braves	OF	Johnny Hopp
May 8, 1945	OF	Buster Adams	Philadelphia Phillies	3B OF	John Antonelli Glenn Crawford
May 23, 1945	P	Red Barrett and $60,000.	Boston Braves	P	Mort Cooper
Jan 5, 1946		$175,000.	New York Giants	C	Walker Cooper
Jan 5, 1946		$30,000.	Pittsburgh Pirates	2B	Jimmy Brown
Feb 5, 1946		Cash	Philadelphia Phillies	P	Al Jurisich
Feb 5, 1946		Cash	Boston Braves	OF	Johnny Wyrostek
Feb 5, 1946		$40,000.	Boston Braves	OF	Johnny Hopp
April 15, 1946		$25,000.	Boston Braves	1B P	Ray Sanders Max Surkont
May 2, 1946	C	Clyde Kluttz	Philadelphia Phillies	SS	Emil Verban
May 14, 1946		Cash	Boston Braves	P	Ernie White
June 9, 1946		Cash	Boston Braves	OF	Danny Litwhiler
July 6, 1946		Cash	Philadelphia Phillies	P	Blix Donnelly
July 8, 1946		Cash	Boston Braves	C	Ken O'Dea
Dec 9, 1946		Cash	Boston Braves	P	Red Barrett
Dec 26, 1946		Cash	Pittsburgh Pirates	C	Clyde Kluttz

DATE	ACQUIRED		FROM	IN EXCHANGE FOR	
Jan 30, 1947		Cash	Brooklyn Dodgers	OF	Walter Sessi
March 21, 1947		Cash	Philadelphia Phillies	OF	Buster Adams
April 18, 1947		Cash	Boston Braves	P	Johnny Beazley
May 3, 1947	OF	Ron Northey	Philadelphia Phillies	OF P	Harry Walker Freddy Schmidt
April 7, 1948	IF	Ralph LaPointe and $30,000.	Philadelphia Phillies	1B	Dick Sisler
May 2, 1948		Cash	Chicago Cubs	3B	Jeff Cross
Nov 8, 1948	1B	Babe Young	Cincinnati Reds	P	Ken Burkhart
Jan 29, 1949		$125,000.	Pittsburgh Pirates	P	Murry Dickson
June 15, 1949		Cash	Pittsburgh Pirates	OF	Ed Sauer
Dec 14, 1949	OF	Harry Walker	Cincinnati Reds	2B OF	Lou Klein Ron Northey
April 27, 1950	OF	Johnny Blatnik	Philadelphia Phillies	P	Ken Johnson
May 3, 1950	SS	Eddie Miller	Philadelphia Phillies		Waiver price
May 1950		Cash	New York Giants	P	Jim Hearn
Sept 7, 1950	OF	Peanuts Lowrey	Cincinnati Reds		Cash
April 27, 1951	OF	Johnny Blatnik	Philadelphia Phillies	P	Ken Johnson
May 14, 1951	3B	Billy Johnson	New York Yankees	1B	Don Bollweg and $15,000.
May 17, 1951	SS	Stan Rojek	Pittsburgh Pirates	OF 1B	Erv Dusak Rocky Nelson
June 15, 1951	P OF	Cliff Chambers Wally Westlake	Pittsburgh Pirates	OF P P C 3B	Bill Howerton Howie Pollet Ted Wilks Joe Garagiola Dick Cole
Aug 1, 1951	C	Bob Scheffing	Cincinnati Reds		Waiver price
Dec 11, 1951	2B	Eddie Stanky (Stanky was named St. Louis manager.)	New York Giants	OF P	Chuck Diering Max Lanier
March 26, 1952	IF	Gene Mauch	Boston Braves		Waiver price
May 3, 1952	P	Bill Werle	Pittsburgh Pirates	P	George Munger
May 13, 1952	1B SS	Dick Sisler Virgil Stallcup	Cincinnati Reds	3B OF	Eddie Kazak Wally Westlake

DATE		ACQUIRED	FROM		IN EXCHANGE FOR
Sept 30, 1952		Waiver price	Philadelphia Phillies	3B	Tommy Glaviano
Oct 1, 1952		Waiver price	St. Louis Browns	P	Bob Habenicht
Oct 1, 1952		Waiver price	St. Louis Browns	1B	Ed Mickelson
May 23, 1953	P	Eddie Erautt	Cincinnati Reds	P	Jackie Collum
June 2, 1953	P	Hal White	St. Louis Browns		Waiver price
June 14, 1953	3B	Pete Castiglione	Pittsburgh Pirates	OF	Hal Rice and cash
June 15, 1953	C	Sal Yvars	New York Giants		$12,500.
Dec 2, 1953	SS	Alex Grammas	Cincinnati Reds	P	Jack Crimian and $100,000.
Feb 23, 1954	P	Vic Raschi	New York Yankees		$85,000.
April 11, 1954	OF P	Bill Virdon Mel Wright minor league OF Emil Tellinger	New York Yankees	OF	Enos Slaughter
April 30, 1954		$12,500.	Chicago Cubs	1B	Steve Bilko
May 7, 1954	P	Carl Scheib	Philadelphia Athletics		Cash
Aug 8, 1954	P	Ben Wade	Brooklyn Dodgers		Waiver price
Dec 8, 1954	P	Frank Smith	Cincinnati Reds	3B P	Ray Jablonski Gerry Staley
Jan 11, 1955	P	Paul LaPalme	Pittsburgh Pirates	P	Ben Wade and cash
June 3, 1955	OF	Pete Whisenant	Milwaukee Braves	C	Del Rice
Sept 8, 1955	P	Ben Flowers	Detroit Tigers	P	Bobby Tiefenauer
Dec 4, 1955	P	Ellis Kinder	Boston Red Sox		Waiver price
Jan 31, 1956	P	Jackie Collum	Cincinnati Reds	P IF	Brooks Lawrence Sonny Senerchia
March 30, 1956	OF	Hank Sauer	Chicago Cubs	OF	Pete Whisenant
April 10, 1956		Waiver price	Cincinnati Reds	P	Frank Smith
May 1, 1956	3B	Milt Smith	Cincinnati Reds	P	Paul LaPalme
May 5, 1956	P	Max Surkont	Pittsburgh Pirates	P	Luis Arroyo
May 11, 1956	3B	Grady Hatton	Boston Red Sox		Cash

DATE		ACQUIRED	FROM		IN EXCHANGE FOR
May 11, 1956	P P	Murry Dickson Herm Wehmeier	Philadelphia Phillies	P P P	Harvey Haddix Ben Flowers Stu Miller
May 14, 1956	3B	Bobby Morgan	Philadelphia Phillies	2B	Solly Hemus
May 16, 1956	OF	Chuck Harmon	Cincinnati Reds	OF SS	Joe Frazier Alex Grammas
May 17, 1956	P OF	Dick Littlefield Bobby Del Greco	Pittsburgh Pirates	OF	Bill Virdon
June 14, 1956	3B C P 1B	Alvin Dark Ray Katt Don Liddle Whitey Lockman	New York Giants	OF 2B P P C	Jackie Brandt Red Schoendienst Gordon Jones Dick Littlefield Bill Sarni
July 11, 1956		Waiver price	Chicago White Sox	P	Ellis Kinder
July 30, 1956	1B	Rocky Nelson	Brooklyn Dodgers		Waiver price
Aug 1, 1956		Cash	Baltimore Orioles	IF	Grady Hatton
Oct 1, 1956		Cash	New York Giants	P	Gordon Jones
Nov 19, 1956	OF	Del Ennis	Philadelphia Phillies	3B OF	Bobby Morgan Rip Repulski
Dec 11, 1956	C P P 3B	Hobie Landrith Jim Davis Sam Jones Eddie Miksis	Chicago Cubs	P P C	Tom Poholsky Jackie Collum Ray Katt minor league P Wally Lammers
Feb 26, 1957	P	Hoyt Wilhelm	New York Giants	1B	Whitey Lockman
April 20, 1957	OF	Jim King	Chicago Cubs	P OF	Ed Mayer Bobby Del Greco
May 10, 1957	OF	Glen Gorbous	Philadelphia Phillies	OF	Chuck Harmon
May 14, 1957		Cash	Pittsburgh Pirates	P	Bob Smith
June 4, 1957		Waiver price	New York Giants	P	Jim Davis
Aug 31, 1957	OF	Irv Noren	Kansas City Athletics		Waiver price
Sept 19, 1957		Waiver price	Baltimore Orioles	IF	Eddie Miksis
Sept 21, 1957		Cash	Cleveland Indians	P	Hoyt Wilhelm
Dec 5, 1957	OF OF	Curt Flood Joe Taylor	Cincinnati Reds	P P	Marty Kutyna Ted Wieand
April 2, 1958	C	Ray Katt	San Francisco Giants	OF	Jim King
April 19, 1958	P	Phil Paine	Milwaukee Braves		Waiver price

DATE		ACQUIRED	FROM		IN EXCHANGE FOR
May 13, 1958		Cash	Detroit Tigers	P	Herm Wehmeier
May 20, 1958	P	Jim Brosnan	Chicago Cubs	3B	Alvin Dark
June 14, 1958	P	Sal Maglie	New York Yankees	P	Joe McClain
June 15, 1958	3B SS	Gene Freese Johnny O'Brien	Pittsburgh Pirates	SS	Dick Schofield and cash
July 2, 1958		Waiver price	Cleveland Indians	P	Morrie Martin
July 9, 1958	P	Chuck Stobbs	Washington Senators		Waiver price
July 25, 1958		Waiver price	Baltimore Orioles	OF	Joe Taylor
Sept 29, 1958	2B	Solly Hemus	Philadelphia Phillies	3B	Gene Freese
Oct 3, 1958	1B P SS	George Crowe Alex Kellner Alex Grammas	Cincinnati Reds	P 3B OF	Bob Mabe Eddie Kasko Del Ennis
Oct 8, 1958	P P	Ernie Broglio Marv Grissom	San Francisco Giants	C P 3B	Hobie Landrith Billy Muffett Benny Valenzuela
Oct 14, 1958	2B P	Jim Brideweser Art Ceccarelli	Baltimore Orioles	3B	Jim Finigan
Dec 3, 1958	OF	Chuck Essegian	Philadelphia Phillies	SS	Ruben Amaro
Dec 4, 1958	OF	Gino Cimoli	Los Angeles Dodgers	OF P	Wally Moon Phil Paine
Feb 2, 1959	IF	Billy Harrell	Cleveland Indians		Waiver price
March 15, 1959	P	Dean Stone	Boston Red Sox	P	Nels Chittum
March 25, 1959	1B 3B	Bill White Ray Jablonski	San Francisco Giants	P P	Sam Jones Don Choate
May 19, 1959	OF	Charlie King	Chicago Cubs	OF	Irv Noren
June 8, 1959	P	Hal Jeffcoat	Cincinnati Reds	P	Jim Brosnan
June 15, 1959	3B	Dick Gray	Los Angeles Dodgers	OF P	Chuck Essegian Lloyd Merritt
July 25, 1959	C	J W Porter	Washington Senators		Waiver price
July 26, 1959		Waiver price	New York Yankees	P	Gary Blaylock
Aug 20, 1959		Waiver price	Kansas City Athletics	3B	Ray Jablonski
Dec 2, 1959	OF	Bob Nieman	Baltimore Orioles	OF	Gene Green
Dec 4, 1959	C	Carl Sawatski	Philadelphia Phillies	OF	Bobby Gene Smith
Dec 15, 1959	2B OF	Daryl Spencer Leon Wagner	San Francisco Giants	2B	Don Blasingame

DATE		ACQUIRED	FROM		IN EXCHANGE FOR
Dec 21, 1959	P	Ron Kline	Pittsburgh Pirates	OF P	Gino Cimoli Tom Cheney
May 19, 1960		Cash	Chicago White Sox	P	Frank Barnes
May 28, 1960	2B P	Julian Javier Ed Bauta	Pittsburgh Pirates	P 3B	Vinegar Bend Mizell Dick Gray
June 15, 1960	OF	Walt Moryn	Chicago Cubs	OF	Jim McKnight
June 15, 1960	OF	John Glenn	Los Angeles Dodgers	P	Jim Donohue
July 29, 1960	P	Bob Grim	Cincinnati Reds		Cash
Aug 2, 1960		Waiver price	Cincinnati Reds	P	Marshall Bridges
Sept 2, 1960	SS	Rocky Bridges	Cleveland Indians		Cash
Sept 7, 1960		Cash	Baltimore Orioles	C	Del Rice
Jan 26, 1961	P	Al Cicotte	Los Angeles Angels	OF P OF	Leon Wagner Cal Browning Ellis Burton and cash
April 10, 1961		Cash	Los Angeles Angels	P	Ron Kline
May 10, 1961	3B	Joe Morgan and cash	Cleveland Indians	OF	Bob Nieman
May 30, 1961	SS OF	Bob Lillis Carl Warwick	Los Angeles Dodgers	SS	Daryl Spencer
June 15, 1961		Cash	Pittsburgh Pirates	OF	Walt Moryn
July 21, 1961		Cash	Kansas City Athletics	P	Mickey McDermott
Oct 13, 1961		Cash	Houston Astros	P	Al Cicotte
Nov 27, 1961	OF	Minnie Minoso	Chicago White Sox	1B	Joe Cunningham
Dec 1, 1961	P	Johnny Kucks	Baltimore Orioles		Minor leaguer Ron Kabbes
March 30, 1962		Cash	Los Angeles Angels	1B	Frank Leja
April 7, 1962	P	Larry Locke	Cleveland Indians		Minor league OF Al Herring
April 28, 1962	P	Don Ferrarese	Philadelphia Phillies	P	Larry Locke and cash
May 7, 1962	P	Bobby Shantz	Houston Astros	OF P	Carl Warwick John Anderson
June 5, 1962	OF P	Bobby Gene Smith Daryl Robertson	Chicago Cubs	OF SS	Don Landrum Alex Grammas
Sept 1, 1962	P	Harvey Branch	Chicago Cubs	P	Paul Toth

DATE		ACQUIRED	FROM		IN EXCHANGE FOR
Oct 17, 1962	OF P C	George Altman Don Cardwell Moe Thacker	Chicago Cubs	P C P	Larry Jackson Jimmie Schaffer Lindy McDaniel
Nov 19, 1962	SS P	Dick Groat Diomedes Olivo	Pittsburgh Pirates	SS P	Julio Gotay Don Cardwell
Dec 15, 1962	P SS	Ron Taylor Jack Kubiszyn	Cleveland Indians	1B	Fred Whitfield
March 25, 1963	P	Bob Humphreys	Detroit Tigers		Cash
March 25, 1963	IF	Leo Burke	Los Angeles Angels		Cash
April 2, 1963		Cash and minor league player to be named later	Washington Senators	OF	Minnie Minoso
June 15, 1963	P	Lew Burdette	Milwaukee Braves	1B P	Gene Oliver Bob Sadowski
June 24, 1963	P	Barney Schultz	Chicago Cubs	IF	Leo Burke
July 29, 1963	OF	Jacke Davis and cash	New York Mets	OF	Duke Carmel
Aug 5, 1963	P	Ken MacKenzie	New York Mets	P	Ed Bauta
Oct 1, 1963	C	Jimmie Coker	San Francisco Giants	P	Ken MacKenzie
Nov 4, 1963	P	Roger Craig	New York Mets	OF P	George Altman Bill Wakefield
Feb 17, 1964	OF	Carl Warwick	Houston Astros	OF P	Jim Beauchamp Chuck Taylor
April 9, 1964	C	Bob Uecker	Milwaukee Braves	C OF	Jimmie Coker Gary Kolb
June 2, 1964	P	Glen Hobbie	Chicago Cubs	P	Lew Burdette
June 13, 1964	OF	Bob Skinner	Cincinnati Reds		Minor league P Jim Saul and cash
June 15, 1964	OF P P	Lou Brock Jack Spring Paul Toth	Chicago Cubs	P P OF	Ernie Broglio Bobby Shantz Doug Clemens
July 7, 1964		Cash	Chicago White Sox	1B	Jeoff Long
Nov 24, 1964	P	Fritz Ackley	Chicago White Sox		Cash
Dec 7, 1964	P 2B	Tracy Stallard Elio Chacon	New York Mets	OF P	Johnny Lewis Gordie Richardson
Dec 14, 1964	P	Bob Purkey	Cincinnati Reds	OF P	Charlie James Roger Craig
Dec 15, 1964	OF	Tito Francona	Cleveland Indians		Cash
April 10, 1965	2B	Bobby Pfeil minor league P Hal Gibson	Chicago Cubs	P	Bob Humphreys

DATE		ACQUIRED	FROM		IN EXCHANGE FOR
May 11, 1965		Waiver price	Chicago Cubs	P	Dave Dowling
June 15, 1965	P P	Hal Woodeshick Chuck Taylor	Houston Astros	P P	Mike Cuellar Ron Taylor
July 24, 1965		Cash	Baltimore Orioles	OF	Carl Warwick
Oct 20, 1965	3B P	Charley Smith Al Jackson	New York Mets	3B	Ken Boyer
Oct 27, 1965	C P OF	Pat Corrales Art Mahaffey Alex Johnson	Philadelphia Phillies	1B SS C	Bill White Dick Groat Bob Uecker
April 7, 1966		Cash	Pittsburgh Pirates	P	Bob Purkey
May 8, 1966	1B	Orlando Cepeda	San Francisco Giants	P	Ray Sadecki
June 22, 1966		Cash	Chicago Cubs	P	Curt Simmons
Dec 8, 1966	OF	Roger Maris	New York Yankees	3B	Charley Smith
Dec 14, 1966	C	Johnny Romano and minor league P Lee White	Chicago White Sox	OF P	Walt Williams Don Dennis
April 1, 1967	SS OF	Ed Bressoud Danny Napoleon and cash	New York Mets	IF P IF	Jerry Buchek Art Mahaffey Tony Martinez
April 10, 1967		Cash	Philadelphia Phillies	OF	Tito Francona
May 14, 1967		Cash	Chicago Cubs	OF	Ted Savage
May 14, 1967	OF	Don Young	Chicago Cubs		Cash
July 16, 1967	P	Jack Lamabe	New York Mets	P	Al Jackson
Aug 1, 1967		Cash	Chicago Cubs	OF	Don Young
Oct 13, 1967	OF	Jim Hicks	Chicago Cubs		Cash
Oct 13, 1967		Cash	Chicago White Sox	1B	George Kernek
Jan 11, 1968	OF	Dick Simpson	Cincinnati Reds	OF	Alex Johnson
Feb 8, 1968	C	Johnny Edwards	Cincinnati Reds	C	Pat Corrales minor league IF Jimmy Williams
April 22, 1968	P P	Pete Mikkelsen Dave Dowling	Chicago Cubs	P P	Jack Lamabe Ron Piche
June 15, 1968	OF	Ron Davis	Houston Astros	OF P	Dick Simpson Hal Gilson
Oct 11, 1968	P C	Dave Giusti Dave Adlesh	Houston Astros	C	Johnny Edwards minor league C Tommy Smith

DATE		ACQUIRED	FROM		IN EXCHANGE FOR
Oct 11, 1968	OF	Vada Pinson	Cincinnati Reds	P OF	Wayne Granger Bobby Tolan
Oct 21, 1968		Cash	Los Angeles Dodgers	P	Pete Mikkelsen
Dec 2, 1968	P	Gary Waslewski	Boston Red Sox	SS	Dick Schofield
Dec 3, 1968	P	Dave Giusti	San Diego Padres	1B OF OF	Danny Breeden Ed Spiezio Ron Davis minor league P Phil Knuckles
March 17, 1969	1B	Joe Torre	Atlanta Braves	1B	Orlando Cepeda
March 25, 1969	IF	Bob Johnson	Atlanta Braves	C	Dave Adlesh
April 3, 1969	1B	Bill White	Philadelphia Phillies	1B IF	Jim Hutto Jerry Buchek
May 22, 1969	1B IF	Bill Davis Jerry Davanon	San Diego Padres	SS C	John Sipin John Ruberto
May 30, 1969	OF	Vic Davalillo	California Angels	OF	Jim Hicks
June 3, 1969	P	Mudcat Grant	Montreal Expos	P	Gary Waslewski
July 12, 1969	OF	Joe Nossek	Oakland Athletics	IF	Bob Johnson
Aug 8, 1969		Cash	Houston Astros	P	Ron Willis
Oct 7, 1969	1B 2B P	Richie Allen Cookie Rojas Jerry Johnson	Philadelphia Phillies	OF C P OF	Curt Flood Tim McCarver Joe Hoerner Byron Browne
		(Flood refused to report to the Philadelphia Phillies and the St. Louis Cardinals sent Willie Montanez and Bob Browning on April 8, 1970 to complete the trade.)			
Oct 21, 1969	C	Carl Taylor minor league OF Frank Vanzin	Pittsburgh Pirates	P C	Dave Giusti Dave Ricketts
Nov 5, 1969	P	George Culver	Cincinnati Reds	P	Ray Washburn
Nov 21, 1969	OF	Jose Cardenal	Cleveland Indians	OF	Vada Pinson
Dec 4, 1969	P	Rich Nye	Chicago Cubs	OF	Boots Day
Dec 5, 1969		Cash	Oakland Athletics	P	Mudcat Grant
Dec 5, 1969	P	Bill Dillman	Baltimore Orioles		Cash
April 2, 1970	P	Billy McCool	San Diego Padres	SS	Steve Huntz
April 8, 1970		Completion of Curt Flood trade of October 7, 1969	Philadelphia Phillies	1B	Willie Montanez minor league P Bob Browning
May 15, 1970		Cash	Montreal Expos	P	Rich Nye

DATE		ACQUIRED	FROM		IN EXCHANGE FOR
May 19, 1970	P	Frank Linzy	San Francisco Giants	P	Jerry Johnson
May 29, 1970	P	Ted Abernathy	Chicago Cubs	IF	Phil Gagliano
June 13, 1970	1B SS	Jim Beauchamp Leon McFadden	Houston Astros	P	George Culver
June 13, 1970	OF	Fred Rico	Kansas City Royals	2B	Cookie Rojas
June 22, 1970	P	Chuck Hartenstein	Pittsburgh Pirates		Cash
July 1, 1970	P	Chris Zachary	Kansas City Royals	P	Ted Abernathy
Aug 14, 1970	P	Frank Bertaina	Baltimore Orioles		Cash
Sept 28, 1970	P	Fred Norman	Los Angeles Dodgers		Cash
Oct 5, 1970	2B C	Ted Sizemore Bob Stinson	Los Angeles Dodgers	1B	Richie Allen
Oct 20, 1970	OF	Herman Hill minor league OF Charlie Wissler	Minnesota Twins	P IF	Sal Campisi Jim Kennedy
Oct 20, 1970	C P	Jerry McNertney George Lauzerique minor league P Jesse Higgins	Milwaukee Brewers	OF P	Carl Taylor Jim Ellis
Oct 21, 1970	SS	Dick Schofield	Boston Red Sox	1B	Jim Campbell
Nov 30, 1970	P	Moe Drabowsky	Baltimore Orioles	IF	Jerry Davanon
Jan 29, 1971	OF P	Matty Alou George Brunet	Pittsburgh Pirates	P OF	Nellie Briles Vic Davalillo
Feb 2, 1971	1B	Bob Burda	Milwaukee Brewers		Minor league P Fred Reahm
June 11, 1971	P	Al Santorini	San Diego Padres	OF P	Leron Lee Fred Norman
June 15, 1971	P	Bob Reynolds	Montreal Expos	P	Mike Torrez
June 25, 1971	P	Daryl Patterson (Patterson was returned to Oakland on October 21, 1971.)	Oakland Athletics		Cash
July 15, 1971	P	Dennis Higgins	Cleveland Indians		Cash
July 29, 1971	IF	Ted Kubiak minor league P Charlie Loseth	Milwaukee Brewers	OF IF P	Jose Cardenal Dick Schofield Bob Reynolds
Sept 1, 1971	P	Stan Williams	Minnesota Twins	OF	Fred Rico and minor league P Dan Ford
Sept 13, 1971	P	Mike Jackson	Kansas City Royals		Cash

DATE	ACQUIRED	FROM	IN EXCHANGE FOR
Oct 18, 1971	OF-1B Art Shamsky P Jim Bibby P Rich Folkers P Charles Hudson	New York Mets	1B Jim Beauchamp P Chuck Taylor P Harry Parker 2B Tom Coulter
Nov 3, 1971	IF Marty Martinez	Houston Astros	C Bob Stinson
Nov 3, 1971	P Joe Grzenda	Texas Rangers	SS Ted Kubiak
Feb 25, 1972	P Rick Wise	Philadelphia Phillies	P Steve Carlton
March 20, 1972	1B Mike Fiore	Boston Red Sox	1B Bob Burda
March 24, 1972	P Tony Cloninger	Cincinnati Reds	2B Julian Javier
March 26, 1972	Minor league P Rich Stonum	Milwaukee Brewers	P Frank Linzy
April 15, 1972	P Scipio Spinks P Lance Clemons	Houston Astros	P Jerry Reuss
May 15, 1972	IF Dwain Anderson	Oakland Athletics	P Don Shaw
May 18, 1972	OF Brant Alyea	Oakland Athletics	IF Marty Martinez
May 19, 1972	OF Bernie Carbo	Cincinnati Reds	1B Joe Hague
June 7, 1972	P Diego Segui	Oakland Athletics	Cash
June 16, 1972	P John Cumberland	San Francisco Giants	Cash
June 20, 1972	IF Rafael Robles	San Diego Padres	1B Mike Fiore P Bob Chlupsa
Aug 27, 1972	OF Bill Voss minor league P Steve Easton	Oakland Athletics	OF Matty Alou
Aug 30, 1972	Minor leaguers IF Joe Lindsey and C Gene Dusen	Oakland Athletics	SS Dal Maxvill
Sept 1, 1972	Cash	San Diego Padres	P Dennis Higgins
Sept 18, 1972	Cash	Cleveland Indians	P Lowell Palmer
Oct 26, 1972	OF Larry Hisle	Los Angeles Dodgers	P Rudy Arroyo minor league P Greg Milliken
Nov 6, 1972	C Tim McCarver	Montreal Expos	OF Jorge Roque
Nov 28, 1972	SS Ray Busse IF Bobby Fenwick	Houston Astros	C Skip Jutze IF Milt Ramirez
Nov 28, 1972	P Pat Jacquez	Cincinnati Reds	OF Bill Voss
Nov 29, 1972	P Wayne Granger	Minnesota Twins	OF Larry Hisle P John Cumberland

DATE		ACQUIRED	FROM		IN EXCHANGE FOR
Jan 24, 1973	P	Mike Nagy	Boston Red Sox	P	Lance Clemons
Feb 1, 1973	P	Mike Thompson	Texas Rangers	P	Charles Hudson
March 31, 1973	P	Mike Thompson	Texas Rangers	P	Mike Nagy
April 5, 1973	P	Alan Foster	California Angels		Cash
May 8, 1973	P	Tom Murphy	Atlanta Braves	P	Al Santorini
June 6, 1973	P C	Mike Nagy John Wockenfuss	Texas Rangers	P	Jim Bibby
June 7, 1973	2B	Dave Campbell	San Diego Padres	IF	Dwain Anderson
June 8, 1973	2B	Stan Papi	Houston Astros	SS	Ray Busse
June 15, 1973	P	Orlando Pena	Baltimore Orioles		Cash
July 16, 1973	P	Jim Kremmel	Texas Rangers	P	Don Durham
July 27, 1973	P 2B	Ed Sprague Roe Skidmore	Cincinnati Reds	IF	Ed Crosby minor league C Gene Dusen
Aug 7, 1973	P	Ken Crosby and cash	New York Yankees	P	Wayne Granger
Aug 18, 1973	OF	Tommie Agee	Houston Astros	2B	Dave Campbell and cash
Aug 29, 1973	P	Eddie Fisher	Chicago White Sox		Cash
Sept 1, 1973	P C	Lew Krausse Larry Haney	Oakland Athletics		Cash
Sept 4, 1973		Cash	Milwaukee Brewers	P	Ed Sprague
Sept 6, 1973	OF	Matty Alou	New York Yankees		Cash
Oct 23, 1973		Cash	Houston Astros	SS	Mick Kelleher
Oct 25, 1973		Cash	San Diego Padres	OF	Matty Alou
Oct 26, 1973	P	Denny O'Toole	Chicago White Sox	P	Jim Kremmel
Oct 26, 1973	OF P	Reggie Smith Ken Tatum	Boston Red Sox	P OF	Rick Wise Bernie Carbo
Oct 26, 1973	P	Sonny Siebert	Texas Rangers	OF	Cirilio Cruz and cash
Dec 5, 1973	P	Pete Richert	Los Angeles Dodgers	OF	Tommie Agee
Dec 6, 1973	C	Jeff Torborg	California Angels	P	John Andrews
Dec 7, 1973	P P P	Lynn McGlothen John Curtis Mike Garman	Boston Red Sox	P P IF	Reggie Cleveland Diego Segui Terry Hughes

DATE	ACQUIRED	FROM	IN EXCHANGE FOR
Dec 8, 1973	IF Bob Heise	Milwaukee Brewers	P Tom Murphy
March 23, 1974	OF Jim Hickman	Chicago Cubs	P Scipio Spinks
March 26, 1974	Cash	Oakland Athletics	C Larry Haney
March 29, 1974	IF Ed Crosby	Philadelphia Phillies	Cash
April 27, 1974	IF Luis Alvarado	Chicago White Sox	P Ken Tatum
June 1, 1974	SS Jack Heidemann	Cleveland Indians	IF Luis Alvarado IF Ed Crosby
June 21, 1974	Cash	Philadelphia Phillies	P Pete Richert
July 31, 1974	OF Doug Howard	California Angels	IF Bob Heise
Aug 5, 1974	OF Richie Scheinblum	Kansas City Royals	Cash
Aug 12, 1974	C Dick Billings	Texas Rangers	Cash
Aug 15, 1974	P Claude Osteen	Houston Astros	Minor league P Ron Selak P Dan Larson
Sept 1, 1974	Cash	Boston Red Sox	C Tim McCarver
Sept 5, 1974	2B Ron Hunt	Montreal Expos	Cash
Sept 10, 1974	Cash	Atlanta Braves	P Mike Thompson
Sept 14, 1974	P Barry Lersch	Atlanta Braves	Cash
Oct 13, 1974	P Ray Sadecki P Tommy Moore	New York Mets	1B-3B Joe Torre
Oct 14, 1974	P Elias Sosa C Ken Rudolph	San Francisco Giants	C Marc Hill
Oct 14, 1974	P Jim Willoughby	San Francisco Giants	2B Tom Heintzelman
Oct 24, 1974	Cash	Houston Astros	OF Jose Cruz
Nov 18, 1974	SS Ed Brinkman C Danny Breeden	San Diego Padres	P Alan Foster P Rich Folkers P Sonny Siebert
	(Part of three-team trade involving San Diego, Detroit, and St. Louis Cardinals.)		
Dec 2, 1974	P Bill Parsons	Oakland Athletics	Cash
Dec 6, 1974	1B-OF Ron Fairly	Montreal Expos	Minor leaguers IF Rudy Kinard and 1B Ed Kurpiel
Dec 11, 1974	IF Teddy Martinez	New York Mets	IF Jack Heidemann OF Mike Vail
Dec 13, 1974	SS Mick Kelleher	Houston Astros	Cash

DATE		ACQUIRED	FROM		IN EXCHANGE FOR
March 29, 1975	1B	Danny Cater	Boston Red Sox	OF	Danny Godby
April 4, 1975	SS	Mario Guerrero	Boston Red Sox	P	Jim Willoughby
April 4, 1975		Cash	Detroit Tigers	P	Ray Bare
May 9, 1975	P	Ron Bryant	San Francisco Giants	OF	Larry Herndon minor league P Luis Gonzalez
May 18, 1975	P	Minor league P Steve Staniland Mike Barlow	Oakland Athletics	IF	Teddy Martinez
May 28, 1975	P OF	Ron Reed Wayne Nordhagen	Atlanta Braves	P P	Elias Sosa Ray Sadecki
June 4, 1975	OF	Willie Davis	Texas Rangers	SS P	Ed Brinkman Tommy Moore
June 13, 1975	P	Mike Wallace	New York Yankees		Cash
June 24, 1975		Cash	San Diego Padres	OF	Don Hahn
June 30, 1975	OF	Buddy Bradford	Chicago White Sox	P	Bill Parsons and cash
July 25, 1975	SS	Larry Lintz	Montreal Expos	OF	Jim Dwyer
Aug 1, 1975	P	Lloyd Allen	Chicago White Sox		Cash
Aug 4, 1975	P	Harry Parker	New York Mets		Cash
Sept 30, 1975	OF	Mike Easler	Houston Astros	P	Mike Barlow
Sept 30, 1975	IF	Luis Alvarado	Cleveland Indians	1B	Doug Howard
Oct 20, 1975	OF	Dick Sharon	San Diego Padres	OF	Willie Davis
Oct 28, 1975	SS	Don Kessinger	Chicago Cubs	P	Mike Garman minor league IF Bobby Hrapmann
Oct 28, 1975	OF	Charlie Chant	Oakland Athletics	SS	Larry Lintz
Dec 8, 1975	P	Pete Falcone	San Francisco Giants	3B	Ken Reitz
Dec 9, 1975	OF	Mike Anderson	Philadelphia Phillies	P	Ron Reed
Dec 12, 1975	IF	Lee Richard	Chicago White Sox	OF P	Buddy Bradford Greg Terlecky
Dec 22, 1975	2B	Vic Harris	Chicago Cubs	SS	Mick Kelleher
Feb 3, 1976	P	Tom Walker	Detroit Tigers		Cash
March 2, 1976	OF	Willie Crawford	Los Angeles Dodgers	2B	Ted Sizemore

DATE		ACQUIRED	FROM		IN EXCHANGE FOR
April 2, 1976	P	Lerrin LaGrow	Detroit Tigers		Cash
April 7, 1976	P	Roric Harrison	Cleveland Indians	P	Harry Parker
April 8, 1976	P	Danny Frisella	San Diego Padres	P	Ken Reynolds and minor leaguer Bob Stewart
May 19, 1976	P	Bill Greif	San Diego Padres	OF	Luis Melendez
May 28, 1976		Cash	Cleveland Indians	P	Card Camper
May 29, 1976		Minor leaguers C Ed Jordan and 1B Ed Kurpiel	California Angels	IF	Mario Guerrero
June 7, 1976	OF	Sam Mejias	Milwaukee Brewers	P	Danny Frisella
June 15, 1976	C OF	Joe Ferguson Bob Detherage minor league IF Fred Tisdale	Los Angeles Dodgers	OF	Reggie Smith
Sept 3, 1976		Minor league IF Ron Farkas	California Angels	OF	Mike Easler
Sept 14, 1976		Cash	Oakland Athletics	1B	Ron Fairly
Oct 20, 1976	P P C	John D'Acquisto Mike Caldwell Dave Rader	San Francisco Giants	OF IF P	Willie Crawford Vic Harris John Curtis
Oct 22, 1976	P	Johnny Sutton	Texas Rangers	P	Mike Wallace
Nov 6, 1976	P IF OF	Steve Dunning Pat Scanlon Tony Scott	Montreal Expos	P P OF	Bill Greif Angel Torres Sam Mejias
Nov 6, 1976		Cash	Detroit Tigers	IF	Luis Alvarado
Nov 23, 1976	P IF	Larry Dierker Jerry Davanon	Montreal Expos	C OF	Joe Ferguson Bob Detherage
Dec 9, 1976	1B OF	Brock Pemberton Leon Brown	New York Mets		Minor league 1B Ed Kurpiel
Dec 10, 1976	3B	Ken Reitz	San Francisco Giants	P	Lynn McGlothen
Feb 28, 1977	P	Buddy Schultz	Chicago Cubs		Minor league P Mark Covert
March 23, 1977	P	Clay Carroll	Chicago White Sox	P	Lerrin LaGrow
March 25, 1977	IF	Tom Sandt	Oakland Athletics		Cash
March 28, 1977	OF	Joel Youngblood	Cincinnati Reds	P	Bill Caudill
March 29, 1977	P	Pat Darcy	Cincinnati Reds	P	Mike Caldwell
March 30, 1977	OF	Benny Ayala	New York Mets	IF	Doug Clarey

DATE	ACQUIRED	FROM	IN EXCHANGE FOR
May 17, 1977	P Clarence Metzger	San Diego Padres	P John D'Acquisto IF Pat Scanlon
June 15, 1977	P Tom Underwood 3B Dane Iorg OF Rick Bosetti	Philadelphia Phillies	OF Bake McBride P Steve Waterbury
June 15, 1977	P Rawley Eastwick	Cincinnati Reds	P Doug Capilla
June 15, 1977	SS Mike Phillips	New York Mets	3B Joel Youngblood
Aug 12, 1977	P Randy Scarbery	Oakland Athletics	P Steve Dunning
Aug 20, 1977	Minor league P Steve Staniland	Chicago White Sox	SS Don Kessinger
Aug 23, 1977	P Randy Wiles	Chicago White Sox	Cash
Aug 31, 1977	OF Nyls Nyman P Dave Hamilton P Silvio Martinez	Chicago White Sox	P Clay Carroll
Sept 7, 1977	3B Taylor Duncan	Baltimore Orioles	Cash
Oct 25, 1977	P Frank Riccelli	San Francisco Giants	OF Jim Dwyer
	(San Francisco received Dwyer on June 15, 1978.)		
Dec 6, 1977	P Pete Vuckovich OF John Scott	Toronto Blue Jays	P Tom Underwood P Victor Cruz
Dec 8, 1977	OF Jerry Morales C Steve Swisher and cash	Chicago Cubs	C Dave Rader OF Hector Cruz
Dec 8, 1977	P Mark Littell C Buck Martinez	Kansas City Royals	P Al Hrabosky
Dec 8, 1977	P George Frazier	Milwaukee Brewers	C Buck Martinez
Dec 9, 1977	Minor league P Ron Selak	Houston Astros	P Randy Wiles
Dec 12, 1977	No compensation (free agent signing)	New York Yankees	P Rawley Eastwick
March 15, 1978	Cash	Toronto Blue Jays	OF Rick Bosetti
April 5, 1978	Cash	New York Mets	P Clarence Metzger
May 26, 1978	OF George Hendrick	San Diego Padres	P Eric Rasmussen
May 28, 1978	Cash	Pittsburgh Pirates	P Dave Hamilton
June 8, 1978	OF Bob Coluccio	Houston Astros	P Frank Riccelli
June 23, 1978	P Roy Thomas	Houston Astros	Cash
June 26, 1978	IF Jose Baez	Seattle Mariners	OF Mike Potter
July 18, 1978	P Rob Dressler	San Francisco Giants	C John Tamargo

DATE		ACQUIRED	FROM		IN EXCHANGE FOR
July 21, 1978	3B	Wayne Garrett	Montreal Expos		Cash
Oct 2, 1978	P	Paul Siebert	New York Mets	OF	Bob Coluccio
Oct 23, 1978	P	Jim Willoughby	Chicago White Sox	OF	John Scott
Dec 4, 1978	P	Bob Sykes and minor league P Jack Murphy	Detroit Tigers	OF P	Jerry Morales Aurelio Lopez
Dec 5, 1978	OF P	Tom Grieve Kim Seaman	New York Mets	P	Pete Falcone
March 10, 1979	OF	Bernie Carbo	Boston Red Sox		No compensation (free agent signing)
June 7, 1979		Cash	Seattle Mariners	P	Rob Dressler
Oct 17, 1979	P	Donnie Moore	Chicago Cubs	2B	Mike Tyson
Nov 9, 1979		Cash	Seattle Mariners	P	Dan O'Brien
Dec 7, 1979	OF	Bobby Bonds	Cleveland Indians	OF P	Jerry Mumphrey John Denny
April 30, 1980	P	Jim Kaat	New York Yankees		Cash
June 2, 1980	P OF	John Martin Al Greene	Detroit Tigers	OF	Jim Lentine
Dec 8, 1980	P P C	Rollie Fingers Bob Shirley Gene Tenace minor league C Bob Geren	San Diego Padres	C C IF P P P P	Terry Kennedy Steve Swisher Mike Phillips John Littlefield John Urrea Kim Seaman Alan Olmsted
Dec 9, 1980	P	Bruce Sutter	Chicago Cubs	OF 3B IF	Leon Durham Ken Reitz Ty Waller
Dec 12, 1980	OF OF P P	Sixto Lezcano David Green Lary Sorensen Dave LaPoint	Milwaukee Brewers	P P C	Pete Vuckovich Rollie Fingers Ted Simmons
Dec 13, 1980	C	Darrell Porter	Kansas City Royals		No compensation (free agent signing)
Feb 16, 1981	C	Rafael Santana	New York Yankees		Cash
June 7, 1981	P	Joaquin Andujar	Houston Astros	OF	Tony Scott
June 7, 1981		Cash	New York Yankees	P	George Frazier
Sept 3, 1981		Cash	Milwaukee Brewers	P	Donnie Moore
Sept 19, 1981	P	Doug Bair	Cincinnati Reds	2B P	Neil Fiala Joe Edelen
Oct 21, 1981	OF	Willie McGee	New York Yankees	P	Bob Sykes

DATE		ACQUIRED	FROM		IN EXCHANGE FOR
Nov 20, 1981	OF	Lonnie Smith	Cleveland Indians	P P	Lary Sorensen Silvio Martinez
		(Part of three-team trade involving Cleveland, Philadelphia, and St. Louis.)			
Dec 7, 1981	P	Mike Stanton	Cleveland Indians		Cash
Dec 10, 1981	SS P P	Ozzie Smith Steve Mura Alan Olmstead	San Diego Padres	OF SS P	Sixto Lezcano Garry Templeton Luis DeLeon
Feb 1, 1982	P	Dan Morogiello	Atlanta Braves	P	Donnie Moore
Feb 8, 1982		Cash	Cleveland Indians	P	Mike Stanton
April 1, 1982	P	Jeff Lahti Minor league P Jose Brito	Cincinnati Reds	P	Bob Shirley
Dec 1, 1982		No compensation (free agent signing)	Pittsburgh Pirates	C	Gene Tenace
Jan 18, 1983	P	Jerry Garvin	Toronto Blue Jays		Cash
Jan 26, 1983			Chicago White Sox	P	Steve Mura
		(Claimed in compensation draft after Chicago lost free agent OF Steve Kemp to Yankees.)			
Jan 28, 1983	C	Jamie Quirk	Kansas City Royals		No compensation (free agent signing)
March 16, 1983		Minor league P Jeff Meadows	Houston Astros	C	George Bjorkman
March 31, 1983		Minor league P Jim Strichek	Cincinnati Reds	IF	Kelly Paris
June 15, 1983	P P	Neil Allen Rick Ownbey	New York Mets	1B	Keith Hernandez
June 15, 1983	C-3B	Floyd Rayford	Baltimore Orioles	OF	Tito Landrum
June 22, 1983	P	Dave Rucker	Detroit Tigers	P	Doug Bair
Aug 2, 1983		Cash	Kansas City Royals	P	Eric Rasmussen
Aug 4, 1983		Cash	Detroit Tigers	P	John Martin
Sept 2, 1983	P	Steve Baker	Oakland Athletics		Minor league Ps Tom Dozier and Jim Strichek
Sept 16, 1983		Cash	Montreal Expos	OF	Gene Roof
Feb 22, 1984	3B	Art Howe	Houston Astros		No compensation (free agent signing)
March 25, 1984	OF	Tito Landrum	Baltimore Orioles		Minor league P Jose Brito
March 30, 1984		Cash	Baltimore Orioles	3B	Floyd Rayford

San Diego Padres

The Best Trades

1. Acquired Tim Lollar, Ruppert Jones, Joe Lefebvre, and Chris Welsh from the New York Yankees for Jerry Mumphrey and John Pacella, April 1, 1981.
2. Acquired George Hendrick from the Cleveland Indians for Johnny Grubb, Fred Kendall, and Hector Torres, December 8, 1976.
3. Acquired Gaylord Perry from the Texas Rangers for Dave Tomlin and $125,000, January 25, 1978.
4. Acquired Sixto Lezcano, Luis DeLeon, and Garry Templeton from the St. Louis Cardinals for Steve Mura, Alan Olmsted, and Ozzie Smith, in a three-part deal covering December 10, 1981, February 11, 1982, and February 19, 1982.
5. Acquired Tito Fuentes and Clarence Metzger from the San Francisco Giants for Derrell Thomas, December 6, 1974.

The Worst Trades

1. Traded George Hendrick to the St. Louis Cardinals for Eric Rasmussen, May 26, 1978.
2. Traded Mike Hargrove to the Cleveland Indians for Paul Dade, June 14, 1979.
3. Traded Gaylord Perry, Tucker Ashford, and Joe Carroll to the Texas Rangers for Willie Montanez, February 15, 1980.
4. Traded Dan Spillner to the Cleveland Indians for Dennis Kinney, June 14, 1978.
5. Traded Fred Norman to the Cincinnati Reds for Gene Locklear, Mike Johnson, and cash, June 12, 1973.

Trader: Jack McKeon

San Diego fans have learned not to bother forming fan clubs for their favorite Padres. Ever since Jack McKeon became general manager of the club, few players have lingered in a San Diego uniform long enough to become known by their first names, much less merit a devoted following.

McKeon isn't called "Trader Jack" or "The Sultan of Swap" for nothing. Almost from the moment he joined the Padres he began remaking them, and remaking them again when results were not immediately forthcoming. While his astute moves have put the Padres among the favorites for the National League West crown, the overall effects of this rapid turnover may be what is keeping them from fulfilling this promise.

Viewed in a vacuum, the majority of these moves look outstanding. While the shortstop swap with St. Louis of Ozzie Smith for Garry Templeton hasn't worked out well owing to Templeton's injuries, the other players involved in the two San Diego–St. Louis deals of 1980–81 tip the scales in the Padres' direction: Terry Kennedy has bloomed into one of the game's top offensive catchers, Luis DeLeon has become an outstanding reliever without anyone outside the Pacific Southwest noticing, and Sixto Lezcano had a strong season before being traded to Philadelphia in '83.

Hardly had the ink dried on the first of the St. Louis trades when McKeon pulled off another blockbuster, this one with the Yankees. He sent Jerry Mumphrey and John Pacella to New York for four players, all of whom would play regularly for the Padres: Ruppert Jones, Joe Lefebvre, Chris Welsh, and Tim Lollar. But problems would affect all four of these ballplayers, and by the end of '83 only Lollar would still be in a Padre uniform. McKeon seemed to have pulled off a real steal by getting second baseman Juan Bonilla from Cleveland for pitcher Bob Lacey, but a stormy confrontation with manager Dick Williams led to Bonilla's being given his outright release before the '84 season. Padres fans could only hold their breath and hope that similar bad luck would not befall Carmelo Martinez, the key acquisition in a three-team trade in which the Padres gave up reliever Gary Lucas.

But regardless of the ultimate outcome of McKeon's deals, his record is far superior to those of his predecessors. In rapid succession the Padres traded away Pat Dobson, Fred Norman, Mike Caldwell, George Hendrick, Dan Spillner, and Mike Hargrove, receiving little in return for each. And while their extravagant free-agent signings greatly enhanced their gate appeal, they did little for the won-lost record. Too many players were signed too unwisely; while Rollie Fingers certainly earned his enormous salary, the same cannot be said for Gene Tenace or Oscar Gamble. The jury is still out on Steve Garvey and Goose Gossage, signed before the 1983 and '84 seasons respectively.

DATE	ACQUIRED	FROM	IN EXCHANGE FOR
Oct 21, 1968	1B Bill Davis	Cleveland Indians	SS Zoilo Versalles
Dec 3, 1968	1B Danny Breeden OF Ed Spiezio OF Ron Davis minor league P Phil Knuckles	St. Louis Cardinals	P Dave Giusti
March 28, 1969	C Chris Cannizzaro P Tommie Sisk	Pittsburgh Pirates	OF Ron Davis IF Bobby Klaus
April 17, 1969	SS Tommy Dean P Leon Everitt	Los Angeles Dodgers	P Al McBean
April 25, 1969	P Joe Niekro P Gary Ross IF Francisco Libran	Chicago Cubs	P Dick Selma
May 22, 1969	SS John Sipin C John Ruberto	St. Louis Cardinals	1B Bill Davis IF Jerry Davanon
June 12, 1969	IF Walt Hriniak IF Van Kelly minor league OF Andy Finlay	Atlanta Braves	OF Tony Gonzalez
June 30, 1969	Cash	Cincinnati Reds	C Danny Breeden
Oct 22, 1969	P Danny Coombs	Houston Astros	Cash
Dec 4, 1969	P Pat Dobson IF Dave Campbell	Detroit Tigers	P Joe Niekro
Dec 5, 1969	C Bob Barton P Ron Herbel IF Bobby Etheridge	San Francisco Giants	P Frank Reberger
March 24, 1970	1B Ramon Webster	Oakland Athletics	IF Roberto Pena
March 30, 1970	P Jerry Nyman	Chicago White Sox	P Tommie Sisk
April 2, 1970	SS Steve Huntz	St. Louis Cardinals	P Billy McCool
May 26, 1970	P Roberto Rodriguez	Oakland Athletics	Cash
June 23, 1970	Cash	Chicago Cubs	P Roberto Rodriguez

DATE		ACQUIRED	FROM		IN EXCHANGE FOR
July 15, 1970	P	Earl Wilson	Detroit Tigers		Cash
Aug 25, 1970	P	Paul Doyle	California Angels		Cash
Sept 1, 1970	OF	Rod Gaspar	New York Mets	P	Ron Herbel
		(San Diego received Gaspar on October 20.)			
Dec 1, 1970	P P P SS	Tom Phoebus Al Severinsen Fred Beene Enzo Hernandez	Baltimore Orioles	P P	Pat Dobson Tom Dukes
Dec 4, 1970	2B	Don Mason minor league P Bill Frost	San Francisco Giants	IF	Steve Huntz
May 13, 1971	OF	Angel Bravo	Cincinnati Reds	OF	Al Ferrara
May 19, 1971	IF	Garry Jestadt	Chicago Cubs	C	Chris Cannizzaro
May 22, 1971	P	Camilo Pascual	Cleveland Indians		Cash
		(Pascual was returned to Cleveland on May 26, 1971.)			
June 11, 1971	OF P	Leron Lee Fred Norman	St. Louis Cardinals	P	Al Santorini
Aug 10, 1971	OF P	John Jeter Ed Acosta	Pittsburgh Pirates	P	Bob Miller
Dec 3, 1971	IF P P	Derrel Thomas Bill Greif Mark Schaeffer	Houston Astros	P	Dave Roberts
April 20, 1972		Cash	Chicago Cubs	P	Tom Phoebus
May 17, 1972	OF P	Curt Blefary Mike Kilkenny minor league OF Greg Schubert	Oakland Athletics	OF	Ollie Brown
June 11, 1972	SS	Fred Stanley	Cleveland Indians	P	Mike Kilkenny
June 11, 1972	C	Pat Corrales	Cincinnati Reds	C	Bob Barton
June 20, 1972	1B P	Mike Fiore Bob Chlupsa	St. Louis Cardinals	IF	Rafael Robles
July 9, 1972	P	Don Eddy and cash	Chicago White Sox	IF	Ed Spiezio
Sept 1, 1972	P	Dennis Higgins	St. Louis Cardinals		Cash
Sept 6, 1972		Cash	Oakland Athletics	C	Larry Haney
Oct 28, 1972	P	Vicente Romo	Chicago White Sox	OF	John Jeter
Nov 30, 1972		Cash	Cincinnati Reds	OF	Larry Stahl
Nov 30, 1972	OF	Dave Marshall	New York Mets	P	Al Severinsen

DATE		ACQUIRED	FROM		IN EXCHANGE FOR
May 26, 1973	IF	Rich Morales	Chicago White Sox		Cash
June 7, 1973	IF	Dwain Anderson	St. Louis Cardinals	2B	Dave Campbell
June 12, 1973	OF P	Gene Locklear Mike Johnson and cash	Cincinnati Reds	P	Fred Norman
June 22, 1973	P	Bob Miller	Detroit Tigers		Cash
Oct 25, 1973	OF	Matty Alou	St. Louis Cardinals		Cash
Oct 25, 1973	1B OF	Willie McCovey Bernie Williams	San Francisco Giants	P	Mike Caldwell
Nov 7, 1973	2B IF	Glenn Beckert Bobby Fenwick	Chicago Cubs	OF	Jerry Morales
Nov 9, 1973	OF P	Bobby Tolan Dave Tomlin	Cincinnati Reds	P	Clay Kirby
Dec 20, 1973	P	Jim McAndrew	New York Mets	P	Steve Simpson
March 28, 1974		Cash	Cleveland Indians	OF	Leron Lee
April 1, 1974		Cash	Atlanta Braves	OF	Ivan Murrell
May 31, 1974	2B	Horace Clarke	New York Yankees		Cash
May 31, 1974	P	Lowell Palmer	New York Yankees		Cash
June 15, 1974	P	Brent Strom minor league P Jerry Lee	Cleveland Indians	P	Steve Arlin
July 11, 1974		Cash	Los Angeles Dodgers	1B	Gail Hopkins
Nov 8, 1974	P	Danny Frisella	Atlanta Braves	OF	Clarence Gaston
Nov 18, 1974	SS P OF	Ed Brinkman Bob Strampe Dick Sharon (Part of three-team trade involving San Diego, Detroit, and St. Louis Cardinals.)	Detroit Tigers	1B	Nate Colbert
Nov 18, 1974	P P P	Alan Foster Rich Folkers Sonny Siebert (Part of three-team trade involving San Diego, Detroit, and St. Louis Cardinals.)	St. Louis Cardinals	SS C	Ed Brinkman Danny Breeden
Dec 6, 1974	2B P	Tito Fuentes Clarence Metzger	San Francisco Giants	IF	Derrel Thomas
April 28, 1975	C	Gerry Moses	Chicago White Sox		Cash
May 16, 1975	IF	Ted Kubiak	Oakland Athletics	P	Sonny Siebert
June 24, 1975	OF	Don Hahn	St. Louis Cardinals		Cash
July 18, 1975		Cash	Chicago White Sox	C	Gerry Moses

DATE		ACQUIRED	FROM		IN EXCHANGE FOR
Sept 17, 1975	IF SS	Bobby Valentine Rudi Meoli	California Angels	P	Gary Ross
Oct 20, 1975	OF	Willie Davis	St. Louis Cardinals	OF	Dick Sharon
Dec 11, 1975	3B	Doug Rader	Houston Astros	P P	Joe McIntosh Larry Hardy
April 5, 1976	OF	Merv Rettenmund	Cincinnati Reds	SS	Rudi Meoli
April 8, 1976	P	Ken Reynolds and minor leaguer Bob Stewart	St. Louis Cardinals	P	Danny Frisella
April 13, 1976		Cash	Chicago Cubs	C	Randy Hundley
May 19, 1976	OF	Luis Melendez	St. Louis Cardinals	P	Bill Greif
July 10, 1976	P	Rick Sawyer	New York Yankees	OF	Gene Locklear
Aug 3, 1976	P	Tom Griffin	Houston Astros		Cash
Aug 30, 1976		Cash	Oakland Athletics	1B	Willie McCovey
Dec 8, 1976	OF	George Hendrick	Cleveland Indians	OF C SS	John Grubb Fred Kendall Hector Torres
Dec 14, 1976	P	Rollie Fingers	Oakland Athletics		No compensation (free agent signing)
Dec 14, 1976	C	Gene Tenace	Oakland Athletics		No compensation (free agent signing)
Jan 6, 1977		No compensation (free agent signing)	San Francisco Giants	1B	Willie McCovey
Feb 16, 1977	UT	Dave Roberts	Toronto Blue Jays	P	Jerry Johnson
Feb 23, 1977		No compensation (free agent signing)	Detroit Tigers	2B	Tito Fuentes
March 21, 1977		Cash	Toronto Blue Jays	P	Ken Reynolds
March 23, 1977		Cash	Milwaukee Brewers	P	Rich Folkers
May 17, 1977	P IF	John D'Acquisto Pat Scanlon	St. Louis Cardinals	P	Clarence Metzger
June 8, 1977		Cash	Toronto Blue Jays	3B	Doug Rader
June 15, 1977	1B	Dave Kingman	New York Mets	IF P	Bobby Valentine Paul Siebert
Sept 6, 1977		Cash	California Angels	1B	Dave Kingman
Sept 29, 1977		Cash	Montreal Expos	P	Rick Sawyer
Nov 29, 1977	OF	Oscar Gamble	Chicago White Sox		No compensation (free agent signing)
Jan 25, 1978	P	Gaylord Perry	Texas Rangers	P	Dave Tomlin and $125,000.

DATE		ACQUIRED	FROM		IN EXCHANGE FOR
Feb 28, 1978	OF	Derrel Thomas	San Francisco Giants	IF	Mike Ivie
May 26, 1978	P	Eric Rasmussen	St. Louis Cardinals	OF	George Hendrick
June 5, 1978	IF	Fernando Gonzalez	Pittsburgh Pirates		Cash
June 5, 1978	P	Gary Lance	Kansas City Royals		Minor league P Steve Hamrick
June 14, 1978	P	Dennis Kinney	Cleveland Indians	P	Dan Spillner
June 22, 1978	P	Bill Laxton	Cleveland Indians	P	Dave Freisleben
Sept 12, 1978		Minor league OF Andy Dyes	Toronto Blue Jays	P	Mark Wiley
Oct 25, 1978	1B 3B C	Mike Hargrove Kurt Bevacqua Bill Fahey	Texas Rangers	OF C	Oscar Gamble Dave Roberts and $300,000.
Nov 14, 1978		No compensation (free agent signing)	Los Angeles Dodgers	IF	Derrel Thomas
March 30, 1979	OF	Dan Briggs	Cleveland Indians	2B	Mike Champion
June 14, 1979	3B	Paul Dade	Cleveland Indians	1B	Mike Hargrove
June 15, 1979	OF	Jay Johnstone	New York Yankees	P	Dave Wehrmeister
Nov 19, 1979	P	Rick Wise	Cleveland Indians		No compensation (free agent signing)
Nov 26, 1979	P	John Curtis	San Francisco Giants		No compensation (free agent signing)
Nov 27, 1979	2B	Dave Cash	Montreal Expos	SS 1B-OF	Bill Almon Dan Briggs
Dec 3, 1979	OF	Von Joshua	Los Angeles Dodgers		Cash
Dec 7, 1979	3B	Aurelio Rodriguez	Detroit Tigers		$200,000.
Feb 15, 1980	1B	Willie Montanez	Texas Rangers	P 3B	Gaylord Perry Tucker Ashford minor league P Joe Carroll
Feb 15, 1980	OF	Jerry Mumphrey	Cleveland Indians	P OF	Bob Owchinko Jim Wilhelm
Aug 4, 1980		Cash	New York Yankees	3B	Aurelio Rodriguez
Aug 5, 1980	OF 3B	Rick Lancellotti Luis Salazar	Pittsburgh Pirates	3B P	Kurt Bevacqua Mark Lee
Aug 11, 1980	OF	Randy Bass	Montreal Expos	P	John D'Acquisto and cash
Aug 31, 1980	IF	Tony Phillips	Montreal Expos	1B	Willie Montanez

DATE		ACQUIRED	FROM		IN EXCHANGE FOR
Dec 8, 1980	C C IF P P P P	Terry Kennedy Steve Swisher Mike Phillips John Littlefield John Urrea Kim Seaman Alan Olmsted	St. Louis Cardinals	P P C	Rollie Fingers Bob Shirley Gene Tenace minor league C Bob Geren
Dec 8, 1980	OF	Dave Edwards	Minnesota Twins	IF	Chuck Baker
Dec 12, 1980	OF	Dave Stegman	Detroit Tigers	P	Dennis Kinney
Dec 15, 1980		No compensation (free agent signing)	New York Yankees	OF	Dave Winfield
Dec 15, 1980	P IF	John Pacella Jose Moreno	New York Mets	P	Randy Jones
March 24, 1981		Cash	Detroit Tigers	C	Bill Fahey
March 27, 1981	P	Bob Lacey minor league P Ray Moretti	Oakland Athletics	3B SS	Kevin Bell Tony Phillips Minor league P Eric Mustard
April 1, 1981	2B	Juan Bonilla	Cleveland Indians	P	Bob Lacey
April 1, 1981	OF OF P P	Ruppert Jones Joe Lefebvre Tim Lollar Chris Welsh	New York Yankees	OF P	Jerry Mumphrey John Pacella
May 10, 1981		Cash	Montreal Expos	IF	Mike Phillips
Sept 9, 1981		Cash	Chicago White Sox	OF	Jerry Turner
Dec 10, 1981	OF SS P	Sixto Lezcano Garry Templeton Luis DeLeon	St. Louis Cardinals	SS P P	Ozzie Smith Steve Mura Alan Olmstead
Jan 27, 1982		Cash	Cleveland Indians	C	Craig Stimac
Feb 22, 1982		Cash	New York Yankees	3B	Barry Evans
April 4, 1982		Cash	Kansas City Royals	P	Mike Armstrong
April 6, 1982	P	John Montefusco	Atlanta Braves		No compensation (free agent signing)
May 17, 1982		Cash	Texas Rangers	1B	Randy Bass
May 22, 1982	2B	Jerry Manuel	Montreal Expos	P	Kim Seaman
June 8, 1982	3B	Joe Pittman	Houston Astros	P	Dan Boone
June 8, 1982	P	Mike Griffin	Montreal Expos	2B	Jerry Manuel
Aug 31, 1982		Cash	California Angels	P	John Curtis

DATE		ACQUIRED	FROM		IN EXCHANGE FOR
Oct 7, 1982	P	Elias Sosa	Detroit Tigers		Cash
Oct 7, 1982		Cash	Montreal Expos	1B	Rick Lancellotti
Oct 15, 1982		Minor league Ps Weldon Swift and Tim Cook	Milwaukee Brewers	P	Tom Tellmann
Nov 18, 1982	P	Ed Whitson	Cleveland Indians	P 1B	Juan Eichelberger Broderick Perkins
Dec 15, 1982	P	Ray Searage	Cleveland Indians		Cash
Dec 21, 1982	1B	Steve Garvey	Los Angeles Dodgers		No compensation (free agent signing)
May 2, 1983	P	Sid Monge	Philadelphia Phillies	OF	Joe Lefebvre
May 4, 1983		Cash	Montreal Expos	P	Chris Welsh
Aug 26, 1983	P 2B	Dennis Rasmussen Eduardo Rodriguez and $200,000.	New York Yankees	P	John Montefusco
Aug 31, 1983	P	Marty Decker minor league Ps Ed Wojna Darren Burroughs and Lance McCullers	Philadelphia Phillies	OF P	Sixto Lezcano Steve Fireovid
Dec 6, 1983	OF	Champ Summers	San Francisco Giants	3B	Joe Pittman minor league OF Tommy Francis
Dec 7, 1983	P	Scott Sanderson	Montreal Expos	P	Gary Lucas
Dec 7, 1983	1B P 3B	Carmelo Martinez Craig Lefferts Allan Ramirez (Part of three-team trade involving Chicago Cubs, San Diego, and Montreal.)	Chicago Cubs	P	Scott Sanderson
Jan 12, 1984	P	Goose Gossage	New York Yankees		No compensation (free agent signing)
March 30, 1984	3B	Graig Nettles	New York Yankees	P	Dennis Rasmussen and a player to be named later
March 31, 1984		No compensation (free agent signing)	San Francisco Giants	OF	Gene Richards

San Francisco Giants

The Best Trades

1. Acquired Jack Sanford from the Philadelphia Phillies for Valmy Thomas and Ruben Gomez, December 3, 1958.
2. Acquired Billy Pierce and Don Larsen from the Chicago White Sox for Eddie Fisher, Dom Zanni, and Bobby Tiefenauer, November 30, 1961.

3. Acquired Mike McCormick from the Washington Senators for Cap Peterson and Bob Priddy, December 3, 1966.
4. Acquired Greg Minton from the Kansas City Royals for Fran Healy, April 2, 1973.
5. Acquired Larry Herndon and Luis Gonzalez from the St. Louis Cardinals for Ron Bryant, May 9, 1975.

The Worst Trades

1. Traded George Foster to the Cincinnati Reds for Frank Duffy and Vern Geishert, May 29, 1971.
2. Traded Orlando Cepeda to the St. Louis Cardinals for Ray Sadecki, May 8, 1966.
3. Traded Gaylord Perry and Frank Duffy to the Cleveland Indians for Sam McDowell, November 29, 1971.
4. Traded Manny Mota and Dick LeMay to the Houston Colt .45s for Joey Amalfitano, November 30, 1962.
5. Traded Bill Hands and Randy Hundley to the Chicago Cubs for Lindy McDaniel, Don Landrum, and Jim Rittwage, December 2, 1965.

Trader: Horace Stoneham

Call the roll, and call it slowly. Bill White. Orlando Cepeda. Leon Wagner. Matty Alou. Felipe Alou. Jesus Alou. Manny Mota. Bobby Bonds. Garry Maddox. Gary Matthews. George Foster.

Horace Stoneham had so many outfielders, he didn't know what to do. So, slowly but surely, he gave them all away, and got next to nothing in return for his generosity. It may be, as some have argued, that the Giants' system was so good at producing outfielders that he came to see them as a constantly renewable commodity. But the well had to run dry eventually, and Giant fans can only rue the teams that might have been.

Stoneham's largesse was not wholly limited to outfielders. He also unloaded such nonoutfielders as Dave Kingman, Jose Pagan, Mike McCormick, Randy Hundley, Bill Hands, Gaylord Perry, Steve Stone, Lindy McDaniel, and Mike Caldwell. But most of the deals involved trading surplus hitting talent for infield or pitching help, and in every case the talent given away far outweighed the return.

The most extreme case was the trade of George Foster for Frank Duffy and Vern Geishert. The Giants wanted Duffy as backup help to shortstop Chris Speier, and the Reds were willing to take either Foster or Bernie Williams, another outfielder toiling in the Giants' farm system. Unfortunately for the Giants, they dug up Foster's Selective Service physical report, which showed that he had been rejected because of a back injury sustained during high school. Fearful that the injury might recur, the Giants elected to make Foster the outfielder in the deal. Duffy was sent packing the following year; Geishert never made it back to the majors; Williams flopped and ended up playing in Japan; Foster was the only man in the 1970s to hit 50 homers in a season.

The rest found themselves odd men out in a too-talented field. Bill White returned from army duty to find his first base job taken by Orlando Cepeda, with Willie McCovey making booming noises down on the farm; White was traded to St. Louis for pitcher Sam Jones. Wagner went to St. Louis for Don Blasingame; by 1962, Wagner was an All-Star for the Angels, and Blasingame was fighting off a rookie named Pete Rose for the Cincinnati second base job. There was no room for Mota, so they sent him to Houston for Joey Amalfitano; twenty years later Mota was still hitting line drives. Felipe Alou went with Ed Bailey, Billy Hoeft, and Ernie Bowman to Milwaukee for Del Crandall, lefty Bob Hendley, and Bob Shaw. Matty was next, off to Pittsburgh for lefty Joe Gibbon and Ozzie Virgil. In Matty's first year with the Pirates, he led the league in batting, hitting .342. Second was brother Felipe, at .327.

(Sandwiched between them, but without enough at bats to qualify for the title, was Mota, at .332.)

Two of the other deals serve to demonstrate their fanatical search for left-handed pitching. In May 1966, they traded Orlando Cepeda to St. Louis for Ray Sadecki. Sadecki proved to be something of a disappointment, particularly in comparison to Cepeda, who won the NL Most Valuable Player Award in his first full year with the Cards. In December 1971, they traded Gaylord Perry to Cleveland for Sam McDowell. Again, this trade paid instant dividends: Perry won the 1972 Cy Young Award in the AL, and would add another 180 wins before he was through. McDowell was out of baseball in two years. (The Giants can consider themselves fortunate that none of the seven players they gave up for Vida Blue became stars; nonetheless, bankrupting the farm system and throwing in an additional $390,000 to acquire a twenty-eight-year-old pitcher whose greatest year had come six years earlier shows questionable judgment.)

Had the Giants been able to hold onto the majority of the talent produced by their farm system in the 1960s, they could well have challenged the Reds and Dodgers for domination of the National League West throughout the 1970s. Even if they had just traded it more wisely, they would have had far more to show for their efforts than just one divisional title. Horace Stoneham's legacy is a large collection of what-ifs.

DATE		ACQUIRED	FROM		IN EXCHANGE FOR
Jan 28, 1958	3B	Jim Finigan and $25,000.	Detroit Tigers	1B 3B	Gail Harris Ozzie Virgil
March 21, 1958		Cash	Chicago White Sox	OF	Don Mueller
March 24, 1958		$30,000.	Baltimore Orioles	IF	Foster Castleman
April 2, 1958	OF	Jim King	St. Louis Cardinals	C	Ray Katt
April 3, 1958	OF	Bob Speake and cash	Chicago Cubs	OF	Bobby Thomson
June 7, 1958		Waiver price	Cleveland Indians	P	Jim Constable
Oct 5, 1958		Cash	Detroit Tigers	P	Pete Burnside
Oct 8, 1958	C P 3B	Hobie Landrith Billy Muffett Benny Valenzuela	St. Louis Cardinals	P P	Ernie Broglio Marv Grissom
Dec 3, 1958	P	Jack Sanford	Philadelphia Phillies	C P	Valmy Thomas Ruben Gomez
Feb 14, 1959		Cash	Baltimore Orioles	1B	Whitey Lockman
March 25, 1959	P P	Sam Jones Don Choate	St. Louis Cardinals	1B 3B	Bill White Ray Jablonski
April 13, 1959		Waiver price	Pittsburgh Pirates	P	Paul Giel
June 14, 1959	C	Jim Hegan	Philadelphia Phillies		Cash
Nov 30, 1959	P P	Billy O'Dell Billy Loes	Baltimore Orioles	OF P C	Jackie Brandt Gordon Jones Roger McCardell
Dec 15, 1959	2B	Don Blasingame	St. Louis Cardinals	2B OF	Daryl Spencer Leon Wagner

DATE		ACQUIRED	FROM		IN EXCHANGE FOR
March 29, 1960	1B	Jim Marshall	Boston Red Sox	P	Al Worthington
April 5, 1960	1B	Dale Long	Chicago Cubs		Cash
May 12, 1960	OF	Dave Philley	Philadelphia Phillies		Cash
Aug 22, 1960		Cash	New York Yankees	1B	Dale Long
Sept 1, 1960		Cash	Baltimore Orioles	OF	Dave Philley
Oct 31, 1960	3B	Alvin Dark	Milwaukee Braves	IF	Andre Rodgers
Dec 3, 1960	OF	Harvey Kuenn	Cleveland Indians	P OF	Johnny Antonelli Willie Kirkland
April 27, 1961	C	Ed Bailey	Cincinnati Reds	C 2B P	Bob Schmidt Don Blasingame Sherman Jones
Oct 13, 1961		Cash	New York Mets	1B	Jim Marshall
Oct 16, 1961		Cash	New York Mets	P	Billy Loes
Nov 26, 1961	SS	Don Buddin	Boston Red Sox	SS	Ed Bressoud
Nov 30, 1961	P P	Billy Pierce Don Larsen	Chicago White Sox	P P P	Eddie Fisher Dom Zanni Bobby Tiefenauer
April 29, 1962	OF	Bob Nieman	Cleveland Indians		Cash
July 13, 1962		Cash	New York Mets	C	Joe Pignatano
Nov 30, 1962	2B	Joey Amalfitano	Houston Astros	P OF	Dick LeMay Manny Mota
Dec 15, 1962	P C P	Jack Fisher Jimmie Coker Billy Hoeft	Baltimore Orioles	P P C	Mike McCormick Stu Miller John Orsino
March 29, 1963	OF	Jacke Davis	Los Angeles Angels	1B	Charlie Dees
Aug 8, 1963	1B	Norm Larker	Milwaukee Braves		Cash
Oct 1, 1963	P	Ken MacKenzie	St. Louis Cardinals	C	Jimmie Coker
Oct 10, 1963		$30,000.	New York Mets	P	Jack Fisher
Dec 3, 1963	C P P	Del Crandall Bob Shaw Bob Hendley	Milwaukee Braves	OF P C SS	Felipe Alou Billy Hoeft Ed Bailey Ernie Bowman
April 14, 1964	OF	Duke Snider	New York Mets		Cash

DATE		ACQUIRED	FROM		IN EXCHANGE FOR
May 20, 1964		Cash	Houston Astros	P	Don Larsen
Nov 21, 1964	C	Jack Hiatt	Los Angeles Angels	OF	Jose Cardenal
Feb 1, 1965	C	Ed Bailey	Milwaukee Braves	P	Billy O'Dell
Feb 11, 1965	P OF	Bob Priddy Bob Burda	Pittsburgh Pirates	C	Del Crandall
May 4, 1965	P	Bill Henry	Cincinnati Reds	P	Jim Duffalo
May 12, 1965		Cash	New York Mets	2B	Chuck Hiller
May 22, 1965	SS	Dick Schofield	Pittsburgh Pirates	SS	Jose Pagan
May 29, 1965	C OF	Dick Bertell Len Gabrielson	Chicago Cubs	OF C P	Harvey Kuenn Ed Bailey Bob Hendley
Aug 18, 1965		Cash	California Angels	P	Jack Sanford
Oct 1, 1965	P 3B	Joe Gibbon Ozzie Virgil	Pittsburgh Pirates	OF	Matty Alou
Dec 2, 1965	P OF P	Lindy McDaniel Don Landrum Jim Rittwage	Chicago Cubs	C P	Randy Hundley Bill Hands
May 8, 1966	P	Ray Sadecki	St. Louis Cardinals	1B	Orlando Cepeda
May 11, 1966		Cash	New York Yankees	SS	Dick Schofield
May 16, 1966		Cash	Atlanta Braves	SS	Gil Garrido
June 10, 1966		Cash	New York Mets	P	Bob Shaw
Dec 3, 1966	P	Mike McCormick	Washington Senators	OF P	Cap Peterson Bob Priddy
Dec 14, 1966	OF	Norm Siebern	California Angels	OF	Len Gabrielson
April 3, 1967	C	Don Bryant	Chicago Cubs		Cash
May 31, 1967	OF	Ty Cline	Atlanta Braves		Cash
June 22, 1967	SS	Dick Groat	Philadelphia Phillies		Cash
July 16, 1967		Cash	Boston Red Sox	OF	Norm Siebern
Feb 13, 1968	2B 2B	Ron Hunt Nate Oliver	Los Angeles Dodgers	C	Tom Haller minor league P Frank Kasmeta
June 27, 1968		Cash	Pittsburgh Pirates	P	Bill Henry
July 12, 1968	P	Bill Monbouquette	New York Yankees	P	Lindy McDaniel

DATE		ACQUIRED	FROM		IN EXCHANGE FOR
Dec 6, 1968	3B	Charley Smith	New York Yankees	IF	Nate Oliver
Dec 21, 1968		Cash	Houston Astros	P	Bill Monbouquette
March 28, 1969		Cash	Chicago Cubs	IF	Charley Smith
June 10, 1969	P	Ron Kline	Pittsburgh Pirates	P	Joe Gibbon
July 5, 1969		Cash	Boston Red Sox	P	Ron Kline
Aug 9, 1969	P	Don McMahon	Detroit Tigers		Cash
Sept 2, 1969		Cash	Detroit Tigers	SS	Cesar Gutierrez
Dec 1, 1969		Cash	Washington Senators	IF	Bob Schroder
Dec 5, 1969	P	Frank Reberger	San Diego Padres	C P IF	Bob Barton Ron Herbel Bobby Etheridge
Dec 12, 1969	IF OF	Bob Heise Jim Gosger	New York Mets	P OF	Ray Sadecki Dave Marshall
Dec 12, 1969	OF OF	Steve Whitaker Dick Simpson	Seattle Pilots	P	Bobby Bolin
April 4, 1970	C	Russ Gibson	Boston Red Sox		Cash
April 6, 1970		Cash	Montreal Expos	C	Jack Hiatt
April 20, 1970		Cash	Montreal Expos	OF	Jim Gosger
May 19, 1970	P	Jerry Johnson	St. Louis Cardinals	P	Frank Linzy
June 9, 1970		Cash	Milwaukee Brewers	OF-1B	Bob Burda
July 20, 1970	P	John Cumberland	New York Yankees	P	Mike McCormick
Dec 4, 1970	IF	Steve Huntz	San Diego Padres	2B	Don Mason minor league P Bill Frost
Dec 30, 1970	3B	Dave McDonald	Montreal Expos	2B	Ron Hunt
March 23, 1971	P	Steve Hamilton	Chicago White Sox	IF	Steve Huntz
May 29, 1971	SS P	Frank Duffy Vern Geishert	Cincinnati Reds	OF	George Foster
June 1, 1971	OF	Floyd Wicker	Milwaukee Brewers	IF	Bob Heise
Nov 29, 1971	P	Sam McDowell	Cleveland Indians	P SS	Gaylord Perry Frank Duffy
Feb 2, 1972		Cash	New York Yankees	SS	Hal Lanier
April 14, 1972		Cash	Los Angeles Dodgers	C	Dick Dietz

DATE		ACQUIRED	FROM		IN EXCHANGE FOR
May 11, 1972	P	Charlie Williams and $50,000.	New York Mets	OF	Willie Mays
June 16, 1972		Cash	St. Louis Cardinals	P	John Cumberland
Nov 28, 1972	P	Tom Bradley	Chicago White Sox	OF P	Ken Henderson Steve Stone
March 6, 1973		Cash	Cleveland Indians	P	Jerry Johnson
April 2, 1973	P	Greg Minton	Kansas City Royals	C	Fran Healy
April 14, 1973	IF	Bruce Miller	California Angels	3B	Alan Gallagher
April 17, 1973		Cash	New York Yankees	3B	Jim Hart
June 7, 1973		Cash	New York Yankees	P	Sam McDowell
Oct 25, 1973	P	Mike Caldwell	San Diego Padres	1B OF	Willie McCovey Bernie Williams
Dec 7, 1973		Cash	Boston Red Sox	P	Juan Marichal
March 19, 1974	C	Ken Rudolph	Chicago Cubs	P	Willie Prall
April 1, 1974	C	John Boccabella	Montreal Expos	P	Don Carrithers
Oct 14, 1974	C	Marc Hill	St. Louis Cardinals	P C	Elias Sosa Ken Rudolph
Oct 14, 1974	2B	Tom Heintzelman	St. Louis Cardinals	P	Jim Willoughby
Oct 22, 1974	OF	Bobby Murcer	New York Yankees	OF	Bobby Bonds
Dec 6, 1974	IF	Derrel Thomas	San Diego Padres	2B P	Tito Fuentes Clarence Metzger
Jan 29, 1975	OF	Von Joshua	Los Angeles Dodgers		Cash
Feb 28, 1975		$150,000.	New York Mets	OF	Dave Kingman
May 3, 1975		Cash	New York Mets	SS	Mike Phillips
May 4, 1975	1B	Willie Montanez	Philadelphia Phillies	OF	Garry Maddox
May 9, 1975	OF	Larry Herndon minor league P Luis Gonzalez	St. Louis Cardinals	P	Ron Bryant
June 11, 1975	SS	Craig Robinson	Atlanta Braves	1B	Ed Goodson
Dec 8, 1975	3B	Ken Reitz	St. Louis Cardinals	P	Pete Falcone
June 2, 1976		Cash	Milwaukee Brewers	OF	Von Joshua

DATE		ACQUIRED	FROM		IN EXCHANGE FOR
June 13, 1976	3B SS	Darrell Evans Marty Perez	Atlanta Braves	1B SS IF	Willie Montanez Craig Robinson Mike Eden
Oct 20, 1976	OF IF P	Willie Crawford Vic Harris John Curtis	St. Louis Cardinals	P P C	John D'Acquisto Mike Caldwell Dave Rader
Nov 17, 1976		No compensation (free agent signing)	Atlanta Braves	OF	Gary Matthews
Dec 6, 1976		Cash	Minnesota Twins	OF	Glenn Adams
Dec 10, 1976	P	Lynn McGlothen	St. Louis Cardinals	3B	Ken Reitz
Jan 6, 1977	1B	Willie McCovey	San Diego Padres		No compensation (free agent signing)
Feb 11, 1977	3B 2B	Bill Madlock Rob Sperring	Chicago Cubs	OF 3B	Bobby Murcer Steve Ontiveros minor league P Andy Muhlstock
March 14, 1977	OF	Terry Whitfield	New York Yankees	SS	Marty Perez
April 27, 1977	SS	Tim Foli	Montreal Expos	SS	Chris Speier
July 27, 1977		Cash	Baltimore Orioles	C	Ken Rudolph
Oct 25, 1977	OF	Jim Dwyer (San Francisco received Dwyer on June 15, 1978.)	St. Louis Cardinals	P	Frank Riccelli
Dec 7, 1977		Cash	New York Mets	SS	Tim Foli
Feb 28, 1978	IF	Mike Ivie	San Diego Padres	OF	Derrel Thomas
March 15, 1978	P	Vida Blue	Oakland Athletics	C OF P P P P SS	Gary Alexander Gary Thomasson Dave Heaverlo Alan Wirth John Henry Johnson Phil Huffman Mario Guerrero and $300,000.
June 15, 1978	OF	Hector Cruz	Chicago Cubs	P	Lynn McGlothen
June 15, 1978	SS	Roger Metzger	Houston Astros		Cash
July 18, 1978	C	John Tamargo	St. Louis Cardinals	P	Rob Dressler
Dec 3, 1978		No compensation (free agent signing)	California Angels	P	Jim Barr
March 15, 1979		Cash	Boston Red Sox	OF	Jim Dwyer
March 27, 1979		Cash	Milwaukee Brewers	1B	Skip James
June 13, 1979	SS	Joe Pettini and cash	Montreal Expos	C	John Tamargo

DATE		ACQUIRED	FROM		IN EXCHANGE FOR
June 28, 1979	P P P	Ed Whitson Fred Breining Al Holland	Pittsburgh Pirates	3B 3B P	Bill Madlock Lenny Randle Dave Roberts
June 28, 1979	P	Pedro Borbon	Cincinnati Reds	OF	Hector Cruz
Nov 1, 1979	C	Milt May	Chicago White Sox		No compensation (free agent signing)
Nov 26, 1979		No compensation (free agent signing)	San Diego Padres	P	John Curtis
Nov 29, 1979	2B	Rennie Stennett	Pittsburgh Pirates		No compensation (free agent signing)
Nov 29, 1979	OF	Jim Wohlford	Milwaukee Brewers		No compensation (free agent signing)
April 6, 1980	P	Allen Ripley	Boston Red Sox		Cash
June 20, 1980		Cash	California Angels	P	Ed Halicki
June 20, 1980		Cash	Seattle Mariners	C	Marc Hill
Dec 8, 1980	3B	Enos Cabell	San Francisco Giants	3B	Enos Cabell
Dec 12, 1980	P	Doyle Alexander	Atlanta Braves	P	John Montefusco minor league OF Craig Landis
Dec 12, 1980	OF OF	Jerry Martin Jesus Figueroa minor league IF Mike Turgeon	Chicago Cubs	2B P	Joe Strain Phil Nastu
Feb 12, 1981		No compensation (free agent signing)	Chicago White Sox	C	Marc Hill
April 20, 1981	1B OF	Dave Bergman Jeff Leonard	Houston Astros	1B	Mike Ivie
Nov 14, 1981	2B	Duane Kuiper	Cleveland Indians	P	Ed Whitson
Dec 7, 1981	P	Doug Capilla	Chicago Cubs	P	Allen Ripley
Dec 9, 1981	P P	Dan Schatzeder Mike Chris	Detroit Tigers	OF	Larry Herndon
Dec 11, 1981	1B	Dorian Boyland	Pittsburgh Pirates	P	Tom Griffin
Dec 11, 1981	P P	Rich Gale Juan Espino	Kansas City Royals	OF	Jerry Martin
March 4, 1982	OF	Champ Summers	Detroit Tigers	1B-3B	Enos Cabell and cash
March 30, 1982	P P P 2B	Renie Martin Craig Chamberlain Atlee Hammaker Brad Wellman	Kansas City Royals	P P	Vida Blue Bob Tufts
March 30, 1982	P OF	Andy McGaffigan Ted Wilborn	New York Yankees	P	Doyle Alexander
April 5, 1982	1B	Reggie Smith	Los Angeles Dodgers		No compensation (free agent signing)

DATE	ACQUIRED	FROM	IN EXCHANGE FOR
June 15, 1982	Cash	Montreal Expos	P Dan Schatzeder
Oct 15, 1982	P Herman Segelke	Chicago Cubs	P Alan Hargesheimer
Dec 14, 1982	P Mike Krukow P Mark Davis minor league OF Charles Penigar	Philadelphia Phillies	2B Joe Morgan P Al Holland
Jan 5, 1983	OF Mike Vail	Cincinnati Reds	P Rich Gale
Feb 2, 1983	SS Chris Smith	Montreal Expos	OF Jim Wohlford
Feb 7, 1983	2B Joel Youngblood	Montreal Expos	No compensation (free agent signing)
May 25, 1983	IF Wallace Johnson	Montreal Expos	OF Mike Vail
Aug 19, 1983	C Steve Nicosia	Pittsburgh Pirates	C Milt May and cash
Sept 30, 1983	Cash	Chicago Cubs	P Mike Chris
Dec 6, 1983	3B Joe Pittman minor league OF Tommy Francis	San Diego Padres	OF Champ Summers
Dec 19, 1983	No compensation (free agent signing)	Detroit Tigers	1B Darrell Evans
Dec 21, 1983	2B Manny Trillo	Montreal Expos	No compensation (free agent signing)
Feb 27, 1984	1B Al Oliver	Montreal Expos	P Fred Breining OF Max Venable P Andy McGaffigan
	(San Francisco sent McGaffigan to Montreal on April 1, 1984, after Breining reported to the Expos with a sore arm.)		
March 24, 1984	OF Alejandro Sanchez	Philadelphia Phillies	1B Dave Bergman
March 31, 1984	OF Gene Richards	San Diego Padres	No compensation (free agent signing)

Baltimore Orioles

The Best Trades

1. Acquired Frank Robinson from the Cincinnati Reds for Milt Pappas, Jack Baldschun, and Dick Simpson, December 9, 1965.
2. Acquired Mike Cuellar, Enzo Hernandez and Elijah Johnson from the Houston Astros for Curt Blefary and John Mason, December 4, 1968.
3. Acquired Mike Torrez and Ken Singleton from the Montreal Expos for Dave McNally, Rich Coggins, and Bill Kirkpatrick, December 4, 1974.
4. Acquired Scott McGregor, Tippy Martinez, Rick Dempsey, Rudy May, and Dave Pagan from the New York Yankees for Doyle Alexander, Ken Holtzman, Grant Jackson, Ellie Hendricks, and Jimmy Freeman, June 15, 1976.

5. Acquired Pat Dobson and Tom Dukes from the San Diego Padres for Tom Phoebus, Fred Beene, Enzo Hernandez, and Al Severinsen, December 1, 1970.

The Worst Trades

1. Traded Vic Wertz to the Cleveland Indians for Bob Chakales, June 1, 1954.
2. Traded Davy Johnson, Pat Dobson, Roric Harrison, and Johnny Oates to the Atlanta Braves for Earl Williams and Taylor Duncan, December 30, 1972.
3. Traded Bob Turley, Don Larsen, Billy Hunter, Mike Blyzka, Darrell Johnson, Jim Fridley, and Dick Kryhoski to the New York Yankees for Gus Triandos, Gene Woodling, Willie Miranda, Hal Smith, Jim McDonald, Harry Byrd, Bill Miller, Kal Segrist, Don Leppert, Ted Del Gurcio, and a player to be named later, November 18 and December 1, 1954.
4. Traded Doug DeCinces and Jeff Schneider to the California Angels for Dan Ford, January 28, 1982.
5. Traded Frank Robinson and Pete Richert to the Los Angeles Dodgers for Doyle Alexander, Bob O'Brien, Sergio Robles, and Royle Stillman, December 2, 1971.

Organization: The Oriole Way

The Baltimore organization prides itself on its stability. It makes very few major player transactions and signs very few free agents from other clubs, preferring to develop players from the farm system and to keep them in Oriole uniforms. They have no objections to paying high salaries on long-term contracts; they'd just rather give them to their own players instead of inheriting someone else's headaches. Eddie Murray and Cal Ripken are both in the million-a-year class without ever having gone through the re-entry draft. (Ripken won't even be eligible for free agency until after the 1987 season.)

While they may not make many deals, those they do make have usually been outstanding. First and foremost, naturally, is the Frank Robinson trade that transformed a young challenging team into an American League champion in four of the subsequent six seasons. But this was hardly the only theft Harry Dalton perpetrated in his years as general manager. Three years later the O's cemented their pitching staff by sending Curt Blefary and a minor league pitcher to Houston for Mike Cuellar and shortstop Enzo Hernandez. And two years after that, Dalton acquired another twenty-game winner, Pat Dobson, for the light-hitting Hernandez in a deal with San Diego. (Hernandez is probably best remembered today for his remarkable 1971 season; in 549 at bats he drove in just 12 runs.)

When Dalton departed to face new challenges in California, Frank Cashen was named general manager. Cashen's first major move was an unfortunate deal with Atlanta in which he gave up Dobson, second baseman Davy Johnson, pitcher Roric Harrison, and catcher Johnny Oates for power-hitting catcher Earl Williams. Manager Earl Weaver had coveted Williams's home run bat, but his work habits left much to be desired. Two years later he was on his way back to Atlanta; in the meantime, Dobson had won 31 games in two seasons for the Braves and Yankees, and Johnson had found home run heaven in Atlanta, belting a career high 43 in 1973.

Cashen more than atoned for that blunder in 1974 in a trade with Montreal. The O's gave up Dave McNally, Bill Kirkpatrick, and Rich Coggins for Ken Singleton and Mike Torrez. McNally retired in June, Kirkpatrick never reported, and Coggins was gone by mid-season. Singleton, on the other hand, became a fixture in the heart of the Baltimore lineup, and Torrez enjoyed his only twenty-win season before being dealt to Oakland. (The Oakland deal stands as a great what-if; the Orioles sent Torrez, Don Baylor, and Paul Mitchell to the A's for Reggie Jackson and Ken Holtzman. The key to this trade was the impending free agency of Baylor and Jackson. Jackson ultimately opted for the bright lights of New York, leaving behind visions of the destruction he might have caused batting between Singleton and Murray.)

Second only to the Robinson deal in its impact on Baltimore fortunes is the deal they pulled with the Yankees in 1976. Holtzman, Doyle Alexander, Grant Jackson, Jimmy Freeman, and Elrod Hendricks were sent to New York for Scott McGregor, Tippy Martinez, Rick Dempsey, Rudy May, and Dave Pagan. The newcomers did next to nothing for the Yankees, while Dempsey, McGregor, and Martinez played crucial roles in the perennially contending Orioles clubs of the late '70s and '80s.

The key to the Baltimore method is the productivity of the farm system. The foundation of their teams has generally been their home-grown players: Jim Palmer, Brooks Robinson, Dave McNally, Boog Powell, Mark Belanger, Bobby Grich, Mike Flanagan, Doug DeCinces, Eddie Murray, and Cal Ripken have all come up through the Oriole chain, learning to play baseball the Oriole way at every level of pro ball. While the club has lost several players to free agency, it has generally only lost those they knew could be replaced. When Wayne Garland demanded a big contract after winning twenty, the Orioles let him go, knowing Flanagan was ready. Grich's departure was eased by the presence of Rich Dauer. Even the loss of Jackson's power was hardly felt when Eddie Murray stepped in as designated hitter; the Orioles' team home run total increased the year after Reggie left. And the O's have occasionally dipped into the free-agent waters, picking up Cy Young winner Steve Stone and outfielder Jim Dwyer at bargain rates.

In all, the Orioles are a perfect model of how to build a winner in a limited market: build primarily from within, trade for players on the rise to provide long-term answers to your problems, and look to the free agent market mostly for needed role-players.

DATE		ACQUIRED	FROM		IN EXCHANGE FOR
Dec 17, 1953	P	Joe Coleman	Philadelphia Athletics	P P	Frank Fanovich Bob Cain
Feb 5, 1954	SS OF	Neil Berry Sam Mele	Chicago White Sox	OF SS	Johnny Groth Johnny Lipon
Feb 10, 1954	P	Vern Bickford	Milwaukee Braves	C	Charlie White and $10,000.
Feb 12, 1954		Cash	Boston Red Sox	OF	Don Lenhardt
Feb 18, 1954	OF	Gil Coan	Washington Senators	OF	Roy Sievers
March 16, 1954	1B	Eddie Waitkus	Philadelphia Phillies		$40,000.
March 28, 1954	C	Ray Murray	Philadelphia Athletics		$25,000.
April 8, 1954	P	Dave Koslo	New York Giants		Cash
April 17, 1954	3B	Bob Kennedy	Cleveland Indians	OF	Jim Dyck
May 11, 1954	IF	Jim Brideweser	New York Yankees		Waiver price
May 25, 1954	OF	Cal Abrams	Pittsburgh Pirates	P	Dick Littlefield
June 1, 1954	P	Bob Chakales	Cleveland Indians	1B	Vic Wertz
July 4, 1954		Waiver price	New York Yankees	P	Marlin Stuart
July 29, 1954		Waiver price	Boston Red Sox	OF	Sam Mele

DATE		ACQUIRED	FROM		IN EXCHANGE FOR
Aug 7, 1954	P	Bob Kuzava	New York Yankees		Waiver price
Nov 18, 1954	P	Harry Byrd	New York Yankees	P	Bob Turley
	P	Jim McDonald		P	Don Larsen
	C	Hal Smith		SS	Billy Hunter
	C	Gus Triandos			
	OF	Gene Woodling			
	SS	Willie Miranda			
		(First part of 18-player trade completed on December 1, 1954.)			
Nov 24, 1954	OF	Charlie Maxwell	Boston Red Sox		Cash
Dec 1, 1954	P	Bill Miller	New York Yankees	P	Mike Blyzka
	3B	Kal Segrist		C	Darrell Johnson
	2B	Don Leppert		OF	Jim Fridley
		minor league OF Ted Del Guercio and a player to be named later		1B	Dick Kryhoski
		(Second part of 18-player trade begun on November 18, 1954.)			
Dec 6, 1954	P	Don Ferrarese	Chicago White Sox	2B	Jim Brideweser
	P	Don Johnson		P	Bob Chakales
	C	Matt Batts		C	Clint Courtney
	SS	Freddie Marsh			
Dec 13, 1954	3B	Billy Cox	Brooklyn Dodgers		Minor leaguers John Jancse and Harry Schwegeman and $50,000.
	P	Preacher Roe			
Jan 3, 1955	OF	Hoot Evers	Detroit Tigers		Cash
March 17, 1955	P	Erv Palica	Brooklyn Dodgers	1B	Frank Kellert and cash
April 13, 1955	P	Jim Wilson	Milwaukee Braves		Cash
May 11, 1955		Cash	Detroit Tigers	OF	Charlie Maxwell
May 11, 1955	P	Art Schallock	New York Yankees		Waiver price
May 23, 1955		Waiver price	Philadelphia Phillies	P	Bob Kuzava
May 30, 1955		Cash	Chicago White Sox	3B	Bob Kennedy
June 6, 1955	P	Harry Dorish	Chicago White Sox	C	Les Moss
June 15, 1955		Waiver price	Chicago White Sox	P	Harry Byrd
June 15, 1955	OF	Dave Pope	Cleveland Indians	OF	Gene Woodling
	OF	Wally Westlake		3B	Billy Cox
		(Cox refused to report and announced retirement. Cleveland received $15,000 to complete trade.)			
June 27, 1955	3B	Hank Majeski	Cleveland Indians	2B	Bobby Young
July 2, 1955	OF	Dave Philley	Cleveland Indians		Waiver price

DATE		ACQUIRED	FROM		IN EXCHANGE FOR
July 8, 1955	P	George Zuverink	Detroit Tigers		Waiver price
July 13, 1955		Minor league P Jim Wright	Cleveland Indians	OF	Hoot Evers
July 16, 1955	OF	Jim Dyck	Cleveland Indians		Cash
July 17, 1955		Waiver price	Chicago White Sox	OF	Gil Coan
July 30, 1955	P	Ed Lopat	New York Yankees		Waiver price
Oct 18, 1955	IF	Bobby Adams	Chicago White Sox	OF	Cal Abrams
April 5, 1956	P	Babe Birrer	Detroit Tigers		Waiver price
April 21, 1956	2B	Billy Gardner	New York Giants		$20,000.
May 11, 1956		$25,000.	Cincinnati Reds	OF	Jim Dyck
May 13, 1956	OF	Hoot Evers	Cleveland Indians	OF	Dave Pope
May 14, 1956	P	Billy Loes	Brooklyn Dodgers		$20,000.
May 14, 1956	P	Johnny Schmitz	Boston Red Sox		Cash
May 14, 1956	P	Sandy Consuegra	Chicago White Sox		Cash
May 21, 1956	OF P P 3B	Bob Nieman Mike Fornieles Connie Johnson George Kell	Chicago White Sox	P OF	Jim Wilson Dave Philley
June 25, 1956		Cash	Boston Red Sox	P	Harry Dorish
June 25, 1956	OF	Dick Williams	Brooklyn Dodgers		Waiver price
July 13, 1956	P	Morrie Martin	Chicago White Sox		Waiver price
Aug 1, 1956	IF	Grady Hatton	St. Louis Cardinals		Cash
Aug 17, 1956	C	Joe Ginsberg	Kansas City Athletics	C	Hal Smith
Oct 11, 1956	P OF	Art Ceccarelli Al Pilarcik	Kansas City Athletics	P OF	Ryne Duren Jim Pisoni
Feb 8, 1957	IF	Jim Brideweser	Detroit Tigers		Cash
May 14, 1957		Waiver price	New York Giants	P	Sandy Consuegra
May 20, 1957	P	Art Houtteman	Cleveland Indians		Cash
June 4, 1957	P	Ken Lehman	Brooklyn Dodgers		$30,000.
June 13, 1957	OF	Jim Busby	Cleveland Indians	OF	Dick Williams

DATE		ACQUIRED	FROM		IN EXCHANGE FOR
June 14, 1957	3B	Billy Goodman	Boston Red Sox	P	Mike Fornieles
Sept 19, 1957	IF	Eddie Miksis	St. Louis Cardinals		Waiver price
Dec 3, 1957	P	Jack Harshman	Chicago White Sox	OF	Tito Francona
	P	Russ Heman		P	Ray Moore
	1B	Jim Marshall		3B	Billy Goodman
	OF	Larry Doby			
Dec 4, 1957		Waiver price	Cincinnati Reds	P	Bill Wight
March 24, 1958	IF	Foster Castleman	San Francisco Giants		$30,000.
June 2, 1958	P	Lou Sleater	Detroit Tigers		Waiver price
July 25, 1958	OF	Joe Taylor	St. Louis Cardinals		Waiver price
Aug 23, 1958		Waiver price	Chicago Cubs	1B	Jim Marshall
Aug 23, 1958	P	Hoyt Wilhelm	Cleveland Indians		Waiver price
Oct 2, 1958		Waiver price	Philadelphia Phillies	P	Ken Lehman
Oct 2, 1958	SS	Chico Carrasquel	Kansas City Athletics	OF	Dick Williams
Oct 14, 1958	3B	Jim Finigan	St. Louis Cardinals	2B	Jim Brideweser
				P	Art Ceccarelli
Dec 2, 1958	2B	Bobby Avila	Cleveland Indians	P	Russ Heman and $30,000.
Dec 15, 1958	IF	Billy Klaus	Boston Red Sox	OF	Jim Busby
Feb 14, 1959	1B	Whitey Lockman	San Francisco Giants		Cash
April 1, 1959	P	Vito Valentinetti	Washington Senators	P	Billy Loes
		(Trade was cancelled on April 8, 1959, by Commissioner Frick due to Loes's sore arm.)			
May 21, 1959		Waiver price	Boston Red Sox	2B	Bobby Avila
May 26, 1959	OF	Albie Pearson	Washington Senators	OF	Lenny Green
June 23, 1959	1B	Walt Dropo	Cincinnati Reds	1B	Whitey Lockman
Sept 6, 1959	P	Rip Coleman	Kansas City Athletics		Waiver price
Nov 30, 1959	OF	Jackie Brandt	San Francisco Giants	P	Billy O'Dell
	P	Gordon Jones		P	Billy Loes
	C	Roger McCardell			
Dec 2, 1959	OF	Gene Green	St. Louis Cardinals	OF	Bob Nieman
Dec 15, 1959	OF	Johnny Powers	Cincinnati Reds		Cash

DATE		ACQUIRED	FROM		IN EXCHANGE FOR
April 3, 1960	C 2B	Clint Courtney Ron Samford	Washington Senators	2B	Billy Gardner
May 12, 1960		Waiver price	Cleveland Indians	OF	Johnny Powers
June 9, 1960	OF	Gene Stephens	Boston Red Sox	OF	Willie Tasby
Sept 1, 1960	OF	Dave Philley	San Francisco Giants		Cash
Sept 7, 1960	C	Del Rice	St. Louis Cardinals		Cash
Dec 15, 1960	OF	Earl Robinson	Los Angeles Dodgers		Cash
Jan 24, 1961	OF OF	Whitey Herzog Russ Snyder	Kansas City Athletics	3B P 1B OF	Wayne Causey Jim Archer Bob Boyd Al Pilarcik
June 8, 1961	1B	Marv Throneberry	Kansas City Athletics	OF	Gene Stephens
Oct 11, 1961	P	Johnny Kucks	Kansas City Athletics		Cash
Oct 16, 1961	P	Robin Roberts	Philadelphia Phillies		Cash
Nov 16, 1961	2B	Johnny Temple	Cleveland Indians	1B C	Ray Barker Harry Chiti and minor leaguer Art Kay
Dec 1, 1961		Minor leaguer Ron Kabbes	St. Louis Cardinals	P	Johnny Kucks
April 20, 1962		Cash	Cincinnati Reds	C	Hank Foiles
May 9, 1962	C	Hobie Landrith and cash	New York Mets	1B	Marv Throneberry
Aug 11, 1962		Cash	Houston Astros	2B	Johnny Temple
Sept 7, 1962		Cash	New York Yankees	P	Hal Brown
Sept 10, 1962	C	Nate Smith	Los Angeles Angels		Cash
Oct 12, 1962		Cash	Houston Astros	OF	Dick Williams
Nov 21, 1962	C	Jimmie Coker	Philadelphia Phillies		Cash
Nov 26, 1962	C	Dick Brown	Detroit Tigers	C OF	Gus Triandos Whitey Herzog
Dec 5, 1962	2B P	Bob Johnson Pete Burnside	Washington Senators	OF 2B	Barry Shetrone Marv Breeding and minor league P Art Quick
Dec 15, 1962	P P C	Mike McCormick Stu Miller John Orsino	San Francisco Giants	P C P	Jack Fisher Jimmie Coker Billy Hoeft

DATE		ACQUIRED	FROM		IN EXCHANGE FOR
Dec 15, 1962	OF	Joe Gaines	Cincinnati Reds	P	Dick Luebke minor league IF Willard Oplinger
Jan 14, 1963	SS OF	Luis Aparicio Al Smith	Chicago White Sox	P 3B SS OF	Hoyt Wilhelm Pete Ward Ron Hansen Dave Nicholson
May 8, 1963		Cash	Washington Senators	C	Hobie Landrith
July 1, 1963		Cash	Kansas City Athletics	C	Charlie Lau
July 14, 1963	P	George Brunet	Houston Astros		Cash
Oct 11, 1963		Cash	Washington Senators	OF	Fred Valentine
Nov 27, 1963	1B	Norm Siebern	Kansas City Athletics	1B	Jim Gentile and cash
Dec 4, 1963	OF	Willie Kirkland	Cleveland Indians	OF	Al Smith and $25,000.
Dec 14, 1963	P	Harvey Haddix	Pittsburgh Pirates		Minor league SS Dick Yencha and cash
March 31, 1964	OF	Lou Piniella	Washington Senators	P	Buster Narum
May 12, 1964		Cash	Houston Astros	P	George Brunet
June 15, 1964	OF	Johnny Weekly and cash	Houston Astros	OF	Joe Gaines
June 15, 1964	C	Charlie Lau	Kansas City Athletics	P	Wes Stock
Aug 12, 1964		Cash	Washington Senators	OF	Willie Kirkland
Sept 5, 1964	OF	Lenny Green	Los Angeles Angels		Cash
Sept 10, 1964	P	Ken Rowe	Los Angeles Dodgers		Cash
April 4, 1965		Minor league P Steve Herman and $20,000.	Washington Senators	P	Mike McCormick
April 24, 1965	P	Don Larsen	Houston Astros	IF	Bob Saverine and cash
July 24, 1965	OF	Carl Warwick	St. Louis Cardinals		Cash
Oct 12, 1965	OF	Woodie Held	Washington Senators	C	John Orsino
Dec 2, 1965	OF	Dick Simpson	California Angels	1B	Norm Siebern
Dec 6, 1965	P	Jack Baldschun	Philadelphia Phillies	OF P	Jackie Brandt Darold Knowles
Dec 9, 1965	OF	Frank Robinson	Cincinnati Reds	P P OF	Milt Pappas Jack Baldschun Dick Simpson

DATE		ACQUIRED	FROM		IN EXCHANGE FOR
March 30, 1966	C	Vic Roznovsky	Chicago Cubs	OF	Carl Warwick
June 12, 1966	P	Eddie Fisher	Chicago White Sox	2B	Jerry Adair and minor league OF Johnny Riddle
Aug 15, 1966		Cash	Boston Red Sox	P	Bill Short
Sept 12, 1966	1B-OF	Dave Roberts	Pittsburgh Pirates		Cash
Dec 15, 1966	P	John Morris	Philadelphia Phillies	P	Dick Hall
May 10, 1967		Cash	New York Mets	IF	Bob Johnson
May 10, 1967		Cash	New York Mets	P	John Miller
May 29, 1967	P	Pete Richert	Washington Senators	1B P	Mike Epstein Frank Bertaina
May 31, 1967		Cash	Atlanta Braves	C	Charlie Lau
June 15, 1967	P	Marcelino Lopez	California Angels	OF	Woodie Held
July 5, 1967	1B	Ray Barker minor league IFs Chet Trail and Joe Brady and cash	New York Yankees	P	Steve Barber
Aug 21, 1967	P	John Buzhardt	Chicago White Sox		Cash
Sept 23, 1967		Cash	Houston Astros	P	John Buzhardt
Nov 28, 1967	P IF	John O'Donoghue Gordon Lund	Cleveland Indians	P	Eddie Fisher minor leaguers P George Scott and IF John Scruggs
Nov 29, 1967	OF P P	Don Buford Bruce Howard Roger Nelson	Chicago White Sox	SS OF OF	Luis Aparicio Russ Snyder John Matias
April 1, 1968		Cash	Atlanta Braves	P	Stu Miller
June 15, 1968	P	Fred Valentine	Washington Senators	P	Bruce Howard
Dec 4, 1968	P SS	Mike Cuellar Enzo Hernandez and minor league IF Elijah Johnson	Houston Astros	OF-1B	Curt Blefary and minor leaguer John Mason
Jan 20, 1969	C	Clay Dalrymple	Philadelphia Phillies	OF	Ron Stone
March 18, 1969	P	Bill Kelso (Kelso was returned to Cincinnati on March 29.)	Cincinnati Reds		Cash
March 31, 1969	IF	Chico Salmon	Seattle Pilots	P IF	Gene Brabender Gordon Lund

DATE		ACQUIRED	FROM		IN EXCHANGE FOR
April 30, 1969	P IF	Gerry Schoen Mike Ferraro	Seattle Pilots	P P	John O'Donoghue Tom Fisher and minor league P Lloyd Fourroux
Dec 5, 1969		Cash	St. Louis Cardinals	P	Bill Dillman
June 15, 1970	P P	Dick Baney Buzz Stephen	Milwaukee Brewers	OF	Dave May
June 15, 1970	P	Moe Drabowsky	Kansas City Royals	IF	Bobby Floyd
Aug 14, 1970		Cash	St. Louis Cardinals	P	Frank Bertaina
Nov 30, 1970	IF	Jerry Davanon	St. Louis Cardinals	P	Moe Drabowsky
Dec 1, 1970	P P	Pat Dobson Tom Dukes	San Diego Padres	P P P SS	Tom Phoebus Al Severinsen Fred Beene Enzo Hernandez
Dec 16, 1970	P 1B OF	Grant Jackson Jim Hutto Sam Parrilla	Philadelphia Phillies	OF	Roger Freed
April 5, 1971	P	Roric Harrison and minor leaguer Marion Jackson	Milwaukee Brewers	P	Marcelino Lopez
May 28, 1971	P	Bill Burbach	New York Yankees	P	Jim Hardin
Dec 2, 1971	P P C 1B	Doyle Alexander Bob O'Brien Sergio Robles Royle Stillman	Los Angeles Dodgers	OF P	Frank Robinson Pete Richert
Dec 9, 1971	P	Bob Reynolds and cash	Milwaukee Brewers	OF	Curt Motton
June 10, 1972	OF	Roger Repoz	California Angels	IF	Jerry Davanon
June 12, 1972	C	Francisco Estrada	California Angels		Cash
Aug 18, 1972	1B	Tommy Davis	Chicago Cubs	C	Ellie Hendricks
Oct 27, 1972	C	Ellie Hendricks	Chicago Cubs	C	Francisco Estrada
Dec 30, 1972	C IF	Earl Williams Taylor Duncan	Atlanta Braves	P P 2B C	Pat Dobson Roric Harrison Davy Johnson Johnny Oates
April 5, 1973	SS	Frank Baker	New York Yankees	IF	Tommy Matchick
May 22, 1973		Cash	Montreal Expos	P	Mickey Scott
June 15, 1973		Cash	St. Louis Cardinals	P	Orlando Pena

DATE		ACQUIRED	FROM		IN EXCHANGE FOR
Dec 4, 1973	P	Ross Grimsley and minor league C Wally Williams	Cincinnati Reds	OF SS	Merv Rettenmund Junior Kennedy and minor league C Bill Wood
Dec 6, 1973		Cash	Texas Rangers	OF-1B	Terry Crowley
Dec 7, 1973		Cash	Philadelphia Phillies	P	Eddie Watt
Sept 11, 1974	UT	Bob Oliver	California Angels	P	Mickey Scott Cash
Sept 16, 1974	OF	Jim Northrup	Montreal Expos		Cash
Sept 16, 1974		Cash	California Angels	P	Larry McCall
Dec 1, 1974		Cash	New York Yankees	UT	Bob Oliver
Dec 3, 1974	1B OF	Lee May Jay Schleuter	Houston Astros	1B IF	Enos Cabell Rob Andrews
Dec 4, 1974	OF P	Ken Singleton Mike Torrez	Montreal Expos	P OF	Dave McNally Rich Coggins minor league P Bill Kirkpatrick
Feb 25, 1975	C	Dave Duncan and minor league OF Al McGrew	Cleveland Indians	1B P	Boog Powell Don Hood
April 17, 1975	P	Jimmy Freeman	Atlanta Braves	C	Earl Williams and cash
May 29, 1975	P	Fred Holdsworth	Detroit Tigers	P	Bob Reynolds
June 15, 1975		Cash	California Angels	C	Andy Etchebarren
June 15, 1975	1B	Tony Muser	Chicago White Sox	P	Jesse Jefferson
April 2, 1976	OF P	Reggie Jackson Ken Holtzman minor leaguer Bill Van Bommell	Oakland Athletics	OF P P	Don Baylor Mike Torrez Paul Mitchell
June 15, 1976	P P P P C	Rudy May Tippy Martinez Dave Pagan Scott McGregor Rick Dempsey	New York Yankees	P P P C P	Ken Holtzman Doyle Alexander Grant Jackson Ellie Hendricks Jimmy Freeman
Sept 9, 1976		Cash	California Angels	IF	Tim Nordbrook
Nov 18, 1976	OF	Pat Kelly	Chicago White Sox	C	Dave Duncan
Nov 19, 1976		No compensation (free agent signing)	Cleveland Indians	P	Wayne Garland

DATE	ACQUIRED	FROM	IN EXCHANGE FOR
Nov 24, 1976	No compensation (free agent signing)	California Angels	2B Bobby Grich
Nov 29, 1976	No compensation (free agent signing)	New York Yankees	OF Reggie Jackson
Jan 20, 1977	OF Elliott Maddox OF-1B Rick Bladt	New York Yankees	OF Paul Blair
June 13, 1977	P Dick Drago	California Angels	P Dyar Miller
July 14, 1977	P Dennis Blair	Montreal Expos	P Fred Holdsworth
July 27, 1977	C Ken Rudolph	San Francisco Giants	Cash
Sept 7, 1977	Cash	St. Louis Cardinals	3B Taylor Duncan
Sept 19, 1977	P Nellie Briles	Texas Rangers	Cash
Nov 30, 1977	No compensation (free agent signing)	New York Yankees	OF Elliott Maddox
Dec 7, 1977	P Don Stanhouse P Joe Kerrigan OF Gary Roenicke	Montreal Expos	P Rudy May P Randy Miller P Bryn Smith
Dec 7, 1977	OF Carlos Lopez P Tommy Moore	Seattle Mariners	P Mike Parrott
Dec 21, 1977	No compensation (free agent signing)	Montreal Expos	P Ross Grimsley
April 4, 1978	Cash	Milwaukee Brewers	P Andy Replogle
Nov 27, 1978	OF John Lowenstein	Texas Rangers	Cash
Nov 29, 1978	P Steve Stone	Chicago White Sox	No compensation (free agent signing)
June 5, 1979	IF Floyd Rayford and cash	California Angels	OF Larry Harlow
Aug 30, 1979	OF Bob Molinaro	Chicago White Sox	Cash
Oct 3, 1979	Cash	Chicago White Sox	OF Bob Molinaro
Nov 17, 1979	No compensation (free agent signing)	Los Angeles Dodgers	P Don Stanhouse
Dec 6, 1979	2B Lenn Sakata	Milwaukee Brewers	P John Flinn
Dec 7, 1979	C Dan Graham	Minnesota Twins	1B Tom Chism
May 13, 1980	Cash	California Angels	C Dave Skaggs
Dec 9, 1980	No compensation (free agent signing)	Kansas City Royals	1B Lee Maye
Dec 23, 1980	OF Jim Dwyer	Boston Red Sox	No compensation (free agent signing)
Dec 23, 1980	1B Jose Morales	Minnesota Twins	No compensation (free agent signing)

DATE		ACQUIRED	FROM		IN EXCHANGE FOR
Dec 29, 1980		No compensation (free agent signing)	Cleveland Indians	OF	Pat Kelly
April 1, 1981	OF	Chris Bourjos and cash	Houston Astros	SS	Kiko Garcia
Dec 11, 1981		No compensation (free agent signing)	Los Angeles Dodgers	SS	Mark Belanger
Jan 28, 1982	OF	Dan Ford	California Angels	3B P	Doug DeCinces Jeff Schneider
Feb 9, 1982	P	Paul Moskau	Cincinnati Reds	3B	Wayne Krenchicki
Feb 19, 1982	OF	Rick Lisi	Texas Rangers	P	Steve Luebber
Feb 24, 1982	P	Craig Minetto	Oakland Athletics		Minor league P Allen Edwards
March 26, 1982	C	Joe Nolan	Cincinnati Reds	OF	Dallas Williams minor league P Brooks Carey
April 3, 1982		Cash	Pittsburgh Pirates	P	Paul Moskau
April 28, 1982	3B	Leo Hernandez	Los Angeles Dodgers	C	Jose Morales
Feb 7, 1983	3B	Aurelio Rodriguez	Chicago White Sox		No compensation (free agent signing)
June 15, 1983	OF	Tito Landrum	St. Louis Cardinals	C-3B	Floyd Rayford
June 30, 1983	SS-3B	Todd Cruz	Seattle Mariners		Cash
Dec 8, 1983	3B	Wayne Gross	Oakland Athletics	P	Tim Stoddard
Dec 21, 1983	P	Bobby Sprowl	Houston Astros	P	Craig Minetto
Feb 6, 1984	P	Tom Underwood	Oakland Athletics		Free agent signing
		(Oakland selected P Tim Belcher of New York Yankees from the compensation pool.)			
March 25, 1984		Minor league P Jose Brito	St. Louis Cardinals	OF	Tito Landrum
March 30, 1984	3B	Floyd Rayford	St. Louis Cardinals		Cash

Boston Red Sox

The Best Trades

1. Acquired Lefty Grove, Rube Walberg, and Max Bishop from the Philadelphia Athletics for $125,000, Bob Kline, and Rabbit Warstler, December 12, 1933.
2. Acquired Joe Cronin from the Washington Senators for $250,000 and Lyn Lary, October 26, 1934.
3. Acquired Jackie Jensen from the Washington Senators for Mickey McDermott and Tommy Umphlett, December 9, 1953.

4. Acquired Vern Stephens and Jack Kramer from the St. Louis Browns for $310,000, Roy Partee, Jim Wilson, Al Widmar, Eddie Pellagrini, Pete Layden, and Joe Ostrowski, November 17, 1947.

5. Acquired Wes Ferrell and Dick Porter from the Cleveland Indians for Bob Weiland, Bob Seeds, and $25,000, May 25, 1934.

The Worst Trades

1. Sold Babe Ruth to the New York Yankees for $125,000 and a $300,000 loan, January 3, 1920.

2. Traded Red Ruffing to the New York Yankees for Cedric Durst and $50,000, May 6, 1930.

3. Traded Sparky Lyle to the New York Yankees for Danny Cater, March 22, 1972.

4. Traded Tris Speaker to the Cleveland Indians for Sad Sam Jones, Fred Thomas, and $55,000, April 12, 1916.

5. Traded Buddy Myer to the Washington Senators for Grant Gillis, Bobby Reeves, Milt Gaston, Hod Lisenbee, and Elliott Bigelow, December 15, 1928.

Trader: Harry Frazee

The Boston Red Sox have known their great years and their lean years. They knew their greatest years first: they won six pennants and five World Series in their first eighteen years. They won only two pennants and no World Series in the fifty that followed.

From 1912 through 1918, the Sox were all but unbeatable. They took four world titles and finished second in the AL twice. They boasted such great stars as Babe Ruth, Tris Speaker, Harry Hooper, Duffy Lewis, Smoky Joe Wood, and Carl Mays. And then came the fall.

It all began when theatrical entrepreneur Harry Frazee purchased the club from Joseph Lannin in 1917. Buying in at the top, Frazee looked at the club as a diversion from his Broadway efforts. But by 1919, with Lannin demanding payment for outstanding notes and with Boston banks refusing him a mortgage on Fenway Park, he was forced to raise cash by selling off his most tangible assets: his players. And, to the eternal chagrin of Boston's loyal rooters, the most willing buyers were the hopelessly mediocre New York Yankees.

The shuttle to New York began with the trade of Duffy Lewis, Ernie Shore and Dutch Leonard for four players and $50,000. Neither Lewis nor Shore quite returned to the form they had shown before World War I, so the deal was not the disaster it could have been. The next two made up for it. Carl Mays, winner of 43 games in the previous two seasons, went away for $40,000 and two pitchers. Babe Ruth went next, for $100,000 and a personal loan to Frazee of $300,000.

The loss of Ruth so upset the Fenway faithful that they vowed to boycott the club and run Frazee out of town, but the deals continued. Waite Hoyt went next in an eight-player deal that gave the Sox the usual collection of has-beens and never-wases along with the obligatory cash. With Hoyt winning 19 and Mays 27, the Yanks took their first pennant in 1921, but lost the Series to the crosstown Giants. Yankee manager Miller Huggins blamed the defeat on a lack of pitching depth, so Frazee forked over pitchers Joe Bush and Sam Jones along with shortstop Everett Scott for three over-the-hill hurlers and the usual fifty grand. A once-great team had been decimated, and the task of dismantling was completed in 1922 when Boston's last quality ballplayers, Joe Dugan, Elmer Smith, and Herb Pennock, boarded the train for New York. The Sox spent the next ten years trying to climb out of the hole their owner had so graciously dug for them, and it wasn't until multimillionaire sportsman Tom Yawkey purchased the club that they made any headway at all.

DATE		ACQUIRED	FROM		IN EXCHANGE FOR
April 1901		Cash	Baltimore Orioles	P	Frank Foreman
Oct 1901		Cash	Cleveland Indians	C	Ossee Schreckengost
April 1902		Cash	Philadelphia Athletics	P	Fred Mitchell
May 30, 1902	1B	Candy LaChance	Cleveland Indians	OF	Piano Legs Hickman
June 1902		Cash			
June 1902		Cash	Baltimore Orioles	P P	George Prentiss Bert Husting
July 1902	P	Long Tom Hughes	Baltimore Orioles		Cash
April 1903		Cash	Chicago White Sox	P	Nick Altrock
Dec 1903	P	Jesse Tannehill	New York Yankees	P	Long Tom Hughes
Jan 16, 1904		Cash	Washington Senators	OF	George Stone
Jan 16, 1904		Cash	Washington Senators	1B	Jake Stahl
June 18, 1904	3B	Bob Unglaub	New York Yankees	OF	Patsy Dougherty
July 4, 1904	OF	Kip Selbach	Washington Senators	OF	Bill O'Neill
Jan 16, 1905	OF	George Stone	Washington Senators		Cash
Jan 16, 1905	OF OF	Jesse Burkett Frank Huelsman	St. Louis Browns	OF	George Stone
Jan 16, 1905		See note	Washington Senators	OF	Frank Huelsman
		(St. Louis reclaimed Huelsmann, who was with Washington on loan, and traded him to Boston. Boston then sent him to Washington as payment for George Stone.)			
May 18, 1905		Waiver price	Detroit Tigers	C	Tom Doran
May 20, 1907	OF	Bunk Congalton	Cleveland Indians		Cash
June 7, 1907	3B	Jack Knight	Philadelphia Athletics	3B	Jimmy Collins
June 22, 1907	P	Beany Jacobson and $1,000.	St. Louis Browns	P	Bill Dinneen
June 29, 1907	C	Deacon McGuire	New York Yankees		Waiver price
		(McGuire was named Boston manager.)			
Aug 1, 1907	P	Cy Morgan	St. Louis Browns		Cash
Aug 11, 1907		Cash	Washington Senators	P	Frank Oberlin

DATE		ACQUIRED	FROM		IN EXCHANGE FOR
Sept 1, 1907		Cash	Chicago White Sox	C	Charlie Armbruster
Oct 1907		Cash	St. Louis Browns	2B	Hobe Ferris
Dec 1907	2B	Frank LaPorte	New York Yankees		Cash
Jan 1908		Cash	Detroit Tigers	P	George Winter
Jan 1908		Cash	Chicago White Sox	C	Al Shaw
April 1908		Cash	Chicago White Sox	SS	Freddy Parent
July 1908	P	Casey Patten	Washington Senators	P 1B	Jesse Tannehill Bob Unglaub
July 1908	1B 2B P	Jake Stahl Harry Niles Charlie Rhodes	New York Yankees	2B	Frank LaPorte
Aug 1908		Cash	Chicago White Sox	OF	Gavvy Cravath
Aug 1908		Cash	Cleveland Indians	C	Deacon McGuire
Aug 1908	P	Jake Thielman	Cleveland Indians		Cash
Sept 1908		Cash	Cleveland Indians	OF	Denny Sullivan
Dec 12, 1908	C	Tubby Spencer	St. Louis Browns	C	Lou Criger
Feb 18, 1909	P P	Charlie Chech Jack Ryan and $12,500.	Cleveland Indians	P	Cy Young
Feb 1909		Waiver price	New York Yankees	SS	John Knight
June 1909	P	Ed Karger	Cincinnati Reds		Waiver price
Aug 1909	P	Jack Chesbro	New York Yankees		Waiver price
Sept 1909	P	Charlie Smith	Washington Senators	OF	Doc Gessler
Feb 1910		Waiver price	Pittsburgh Pirates	P	Elmer Steele
May 1910		Cash	Philadelphia Athletics	C	Pat Donahue
May 1910	3B	Clyde Engle	New York Yankees	OF	Harry Wolter
May 1910		Cash	Chicago White Sox	2B	Charlie French
May 1910		Cash	Cleveland Indians	2B	Harry Niles
May 1910	C	Red Kleinow	New York Yankees		Cash
Aug 9, 1910	P 3B	Frank Smith Billy Purtell	Chicago White Sox	OF 2B	Harry Lord Amby McConnell

DATE		ACQUIRED	FROM		IN EXCHANGE FOR
April 1911		Cash	Chicago Cubs	P	Charlie Smith
May 11, 1911		Cash	Cincinnati Reds	P	Frank Smith
May 1911	1B	Hap Myers	St. Louis Browns		Cash
May 1911		Waiver price	Philadelphia Phillies	C	Tom Madden
June 2, 1911	1B	Del Gainor	Detroit Tigers		Waiver price
June 1911		Waiver price	Philadelphia Phillies	C	Red Kleinow
June 1911		Cash	St. Louis Browns	P	Walter Moser
July 1911	P	Judge Nagle	Pittsburgh Pirates		Cash
Jan 1912		Waiver price	Washington Senators	C	Rip Williams
May 8, 1912		Cash	Chicago White Sox	1B	Jack Fournier
May 1912	SS	Neal Ball	Cleveland Indians		Cash
July 22, 1912		Cash	Chicago White Sox	P	Eddie Cicotte
Jan 1913	OF	Wally Rehg	Pittsburgh Pirates		Waiver price
July 1913		Cash	Chicago White Sox	P	Buck O'Brien
May 13, 1914		Cash	New York Yankees	C	Les Nunamaker
May 27, 1914	P	Guy Cooper	New York Yankees		Cash
June 2, 1914	1B	Del Gainor	Detroit Tigers		Waiver price
July 16, 1914	1B	Dick Hoblitzell	Cincinnati Reds		Waiver price
Aug 20, 1914	P	Vean Gregg	Cleveland Indians	P P C	Adam Johnson Fritz Coumbe Ben Egan
May 1915	2B	Bill Rodgers	Cleveland Indians		Cash
June 13, 1915	P	Herb Pennock	Philadelphia Athletics		Waiver price
June 1915		Cash	Cincinnati Reds	2B	Bill Rodgers
July 2, 1915	SS	Jack Barry	Philadelphia Athletics		$8,000.
Dec 1915	C	Sam Agnew	St. Louis Browns		Cash
April 8, 1916	OF	Tilly Walker	St. Louis Browns		Cash

DATE		ACQUIRED	FROM		IN EXCHANGE FOR
April 12, 1916	P 2B	Sad Sam Jones Fred Thomas and $55,000.	Cleveland Indians	OF	Tris Speaker
May 1916		Cash	Cleveland Indians	P	Marty McHale
Sept 2, 1916	OF	Jimmy Walsh	Philadelphia Athletics	C	Ray Haley
Feb 24, 1917		$15,000.	Cleveland Indians	P	Joe Wood
Dec 14, 1917	OF P C	Amos Strunk Joe Bush Wally Schang	Philadelphia Athletics	P OF C	Vean Gregg Merlin Kopp Pinch Thomas and $60,000.
Jan 10, 1918	1B	Stuffy McInnis	Philadelphia Athletics	3B OF C	Larry Gardner Tilly Walker Hick Cady
April 1918	2B	Dave Shean	Cincinnati Reds	P	Rube Foster
		(Foster refused to report to Cincinnati; Cincinnati received cash instead.)			
June 1, 1918		Cash	Cleveland Indians	C	Pinch Thomas
July 1918	SS	Jack Coffey	Detroit Tigers		Cash
Dec 18, 1918	OF P P C	Frank Gilhooley Slim Love Ray Caldwell Roxy Walters and $15,000.	New York Yankees	P OF P	Ernie Shore Duffy Lewis Dutch Leonard
		(Leonard refused to report to New York, and remained Boston property.)			
Jan 17, 1919	C P	Eddie Ainsmith George Dumont	Washington Senators	IF	Hal Janvrin and cash
Jan 17, 1919	3B	Ossie Vitt	Detroit Tigers	C OF P	Eddie Ainsmith Chick Shorten Slim Love
Jan 1919		Cash	Washington Senators	C	Sam Agnew
Jan 1919		$7,500.	Detroit Tigers	P	Dutch Leonard
Jan 1919		Cash	Pittsburgh Pirates	3B	Walter Barbare
Jan 1919		Cash	Philadelphia Athletics	3B	Fred Thomas
May 1919	OF	Bill Lamar	New York Yankees		Cash
June 27, 1919	OF OF	Braggo Roth Red Shannon	Philadelphia Athletics	OF SS	Amos Strunk Jack Barry
		(Barry refused to report, and retired.)			
July 29, 1919	P P	Allan Russell Bob McGraw and $40,000.	New York Yankees	P	Carl Mays
Aug 1919	P	Bill James	Detroit Tigers		Cash

DATE		ACQUIRED	FROM		IN EXCHANGE FOR
Aug 1919		Cash	Chicago White Sox	P	Bill James
Jan 3, 1920		$125,000 and a $300,000 loan to Boston owner Harry Frazee	New York Yankees	OF	Babe Ruth
Jan 20, 1920	OF P 3B	Mike Menosky Harry Harper Eddie Foster	Washington Senators	OF SS	Braggo Roth Red Shannon
Jan 1920	OF	Tim Hendryx	St. Louis Browns		Cash
March 1920		Cash	Brooklyn Dodgers	OF	Bill Lamar
May 1920	OF	Gene Bailey	Boston Braves		Cash
June 1920	P	Elmer Myers	Cleveland Indians		Waiver price
July 1920	OF	Jigger Statz	New York Giants		Cash
Dec 15, 1920	C 2B OF P	Muddy Ruel Del Pratt Sammy Vick Hank Thormahlen	New York Yankees	P P C IF	Waite Hoyt Harry Harper Wally Schang Mike McNally
Jan 1921	P	Allen Sothoron	St. Louis Browns		Waiver price
March 4, 1921	OF OF	Shano Collins Nemo Leibold	Chicago White Sox	OF	Harry Hooper
April 1921		Waiver price	Cleveland Indians	P	Allen Sothoron
Dec 20, 1921	SS P P P	Roger Peckinpaugh Jack Quinn Rip Collins Bill Piercy	New York Yankees	SS P P	Everett Scott Joe Bush Sad Sam Jones
Dec 24, 1921	1B 1B OF	George Burns Joe Harris Elmer Smith	Cleveland Indians	1B	Stuffy McInnis
Jan 10, 1922	3B OF	Joe Dugan Frank O'Rourke (Part of three-team trade involving Boston, Philadelphia, and Washington.)	Washington Senators	SS	Roger Peckinpaugh
Feb 24, 1922	P	Alex Ferguson	New York Yankees		Waiver price
July 23, 1922	OF OF SS P	Chick Fewster Elmer Miller Johnny Mitchell Lefty O'Doul and $50,000.	New York Yankees	3B OF	Joe Dugan Elmer Smith
Aug 15, 1922		Waiver price	St. Louis Browns	3B	Eddie Foster
Oct 24, 1922		Waiver price	Detroit Tigers	OF	Frank O'Rourke

DATE		ACQUIRED	FROM		IN EXCHANGE FOR
Oct 30, 1922	P P IF OF	Carl Holling Howard Ehmke Danny Clark Babe Herman and $25,000.	Detroit Tigers	2B P	Del Pratt Rip Collins
Jan 3, 1923	C	Al DeVormer and cash	New York Yankees	P OF	George Pipgras Harvey Hendrick
Jan 30, 1923	OF IF P	Camp Skinner Norm McMillan George Murray and $50,000.	New York Yankees	P	Herb Pennock
Feb 10, 1923	C IF OF	Val Picinich Howard Shanks Ed Goebel	Washington Senators	C P	Muddy Ruel Allan Russell
April 20, 1923	OF	Ira Flagstead	Detroit Tigers		Cash
May 26, 1923		Waiver price	Washington Senators	OF	Nemo Leibold
Nov 1923		Cash	Brooklyn Dodgers	SS	Johnny Mitchell
Dec 1923	3B	Homer Ezzell	St. Louis Browns	2B	Norm McMillan
Jan 7, 1924	P C OF 2B	Danny Boone Steve O'Neill Joe Connolly Bill Wambsganss	Cleveland Indians	1B C UT	George Burns Roxy Walters Chick Fewster
March 12, 1924	OF	Bobby Veach	Detroit Tigers		Cash
Sept 10, 1924	P	Ted Wingfield	Washington Senators		Cash
Dec 10, 1924	3B	Mike McNally	New York Yankees	3B	Howard Shanks
Dec 11, 1924	3B	Doc Prothro	Washington Senators	3B	Mike McNally
Dec 12, 1924		Waiver price	New York Yankees	C	Steve O'Neill
April 26, 1925	P OF	Paul Zahniser Roy Carlyle	Washington Senators	1B	Joe Harris
May 5, 1925	P	Ray Francis and $9,000.	New York Yankees	OF P	Bobby Veach Alex Ferguson
July 10, 1925		Waiver price	Philadelphia Athletics	P	Jack Quinn
July 11, 1925	OF	John Bischoff	Chicago White Sox		Cash
Dec 9, 1925	3B	Fred Haney	Detroit Tigers	OF IF	Tex Vache Homer Ezzell
Dec 12, 1925		$4,000.	Philadelphia Athletics	2B	Bill Wambsganss
Feb 10, 1926		$7,500.	Cincinnati Reds	C	Val Picinich
April 7, 1926	SS	Topper Rigney	Detroit Tigers		Cash

DATE		ACQUIRED	FROM		IN EXCHANGE FOR
June 15, 1926	P P OF	Fred Heimach Slim Harriss Baby Doll Jacobson	Philadelphia Athletics	OF P	Tom Jenkins Howard Ehmke
June 15, 1926		Waiver price	New York Yankees	OF	Roy Carlyle
July 31, 1926	OF	Jack Tobin	Washington Senators		Cash
Nov 1926	OF	Frank Welch	Philadelphia Athletics		Cash
May 2, 1927	3B	Buddy Myer	Washington Senators	SS	Topper Rigney
June 12, 1927		Cash	Cleveland Indians	OF	Baby Doll Jacobson
July 12, 1927		Cash	Chicago Cubs	3B	Fred Haney
Dec 15, 1927	OF	Ken Williams	St. Louis Browns		$10,000.
Dec 1927		Waiver price	Cleveland Indians	C	Grover Hartley
April 25, 1928	SS	Wally Gerber	St. Louis Browns	P	Hal Wiltse
Dec 15, 1928	P P 2B 3B OF	Milt Gaston Hod Lisenbee Bobby Reeves Grant Gillis Elliott Bigelow	Washington Senators	3B	Buddy Myer
Dec 1928	P	Bill Bayne	Cleveland Indians		Cash
May 23, 1929	OF	Bill Barrett	Chicago White Sox	OF	Doug Taitt
Dec 1929	OF	Tom Oliver	Philadelphia Athletics		Cash
Jan 29, 1930		Waiver price	New York Yankees	OF	Ken Williams
April 30, 1930	OF	Earl Webb	Washington Senators	OF	Bill Barrett
May 6, 1930	OF	Cedric Durst and $50,000.	New York Yankees	P	Red Ruffing
Dec 15, 1930	C	Muddy Ruel	Washington Senators		Cash
Jan 1931		Waiver price	Pittsburgh Pirates	2B	Bill Regan
Jan 1931		Waiver price	Philadelphia Athletics	C	Johnnie Heving
Feb 3, 1931		Cash	Philadelphia Athletics	1B	Phil Todt
Aug 31, 1931	2B	Marty McManus	Detroit Tigers	C	Muddy Ruel

DATE		ACQUIRED	FROM		IN EXCHANGE FOR
Dec 2, 1931	P	Bob Weiland	Chicago White Sox	P	Milt Gaston
Jan 7, 1932	SS	Barney Friberg	Philadelphia Phillies		Waiver price
April 29, 1932	C OF OF	Bennie Tate Smead Jolley Cliff Watwood	Chicago White Sox	C	Charlie Berry
April 30, 1932		Cash	Chicago White Sox	OF	Jack Rothrock
May 1, 1932	P	Gordon Rhodes	New York Yankees	P	Wilcy Moore
June 5, 1932	P P	Ivy Andrews Hank Johnson and $50,000.	New York Yankees	P	Danny MacFayden
June 10, 1932	P	Pete Appleton	Cleveland Indians	P	Jack Russell
June 12, 1932	1B OF	Dale Alexander Roy Johnson	Detroit Tigers	OF	Earl Webb
Dec 15, 1932	2B SS OF OF	Johnny Hodapp Greg Mulleavy Bob Fothergill Bob Seeds	Chicago White Sox	P SS	Ed Durham Hal Rhyne
Jan 7, 1933	SS	Barney Friberg	Philadelphia Phillies		Waiver price
May 9, 1933	C P	Rick Ferrell Lloyd Brown	St. Louis Browns	C	Merv Shea and cash
May 12, 1933	3B P	Bill Werber George Pipgras	New York Yankees		$100,000.
Oct 12, 1933	2B	Bill Cissell	Cleveland Indians	P	Lloyd Brown
Dec 12, 1933	P P 2B	Lefty Grove Rube Walberg Max Bishop	Philadelphia Athletics	P SS	Bob Kline Rabbit Warstler and $125,000.
Dec 14, 1933	OF	Carl Reynolds	St. Louis Browns	P OF	Ivy Andrews Smead Jolley and cash
May 15, 1934	SS	Lyn Lary	New York Yankees	IF	Freddie Muller and $20,000.
May 25, 1934	P OF	Wes Ferrell Dick Porter	Cleveland Indians	P OF	Bob Weiland Bob Seeds and $25,000.
June 14, 1934		Cash	Philadelphia Phillies	3B	Bucky Walters
June 23, 1934	P	Flint Rhem	St. Louis Cardinals		Cash
June 30, 1934	P	Joe Cascarella	Philadelphia Athletics		Cash
Sept 24, 1934		Cash	Detroit Tigers	P	Spike Merena
Oct 26, 1934	SS	Joe Cronin	Washington Senators	SS	Lyn Lary and $225,000.

DATE		ACQUIRED	FROM		IN EXCHANGE FOR
May 1, 1935	OF 2B	Bing Miller Dib Williams	Philadelphia Athletics		$50,000.
May 21, 1935	2B	Oscar Melillo	St. Louis Browns	OF	Moose Solters and cash
Dec 10, 1935	1B P	Jimmie Foxx Johnny Marcum	Philadelphia Athletics	P	Gordon Rhodes minor league C George Savino and $150,000.
Dec 17, 1935	OF	Heinie Manush	Washington Senators	OF OF	Carl Reynolds Roy Johnson
Jan 4, 1936	OF SS	Doc Cramer Eric McNair	Philadelphia Athletics	P 2B	Hank Johnson Al Niemiec and $75,000.
June 13, 1936	P	Jack Russell	Washington Senators	P	Joe Cascarella
July 1936	P	Mike Meola	St. Louis Browns		Cash
July 1936		Waiver price	Pittsburgh Pirates	P	Johnny Welch
Dec 9, 1936	3B	Pinky Higgins	Philadelphia Athletics	3B	Bill Werber
Dec 1936		Cash	Cleveland Indians	2B	John Kroner
Feb 17, 1937		Cash	New York Yankees	1B	Babe Dahlgren
June 11, 1937	OF P	Ben Chapman Bobo Newsom	Washington Senators	P C OF	Wes Ferrell Rick Ferrell Mel Almada
Oct 2, 1937	OF	Joe Vosmik	St. Louis Browns	P SS OF	Bobo Newsom Red Kress Buster Mills
Aug 1938	P	Joe Heving	Cleveland Indians		Cash
Dec 15, 1938	P SS	Denny Galehouse Tommy Irwin	Cleveland Indians	OF	Ben Chapman
Dec 15, 1938	P P 3B	Eldon Auker Jake Wade Chet Morgan	Detroit Tigers	3B P	Pinky Higgins Archie McKain
Dec 21, 1938	2B	Boze Berger	Chicago White Sox	SS	Eric McNair
Feb 1939	P	Monte Weaver	Washington Senators		Cash
May 8, 1939	OF	Lou Finney	Philadelphia Athletics		Cash
Sept 1939		Cash	St. Louis Browns	P	Jake Wade
Dec 8, 1939	3B	Marv Owen	Chicago White Sox		Cash
Dec 26, 1939		Waiver price	Brooklyn Dodgers	2B	Boze Berger
Feb 8, 1940		Cash	St. Louis Browns	P	Eldon Auker

DATE		ACQUIRED	FROM		IN EXCHANGE FOR
Feb 12, 1940		$25,000.	Brooklyn Dodgers	OF	Joe Vosmik
Aug 30, 1940	3B	Charley Gelbert	Washington Senators		Waiver price
Nov 20, 1940		Cash	St. Louis Browns	P	Denny Galehouse
Dec 3, 1940		Cash	St. Louis Browns	P	Fritz Ostermueller
Dec 12, 1940	OF	Pete Fox	Detroit Tigers		Cash
Dec 12, 1940	OF	Gee Walker	Washington Senators	OF	Doc Cramer
Dec 12, 1940	C 2B P	Frankie Pytlak Odell Hale Joe Dobson	Cleveland Indians	C P OF	Gene Desautels Jim Bagby Gee Walker
Feb 3, 1941		Cash	Cleveland Indians	P	Joe Heving
June 19, 1941		Waiver price	New York Giants	2B	Odell Hale
June 30, 1941	P	Nels Potter	Philadelphia Athletics		Cash
Dec 10, 1941	P	Mace Brown	Brooklyn Dodgers		Cash
Dec 13, 1941	P OF	Ken Chase Johnny Welaj	Washington Senators	OF P	Stan Spence Jack Wilson
June 1, 1942		Waiver price	Chicago Cubs	1B	Jimmie Foxx
Dec 4, 1943	OF	Bob Johnson	Washington Senators		Cash
April 13, 1944		Waiver price	Philadelphia Phillies	1B	Tony Lupien
May 7, 1944	C	Hal Wagner	Philadelphia Athletics	OF	Ford Garrison
June 11, 1944		Cash	Philadelphia Phillies	C	Johnny Peacock
Dec 1944	C	Billy Holm	Chicago Cubs		Cash
May 31, 1945		Waiver price	Philadelphia Phillies	P	Oscar Judd
July 27, 1945		Cash	St. Louis Browns	OF	Lou Finney
Dec 12, 1945		Cash	Philadelphia Phillies	SS	Skeeter Newsome
Jan 3, 1946	1B	Rudy York	Detroit Tigers	SS	Eddie Lake
Jan 22, 1946		Cash	Philadelphia Phillies	3B	Jim Tabor
May 19, 1946	3B	Pinky Higgins	Detroit Tigers		Cash
June 18, 1946	P	Bill Zuber	New York Yankees		Cash

DATE		ACQUIRED	FROM		IN EXCHANGE FOR
July 23, 1946	OF	Wally Moses	Chicago White Sox		Cash
Dec 12, 1946	P	Jim Bagby	Cleveland Indians	P	Vic Johnson and cash
Feb 10, 1947		Cash	Pittsburgh Pirates	P	Jim Bagby
April 2, 1947		Cash	Cleveland Indians	OF	Catfish Metkovich
May 14, 1947		Cash	Washington Senators	OF	Tom McBride
May 20, 1947	C	Birdie Tebbetts	Detroit Tigers	C	Hal Wagner
June 14, 1947	1B	Jake Jones	Chicago White Sox	1B	Rudy York
June 20, 1947	P	Denny Galehouse	St. Louis Browns		Cash
Nov 17, 1947	SS P	Vern Stephens Jack Kramer	St. Louis Browns	C P P OF OF P	Roy Partee Jim Wilson Al Widmar Eddie Pellagrini Pete Layden Joe Ostrowski and $310,000.
Nov 18, 1947	P 3B	Ellis Kinder Billy Hitchcock	St. Louis Browns	SS P 1B	Sam Dente Clem Dreisewerd Bill Sommers and $65,000.
Dec 10, 1947	OF	Stan Spence	Washington Senators	OF 3B	Leon Culberson Al Kozar
March 26, 1948		Cash	Pittsburgh Pirates	SS	Don Gutteridge
May 8, 1949	OF	Al Zarilla	St. Louis Browns	OF	Stan Spence and cash
June 13, 1949	P	Walt Masterson	Washington Senators	OF P	Sam Mele Mickey Harris
Oct 8, 1949	C	Buddy Rosar	Philadelphia Athletics	3B	Billy Hitchcock
March 26, 1950		Cash	New York Giants	P	Jack Kramer
May 8, 1950	OF	Clyde Vollmer	Washington Senators	OF SS	Tommy O'Brien Merrill Combs
May 9, 1950		Cash	St. Louis Browns	P	Harry Dorish
Dec 10, 1950	P P	Ray Scarborough Bill Wight	Chicago White Sox	P P OF	Joe Dobson Dick Littlefield Al Zarilla
Dec 13, 1950	C	Mike Guerra	Philadelphia Athletics		Cash
Feb 5, 1951	C	Al Evans	Washington Senators		Waiver price

DATE		ACQUIRED	FROM		IN EXCHANGE FOR
May 17, 1951	C	Les Moss	St. Louis Browns	C P P	Matt Batts Jim Suchecki Jim McDonald and $100,000.
Aug 6, 1951	C	Aaron Robinson	Detroit Tigers		Waiver price
Nov 13, 1951	P OF	Randy Gumpert Don Lenhardt	Chicago White Sox	2B P	Mel Hoderlein Chuck Stobbs
Nov 28, 1951	OF C	Ken Wood Gus Niarhos	St. Louis Browns	C OF	Les Moss Tom Wright
May 3, 1952		Waiver price	Philadelphia Athletics	3B	Hal Bevan
May 12, 1952	C	Del Wilber	Philadelphia Phillies		Cash
June 3, 1952	P 3B SS OF	Dizzy Trout George Kell Johnny Lipon Hoot Evers	Detroit Tigers	1B P 3B SS OF	Walt Dropo Bill Wight Fred Hatfield Johnny Pesky Don Lenhardt
June 9, 1952	OF	Archie Wilson	Washington Senators	OF	Ken Wood
June 10, 1952	P	Sid Hudson	Washington Senators	P P	Randy Gumpert Walt Masterson
June 25, 1952	OF	Paul Lehner	Cleveland Indians		Waiver price
June 30, 1952	OF	George Schmees	St. Louis Browns		Waiver price
Aug 22, 1952		Cash	New York Yankees	P	Ray Scarborough
Aug 31, 1952	OF	Al Zarilla	St. Louis Browns		Cash
Feb 9, 1953	P P P	Hal Brown Marv Grissom Bill Kennedy	Chicago White Sox	SS	Vern Stephens
April 22, 1953		Cash	Washington Senators	OF	Clyde Vollmer
May 12, 1953	3B	Floyd Baker	Washington Senators		Cash
July 1, 1953		Waiver price	New York Giants	P	Marv Grissom
Sept 8, 1953		Cash	St. Louis Browns	SS	Johnny Lipon
Dec 9, 1953	OF	Jackie Jensen	Washington Senators	P OF	Mickey McDermott Tommy Umphlett
Feb 12, 1954	OF	Don Lenhardt	Baltimore Orioles		Cash
May 18, 1954		Waiver price	New York Giants	OF	Hoot Evers
May 23, 1954	3B	Grady Hatton and $100,000.	Chicago White Sox	3B	George Kell
July 18, 1954		Cash	Philadelphia Phillies	3B	Floyd Baker

DATE		ACQUIRED	FROM		IN EXCHANGE FOR
July 29, 1954	OF	Sam Mele	Baltimore Orioles		Waiver price
Nov 24, 1954		Cash	Baltimore Orioles	OF	Charlie Maxwell
Dec 14, 1954	SS	Billy Klaus	New York Giants	C	Del Wilber
May 10, 1955		Cash	Cincinnati Reds	P	Hersh Freeman
June 23, 1955		Cash	Cincinnati Reds	OF	Sam Mele
Nov 8, 1955	P	Bob Porterfield	Washington Senators	OF	Karl Olson
	P	Johnny Schmitz		P	Dick Brodowski
	1B	Mickey Vernon		P	Tex Clevenger
	OF	Tommy Umphlett		OF	Neil Chrisley and minor league P Al Curtis
Dec 4, 1955		Waiver price	St. Louis Cardinals	P	Ellis Kinder
May 11, 1956		Cash	St. Louis Cardinals	3B	Grady Hatton
May 14, 1956		Cash	Baltimore Orioles	P	Johnny Schmitz
June 25, 1956	P	Harry Dorish	Baltimore Orioles		Cash
April 13, 1957	P	Russ Meyer	Cincinnati Reds		Waiver price
April 29, 1957	P	Dean Stone	Washington Senators	2B	Milt Bolling
	P	Bob Chakales		P	Russ Kemmerer
				OF	Faye Throneberry
April 30, 1957	OF	Karl Olson	Washington Senators		Cash
April 30, 1957	1B	Jack Phillips	Detroit Tigers	OF	Karl Olson
June 14, 1957	P	Mike Fornieles	Baltimore Orioles	3B	Billy Goodman
Jan 23, 1958	2B	Pete Runnels	Washington Senators	OF	Albie Pearson
				OF	Norm Zauchin
Jan 29, 1958		Waiver price	Cleveland Indians	1B	Mickey Vernon
March 26, 1958		Waiver price	Cleveland Indians	P	Chuck Churn
May 1, 1958	C	Lou Berberet	Washington Senators	2B	Ken Aspromonte
May 7, 1958		Cash	Pittsburgh Pirates	P	Bob Porterfield
May 12, 1958		Waiver price	Detroit Tigers	P	George Susce
June 24, 1958	P	Bud Byerly	Washington Senators	P	Jack Spring
Dec 2, 1958	P	Herb Moford	Detroit Tigers	C	Lou Berberet

DATE		ACQUIRED	FROM		IN EXCHANGE FOR
Dec 2, 1958	1B OF	Vic Wertz Gary Geiger	Cleveland Indians	OF	Jimmy Piersall
Dec 15, 1958	OF	Jim Busby	Baltimore Orioles	IF	Billy Klaus
March 9, 1959	OF	Chuck Tanner	Chicago Cubs	P	Riverboat Smith
March 15, 1959	P	Nels Chittum	St. Louis Cardinals	P	Dean Stone
May 2, 1959	P	Billy Hoeft	Detroit Tigers	P 2B	Dave Sisler Ted Lepcio
May 21, 1959	2B	Bobby Avila	Baltimore Orioles		Waiver price
June 11, 1959	P 2B	Dick Hyde Herb Plews	Washington Senators	2B P	Billy Consolo Murray Wall
		(Hyde was returned to Washington and Wall was returned to Boston.)			
July 21, 1959		Waiver price	Milwaukee Braves	2B	Bobby Avila
July 30, 1959		Waiver price	Cleveland Indians	P	Jack Harshman
Nov 3, 1959	1B	Ron Jackson	Chicago White Sox	P	Frank Baumann
Nov 21, 1959	P 1B	Dave Hillman Jim Marshall	Chicago Cubs	1B	Dick Gernert
Dec 3, 1959	P	Tom Sturdivant	Kansas City Athletics	C	Pete Daley
Jan 8, 1960	SS	Ray Webster	Cleveland Indians	P	Leo Kiely
March 16, 1960	C	Russ Nixon	Cleveland Indians	C 1B	Sammy White Jim Marshall
		(Trade was cancelled when White decided to retire.)			
March 29, 1960	P	Al Worthington	San Francisco Giants	1B	Jim Marshall
May 6, 1960	OF	Rip Repulski	Los Angeles Dodgers	P	Nels Chittum
May 17, 1960	1B	Ray Boone	Milwaukee Braves	1B	Ron Jackson
June 9, 1960	OF	Willie Tasby	Baltimore Orioles	OF	Gene Stephens
June 13, 1960	C OF	Russ Nixon Carroll Hardy	Cleveland Indians	OF P	Marty Keough Ted Bowsfield
Dec 15, 1960	P	Gene Conley	Philadelphia Phillies	P	Frank Sullivan
June 15, 1961		Cash	Milwaukee Braves	C	Sammy White
Sept 8, 1961		Waiver price	Detroit Tigers	1B	Vic Wertz
Nov 26, 1961	SS	Ed Bressoud	San Francisco Giants	SS	Don Buddin
March 24, 1962	OF	Dave Philley	Houston Astros	P	Tom Borland
May 8, 1962		Cash	Cincinnati Reds	P	Ted Wills

DATE		ACQUIRED	FROM		IN EXCHANGE FOR
June 12, 1962	2B	Billy Gardner	New York Yankees	OF	Tommy Umphlett and cash
Sept 7, 1962		Waiver price	New York Mets	P	Galen Cisco
Nov 20, 1962	P 1B	Jack Lamabe Dick Stuart	Pittsburgh Pirates	C P	Jim Pagliaroni Don Schwall
Nov 26, 1962	OF	Roman Mejias	Houston Astros	1B	Pete Runnels
Dec 10, 1962	OF	Dick Williams	Houston Astros	OF	Carroll Hardy
Dec 11, 1962	3B	Felix Mantilla	New York Mets	P 2B SS	Tracy Stallard Pumpsie Green Al Moran
June 14, 1963		Cash	Minnesota Twins	P	Mike Fornieles
June 4, 1964	OF	Lee Thomas	Los Angeles Angels	OF	Lu Clinton
Nov 29, 1964	P	Dennis Bennett	Philadelphia Phillies	1B	Dick Stuart
Sept 14, 1965	P	Darrell Brandon	Houston Astros	P	Jack Lamabe
Oct 4, 1965	2B OF	George Smith George Thomas	Detroit Tigers	P	Bill Monbouquette
Nov 30, 1965	OF	Joe Christopher	New York Mets	SS	Ed Bressoud
Dec 15, 1965	P P	Bob Sadowski Dan Osinski	Milwaukee Braves	OF P P	Lee Thomas Arnie Earley Jay Ritchie
April 3, 1966	SS	Eddie Kasko	Houston Astros	2B	Felix Mantilla
April 6, 1966	P	Dick Stigman and minor league 1B Jose Calero	Minnesota Twins	C 2B	Russ Nixon Chuck Schilling
June 2, 1966	P P	Don McMahon Lee Stange	Cleveland Indians	P	Dick Radatz
June 13, 1966	P P OF	John Wyatt Rollie Sheldon Jose Tartabull	Kansas City Athletics	OF P P	Jim Gosger Ken Sanders Guido Grilli
June 14, 1966	P OF	Julio Navarro Don Demeter	Detroit Tigers	P OF	Earl Wilson Joe Christopher
Aug 15, 1966	P	Bill Short	Baltimore Orioles		Cash
Aug 15, 1966	P	Hank Fischer	Cincinnati Reds	P P	Dick Stigman Bill Stafford
		(Cincinnati received Stigman and Stafford on December 15, 1966.)			
Sept 7, 1966	P	Garry Roggenburk	Minnesota Twins		Cash
Oct 17, 1966		Cash	Pittsburgh Pirates	P	Bill Short

DATE		ACQUIRED	FROM		IN EXCHANGE FOR
June 3, 1967	2B	Jerry Adair	Chicago White Sox	P	Don McMahon minor league P Bob Snow
June 4, 1967	P	Gary Bell	Cleveland Indians	OF OF	Tony Horton Don Demeter
June 24, 1967	OF	Al Yates and cash	New York Mets	P	Dennis Bennett
July 16, 1967	OF	Norm Siebern	San Francisco Giants		Cash
Aug 3, 1967	C	Elston Howard	New York Yankees	P P	Ron Klimkowski Pete Magrini
Aug 8, 1967		Cash	New York Yankees	C	Bob Tillman
Nov 30, 1967	P	Ray Culp	Chicago Cubs		Minor league OF Bill Schlessinger and cash
Dec 15, 1967	P OF	Dick Ellsworth Gene Oliver	Philadelphia Phillies	C	Mike Ryan and cash
May 18, 1968		Cash	New York Yankees	P	John Wyatt
June 27, 1968	P	Juan Pizarro	Pittsburgh Pirates		Cash
June 27, 1968		Cash	Chicago Cubs	C	Gene Oliver
July 31, 1968	OF	Floyd Robinson	Oakland Athletics		Cash
Dec 2, 1968	SS	Dick Schofield	St. Louis Cardinals	P	Gary Waslewski
April 19, 1969	P C P	Sonny Siebert Joe Azcue Vicente Romo	Cleveland Indians	OF-1B P P	Ken Harrelson Juan Pizarro Dick Ellsworth
May 5, 1969	OF	Don Lock	Philadelphia Phillies	OF	Rudy Schlesinger
May 7, 1969		Cash	Oakland Athletics	OF	Jose Tartabull
June 15, 1969	C	Tom Satriano	California Angels	C	Joe Azcue
June 23, 1969		Cash	Seattle Pilots	P	Garry Roggenburk
July 5, 1969	P	Ron Kline	San Francisco Giants		Cash
Sept 6, 1969	P	Gary Wagner	Philadelphia Phillies	P	Mike Jackson
Nov 25, 1969		Cash	Philadelphia Phillies	P	Fred Wenz
Dec 13, 1969	C P	Don Pavletich Gary Peters	Chicago White Sox	IF P	Syd O'Brien minor league P Billy Farmer Gerry Janeski
		(Janeski replaced Farmer, who retired.)			
Dec 13, 1969	IF	Tommy Matchick	Detroit Tigers	3B	Dalton Jones

DATE		ACQUIRED	FROM		IN EXCHANGE FOR
April 4, 1970		Cash	San Francisco Giants	C	Russ Gibson
May 28, 1970	1B	Mike Fiore	Kansas City Royals	IF	Tommy Matchick
June 8, 1970	P	Cal Koonce	New York Mets		Cash
June 26, 1970	1B	John Kennedy	Milwaukee Brewers		Cash
June 29, 1970		Cash	Chicago White Sox	P	Lee Stange
Sept 10, 1970	P	Bobby Bolin	Milwaukee Brewers		Cash
Oct 11, 1970	P OF 2B	Ken Tatum Jarvis Tatum Doug Griffin	California Angels	OF P C	Tony Conigliaro Ray Jarvis Gerry Moses
Oct 21, 1970	1B	Jim Campbell	St. Louis Cardinals	SS	Dick Schofield
Dec 1, 1970	SS	Luis Aparicio	Chicago White Sox	2B SS	Mike Andrews Luis Alvarado
Dec 3, 1970	IF	Phil Gagliano	Chicago Cubs	3B	Carmen Fanzone
March 31, 1971	C P	Duane Josephson Danny Murphy	Chicago White Sox	P 1B	Vicente Romo Tony Muser
Oct 11, 1971	P P OF OF	Marty Pattin Lew Krausse Tommy Harper Pat Skrable	Milwaukee Brewers	OF OF P P 1B C	Billy Conigliaro Joe LaHoud Jim Lonborg Ken Brett George Scott Don Pavletich
March 20, 1972	1B	Bob Burda	St. Louis Cardinals	1B	Mike Fiore
March 20, 1972	OF	Bobby Pfeil	Milwaukee Brewers		Cash
March 22, 1972	OF	Danny Cater	New York Yankees	P	Sparky Lyle
Aug 15, 1972	OF	Andy Kosco	California Angels	OF	Chris Coletta
Sept 2, 1972	P	Bob Veale	Pittsburgh Pirates		Cash
Jan 24, 1973	P	Lance Clemons	St. Louis Cardinals	P	Mike Nagy
March 27, 1973	P	Mel Behney	Cincinnati Reds	IF OF	Phil Gagliano Andy Kosco
May 4, 1973		Cash	Texas Rangers	P	Sonny Siebert
Oct 23, 1973	2B	Dick McAuliffe	Detroit Tigers	OF	Ben Oglivie
Oct 24, 1973	P	Dick Drago	Kansas City Royals	P	Marty Pattin
Oct 26, 1973	P OF	Rick Wise Bernie Carbo	St. Louis Cardinals	OF P	Reggie Smith Ken Tatum

DATE		ACQUIRED	FROM		IN EXCHANGE FOR
Dec 7, 1973	P	Juan Marichal	San Francisco Giants		Cash
Dec 7, 1973	P P IF	Reggie Cleveland Diego Segui Terry Hughes	St. Louis Cardinals	P P P	Lynn McGlothen John Curtis Mike Garman
Dec 10, 1973		Cash	Kansas City Royals	SS	Buddy Hunter
March 26, 1974	2B	Chuck Goggin	Atlanta Braves	C	Vic Correll
March 26, 1974	C	Bob Didier	Detroit Tigers		Cash
Sept 1, 1974	C	Tim McCarver	St. Louis Cardinals		Cash
Sept 7, 1974	1B	Deron Johnson	Milwaukee Brewers		Cash
Dec 2, 1974	IF	Bob Heise	California Angels	OF	Tommy Harper
March 29, 1975	OF	Danny Godby	St. Louis Cardinals	1B	Danny Cater
April 4, 1975	P	Jim Willoughby	St. Louis Cardinals	SS	Mario Guerrero
June 14, 1975	2B	Denny Doyle	California Angels		Cash
Sept 22, 1975	1B	Deron Johnson	Chicago White Sox		Minor league C Chuck Erickson and cash
Nov 17, 1975	P	Ferguson Jenkins	Texas Rangers	OF P P	Juan Beniquez Steve Barr Craig Skok
Dec 12, 1975	P	Tom House	Atlanta Braves	P	Roger Moret
March 3, 1976	OF OF IF	John Balaz Dick Sharon Dave Machemer	California Angels	P	Dick Drago
April 19, 1976		Cash	Philadelphia Phillies	C	Tim Blackwell
June 3, 1976	P OF	Tom Murphy Bobby Darwin	Milwaukee Brewers	OF	Bernie Carbo
Nov 6, 1976	P	Bill Campbell	Minnesota Twins		No compensation (free agent signing)
Dec 6, 1976	1B OF	George Scott Bernie Carbo	Milwaukee Brewers	1B	Cecil Cooper
Dec 6, 1976		Cash	Kansas City Royals	IF	Bob Heise
May 28, 1977	P	Ramon Hernandez	Chicago Cubs	OF	Bobby Darwin
May 28, 1977		Cash	Seattle Mariners	P	Tom House
July 27, 1977		Cash	Toronto Blue Jays	P	Tom Murphy

DATE		ACQUIRED	FROM		IN EXCHANGE FOR
Sept 19, 1977	3B	Bob Bailey	Cincinnati Reds		Minor league P Frank Newcomer and cash
Nov 23, 1977	P	Mike Torrez	New York Yankees		No compensation (free agent signing)
Dec 8, 1977	2B	Jerry Remy	California Angels	P	Don Aase
Dec 9, 1977	OF	Garry Hancock	Cleveland Indians	1B	Jack Baker
Dec 14, 1977	P	John Poloni and cash	Texas Rangers	P	Ferguson Jenkins
Dec 21, 1977		No compensation (free agent signing)	California Angels	OF	Rick Miller
Jan 30, 1978		Minor league Ps Mike Burns and Frank Harris and cash	Detroit Tigers	IF	Steve Dillard
March 24, 1978	SS	Frank Duffy	Cleveland Indians	P	Rick Kreuger
March 29, 1978	IF	Len Foster	New York Mets	P	Jim Burton
April 5, 1978		Cash	Philadelphia Phillies	IF	Ramon Aviles
April 5, 1978		Cash	Chicago White Sox	P	Jim Willoughby
April 18, 1978		Cash	Texas Rangers	P	Reggie Cleveland
June 15, 1978		Cash	Cleveland Indians	OF	Bernie Carbo
July 24, 1978	P	Andy Hassler	Kansas City Royals		Cash
Oct 27, 1978	OF	Mike Easler	Pittsburgh Pirates		Cash
Nov 13, 1978		No compensation (free agent signing)	New York Yankees	P	Luis Tiant
Dec 7, 1978	IF	Stan Papi	Montreal Expos	P	Bill Lee
Jan 20, 1979	P	Steve Renko	Oakland Athletics		No compensation (free agent signing)
March 10, 1979		No compensation (free agent signing)	St. Louis Cardinals	OF	Bernie Carbo
March 15, 1979	OF	Jim Dwyer	San Francisco Giants		Cash
March 15, 1979		Minor league OF George Hill and P Martin Rivas and cash	Pittsburgh Pirates	OF	Mike Easler
June 13, 1979	1B	Bob Watson	Houston Astros	P P	Pete Ladd Bobby Sprowl and cash
June 13, 1979	OF	Tom Poquette	Kansas City Royals	1B	George Scott

DATE		ACQUIRED	FROM		IN EXCHANGE FOR
June 15, 1979		Cash	New York Mets	P	Andy Hassler
Aug 17, 1979	2B	Ted Sizemore	Chicago Cubs	C	Mike O'Berry and cash
Nov 8, 1979		No compensation (free agent signing)	New York Yankees	1B	Bob Watson
Nov 20, 1979	1B	Tony Perez	Montreal Expos		No compensation (free agent signing)
Nov 27, 1979	P	Skip Lockwood	New York Mets		No compensation (free agent signing)
March 30, 1980	C	Dave Rader	Philadelphia Phillies	2B	Stan Papi and cash
April 6, 1980		Cash	San Francisco Giants	P	Allen Ripley
May 12, 1980	P	Jack Billingham	Detroit Tigers		Cash
June 20, 1980		Cash	Cleveland Indians	IF	Jack Brohamer
Dec 10, 1980	3B OF P	Carney Lansford Rick Miller Mark Clear	California Angels	SS 3B	Rick Burleson Butch Hobson
Dec 23, 1980		No compensation (free agent signing)	Baltimore Orioles	OF	Jim Dwyer
Jan 23, 1981	P P OF	Frank Tanana Jim Dorsey Joe Rudi	California Angels	OF P	Fred Lynn Steve Renko
March 9, 1981		No compensation (free agent signing)	Chicago White Sox	C	Carlton Fisk
April 8, 1981	P	Manny Sarmiento	Seattle Mariners	P	Dick Drago
Aug 12, 1981		Cash	Texas Rangers	OF	Tom Poquette
Oct 23, 1981		Cash	Pittsburgh Pirates	P	Manny Sarmiento
Dec 4, 1981		No compensation (free agent signing)	Oakland Athletics	1B	Joe Rudi
Dec 8, 1981		No compensation (free agent signing)	Chicago Cubs	P	Bill Campbell
Jan 6, 1982		No compensation (free agent signing)	Texas Rangers	P	Frank Tanana
April 9, 1982	P	John Henry Johnson	Texas Rangers	P	Mike Smithson
Nov 15, 1982		No compensation (free agent signing)	Oakland Athletics	P	Tom Burgmeier
Dec 6, 1982	OF C	Tony Armas Jeff Newman	Oakland Athletics	3B OF	Carney Lansford Garry Hancock minor league P Jerry King
Dec 10, 1982	P	Doug Bird	Chicago Cubs	P	Chuck Rainey
Jan 14, 1983		Minor league 3B Mike Davis	New York Mets	P	Mike Torrez

DATE		ACQUIRED	FROM		IN EXCHANGE FOR
Jan 17, 1983	P	Brian Kingman	Oakland Athletics		Cash
Dec 6, 1983	OF	Mike Easler	Pittsburgh Pirates	P	John Tudor
March 24, 1984		Minor league Ps Mike Poindexter and Paul Perry	Cleveland Indians	P	Luis Aponte

California Angels

The Best Trades

1. Acquired Nolan Ryan, Don Rose, Leroy Stanton, and Francisco Estrada from the New York Mets for Jim Fregosi, December 10, 1971.
2. Acquired Doug DeCinces and Jeff Schneider from the Baltimore Orioles for Dan Ford, January 28, 1982.
3. Acquired Fred Lynn and Steve Renko from the Boston Red Sox for Frank Tanana, Joe Rudi, and Jim Dorsey, January 23, 1981.
4. Acquired Rudy May and Costen Shockley from the Philadelphia Phillies for Bo Belinsky, December 3, 1964.
5. Acquired Alex Johnson and Chico Ruiz from the Cincinnati Reds for Pedro Borbon, Jim McGlothlin, and Vern Geishert, November 25, 1969.

The Worst Trades

1. Traded Mickey Rivers and Ed Figueroa to the New York Yankees for Bobby Bonds, December 11, 1975.
2. Traded Jason Thompson to the Pittsburgh Pirates for Ed Ott and Mickey Mahler, April 1, 1981.
3. Traded Carney Lansford, Rick Miller, and Mark Clear to the Boston Red Sox for Rick Burleson and Butch Hobson, December 10, 1980.
4. Traded Willie Aikens and Rance Mulliniks to the Kansas City Royals for Al Cowens, Todd Cruz, and Craig Eaton, December 6, 1979.
5. Traded Tom Brunansky, Mike Walters, and $400,000 to the Minnesota Twins for Doug Corbett and Rob Wilfong, May 12, 1982.

Owner: Gene Autry

Sometimes it costs more than gas money to sit and spin your wheels. The California (formerly Los Angeles) Angels were one of the most successful expansion teams ever, finishing third in the ten-team American League in just their second year of operation. Now in their twenty-fourth season, the Angels have won just two divisional flags, and have never been in a World Series, despite prodigious bouts of spending by their owner, Gene Autry.

Autry was first in line to greet the original group of free agents when they came out through the re-entry draft of 1976. Autry signed Bobby Grich and Don Baylor from the Baltimore Orioles, and Joe Rudi from the Oakland A's. The improvements made the Angels a consensus choice to win the AL West flag, but injuries limited Grich to 52 games and Rudi to 64 as the Angels won two fewer games than the year before. Undaunted, Autry continued to spend freely, giving million-dollar contracts to free agents including Reggie Jackson, Lyman Bostock, Bruce Kison, Rick Miller, Jim Barr, Freddie Patek, Tom Griffin, Geoff Zahn, Juan Beniquez, John D'Acquisto, and Billy Travers. In addition, Autry made trades for players about to become free agents, not only paying them huge sums to forgo the open market but giving up players as well. He sent Ken Landreaux, Dave Engle, and two pitchers to Minnesota for Rod Carew; and Frank Tanana, Joe Rudi, and Jim Dorsey to Boston for Fred Lynn and Steve Renko.

Even by Steinbrenner's standards, Autry's spending has been lavish; unfortunately for the Singing Cowboy, his results haven't come near the Yankees'. Baylor and Grich were the two leaders of the club that won divisional titles in '79 and '82, but both times the Angels fell in the League Championship Series. To accommodate the players they've signed, the Angels have traded away a steady stream of young talent. In just the last five years they traded away what could have been an infield of Willie Aikens or Jason Thompson at first, Jerry Remy at second, Dickie Thon at shortstop, and Carney Lansford at third, with an outfield of Dan Ford in left, Ken Landreaux in center, and Tom Brunansky in right.

The Angels have made some profitable trades, including the famed Nolan Ryan for Jim Fregosi deal. They got Doug DeCinces for Dan Ford, and Brian Downing for a fading Bobby Bonds. But more of their trades have been dreadful. To get that same Bobby Bonds, they gave the Yankees Mickey Rivers and Ed Figueroa. They gave up Dickie Thon for Ken Forsch. And a little-noticed throw-in in that Brian Downing trade was pitcher Rich Dotson, now a mainstay of the White Sox rotation. On the whole, it can be safely said that the Angels would be better off if they had never made a trade and kept Mr. Autry's checkbook closed.

DATE		ACQUIRED	FROM		IN EXCHANGE FOR
June 15, 1965	OF	Bubba Morton and cash	Cleveland Indians	C	Phil Roof
		(California received Morton on September 15, 1965.)			
July 6, 1965	OF	Al Spangler	Houston Astros	P	Don Lee
July 28, 1965		Cash	Cincinnati Reds	P	Larry Locke
Aug 18, 1965	P	Jack Sanford	San Francisco Giants		Cash
Sept 9, 1965		Waiver price	Cleveland Indians	OF	Lu Clinton
		(Clinton was claimed on waivers by Kansas City and played one game for them before Cleveland's claim was upheld.)			
Dec 2, 1965	1B	Norm Siebern	Baltimore Orioles	OF	Dick Simpson
Dec 15, 1965		Minor league C Ed Pacheco and cash	Houston Astros	P	Barry Latman
Feb 15, 1966	C	Ed Bailey	Chicago Cubs		Cash
May 27, 1966	P	Howie Reed	Los Angeles Dodgers	P	Dick Egan
June 3, 1966	P	Larry Locke	Cincinnati Reds		Cash
Dec 2, 1966	OF 1B P	Jimmie Hall Don Mincher Pete Cimino	Minnesota Twins	P SS	Dean Chance Jackie Hernandez
Dec 14, 1966	OF	Len Gabrielson	San Francisco Giants	OF	Norm Siebern

DATE		ACQUIRED	FROM		IN EXCHANGE FOR
Dec 15, 1966	P	Nick Willhite	Los Angeles Dodgers	P	Bob Lee
Feb 16, 1967	2B	Chuck Cottier	Washington Senators		Cash
April 10, 1967	C	Orlando McFarlane	Detroit Tigers		Cash
May 6, 1967	1B	Bill Skowron	Chicago White Sox	OF	Cotton Nash and cash
May 10, 1967	IF	Johnny Werhas	Los Angeles Dodgers	1B	Len Gabrielson
June 10, 1967	P	Jack Hamilton	New York Mets	P	Nick Willhite
June 15, 1967	OF	Roger Repoz	Kansas City Athletics	P OF	Jack Sanford Jackie Warner
June 15, 1967	OF	Woodie Held	Baltimore Orioles	P	Marcelino Lopez
July 24, 1967	C-1B	Hawk Taylor	New York Mets	2B	Don Wallace and cash
Aug 2, 1967	P	Curt Simmons	Chicago Cubs		Cash
Aug 7, 1967	P	Jim Weaver	Houston Astros	SS	Hector Torres
Nov 29, 1967	OF	Chuck Hinton	Cleveland Indians	OF	Jose Cardenal
Nov 29, 1967	P	Sammy Ellis	Cincinnati Reds	P P	Bill Kelso Jorge Rubio
June 15, 1968	OF	Vic Davalillo	Cleveland Indians	OF	Jimmie Hall
July 20, 1968	IF	Wayne Causey	Chicago White Sox	OF	Woodie Held
July 29, 1968		Cash	Atlanta Braves	IF	Wayne Causey
Oct 8, 1968	P	Eddie Fisher	Cleveland Indians	P	Jack Hamilton
Dec 12, 1968	P	Hoyt Wilhelm	Kansas City Royals	OF-C C	Ed Kirkpatrick Dennis Paepke
Jan 20, 1969	OF	Bill Voss minor league P Andy Rubicotta	Chicago White Sox	P	Sammy Ellis
April 4, 1969	OF	Lou Johnson	Cleveland Indians	OF	Chuck Hinton
April 4, 1969	P	Phil Ortega	Washington Senators		Cash
May 14, 1969	2B P	Sandy Alomar Bob Priddy	Chicago White Sox	IF	Bobby Knoop
May 30, 1969	OF	Jim Hicks	St. Louis Cardinals	OF	Vic Davalillo
June 15, 1969	C	Joe Azcue	Boston Red Sox	C	Tom Satriano
July 26, 1969	OF	Billy Cowan	New York Yankees		Cash

DATE		ACQUIRED	FROM		IN EXCHANGE FOR
July 31, 1969		Cash	Seattle Pilots	P	George Brunet
Sept 8, 1969		Cash	Atlanta Braves	P	Hoyt Wilhelm
Sept 9, 1969		Cash	Atlanta Braves	P	Bob Priddy
Oct 24, 1969	P	Mel Queen	Cincinnati Reds		Cash
Nov 25, 1969	OF IF	Alex Johnson Chico Ruiz	Cincinnati Reds	P P P	Pedro Borbon Jim McGlothlin Vern Geishert
Nov 27, 1969	P	Paul Doyle	Atlanta Braves		Cash
Jan 14, 1970	P	Jack Fisher	Cincinnati Reds	P	Bill Harrelson minor league IF Dan Loomer
April 17, 1970	SS	Ray Oyler	Oakland Athletics		Cash
April 27, 1970	3B	Ken McMullen	Washington Senators	3B OF	Aurelio Rodriguez Rick Reichardt
May 16, 1970	OF	Tommie Reynolds	Oakland Athletics		Cash
July 9, 1970	P	Archie Reynolds	Chicago Cubs	P	Juan Pizarro
Aug 25, 1970		Cash	San Diego Padres	P	Paul Doyle
Aug 31, 1970	OF	Tony Gonzalez	Atlanta Braves		Cash
Oct 11, 1970	OF P C	Tony Conigliaro Ray Jarvis Gerry Moses	Boston Red Sox	P OF 2B	Ken Tatum Jarvis Tatum Doug Griffin
Oct 21, 1970		Minor league C John Burns	Atlanta Braves	SS	Marty Perez
Nov 30, 1970	OF 2B P	Ken Berry Syd O'Brien Billy Wynne	Chicago White Sox	OF C P	Jay Johnstone Tom Egan Tom Bradley
Dec 15, 1970	P	Jim Maloney	Cincinnati Reds	P	Greg Garrett
Jan 28, 1971	P	Gene Brabender	Milwaukee Brewers	OF	Bill Voss
March 13, 1971	C	Jeff Torborg	Los Angeles Dodgers		Cash
March 15, 1971		Cash	Chicago White Sox	P	Steve Kealey
Oct 5, 1971	OF OF P	Vada Pinson Frank Baker Alan Foster	Cleveland Indians	OF C	Alex Johnson Gerry Moses
Nov 30, 1971	SS	Leo Cardenas	Minnesota Twins	P	Dave LaRoche

DATE		ACQUIRED	FROM		IN EXCHANGE FOR
Dec 10, 1971	P P OF C	Nolan Ryan Don Rose Leroy Stanton Francisco Estrada	New York Mets	SS	Jim Fregosi
Jan 26, 1972	1B	Andy Kosco	Milwaukee Brewers	OF	Tommie Reynolds
May 5, 1972	1B	Bob Oliver	Kansas City Royals	P	Tom Murphy
June 10, 1972	IF	Jerry Davanon	Baltimore Orioles	OF	Roger Repoz
June 12, 1972		Cash	Baltimore Orioles	C	Francisco Estrada
July 28, 1972	C OF	Paul Ratliff Ron Clark	Milwaukee Brewers	IF C	Syd O'Brien Joe Azcue
July 29, 1972	C	Jack Hiatt	Houston Astros		Cash
Aug 15, 1972	OF	Chris Coletta	Boston Red Sox	OF	Andy Kosco
Aug 17, 1972	IF C	Bruce Miller Bruce Kimm	Chicago White Sox	P	Eddie Fisher
Sept 6, 1972	P	Bill Gilbreth	Detroit Tigers		Cash
Nov 28, 1972	OF P P IF OF	Frank Robinson Bill Singer Mike Strahler Billy Grabarkewitz Bobby Valentine	Los Angeles Dodgers	P 3B	Andy Messersmith Ken McMullen
Jan 29, 1973		Cash	Philadelphia Phillies	P	Rickey Clark
April 2, 1973	1B	Tom McCraw and minor league 2B Bob Marcano	Cleveland Indians	SS	Leo Cardenas
April 5, 1973		Cash	St. Louis Cardinals	P	Alan Foster
April 14, 1973	3B	Alan Gallagher	San Francisco Giants	IF	Bruce Miller
May 20, 1973	1B P C	Mike Epstein Rich Hand Rick Stelmaszek	Texas Rangers	1B P	Jim Spencer Lloyd Allen
June 15, 1973	OF	Richie Scheinblum	Cincinnati Reds	P	Terry Wilshusen minor league P Thor Skogan
Aug 14, 1973	2B P OF	Denny Doyle Aurelio Monteagudo Chris Coletta	Philadelphia Phillies	2B	Billy Grabarkewitz
Oct 22, 1973	C P P OF OF	Elly Rodriguez Skip Lockwood Gary Ryerson Ollie Brown Joe LaHoud	Milwaukee Brewers	P P OF C	Clyde Wright Steve Barber Ken Berry Art Kusnyer and cash
Dec 6, 1973	P	John Andrews	St. Louis Cardinals	C	Jeff Torborg

DATE		ACQUIRED	FROM		IN EXCHANGE FOR
Feb 23, 1974	P	Barry Raziano and cash	Kansas City Royals	OF	Vada Pinson
March 28, 1974		Cash	Houston Astros	OF	Ollie Brown
April 4, 1974	P	Bill Stoneman	Montreal Expos		Cash
April 30, 1974	3B	Paul Schaal	Kansas City Royals	OF	Richie Scheinblum
June 15, 1974		Cash	New York Yankees	P	Rudy May
July 8, 1974		Cash	New York Yankees	2B	Sandy Alomar
July 17, 1974		Cash	Cleveland Indians	1B	Tom McCraw
July 28, 1974	P	Horacio Pina	Chicago Cubs	C	Rick Stelmaszek
July 29, 1974		Cash	Milwaukee Brewers	P	Dick Selma
		(Selma was returned to California on August 12, 1974.)			
July 31, 1974	IF	Bob Heise	St. Louis Cardinals	OF	Doug Howard
Sept 11, 1974	P	Mickey Scott Cash	Baltimore Orioles	UT	Bob Oliver
Sept 12, 1974	C OF	Ken Suarez Rusty Torres and cash	Cleveland Indians	OF	Frank Robinson
Sept 16, 1974	P	Larry McCall	Baltimore Orioles		Cash
Dec 2, 1974	OF	Tommy Harper	Boston Red Sox	IF	Bob Heise
Dec 3, 1974	IF	Bill Sudakis	New York Mets	P	Skip Lockwood
March 22, 1975	C	Ike Hampton	New York Mets	P	Ken Sanders
June 14, 1975		Cash	Boston Red Sox	2B	Denny Doyle
June 15, 1975	C	Andy Etchebarren	Baltimore Orioles		Cash
July 15, 1975	P	Jim Brewer	Los Angeles Dodgers		Cash
July 31, 1975	OF-1B	Adrian Garrett	Chicago Cubs		Cash
Aug 13, 1975		Cash	Oakland Athletics	OF	Tommy Harper
Sept 17, 1975	P	Gary Ross	San Diego Padres	IF SS	Bobby Valentine Rudi Meoli
Dec 10, 1975	1B	Jim Spencer and $100,000.	Texas Rangers	P	Bill Singer
Dec 11, 1975	OF	Bobby Bonds	New York Yankees	OF P	Mickey Rivers Ed Figueroa

DATE		ACQUIRED	FROM		IN EXCHANGE FOR
Dec 11, 1975	3B P	Bill Melton Steve Dunning	Chicago White Sox	1B OF	Jim Spencer Morris Nettles
Feb 20, 1976	C	Ed Herrmann	New York Yankees		Cash
March 3, 1976	P	Dick Drago	Boston Red Sox	OF OF IF	John Balaz Dick Sharon Dave Machemer
March 31, 1976	OF	Jesus Alvarez and cash	Los Angeles Dodgers	C	Elly Rodriguez
April 8, 1976	P	Wayne Simpson	Philadelphia Phillies		Cash
May 29, 1976	IF	Mario Guerrero	St. Louis Cardinals		Minor leaguers C Ed Jordan and 1B Ed Kurpiel
June 6, 1976	C P	Terry Humphrey Mike Barlow	Houston Astros	C	Ed Herrmann
June 15, 1976		Cash	Texas Rangers	OF	Joe LaHoud
July 5, 1976		Cash	Kansas City Royals	P	Andy Hassler
July 14, 1976	1B	Tony Solaita	Kansas City Royals		Cash
Sept 3, 1976	OF	Mike Easler	St. Louis Cardinals		Minor league IF Ron Farkas
Sept 9, 1976	IF	Tim Nordbrook	Baltimore Orioles		Cash
Sept 20, 1976		Cash	Kansas City Royals	OF	Tommy Davis
Nov 16, 1976	OF	Don Baylor	Oakland Athletics		No compensation (free agent signing)
Nov 17, 1976	OF	Joe Rudi	Oakland Athletics		No compensation (free agent signing)
Nov 21, 1976	OF	Lyman Bostock	Minnesota Twins		No compensation (free agent signing)
Nov 24, 1976	2B	Bobby Grich	Baltimore Orioles		No compensation (free agent signing)
Dec 3, 1976	P	Stan Perzanowski and cash	Cleveland Indians	3B	Bill Melton
April 4, 1977		Minor league P Randy Sealy	Pittsburgh Pirates	OF	Mike Easler
May 11, 1977	P P	Dave LaRoche Dave Schuler	Cleveland Indians	1B P	Bruce Bochte Sid Monge and $250,000.
June 13, 1977	P	Dyar Miller	Baltimore Orioles	P	Dick Drago
June 15, 1977	P	Ken Brett	Chicago White Sox	P P IF	Don Kirkwood John Verhoeven John Flannery
June 15, 1977	P	Gary Nolan	Cincinnati Reds		Minor league IF Craig Henderson
July 13, 1977	P	Tom Walker	Montreal Expos		Cash

DATE		ACQUIRED	FROM		IN EXCHANGE FOR
Sept 6, 1977	1B	Dave Kingman	San Diego Padres		Cash
Sept 15, 1977		Cash	New York Yankees	1B	Dave Kingman
Sept 16, 1977	OF	Carlos May	New York Yankees		Cash
Dec 5, 1977	C P P	Brian Downing Chris Knapp Dave Frost	Chicago White Sox	OF OF P	Bobby Bonds Thad Bosley Rich Dotson
Dec 8, 1977	P	Don Aase	Boston Red Sox	2B	Jerry Remy
Dec 8, 1977	1B	Ron Fairly	Toronto Blue Jays	C 1B	Dale Kelly Butch Alberts
Dec 15, 1977		Cash	Milwaukee Brewers	C	Andy Etchebarren
Dec 21, 1977	OF	Rick Miller	Boston Red Sox		No compensation (free agent signing)
April 13, 1978		Cash	Toronto Blue Jays	P	Balor Moore
July 28, 1978		Cash	New York Mets	OF	Gil Flores
Dec 3, 1978	P	Jim Barr	San Francisco Giants		No compensation (free agent signing)
Dec 4, 1978	OF	Dan Ford	Minnesota Twins	1B DH	Ron Jackson Danny Goodwin
Dec 5, 1978		Cash	Montreal Expos	1B	Tony Solaita
Feb 3, 1979	1B	Rod Carew	Minnesota Twins	OF 3B P P	Ken Landreaux Dave Engle Paul Hartzell Brad Havens
May 4, 1979	SS	Bert Campaneris	Texas Rangers	3B	Dave Chalk
June 5, 1979	OF	Larry Harlow	Baltimore Orioles	IF	Floyd Rayford and cash
June 6, 1979		Cash	Toronto Blue Jays	P	Dyar Miller
Aug 29, 1979	P	John Montague	Seattle Mariners	SS	Jim Anderson
Sept 20, 1979	OF	Ralph Garr	Chicago White Sox		Cash
Nov 16, 1979	P	Bruce Kison	Pittsburgh Pirates		No compensation (free agent signing)
Nov 19, 1979		No compensation (free agent signing)	Houston Astros	P	Nolan Ryan
Dec 5, 1979	SS	Freddie Patek	Kansas City Royals		No compensation (free agent signing)
Dec 6, 1979	OF SS P	Al Cowens Todd Cruz Craig Eaton	Kansas City Royals	IF 1B	Rance Mulliniks Willie Aikens
May 13, 1980	C	Dave Skaggs	Baltimore Orioles		Cash

DATE		ACQUIRED	FROM		IN EXCHANGE FOR
May 27, 1980	1B	Jason Thompson	Detroit Tigers	OF	Al Cowens
June 3, 1980	P	Dave Lemanczyk	Toronto Blue Jays	P	Ken Schrom
June 10, 1980	P	Andy Hassler	Pittsburgh Pirates		Cash
June 12, 1980	P	Randy Scarbery	Chicago White Sox	SS	Todd Cruz
June 20, 1980	P	Ed Halicki	San Francisco Giants		Cash
Nov 3, 1980	P	John D'Acquisto	Montreal Expos		No compensation (free agent signing)
Dec 2, 1980	P	Geoff Zahn	Minnesota Twins		No compensation (free agent signing)
Dec 10, 1980	SS 3B	Rick Burleson Butch Hobson	Boston Red Sox	3B OF P	Carney Lansford Rick Miller Mark Clear
Dec 29, 1980	OF	Juan Beniquez	Seattle Mariners		No compensation (free agent signing)
Jan 23, 1981	OF P	Fred Lynn Steve Renko	Boston Red Sox	P P OF	Frank Tanana Jim Dorsey Joe Rudi
Jan 26, 1981	P	Bill Travers	Milwaukee Brewers		No compensation (free agent signing)
April 1, 1981	P	Ken Forsch	Houston Astros	2B	Dickie Thon
April 1, 1981	C P	Ed Ott Mickey Mahler	Pittsburgh Pirates	1B	Jason Thompson
Dec 6, 1981	C	Bob Boone	Philadelphia Phillies		Cash
Dec 11, 1981	SS	Tim Foli	Pittsburgh Pirates	C-OF	Brian Harper
Dec 17, 1981	1B	Craig Cacek	Pittsburgh Pirates		Cash
Jan 22, 1982	OF	Reggie Jackson	New York Yankees		No compensation (free agent signing)
Jan 28, 1982	3B P	Doug DeCinces Jeff Schneider	Baltimore Orioles	OF	Dan Ford
Feb 20, 1982		No compensation (free agent signing)	Kansas City Royals	P	Dave Frost
March 24, 1982	P	Bill Castro	New York Yankees	3B	Butch Hobson
April 20, 1982	1B	Ron Jackson	Detroit Tigers		No compensation (free agent signing)
April 21, 1982	SS	Mick Kelleher	Detroit Tigers		Cash
May 12, 1982	P 2B	Doug Corbett Rob Wilfong	Minnesota Twins	OF P	Tom Brunansky Mike Walters and $400,000.
Aug 31, 1982	P	John Curtis	San Diego Padres		Cash

DATE		ACQUIRED	FROM		IN EXCHANGE FOR
Aug 31, 1982	P	Tommy John	New York Yankees	P	Dennis Rasmussen
Jan 10, 1983	C	Mike O'Berry	Cincinnati Reds	1B	John Harris
Jan 24, 1983	OF	Ellis Valentine	New York Mets		No compensation (free agent signing)
Feb 9, 1983		No compensation (free agent signing)	Kansas City Royals	P	Steve Renko
Dec 7, 1983	P	Curt Kaufman and cash	New York Yankees	SS	Tim Foli
Dec 8, 1983	P	Frank LaCorte	Houston Astros		No compensation (free agent signing)
Dec 8, 1983		No compensation (free agent signing)	New York Yankees	C	Mike O'Berry
Dec 19, 1983		Minor league P Mike Browning	New York Yankees	P	Curt Brown
Dec 20, 1983	P	Jim Slaton	Milwaukee Brewers	OF	Bobby Clark
Feb 6, 1984	SS	Rob Picciolo	Milwaukee Brewers		No compensation (free agent signing)

Chicago White Sox

The Best Trades

1. Acquired Nellie Fox from the Philadelphia Athletics for Joe Tipton, October 19, 1949.
2. Acquired Billy Pierce and $10,000 from the Detroit Tigers for Aaron Robinson, November 10, 1948.
3. Acquired Joe Jackson from the Cleveland Indians for Braggo Roth, Larry Chappell, Ed Klepfer, and $31,500, August 21, 1915.
4. Acquired LaMarr Hoyt, Oscar Gamble, Bob Polinsky, and $200,000 from the New York Yankees for Bucky Dent, April 5, 1977.
5. Acquired Wilbur Wood from the Pittsburgh Pirates for Juan Pizarro, October 12, 1966.

The Worst Trades

1. Traded Eddie Lopat to the New York Yankees for Aaron Robinson, Fred Bradley, and Bill Wight, February 24, 1948.
2. Traded Johnny Callison to the Philadelphia Phillies for Gene Freese, December 29, 1959.
3. Traded Bibb Falk to the Cleveland Indians for Martin Autry, February 28, 1929.
4. Traded Tommie Agee and Al Weis to the New York Mets for Tommy Davis, Jack Fisher, Billy Wynne, and Dick Booker, December 15, 1967.
5. Traded Goose Gossage and Terry Forster to the Pittsburgh Pirates for Richie Zisk and Silvio Martinez, December 10, 1976.

Trader: Frank Lane

There have been some big wheelers and dealers in baseball, among them Branch Rickey, Larry MacPhail, Bill Veeck, and in recent years Whitey Herzog. But they were all pikers by comparison to Frantic Frank Lane, the master dealer of them all.

Impatient, impulsive, and impersonal, Lane had no time for the long and tedious process of building a farm system. He traded. And traded again. In his twelve years as general manager of four different clubs, he made over 300 trades involving some 400 players — and that only counts trades involving major league teams.

With one exception, every club Lane took over improved its standing. He took a last place Chicago team and boosted it up to third, a second division St. Louis Cardinals team and advanced them to second, and a fourth place Cleveland squad that he moved up to second (though Indians fans will never forgive him for trading away Rocky Colavito). Only in Kansas City did he fail to improve a team; there he was fired before the end of his first year.

Just a few days after the White Sox hired Lane, he pulled off one of their best deals ever, getting young southpaw Billy Pierce and $10,000 from Detroit for veteran catcher Aaron Robinson. Pierce became one of the American League's top starters, and Robinson faded quickly from view. Lane always claimed he was lucky, because the pitcher he really wanted was Ted Gray, but Detroit wouldn't let him go. In his first year with the Sox, Lane pulled off forty-nine deals, and the forty-ninth was a very special one: it landed second baseman Nellie Fox from the Philadelphia Athletics for catcher Joe Tipton. Connie Mack agreed to let Fox go because he doubted that the 160-pounder had enough stamina to withstand the rigors of a 154-game season. Mr. Mack was never more wrong; Fox played 152 or more games for eleven straight seasons, and ended his career second only to Luke Appling on the White Sox all-time lists in games, at bats, hits, doubles, triples, runs, and total bases.

Another splendid Lane acquisition was shortstop Chico Carrasquel, whom he purchased from the Brooklyn chain for a modest sum. Chico teamed with Fox for six years to form a deft double play combination. Lane also maneuvered the three-team deal that landed Minnie Minoso, one of the most popular players ever to wear the Chicago uniform. But often Lane seemed to be dealing for the sake of dealing. He made innumerable deals with the St. Louis Browns, at one point trading infielder Willie Miranda to St. Louis twice within six months. All of these deals helped build the Chicago White Sox team that became known as the Go-Go Sox. Ironically, Lane made the deal that probably put them over the top in 1959: in December 1957, Chicago traded Minnie Minoso to Cleveland for Early Wynn and Al Smith. Wynn was 22–10 for the '59 White Sox. Of course, the effect wasn't what Lane had in mind when he made the deal; it was his first trade as general manager of the Indians.

DATE		ACQUIRED	FROM		IN EXCHANGE FOR
May 1901		Cash	Cleveland Indians	OF	Erwin Harvey
July 1901	P	Wiley Piatt	Philadelphia Athletics		Cash
July 1901	3B	Jimmy Burke	Milwaukee Brewers		Cash
Sept 1901		Cash	Pittsburgh Pirates	3B	Jimmy Burke
Sept 1901	OF	Pop Foster	Washington Senators		Cash
Feb 1902		Cash	St. Louis Browns	C	Joe Sugden
May 5, 1902		Cash	Baltimore Orioles	P OF	John Katoll Herm McFarland

DATE		ACQUIRED	FROM		IN EXCHANGE FOR
May 1902	P	Dummy Leitner	Cleveland Indians		Cash
April 1903	C	Jack Slattery	Cleveland Indians		Cash
April 1903	P	Nick Altrock	Boston Red Sox		Cash
May 1903		Cash	Cincinnati Reds	OF	Cozy Dolan
June 1903	OF	Ducky Holmes	Washington Senators	P	Davey Dunkle
June 1903		Cash	Cincinnati Reds	2B	Tom Daly
May 30, 1904		Cash	Detroit Tigers	OF	Frank Huelsman
Feb 1905	C	Frank Roth	St. Louis Browns	C	Branch Rickey
Feb 1906	OF	Rube Vinson	Cleveland Indians		Cash
May 9, 1906	OF	Ed Hahn	New York Yankees		Cash
June 6, 1906	OF	Patsy Dougherty	New York Yankees		Cash
March 1907	1B	Jake Stahl	Washington Senators		Cash
		(Stahl refused to report and was sold by Chicago to the New York Yankees.)			
Aug 1, 1907	1B	Piano Legs Hickman	Washington Senators		Cash
Sept 1, 1907	C	Charlie Armbruster	Boston Red Sox		Cash
Oct 1907		Cash	New York Yankees	1B	Jake Stahl
Nov 1907		Cash	Cleveland Indians	OF	Piano Legs Hickman
Jan 1908	1B	John Anderson	Washington Senators		Cash
Jan 1908	C	Al Shaw	Boston Red Sox		Cash
April 1908	SS	Freddy Parent	Boston Red Sox		Cash
May 1908	C	Ossee Schreckengost	Philadelphia Athletics		Cash
Aug 1908	OF	Gavvy Cravath	Boston Red Sox		Cash
Aug 1908		Cash	Washington Senators	1B	Jiggs Donahue
May 16, 1909	P	Bill Burns	Washington Senators	P OF 1B	Nick Altrock Gavvy Cravath Jiggs Donahue
April 1910		Cash	Cincinnati Reds	P	Bill Burns
May 1910	OF	George Browne	Washington Senators		Cash

DATE		ACQUIRED	FROM		IN EXCHANGE FOR
May 1910	2B	Charlie French	Boston Red Sox		Cash
Aug 9, 1910	OF 2B	Harry Lord Amby McConnell	Boston Red Sox	P 3B	Frank Smith Billy Purtell
Jan 1911	OF	Matty McIntyre	Detroit Tigers		Cash
April 1911		Cash	St. Louis Browns	OF	Paul Meloan
Jan 1912	C	Ted Easterly	Cleveland Indians		Cash
Jan 1912		Cash	New York Yankees	3B	Del Paddock
May 8, 1912	1B	Jack Fournier	Boston Red Sox		Cash
May 1912		Cash	Philadelphia Athletics	P	Jim Crabb
July 22, 1912	P	Eddie Cicotte	Boston Red Sox		Cash
Dec 1912	OF	Davy Jones	Detroit Tigers		Cash
June 23, 1913	1B 1B	Babe Borton Hal Chase	New York Yankees	2B	Rollie Zeider
July 1913	P	Buck O'Brien	Boston Red Sox		Cash
April 1914	OF	Ray Demmitt	Detroit Tigers		Cash
Dec 8, 1914	2B	Eddie Collins	Philadelphia Athletics		$50,000.
Jan 1915	C	Jack Lapp	Philadelphia Athletics		Cash
Feb 1915		Cash	New York Yankees	P	George Mogridge
July 7, 1915	OF	Nemo Leibold	Cleveland Indians		Waiver price
July 15, 1915	OF	Eddie Murphy	Philadelphia Athletics		$13,500.
July 1915		Cash	New York Giants	3B	Howard Baker
Aug 21, 1915	OF	Joe Jackson	Cleveland Indians	OF OF P	Braggo Roth Larry Chappell Ed Klepfer and $31,500.
Dec 1915		Cash	Cleveland Indians	C	Tom Daly
Feb 25, 1917	1B	Chick Gandil	Cleveland Indians		$3,500.
July 14, 1917		Cash	St. Louis Browns	P	Speed Martin
Sept 1917	3B	Bobby Byrne	Philadelphia Phillies		Waiver price
April 1918		Cash	Cincinnati Reds	P	Roy Mitchell

DATE		ACQUIRED	FROM		IN EXCHANGE FOR
May 1919	P	Grover Lowdermilk	St. Louis Browns		Cash
Aug 1919	P	Erskine Mayer	Pittsburgh Pirates		Waiver price
Aug 1919	P	Bill James	Boston Red Sox		Cash
Aug 1919	P	Wynn Noyes	Philadelphia Athletics		Cash
Sept 1919	P	Pat Ragan	New York Giants		Waiver price
Dec 1919		Cash	Detroit Tigers	3B	Babe Pinelli
July 23, 1920	OF	Amos Strunk	Philadelphia Athletics		Waiver price
March 4, 1921	OF	Harry Hooper	Boston Red Sox	OF OF	Shano Collins Nemo Leibold
May 1921		Cash	St. Louis Browns	P	Joe Bennett
Dec 1921	P	Ferdie Schupp	Brooklyn Dodgers		Cash
Feb 4, 1922	P	Jose Acosta	Philadelphia Athletics		Cash
May 1922	P	Henry Courtney	Washington Senators		Cash
May 12, 1923	P	Sloppy Thurston	St. Louis Browns		Cash
May 31, 1923		Waiver price	New York Yankees	SS	Ernie Johnson
July 6, 1923	P	Leon Cadore	Brooklyn Dodgers		Waiver price
April 30, 1924		Waiver price	Philadelphia Athletics	OF	Amos Strunk
July 11, 1925		Cash	Boston Red Sox	OF	John Bischoff
July 1925	P	Jim Joe Edwards	Cleveland Indians		Cash
Aug 1925	SS	Moe Berg	Brooklyn Dodgers		Cash
Dec 31, 1925		Waiver price	St. Louis Browns	P	Charlie Robertson
July 6, 1926		Waiver price	Cincinnati Reds	SS	Everett Scott
Jan 13, 1927	2B	Aaron Ward	New York Yankees	C 2B	Johnny Grabowski Ray Morehart
Jan 15, 1927	SS	Roger Peckinpaugh	Washington Senators	P P	Sloppy Thurston Leo Mangum
June 15, 1927	OF	Bernie Neis	Cleveland Indians		Cash
March 4, 1928		Waiver price	Cleveland Indians	2B	Aaron Ward

DATE		ACQUIRED	FROM		IN EXCHANGE FOR
Feb 28, 1929	C	Martin Autry	Cleveland Indians	OF	Bibb Falk
May 23, 1929	OF	Doug Taitt	Boston Red Sox	OF	Bill Barrett
June 22, 1929	3B	Frank Sigafoos	Detroit Tigers		Cash
Sept 27, 1929	P	Dutch Henry	New York Giants		Waiver price
June 13, 1930	OF	Red Barnes	Washington Senators	1B	Dave Harris
June 16, 1930	P C	Garland Braxton Bennie Tate	Washington Senators	1B	Art Shires
July 18, 1930	OF	Bob Fothergill	Detroit Tigers		Waiver price
July 21, 1930		Cash	St. Louis Browns	OF	Alex Metzler
Nov 1930		Cash	Cleveland Indians	SS	Bill Hunnefield
April 2, 1931		Waiver price	Cleveland Indians	C	Moe Berg
April 3, 1931	1B	Lu Blue	St. Louis Browns		$15,000.
May 17, 1931	1B	Lew Fonseca	Cleveland Indians	3B	Willie Kamm
July 13, 1931		Waiver price	St. Louis Browns	P	Garland Braxton
Nov 1931	P	Sad Sam Jones	Washington Senators		Waiver price
Dec 2, 1931	P	Milt Gaston	Boston Red Sox	P	Bob Weiland
Dec 4, 1931	2B P P	Jackie Hayes Bump Hadley Sad Sam Jones	Washington Senators	OF 2B	Carl Reynolds John Kerr
April 24, 1932	2B OF	Johnny Hodapp Bob Seeds	Cleveland Indians	3B P	Bill Cissell Jim Moore
April 27, 1932	SS	Red Kress	St. Louis Browns	OF P	Bruce Campbell Bump Hadley
April 29, 1932	C	Charlie Berry	Boston Red Sox	C OF OF	Bennie Tate Smead Jolley Cliff Watwood
April 30, 1932	OF	Jack Rothrock	Boston Red Sox		Cash
June 11, 1932		Cash	Washington Senators	P	Tommy Thomas
Sept 9, 1932	P	Chad Kimsey	St. Louis Browns		Cash
Sept 28, 1932	OF 2B OF	Al Simmons Jimmy Dykes Mule Haas	Philadelphia Athletics		$100,000.

DATE		ACQUIRED	FROM		IN EXCHANGE FOR
Dec 15, 1932	P SS	Ed Durham Hal Rhyne	Boston Red Sox	2B SS OF OF	Johnny Hodapp Greg Mulleavy Bob Fothergill Bob Seeds
May 14, 1933	OF	Earl Webb	Detroit Tigers		Waiver price
June 2, 1933	P	Whit Wyatt	Detroit Tigers	P	Vic Frazier
Dec 11, 1933	C	Merv Shea	St. Louis Browns		Cash
Dec 12, 1933	P C	George Earnshaw Johnny Pasek	Philadelphia Athletics	C	Charlie Berry and $20,000.
May 9, 1934	SS	Bob Boken	Washington Senators	SS	Red Kress
May 16, 1934		Cash	Brooklyn Dodgers	P	George Earnshaw
May 17, 1934	P	Carl Fischer	Detroit Tigers		Cash
May 1934	C	Ed Madjeski	Philadelphia Athletics		Cash
June 27, 1934	3B	Marty Hopkins	Philadelphia Phillies		Waiver price
Jan 22, 1935	C	Luke Sewell	St. Louis Browns		Cash
June 4, 1935	2B	Tony Piet	Cincinnati Reds		Cash
June 16, 1935	P	Jack Salveson	Pittsburgh Pirates		Cash
Sept 20, 1935	C	Frank Grube	St. Louis Browns		Cash
Dec 10, 1935		$75,000.	Detroit Tigers	OF	Al Simmons
April 11, 1936	P	Clint Brown	Cleveland Indians		Cash
May 4, 1936	OF	Dixie Walker	New York Yankees		Waiver price
May 5, 1936	P	Sugar Cain	St. Louis Browns	P	Les Tietje
July 20, 1936	P	Bill Dietrich	Washington Senators		Waiver price
Dec 10, 1936	P	Thornton Lee	Cleveland Indians	P	Jack Salveson
		(Part of three-team trade involving Chicago, Cleveland, and Washington.)			
April 1937	2B	Boze Berger	Cleveland Indians		Cash
Dec 2, 1937	3B C OF	Marv Owen Mike Tresh Gee Walker	Detroit Tigers	P 2B OF	Vern Kennedy Tony Piet Dixie Walker
March 18, 1938	1B	Joe Kuhel	Washington Senators	1B	Zeke Bonura
May 2, 1938	P	Frank Gabler	Boston Braves		Cash

DATE		ACQUIRED	FROM		IN EXCHANGE FOR
June 11, 1938	P	Jack Knott	St. Louis Browns	P	Billy Cox
Dec 19, 1938		Cash	Brooklyn Dodgers	C	Luke Sewell
Dec 21, 1938	SS	Eric McNair	Boston Red Sox	2B	Boze Berger
April 27, 1939	P	Eddie Smith	Philadelphia Athletics		Waiver price
April 27, 1939		Cash	St. Louis Browns	OF	Tommy Thompson
June 2, 1939	P	Johnny Marcum	St. Louis Browns	P	John Whitehead
Dec 8, 1939	OF	Moose Solters	St. Louis Browns	OF	Rip Radcliff
Dec 8, 1939		Cash	Boston Red Sox	3B	Marv Owen
Dec 8, 1939	OF P	Taffy Wright Pete Appleton	Washington Senators	OF	Gee Walker
Jan 10, 1940	SS	Skeeter Webb	Cleveland Indians	2B IF	Ollie Bejma John Gerlach
April 30, 1940	P	Buck Ross	Philadelphia Athletics		Cash
April 30, 1940	OF	Myril Hoag	St. Louis Browns		Cash
Dec 16, 1940	2B	Dario Lodigiani	Philadelphia Athletics	P	Jack Knott
Dec 18, 1940		Waiver price	Detroit Tigers	SS	Eric McNair
Dec 31, 1940	SS	Bill Knickerbocker	New York Yankees	C	Ken Silvestri
Jan 4, 1941	P	Joe Haynes	Washington Senators		Cash
Feb 7, 1941	P	John Humphries	Cleveland Indians	P	Clint Brown
May 29, 1941		Cash	Cleveland Indians	OF	Larry Rosenthal
Dec 9, 1941	OF	Wally Moses	Philadelphia Athletics	OF P	Mike Kreevich Jack Hallett
April 3, 1942		Waiver price	Philadelphia Athletics	SS	Bill Knickerbocker
Aug 11, 1943		Cash	Cleveland Indians	3B	Jimmy Grant
Nov 6, 1943	1B	Hal Trosky	Cleveland Indians		Cash
Nov 24, 1943		Cash	Washington Senators	1B	Joe Kuhel
June 27, 1944		Cash	Cleveland Indians	OF	Myril Hoag
July 31, 1944		Cash	St. Louis Browns	C	Tom Turner

DATE		ACQUIRED	FROM		IN EXCHANGE FOR
Dec 12, 1944	SS	Joe Orengo	Detroit Tigers	SS	Skeeter Webb
Dec 12, 1944	OF	Oris Hockett	Cleveland Indians	OF	Eddie Carnett
Dec 15, 1944	P	Johnny Johnson	New York Yankees	P	Jake Wade
Dec 30, 1944	3B	Floyd Baker	St. Louis Browns		Cash
Jan 2, 1946	P SS	Alex Carrasquel Fred Vaughn	Washington Senators		Cash
June 6, 1946	P	Al Hollingsworth	St. Louis Browns		Waiver price
June 1946	C	Frankie Hayes	Cleveland Indians	C	Tom Jordan
July 23, 1946		Cash	Boston Red Sox	OF	Wally Moses
Dec 13, 1946	SS	Jack Wallaesa	Philadelphia Athletics		Cash
March 22, 1947	P	Hi Bithorn	Pittsburgh Pirates		Waiver price
June 14, 1947	1B	Rudy York	Boston Red Sox	1B	Jake Jones
Jan 27, 1948	C	Ralph Weigel	Cleveland Indians	OF	Thurman Tucker
Feb 24, 1948	C P P	Aaron Robinson Fred Bradley Bill Wight	New York Yankees	P	Ed Lopat
June 2, 1948	P OF	Al Gettel Pat Seerey	Cleveland Indians	3B	Bob Kennedy
June 9, 1948	P	Marino Pieretti	Washington Senators	P	Earl Harrist
July 28, 1948	P	Randy Gumpert	New York Yankees		Cash
Oct 2, 1948	P P	Bob Kuzava Ernie Groth	Cleveland Indians	P	Frank Papish
Nov 10, 1948	P	Billy Pierce and $10,000.	Detroit Tigers	C	Aaron Robinson
Nov 15, 1948		Cash	Philadelphia Athletics	OF	Taffy Wright
Nov 22, 1948	C	Joe Tipton	Cleveland Indians	P	Joe Haynes
Dec 14, 1948	1B	Steve Souchock	New York Yankees	OF	Jim Delsing
Jan 12, 1949		Cash	Cleveland Indians	C	Mike Tresh
Jan 17, 1949	P	Bill Bevens	New York Yankees		Cash
		(Bevens was returned to New York Yankees on March 28, 1949.)			
Jan 26, 1949		Waiver price	Detroit Tigers	1B	Tony Lupien
April 15, 1949		Cash	Washington Senators	C	Ralph Weigel

DATE		ACQUIRED	FROM		IN EXCHANGE FOR
May 7, 1949	OF	Vern Rapp	Detroit Tigers	3B	Don Kolloway
May 11, 1949	P	Clyde Shoun	Boston Braves		Cash
June 8, 1949	1B	Charlie Kress	Cincinnati Reds		Cash
July 12, 1949		Cash	Washington Senators	P	Al Gettel
July 21, 1949	P	Mickey Haefner	Washington Senators		Cash
Sept 26, 1949	C	Bill Salkeld	Boston Braves		Cash
Oct 19, 1949	2B	Nellie Fox	Philadelphia Athletics	C	Joe Tipton
Dec 14, 1949	3B	Hank Majeski	Philadelphia Athletics	P	Eddie Klieman
Feb 2, 1950	C	Phil Masi	Pittsburgh Pirates		Cash
April 16, 1950		Waiver price	Cleveland Indians	P	Marino Pieretti
May 29, 1950	OF	Marv Rickert	Pittsburgh Pirates		Cash
May 31, 1950	2B P 1B	Al Kozar Ray Scarborough Eddie Robinson	Washington Senators	P 2B OF	Bob Kuzava Cass Michaels John Ostrowski
June 27, 1950	C	Gus Niarhos	New York Yankees		$10,000.
July 1, 1950		Cash	St. Louis Browns	P	Jack Bruner
July 5, 1950	P	Lou Kretlow	St. Louis Browns		Waiver price
Aug 8, 1950		Cash	Boston Braves	P	Mickey Haefner
Nov 11, 1950		Waiver price	Cleveland Indians	C	Herb Adams
Dec 10, 1950	P P OF	Joe Dobson Dick Littlefield Al Zarilla	Boston Red Sox	P P	Ray Scarborough Bill Wight
Dec 11, 1950	OF	Bud Stewart	Washington Senators	OF	Mike McCormick
April 30, 1951	OF OF	Paul Lehner Minnie Minoso (Part of three-team trade involving Chicago White Sox, Philadelphia A's, and Cleveland.)	Philadelphia Athletics	OF OF	Gus Zernial Dave Philley
May 16, 1951	2B	Bob Dillinger	Pittsburgh Pirates		Cash
May 29, 1951		Waiver price	St. Louis Browns	P	Bob Mahoney
June 4, 1951	SS	Kermit Wahl	Philadelphia Athletics	3B	Hank Majeski
June 4, 1951	OF	Don Lenhardt	St. Louis Browns	OF SS	Paul Lehner Kermit Wahl and cash

DATE	ACQUIRED		FROM	IN EXCHANGE FOR	
July 31, 1951	OF	Ray Coleman	St. Louis Browns		Waiver price
Sept 20, 1951	1B	Rocky Nelson	Pittsburgh Pirates		Waiver price
Oct 24, 1951	SS	Willie Miranda	Washington Senators	3B	Floyd Baker
Nov 13, 1951	2B	Mel Hoderlein	Boston Red Sox	P	Randy Gumpert
	P	Chuck Stobbs		OF	Don Lenhardt
Nov 27, 1951	P	Al Widmar	St. Louis Browns	SS	Joe DeMaestri
	C	Sherm Lollar		P	Dick Littlefield
	SS	Tom Upton		C	Gus Niarhos
				1B	Gordon Goldsberry
				OF	Jim Rivera
Nov 27, 1951	SS	Sam Dente	Washington Senators	SS	Tom Upton
March 13, 1952	P	Bill Kennedy	St. Louis Browns		Cash
May 3, 1952	OF	Sam Mele	Washington Senators	OF	Jim Busby
				2B	Mel Hoderlein
May 5, 1952	P	Jim Suchecki	Pittsburgh Pirates		Waiver price
June 15, 1952	OF	Tom Wright	St. Louis Browns	SS	Willie Miranda
	3B	Leo Thomas		OF	Al Zarilla
June 16, 1952		Cash	St. Louis Browns	P	Ken Holcombe
June 28, 1952	SS	Willie Miranda	St. Louis Browns		Waiver price
July 28, 1952	OF	Jim Rivera	St. Louis Browns	C	J W Porter
	C	Darrell Johnson		OF	Ray Coleman
Aug 27, 1952	P	Hal Hudson	St. Louis Browns		Waiver price
Sept 1, 1952	OF	Hank Edwards	Cincinnati Reds	P	Howie Judson
Oct 16, 1952	SS	Joe DeMaestri	St. Louis Browns	SS	Willie Miranda
	P	Tommy Byrne		OF	Hank Edwards
Dec 10, 1952	P	Mike Fornieles	Washington Senators	P	Chuck Stobbs
Jan 20, 1953	SS	Freddie Marsh	St. Louis Browns	SS	Dixie Upright and $25,000.
Jan 27, 1953	1B	Ferris Fain	Philadelphia Athletics	SS	Joe DeMaestri
		minor league		1B	Eddie Robinson
		2B Bob Wilson		1B	Ed McGhee
Feb 9, 1953	SS	Vern Stephens	Boston Red Sox	P	Hal Brown
				P	Marv Grissom
				P	Bill Kennedy
March 7, 1953	P	Earl Harrist	St. Louis Browns		Cash
March 18, 1953	P	Gene Bearden	St. Louis Browns		Waiver price
May 12, 1953	OF	Allie Clark	Philadelphia Athletics		Waiver price

DATE		ACQUIRED	FROM		IN EXCHANGE FOR
May 12, 1953	P	Sandy Consuegra	Washington Senators		Cash
May 23, 1953		Waiver price	Detroit Tigers	P	Earl Harrist
June 11, 1953		Cash	Washington Senators	P	Tommy Byrne
June 13, 1953	P OF	Virgil Trucks Bob Elliott	St. Louis Browns	C P	Darrell Johnson Lou Kretlow and $75,000.
July 20, 1953		Waiver price	St. Louis Browns	SS	Vern Stephens
Aug 25, 1953	IF	Connie Ryan	Philadelphia Phillies		Waiver price
Sept 1, 1953	SS	Neil Berry	St. Louis Browns		Waiver price
Nov 30, 1953	C	Carl Sawatski	Chicago Cubs		Waiver price
Dec 8, 1953	2B	Cass Michaels	Philadelphia Athletics		Cash
Dec 10, 1953	OF	Willard Marshall	Cincinnati Reds	P 2B 3B	Saul Rogovin Connie Ryan Rocky Krsnich
Feb 5, 1954	OF SS	Johnny Groth Johnny Lipon	Baltimore Orioles	SS OF	Neil Berry Sam Mele
April 18, 1954	3B	Grady Hatton	Cincinnati Reds	SS	Johnny Lipon
May 10, 1954	OF	Stan Jok	Philadelphia Phillies		Waiver price
May 23, 1954	3B	George Kell	Boston Red Sox	3B	Grady Hatton and $100,000.
May 27, 1954		Waiver price	Washington Senators	OF	Tom Wright
May 29, 1954	C	Matt Batts	Detroit Tigers	C	Red Wilson
June 11, 1954	1B P	Ed McGhee Morrie Martin	Philadelphia Athletics	P P OF	Sonny Dixon Al Sima Bill Wilson and $20,000.
June 11, 1954	P	Sonny Dixon	Washington Senators	P	Gus Keriazakos
Sept 30, 1954	3B	Bill Serena	Chicago Cubs		Waiver price
Dec 6, 1954	1B P OF	Walt Dropo Ted Gray Bob Nieman	Detroit Tigers	P 1B 1B	Leo Cristante Ferris Fain Jack Phillips
Dec 6, 1954	2B P C	Jim Brideweser Bob Chakales Clint Courtney	Baltimore Orioles	P P C SS	Don Ferrarese Don Johnson Matt Batts Freddie Marsh

DATE		ACQUIRED	FROM		IN EXCHANGE FOR
Feb 10, 1955	OF	Lloyd Merriman	Cincinnati Reds		Cash
May 30, 1955	3B	Bob Kennedy	Baltimore Orioles		Cash
June 6, 1955	C	Les Moss	Baltimore Orioles	P	Harry Dorish
June 7, 1955	OF	Jim Busby	Washington Senators	P C OF	Bob Chakales Clint Courtney Johnny Groth
June 15, 1955	P	Harry Byrd	Baltimore Orioles		Waiver price
July 17, 1955	OF	Gil Coan	Baltimore Orioles		Waiver price
July 26, 1955	2B	Bobby Adams	Cincinnati Reds		Cash
Aug 26, 1955		Waiver price	New York Giants	OF	Gil Coan
Oct 18, 1955	OF	Cal Abrams	Baltimore Orioles	IF	Bobby Adams
Oct 25, 1955	OF	Larry Doby	Cleveland Indians	OF SS	Jim Busby Chico Carrasquel
Nov 30, 1955	3B	Bubba Phillips	Detroit Tigers	P	Virgil Trucks
April 16, 1956		Cash	Pittsburgh Pirates	P	Howie Pollet
May 14, 1956		Cash	Baltimore Orioles	P	Sandy Consuegra
May 15, 1956	3B OF	Fred Hatfield Jim Delsing	Detroit Tigers	2B P 3B	Jim Brideweser Harry Byrd Bob Kennedy
May 21, 1956	P OF	Jim Wilson Dave Philley	Baltimore Orioles	OF P P 3B	Bob Nieman Mike Fornieles Connie Johnson George Kell
May 28, 1956	P	Gerry Staley	New York Yankees		Waiver price
June 22, 1956	P	Paul LaPalme	Cincinnati Reds		Waiver price
July 11, 1956	P	Ellis Kinder	St. Louis Cardinals		Waiver price
July 13, 1956		Waiver price	Baltimore Orioles	P	Morrie Martin
Sept 17, 1956	P	Dick Marlowe	Detroit Tigers		Waiver price
May 20, 1957		Cash	Brooklyn Dodgers	3B	Bob Kennedy
June 14, 1957	1B	Earl Torgeson	Detroit Tigers	OF	Dave Philley

DATE		ACQUIRED	FROM		IN EXCHANGE FOR
Dec 3, 1957	OF	Tito Francona	Baltimore Orioles	P	Jack Harshman
	P	Ray Moore		P	Russ Heman
	3B	Billy Goodman		1B	Jim Marshall
				OF	Larry Doby
Dec 4, 1957	P	Early Wynn	Cleveland Indians	3B	Fred Hatfield
	P	Al Smith		OF	Minnie Minoso
March 21, 1958	OF	Don Mueller	San Francisco Giants		Cash
April 1, 1958	P	Buddy Daley	Cleveland Indians	OF	Larry Doby
	OF	Dick Williams		P	Don Ferrarese
	OF	Gene Woodling			
April 30, 1958	P	Tom Qualters	Philadelphia Phillies		Cash
June 15, 1958	3B	Ray Boone	Detroit Tigers	P	Bill Fischer
	P	Bob Shaw		OF	Tito Francona
June 23, 1958	P	Turk Lown	Cincinnati Reds		Waiver price
June 24, 1958		Waiver price	Cincinnati Reds	1B	Walt Dropo
May 1, 1959	OF	Del Ennis	Cincinnati Reds	P	Don Rudolph
				OF	Lou Skizas
May 2, 1959	OF	Harry Simpson	Kansas City Athletics	3B	Ray Boone
May 13, 1959	OF	Larry Doby	Detroit Tigers		$30,000.
Aug 25, 1959	1B	Ted Kluszewski	Pittsburgh Pirates	OF	Harry Simpson
					minor league IF Bob Sagers
Nov 3, 1959	P	Frank Baumann	Boston Red Sox	1B	Ron Jackson
Dec 6, 1959	C	Dick Brown	Cleveland Indians	C	Johnny Romano
	P	Don Ferrarese		3B	Bubba Phillips
	P	Jake Striker		1B	Norm Cash
	OF	Minnie Minoso			
Dec 9, 1959	3B	Gene Freese	Philadelphia Phillies	OF	Johnny Callison
April 4, 1960	OF	Roy Sievers	Washington Senators	C	Earl Battey
				1B	Don Mincher and $150,000.
April 18, 1960	P	Herb Score	Cleveland Indians	P	Barry Latman
May 18, 1960	P	Russ Kemmerer	Washington Senators		Cash
May 19, 1960	P	Frank Barnes	St. Louis Cardinals		Cash
June 11, 1960	P	Bob Rush	Milwaukee Braves		Cash
June 13, 1960		Cash	Washington Senators	P	Ray Moore
Aug 13, 1960	C	Earl Averill	Chicago Cubs		Minor league C Don Prohovich and cash

DATE		ACQUIRED	FROM		IN EXCHANGE FOR
Nov 28, 1960		Cash	Milwaukee Braves	C	Dick Brown
Dec 15, 1960	P P	Juan Pizarro Cal McLish	Cincinnati Reds	3B	Gene Freese
April 3, 1961	2B	Ted Lepcio	Philadelphia Phillies		Cash
May 10, 1961	OF	Wes Covington	Milwaukee Braves		Waiver price
June 10, 1961	P P 3B OF	Ray Herbert Don Larsen Andy Carey Al Pilarcik	Kansas City Athletics	OF P P OF	Wes Covington Bob Shaw Gerry Staley Stan Johnson
Nov 27, 1961	1B	Joe Cunningham	St. Louis Cardinals	OF	Minnie Minoso
Nov 28, 1961	P 3B	John Buzhardt Charley Smith	Philadelphia Phillies	OF	Roy Sievers
Nov 30, 1961	P P P	Eddie Fisher Dom Zanni Bobby Tiefenauer	San Francisco Giants	P P	Billy Pierce Don Larsen
Dec 15, 1961	3B-OF P	Bob Sadowski Taylor Phillips minor league IF Lou Vassie	Philadelphia Phillies	P 3B P	Frank Barnes Andy Carey Cal McLish
		(Carey refused to report, and the Phillies received McLish in exchange for Vassie to complete the trade on March 24, 1962.)			
March 24, 1962		Minor leaguers IF Ramon Conde and 1B Jim Koranda	Los Angeles Dodgers	3B	Andy Carey
June 22, 1962	P	Dean Stone	Houston Astros	P	Russ Kemmerer
June 25, 1962	OF	Charlie Maxwell	Detroit Tigers	OF	Bob Farley
Jan 14, 1963	P 3B SS OF	Hoyt Wilhelm Pete Ward Ron Hansen Dave Nicholson	Baltimore Orioles	SS OF	Luis Aparicio Al Smith
April 8, 1963		Waiver price	Detroit Tigers	P	Denny McLain
May 5, 1963	P	Jim Brosnan	Cincinnati Reds	P	Dom Zanni
June 28, 1963	OF	Jim Lemon	Philadelphia Phillies		Cash
Dec 10, 1963	P P-OF	Jim Golden Danny Murphy and cash	Houston Astros	2B	Nellie Fox
March 18, 1964	P	Don Mossi	Detroit Tigers		Cash
March 31, 1964		Cash	New York Mets	P	Mike Joyce
April 23, 1964	SS	Chico Fernandez minor league C Bobby Caton and cash	New York Mets	3B	Charley Smith

DATE		ACQUIRED	FROM		IN EXCHANGE FOR
July 7, 1964	1B	Jeoff Long	St. Louis Cardinals		Cash
July 13, 1964	1B P	Bill Skowron Carl Bouldin	Washington Senators	1B P	Joe Cunningham Frank Kreutzer
Sept 12, 1964	C	Smoky Burgess	Pittsburgh Pirates		Waiver price
Oct 15, 1964	C	Bill Heath minor league P Joel Gibson	Philadelphia Phillies	P	Rudy May
Nov 24, 1964		Cash	St. Louis Cardinals	P	Fritz Ackley
Dec 1, 1964	OF	Danny Cater	Philadelphia Phillies	P	Ray Herbert
Dec 1, 1964	C	Jimmie Schaffer	Chicago Cubs	P	Frank Baumann
Jan 20, 1965	OF	Rocky Colavito	Kansas City Athletics	OF OF P	Jim Landis Mike Hershberger Fred Talbot
		(Part of three-team trade involving Kansas City, Cleveland, and Chicago White Sox.)			
Jan 20, 1965	P OF C	Tommy John Tommie Agee Johnny Romano	Cleveland Indians	OF C	Rocky Colavito Cam Carreon
		(Part of three-team trade involving Kansas City, Cleveland, and Chicago White Sox.)			
July 8, 1965	P	Frank Lary	New York Mets	C	Jimmie Schaffer
Aug 25, 1965	3B	Gene Freese	Pittsburgh Pirates		Cash
Dec 1, 1965	P	Jack Lamabe minor league P Ray Cordeiro and cash	Houston Astros	OF C	Dave Nicholson Bill Heath
May 27, 1966	3B	Wayne Causey	Kansas City Athletics	1B	Danny Cater
June 12, 1966	2B	Jerry Adair and minor league OF Johnny Riddle	Baltimore Orioles	P	Eddie Fisher
July 20, 1966	SS	Jim Mahoney and cash	Houston Astros	3B	Gene Freese
Oct 12, 1966	P	Wilbur Wood	Pittsburgh Pirates	P	Juan Pizarro
Dec 14, 1966	OF P	Walt Williams Don Dennis	St. Louis Cardinals	C	Johnny Romano and minor league P Lee White
Dec 15, 1966	P	Jim O'Toole	Cincinnati Reds	OF	Floyd Robinson
April 26, 1967		Cash	New York Mets	P	Jack Lamabe
May 6, 1967	OF	Cotton Nash and cash	California Angels	1B	Bill Skowron
May 22, 1967	IF	Jimmy Stewart	Chicago Cubs		Cash

DATE	ACQUIRED	FROM	IN EXCHANGE FOR
June 3, 1967	P Don McMahon minor league P Bob Snow	Boston Red Sox	2B Jerry Adair
June 15, 1967	OF Jim King	Washington Senators	OF Ed Stroud
July 22, 1967	3B Ken Boyer	New York Mets	C J. C. Martin
July 29, 1967	OF Rocky Colavito	Cleveland Indians	OF Jim King IF Marv Staehle
Aug 15, 1967	2B Sandy Alomar	New York Mets	Cash
Aug 21, 1967	Cash	Baltimore Orioles	P John Buzhardt
Oct 13, 1967	1B George Kernek	St. Louis Cardinals	Cash
Nov 29, 1967	SS Luis Aparicio OF Russ Snyder OF John Matias	Baltimore Orioles	OF Don Buford P Bruce Howard P Roger Nelson
Dec 15, 1967	OF Tommy Davis P Jack Fisher P Billy Wynne minor league C Dick Booker	New York Mets	OF Tommie Agee 2B Al Weis
Feb 9, 1968	Minor league OFs Tom Murray and Levi Brown	Houston Astros	OF Lee Thomas
Feb 13, 1968	2B Tim Cullen P Buster Narum P Bob Priddy	Washington Senators	P Dennis Higgins P Steve Jones SS Ron Hansen
March 26, 1968	Cash	Los Angeles Dodgers	OF Rocky Colavito
June 13, 1968	OF Leon Wagner	Cleveland Indians	OF Russ Snyder
July 20, 1968	OF Woodie Held	California Angels	IF Wayne Causey
July 21, 1968	P Dennis Ribant	Detroit Tigers	P Don McMahon
Aug 2, 1968	SS Ron Hansen	Washington Senators	2B Tim Cullen
Sept 30, 1968	IF Bob Christian	Detroit Tigers	Cash
Dec 5, 1968	Cash	Cincinnati Reds	OF Leon Wagner
Dec 5, 1968	C Don Pavletich P Don Secrist	Cincinnati Reds	P Jack Fisher
Jan 20, 1969	P Sammy Ellis	California Angels	OF Bill Voss minor league P Andy Rubicotta
May 14, 1969	IF Bobby Knoop	California Angels	2B Sandy Alomar P Bob Priddy
June 8, 1969	P Gary Bell	Seattle Pilots	P Bob Locker

DATE		ACQUIRED	FROM		IN EXCHANGE FOR
June 13, 1969	P	Jack Hamilton	Cleveland Indians	P	Sammy Ellis
Aug 25, 1969		Cash	Washington Senators	P	Cisco Carlos
Dec 13, 1969	IF	Syd O'Brien	Boston Red Sox	C	Don Pavletich
		minor league P Billy Farmer		P	Gary Peters
	P	Gerry Janeski (Janeski replaced Farmer, who retired.)			
Dec 15, 1969	P	Jerry Arrigo	Cincinnati Reds	OF	Angel Bravo
Dec 18, 1969	P	Mickey Scott and cash	New York Yankees	OF	Pete Ward
Feb 28, 1970		Cash	New York Yankees	SS	Ron Hansen
March 30, 1970	P	Tommie Sisk	San Diego Padres	P	Jerry Nyman
June 15, 1970	P	Barry Moore	Cleveland Indians	OF	Buddy Bradford
	P	Bob Miller			
June 29, 1970	P	Lee Stange	Boston Red Sox		Cash
Sept 1, 1970	P	Bob Miller	Chicago Cubs		Cash
Sept 9, 1970	P	Steve Hamilton	New York Yankees		Cash
Sept 10, 1970	OF	Lee Maye	Washington Senators		Cash
Oct 13, 1970	OF	Pat Kelly	Kansas City Royals	1B	Gail Hopkins
	P	Don O'Riley		OF	John Matias
Nov 30, 1970	P	Pat Jacquez	Chicago Cubs	OF	Jose Ortiz
	P	Dave Lemonds		1B	Ossie Blanco
	1B	Roe Skidmore			
Nov 30, 1970	OF	Jay Johnstone	California Angels	OF	Ken Berry
	C	Tom Egan		2B	Syd O'Brien
	P	Tom Bradley		P	Billy Wynne
Dec 1, 1970	2B	Mike Andrews	Boston Red Sox	SS	Luis Aparicio
	SS	Luis Alvarado			
Feb 9, 1971	OF	Rick Reichardt	Washington Senators	P	Gerry Janeski
March 15, 1971	P	Steve Kealey	California Angels		Cash
March 23, 1971	IF	Steve Huntz	San Francisco Giants	P	Steve Hamilton
March 24, 1971	IF	Luis Alcaraz and cash	Kansas City Royals	2B	Bobby Knoop
March 29, 1971	OF	Ed Stroud	Washington Senators	1B	Tom McCraw
March 31, 1971	P	Vicente Romo	Boston Red Sox	C	Duane Josephson
	1B	Tony Muser		P	Danny Murphy
June 30, 1971		Cash	Milwaukee Brewers	P	Floyd Weaver

DATE		ACQUIRED	FROM		IN EXCHANGE FOR
Oct 13, 1971	OF	Jim Lyttle	New York Yankees	P	Rich Hinton
Dec 2, 1971	1B	Richie Allen	Los Angeles Dodgers	P IF	Tommy John Steve Huntz
Dec 2, 1971	P	Stan Bahnsen	New York Yankees	2B	Rich McKinney
Feb 5, 1972	P	Pete Hamm	Minnesota Twins		Cash
June 2, 1972	P	Phil Regan	Chicago Cubs		Cash
July 9, 1972	IF	Ed Spiezio	San Diego Padres	P	Don Eddy and cash
Aug 17, 1972	P	Eddie Fisher	California Angels	IF C	Bruce Miller Bruce Kimm
Oct 19, 1972	IF	Eddie Leon	Cleveland Indians	OF	Walt Williams
Oct 28, 1972	OF	John Jeter	San Diego Padres	P	Vicente Romo
Nov 28, 1972	OF P	Ken Henderson Steve Stone	San Francisco Giants	P	Tom Bradley
Feb 1, 1973	OF	Joe Keough	Kansas City Royals	OF	Jim Lyttle
May 26, 1973		Cash	San Diego Padres	IF	Rich Morales
Aug 15, 1973	P	Jim Kaat	Minnesota Twins		Cash
Aug 29, 1973	P	Jim McGlothlin	Cincinnati Reds	P	Steve Kealey
Aug 29, 1973		Cash	St. Louis Cardinals	P	Eddie Fisher
Oct 23, 1973	IF	Hector Torres	Houston Astros	P	Dan Neumeier
Oct 26, 1973	P	Jim Kremmel	St. Louis Cardinals	P	Denny O'Toole
Dec 11, 1973	3B	Ron Santo	Chicago Cubs	P P C P	Steve Stone Ken Frailing Steve Swisher Jim Kremmel
April 27, 1974	P	Ken Tatum	St. Louis Cardinals	IF	Luis Alvarado
July 1, 1974	P	Lloyd Allen	Texas Rangers		Cash
July 11, 1974		Cash	Pittsburgh Pirates	C	Chuck Brinkman
Oct 25, 1974	P	Roger Nelson	Cincinnati Reds		Cash
Dec 3, 1974		Player to be named later and cash (Chicago received Jim Essian, May 15, 1975.)	Atlanta Braves	1B	Richie Allen
Dec 5, 1974	P	Cecil Upshaw	New York Yankees	SS	Eddie Leon

DATE		ACQUIRED	FROM		IN EXCHANGE FOR
Feb 25, 1975	P	Steve Dunning	Texas Rangers	P	Stan Perzanowski
Feb 25, 1975	P	Milt Wilcox	Cleveland Indians	P OF	Dave LaRoche Brock Davis
March 17, 1975		Cash	Philadelphia Phillies	P	Cecilio Acosta
April 1, 1975		Minor leaguers Ken Bennett Terry Quinn Fred Anyzeski John Narron and cash	New York Yankees	C	Ed Herrmann
April 28, 1975		Cash	San Diego Padres	C	Gerry Moses
May 8, 1975	OF	Bob Coluccio	Milwaukee Brewers	OF	Bill Sharp
May 15, 1975	C	Jim Essian	Atlanta Braves		Completion of Richie Allen trade of December 3, 1974.
June 15, 1975	P OF	Dave Hamilton Chet Lemon	Oakland Athletics	P P	Stan Bahnsen Skip Pitlock
June 15, 1975	P	Jesse Jefferson	Baltimore Orioles	1B	Tony Muser
June 30, 1975	P	Bill Parsons and cash	St. Louis Cardinals	OF	Buddy Bradford
July 18, 1975		Cash	Montreal Expos	OF	Jim Lyttle
July 18, 1975	C	Gerry Moses	San Diego Padres		Cash
Aug 1, 1975		Cash	St. Louis Cardinals	P	Lloyd Allen
Sept 22, 1975		Minor league C Chuck Erickson and cash	Boston Red Sox	1B	Deron Johnson
Dec 10, 1975	P P OF	Dick Ruthven Roy Thomas Alan Bannister	Philadelphia Phillies	P SS	Jim Kaat Mike Buskey
Dec 11, 1975	1B OF	Jim Spencer Morris Nettles	California Angels	3B P	Bill Melton Steve Dunning
Dec 12, 1975	OF P	Buddy Bradford Greg Terlecky	St. Louis Cardinals	IF	Lee Richard
Dec 12, 1975	OF IF	Ralph Garr Larvell Blanks	Atlanta Braves	OF P P	Ken Henderson Dick Ruthven Danny Osborn
Dec 12, 1975	2B	Jack Brohamer	Cleveland Indians	IF	Larvell Blanks
Dec 12, 1975	P	Clay Carroll	Cincinnati Reds	P	Rich Hinton minor league OF Jeff Sovern
May 18, 1976	P OF	Ken Brett Rich Coggins	New York Yankees	OF	Carlos May
June 15, 1976	P	Blue Moon Odom	Atlanta Braves	C	Pete Varney

DATE		ACQUIRED	FROM		IN EXCHANGE FOR
July 14, 1976	OF	Wayne Nordhagen	Philadelphia Phillies	OF	Rich Coggins
Oct 21, 1976	P	Larry Anderson	Toronto Blue Jays	C	Phil Roof
Nov 6, 1976	OF	Tom Spencer	Cincinnati Reds	IF	Hugh Yancy
Nov 18, 1976	C	Dave Duncan	Baltimore Orioles	OF	Pat Kelly
Nov 24, 1976	P	Steve Stone	Chicago Cubs		No compensation (free agent signing)
Nov 26, 1976	3B	Eric Soderholm	Minnesota Twins		No compensation (free agent signing)
Dec 10, 1976	OF P	Richie Zisk Silvio Martinez	Pittsburgh Pirates	P P	Terry Forster Goose Gossage
March 23, 1977	P	Lerrin LaGrow	St. Louis Cardinals	P	Clay Carroll
April 5, 1977	OF P	Oscar Gamble LaMarr Hoyt minor league P Bob Polinsky and $200,000.	New York Yankees	SS	Bucky Dent
June 13, 1977		Cash	Pittsburgh Pirates	OF	Jerry Hairston
June 15, 1977	P P IF	Don Kirkwood John Verhoeven John Flannery	California Angels	P	Ken Brett
Aug 18, 1977	P	Steve Renko	Chicago Cubs	P	Larry Anderson and cash
Aug 20, 1977	SS	Don Kessinger	St. Louis Cardinals		Minor league P Steve Staniland
Aug 23, 1977		Cash	St. Louis Cardinals	P	Randy Wiles
Aug 30, 1977		Cash	Toronto Blue Jays	SS	Tim Nordbrook
Aug 31, 1977	P	Clay Carroll	St. Louis Cardinals	OF P P	Nyls Nyman Dave Hamilton Silvio Martinez
Sept 2, 1977	OF	Henry Cruz	Los Angeles Dodgers		Cash
Sept 8, 1977	C	Bill Nahorodny	Philadelphia Phillies		Cash
Sept 22, 1977	OF	Bob Molinaro	Detroit Tigers		Cash
Nov 9, 1977		No compensation (free agent signing)	Texas Rangers	OF	Richie Zisk
Nov 17, 1977	OF	Ron Blomberg	New York Yankees		No compensation (free agent signing)
Nov 28, 1977	SS	Greg Pryor	Texas Rangers		No compensation (free agent signing)
Nov 29, 1977		No compensation (free agent signing)	San Diego Padres	OF	Oscar Gamble

DATE		ACQUIRED	FROM		IN EXCHANGE FOR
Dec 5, 1977	OF OF P	Bobby Bonds Thad Bosley Rich Dotson	California Angels	C P P	Brian Downing Chris Knapp Dave Frost
Dec 12, 1977	P	Stan Thomas minor league P Ed Ricks and cash	New York Yankees	1B OF	Jim Spencer Cirilio Cruz minor league P Bob Polinsky
Feb 15, 1978	1B	Frank Ortenzio (Ortenzio was returned to Montreal on April 4, 1978.)	Montreal Expos		Cash
March 30, 1978	P	Pablo Torrealba	Oakland Athletics	P C	Steve Renko Jim Essian
April 5, 1978	P	Jim Willoughby	Boston Red Sox		Cash
April 11, 1978		Cash	Toronto Blue Jays	P	Don Kirkwood
May 16, 1978	OF OF	Claudell Washington Rusty Torres	Texas Rangers	OF	Bobby Bonds
Oct 23, 1978	OF	John Scott	St. Louis Cardinals	P	Jim Willoughby
Nov 29, 1978		No compensation (free agent signing)	Baltimore Orioles	P	Steve Stone
April 13, 1979	3B	Jim Morrison	Philadelphia Phillies	P	Jack Kucek
May 11, 1979		Cash	Los Angeles Dodgers	P	Lerrin LaGrow
May 27, 1979	C	Milt May	Detroit Tigers		Cash
June 15, 1979	P 1B	Ed Farmer Gary Holle	Texas Rangers	3B	Eric Soderholm
July 6, 1979	3B	Juan Bernhardt	Seattle Mariners	P	Rich Hinton
Aug 30, 1979		Cash	Baltimore Orioles	OF	Bob Molinaro
Sept 20, 1979		Cash	California Angels	OF	Ralph Garr
Oct 3, 1979	OF	Bob Molinaro	Baltimore Orioles		Cash
Nov 1, 1979		No compensation (free agent signing)	San Francisco Giants	C	Milt May
Dec 3, 1979		Minor league P Rick Wieters	Atlanta Braves	C	Bill Nahorodny
Dec 12, 1979	P	Bill Atkinson	Montreal Expos		Cash
Dec 19, 1979		No compensation (free agent signing)	Cleveland Indians	OF	Jorge Orta
Jan 15, 1980	OF	Joe Zdeb	Kansas City Royals	P	Ed Bane
June 7, 1980		Minor league OF Jesse Anderson	New York Mets	OF	Claudell Washington
June 12, 1980	SS	Todd Cruz	California Angels	P	Randy Scarbery

DATE		ACQUIRED	FROM		IN EXCHANGE FOR
June 13, 1980	C	Ron Pruitt	Cleveland Indians	UT	Alan Bannister
Nov 20, 1980	C	Jim Essian	Oakland Athletics		No compensation (free agent signing)
Dec 6, 1980	OF	Ron LeFlore	Montreal Expos		No compensation (free agent signing)
Dec 12, 1980	2B	Tony Bernazard	Montreal Expos	P	Rich Wortham
Feb 4, 1981	SS	Bill Almon	New York Mets		No compensation (free agent signing)
Feb 12, 1981	C	Marc Hill	San Francisco Giants		No compensation (free agent signing)
March 9, 1981	C	Carlton Fisk	Boston Red Sox		No compensation (free agent signing)
March 28, 1981	P	Dennis Lamp	Chicago Cubs	P	Ken Kravec
March 30, 1981	OF	Greg Luzinski	Philadelphia Phillies		Cash
April 1, 1981	OF	John Poff	Milwaukee Brewers	OF	Thad Bosley
April 1, 1981	2B	Jay Loviglio	Philadelphia Phillies	P	Mike Proly
Aug 15, 1981	P	Lynn McGlothen	Chicago Cubs	UT	Bob Molinaro
		(Cubs received Molinaro on March 29, 1982.)			
Aug 30, 1981	P	Jerry Koosman	Minnesota Twins		Minor league SS Ivan Mesa minor league 3B Ronnie Perry
				OF	Randy Johnson and cash
Sept 9, 1981	OF	Jerry Turner	San Diego Padres		Cash
Oct 30, 1981		Minor league IF Jose Castillo	Philadelphia Phillies	P 1B	Dewey Robinson Gary Holle
Nov 27, 1981	OF	Steve Kemp	Detroit Tigers	OF	Chet Lemon
Dec 11, 1981	OF	Tom Paciorek	Seattle Mariners	SS C OF	Todd Cruz Jim Essian Rod Allen
Jan 15, 1982		No compensation (free agent signing)	Texas Rangers	1B	Lamar Johnson
Jan 28, 1982		Free agent signing	Philadelphia Phillies	P	Ed Farmer
		(Chicago selected Joel Skinner of Pittsburgh from the compensation pool.)			
Feb 2, 1982	C	Joel Skinner	Pittsburgh Pirates		
		(Claimed in compensation draft after Chicago lost free agent P Ed Farmer to Philadelphia.)			
March 21, 1982	IF P	Vance Law Ernie Camacho	Pittsburgh Pirates	P P	Ross Baumgarten Butch Edge
March 24, 1982	P	Jeff Schattinger	Kansas City Royals	IF	Greg Pryor

DATE	ACQUIRED	FROM	IN EXCHANGE FOR
March 30, 1982	OF Rudy Law	Los Angeles Dodgers	Minor league P Bert Geiger OF Cecil Espy
April 2, 1982	3B Aurelio Rodriguez	Toronto Blue Jays	OF Wayne Nordhagen
June 14, 1982	P Eddie Solomon	Pittsburgh Pirates	3B Jim Morrison
Aug 21, 1982	P Sparky Lyle	Philadelphia Phillies	Cash
Aug 23, 1982	P Jim Kern	Cincinnati Reds	Minor leaguers 3B Wade Rowdon and OF Leo Garcia
Aug 30, 1982	P Warren Brusstar	Philadelphia Phillies	Cash
Nov 29, 1982	Cash	Chicago Cubs	2B Jay Loviglio
Dec 9, 1982	No compensation (free agent signing)	New York Yankees	OF Steve Kemp
Dec 10, 1982	OF Ty Waller	Chicago Cubs	P Reggie Patterson
Dec 13, 1982	P Floyd Bannister	Seattle Mariners	No compensation (free agent signing)
Jan 18, 1983	No compensation (free agent signing)	Oakland Athletics	SS Bill Almon
Jan 25, 1983	SS Scott Fletcher 3B Pat Tabler P Randy Martz P Dick Tidrow	Chicago Cubs	P Steve Trout P Warren Brusstar
Jan 26, 1983	P Steve Mura	St. Louis Cardinals	
	(Claimed in compensation draft after Chicago lost free agent OF Steve Kemp to Yankees.)		
Feb 7, 1983	No compensation (free agent signing)	Baltimore Orioles	3B Aurelio Rodriguez
April 1, 1983	SS Jerry Dybzinski	Cleveland Indians	3B Pat Tabler
June 15, 1983	2B Julio Cruz	Seattle Mariners	2B Tony Bernazard
June 21, 1983	Minor league IF Mike Sodders	Minnesota Twins	OF Rusty Kuntz
July 16, 1983	Cash	Chicago Cubs	OF Thad Bosley
Aug 25, 1983	OF Miguel Dilone	Cleveland Indians	P Rich Barnes
Sept 7, 1983	P Randy Niemann	Pittsburgh Pirates	OF Miguel Dilone minor league P Mike Maitland
Nov 21, 1983	C Steve Christmas	Cincinnati Reds	3B Fran Mullins
Nov 28, 1983	IF Kelly Paris	Cincinnati Reds	Cash

DATE		ACQUIRED	FROM		IN EXCHANGE FOR
Dec 5, 1983	P	Ron Reed	Philadelphia Phillies	P	Jerry Koosman
Jan 10, 1984		Free agent signing	Toronto Blue Jays	P	Dennis Lamp
		Chicago selected Tom Seaver of the New York Mets from the compensation pool.			
Jan 20, 1984	P	Tom Seaver	New York Mets		
		(Claimed in compensation draft after Chicago lost free agent P Dennis Lamp to Toronto.)			
Jan 21, 1984	P	Tom Brennan	Cleveland Indians		Player to be named later
Jan 27, 1984		No compensation (free agent signing)	New York Mets	P	Dick Tidrow

Cleveland Indians

The Best Trades

1. Acquired Tris Speaker from the Boston Red Sox for Sad Sam Jones, Fred Thomas, and $55,000, April 12, 1916.
2. Acquired Gaylord Perry and Frank Duffy from the San Francisco Giants for Sam McDowell, November 29, 1971.
3. Acquired Joe Jackson from the Philadelphia Athletics for Bris Lord, July 25, 1910.
4. Acquired Andre Thornton from the Montreal Expos for Jackie Brown, December 10, 1976.
5. Acquired Charlie Jamieson, Larry Gardner, and Elmer Myers from the Philadelphia Athletics for Braggo Roth, March 1, 1919.

The Worst Trades

1. Traded Pedro Guerrero to the Los Angeles Dodgers for Bruce Ellingsen, April 3, 1974.
2. Traded Graig Nettles and Gerry Moses to the New York Yankees for Charlie Spikes, Rusty Torres, John Ellis, and Jerry Kenney, November 27, 1972.
3. Traded Mudcat Grant to the Minnesota Twins for Lee Stange and George Banks, June 15, 1964.
4. Traded Joe Rudi and Phil Roof to the Kansas City Athletics for Jim Landis, October 1, 1965.
5. Traded Joe Jackson to the Chicago White Sox for Braggo Roth, Ed Klepfer, Larry Chappell, and $31,500, August 21, 1915.

Trader: Bill Veeck

To some, Bill Veeck was the master of the bizarre. To others, he was an insult to the dignity of the game of baseball, a sentence that lies on a fairly shaky premise at best. But none can deny that he was a man who brought a true sense of personal style to the game, and that many of his ideas were far ahead of their time.

Veeck was a tireless worker who thought nothing of putting in eighteen- and twenty-hour days, seven days a week. His two most prominent hobbies were buying and selling franchises and buying, selling, and trading ballplayers. Veeck owned three different major league clubs in his career (four if we count his two Chicago White Sox regimes separately; three if we don't count the St. Louis Browns as major league). But his first and probably greatest achievement came in building the Cleveland Indians into a World Series winner in the three years after he bought them.

A series of shrewd trades changed the Tribe from a second division club into a champion. Of the twenty-five players on the club in June 1946, eight were still with them two years later. Veeck particularly relished making deals with the New York Yankees, whom he regarded as the Goliath of baseball, just waiting for a hard-working David to come along and knock him off. Joe Gordon, the acrobatic second baseman who solidified the infield, was acquired from the Yanks, though at a cost of Allie Reynolds. Allie Clark, who hit .310 as a part-time outfielder, came in exchange for Red Embree. Gene Bearden, the knuckleballing sensation of the '48 season, was part of a package picked up for Ray Mack and Sherm Lollar, neither of whom would be wearing pinstripes for long.

Veeck's frenzied dealing kept the fans on their toes; they never quite knew who would be taking the field, and turned out in record numbers to find out. At first he made trades as much to draw fans as to help the team, but as the '48 pennant drew near, it became clear what a strong club he had constructed. The Indians led for much of the season, and won the first playoff game in American League history over the Boston Red Sox for the title, Cleveland's first since 1920. A year later, Veeck sold the team; his next venture, the St. Louis Browns, would prove far less enjoyable than his years with the Tribe.

Trader: Gabe Paul

A baseball man all his life, Gabe Paul has never held or wanted a job in any other field. He began learning the business as a teenager and, in his own words, "I'm still learning." Paul has been around the front offices of the Cincinnati Reds, Cleveland Indians, and New York Yankees for over fifty years, with more than thirty years as general manager, president, and chief operating officer. He himself estimates that he has made in the neighborhood of 500 trades; some he'd rather forget, but on the whole his batting average is quite respectable.

In his latest rebuilding effort with the Indians, Paul has relied almost entirely on trades to pluck the best prospects from his rivals' farm systems. Every player in the Indians' starting lineup in 1983 with the exception of part-time catcher Chris Bando, and including the top four starters and reliever Dan Spillner, was acquired by trade. And the most lucrative deal was probably the deal he was most criticized for: the trade of Von Hayes for five players. Hayes was fresh from a promising rookie season and bore the tag of a potential superstar. Nonetheless, Paul traded him to the Philadelphia Phillies for a package of talent that included second baseman Manny Trillo, shortstop Julio Franco, catcher Jerry Willard, outfielder George Vukovich, and pitcher Jay Baller. While Hayes disappointed Phillies fans, who derisively nicknamed him "Five for One," Franco moved smartly into the starting shortstop job, Willard began challenging for a regular assignment behind the plate, and Vukovich took over in right field.

The Cleveland youth movement continued with two more decisive trades: veteran starter Len Barker was sent to Atlanta for Brett Butler, Brook Jacoby, and Rick Behenna; and Toby Harrah was traded to the Yankees for Otis Nixon and George Frazier. For the first time in many years, the Indians were making a firm commitment to youth in an effort to reverse the rudderless drift of the organization. Instead of trading young players for proven but limited talents, the Indians are cashing in the talent they possess for future, potentially unlimited talent. The 1984 Opening Day lineup contained only one player who was with the Tribe two years earlier, and the team will be on the rise in the years to come — if they know when to stop making deals.

DATE		ACQUIRED	FROM		IN EXCHANGE FOR
Jan 1901	P	Bill Hoffer	Pittsburgh Pirates		Cash
April 23, 1901		Cash	Philadelphia Athletics	P	Bock Baker
May 1901	OF	Erwin Harvey	Chicago White Sox		Cash
May 1901	OF	Jack O'Brien	Washington Senators		Cash
May 1901	P	Dave Dowling	Milwaukee Brewers		Cash
June 1901	C	Joe Connor	Milwaukee Brewers		Cash
Oct 1901	C	Ossee Schreckengost	Boston Red Sox		Cash
May 16, 1902	OF	Elmer Flick	Philadelphia Athletics		Cash
May 30, 1902	OF	Piano Legs Hickman	Boston Red Sox	1B	Candy LaChance
May 30, 1902		Player to be named later (Cleveland received P Red Donahue in June, 1903.)	St. Louis Browns	OF	Charlie Hemphill
May 1902		Cash	Chicago White Sox	P	Dummy Leitner
June 1902	P	Bill Bernhard	Philadelphia Athletics	C 2B	Ossee Schreckengost Frank Bonner
June 1902	2B	Nap Lajoie	Philadelphia Athletics		Cash
Feb 1903		Cash	Philadelphia Athletics	3B	Ollie Pickering
April 1903		Cash	Chicago White Sox	C	Jack Slattery
June 1903	P	Red Donahue	St. Louis Browns		Completes Charlie Hemphill trade of May, 1902.
Jan 1904	OF	Billy Lush	Detroit Tigers	P P	Jesse Stovall Ed Killian
Aug 7, 1904	1B C	Charlie Carr Fritz Buelow	Detroit Tigers	1B	Piano Legs Hickman
Aug 1, 1905		Cash	Detroit Tigers	C	Nig Clarke
Aug 11, 1905	C	Nig Clarke	Detroit Tigers		Cash
Jan 1906	P	Jack Townsend	Washington Senators		Cash
Feb 1906		Cash	Washington Senators	C	Howard Wakefield
Feb 1906		Cash	Chicago White Sox	OF	Rube Vinson
Feb 1906		Cash	Detroit Tigers	P	Red Donahue

DATE		ACQUIRED	FROM		IN EXCHANGE FOR
Feb 1906		Cash	Cincinnati Reds	1B	Charlie Carr
Aug 15, 1906	C	Malachi Kittredge	Washington Senators		Cash
Dec 1906	2B	Pete O'Brien	St. Louis Browns	C	Fritz Buelow
Dec 1906		Cash	Detroit Tigers	1B	Claude Rossman
Feb 1907	C	Howard Wakefield	Washington Senators		Cash
May 16, 1907	P	Walter Clarkson	New York Yankees	P	Earl Moore
May 20, 1907		Cash	Boston Red Sox	OF	Bunk Congalton
Aug 11, 1907	2B	Rabbit Nill	Washington Senators	2B C	Pete O'Brien Howard Wakefield
Nov 1907		Cash	New York Yankees	OF	Frank Delahanty
Nov 1907	OF	Piano Legs Hickman	Chicago White Sox		Cash
Jan 1908		Cash	New York Yankees	3B	Mike Donovan
Aug 1908	C	Deacon McGuire	Boston Red Sox		Cash
Aug 1908	P 2B	Cy Falkenberg Dave Altizer	Washington Senators		Cash
Aug 1908		Cash	Boston Red Sox	P	Jake Thielman
Sept 1908	OF	Denny Sullivan	Boston Red Sox		Cash
Feb 18, 1909	P	Cy Young	Boston Red Sox	P P	Charlie Chech Jack Ryan and $12,500.
May 1909	SS	Neal Ball	New York Yankees		Cash
May 1910	2B	Harry Niles	Boston Red Sox		Cash
May 1910	3B	Morrie Rath	Philadelphia Athletics		Cash
July 25, 1910	OF	Joe Jackson	Philadelphia Athletics	OF	Bris Lord
Sept 1910	C	Pat Donahue	Philadelphia Athletics		Cash
Sept 1910		Cash	Boston Braves	OF	Art Krueger
Sept 1910		Cash	St. Louis Browns	P	Fred Linke
Oct 1910	1B	Art Griggs	St. Louis Browns	C	Nig Clarke
July 1911		Waiver price	Boston Braves	P	Cy Young

DATE		ACQUIRED	FROM		IN EXCHANGE FOR
Aug 20, 1911	C	Steve O'Neill	Philadelphia Athletics		Cash
Dec 1911	C	Paddy Livingston	Philadelphia Athletics		Cash
Dec 1911	P	Lefty George	St. Louis Browns	1B	George Stovall
Jan 1912		Cash	Chicago White Sox	C	Ted Easterly
March 1912		Waiver price	New York Yankees	C	Gus Fisher
May 1912		Cash	Boston Red Sox	SS	Neal Ball
July 1912	P	Harry Krause	Philadelphia Athletics		Cash
May 20, 1913	OF OF	Bill Stumpf Jack Lelivelt	New York Yankees	SS	Roger Peckinpaugh
Jan 1914	OF	Roy Wood	Pittsburgh Pirates		Cash
Aug 20, 1914	P P C	Adam Johnson Fritz Coumbe Ben Egan	Boston Red Sox	P	Vean Gregg
Dec 14, 1914		Cash	Cincinnati Reds	SS	Ivy Olson
Jan 1915		Waiver price	Philadelphia Athletics	2B	Nap Lajoie
Feb 1915		$7,500.	Pittsburgh Pirates	2B	Doc Johnston
May 1915		Cash	Boston Red Sox	2B	Bill Rodgers
June 1915		Cash	Detroit Tigers	P	Bill Steen
July 7, 1915		Waiver price	Chicago White Sox	OF	Nemo Leibold
Aug 21, 1915	OF OF P	Braggo Roth Larry Chappell Ed Klepfer and $31,500.	Chicago White Sox	OF	Joe Jackson
Dec 1915	C	Tom Daly	Chicago White Sox		Cash
Jan 1916	2B	Ivan Howard	St. Louis Browns		Cash
Feb 10, 1916	SS	Clyde Engle	Buffalo (Federal League)		Cash
Feb 15, 1916	1B	Chick Gandil	Washington Senators		$7,500.
April 12, 1916	OF	Tris Speaker	Boston Red Sox	P 2B	Sad Sam Jones Fred Thomas and $55,000.
May 1916		Cash	Boston Braves	OF	Larry Chappell

DATE		ACQUIRED	FROM		IN EXCHANGE FOR
May 1916	P	Marty McHale	Boston Red Sox		Cash
May 1916	OF	Marty Kavanagh	Detroit Tigers		Cash
June 20, 1916		Waiver price	Detroit Tigers	P	Willie Mitchell
Aug 18, 1916	P OF	Joe Boehling Danny Moeller	Washington Senators	OF 3B	Elmer Smith Joe Leonard
Aug 1916	P	Grover Lowdermilk	Detroit Tigers		Cash
Feb 24, 1917	P	Joe Wood	Boston Red Sox		$15,000.
Feb 25, 1917		$3,500.	Chicago White Sox	1B	Chick Gandil
June 13, 1917	OF	Elmer Smith	Washington Senators		$4,000.
Oct 1917		Waiver price	St. Louis Browns	P	Grover Lowdermilk
Feb 15, 1918	P	Bob Groom	St. Louis Browns		Waiver price
June 1, 1918	C	Pinch Thomas	Boston Red Sox		Cash
June 1918		Cash	St. Louis Cardinals	OF	Marty Kavanagh
June 1918		Waiver price	Pittsburgh Pirates	3B	Gus Getz
June 1918	P	Ad Brennan	Washington Senators		Cash
Jan 1919		Waiver price	Philadelphia Athletics	SS	Terry Turner
March 1, 1919	3B P OF	Larry Gardner Elmer Myers Charlie Jamieson	Philadelphia Athletics	OF	Braggo Roth
March 1919	C	Les Nunamaker	St. Louis Browns	C	Josh Billings
Dec 1919		Cash	Philadelphia Phillies	P	Johnny Enzmann
May 29, 1920	OF	George Burns	Philadelphia Athletics		Cash
June 1920		Waiver price	Boston Red Sox	P	Elmer Myers
April 1921	P	Allen Sothoron	Boston Red Sox		Waiver price
June 2, 1921	P	Dave Keefe	Philadelphia Athletics		Waiver price
Dec 24, 1921	1B	Stuffy McInnis	Boston Red Sox	1B 1B OF	George Burns Joe Harris Elmer Smith
Feb 16, 1922		Cash	Philadelphia Athletics	1B	Doc Johnston
April 1922		Cash	Pittsburgh Pirates	2B	Jack Hammond

DATE		ACQUIRED	FROM		IN EXCHANGE FOR
Sept 18, 1922	P	Sherry Smith	Brooklyn Dodgers		Waiver price
Nov 5, 1922		Waiver price	Pittsburgh Pirates	P	Jim Bagby
Jan 8, 1923	IF	Frank Brower	Washington Senators	OF	Joe Evans
Jan 1923		Waiver price	Boston Braves	1B	Stuffy McInnis
Jan 7, 1924	1B C UT	George Burns Roxy Walters Chick Fewster	Boston Red Sox	P C OF 2B	Danny Boone Steve O'Neill Joe Connolly Bill Wambsganss
June 3, 1924	3B	Frank Ellerbe	St. Louis Browns		Cash
Dec 12, 1924	P OF	Byron Speece Carr Smith	Washington Senators	P	Stan Coveleski
July 1925	P	Bert Cole	Detroit Tigers		Cash
July 1925		Cash	Chicago White Sox	P	Jim Joe Edwards
Jan 1926		Cash	Brooklyn Dodgers	2B	Chick Fewster
Feb 1926	3B	Ernie Padgett	Boston Braves		Cash
June 12, 1927	OF	Baby Doll Jacobson	Boston Red Sox		Cash
June 15, 1927		Cash	Chicago White Sox	OF	Bernie Neis
Aug 5, 1927		Waiver price	Philadelphia Athletics	OF	Baby Doll Jacobson
Dec 1927	C	Grover Hartley	Boston Red Sox		Waiver price
March 4, 1928	2B	Aaron Ward	Chicago White Sox		Waiver price
May 10, 1928		Cash	St. Louis Browns	OF	Frank Wilson
July 7, 1928		Waiver price	New York Giants	P	Garland Buckeye
July 10, 1928	P	Johnny Miljus	Pittsburgh Pirates		Waiver price
Dec 11, 1928	2B P	Jackie Tavener Ken Holloway	Detroit Tigers	P	George Uhle
Dec 1928		Cash	Boston Red Sox	P	Bill Bayne
Jan 5, 1929		Cash	Philadelphia Athletics	OF	Homer Summa
Feb 28, 1929	OF	Bibb Falk	Chicago White Sox	C	Martin Autry
June 7, 1929	1B	Joe Hauser	Philadelphia Athletics		Waiver price
July 20, 1930		Cash	New York Yankees	P	Ken Holloway

DATE		ACQUIRED	FROM		IN EXCHANGE FOR
Nov 1930	SS	Bill Hunnefield	Chicago White Sox		Cash
April 2, 1931	C	Moe Berg	Chicago White Sox		Waiver price
May 17, 1931	3B	Willie Kamm	Chicago White Sox	1B	Lew Fonseca
May 28, 1931		Waiver price	Boston Braves	2B	Bill Hunnefield
April 24, 1932	3B P	Bill Cissell Jim Moore	Chicago White Sox	2B OF	Johnny Hodapp Bob Seeds
June 6, 1932	SS	Joe Boley	Philadelphia Athletics		Cash
June 10, 1932	P	Jack Russell	Boston Red Sox	P	Pete Appleton
Dec 15, 1932	1B	Harley Boss	Washington Senators	P OF	Jack Russell Bruce Connatser
Jan 7, 1933	C	Roy Spencer	Washington Senators	C	Luke Sewell
Oct 12, 1933	P	Lloyd Brown	Boston Red Sox	2B	Bill Cissell
May 25, 1934	P OF	Bob Weiland Bob Seeds and $25,000.	Boston Red Sox	P OF	Wes Ferrell Dick Porter
Nov 20, 1934	OF	Bruce Campbell	St. Louis Browns	3B P	Johnny Burnett Bob Weiland and cash
Dec 1934	C	Eddie Phillips	Washington Senators		Cash
Dec 1934		Cash	Detroit Tigers	OF	Bob Seeds
May 14, 1935	P	Lefty Stewart	Washington Senators	P	Belve Bean
Dec 11, 1935	P	Johnny Allen	New York Yankees	P P	Monte Pearson Steve Sundra
Jan 27, 1936	P	George Blaeholder	Philadelphia Athletics		Waiver price
Jan 29, 1936	C	Billy Sullivan	Cincinnati Reds		Cash
April 11, 1936		Cash	Chicago White Sox	P	Clint Brown
Dec 10, 1936	P	Jack Salveson	Chicago White Sox	P	Thornton Lee
		(Part of three-team trade involving Chicago, Cleveland, and Washington.)			
Dec 10, 1936	P	Earl Whitehill	Washington Senators	P	Jack Salveson
		(Part of three-team trade involving Chicago, Cleveland, and Washington.)			
Dec 1936	2B	John Kroner	Boston Red Sox		Cash

DATE	ACQUIRED	FROM	IN EXCHANGE FOR
Jan 17, 1937	P Ivy Andrews SS Lyn Lary OF Moose Solters	St. Louis Browns	SS Bill Knickerbocker OF Joe Vosmik P Oral Hildebrand
April 1937	Cash	Chicago White Sox	2B Boze Berger
May 1937	Cash	Washington Senators	P Carl Fischer
Aug 14, 1937	$7,500.	New York Yankees	P Ivy Andrews
Feb 10, 1938	C Rollie Hemsley	St. Louis Browns	P Ed Cole 2B Roy Hughes C Billy Sullivan
Aug 1938	Cash	Boston Red Sox	P Joe Heving
Nov 1938	OF Johnny Broaca	New York Yankees	Waiver price
Dec 15, 1938	OF Ben Chapman	Boston Red Sox	P Denny Galehouse SS Tommy Irwin
May 3, 1939	Cash	Brooklyn Dodgers	SS Lyn Lary
June 14, 1939	P Harry Eisenstat and cash	Detroit Tigers	OF Earl Averill
Aug 2, 1939	Waiver price	St. Louis Browns	OF Moose Solters
Sept 25, 1939	P Nate Andrews	St. Louis Cardinals	Cash
Jan 10, 1940	2B Ollie Bejma IF John Gerlach	Chicago White Sox	SS Skeeter Webb
Jan 20, 1940	OF Beau Bell	Detroit Tigers	OF Bruce Campbell
April 21, 1940	Cash	Washington Senators	P Bill Zuber
Dec 12, 1940	C Gene Desautels P Jim Bagby OF Gee Walker	Boston Red Sox	C Frankie Pytlak 2B Odell Hale P Joe Dobson
Dec 24, 1940	$20,000.	St. Louis Browns	P Johnny Allen
Dec 24, 1940	P Joe Krakauskas	Washington Senators	OF Ben Chapman
Feb 3, 1941	P Joe Heving	Boston Red Sox	Cash
Feb 7, 1941	P Clint Brown	Chicago White Sox	P John Humphries
May 29, 1941	OF Larry Rosenthal	Chicago White Sox	Cash
Aug 9, 1941	OF Chubby Dean	Philadelphia Athletics	Waiver price
Sept 22, 1941	P Tom Ferrick	Philadelphia Athletics	Waiver price
Dec 4, 1941	Cash	Cincinnati Reds	C Rollie Hemsley

DATE		ACQUIRED	FROM		IN EXCHANGE FOR
Dec 11, 1941	P	Vern Kennedy	Washington Senators		Cash
March 26, 1942		Cash	Cincinnati Reds	OF	Gee Walker
Dec 17, 1942	OF C	Roy Cullenbine Buddy Rosar	New York Yankees	OF 2B	Roy Weatherly Oscar Grimes
Aug 11, 1943	3B	Jimmy Grant	Chicago White Sox		Cash
Aug 27, 1943		Cash	St. Louis Browns	P	Al Milnar
Nov 6, 1943		Cash	Chicago White Sox	1B	Hal Trosky
June 27, 1944	OF	Myril Hoag	Chicago White Sox		Cash
July 28, 1944		Cash	Philadelphia Phillies	P	Vern Kennedy
Dec 12, 1944	OF	Eddie Carnett	Chicago White Sox	OF	Oris Hockett
April 27, 1945	OF 2B	Don Ross Dutch Meyer	Detroit Tigers	OF	Roy Cullenbine
May 29, 1945	C	Frankie Hayes	Philadelphia Athletics	C	Buddy Rosar
Oct 2, 1945	P	Don Black	Philadelphia Athletics		Cash
Dec 14, 1945	OF	George Case	Washington Senators	OF	Jeff Heath
May 1946	1B	Heinz Becker	Chicago Cubs	1B	Mickey Rocco
May 1946	P	Joe Berry	Philadelphia Athletics		Cash
June 24, 1946		Cash	St. Louis Browns	P	Tom Ferrick
June 1946	C	Tom Jordan	Chicago White Sox	C	Frankie Hayes
Oct 19, 1946	2B 3B	Joe Gordon Eddie Bockman	New York Yankees	P	Allie Reynolds
Dec 7, 1946		Cash	St. Louis Browns	2B	Rusty Peters
Dec 7, 1946	C	Al Lopez	Pittsburgh Pirates	OF	Gene Woodling
Dec 12, 1946	P	Vic Johnson and cash	Boston Red Sox	P	Jim Bagby
Dec 20, 1946	OF P P	Hal Peck Al Gettel Gene Bearden	New York Yankees	C 2B	Sherm Lollar Ray Mack
March 4, 1947	P	Roger Wolff	Washington Senators	OF	George Case
April 2, 1947	OF	Catfish Metkovich	Boston Red Sox		Cash
June 14, 1947		Cash	Pittsburgh Pirates	P	Roger Wolff

DATE		ACQUIRED	FROM		IN EXCHANGE FOR
Oct 10, 1947	OF	Allie Clark	New York Yankees	P	Red Embree
Nov 20, 1947	P OF	Bob Muncrief Walt Judnich	St. Louis Browns	OF P OF	Dick Kokos Bryan Stephens Joe Frazier and $25,000.
Dec 4, 1947	1B	Elbie Fletcher	Pittsburgh Pirates	1B	Les Fleming
Dec 9, 1947	2B	Johnny Berardino	St. Louis Browns	OF-1B	Catfish Metkovich and $50,000.
		(Metkovich was returned to Cleveland because of a broken finger and the St. Louis Browns received another $15,000 to complete the trade.)			
Jan 16, 1948		Cash	Pittsburgh Pirates	3B	Eddie Bockman
Jan 16, 1948		Cash	New York Giants	IF	Jack Conway
Jan 27, 1948	OF	Thurman Tucker	Chicago White Sox	C	Ralph Weigel
April 3, 1948	P	Russ Christopher	Philadelphia Athletics		Cash
April 12, 1948	P	Butch Wensloff	New York Yankees		Cash
June 2, 1948	3B	Bob Kennedy	Chicago White Sox	P OF	Al Gettel Pat Seerey
June 15, 1948	P	Sam Zoldak	St. Louis Browns	P	Bill Kennedy and $100,000.
Oct 2, 1948	P	Frank Papish	Chicago White Sox	P P	Bob Kuzava Ernie Groth
Nov 20, 1948		$20,000.	Pittsburgh Pirates	P	Bob Muncrief
Nov 22, 1948	P	Joe Haynes	Chicago White Sox	C	Joe Tipton
Dec 14, 1948	1B P	Mickey Vernon Early Wynn	Washington Senators	P P 1B	Joe Haynes Eddie Klieman Eddie Robinson
Jan 12, 1949	C	Mike Tresh	Chicago White Sox		Cash
Feb 9, 1949		Waiver price	Pittsburgh Pirates	OF	Walt Judnich
April 20, 1949	P	Al Benton	Detroit Tigers		Cash
Dec 14, 1949		Cash	Pittsburgh Pirates	P	Frank Papish
April 16, 1950	P	Marino Pieretti	Chicago White Sox		Waiver price
June 14, 1950	P	Dick Weik	Washington Senators	1B	Mickey Vernon
Aug 2, 1950		Waiver price	Washington Senators	P	Gene Bearden
Nov 11, 1950	C	Herb Adams	Chicago White Sox		Waiver price

DATE		ACQUIRED	FROM		IN EXCHANGE FOR
April 1, 1951	2B SS	Snuffy Stirnweiss Merrill Combs and $35,000.	St. Louis Browns	2B	Freddie Marsh
April 30, 1951	P	Lou Brissie	Philadelphia Athletics	P C OF	Sam Zoldak Ray Murray Minnie Minoso
		(Part of three-team trade involving Cleveland, Philadelphia A's, and Chicago White Sox.)			
May 10, 1951	OF	Sam Chapman	Philadelphia Athletics	OF 2B	Allie Clark Lou Klein
July 19, 1951	OF	Paul Lehner	St. Louis Browns		Waiver price
July 21, 1951	OF	Barney McCosky	Cincinnati Reds		Waiver price
April 22, 1952	P	Mickey Harris	Washington Senators		Waiver price
June 10, 1952	3B	Hank Majeski	Philadelphia Athletics		Cash
June 23, 1952	C	Joe Tipton	Philadelphia Athletics		Waiver price
June 25, 1952		Waiver price	Boston Red Sox	OF	Paul Lehner
Aug 7, 1952	OF	Wally Westlake	Cincinnati Reds		Cash
Aug 18, 1952	SS P	George Strickland Ted Wilks	Pittsburgh Pirates	2B P	Johnny Berardino Charlie Ripple and $50,000.
Dec 19, 1952	P	Bob Hooper	Philadelphia Athletics	P	Dick Rozek minor league 2B Bob Wilson
May 3, 1953	C	Hank Foiles	Cincinnati Reds		Cash
June 15, 1953	P SS P C	Art Houtteman Owen Friend Bill Wight Joe Ginsberg	Detroit Tigers	3B P P P	Ray Boone Al Aber Steve Gromek Dick Weik
Jan 20, 1954	C	Mickey Grasso	Washington Senators	C	Joe Tipton
Feb 19, 1954	OF	Dave Philley	Philadelphia Athletics	P P	Bill Upton Lee Wheat
April 17, 1954	OF	Jim Dyck	Baltimore Orioles	3B	Bob Kennedy
May 12, 1954		Cash	Washington Senators	OF	Jim Lemon
June 1, 1954	1B	Vic Wertz	Baltimore Orioles	P	Bob Chakales
Nov 16, 1954	OF	Ralph Kiner	Chicago Cubs	P OF	Sam Jones Gale Wade and $60,000.
April 7, 1955		Waiver price	Detroit Tigers	IF	Harry Malmberg
April 13, 1955		Cash	Cincinnati Reds	P	Bob Hooper

DATE		ACQUIRED	FROM		IN EXCHANGE FOR
May 11, 1955		Cash	Kansas City Athletics	OF	Harry Simpson
June 15, 1955	OF 3B	Gene Woodling Billy Cox (Cox refused to report and announced retirement. Cleveland received $15,000 to complete trade.)	Baltimore Orioles	OF OF	Dave Pope Wally Westlake
June 27, 1955	2B	Bobby Young	Baltimore Orioles	3B	Hank Majeski
July 2, 1955		Waiver price	Baltimore Orioles	OF	Dave Philley
July 13, 1955	OF	Hoot Evers	Baltimore Orioles		Minor league P Jim Wright
July 16, 1955		Cash	Baltimore Orioles	OF	Jim Dyck
July 31, 1955	P	Sal Maglie	New York Giants		Waiver price
Oct 25, 1955	OF SS	Jim Busby Chico Carrasquel	Chicago White Sox	OF	Larry Doby
May 13, 1956	OF	Dave Pope	Baltimore Orioles	OF	Hoot Evers
May 15, 1956		Cash	Brooklyn Dodgers	P	Sal Maglie
May 15, 1956	1B	Preston Ward	Pittsburgh Pirates	C	Hank Foiles
May 16, 1956		Cash	Kansas City Athletics	P	Jose Santiago
July 29, 1956		Cash	Brooklyn Dodgers	OF	Dale Mitchell
May 15, 1957		Cash	Washington Senators	OF	Bob Usher
May 20, 1957		Cash	Baltimore Orioles	P	Art Houtteman
June 13, 1957	OF	Dick Williams	Baltimore Orioles	OF	Jim Busby
Aug 24, 1957	P	Vito Valentinetti	Chicago Cubs		Cash
Sept 21, 1957	P	Hoyt Wilhelm	St. Louis Cardinals		Cash
Dec 4, 1957	3B OF	Fred Hatfield Minnie Minoso	Chicago White Sox	P P	Early Wynn Al Smith
Jan 29, 1958	1B	Mickey Vernon	Boston Red Sox		Waiver price
Feb 18, 1958	P C	Hal Woodeshick J W Porter	Detroit Tigers	C P	Jim Hegan Hank Aguirre
Feb 25, 1958	2B	Milt Bolling	Washington Senators		Minor league P Pete Mesa
March 26, 1958	P	Chuck Churn	Boston Red Sox		Waiver price
March 27, 1958	P	Pete Wojey and $20,000.	Detroit Tigers	2B P	Milt Bolling Vito Valentinetti

DATE		ACQUIRED	FROM		IN EXCHANGE FOR
April 1, 1958	OF	Larry Doby	Chicago	P	Buddy Daley
	P	Don Ferrarese	White Sox	OF	Dick Williams
				OF	Gene Woodling
April 17, 1958	P	Arnie Portocarrero	Kansas City Athletics	P	Buddy Daley
April 23, 1958	P	Bob Kelly	Cincinnati Reds	3B	Fred Hatfield
June 7, 1958	P	Jim Constable	San Francisco Giants		Waiver price
June 12, 1958	SS	Billy Hunter	Kansas City Athletics	SS	Chico Carrasquel
June 15, 1958	OF	Woodie Held	Kansas City	OF	Roger Maris
	1B	Vic Power	Athletics	P	Dick Tomanek
				1B	Preston Ward
July 2, 1958	P	Morrie Martin	St. Louis Cardinals		Waiver price
July 12, 1958		Waiver price	Washington Senators	P	Jim Constable
Aug 4, 1958	3B	Randy Jackson	Los Angeles Dodgers		Cash
Aug 23, 1958		Waiver price	Baltimore Orioles	P	Hoyt Wilhelm
Oct 27, 1958	IF	Ossie Alvarez	Washington Senators	C	J W Porter
Nov 20, 1958	2B	Billy Martin	Detroit	P	Don Mossi
	P	Al Cicotte	Tigers	P	Ray Narleski
				IF	Ossie Alvarez
Dec 2, 1958	P	Russ Heman and $30,000.	Baltimore Orioles	2B	Bobby Avila
Dec 2, 1958	OF	Jimmy Piersall	Boston	1B	Vic Wertz
			Red Sox	OF	Gary Geiger
Jan 23, 1959	P	Johnny Briggs	Chicago	C	Earl Averill
	OF	Jim Bolger	Cubs		
Feb 2, 1959		Waiver price	St. Louis Cardinals	IF	Billy Harrell
March 21, 1959	OF	Tito Francona	Detroit Tigers	OF	Larry Doby
April 11, 1959	P	Humberto Robinson	Milwaukee Braves	1B	Mickey Vernon
May 4, 1959	P	Riverboat Smith	Chicago Cubs	3B	Randy Jackson
May 16, 1959	P	Granny Hamner	Philadelphia Phillies	P	Humberto Robinson
May 25, 1959	C	Ed Fitz Gerald	Washington	P	Hal Woodeshick
			Senators	C	Hal Naragon
June 6, 1959	3B	Willie Jones	Cincinnati Reds	OF	Jim Bolger and cash
July 1, 1959		Cash	Cincinnati Reds	3B	Willie Jones
July 30, 1959	P	Jack Harshman	Boston Red Sox		Waiver price

DATE	ACQUIRED	FROM	IN EXCHANGE FOR
Dec 6, 1959	C Johnny Romano 3B Bubba Phillips 1B Norm Cash	Chicago White Sox	C Dick Brown P Don Ferrarese P Jake Striker OF Minnie Minoso
Jan 8, 1960	P Leo Kiely	Boston Red Sox	SS Ray Webster
March 16, 1960	C Sammy White 1B Jim Marshall (Trade was cancelled when White decided to retire.)	Boston Red Sox	C Russ Nixon
April 5, 1960	P Bob Grim	Kansas City Athletics	P Leo Kiely
April 11, 1960	P Johnny Klippstein	Los Angeles Dodgers	$25,000.
April 12, 1960	3B Steve Demeter	Detroit Tigers	1B Norm Cash
April 17, 1960	SS Harvey Kuenn	Detroit Tigers	OF Rocky Colavito
April 18, 1960	P Barry Latman	Chicago White Sox	P Herb Score
April 29, 1960	OF Pete Whisenant	Cincinnati Reds	Cash
May 12, 1960	OF Johnny Powers	Baltimore Orioles	Waiver price
May 15, 1960	2B Ken Aspromonte	Washington Senators	OF Pete Whisenant
May 18, 1960	Cash	Cincinnati Reds	P Bob Grim
June 2, 1960	C Hank Foiles	Pittsburgh Pirates	OF Johnny Powers
June 13, 1960	OF Marty Keough P Ted Bowsfield	Boston Red Sox	C Russ Nixon OF Carroll Hardy
July 26, 1960	IF Rocky Bridges C Red Wilson	Detroit Tigers	C Hank Foiles
July 29, 1960	P Don Newcombe	Cincinnati Reds	Cash
July 30, 1960	Cash	Kansas City Athletics	P Johnny Briggs
Aug 9, 1960	3B Joe Morgan	Philadelphia Phillies	Cash
Aug 10, 1960	MGR Jimmy Dykes	Detroit Tigers	MGR Joe Gordon
Sept 2, 1960	Cash	St. Louis Cardinals	SS Rocky Bridges
Dec 3, 1960	P Johnny Antonelli OF Willie Kirkland	San Francisco Giants	OF Harvey Kuenn
May 3, 1961	OF Chuck Essegian	Kansas City Athletics	Cash
May 10, 1961	OF Bob Nieman	St. Louis Cardinals	3B Joe Morgan and cash
June 5, 1961	Cash	Los Angeles Angels	P Russ Heman

DATE		ACQUIRED	FROM		IN EXCHANGE FOR
July 4, 1961		Cash	Milwaukee Braves	P	Johnny Antonelli
July 7, 1961	P	Joe Schaffernoth	Chicago Cubs		Cash
July 26, 1961		Cash	New York Yankees	1B	Bob Hale
Oct 5, 1961	P C SS	Dick Donovan Gene Green Jim Mahoney	Washington Senators	OF	Jimmy Piersall
Oct 14, 1961		Cash	Washington Senators	P	Joe Schaffernoth
Oct 14, 1961		Cash	Washington Senators	P	Dave Tyriver
Nov 16, 1961	1B C	Ray Barker Harry Chiti and minor leaguer Art Kay	Baltimore Orioles	2B	Johnny Temple
March 20, 1962	P OF	Ken Lehman Tony Curry	Philadelphia Phillies	OF	Mel Roach
April 2, 1962	P	Pedro Ramos	Minnesota Twins	P 1B	Dick Stigman Vic Power
April 7, 1962		Minor league OF Al Herring	St. Louis Cardinals	P	Larry Locke
April 26, 1962		Cash	New York Mets	C	Harry Chiti
April 29, 1962		Cash	San Francisco Giants	OF	Bob Nieman
May 3, 1962	OF	Willie Tasby	Washington Senators	P P	Steve Hamilton Don Rudolph
June 24, 1962	P	Bob Hartman	Milwaukee Braves	2B	Ken Aspromonte and cash
July 2, 1962	3B	Marlan Coughtry	Kansas City Athletics		Cash
Aug 20, 1962	P P	Georges Maranda Jackie Collum and cash	Minnesota Twins	P	Ruben Gomez
Nov 27, 1962	P	Ron Nischwitz	Detroit Tigers	P 3B	Gordon Seyfried Bubba Phillips
Nov 27, 1962	1B P	Joe Adcock Jack Curtis	Milwaukee Braves	OF OF P	Ty Cline Don Dillard Frank Funk
Nov 27, 1962		Cash	New York Mets	P	Wynn Hawkins
Dec 15, 1962	1B	Fred Whitfield	St. Louis Cardinals	P SS	Ron Taylor Jack Kubiszyn
Feb 27, 1963	P	Jerry Walker	Kansas City Athletics	OF	Chuck Essegian
April 2, 1963	OF	Ellis Burton	Houston Astros		Cash
April 8, 1963		Cash	Minnesota Twins	P	Bill Dailey

DATE		ACQUIRED	FROM		IN EXCHANGE FOR
May 2, 1963	P	Jack Kralick	Minnesota Twins	P	Jim Perry
May 25, 1963	C SS	Joe Azcue Dick Howser	Kansas City Athletics	C	Doc Edwards and $100,000.
May 31, 1963		Waiver price	Washington Senators	P	Casey Cox
Aug 1, 1963	C	Sammy Taylor	Cincinnati Reds	OF	Gene Green
Sept 30, 1963	P	Don McMahon	Houston Astros		Cash
Dec 2, 1963	OF	Leon Wagner	Los Angeles Angels	1B P	Joe Adcock Barry Latman
Dec 4, 1963	OF	Al Smith and $25,000.	Baltimore Orioles	OF	Willie Kirkland
Dec 14, 1963		Cash	Pittsburgh Pirates	P	Bob Allen
April 1, 1964	OF	Chico Salmon	Milwaukee Braves	3B	Mike de la Hoz
June 11, 1964	2B	Jerry Kindall	Los Angeles Angels	SS	Billy Moran
		(Part of three-team trade involving Los Angeles Angels, Cleveland, and Minnesota.)			
June 15, 1964	3B P	George Banks Lee Stange	Minnesota Twins	P	Mudcat Grant
Sept 5, 1964	P P	Ralph Terry Buddy Daley and $75,000.	New York Yankees	P	Pedro Ramos
Dec 1, 1964	OF	Chuck Hinton	Washington Senators	1B OF	Bob Chance Woodie Held
Dec 15, 1964		Cash	St. Louis Cardinals	OF	Tito Francona
Jan 20, 1965	OF C	Rocky Colavito Cam Carreon	Chicago White Sox	P OF C	Tommy John Tommie Agee Johnny Romano
		(Part of three-team trade involving Kansas City, Cleveland, and Chicago White Sox.)			
Feb 15, 1965	P	Bill Edgerton	Kansas City Athletics		Waiver price
March 30, 1965	P	Stan Williams	New York Yankees		Cash
April 9, 1965		Waiver price	Kansas City Athletics	P	Bill Edgerton
April 14, 1965		Cash	Chicago Cubs	P	Ted Abernathy
May 10, 1965	2B	Pedro Gonzalez	New York Yankees	1B	Ray Barker
June 15, 1965	C	Phil Roof	California Angels	OF	Bubba Morton and cash
		(California received Morton on September 15, 1965.)			
Sept 9, 1965	OF	Lu Clinton	California Angels		Waiver price
		(Clinton was claimed on waivers by Kansas City and played one game for them before Cleveland's claim was upheld.)			

DATE		ACQUIRED	FROM		IN EXCHANGE FOR
Oct 1, 1965	OF	Jim Landis	Kansas City Athletics	C OF	Phil Roof Joe Rudi
Nov 29, 1965		Cash	New York Mets	OF	Al Luplow
Jan 14, 1966	C	Doc Edwards	New York Yankees	OF	Lu Clinton
April 5, 1966		Cash	Washington Senators	P	Al Closter
April 6, 1966	P	John O'Donoghue and cash	Kansas City Athletics	P	Ralph Terry
June 2, 1966	P	Dick Radatz	Boston Red Sox	P P	Don McMahon Lee Stange
July 19, 1966	1B	Jim Gentile	Houston Astros	OF	Tony Curry
Dec 20, 1966		Minor league P Gil Downs	New York Yankees	SS	Dick Howser
Jan 4, 1967	OF C	Lee Maye Ken Retzer	Houston Astros	OF P C	Jim Landis Jim Weaver Doc Edwards
April 25, 1967	OF	Bob Raudman and cash	Chicago Cubs	P	Dick Radatz
May 1, 1967		Cash	New York Yankees	P	Jack Kralick
May 6, 1967	P	Orlando Pena	Detroit Tigers		Cash
June 4, 1967	OF OF	Tony Horton Don Demeter	Boston Red Sox	P	Gary Bell
July 20, 1967	P	Gary Kroll	Houston Astros		Cash
July 29, 1967	OF IF	Jim King Marv Staehle	Chicago White Sox	OF	Rocky Colavito
Nov 21, 1967	OF	Tommy Harper	Cincinnati Reds	P 1B	George Culver Fred Whitfield
Nov 28, 1967	P	Eddie Fisher minor leaguers P George Scott and IF John Scruggs	Baltimore Orioles	P IF	John O'Donoghue Gordon Lund
Nov 29, 1967	OF	Jose Cardenal	California Angels	OF	Chuck Hinton
March 30, 1968	P	Rob Gardner	Chicago Cubs	P	Bobby Tiefenauer
June 13, 1968	OF	Russ Snyder	Chicago White Sox	OF	Leon Wagner
June 15, 1968	OF	Jimmie Hall	California Angels	OF	Vic Davalillo
June 28, 1968	OF	Lou Johnson	Chicago Cubs	OF	Willie Smith
Oct 8, 1968	P	Jack Hamilton	California Angels	P	Eddie Fisher
Oct 21, 1968	SS	Zoilo Versalles	San Diego Padres	1B	Bill Davis

DATE	ACQUIRED	FROM	IN EXCHANGE FOR
March 31, 1969	OF Cap Peterson	Washington Senators	Minor league P George Woodson
April 4, 1969	OF Chuck Hinton	California Angels	OF Lou Johnson
April 14, 1969	Cash	New York Yankees	OF Jimmie Hall
April 19, 1969	OF-1B Ken Harrelson P Juan Pizarro P Dick Ellsworth	Boston Red Sox	P Sonny Siebert C Joe Azcue P Vicente Romo
June 13, 1969	P Sammy Ellis	Chicago White Sox	P Jack Hamilton
June 20, 1969	Cash	Washington Senators	OF Lee Maye
July 26, 1969	Cash	Washington Senators	SS Zoilo Versalles
Sept 21, 1969	Cash	Oakland Athletics	P Juan Pizarro
Nov 21, 1969	OF Vada Pinson	St. Louis Cardinals	OF Jose Cardenal
Dec 5, 1969	P Dennis Higgins P Barry Moore	Washington Senators	IF Dave Nelson P Horacio Pina P Ron Law
Dec 10, 1969	P Dean Chance P Bob Miller 3B Graig Nettles OF Ted Uhlaender	Minnesota Twins	P Luis Tiant P Stan Williams
April 4, 1970	OF Roy Foster IF Frank Coggins and cash	Milwaukee Brewers	3B Max Alvis OF Russ Snyder
May 22, 1970	P Fred Lasher	Detroit Tigers	OF Rusty Nagelson P Billy Rohr
June 15, 1970	OF Buddy Bradford	Chicago White Sox	P Barry Moore P Bob Miller
Aug 7, 1970	Cash	Milwaukee Brewers	P Dick Ellsworth
Sept 18, 1970	Cash	New York Mets	P Dean Chance
Oct 23, 1970	Cash	Washington Senators	OF Richie Scheinblum
Dec 11, 1970	P Alan Foster P Ray Lamb	Los Angeles Dodgers	C Duke Sims
April 24, 1971	Cash	Oakland Athletics	SS Larry Brown
May 8, 1971	IF Kurt Bevacqua	Cincinnati Reds	OF Buddy Bradford
May 22, 1971	Cash	San Diego Padres	P Camilo Pascual
	(Pascual was returned to Cleveland on May 26, 1971.)		
July 15, 1971	Cash	St. Louis Cardinals	P Dennis Higgins

DATE	ACQUIRED		FROM	IN EXCHANGE FOR	
Oct 5, 1971	OF	Alex Johnson	California Angels	OF	Vada Pinson
	C	Gerry Moses		OF	Frank Baker
				P	Alan Foster
Nov 29, 1971	P	Gaylord Perry	San Francisco Giants	P	Sam McDowell
	SS	Frank Duffy			
Dec 2, 1971	OF	Del Unser	Texas Rangers	OF	Roy Foster
	P	Denny Riddleberger		C	Ken Suarez
	P	Gary Jones		P	Mike Paul
		minor league P Terry Lee		P	Rich Hand
Dec 6, 1971	P	Milt Wilcox	Cincinnati Reds	OF	Ted Uhlaender
March 29, 1972	P	Marcelino Lopez	Milwaukee Brewers		Cash
April 3, 1972	OF	Roy Foster	Texas Rangers	OF	Ted Ford
	1B	Tom McCraw			
June 11, 1972	P	Mike Kilkenny	San Diego Padres	SS	Fred Stanley
July 10, 1972	P	Tom Hilgendorf	Kansas City Royals	OF	Jim Clark
July 11, 1972	P	Bill Butler	Kansas City Royals		Cash
Sept 18, 1972	P	Lowell Palmer	St. Louis Cardinals		Cash
Oct 19, 1972	OF	Walt Williams	Chicago White Sox	IF	Eddie Leon
Nov 2, 1972	P	Mike Hedlund	Kansas City Royals	IF	Kurt Bevacqua
Nov 27, 1972	C	John Ellis	New York Yankees	3B	Graig Nettles
	IF	Jerry Kenney		C	Gerry Moses
	OF	Charlie Spikes			
	OF	Rusty Torres			
Nov 27, 1972	P	Brent Strom	New York Mets	P	Phil Hennigan
	P	Bob Rauch			
Nov 30, 1972	IF	Tom Ragland	Texas Rangers	P	Vince Colbert
Nov 30, 1972	OF	Oscar Gamble	Philadelphia Phillies	OF	Del Unser
	OF	Roger Freed			minor league IF Terry Wedgewood
March 6, 1973	P	Jerry Johnson	San Francisco Giants		Cash
March 8, 1973	P	Rich Hinton	Texas Rangers	OF	Alex Johnson
	P	Vince Colbert			
March 24, 1973	OF	George Hendrick	Oakland Athletics	C	Ray Fosse
	C	Dave Duncan		SS	Jack Heidemann
April 2, 1973	SS	Leo Cardenas	California Angels	1B	Tom McCraw and minor league 2B Bob Marcano
May 10, 1973	P	Dick Bosman	Texas Rangers	P	Steve Dunning
	OF	Ted Ford			
June 12, 1973	P	Mike Kekich	New York Yankees	P	Lowell Palmer

DATE		ACQUIRED	FROM		IN EXCHANGE FOR
June 15, 1973	P 3B	Tom Timmerman Kevin Collins	Detroit Tigers	P	Ed Farmer
Aug 3, 1973	P	Ken Sanders	Minnesota Twins		Cash
Nov 3, 1973	P	Cecil Upshaw	Houston Astros	P	Jerry Johnson
Dec 7, 1973	P	Bob Johnson	Pittsburgh Pirates		Minor league OF Burnel Flowers
Feb 12, 1974	C	Ken Suarez	Texas Rangers	SS	Leo Cardenas
March 19, 1974	P	Jim Perry (Part of three-team trade involving Detroit, Cleveland, and New York Yankees.)	Detroit Tigers	P OF	Rick Sawyer Walt Williams
March 23, 1974	P	Bill Gogolewski	Texas Rangers	P	Steve Hargan
March 25, 1974	IF	Jack Heidemann	Oakland Athletics		Cash
March 28, 1974	OF	Leron Lee	San Diego Padres		Cash
April 3, 1974	P	Bruce Ellingsen	Los Angeles Dodgers	IF	Pedro Guerrero
April 27, 1974	P P P P	Fritz Peterson Steve Kline Fred Beene Tom Buskey	New York Yankees	1B P P	Chris Chambliss Dick Tidrow Cecil Upshaw
June 1, 1974	IF IF	Luis Alvarado Ed Crosby	St. Louis Cardinals	SS	Jack Heidemann
June 5, 1974	1B	Joe Lis	Minnesota Twins		Cash
June 15, 1974	P	Steve Arlin	San Diego Padres	P	Brent Strom minor league P Jerry Lee
July 1, 1974		Cash	Texas Rangers	P	Bob Johnson
July 17, 1974	1B	Tom McCraw	California Angels		Cash
Sept 12, 1974	OF	Frank Robinson	California Angels	C OF	Ken Suarez Rusty Torres and cash
Feb 25, 1975	1B P	Boog Powell Don Hood	Baltimore Orioles	C	Dave Duncan and minor league OF Al McGrew
Feb 25, 1975	P OF	Dave LaRoche Brock Davis	Chicago White Sox	P	Milt Wilcox
March 6, 1975		Minor league OF Nelson Garcia	Philadelphia Phillies	P	Tom Hilgendorf
May 20, 1975	P	Blue Moon Odom and cash	Oakland Athletics	P P	Dick Bosman Jim Perry
June 7, 1975	P	Roric Harrison	Atlanta Braves	P SS	Blue Moon Odom Bob Belloir

DATE		ACQUIRED	FROM		IN EXCHANGE FOR
June 13, 1975	P P P	Jim Bibby Jackie Brown Rick Waits and $100,000.	Texas Rangers	P	Gaylord Perry
Aug 26, 1975	P	Bob Reynolds	Detroit Tigers		Cash
Sept 30, 1975	1B	Doug Howard	St. Louis Cardinals	IF	Luis Alvarado
Nov 22, 1975	P	Pat Dobson	New York Yankees	OF	Oscar Gamble
Dec 9, 1975	C	Ray Fosse	Oakland Athletics		Cash
Dec 9, 1975	P C	Stan Thomas Ron Pruitt	Texas Rangers	C	John Ellis
Dec 12, 1975	IF	Larvell Blanks	Chicago White Sox	2B	Jack Brohamer
April 7, 1976	P	Harry Parker	St. Louis Cardinals	P	Roric Harrison
May 28, 1976	P	Stan Perzanowski and cash	Texas Rangers	P	Fritz Peterson
May 28, 1976	P	Card Camper	St. Louis Cardinals		Cash
Nov 5, 1976	P	Al Fitzmorris	Toronto Blue Jays	C 1B	Alan Ashby Doug Howard
Nov 19, 1976	P	Wayne Garland	Baltimore Orioles		No compensation (free agent signing)
Dec 3, 1976	3B	Bill Melton	California Angels	P	Stan Perzanowski and cash
Dec 6, 1976	OF	Rico Carty	Toronto Blue Jays	OF C	John Lowenstein Rick Cerone
Dec 8, 1976	OF C SS	John Grubb Fred Kendall Hector Torres	San Diego Padres	OF	George Hendrick
Dec 10, 1976	1B	Andre Thornton	Montreal Expos	P	Jackie Brown
March 29, 1977	OF	John Lowenstein	Toronto Blue Jays	SS	Hector Torres
May 11, 1977	1B P	Bruce Bochte Sid Monge and $250,000.	California Angels	P P	Dave LaRoche Dave Schuler
Sept 9, 1977	P	Bill Laxton and cash	Seattle Mariners	C	Ray Fosse
Dec 5, 1977	IF	Dave Rosello	Chicago Cubs		Minor leaguers P Norm Churchill and OF Bruce Compton
Dec 9, 1977	SS	Tom Veryzer	Detroit Tigers	OF	Charlie Spikes
Dec 9, 1977	1B	Jack Baker	Boston Red Sox	OF	Garry Hancock
Dec 20, 1977		No compensation (free agent signing)	Seattle Mariners	1B	Bruce Bochte

DATE		ACQUIRED	FROM		IN EXCHANGE FOR
Feb 28, 1978	OF P	Willie Horton David Clyde	Texas Rangers	P OF	Tom Buskey John Lowenstein
March 15, 1978		No compensation (free agent signing)	Pittsburgh Pirates	P	Jim Bibby
March 24, 1978	P	Rick Kreuger	Boston Red Sox	SS	Frank Duffy
March 26, 1978	OF	Mike Vail	New York Mets		Cash
June 14, 1978	P	Dan Spillner	San Diego Padres	P	Dennis Kinney
June 15, 1978	OF	Joe Wallis	Chicago Cubs	OF	Mike Vail
June 15, 1978	C	Gary Alexander	Oakland Athletics	OF	Joe Wallis
June 15, 1978	OF	Bernie Carbo	Boston Red Sox		Cash
June 22, 1978	P	Dave Freisleben	San Diego Padres	P	Bill Laxton
June 26, 1978	P	Paul Reuschel	Chicago Cubs	P	Denny DeBarr
Aug 31, 1978	P	Bobby Cuellar minor league OF Dave Rivera	Texas Rangers	OF	John Grubb
Oct 3, 1978	OF P	Bobby Bonds Len Barker	Texas Rangers	P IF	Jim Kern Larvell Blanks
Nov 3, 1978	OF	Sheldon Mallory	Toronto Blue Jays	P	Dave Freisleben
Dec 5, 1978	P	Victor Cruz	Toronto Blue Jays	SS	Alfredo Griffin minor league 3B Phil Lansford
Dec 8, 1978	3B	Toby Harrah	Texas Rangers	3B	Buddy Bell
March 30, 1979	2B	Mike Champion	San Diego Padres	OF	Dan Briggs
June 14, 1979	1B	Mike Hargrove	San Diego Padres	3B	Paul Dade
June 15, 1979	C	Cliff Johnson	New York Yankees	P	Don Hood
Nov 19, 1979		No compensation (free agent signing)	San Diego Padres	P	Rick Wise
Dec 6, 1979	P P	Rafael Vasquez Bud Anderson and minor league P Bob Pietburgo	Seattle Mariners	3B	Ted Cox
Dec 7, 1979	OF P	Jerry Mumphrey John Denny	St. Louis Cardinals	OF	Bobby Bonds
Dec 19, 1979	OF	Jorge Orta	Chicago White Sox		No compensation (free agent signing)
Dec 21, 1979	OF	Larry Littleton and minor league P John Burden	Pittsburgh Pirates	P	Larry Andersen

DATE	ACQUIRED	FROM	IN EXCHANGE FOR
Jan 4, 1980	P Larry McCall 1B Gary Gray minor league 3B-OF Mike Bucci	Texas Rangers	P David Clyde OF Jim Norris
Feb 15, 1980	P Bob Owchinko OF Jim Wilhelm	San Diego Padres	OF Jerry Mumphrey
Feb 15, 1980	P Don Collins	Atlanta Braves	Minor league P Gary Melson
May 7, 1980	OF Miguel Dilone	Chicago Cubs	Cash
June 13, 1980	UT Alan Bannister	Chicago White Sox	C Ron Pruitt
June 20, 1980	IF Jack Brohamer	Boston Red Sox	Cash
June 23, 1980	OF Karl Pagel and cash	Chicago Cubs	C Cliff Johnson
July 11, 1980	P Ross Grimsley	Montreal Expos	IF Dave Oliver
Dec 9, 1980	P Bert Blyleven C Manny Sanguillen	Pittsburgh Pirates	C Gary Alexander P Victor Cruz P Rafael Vasquez P Bob Owchinko
Dec 29, 1980	OF Pat Kelly	Baltimore Orioles	No compensation (free agent signing)
March 26, 1981	OF Rodney Craig	Seattle Mariners	1B Wayne Cage
April 1, 1981	P Bob Lacey	San Diego Padres	2B Juan Bonilla
April 3, 1981	SS Mike Fischlin	Houston Astros	OF Jim Lentine and cash
April 6, 1981	P Ed Glynn	New York Mets	Minor league P Dominick Bullinger
Aug 25, 1981	P Dennis Lewallyn	Texas Rangers	Cash
Sept 8, 1981	Cash	Texas Rangers	P Bob Lacey
Nov 14, 1981	P Ed Whitson	San Francisco Giants	2B Duane Kuiper
Nov 20, 1981	OF Lonnie Smith P Scott Munninghoff (Part of three-team trade involving Cleveland, Philadelphia, and St. Louis.)	Philadelphia Phillies	C Bo Diaz
Nov 20, 1981	P Lary Sorensen P Silvio Martinez (Part of three-team trade involving Cleveland, Philadelphia, and St. Louis.)	St. Louis Cardinals	OF Lonnie Smith
Dec 7, 1981	Cash	St. Louis Cardinals	P Mike Stanton
Dec 9, 1981	P Rick Sutcliffe 2B Jack Perconte	Los Angeles Dodgers	OF Jorge Orta P Larry White C Jack Fimple
Jan 8, 1982	P Ray Searage	New York Mets	SS Tom Veryzer

DATE		ACQUIRED	FROM		IN EXCHANGE FOR
Jan 27, 1982	C	Craig Stimac	San Diego Padres		Cash
Feb 8, 1982	P	Mike Stanton	St. Louis Cardinals		Cash
Feb 16, 1982	OF	Bake McBride	Philadelphia Phillies	P	Sid Monge
July 3, 1982	SS	Larry Milbourne	Minnesota Twins	OF	Larry Littleton
Sept 12, 1982	OF P	Wil Culmer Jerry Reed minor league P Roy Smith	Philadelphia Phillies	P	John Denny
Nov 18, 1982	P 1B	Juan Eichelberger Broderick Perkins	San Diego Padres	P	Ed Whitson
Dec 9, 1982	2B OF P SS	Manny Trillo George Vukovich Jay Baller Julio Franco minor league C Jerry Willard	Philadelphia Phillies	OF	Von Hayes
Dec 9, 1982		Player to be named later	Philadelphia Phillies	SS	Larry Milbourne
Dec 15, 1982		Cash	San Diego Padres	P	Ray Searage
Jan 21, 1983	C	Jim Essian	Seattle Mariners		Cash
April 1, 1983	3B	Pat Tabler	Chicago White Sox	SS	Jerry Dybzinski
June 6, 1983	OF P P	Gorman Thomas Jamie Easterly Ernie Camacho	Milwaukee Brewers	OF P	Rick Manning Rick Waits
Aug 17, 1983		Minor league OF Don Carter and $300,000.	Montreal Expos	2B	Manny Trillo
Aug 25, 1983	P	Rich Barnes	Chicago White Sox	OF	Miguel Dilone
Aug 28, 1983	P OF 3B	Rick Behenna Brett Butler Brook Jacoby and $150,000. (Butler and Jacoby were sent to Cleveland at the end of the season.)	Atlanta Braves	P	Len Barker
Dec 6, 1983	SS	Luis Quinones	Oakland Athletics	C	Jim Essian
Dec 7, 1983	2B	Tony Bernazard	Seattle Mariners	OF 2B	Gorman Thomas Jack Perconte
Jan 21, 1984		Player to be named later	Chicago White Sox	P	Tom Brennan
Jan 23, 1984		No compensation (free agent signing)	Oakland Athletics	P	Lary Sorensen
Feb 4, 1984	P OF	Danny Boitano Otis Nixon	New York Yankees	3B	Toby Harrah and a player to be named later

DATE		ACQUIRED	FROM		IN EXCHANGE FOR
March 24, 1984	P	Luis Aponte	Boston Red Sox		Minor league Ps Mike Poindexter and Paul Perry
March 25, 1984		Cash	Houston Astros	OF	Alan Bannister
April 1, 1984	C	Juan Espino	New York Yankees		Cash

Detroit Tigers

The Best Trades

1. Acquired Norm Cash from the Cleveland Indians for Steve Demeter, April 12, 1960.
2. Acquired George Kell from the Philadelphia Athletics for Barney McCosky, May 18, 1946.
3. Acquired Joe Coleman, Ed Brinkman, Aurelio Rodriguez, and Jim Hannan from the Washington Senators for Denny McLain, Don Wert, Norm McRae, and Elliott Maddox, October 9, 1970.
4. Acquired Mickey Cochrane from the Philadelphia Athletics for $100,000 and Johnny Pasek, December 12, 1933.
5. Acquired Larry Herndon from the San Francisco Giants for Dan Schatzeder and Mike Chris, December 9, 1981.

The Worst Trades

1. Traded Billy Pierce and $10,000 to the Chicago White Sox for Aaron Robinson, November 10, 1948.
2. Traded Jim Bunning and Gus Triandos to the Philadelphia Phillies for Don Demeter and Jack Hamilton, December 4, 1963.
3. Traded Ben Oglivie to the Milwaukee Brewers for Jim Slaton and Rich Folkers, December 9, 1977.
4. Traded Heinie Manush and Lu Blue to the St. Louis Browns for Chick Galloway, Elam Vangilder, and Harry Rice, December 2, 1927.
5. Traded Dale Alexander and Roy Johnson to the Boston Red Sox for Earl Webb, June 12, 1932.

Organization: A Change in the Wind?

Before the 1984 season, the Detroit Tigers were sold by John Fetzer, who had held controlling interest in the club for twenty-seven years, to Domino's Pizza magnate Tom Monaghan. The acquisition of the club by Monaghan may mark a turning point in the history of the franchise, which had been known for its low profile and solid conservatism.

The most significant sign of the new aggressive attitude was the signing of Darrell Evans, the most sought-after free agent in the '83 re-entry draft. Evans signed a three-year contract worth $2.25 million; he was the first free agent ever signed by Detroit. Fetzer had steadfastly refused to enter the free-agent sweepstakes. "I could be a hero to the fans if I went out and spent a million here and a million there," he maintained, "but who is going to pay the price when the chips are down and the day of reckoning comes, as it surely will? It seems to me a ballclub that puts $20 million in deferred payments on its books for the sake of winning a pennant this year is not prudent."

The Tigers have always been a team of home-grown stars. Their greatest players — Ty Cobb, Harry Heilmann, Hank Greenberg, Rudy York, Charlie Gehringer, Hal Newhouser, Dizzy Trout, Harvey Kuenn, Al Kaline, Mickey Lolich — all first played in the majors for Detroit. Of their current stars, Lance Parrish, Lou Whitaker, Alan Trammell, Jack Morris, and Dan Petry are all products of the Tiger farm system. While a few key players in Tigers history have come from other squads — George Kell, Mickey Cochrane, Norm Cash, Rocky Colavito, Denny McLain, Larry Herndon — they are the exception. The Tigers have, in fact, had little success through the years in the trade mart.

Their bad luck started early with the trade of Kid Elberfeld to New York for Herman Long and Ernie Courtney. Elberfeld went on to become an all-star shortstop for the Highlanders, while Courtney didn't last and Long faded fast. They traded Howard Ehmke, two players, and $25,000 to Philadelphia for Del Pratt and Rip Collins, only to watch Ehmke become one of the league's top hurlers. In 1927, they sent Heinie Manush, on his way to Cooperstown, along with first baseman Lu Blue to the Browns for three nonentities. Other ill-advised moves include Billy Pierce to Chicago for Aaron Robinson, Jim Bunning and Gus Triandos to Philadelphia for Don Demeter and Jack Hamilton, Phil Regan to Los Angeles for Dick Tracewski, and Ben Oglivie to Milwaukee for Jim Slaton, who promptly returned to Milwaukee as a free agent. Their trade of twenty-five-year-old outfielder Glenn Wilson along with useful utility man John Wockenfuss to the Phils for Dave Bergman and Willie Hernandez just prior to the 1984 season could provide the answer to a bullpen problem; it could also turn out to be a giveaway of a talented young player. The new regime must show it can avoid repeating the mistakes of the old one.

DATE		ACQUIRED	FROM		IN EXCHANGE FOR
Jan 1901	1B	Pop Dillon	Pittsburgh Pirates		Cash
April 1901		Cash	Philadelphia Athletics	SS	Harry Lockhead
May 1902		Cash	Baltimore Orioles	OF	Harry Arndt
June 1902		Cash	Baltimore Orioles	P	John Cronin
July 1902		Cash	Baltimore Orioles	1B	Pop Dillon
Sept 1902		Cash	Baltimore Orioles	1B	Sport McAllister
		(Baltimore returned McAllister to Detroit later in September.)			
Dec 1902		Cash	St. Louis Browns	P	Ed Siever
Feb 1903		Cash	Washington Senators	OF	Ducky Holmes
June 10, 1903	SS IF	Herman Long Ernie Courtney	New York Yankees	SS	Kid Elberfeld
Jan 1904	P P	Jesse Stovall Ed Killian	Cleveland Indians	OF	Billy Lush
Jan 1904		Cash	New York Yankees	C	Deacon McGuire
April 30, 1904	2B	Bobby Lowe	Pittsburgh Pirates		Cash
May 30, 1904	OF	Frank Huelsman	Chicago White Sox		Cash

DATE		ACQUIRED	FROM		IN EXCHANGE FOR
June 16, 1904		Cash	St. Louis Browns	OF	Frank Huelsman
July 25, 1904	C	Monte Beville	New York Yankees	C	Frank McManus
Aug 7, 1904	1B	Piano Legs Hickman	Cleveland Indians	1B C	Charlie Carr Fritz Buelow
Aug 10, 1904	3B C	Bill Coughlin Lew Drill	Washington Senators		$7,500.
Oct 1904	OF	Duff Cooley	Boston Braves		Waiver price
May 18, 1905	C	Tom Doran	Boston Red Sox		Waiver price
July 6, 1905		Cash	Washington Senators	1B	Piano Legs Hickman
Aug 1, 1905	C	Nig Clarke	Cleveland Indians		Cash
Aug 10, 1905	C	John Warner	St. Louis Cardinals		Cash
Aug 11, 1905		Cash	Cleveland Indians	C	Nig Clarke
Dec 1905		Cash	Washington Senators	P	Frank Kitson
Dec 1905	OF	Duff Cooley	Boston Braves		Cash
Feb 1906	P	Red Donahue	Cleveland Indians		Cash
Feb 1906		Waiver price	Cincinnati Reds	OF	Jimmy Barrett
Aug 13, 1906		Cash	Washington Senators	C	John Warner
Dec 1906	1B	Claude Rossman	Cleveland Indians		Cash
Dec 12, 1907	C	Ira Thomas	New York Yankees		Cash
Jan 1908	P	George Winter	Boston Red Sox		Cash
Dec 8, 1908		Cash	Philadelphia Athletics	C	Ira Thomas
Jan 1909	3B	George Moriarty	New York Yankees		Cash
Aug 13, 1909	2B	Jim Delahanty	Washington Senators	2B C	Germany Schaefer Red Killefer
Aug 20, 1909	1B	Tom Jones	St. Louis Browns	1B	Claude Rossman
April 1910		Cash	Washington Senators	C	Heinie Beckendorf
Jan 1911		Cash	Chicago White Sox	OF	Matty McIntyre
June 2, 1911		Waiver price	Boston Red Sox	1B	Del Gainor

DATE		ACQUIRED	FROM		IN EXCHANGE FOR
May 1912	P	Joe Lake	St. Louis Browns		Cash
Aug 1912		Cash	Cincinnati Reds	P	Ralph Works
Nov 16, 1912		Cash	Cincinnati Reds	IF	Red Corriden
Dec 1912		Cash	Chicago White Sox	OF	Davy Jones
May 17, 1913		Waiver price	Washington Senators	P	George Mullin
June 1913		Cash	Boston Braves	3B	Charlie Deal
April 1914		Cash	Chicago White Sox	OF	Ray Demmitt
June 2, 1914		Waiver price	Boston Red Sox	1B	Del Gainor
July 14, 1914		Waiver price	St. Louis Browns	2B	Ivan Howard
Jan 7, 1915		Waiver price	New York Yankees	IF	Hugh High
Jan 7, 1915		Waiver price	New York Yankees	1B	Wally Pipp
June 1915	P	Bill Steen	Cleveland Indians		Cash
Aug 18, 1915	P P	Bill James Grover Lowdermilk	St. Louis Browns	OF	Baby Doll Jacobson
Feb 10, 1916	OF P	Jack Dalton Howard Ehmke	Buffalo (Federal League)		Cash
May 30, 1916	P	Earl Hamilton	St. Louis Browns		Cash
May 1916		Cash	Cleveland Indians	OF	Marty Kavanagh
June 20, 1916	P	Willie Mitchell	Cleveland Indians		Waiver price
June 22, 1916		Waiver price	St. Louis Browns	P	Earl Hamilton
Aug 1916		Cash	Cleveland Indians	P	Grover Lowdermilk
Sept 1917	SS	Tony DeFate	St. Louis Cardinals		Waiver price
March 8, 1918		Cash	New York Yankees	1B	George Burns
May 1918		Cash	New York Yankees	P	Happy Finneran
July 1918		Cash	Boston Red Sox	SS	Jack Coffey
Aug 1918	OF	Marty Kavanagh	St. Louis Cardinals		Cash

DATE		ACQUIRED	FROM		IN EXCHANGE FOR
Jan 17, 1919	C OF P	Eddie Ainsmith Chick Shorten Slim Love	Boston Red Sox	3B	Ossie Vitt
Jan 1919	P	Dutch Leonard	Boston Red Sox		$7,500.
April 1919		Cash	Philadelphia Athletics	2B	Snooks Dowd
July 5, 1919	P	Doc Ayers	Washington Senators	P	Eric Erickson
July 1919		Waiver price	Pittsburgh Pirates	OF	Fred Nicholson
Aug 1919		Cash	Boston Red Sox	P	Bill James
Dec 1919	3B	Babe Pinelli	Chicago White Sox		Cash
June 1921	P	Pol Perritt	New York Giants		Cash
Aug 20, 1921		Waiver price	Washington Senators	SS	Donie Bush
Dec 14, 1921		Waiver price	St. Louis Browns	OF	Chick Shorten
Dec 29, 1921	2B	George Cutshaw	Pittsburgh Pirates		Waiver price
March 1922		Waiver price	Philadelphia Athletics	2B	Ralph Young
July 1922	P	Roy Moore	Philadelphia Athletics		Cash
Oct 24, 1922	OF	Frank O'Rourke	Boston Red Sox		Waiver price
Oct 30, 1922	2B P	Del Pratt Rip Collins	Boston Red Sox	P P IF OF	Carl Holling Howard Ehmke Danny Clark Babe Herman and $25,000.
Nov 24, 1922	P	Ray Francis	Washington Senators	SS	Chick Gagnon
April 20, 1923		Cash	Boston Red Sox	OF	Ira Flagstead
March 12, 1924		Cash	Boston Red Sox	OF	Bobby Veach
July 1925		Cash	Cleveland Indians	P	Bert Cole
Dec 9, 1925	OF IF	Tex Vache Homer Ezzell	Boston Red Sox	3B	Fred Haney
April 7, 1926		Cash	Boston Red Sox	SS	Topper Rigney
June 7, 1926	P	Wilbur Cooper	Chicago Cubs		Waiver price

DATE		ACQUIRED	FROM		IN EXCHANGE FOR
Jan 15, 1927	2B IF C	Marty McManus Bobby LaMotte Pinky Hargrave	St. Louis Browns	P IF 2B IF	Lefty Stewart Frank O'Rourke Billy Mullen Otto Miller
Dec 2, 1927	SS P OF	Chick Galloway Elam Vangilder Harry Rice	St. Louis Browns	OF 1B	Heinie Manush Lu Blue
Dec 11, 1928	P	George Uhle	Cleveland Indians	2B P	Jackie Tavener Ken Holloway
Dec 19, 1928	2B	Bucky Harris (Harris was named Detroit manager.)	Washington Senators	SS	Jack Warner
June 22, 1929		Cash	Chicago White Sox	3B	Frank Sigafoos
Oct 14, 1929		Cash	Cincinnati Reds	OF	Harry Heilmann
May 30, 1930	P SS	Waite Hoyt Mark Koenig	New York Yankees	P SS OF	Ownie Carroll Yats Wuestling Harry Rice
June 1930		Waiver price	Philadelphia Phillies	C	Tony Rensa
July 18, 1930		Waiver price	Chicago White Sox	OF	Bob Fothergill
Sept 10, 1930		Cash	Washington Senators	C	Pinky Hargrave
June 30, 1931		Cash	Philadelphia Athletics	P	Waite Hoyt
Aug 31, 1931	C	Muddy Ruel	Boston Red Sox	2B	Marty McManus
June 12, 1932	OF	Earl Webb	Boston Red Sox	1B OF	Dale Alexander Roy Johnson
Dec 14, 1932	P P	Firpo Marberry Carl Fischer	Washington Senators	P	Earl Whitehill
Dec 1932		Waiver price	St. Louis Browns	C	Muddy Ruel
April 21, 1933		$20,000.	New York Giants	P	George Uhle
May 14, 1933		Waiver price	Chicago White Sox	OF	Earl Webb
June 2, 1933	P	Vic Frazier	Chicago White Sox	P	Whit Wyatt
Dec 12, 1933	C	Mickey Cochrane	Philadelphia Athletics	C	Johnny Pasek and $100,000.
Dec 20, 1933	OF	Goose Goslin	Washington Senators	OF	John Stone
Dec 1933		Cash	Brooklyn Dodgers	P	Art Herring
May 17, 1934		Cash	Chicago White Sox	P	Carl Fischer
Aug 4, 1934	P	General Crowder	Washington Senators		Waiver price

DATE		ACQUIRED	FROM		IN EXCHANGE FOR
Sept 24, 1934	P	Spike Merena	Boston Red Sox		Cash
Dec 1934	OF	Bob Seeds	Cleveland Indians		Cash
Dec 10, 1935	OF	Al Simmons	Chicago White Sox		$75,000.
April 30, 1936	1B	Jack Burns	St. Louis Browns	P	Chief Hogsett
April 1, 1937	OF	Babe Herman	Cincinnati Reds		Cash
April 4, 1937		$15,000.	Washington Senators	OF	Al Simmons
June 10, 1937	C	Cliff Bolton	Washington Senators		Waiver price
June 1937		Cash	Boston Braves	3B	Gil English
July 9, 1937	SS	Charley Gelbert	Cincinnati Reds		Waiver price
Dec 2, 1937	P 2B OF	Vern Kennedy Tony Piet Dixie Walker	Chicago White Sox	3B C OF	Marv Owen Mike Tresh Gee Walker
Jan 1938	P	Al Benton	Philadelphia Athletics		Cash
Sept 14, 1938		Waiver price	Brooklyn Dodgers	C	Ray Hayworth
Sept 14, 1938		Cash	Brooklyn Dodgers	3B	Don Ross
Dec 15, 1938	3B P	Pinky Higgins Archie McKain	Boston Red Sox	P P 3B	Eldon Auker Jake Wade Chet Morgan
Jan 1939		Waiver price	Brooklyn Dodgers	P	Boots Poffenberger
May 9, 1939		Cash	New York Giants	P	Red Lynn
May 13, 1939	OF P SS P	Beau Bell Bobo Newsom Red Kress Jim Walkup	St. Louis Browns	P P P P OF 3B	Vern Kennedy Bob Harris George Gill Roxie Lawson Chet Laabs Mark Christman
May 18, 1939	P	Bud Thomas	Washington Senators		Waiver price
June 14, 1939	OF	Earl Averill	Cleveland Indians	P	Harry Eisenstat and cash
July 24, 1939		Waiver price	Brooklyn Dodgers	OF	Dixie Walker
Sept 12, 1939	P	Cotton Pippen	Philadelphia Athletics		Waiver price
Dec 6, 1939	SS	Dick Bartell	Chicago Cubs	SS	Billy Rogell

DATE		ACQUIRED	FROM		IN EXCHANGE FOR
Dec 9, 1939	OF	Wally Moses	Philadelphia Athletics	2B P	Benny McCoy Slick Coffman
		(Commissioner Landis ruled that Detroit had kept McCoy covered up in the minors and declared him a free agent, cancelling the deal. McCoy then signed with Philadelphia for a $10,000 bonus.)			
Jan 20, 1940	OF	Bruce Campbell	Cleveland Indians	OF	Beau Bell
Jan 30, 1940	C	Billy Sullivan	St. Louis Browns	P	Slick Coffman
Feb 23, 1940	P	Lynn Nelson	Philadelphia Athletics		Waiver price
Dec 12, 1940		Cash	Boston Red Sox	OF	Pete Fox
Dec 18, 1940	SS	Eric McNair	Chicago White Sox		Waiver price
May 5, 1941	OF	Rip Radcliff	St. Louis Browns		$25,000.
Aug 4, 1941		Cash	St. Louis Browns	P	Archie McKain
Dec 12, 1941	2B OF	Jimmy Bloodworth Doc Cramer	Washington Senators	2B OF	Frank Croucher Bruce Campbell
March 13, 1942		Cash	Brooklyn Dodgers	C	Billy Sullivan
March 31, 1942		$40,000.	Washington Senators	P	Bobo Newsom
April 30, 1942		Cash	Brooklyn Dodgers	P	Schoolboy Rowe
July 17, 1942	P	Jack Wilson	Washington Senators	SS	Eric McNair
		(McNair refused to report.)			
July 25, 1942		Cash	Philadelphia Athletics	SS	Eric McNair
Oct 11, 1943	2B C	Don Heffner Bob Swift	Philadelphia Athletics	OF	Rip Radcliff
Aug 13, 1944		Cash	Philadelphia Athletics	OF	Charlie Metro
Dec 12, 1944	SS	Skeeter Webb	Chicago White Sox	SS	Joe Orengo
April 27, 1945	OF	Roy Cullenbine	Cleveland Indians	OF 2B	Don Ross Dutch Meyer
Aug 8, 1945	P	George Caster	St. Louis Browns		Waiver price
Aug 1945	P	Jim Tobin	Boston Braves		Cash
Jan 3, 1946	SS	Eddie Lake	Boston Red Sox	1B	Rudy York
May 16, 1946		Cash	Washington Senators	IF	Billy Hitchcock
May 18, 1946	3B	George Kell	Philadelphia Athletics	OF	Barney McCosky
May 19, 1946		Cash	Boston Red Sox	3B	Pinky Higgins

DATE		ACQUIRED	FROM		IN EXCHANGE FOR
Dec 12, 1946		Cash	Pittsburgh Pirates	2B	Jimmy Bloodworth
Jan 18, 1947		$75,000.	Pittsburgh Pirates	1B	Hank Greenberg
May 20, 1947	C	Hal Wagner	Boston Red Sox	C	Birdie Tebbetts
Sept 13, 1948		Waiver price	Philadelphia Phillies	C	Hal Wagner
Nov 10, 1948	C	Aaron Robinson	Chicago White Sox	P	Billy Pierce and $10,000.
Jan 20, 1949	OF	Don Lund	St. Louis Browns		$15,000.
Jan 26, 1949	1B	Tony Lupien	Chicago White Sox		Waiver price
April 20, 1949		Cash	Cleveland Indians	P	Al Benton
May 7, 1949	3B	Don Kolloway	Chicago White Sox	OF	Vern Rapp
Dec 1, 1949		Waiver price	St. Louis Browns	P	Stubby Overmire
Dec 14, 1949	2B	Gerry Priddy	St. Louis Browns	P	Lou Kretlow and $100,000.
Dec 17, 1949	1B	Dick Kryhoski	New York Yankees	OF	Dick Wakefield
Feb 15, 1950	P	Paul Calvert	Washington Senators		Waiver price
Aug 3, 1950	P	Hank Borowy	Pittsburgh Pirates		$15,000.
April 26, 1951	P	Gene Bearden	Washington Senators		Waiver price
Aug 6, 1951		Waiver price	Boston Red Sox	C	Aaron Robinson
Feb 14, 1952	P 1B OF	Dick Littlefield Ben Taylor Cliff Mapes	St. Louis Browns	P P 1B	Gene Bearden Bob Cain Dick Kryhoski
March 21, 1952	P	Ken Johnson	Philadelphia Phillies		Waiver price
June 3, 1952	1B P 3B SS OF	Walt Dropo Bill Wight Fred Hatfield Johnny Pesky Don Lenhardt	Boston Red Sox	P 3B SS OF	Dizzy Trout George Kell Johnny Lipon Hoot Evers
Aug 14, 1952	OF P P P	Jim Delsing Ned Garver Dave Madison Bill Black	St. Louis Browns	P P OF OF	Dick Littlefield Marlin Stuart Don Lenhardt Vic Wertz
Oct 27, 1952	OF	Rufus Crawford	St. Louis Browns	SS OF	Neil Berry Cliff Mapes and $25,000.
Dec 4, 1952	SS OF C	Owen Friend Bob Nieman J W Porter	St. Louis Browns	P P OF	Virgil Trucks Hal White Johnny Groth

DATE		ACQUIRED	FROM		IN EXCHANGE FOR
Jan 29, 1953	3B	Billy Hitchcock	Philadelphia Athletics	3B	Don Kolloway
April 7, 1953	3B	George Freese	St. Louis Browns		Cash
May 23, 1953	P	Earl Harrist	Chicago White Sox		Waiver price
June 15, 1953	3B P P P	Ray Boone Al Aber Steve Gromek Dick Weik	Cleveland Indians	P SS P C	Art Houtteman Owen Friend Bill Wight Joe Ginsberg
July 10, 1953	P	Ralph Branca	Brooklyn Dodgers		Waiver price
May 29, 1954	C	Red Wilson	Chicago White Sox	C	Matt Batts
June 9, 1954	1B	Wayne Belardi	Brooklyn Dodgers	1B C P	Charlie Kress Johnny Bucha Ernie Nevel and cash
June 14, 1954	3B	Mel Hoderlein	Washington Senators	3B	Johnny Pesky
July 29, 1954	OF	Hoot Evers	New York Giants		Waiver price
Dec 6, 1954	P 1B 1B	Leo Cristante Ferris Fain Jack Phillips	Chicago White Sox	1B P OF	Walt Dropo Ted Gray Bob Nieman
Dec 29, 1954	P	Bob Schultz	Pittsburgh Pirates		Cash
Jan 3, 1955		Cash	Baltimore Orioles	OF	Hoot Evers
April 7, 1955	IF	Harry Malmberg	Cleveland Indians		Waiver price
April 8, 1955	SS	Ron Samford	New York Giants		Waiver price
May 11, 1955	OF	Charlie Maxwell	Baltimore Orioles		Cash
May 11, 1955		Cash	Kansas City Athletics	P	Ray Herbert
June 15, 1955	1B	Earl Torgeson	Philadelphia Phillies		Cash
July 8, 1955		Waiver price	Baltimore Orioles	P	George Zuverink
Sept 8, 1955	P	Bobby Tiefenauer	St. Louis Cardinals	P	Ben Flowers
Nov 30, 1955	P	Virgil Trucks	Chicago White Sox	3B	Bubba Phillips
April 5, 1956		Waiver price	Baltimore Orioles	P	Babe Birrer
May 11, 1956	P	Walt Masterson	Washington Senators		Waiver price

DATE		ACQUIRED	FROM		IN EXCHANGE FOR
May 15, 1956	2B	Jim Brideweser	Chicago	3B	Fred Hatfield
	P	Harry Byrd	White Sox	OF	Jim Delsing
	3B	Bob Kennedy			
Sept 17, 1956		Waiver price	Chicago White Sox	P	Dick Marlowe
Dec 5, 1956	IF	Jim Finigan	Kansas City	P	Ned Garver
	P	Jack Crimian	Athletics	P	Gene Host
	P	Bill Harrington		P	Virgil Trucks
	1B	Eddie Robinson		1B	Wayne Belardi and $20,000.
Feb 8, 1957		Cash	Baltimore Orioles	IF	Jim Brideweser
Feb 12, 1957	2B	Jack Dittmer	Milwaukee Braves	OF	Charlie King Cash
April 30, 1957	OF	Karl Olson	Boston Red Sox	1B	Jack Phillips
June 14, 1957	OF	Dave Philley	Chicago White Sox	1B	Earl Torgeson
Aug 1, 1957	OF	Johnny Groth	Kansas City Athletics		Cash
Aug 27, 1957		Waiver price	Kansas City Athletics	P	Al Aber
Nov 20, 1957	2B	Billy Martin	Kansas City	OF	Bill Tuttle
	OF	Gus Zernial	Athletics	OF	Jim Small
	P	Tom Morgan		P	Duke Maas
	OF	Lou Skizas		P	John Tsitouris
	P	Mickey McDermott		C	Frank House
	C	Tim Thompson		1B	Kent Hadley
				1B	Jim McManus
Dec 11, 1957		Cash	Philadelphia Phillies	OF	Dave Philley
Jan 28, 1958	1B	Gail Harris	San Francisco	3B	Jim Finigan
	3B	Ozzie Virgil	Giants		and $25,000.
Feb 18, 1958	C	Jim Hegan	Cleveland	P	Hal Woodeshick
	P	Hank Aguirre	Indians	C	J W Porter
March 27, 1958	2B	Milt Bolling	Cleveland	P	Pete Wojey
	P	Vito Valentinetti	Indians		and $20,000.
April 3, 1958	OF	Stan Palys	Cincinnati Reds		Waiver price
May 12, 1958	P	George Susce	Boston Red Sox		Waiver price
May 13, 1958	P	Herm Wehmeier	St. Louis Cardinals		Cash
May 24, 1958	OF	Bob Hazle	Milwaukee Braves		Cash
June 2, 1958		Waiver price	Baltimore Orioles	P	Lou Sleater
June 15, 1958	P	Bill Fischer	Chicago	3B	Ray Boone
	OF	Tito Francona	White Sox	P	Bob Shaw
June 23, 1958	P	Al Cicotte	Washington Senators	P	Vito Valentinetti

DATE		ACQUIRED	FROM		IN EXCHANGE FOR
July 27, 1958		Minor league OF John Turk and cash	Philadelphia Phillies	C	Jim Hegan
Sept 11, 1958		Waiver price	Washington Senators	P	Bill Fischer
Oct 5, 1958	P	Pete Burnside	San Francisco Giants		Cash
Nov 20, 1958	P P IF	Don Mossi Ray Narleski Ossie Alvarez	Cleveland Indians	2B P	Billy Martin Al Cicotte
Dec 2, 1958	C	Lou Berberet	Boston Red Sox	P	Herb Moford
Dec 6, 1958	3B SS OF	Eddie Yost Rocky Bridges Neil Chrisley	Washington Senators	2B 2B OF	Reno Bertoia Ron Samford Jim Delsing
March 21, 1959	OF	Larry Doby	Cleveland Indians	OF	Tito Francona
May 2, 1959	P 2B	Dave Sisler Ted Lepcio	Boston Red Sox	P	Billy Hoeft
May 13, 1959		$30,000.	Chicago White Sox	OF	Larry Doby
June 13, 1959	P	Bob Smith	Pittsburgh Pirates		Waiver price
Oct 15, 1959	P C 2B	Don Kaiser Mike Roarke Casey Wise	Milwaukee Braves	C P	Charlie Lau Don Lee
Dec 5, 1959	SS P	Chico Fernandez Ray Semproch	Philadelphia Phillies	OF 2B	Ken Walters Ted Lepcio minor league P Alex Cosmidis
April 12, 1960	1B	Norm Cash	Cleveland Indians	3B	Steve Demeter
April 17, 1960	OF	Rocky Colavito	Cleveland Indians	SS	Harvey Kuenn
May 7, 1960	OF	Sandy Amoros	Los Angeles Dodgers	1B	Gail Harris
June 15, 1960	P	Clem Labine	Los Angeles Dodgers	P	Ray Semproch and cash
July 22, 1960	P	Bill Fischer	Washington Senators	P	Tom Morgan
July 26, 1960	C	Harry Chiti	Kansas City Athletics		Cash
July 26, 1960	C	Hank Foiles	Cleveland Indians	IF C	Rocky Bridges Red Wilson
Aug 10, 1960	MGR	Joe Gordon	Cleveland Indians	MGR	Jimmy Dykes
Aug 31, 1960	1B	Dick Gernert	Chicago Cubs		Cash
Dec 7, 1960	OF P C 2B	Bill Bruton Terry Fox Dick Brown Chuck Cottier	Milwaukee Braves	2B OF	Frank Bolling Neil Chrisley

DATE		ACQUIRED	FROM		IN EXCHANGE FOR
June 5, 1961	P	Hal Woodeshick	Washington Senators	2B	Chuck Cottier
June 7, 1961	P	Jerry Casale	Los Angeles Angels	P	Jim Donohue
June 26, 1961		Cash	Los Angeles Angels	OF	George Thomas
Aug 2, 1961	P 3B	Gerry Staley Reno Bertoia	Kansas City Athletics	3B P	Ozzie Virgil Bill Fischer
Aug 10, 1961	P	Ron Kline	Los Angeles Angels		Waiver price
Sept 8, 1961	1B	Vic Wertz	Boston Red Sox		Waiver price
Dec 1, 1961	P	Sam Jones	Houston Astros	P P	Bob Bruce Manny Montejo
May 7, 1962		Cash	Kansas City Athletics	OF	George Alusik
June 25, 1962	OF	Bob Farley	Chicago White Sox	OF	Charlie Maxwell
July 20, 1962	3B	Don Buddin	Houston Astros		Cash
Nov 26, 1962	C OF	Gus Triandos Whitey Herzog	Baltimore Orioles	C	Dick Brown
Nov 27, 1962	P 3B	Gordon Seyfried Bubba Phillips	Cleveland Indians	P	Ron Nischwitz
Nov 28, 1962	P	Bob Anderson	Chicago Cubs	1B	Steve Boros
March 18, 1963		Cash	Washington Senators	P	Ron Kline
March 25, 1963		Cash	St. Louis Cardinals	P	Bob Humphreys
April 8, 1963	P	Denny McLain	Chicago White Sox		Waiver price
May 4, 1963	P	Tom Sturdivant	Pittsburgh Pirates		Cash
May 4, 1963		Cash	Milwaukee Braves	OF	Bubba Morton
May 8, 1963	OF	Lou Johnson and cash	Milwaukee Braves	SS	Chico Fernandez
May 23, 1963		Cash	Kansas City Athletics	P	Tom Sturdivant
June 15, 1963	OF 3B	George Thomas and cash Frank Kostro	Los Angeles Angels	P	Paul Foytack
Nov 18, 1963	2B P P	Jerry Lumpe Ed Rakow Dave Wickersham	Kansas City Athletics	OF P	Rocky Colavito Bob Anderson and $50,000.
Dec 4, 1963	OF P	Don Demeter Jack Hamilton	Philadelphia Phillies	P C	Jim Bunning Gus Triandos

DATE		ACQUIRED	FROM		IN EXCHANGE FOR
March 18, 1964		Cash	Chicago White Sox	P	Don Mossi
April 9, 1964	P	Larry Sherry	Los Angeles Dodgers	OF	Lou Johnson and $10,000.
April 11, 1964		Waiver price	Washington Senators	P	Pete Craig
April 28, 1964	P	Julio Navarro	Los Angeles Angels	P-OF	Willie Smith
May 9, 1964		Cash	Washington Senators	P	Alan Koch
May 30, 1964		Cash	New York Mets	P	Frank Lary
March 27, 1965		Cash	Chicago Cubs	P	Bill Faul
June 23, 1965	P	Orlando Pena	Kansas City Athletics		Cash
Oct 4, 1965	P	Bill Monbouquette	Boston Red Sox	2B OF	George Smith George Thomas
Oct 14, 1965		Cash	New York Mets	P	Jack Hamilton
Dec 15, 1965	SS	Dick Tracewski	Los Angeles Dodgers	P	Phil Regan
May 10, 1966		Cash	Philadelphia Phillies	P	Terry Fox
May 10, 1966	P	Johnny Podres	Los Angeles Dodgers		Cash
June 14, 1966	P OF	Earl Wilson Joe Christopher	Boston Red Sox	P OF	Julio Navarro Don Demeter
Dec 19, 1966	C	Chris Cannizzaro	New York Mets		Cash
April 7, 1967	C	Jim Price	Pittsburgh Pirates		Cash
April 10, 1967		Cash	California Angels	C	Orlando McFarlane
May 6, 1967		Cash	Cleveland Indians	P	Orlando Pena
June 23, 1967		Cash	Cincinnati Reds	2B	Jake Wood
June 29, 1967	OF	Jim Landis	Houston Astros	P	Larry Sherry
Aug 17, 1967	3B	Eddie Mathews	Houston Astros	P	Fred Gladding
Nov 28, 1967	P	Dennis Ribant	Pittsburgh Pirates	P	Dave Wickersham
Nov 29, 1967		Cash	Pittsburgh Pirates	C	Chris Cannizzaro
April 3, 1968		Cash	Los Angeles Dodgers	P	Hank Aguirre
June 15, 1968	P	John Wyatt	New York Yankees		Cash

DATE		ACQUIRED	FROM		IN EXCHANGE FOR
July 21, 1968	P	Don McMahon	Chicago White Sox	P	Dennis Ribant
Aug 31, 1968	P	Roy Face	Pittsburgh Pirates		Cash
Sept 30, 1968		Cash	Chicago White Sox	IF	Bob Christian
Sept 30, 1968		Cash	New York Yankees	P	Jim Rooker
March 25, 1969		Cash	Montreal Expos	1B	Don Pepper
June 14, 1969	OF	Tom Tresh	New York Yankees	OF	Ron Woods
June 15, 1969		Cash	Montreal Expos	P	Dick Radatz
Aug 9, 1969		Cash	San Francisco Giants	P	Don McMahon
Sept 2, 1969	SS	Cesar Gutierrez	San Francisco Giants		Cash
Dec 3, 1969	P	Jerry Robertson	Montreal Expos	P	Joe Sparma
Dec 4, 1969	P	Joe Niekro	San Diego Padres	P IF	Pat Dobson Dave Campbell
Dec 13, 1969	3B	Dalton Jones	Boston Red Sox	IF	Tommy Matchick
May 22, 1970	OF P	Rusty Nagelson Billy Rohr	Cleveland Indians	P	Fred Lasher
July 15, 1970		Cash	San Diego Padres	P	Earl Wilson
Oct 9, 1970	P SS 3B P	Joe Coleman Ed Brinkman Aurelio Rodriguez Jim Hannan	Washington Senators	P 3B P OF	Denny McLain Don Wert Norm McRae Elliott Maddox
March 29, 1971	P	Bill Zepp	Minnesota Twins	IF	Bob Adams and minor league P Art Clifford
March 30, 1971	P P	Dean Chance Bill Denehy	New York Mets	P	Jerry Robertson
May 11, 1971	P IF	John Gelnar Jose Herrera	Milwaukee Brewers	P	Jim Hannan
May 22, 1971	2B	John Donaldson	Oakland Athletics	P	Daryl Patterson
June 12, 1971	2B	Tony Taylor	Philadelphia Phillies		Minor league Ps Mike Fremuth and Carl Cavanaugh
July 30, 1971	P	Ron Perranoski	Minnesota Twins		Cash
Dec 2, 1971	C	Tom Haller	Los Angeles Dodgers		Minor league P Bernie Beckman and cash
March 24, 1972		Cash	Montreal Expos	SS	Cesar Gutierrez
May 9, 1972	1B	Reggie Sanders	Oakland Athletics	P	Mike Kilkenny

DATE		ACQUIRED	FROM		IN EXCHANGE FOR
May 30, 1972	P	Norm McRae	Texas Rangers	3B	Dalton Jones
Aug 2, 1972	P	Woodie Fryman	Philadelphia Phillies		Cash
Aug 31, 1972	1B	Frank Howard	Texas Rangers		Cash
Sept 6, 1972		Cash	California Angels	P	Bill Gilbreth
Oct 25, 1972		Cash	Philadelphia Phillies	C P	Tom Haller Don Leshnock
Nov 30, 1972	1B	Rich Reese	Minnesota Twins		Cash
Nov 30, 1972	OF	Dick Sharon	Pittsburgh Pirates	P P	Jim Foor Norm McRae
March 27, 1973	P	Jim Perry	Minnesota Twins	P	Dan Fife and cash
April 2, 1973	C	Charlie Sands	Pittsburgh Pirates	P	Chris Zachary
May 14, 1973	C	Bob Didier	Atlanta Braves	C	Gene Lamont
June 15, 1973	P	Ed Farmer	Cleveland Indians	P 3B	Tom Timmerman Kevin Collins
June 22, 1973		Cash	San Diego Padres	P	Bob Miller
Aug 7, 1973		Cash	Atlanta Braves	P	Joe Niekro
Sept 23, 1973		Cash	New York Mets	P	Bob Miller
Sept 24, 1973		Cash	New York Yankees	C	Duke Sims
Oct 23, 1973	OF	Ben Oglivie	Boston Red Sox	2B	Dick McAuliffe
Nov 3, 1973	P	Jim Ray and minor league SS Gary Strickland	Houston Astros	P	Fred Scherman Cash
Dec 5, 1973	P	Luke Walker	Pittsburgh Pirates		Cash
Dec 6, 1973	P	Ray Newman	Milwaukee Brewers	P	Mike Strahler
March 19, 1974	P OF	Rick Sawyer Walt Williams	Cleveland Indians	P	Jim Perry

(Part of three-team trade involving Detroit, Cleveland, and New York Yankees.)

DATE		ACQUIRED	FROM		IN EXCHANGE FOR
March 19, 1974	C	Gerry Moses	New York Yankees	P OF P	Rick Sawyer Walt Williams Ed Farmer
		(Part of three-team trade involving Detroit, New York Yankees, and Cleveland.)			
March 26, 1974		Cash	Boston Red Sox	C	Bob Didier
Aug 7, 1974		Cash	Montreal Expos	OF	Jim Northrup
Nov 18, 1974	1B	Nate Colbert	San Diego Padres	SS P OF	Ed Brinkman Bob Strampe Dick Sharon
		(Part of three-team trade involving San Diego, Detroit, and St. Louis Cardinals.)			
Dec 4, 1974	P C	Tom Walker Terry Humphrey	Montreal Expos	P	Woodie Fryman
Dec 6, 1974		Cash	Pittsburgh Pirates	P	Jim Ray
Jan 30, 1975		Cash	New York Mets	C	Gerry Moses
March 29, 1975	1B	Jack Pierce	Atlanta Braves	1B	Reggie Sanders
April 4, 1975	P	Ray Bare	St. Louis Cardinals		Cash
May 29, 1975	P	Bob Reynolds	Baltimore Orioles	P	Fred Holdsworth
June 15, 1975		Cash	Montreal Expos	1B	Nate Colbert
Aug 26, 1975		Cash	Cleveland Indians	P	Bob Reynolds
Dec 6, 1975	C P P	Milt May Dave Roberts Jim Crawford	Houston Astros	OF C P P	Leon Roberts Terry Humphrey Gene Pentz Mark Lemongello
Dec 12, 1975	1B P	Rusty Staub Bill Laxton	New York Mets	P OF	Mickey Lolich Bobby Baldwin
Feb 3, 1976		Cash	St. Louis Cardinals	P	Tom Walker
April 2, 1976		Cash	St. Louis Cardinals	P	Lerrin LaGrow
June 8, 1976		Cash	Chicago Cubs	P	Joe Coleman
June 10, 1976	2B	Pedro Garcia	Milwaukee Brewers	2B	Gary Sutherland
Nov 6, 1976	IF	Luis Alvarado	St. Louis Cardinals		Cash
Feb 23, 1977	2B	Tito Fuentes	San Diego Padres		No compensation (free agent signing)
Feb 25, 1977		Cash	New York Mets	IF	Luis Alvarado
		(Alvarado was returned to Detroit on April 27, 1977.)			
April 12, 1977	P	Steve Foucault	Texas Rangers	OF	Willie Horton

DATE		ACQUIRED	FROM		IN EXCHANGE FOR
July 30, 1977		Cash	Chicago Cubs	P	Dave Roberts
Sept 22, 1977		Cash	Chicago White Sox	OF	Bob Molinaro
Dec 9, 1977	OF	Charlie Spikes	Cleveland Indians	SS	Tom Veryzer
Dec 9, 1977	P P	Jim Slaton Rich Folkers	Milwaukee Brewers	OF	Ben Oglivie
Jan 30, 1978	IF	Steve Dillard	Boston Red Sox		Minor league Ps Mike Burns and Frank Harris and cash
Jan 30, 1978		Cash	Montreal Expos	2B	Tito Fuentes
Feb 23, 1978		Cash	Toronto Blue Jays	P	Steve Grilli
March 6, 1978	P	Jack Billingham	Cincinnati Reds	P	George Cappuzzello minor league OF John Valle
Aug 16, 1978		Cash	Kansas City Royals	P	Steve Foucault
Nov 29, 1978		No compensation (free agent signing)	Milwaukee Brewers	P	Jim Slaton
Dec 4, 1978	OF P	Jerry Morales Aurelio Lopez	St. Louis Cardinals	P	Bob Sykes and minor league P Jack Murphy
Jan 27, 1979		No compensation (free agent signing)	Seattle Mariners	DH	Willie Horton
March 13, 1979	P	Mardie Cornejo	New York Mets	P	Ed Glynn
March 20, 1979	IF	Ed Putman	Chicago Cubs	2B	Steve Dillard
May 25, 1979	OF	Champ Summers	Cincinnati Reds	P	Sheldon Burnside
May 27, 1979		Cash	Chicago White Sox	C	Milt May
July 20, 1979		Minor league C Randy Schafer and cash	Montreal Expos	DH	Rusty Staub
Aug 30, 1979		Cash	Chicago Cubs	C	Bruce Kimm
Oct 31, 1979	1B	Richie Hebner	New York Mets	OF 3B	Jerry Morales Phil Mankowski
Dec 5, 1979	P	Jeff Holly	Minnesota Twins	P	Fernando Arroyo
Dec 7, 1979		$200,000.	San Diego Padres	3B	Aurelio Rodriguez
Dec 7, 1979	P	Dan Schatzeder	Montreal Expos	OF	Ron LeFlore
March 15, 1980	C	Duffy Dyer	Montreal Expos	IF	Jerry Manuel

DATE		ACQUIRED	FROM		IN EXCHANGE FOR
May 12, 1980		Cash	Boston Red Sox	P	Jack Billingham
May 27, 1980	OF	Al Cowens	California Angels	1B	Jason Thompson
May 29, 1980	2B	Stan Papi	Philadelphia Phillies		Cash
June 2, 1980	OF	Jim Lentine	St. Louis Cardinals	P OF	John Martin Al Greene
Dec 10, 1980	P	Kevin Saucier	Texas Rangers	SS	Mark Wagner
Dec 12, 1980	P	Dennis Kinney	San Diego Padres	OF	Dave Stegman
March 24, 1981	C	Bill Fahey	San Diego Padres		Cash
April 1, 1981	IF	Mick Kelleher	Chicago Cubs		Cash
Aug 23, 1981	1B	Ron Jackson	Minnesota Twins	OF	Tim Corcoran
Nov 27, 1981	OF	Chet Lemon	Chicago White Sox	OF	Steve Kemp
Dec 9, 1981	OF	Larry Herndon	San Francisco Giants	P P	Dan Schatzeder Mike Chris
Jan 30, 1982	OF	Jerry Turner	Chicago Cubs		No compensation (free agent signing)
March 1, 1982	3B C	Jeff Cox Scott Meyer	Oakland Athletics	OF	Darrell Brown minor league Ps Mark Fellows and Jack Smith
March 4, 1982	1B-3B	Enos Cabell and cash	San Francisco Giants	OF	Champ Summers
March 23, 1982	OF	Eddie Miller	Atlanta Braves	P	Roger Weaver
March 28, 1982		Cash	Seattle Mariners	OF	Al Cowens
March 30, 1982	P	Elias Sosa	Montreal Expos		Cash
April 20, 1982		No compensation (free agent signing)	California Angels	1B	Ron Jackson
April 21, 1982		Cash	California Angels	SS	Mick Kelleher
Aug 16, 1982		Cash	Pittsburgh Pirates	1B-OF	Richie Hebner
Sept 7, 1982	2B	German Barranca	Cincinnati Reds		Cash
Oct 7, 1982		Cash	San Diego Padres	P	Elias Sosa
March 24, 1983	P	John Grubb	Texas Rangers	P	Dave Tobik
March 25, 1983	C	Sal Butera	Minnesota Twins		Minor league C Stine Poole and cash

DATE		ACQUIRED	FROM		IN EXCHANGE FOR
May 4, 1983		Cash	Montreal Expos	P	Bob James
June 22, 1983	P	Doug Bair	St. Louis Cardinals	P	Dave Rucker
June 30, 1983	IF	Wayne Krenchicki	Cincinnati Reds	P	Pat Underwood
Aug 4, 1983	P	John Martin	St. Louis Cardinals		Cash
Aug 23, 1983	P	Glenn Abbott	Seattle Mariners		$100,000.
Nov 21, 1983		Cash	Cincinnati Reds	IF	Wayne Krenchicki
Dec 8, 1983	OF	Rusty Kuntz	Minnesota Twins	P	Larry Pashnick
Dec 19, 1983	1B	Darrell Evans	San Francisco Giants		No compensation (free agent signing)
Feb 14, 1984		No compensation (free agent signing)	Houston Astros	1B	Enos Cabell
March 24, 1984	P 1B	Willie Hernandez Dave Bergman	Philadelphia Phillies	C OF	John Wockenfuss Glenn Wilson
March 30, 1984	OF	Dallas Williams	Cincinnati Reds		Minor league P Charlie Nail

Kansas City Athletics

The Best Trades

1. Acquired Joe Rudi and Phil Roof from the Cleveland Indians for Jim Landis, October 1, 1965.
2. Acquired Diego Segui from the Washington Senators for Jim Duckworth, July 30, 1966.
3. Acquired Rocky Colavito, Bob Anderson, and $50,000 from the Detroit Tigers for Jerry Lumpe, Dave Wickersham, and Ed Rakow, November 18, 1963.
4. Acquired Buddy Daley from the Cleveland Indians for Arnie Portocarrero, April 17, 1958.
5. Acquired Roger Maris, Dick Tomanek, and Preston Ward from the Cleveland Indians for Woodie Held and Vic Power, June 15, 1958.

The Worst Trades

1. Traded Roger Maris, Kent Hadley and Joe DeMaestri to the New York Yankees for Hank Bauer, Don Larsen, and Norm Siebern, December 11, 1959.
2. Traded Ralph Terry and Hector Lopez to the New York Yankees for Johnny Kucks, Tom Sturdivant and Jerry Lumpe, May 26, 1959.
3. Traded Ed Charles to the New York Mets for Larry Elliot and $50,000, May 10, 1967.
4. Traded Ken Harrelson to the Washington Senators for Jim Duckworth, June 23, 1966.
5. Traded Murry Dickson to the New York Yankees for Zeke Bella and cash, August 22, 1958.

The Strange Case of the Major League Farm Team

The first Kansas City franchise in the major leagues was a sorry crew left over from Connie Mack's once-proud Philadelphia Athletics. The A's quickly came to bear the label "Yankee Farm Club" because of the numerous controversial, and in some cases scandalous, trades made between the two clubs.

The "Farm Club" accusation was well founded. Kansas City had been the location of a minor league Yankee farm team for eighteen years, and its management never seemed to understand that their role had changed when they were granted a major league franchise. In the first five years of its existence, Kansas City made sixteen trades with New York involving fifty-nine players. Many of them went back and forth between the two like yo-yos — or like players shuttling from the Yankees to their Columbus farm team today. Typical of these maneuvers were the deals involving Clete Boyer, Enos Slaughter, Murry Dickson, Ralph Terry, and Roger Maris.

Boyer was signed by the Athletics in May of 1955 for a $40,000 bonus. At the time, the bonus rules stated that a player receiving a bonus in excess of $4,000 had to remain with the parent club for at least two seasons before he could be optioned to the minor leagues. After sitting on the A's bench for two years, Boyer was traded to the Yankees. It was later admitted that the A's had signed Boyer on behalf of the Yankees, with the understanding that he would be turned over to New York as soon as the two-year period was through.

The Yankees frequently used the Athletics to keep a player sharp or to let him develop away from pennant pressure so that he would be ready when they needed him. The Yanks sent Enos Slaughter to K.C. with the former in mind in May 1955; fifteen months later, they reacquired him for the '56 stretch run. Ralph Terry fell into the latter category; the experience he received facing big league hitters from '57 to '59 helped him prepare for his role on the Yankee pennant winners of 1960–64.

It didn't matter to owner Arnold Johnson how his team stood; when the Yankees called, he was always obliging. In August 1958, the A's were enjoying their finest season in Kansas City, standing in sixth place, but just two and a half games out of fourth. Suddenly, they traded the second biggest winner on their pitching staff, Murry Dickson, to the Yanks for a player to be named later. That player, an obscure minor leaguer named Zeke Bella, did not report until after the season was over. But the biggest and most controversial of the deals sent Roger Maris to New York for Hank Bauer, Norm Siebern, and Don Larsen. Frank Lane had drawn some criticism when he traded Maris from Cleveland to Kansas City; knowledgeable baseball men knew that this put him on an inexorable path to the Bronx. Sure enough, that's where he wound up, winning Most Valuable Player Awards in his first two seasons with the Yankees, breaking Babe Ruth's home run record along the way.

The worst of these abuses were halted when Charlie Finley bought the team from Arnold Johnson's estate in the winter of 1960–61. Finley had unpleasant ideas of his own, cutting out for Oakland at the first convenient opportunity. But the people of Kansas City were lucky; a first-class organization was just around the corner.

DATE		ACQUIRED	FROM		IN EXCHANGE FOR
March 30, 1955	1B P P	Dick Kryhoski Ewell Blackwell Tom Gorman	New York Yankees		$50,000.
April 28, 1955	P	Lou Sleater	New York Yankees		Cash
May 11, 1955	P OF	Johnny Sain Enos Slaughter	New York Yankees	P	Sonny Dixon and cash
May 11, 1955	P	Ray Herbert	Detroit Tigers		Cash
May 11, 1955	OF	Harry Simpson	Cleveland Indians		Cash

DATE	ACQUIRED	FROM	IN EXCHANGE FOR
Sept 12, 1955	P Glenn Cox	Brooklyn Dodgers	Waiver price
Sept 14, 1955	OF Tom Saffell	Pittsburgh Pirates	Waiver price
April 16, 1956	OF Johnny Groth	Washington Senators	Cash
April 16, 1956	C Tim Thompson	Brooklyn Dodgers	P Lee Wheat OF Tom Saffell and cash
May 16, 1956	P Jose Santiago	Cleveland Indians	Cash
June 14, 1956	OF Lou Skizas 1B Eddie Robinson	New York Yankees	P Moe Burtschy OF Bill Renna and cash
June 23, 1956	P Jack McMahan	Pittsburgh Pirates	2B Spook Jacobs
Aug 17, 1956	C Hal Smith	Baltimore Orioles	C Joe Ginsberg
Aug 25, 1956	Waiver price	New York Yankees	OF Enos Slaughter
Oct 11, 1956	P Ryne Duren OF Jim Pisoni	Baltimore Orioles	P Art Ceccarelli OF Al Pilarcik
Oct 15, 1956	P Ben Flowers	Philadelphia Phillies	Waiver price
Oct 16, 1956	OF Bob Cerv	New York Yankees	Cash
Dec 5, 1956	P Ned Garver P Gene Host P Virgil Trucks 1B Wayne Belardi and $20,000.	Detroit Tigers	IF Jim Finigan P Jack Crimian P Bill Harrington 1B Eddie Robinson
Feb 19, 1957	SS Billy Hunter P Rip Coleman P Tom Morgan P Mickey McDermott 2B Milt Graff OF Irv Noren (New York received Roberts on April 4, and Boyer on June 4, 1957.)	New York Yankees	P Art Ditmar P Bobby Shantz P Jack McMahan 1B Wayne Belardi 2B Curt Roberts 3B Clete Boyer
April 5, 1957	P Jack Urban	New York Yankees	Continuation of Billy Hunter trade of February 19, 1957.
June 15, 1957	2B Billy Martin P Ralph Terry OF Woodie Held	New York Yankees	P Ryne Duren OF Jim Pisoni OF Harry Simpson
Aug 1, 1957	Cash	Detroit Tigers	OF Johnny Groth
Aug 27, 1957	P Al Aber	Detroit Tigers	Waiver price
Aug 31, 1957	Waiver price	St. Louis Cardinals	OF Irv Noren

DATE	ACQUIRED	FROM	IN EXCHANGE FOR
Nov 20, 1957	OF Bill Tuttle OF Jim Small P Duke Maas P John Tsitouris C Frank House 1B Kent Hadley 1B Jim McManus	Detroit Tigers	2B Billy Martin OF Gus Zernial P Tom Morgan OF Lou Skizas P Mickey McDermott C Tim Thompson
April 17, 1958	P Buddy Daley	Cleveland Indians	P Arnie Portocarrero
May 14, 1958	OF Whitey Herzog	Washington Senators	Cash
June 12, 1958	SS Chico Carrasquel	Cleveland Indians	SS Billy Hunter
June 15, 1958	OF Roger Maris P Dick Tomanek 1B Preston Ward	Cleveland Indians	OF Woodie Held 1B Vic Power
June 15, 1958	P Bob Grim OF Harry Simpson	New York Yankees	P Duke Maas P Virgil Trucks
June 23, 1958	Waiver price	Cincinnati Reds	P Alex Kellner
Aug 22, 1958	OF Zeke Bella and cash	New York Yankees	P Murry Dickson
Oct 2, 1958	OF Dick Williams	Baltimore Orioles	SS Chico Carrasquel
April 8, 1959	P Mark Freeman	New York Yankees	P Jack Urban
	(Freeman was returned to the Yankees on May 8, 1959.)		
April 12, 1959	OF Russ Snyder SS Tommy Carroll	New York Yankees	IF Mike Baxes OF Bob Martyn
May 2, 1959	3B Ray Boone	Chicago White Sox	OF Harry Simpson
May 9, 1959	P Murry Dickson	New York Yankees	Cash
May 26, 1959	P Johnny Kucks P Tom Sturdivant 2B Jerry Lumpe	New York Yankees	OF Hector Lopez P Ralph Terry
Aug 20, 1959	3B Ray Jablonski	St. Louis Cardinals	Waiver price
Aug 20, 1959	Waiver price	Milwaukee Braves	1B Ray Boone
Sept 6, 1959	Waiver price	Baltimore Orioles	P Rip Coleman
Oct 12, 1959	P Bob Trowbridge	Milwaukee Braves	Cash
Nov 21, 1959	P Tom Acker	Cincinnati Reds	C Frank House
Dec 3, 1959	C Pete Daley	Boston Red Sox	P Tom Sturdivant
Dec 11, 1959	OF Hank Bauer P Don Larsen OF Norm Siebern	New York Yankees	OF Roger Maris SS Joe DeMaestri 1B Kent Hadley
Dec 15, 1959	C Hank Foiles	Pittsburgh Pirates	Cash

DATE		ACQUIRED	FROM		IN EXCHANGE FOR
Dec 15, 1959	2B P	Ken Hamlin Dick Hall	Pittsburgh Pirates	C	Hal Smith
April 5, 1960	P	Leo Kiely	Cleveland Indians	P	Bob Grim
May 11, 1960	P	Bob Giggie	Milwaukee Braves	P	George Brunet
May 19, 1960	3B	Andy Carey	New York Yankees	OF	Bob Cerv
June 1, 1960	C	Danny Kravitz	Pittsburgh Pirates	C	Hank Foiles Cash
July 26, 1960		Cash	Detroit Tigers	C	Harry Chiti
July 30, 1960	P	Johnny Briggs	Cleveland Indians		Cash
Oct 15, 1960	C	Dutch Dotterer	Cincinnati Reds	C	Danny Kravitz
Dec 29, 1960	C	Haywood Sullivan	Washington Senators	P	Marty Kutyna and cash
Jan 24, 1961	3B P 1B OF	Wayne Causey Jim Archer Bob Boyd Al Pilarcik	Baltimore Orioles	OF OF	Whitey Herzog Russ Snyder
Jan 31, 1961	C	Joe Pignatano	Los Angeles Dodgers		Cash
March 30, 1961	P	Ed Rakow	Los Angeles Dodgers	P	Howie Reed and cash
May 3, 1961		Cash	Cleveland Indians	OF	Chuck Essegian
June 1, 1961	P 3B	Paul Giel Reno Bertoia (Giel was returned to Minnesota for a cash payment.)	Minnesota Twins	OF	Bill Tuttle
June 8, 1961	OF	Gene Stephens	Baltimore Orioles	1B	Marv Throneberry
June 10, 1961	OF P P OF	Wes Covington Bob Shaw Gerry Staley Stan Johnson	Chicago White Sox	P	Ray Herbert
June 10, 1961		Cash	Milwaukee Braves	1B P 3B OF	Bob Boyd Don Larsen Andy Carey Al Pilarcik
July 2, 1961	OF	Bobby Del Greco	Philadelphia Phillies	OF	Wes Covington
July 21, 1961	P	Mickey McDermott	St. Louis Cardinals		Cash
July 21, 1961		Cash	Cincinnati Reds	P	Ken Johnson
Aug 2, 1961	3B P	Ozzie Virgil Bill Fischer	Detroit Tigers	P 3B	Gerry Staley Reno Bertoia
Oct 11, 1961		Cash	Baltimore Orioles	P	Johnny Kucks

DATE		ACQUIRED	FROM		IN EXCHANGE FOR
April 10, 1962	P	Danny McDevitt	Minnesota Twins		Cash
May 7, 1962	OF	George Alusik	Detroit Tigers		Cash
May 12, 1962	3B	Marlan Coughtry	Los Angeles Angels	OF	Gordie Windhorn
June 26, 1962	IF	Billy Consolo	Los Angeles Angels		Cash
July 2, 1962		Cash	Cleveland Indians	3B	Marlan Coughtry
Aug 13, 1962	P	Moe Drabowsky	Cincinnati Reds		Cash
Nov 30, 1962	P	Ted Bowsfield	Los Angeles Angels	P	Dan Osinski
Feb 27, 1963	OF	Chuck Essegian	Cleveland Indians	P	Jerry Walker
May 23, 1963	P	Tom Sturdivant	Detroit Tigers		Cash
May 25, 1963	C	Doc Edwards and $100,000.	Cleveland Indians	C SS	Joe Azcue Dick Howser
July 1, 1963	C	Charlie Lau	Baltimore Orioles		Cash
July 23, 1963	OF	Gordie Windhorn	Los Angeles Angels	P	Dan Osinski
Nov 18, 1963	OF P	Rocky Colavito Bob Anderson and $50,000.	Detroit Tigers	2B P P	Jerry Lumpe Ed Rakow Dave Wickersham
Nov 27, 1963	1B	Jim Gentile and cash	Baltimore Orioles	1B	Norm Siebern
Dec 15, 1963	OF	Nelson Mathews	Chicago Cubs	P	Fred Norman
June 15, 1964	P	Wes Stock	Baltimore Orioles	C	Charlie Lau
July 29, 1964	P	Bob Meyer	Los Angeles Angels		Cash
Jan 20, 1965	OF OF P	Jim Landis Mike Hershberger Fred Talbot (Part of three-team trade involving Kansas City, Cleveland, and Chicago White Sox.)	Chicago White Sox	OF	Rocky Colavito
Feb 15, 1965		Waiver price	Cleveland Indians	P	Bill Edgerton
April 9, 1965	P	Bill Edgerton	Cleveland Indians		Waiver price
May 3, 1965	C P	Johnny Blanchard Rollie Sheldon	New York Yankees	C	Doc Edwards
June 4, 1965	P 2B	Jess Hickman Ernie Fazio (Kansas City received Fazio on October 15.)	Houston Astros	1B	Jim Gentile
June 23, 1965		Cash	Detroit Tigers	P	Orlando Pena

DATE		ACQUIRED	FROM		IN EXCHANGE FOR
Sept 9, 1965		Cash	Milwaukee Braves	C	Johnny Blanchard
Oct 1, 1965	C OF	Phil Roof Joe Rudi	Cleveland Indians	OF	Jim Landis
April 6, 1966	P	Ralph Terry	Cleveland Indians	P	John O'Donoghue and cash
April 13, 1966		Cash	Washington Senators	P	Diego Segui
May 11, 1966	OF	Joe Nossek	Minnesota Twins		Cash
May 17, 1966		Cash	Houston Astros	P	Aurelio Monteagudo
May 27, 1966	1B	Danny Cater	Chicago White Sox	3B	Wayne Causey
June 10, 1966	P OF P	Gil Blanco Roger Repoz Bill Stafford	New York Yankees	P C	Fred Talbot Billy Bryan
June 13, 1966	OF P P	Jim Gosger Ken Sanders Guido Grilli	Boston Red Sox	P P OF	John Wyatt Rollie Sheldon Jose Tartabull
June 23, 1966	P	Jim Duckworth	Washington Senators	OF	Ken Harrelson
July 30, 1966	P	Diego Segui	Washington Senators	P	Jim Duckworth
Aug 6, 1966		Cash	New York Mets	P	Ralph Terry
Oct 14, 1966		Waiver price	New York Mets	OF	Larry Stahl
May 10, 1967	OF	Larry Elliot and $50,000.	New York Mets	3B	Ed Charles
June 9, 1967	OF	Ken Harrelson	Washington Senators		Cash
June 15, 1967	P OF	Jack Sanford Jackie Warner	California Angels	OF	Roger Repoz
Aug 14, 1967		Cash	New York Mets	P	Joe Grzenda
Oct 20, 1967	OF P	Floyd Robinson Darrell Osteen	Cincinnati Reds	P	Ron Tompkins

Kansas City Royals

The Best Trades

1. Acquired Amos Otis and Bob Johnson from the New York Mets for Joe Foy, December 3, 1969.
2. Acquired Freddie Patek, Bruce Dal Canton, and Jerry May from the Pittsburgh Pirates

for Bob Johnson, Jackie Hernandez, and Jim Campanis, December 2, 1970.

3. Acquired Hal McRae and Wayne Simpson from the Cincinnati Reds for Richie Scheinblum and Roger Nelson, November 30, 1972.
4. Acquired Larry Gura from the New York Yankees for Fran Healy, May 16, 1976.
5. Acquired John Mayberry and Dave Grangaard from the Houston Astros for Jim York and Lance Clemons, December 2, 1971.

The Worst Trades

1. Traded Lou Piniella and Ken Wright to the New York Yankees for Lindy McDaniel, December 7, 1973.
2. Traded Greg Minton to the San Francisco Giants for Fran Healy, April 2, 1973.
3. Traded Atlee Hammaker, Brad Wellman, Renie Martin, and Craig Chamberlain to the San Francisco Giants for Vida Blue and Bob Tufts, March 30, 1982.
4. Traded Tom Burgmeier to the Minnesota Twins for Ken Gill, October 24, 1973.
5. Traded Bill Laskey and Rich Gale to the San Francisco Giants for Jerry Martin, December 11, 1981.

Trader: Cedric Tallis

Of all the expansion teams created through the '60s and '70s, the Kansas City Royals have had the greatest success. The Royals drafted smartly, built impressively, and pulled off some of the most remarkable trades of the past fifteen years. Their rapid rise owes much to the trading record of their first general manager, Cedric Tallis.

Expansion teams have too often tried to begin with aging stars in the hope of filling the seats while developing a farm system. The Royals knew better than to trade for such players; they focussed on the rising young players who were, for one reason or other, unwanted by their teams. They could have been unwanted because their position was already filled, or because they were seen as potential troublemakers; either way, the Royals would find themselves with a good ballplayer at very low cost.

Tallis's first big trade was the acquisition of Lou Piniella from the Seattle Pilots for Steve Whitaker and John Gelnar. All Piniella did for them was bat .282 and win the Rookie of the Year Award. That December Tallis pulled off his biggest heist, unloading third baseman Joe Foy to the Mets for Amos Otis. The Mets were blind to Otis's potential as an outfielder, since they were trying to pound him into their third base hole. Otis solved the Royals' center field questions for thirteen solid seasons.

Six months later, Tallis went shopping for a double play combination. He lifted second baseman Cookie Rojas from St. Louis for minor leaguer Fred Rico, and the following December got shortstop Freddie Patek from Pittsburgh in a six-player deal. Rojas and Patek anchored the Royals' infield for the next five seasons, until Frank White was ready to take over at second. Their next need was for a big power hitter in the heart of the lineup; enter John Mayberry, picked up from Houston for two very minor pitchers, Jim York and Lance Clemons. Still need more offense? How about Hal McRae? The man who now holds almost all the career designated hitter records cost Kansas City pitcher Roger Nelson and outfielder Richie Scheinblum.

Tallis was mysteriously dismissed on June 11, 1974, and Joe Burke was given the job. Under Burke, the Royals have tended to emphasize stability, building the club from the farm system (though the very good trades that brought them Willie Aikens and Larry Gura, as well as the very bad one that brought them Vida Blue, are exceptions). This has been a luxury that the Royals could afford thanks to the foundation laid for the franchise by Tallis's extraordinary hot streak.

DATE		ACQUIRED	FROM		IN EXCHANGE FOR
Oct 17, 1968	1B	Chuck Harrison	Houston Astros		Cash
Oct 18, 1968	P	John Gelnar	Pittsburgh Pirates		Cash
Oct 21, 1968	P	Dave Wickersham	Pittsburgh Pirates		Cash
Dec 5, 1968	C	Jim Campanis	Los Angeles Dodgers		Two minor leaguers
Dec 12, 1968	OF-C C	Ed Kirkpatrick Dennis Paepke	California Angels	P	Hoyt Wilhelm
Dec 16, 1968	C C	Buck Martinez Tommy Smith and minor league IF Mickey Sinnerud	Houston Astros		Minor league C John Jones
March 25, 1969	2B	Juan Rios	Montreal Expos		Cash
April 1, 1969	OF	Lou Piniella	Seattle Pilots	OF P	Steve Whitaker John Gelnar
Oct 21, 1969	OF	Ron Tompkins	Atlanta Braves	P	Dave Wickersham
Dec 3, 1969	3B P	Amos Otis Bob Johnson	New York Mets	3B	Joe Foy
May 28, 1970	IF	Tommy Matchick	Boston Red Sox	1B	Mike Fiore
June 13, 1970	2B	Cookie Rojas	St. Louis Cardinals	OF	Fred Rico
June 15, 1970	IF	Bobby Floyd	Baltimore Orioles	P	Moe Drabowsky
July 1, 1970	P	Ted Abernathy	St. Louis Cardinals	P	Chris Zachary
Sept 15, 1970		Cash	Milwaukee Brewers	IF	Juan Rios
Oct 13, 1970	1B OF	Gail Hopkins John Matias	Chicago White Sox	OF P	Pat Kelly Don O'Riley
Dec 2, 1970	SS P C	Freddie Patek Bruce Dal Canton Jerry May	Pittsburgh Pirates	P SS C	Bob Johnson Jackie Hernandez Jim Campanis
Feb 2, 1971	OF	Carl Taylor	Milwaukee Brewers	C	Elly Rodriguez
March 15, 1971		Cash	New York Mets	OF	George Spriggs
March 24, 1971	2B	Bobby Knoop	Chicago White Sox	IF	Luis Alcaraz and cash
May 11, 1971	OF	Ted Savage	Milwaukee Brewers	IF	Tommy Matchick
Sept 3, 1971		Cash	Pittsburgh Pirates	OF	Carl Taylor
Sept 13, 1971		Cash	St. Louis Cardinals	P	Mike Jackson
Dec 2, 1971	1B	John Mayberry minor league IF Dave Grangaard	Houston Astros	P P	Jim York Lance Clemons
May 5, 1972	P	Tom Murphy	California Angels	1B	Bob Oliver

DATE		ACQUIRED	FROM		IN EXCHANGE FOR
July 10, 1972	OF	Jim Clark	Cleveland Indians	P	Tom Hilgendorf
July 11, 1972		Cash	Cleveland Indians	P	Bill Butler
Oct 25, 1972	P	Gene Garber	Pittsburgh Pirates	P	Jim Rooker
Nov 2, 1972	IF	Kurt Bevacqua	Cleveland Indians	P	Mike Hedlund
Nov 30, 1972	OF P	Hal McRae Wayne Simpson	Cincinnati Reds	P OF	Roger Nelson Richie Scheinblum
Feb 1, 1973	OF	Jim Lyttle	Chicago White Sox	OF	Joe Keough
April 2, 1973	C	Fran Healy	San Francisco Giants	P	Greg Minton
May 14, 1973		Cash	New York Mets	C	Jerry May
July 10, 1973		Cash	Montreal Expos	OF	Jim Lyttle
July 18, 1973	P	Joe Hoerner	Atlanta Braves		Cash
Oct 24, 1973		Minor leaguer Ken Gill	Minnesota Twins	P	Tom Burgmeier
Oct 24, 1973	P	Marty Pattin	Boston Red Sox	P	Dick Drago
Dec 4, 1973	P IF	Nellie Briles Fernando Gonzalez	Pittsburgh Pirates	C IF	Ed Kirkpatrick Kurt Bevacqua minor league 1B Winston Cole
Dec 7, 1973	P	Lindy McDaniel	New York Yankees	OF P	Lou Piniella Ken Wright
Dec 10, 1973	SS	Buddy Hunter	Boston Red Sox		Cash
Feb 23, 1974	OF	Vada Pinson	California Angels	P	Barry Raziano and cash
March 28, 1974	P	Jim Foor	Pittsburgh Pirates	P	Wayne Simpson
April 30, 1974	OF	Richie Scheinblum	California Angels	3B	Paul Schaal
May 5, 1974		Cash	New York Yankees	IF	Fernando Gonzalez
July 8, 1974	IF	Kurt Bevacqua	Pittsburgh Pirates		Minor league IF Cal Meier and cash
Aug 5, 1974		Cash	St. Louis Cardinals	OF	Richie Scheinblum
March 6, 1975		Cash	Milwaukee Brewers	UT	Kurt Bevacqua
March 31, 1975	C	Bob Stinson	Montreal Expos		Cash
June 30, 1975	P	Ray Sadecki and cash	Atlanta Braves	P	Bruce Dal Canton

(Two minor league pitchers were assigned to Atlanta farm team on September 4, 1975 to complete the trade.)

DATE		ACQUIRED	FROM		IN EXCHANGE FOR
Nov 12, 1975	2B	Dave Nelson	Texas Rangers	P	Nellie Briles
Dec 12, 1975		Cash	Montreal Expos	2B	Rodney Scott
May 7, 1976	P	Tom Hall	New York Mets		Minor league IF Bryan Jones and cash
May 16, 1976	P	Larry Gura	New York Yankees	C	Fran Healy
July 5, 1976	P	Andy Hassler	California Angels		Cash
July 14, 1976		Cash	California Angels	1B	Tony Solaita
Sept 17, 1976	P	Ken Sanders	New York Mets		Cash
Sept 20, 1976	OF	Tommy Davis	California Angels		Cash
Dec 6, 1976	P C	Jim Colborn Darrell Porter	Milwaukee Brewers	OF C P	Jim Wohlford Jamie Quirk Bob McClure
Dec 6, 1976	IF	Bob Heise	Boston Red Sox		Cash
Dec 8, 1976	1B	Pete LaCock	Chicago Cubs	OF	Sheldon Mallory
		(Part of three-team trade involving Kansas City, Chicago Cubs, and New York Mets.)			
Dec 8, 1977	P	Al Hrabosky	St. Louis Cardinals	P C	Mark Littell Buck Martinez
April 4, 1978		Cash	Toronto Blue Jays	1B	John Mayberry
June 1, 1978	OF	Steve Braun	Seattle Mariners	P	Jim Colborn
June 5, 1978		Minor league P Steve Hamrick	San Diego Padres	P	Gary Lance
July 24, 1978		Cash	Boston Red Sox	P	Andy Hassler
Aug 3, 1978	C	Jamie Quirk	Milwaukee Brewers		Minor league P Gerry Ako and cash
Aug 16, 1978	P	Steve Foucault	Detroit Tigers		Cash
Feb 26, 1979	P	Ed Rodriguez	Milwaukee Brewers		Cash
April 3, 1979	SS	Todd Cruz	Philadelphia Phillies	P	Doug Bird
April 27, 1979	2B	Keith Drumright	Houston Astros	P	George Throop
June 13, 1979	1B	George Scott	Boston Red Sox	OF	Tom Poquette
Oct 24, 1979	P	Lance Rautzhan	Milwaukee Brewers		Minor league OF Kevin Gillen

DATE		ACQUIRED	FROM		IN EXCHANGE FOR
Nov 20, 1979		No compensation (free agent signing)	Atlanta Braves	P	Al Hrabosky
Dec 5, 1979		No compensation (free agent signing)	California Angels	SS	Freddie Patek
Dec 6, 1979	IF 1B	Rance Mulliniks Willie Aikens	California Angels	OF SS P	Al Cowens Todd Cruz Craig Eaton
Jan 15, 1980	P	Ed Bane	Chicago White Sox	OF	Joe Zdeb
June 17, 1980	P	Kevin Kobel	New York Mets	P	Randy McGilberry
Dec 9, 1980	1B	Lee Maye	Baltimore Orioles		No compensation (free agent signing)
Dec 13, 1980		No compensation (free agent signing)	St. Louis Cardinals	C	Darrell Porter
Jan 21, 1981	OF	Cesar Geronimo	Cincinnati Reds	IF	German Barranca
Feb 5, 1981	C	Jerry Grote	Los Angeles Dodgers		No compensation (free agent signing)
March 31, 1981	P	Juan Berenguer	New York Mets	OF	Marvell Wynne minor league P John Skinner
Aug 8, 1981		Cash	Toronto Blue Jays	P	Juan Berenguer
Oct 23, 1981	P	Bud Black	Seattle Mariners	3B	Manny Castillo
Dec 11, 1981	P	Scott Brown	Cincinnati Reds	OF	Clint Hurdle
Dec 11, 1981	OF	Jerry Martin	San Francisco Giants	P P	Rich Gale Juan Espino
Jan 14, 1982	P	Grant Jackson	Montreal Expos	1B	Ken Phelps
Jan 15, 1982	OF	Tom Poquette	Texas Rangers		No compensation (free agent signing)
Feb 20, 1982	P	Dave Frost	California Angels		No compensation (free agent signing)
March 24, 1982	1B	Dennis Werth	New York Yankees		Minor league P Scott Behan
March 24, 1982	IF	Greg Pryor	Chicago White Sox	P	Jeff Schattinger
March 25, 1982	P	Phil Huffman	Toronto Blue Jays	SS	Rance Mulliniks
March 30, 1982	P P	Vida Blue Bob Tufts	San Francisco Giants	P P P 2B	Renie Martin Craig Chamberlain Atlee Hammaker Brad Wellman
April 4, 1982	P	Mike Armstrong	San Diego Padres		Cash
April 28, 1982	OF	Steve Hammond	Atlanta Braves		Cash
Jan 28, 1983		No compensation (free agent signing)	St. Louis Cardinals	C	Jamie Quirk

DATE		ACQUIRED	FROM		IN EXCHANGE FOR
Feb 5, 1983	OF	Leon Roberts	Toronto Blue Jays		Minor league 1B Cecil Fielder
Feb 9, 1983	P	Steve Renko	California Angels		No compensation (free agent signing)
Aug 2, 1983	P	Eric Rasmussen	St. Louis Cardinals		Cash
Dec 7, 1983	1B P	Steve Balboni Roger Erickson	New York Yankees	P	Mike Armstrong minor league C Duane Dewey
Dec 7, 1983	P	Joe Beckwith	Los Angeles Dodgers		Minor leaguers C Joe Szeneley P Jose Torres and P John Serritella
Dec 19, 1983		No compensation (free agent signing)	Pittsburgh Pirates	OF	Amos Otis
Dec 20, 1983	OF	Jorge Orta	Toronto Blue Jays	1B	Willie Aikens
March 30, 1984	P	Alan Hargesheimer and a player to be named later	Chicago Cubs	C P	Don Werner Dick Botelho
April 1, 1984	3B	Tucker Ashford	New York Mets		Minor league P Tom Edens

Los Angeles Angels

DATE		ACQUIRED	FROM		IN EXCHANGE FOR
Jan 3, 1961	P	Tom Morgan	Washington Senators		Cash
Jan 4, 1961	IF	Leo Burke	Washington Senators		Cash
Jan 26, 1961	OF P OF	Leon Wagner Cal Browning Ellis Burton and cash	St. Louis Cardinals	P	Al Cicotte
April 1, 1961	OF	Lou Johnson	Chicago Cubs	OF	Jim McAnany
April 7, 1961	P	Ray Semproch	Washington Senators		Cash
April 10, 1961	P	Ron Kline	St. Louis Cardinals		Cash
May 8, 1961	OF P P	Lee Thomas Ryne Duren Johnny James	New York Yankees	P OF	Tex Clevenger Bob Cerv
June 5, 1961	P	Russ Heman	Cleveland Indians		Cash
June 7, 1961	P	Jim Donohue	Detroit Tigers	P	Jerry Casale
June 26, 1961	OF	George Thomas	Detroit Tigers		Cash

DATE		ACQUIRED	FROM		IN EXCHANGE FOR
Aug 10, 1961		Waiver price	Detroit Tigers	P	Ron Kline
Oct 10, 1961	P	George Witt	Pittsburgh Pirates		Cash
March 30, 1962	1B	Frank Leja	St. Louis Cardinals		Cash
May 8, 1962	IF	Billy Consolo	Philadelphia Phillies		Cash
May 12, 1962	OF	Gordie Windhorn	Kansas City Athletics	3B	Marlan Coughtry
May 29, 1962	P	Don Lee	Minnesota Twins	P	Jim Donohue
June 26, 1962		Cash	Kansas City Athletics	IF	Billy Consolo
Sept 10, 1962		Cash	Baltimore Orioles	C	Nate Smith
Oct 29, 1962	P	Bob Turley	New York Yankees		Cash
Nov 30, 1962	P	Dan Osinski	Kansas City Athletics	P	Ted Bowsfield
Dec 11, 1962	OF	Jacke Davis	Philadelphia Phillies	C	Earl Averill
March 14, 1963		Cash	Philadelphia Phillies	P	Ryne Duren
March 25, 1963		Cash	St. Louis Cardinals	IF	Leo Burke
March 29, 1963	1B	Charlie Dees	San Francisco Giants	OF	Jacke Davis
June 15, 1963	P	Paul Foytack	Detroit Tigers	OF 3B	George Thomas and cash Frank Kostro
July 23, 1963	P	Dan Osinski	Kansas City Athletics	OF	Gordie Windhorn
Sept 12, 1963		Cash	Washington Senators	OF	Ken Hunt
Dec 2, 1963	1B P	Joe Adcock Barry Latman	Cleveland Indians	OF	Leon Wagner
April 28, 1964	P-OF	Willie Smith	Detroit Tigers	P	Julio Navarro
May 15, 1964		Cash	Chicago Cubs	P	Jack Spring
June 4, 1964	OF	Lu Clinton	Boston Red Sox	OF	Lee Thomas
June 11, 1964	SS	Billy Moran	Cleveland Indians	2B	Jerry Kindall
		(Part of three-team trade involving Los Angeles Angels, Cleveland, and Minnesota.)			
June 11, 1964	OF 1B	Lenny Green Vic Power	Minnesota Twins	SS OF	Billy Moran Frank Kostro
		(Part of three-team trade involving Los Angeles Angels, Minnesota, and Cleveland.)			
June 12, 1964	P	Bob Meyer	New York Yankees		Cash

DATE		ACQUIRED	FROM		IN EXCHANGE FOR
July 29, 1964		Cash	Kansas City Athletics	P	Bob Meyer
Aug 18, 1964	P	George Brunet	Houston Astros		Cash
Sept 5, 1964		Cash	Baltimore Orioles	OF	Lenny Green
Sept 9, 1964	P	Marcelino Lopez and cash	Philadelphia Phillies	1B	Vic Power
Oct 14, 1964	C P	Phil Roof Ron Piche	Milwaukee Braves	P	Dan Osinski
Oct 15, 1964	P	Larry Locke	Philadelphia Phillies		Cash
Nov 21, 1964	OF	Jose Cardenal	San Francisco Giants	C	Jack Hiatt
Nov 30, 1964	1B	Vic Power	Philadelphia Phillies		Cash
Dec 3, 1964	1B P	Costen Shockley Rudy May	Philadelphia Phillies	P	Bo Belinsky

Milwaukee Brewers

The Best Trades

1. Acquired Cecil Cooper from the Boston Red Sox for George Scott and Bernie Carbo, December 6, 1976.
2. Acquired Rollie Fingers, Pete Vuckovich, and Ted Simmons from the St. Louis Cardinals for Sixto Lezcano, David Green, Lary Sorensen, and Dave LaPoint, December 12, 1980.
3. Acquired Ben Oglivie from the Detroit Tigers for Jim Slaton and Rich Folkers, December 9, 1977.
4. Acquired Mike Caldwell from the Cincinnati Reds for Dick O'Keefe and Garry Pyka, June 15, 1977.

The Worst Trades

1. Traded Darrell Porter and Jim Colborn to the Kansas City Royals for Bob McClure, Jim Wohlford, and Jamie Quirk, December 6, 1976.
2. Traded Al Downing to the Los Angeles Dodgers for Andy Kosco, February 10, 1971.
3. Traded Frank DiPino, Mike Madden, Kevin Bass, and cash to the Houston Astros for Don Sutton, August 30, 1982.

Trader: Harry Dalton and The Deal

Writers dubbed the 1982 World Series the six-pack series in honor of those foaming metropolises, St. Louis and Milwaukee. But the series was actually brewed in December 1980 when the two clubs consummated one of the biggest trades of recent years, with Rollie Fingers, Pete Vuckovich, and Ted Simmons going to Milwaukee, and Sixto Lezcano, Lary Sorenson, Dave LaPoint, and David Green heading to the Cardinals.

The trade proved to be one of those rare transactions that really does help both clubs. The Brewers would never have won their half-title without Fingers in '81, or made it to the Series without Vuckovich and Simmons in '82. The Cardinals dealt Sorenson and Lezcano in trades that netted them Ozzie and Lonnie Smith, and they expect Green and LaPoint to play key roles for them through the '80s.

At the time of the trade, Milwaukee desperately needed a reliever. They had gone as far as their hitting could carry them, finishing third in 1980, and felt their greatest need was a man who could shut teams down in the late innings. They wanted either Fingers of the Padres or Bruce Sutter of the Cubs, but Whitey Herzog struck first, and quickly acquired both. "We knew the Cardinals wouldn't keep both," recalls Harry Dalton, the Brewers' general manager. "That's when we started talking about Fingers. We were also seeking another starting pitcher and a catcher with some power, and we knew that Vuckovich and Simmons might be available." The Cardinals had just signed Darrell Porter, and Simmons was very unhappy about Herzog's plans to move him to first base.

The deal was held up for several days by Herzog's insistence that David Green be part of the deal. Scouts were touting Green as a talent on the level of a Roberto Clemente, and Dalton was loath to give him up. But he reluctantly agreed after learning that the Yankees were also taking a long look at Simmons and Vuckovich.

It took a few years for Green to establish himself in the Cardinal lineup, but the new Brewers paid instant dividends. Fingers won both the Cy Young and Most Valuable Player Awards in strike-shortened '81, and Vuckovich took Cy Young honors in '82, compiling a 32–10 record in the two seasons. Arm woes have kept both Vuckovich and Fingers inactive since '82, but Simmons has kept on hitting, crashing 23 homers and driving in 97 runs in '82, and cracked the top ten in batting in '83 with his .308 average.

But productive trades are nothing new to Dalton. As director of player personnel for the Orioles in the 1960s, he engineered the trade that brought Frank Robinson and a world championship to Baltimore. After leaving the O's to take a position with the California Angels, one of his first moves was to acquire Nolan Ryan. And his first deal after joining Milwaukee was to send pitchers Jim Slaton and Rich Folkers to Detroit for outfielder Ben Oglivie. His enviable record makes picking up back-to-back Cy Young Award winners in the same deal look almost routine.

DATE	ACQUIRED	FROM	IN EXCHANGE FOR
Jan 15, 1970	OF Mike Hershberger P Lew Krausse C Phil Roof P Ken Sanders	Oakland Athletics	1B Don Mincher IF Ron Clark
April 4, 1970	3B Max Alvis OF Russ Snyder	Cleveland Indians	OF Roy Foster IF Frank Coggins and cash
April 5, 1970	OF Ted Savage	Cincinnati Reds	Cash
May 11, 1970	OF Hank Allen IF Ron Theobald	Washington Senators	OF Wayne Comer
May 18, 1970	IF Roberto Pena	Oakland Athletics	2B John Donaldson
June 9, 1970	OF-1B Bob Burda	San Francisco Giants	Cash
June 11, 1970	P Al Downing OF Tito Francona	Oakland Athletics	OF Steve Hovley
June 15, 1970	Cash	Montreal Expos	P John O'Donoghue

DATE		ACQUIRED	FROM		IN EXCHANGE FOR
June 15, 1970	OF	Dave May	Baltimore Orioles	P P	Dick Baney Buzz Stephen
June 15, 1970		Cash	Oakland Athletics	P	Bob Locker
June 26, 1970		Cash	Boston Red Sox	1B	John Kennedy
Aug 7, 1970	P	Dick Ellsworth	Cleveland Indians		Cash
Sept 10, 1970		Cash	Boston Red Sox	P	Bobby Bolin
Sept 15, 1970	IF	Juan Rios	Kansas City Royals		Cash
Oct 20, 1970	OF P	Carl Taylor Jim Ellis	St. Louis Cardinals	C P	Jerry McNertney George Lauzerique minor league P Jesse Higgins
Dec 2, 1970	C	Bob Tillman	Atlanta Braves	OF	Hank Allen minor leaguers P Paul Click and IF John Ryan
Jan 28, 1971	OF	Bill Voss	California Angels	P	Gene Brabender
Feb 2, 1971		Minor league P Fred Reahm	St. Louis Cardinals	1B	Bob Burda
Feb 2, 1971	C	Elly Rodriguez	Kansas City Royals	OF	Carl Taylor
Feb 10, 1971	OF	Andy Kosco	Los Angeles Dodgers	P	Al Downing
April 5, 1971	P	Marcelino Lopez	Baltimore Orioles	P	Roric Harrison and minor leaguer Marion Jackson
April 22, 1971	OF	John Briggs	Philadelphia Phillies	P OF	Ray Peters Pete Koegel
May 11, 1971	IF	Tommy Matchick	Kansas City Royals	OF	Ted Savage
May 11, 1971	P	Jim Hannan	Detroit Tigers	P IF	John Gelnar Jose Herrera
June 1, 1971	IF	Bob Heise	San Francisco Giants	OF	Floyd Wicker
June 7, 1971	1B OF	Frank Tepedino Bobby Mitchell	New York Yankees	OF	Danny Walton
June 14, 1971		Cash	Oakland Athletics	1B	Mike Hegan
June 30, 1971	P	Floyd Weaver	Chicago White Sox		Cash
July 8, 1971	C	Paul Ratliff	Minnesota Twins	C	Phil Roof
July 29, 1971	OF IF P	Jose Cardenal Dick Schofield Bob Reynolds	St. Louis Cardinals	IF	Ted Kubiak minor league P Charlie Loseth

DATE		ACQUIRED	FROM		IN EXCHANGE FOR
Oct 11, 1971	OF	Billy Conigliaro	Boston	P	Marty Pattin
	OF	Joe LaHoud	Red Sox	P	Lew Krausse
	P	Jim Lonborg		OF	Tommy Harper
	P	Ken Brett		OF	Pat Skrable
	1B	George Scott			
	C	Don Pavletich			
Dec 3, 1971	OF	Brock Davis	Chicago	OF	Jose Cardenal
	P	Jim Colborn	Cubs		
	P	Earl Stephenson			
Dec 9, 1971	OF	Curt Motton	Baltimore	P	Bob Reynolds
			Orioles		and cash
Jan 26, 1972	OF	Tommie Reynolds	California	1B	Andy Kosco
			Angels		
Feb 8, 1972	IF	Bobby Pfeil	Philadelphia		Minor league
			Phillies		3B Chico Vaughns
March 20, 1972		Cash	Boston	OF	Bobby Pfeil
			Red Sox		
March 26, 1972	P	Frank Linzy	St. Louis		Minor league
			Cardinals		P Rich Stonum
March 29, 1972		Cash	Cleveland	P	Marcelino Lopez
			Indians		
June 20, 1972	OF	Ron Clark	Oakland	OF	Bill Voss
			Athletics		
June 29, 1972	OF	Ollie Brown	Oakland		Cash
			Athletics		
July 28, 1972	IF	Syd O'Brien	California	C	Paul Ratliff
	C	Joe Azcue	Angels	OF	Ron Clark
Sept 13, 1972	P	Chuck Taylor	New York		Cash
			Mets		
Oct 31, 1972	3B	Don Money	Philadelphia	P	Jim Lonborg
	IF	John Vukovich	Phillies	P	Ken Sanders
	P	Billy Champion		P	Ken Brett
				P	Earl Stephenson
Feb 14, 1973		Cash	Oakland	OF	Billy Conigliaro
			Athletics		
March 27, 1973	P	Ken Reynolds	Minnesota	3B	Mike Ferraro
			Twins		
April 24, 1973	SS	Tim Johnson	Los Angeles		Cash
			Dodgers		
May 31, 1973	P	Rob Gardner	Oakland		Cash
			Athletics		
		(Deal was cancelled and Gardner was returned to Oakland.)			
Sept 4, 1973	P	Ed Sprague	St. Louis		Cash
			Cardinals		
Oct 22, 1973	P	Clyde Wright	California	C	Elly Rodriguez
	P	Steve Barber	Angels	P	Skip Lockwood
	OF	Ken Berry		P	Gary Ryerson
	C	Art Kusnyer		OF	Ollie Brown
		and cash		OF	Joe LaHoud
Oct 27, 1973		Cash	Los Angeles	SS	Rick Auerbach
			Dodgers		
Nov 7, 1973	P	Bill Wilson	Philadelphia	P	Frank Linzy
			Phillies		

DATE	ACQUIRED		FROM	IN EXCHANGE FOR	
Dec 6, 1973	P	Mike Strahler	Detroit Tigers	P	Ray Newman
Dec 7, 1973	OF	Felipe Alou	Montreal Expos		Cash
Dec 8, 1973	P	Tom Murphy	St. Louis Cardinals	IF	Bob Heise
May 13, 1974	1B	Mike Hegan	New York Yankees		Cash
June 24, 1974	1B	Deron Johnson	Oakland Athletics	P	Bill Parsons and cash
July 29, 1974	P	Dick Selma	California Angels		Cash
		(Selma was returned to California on August 12, 1974.)			
Sept 7, 1974		Cash	Boston Red Sox	1B	Deron Johnson
Oct 22, 1974	P	Pat Osborn	Cincinnati Reds	IF	John Vukovich
Nov 2, 1974	OF	Hank Aaron	Atlanta Braves	OF	Dave May minor league P Roger Alexander
Dec 5, 1974	P	Pete Broberg	Texas Rangers	P	Clyde Wright
March 6, 1975	UT	Kurt Bevacqua	Kansas City Royals		Cash
May 8, 1975	OF	Bill Sharp	Chicago White Sox	OF	Bob Coluccio
June 14, 1975	OF	Bobby Darwin	Minnesota Twins	OF	John Briggs
June 2, 1976	OF	Von Joshua	San Francisco Giants		Cash
June 3, 1976	OF	Bernie Carbo	Boston Red Sox	P OF	Tom Murphy Bobby Darwin
June 7, 1976	P	Danny Frisella	St. Louis Cardinals	OF	Sam Mejias
June 10, 1976	2B	Gary Sutherland	Detroit Tigers	2B	Pedro Garcia
June 22, 1976	IF	Jack Heidemann	New York Mets		Minor league P Tom Deidel
Nov 19, 1976	3B	Sal Bando	Oakland Athletics		No compensation (free agent signing)
Dec 6, 1976	OF C P	Jim Wohlford Jamie Quirk Bob McClure	Kansas City Royals	P C	Jim Colborn Darrell Porter
Dec 6, 1976	1B	Cecil Cooper	Boston Red Sox	1B OF	George Scott Bernie Carbo
Dec 6, 1976	C	Larry Haney	Oakland Athletics		Cash
Feb 25, 1977	3B	Ken McMullen	Oakland Athletics		Cash
March 21, 1977	OF	Steve Brye	Minnesota Twins		Cash

DATE		ACQUIRED	FROM		IN EXCHANGE FOR
March 23, 1977	P	Rich Folkers	San Diego Padres		Cash
June 15, 1977	P	Mike Caldwell	Cincinnati Reds		Minor leaguers P Dick O'Keefe and IF Garry Pyka
Aug 20, 1977	1B	Ed Kirkpatrick	Texas Rangers	OF	Gorman Thomas
Nov 17, 1977	OF	Larry Hisle	Minnesota Twins		No compensation (free agent signing)
Nov 21, 1977		No compensation (free agent signing)	New York Mets	P	Tom Hausman
Dec 8, 1977	C	Buck Martinez	St. Louis Cardinals	P	George Frazier
Dec 9, 1977	OF	Ben Oglivie	Detroit Tigers	P P	Jim Slaton Rich Folkers
Dec 15, 1977	C	Andy Etchebarren	California Angels		Cash
Feb 8, 1978	OF	Gorman Thomas	Texas Rangers		Cash
April 4, 1978	P	Andy Replogle	Baltimore Orioles		Cash
April 29, 1978	IF	Tim Nordbrook	Toronto Blue Jays	SS	Tim Johnson
May 17, 1978	OF	Dave May	Texas Rangers		Cash
Aug 3, 1978		Minor league P Gerry Ako and cash	Kansas City Royals	C	Jamie Quirk
Sept 13, 1978		Cash	Pittsburgh Pirates	OF	Dave May
Nov 29, 1978	P	Jim Slaton	Detroit Tigers		No compensation (free agent signing)
Dec 15, 1978	P	Reggie Cleveland	Texas Rangers	P 1B	Ed Farmer Gary Holle and cash
Feb 26, 1979		Cash	Kansas City Royals	P	Ed Rodriguez
March 27, 1979	1B	Skip James	San Francisco Giants		Cash
March 28, 1979	P	Danny Boitano	Philadelphia Phillies	P	Gary Beare
May 11, 1979	P	Lance Rautzhan	Los Angeles Dodgers		Cash
June 7, 1979	P	Paul Mitchell	Seattle Mariners	P	Randy Stein
Oct 24, 1979		Minor league OF Kevin Gillen	Kansas City Royals	P	Lance Rautzhan
Oct 26, 1979	P	Dwight Bernard	New York Mets	P	Mark Bomback
Nov 29, 1979		No compensation (free agent signing)	San Francisco Giants	OF	Jim Wohlford

DATE		ACQUIRED	FROM		IN EXCHANGE FOR
Dec 6, 1979	P	John Flinn	Baltimore Orioles	2B	Lenn Sakata
July 11, 1980		No compensation (free agent signing)	New York Mets	SS	Bill Almon
Sept 1, 1980	OF	John Poff	Philadelphia Phillies		Cash
Sept 22, 1980	P	Jamie Easterly	Montreal Expos		Cash
Dec 12, 1980	P P C	Pete Vuckovich Rollie Fingers Ted Simmons	St. Louis Cardinals	OF OF P P	Sixto Lezcano David Green Lary Sorensen Dave LaPoint
Dec 23, 1980	3B	Roy Howell	Toronto Blue Jays		No compensation (free agent signing)
Jan 26, 1981		No compensation (free agent signing)	California Angels	P	Bill Travers
March 1, 1981	P	Randy Lerch	Philadelphia Phillies	OF	Dick Davis
April 1, 1981	OF	Thad Bosley	Chicago White Sox	OF	John Poff
May 10, 1981	OF	Gil Kubski	Toronto Blue Jays	C	Buck Martinez
Sept 3, 1981	P	Donnie Moore	St. Louis Cardinals		Cash
Oct 23, 1981	P	Pete Ladd	Houston Astros	P	Rickey Keeton
March 5, 1982	P	Mike Parrott	Seattle Mariners	OF	Thad Bosley
May 14, 1982	SS	Rob Picciolo	Oakland Athletics	P	Mike Warren minor league 1B John Evans
Aug 11, 1982	P	Doc Medich	Texas Rangers		Cash
Aug 14, 1982		Cash	Montreal Expos	P	Randy Lerch
Aug 30, 1982	P	Don Sutton	Houston Astros	OF P P	Kevin Bass Frank DiPino Mike Madden and cash
Oct 15, 1982	P	Tom Tellmann	San Diego Padres		Minor league Ps Weldon Swift and Tim Cook
April 1, 1983		Minor league P Rich Buonotony and cash	Chicago Cubs	C	Steve Lake
June 6, 1983	OF P	Rick Manning Rick Waits	Cleveland Indians	OF P P	Gorman Thomas Jamie Easterly Ernie Camacho
Dec 8, 1983	C	Jim Sundberg	Texas Rangers	C	Ned Yost minor league P Dan Scarpetta
Dec 20, 1983	OF	Bobby Clark	California Angels	P	Jim Slaton

DATE		ACQUIRED	FROM		IN EXCHANGE FOR
Feb 6, 1984		No compensation (free agent signing)	California Angels	SS	Rob Picciolo
Feb 19, 1984	1B	Kelvin Moore	New York Mets		Minor league IF Billy Max

Minnesota Twins

The Best Trades

1. Acquired Mudcat Grant from the Cleveland Indians for Lee Stange and George Banks, June 15, 1964.
2. Acquired Larry Hisle and John Cumberland from the St. Louis Cardinals for Wayne Granger, November 29, 1972.
3. Acquired Cesar Tovar from the Cincinnati Reds for Jerry Arrigo, December 4, 1964.
4. Acquired Tom Brunansky, Mike Walters, and $400,000 from the California Angels for Doug Corbett and Rob Wilfong, May 12, 1982.
5. Acquired Roy Smalley, Bill Singer, Mike Cubbage, Jim Gedeon, and $250,000 from the Texas Rangers for Bert Blyleven and Danny Thompson, June 1, 1976.

The Worst Trades

1. Traded Rick Dempsey to the New York Yankees for Danny Walton, October 27, 1972.
2. Traded Butch Wynegar and Roger Erickson to the New York Yankees for John Pacella, Pete Filson, Larry Milbourne, and cash, May 12, 1982.
3. Traded Graig Nettles, Dean Chance, Bob Miller, and Ted Uhlaender to the Cleveland Indians for Stan Williams and Luis Tiant, December 10, 1969.
4. Traded Jim Perry to the Detroit Tigers for Dan Fife and cash, March 27, 1973.
5. Traded Dave LaRoche to the California Angels for Leo Cardenas, November 30, 1971.

Owner: Calvin Griffith

"Poor Cal Griffith," you hear all around baseball. Any day he's going to be driven out of the game by the multimillionaire owners like George Steinbrenner and Gene Autry. The Griffith family is supposed to fold its tent and give up the Twins, or at least start paying the huge salaries that others are paying out for the privilege of staying in the game.

Calvin doesn't see it that way. He thinks some of the sympathy should be reserved for the owners who are heading for bankruptcy under the weight of long-term contracts at grotesquely inflated rates. "There's no way we can make it by competing with the big-money clubs," Griffith will tell you. "We have to sign good young players and develop them fast enough to get six good years out of them before they can turn free agents under the new rules. We don't have the millions behind us to invest, as some clubs do. So we have to take what resources we have and go from there. We think we can do it, or we wouldn't be here."

One of the club's most important resources is Griffith's confidence in his scouting staff, and his own judgment of talent. He was raised in the game by the Old Fox himself, uncle Clark Griffith, beginning back in the 1920s. He has held virtually every job in baseball, starting as a batboy and working his way up as a catcher in college, a minor league manager, farm director, and finally, club president. He found a steady stream of great hitters and built the once-sorry Washington Senators squad into the perennially contending Minnesota Twins team of the '60s and early '70s.

Griffith stands firmly by the old values of building from the farm. Every year the Twins are threatened with the loss of players seeking more money. Griffith's strategy has been to deal his high-priced players before they can become free agents, replacing them with eager home-grown talent, or with the cream of other systems acquired in those trades. And even when free agents have left the Twins, few have had seasons as productive as those they left behind in Minnesota.

It is hard to imagine how a team can survive the loss of such players to free agency as Larry Hisle, Lyman Bostock, Bill Campbell, Dave Goltz, and Geoff Zahn, and the forced trading of Rod Carew, Roy Smalley, Butch Wynegar, and Doug Corbett. But Griffith has dealt shrewdly, picking up as prospects Ken Landreaux, Tom Brunansky, and Dave Engle, while the farm system was turning out Kent Hrbek, Gary Gaetti, John Castino, and Tim Teufel. Calvin's best deal may have been the one in which he sent Bert Blyleven, his unhappy right-handed pitching ace, to Texas along with shortstop Danny Thompson for a package that included Smalley, Bill Singer, Mike Cubbage, and $250,000. Blyleven lasted just one and a half seasons in Texas before being sent on to Pittsburgh, while Smalley soon developed into an All-Star shortstop, outstanding both in the field and at the plate. And when Smalley's demands became too great, Griffith sent him to the Yankees for reliever Ron Davis and a pair of youngsters, Paul Boris and Greg Gagne.

How long can Griffith last? The answer seems to be as long as the system can produce good young talent. Can he win a pennant with his methods? That's a tougher question, but with groups in Tampa and other cities hungry for major league franchises offering him fabulous sums of money, Calvin Griffith himself may turn out to be the highest-priced free agent of them all.

DATE		ACQUIRED	FROM		IN EXCHANGE FOR
June 1, 1961	2B	Billy Martin	Milwaukee Braves	IF	Billy Consolo
June 1, 1961	OF	Bill Tuttle	Kansas City Athletics	P 3B	Paul Giel Reno Bertoia
		(Giel was returned to Minnesota for a cash payment.)			
Jan 30, 1962	C	Jerry Zimmerman	Cincinnati Reds	OF	Dan Dobbek
April 2, 1962	P 1B	Dick Stigman Vic Power	Cleveland Indians	P	Pedro Ramos
April 10, 1962		Cash	Kansas City Athletics	P	Danny McDevitt
May 29, 1962	P	Jim Donohue	Los Angeles Angels	P	Don Lee
Aug 20, 1962	P	Ruben Gomez	Cleveland Indians	P P	Georges Maranda Jackie Collum and cash
April 8, 1963	P	Bill Dailey	Cleveland Indians		Cash
May 2, 1963	P	Jim Perry	Cleveland Indians	P	Jack Kralick
May 4, 1963		Cash	Philadelphia Phillies	OF	Jim Lemon
May 16, 1963	OF	Wally Post	Cincinnati Reds		Cash
June 14, 1963	P	Mike Fornieles	Boston Red Sox		Cash

DATE		ACQUIRED	FROM		IN EXCHANGE FOR
June 11, 1964	SS OF	Billy Moran Frank Kostro	Los Angeles Angels	OF 1B	Lenny Green Vic Power
		(Part of three-team trade involving Los Angeles Angels, Minnesota, and Cleveland.)			
June 15, 1964	P	Mudcat Grant	Cleveland Indians	3B P	George Banks Lee Stange
June 29, 1964	P	Johnny Klippstein	Philadelphia Phillies		Cash
Aug 7, 1964	P	Gary Kroll	Philadelphia Phillies	3B OF	Wayne Graham Frank Thomas
Oct 15, 1964	C	Ken Retzer	Washington Senators	C	Joe McCabe
Dec 4, 1964	OF	Cesar Tovar	Cincinnati Reds	P	Jerry Arrigo
April 6, 1966	C 2B	Russ Nixon Chuck Schilling	Boston Red Sox	P	Dick Stigman and minor league 1B Jose Calero
May 11, 1966		Cash	Kansas City Athletics	OF	Joe Nossek
Sept 7, 1966		Cash	Boston Red Sox	P	Garry Roggenburk
Dec 2, 1966	P SS	Dean Chance Jackie Hernandez	California Angels	OF 1B P	Jimmie Hall Don Mincher Pete Cimino
Dec 3, 1966	P	Ron Kline	Washington Senators	2B P	Bernie Allen Camilo Pascual
Nov 28, 1967	C P P	Johnny Roseboro Ron Perranoski Bob Miller	Los Angeles Dodgers	P SS	Mudcat Grant Zoilo Versalles
Nov 29, 1967	P	Joe Grzenda	New York Mets		Cash
Dec 2, 1967	1B	Bob Oliver	Pittsburgh Pirates	P	Ron Kline
Nov 21, 1968	SS	Leo Cardenas	Cincinnati Reds	P	Jim Merritt
Feb 24, 1969		Cash	Oakland Athletics	P	Jim Roland
July 8, 1969	P	Darrell Brandon	Seattle Pilots		Cash
Dec 10, 1969	P P	Luis Tiant Stan Williams	Cleveland Indians	P P 3B OF	Dean Chance Bob Miller Graig Nettles Ted Uhlaender
March 21, 1970	OF	Brant Alyea	Washington Senators	P P	Joe Grzenda Charley Walters
Oct 20, 1970	P IF	Sal Campisi Jim Kennedy	St. Louis Cardinals	OF	Herman Hill minor league OF Charlie Wissler
March 29, 1971	IF	Bob Adams and minor league P Art Clifford	Detroit Tigers	P	Bill Zepp
July 8, 1971	C	Phil Roof	Milwaukee Brewers	C	Paul Ratliff

DATE		ACQUIRED	FROM		IN EXCHANGE FOR
July 30, 1971		Cash	Detroit Tigers	P	Ron Perranoski
Sept 1, 1971	OF	Fred Rico and minor league P Dan Ford	St. Louis Cardinals	P	Stan Williams
Oct 22, 1971	OF	Bobby Darwin	Los Angeles Dodgers	OF	Paul Powell
Nov 30, 1971	P	Dave LaRoche	California Angels	SS	Leo Cardenas
Dec 3, 1971	P	Wayne Granger	Cincinnati Reds	P	Tom Hall
Feb 5, 1972		Cash	Chicago White Sox	P	Pete Hamm
Oct 27, 1972	OF	Danny Walton	New York Yankees	C	Rick Dempsey
Nov 29, 1972	OF P	Larry Hisle John Cumberland	St. Louis Cardinals	P	Wayne Granger
Nov 30, 1972	P P	Bill Hands Joe Decker minor league P Bob Maneely	Chicago Cubs	P	Dave LaRoche
Nov 30, 1972	P P OF	Ken Sanders Ken Reynolds Joe Lis	Philadelphia Phillies	OF	Cesar Tovar
Nov 30, 1972		Cash	Detroit Tigers	1B	Rich Reese
March 27, 1973	3B	Mike Ferraro	Milwaukee Brewers	P	Ken Reynolds
March 27, 1973	P	Dan Fife and cash	Detroit Tigers	P	Jim Perry
Aug 3, 1973		Cash	Cleveland Indians	P	Ken Sanders
Aug 15, 1973		Cash	Chicago White Sox	P	Jim Kaat
Oct 24, 1973	P	Tom Burgmeier	Kansas City Royals		Minor leaguer Ken Gill
Dec 6, 1973	C	Randy Hundley	Chicago Cubs	C	George Mitterwald
May 4, 1974	P	Mike Pazik	New York Yankees	P	Dick Woodson
June 5, 1974		Cash	Cleveland Indians	1B	Joe Lis
Aug 19, 1974	1B	Pat Bourque	Oakland Athletics	1B-OF	Jim Holt
Sept 9, 1974		Cash	Texas Rangers	P	Bill Hands
Oct 23, 1974	OF	Dan Ford minor league P Denny Myers	Oakland Athletics	1B	Pat Bourque

DATE		ACQUIRED	FROM		IN EXCHANGE FOR
June 14, 1975	OF	John Briggs	Milwaukee Brewers	OF	Bobby Darwin
Oct 24, 1975	C	Larry Cox	Philadelphia Phillies	SS	Sergio Ferrer
June 1, 1976	P SS 3B P	Bill Singer Roy Smalley Mike Cubbage Jim Gideon and $250,000.	Texas Rangers	P SS	Bert Blyleven Danny Thompson
Nov 6, 1976		No compensation (free agent signing)	Boston Red Sox	P	Bill Campbell
Nov 21, 1976		No compensation (free agent signing)	California Angels	OF	Lyman Bostock
Nov 26, 1976		No compensation (free agent signing)	Chicago White Sox	3B	Eric Soderholm
Dec 6, 1976	OF	Glenn Adams	San Francisco Giants		Cash
March 21, 1977		Cash	Milwaukee Brewers	OF	Steve Brye
March 31, 1977	P	Ron Schueler	Philadelphia Phillies		Cash
April 6, 1977	P	Don Carrithers	Montreal Expos		Cash
May 2, 1977	P	Dave Johnson	Seattle Mariners		Cash
Nov 17, 1977		No compensation (free agent signing)	Milwaukee Brewers	OF	Larry Hisle
Nov 23, 1977	P	Dennis Lewallyn	Los Angeles Dodgers		Cash
		(Lewallyn was returned to the Dodgers on April 15, 1978.)			
March 29, 1978	UT	Jose Morales	Montreal Expos		Cash
Dec 4, 1978	1B DH	Ron Jackson Danny Goodwin	California Angels	OF	Dan Ford
Dec 8, 1978	P	Jerry Koosman	New York Mets	P	Jesse Orosco minor league P Greg Field
Dec 13, 1978	P	Mike Bacsik	Texas Rangers	P	Mac Scarce
Feb 3, 1979	OF 3B P P	Ken Landreaux Dave Engle Paul Hartzell Brad Havens	California Angels	1B	Rod Carew
March 29, 1979		Cash	Seattle Mariners	C	Terry Bulling
July 25, 1979		Cash	Toronto Blue Jays	1B	Craig Kusick
Nov 15, 1979		No compensation (free agent signing)	Los Angeles Dodgers	P	Dave Goltz
Dec 5, 1979	P	Fernando Arroyo	Detroit Tigers	P	Jeff Holly

DATE		ACQUIRED	FROM		IN EXCHANGE FOR
Dec 7, 1979	IF	Pete Mackanin	Philadelphia Phillies	P	Paul Thormodsgard
Dec 7, 1979	1B	Tom Chism	Baltimore Orioles	C	Dan Graham
Dec 2, 1980		No compensation (free agent signing)	California Angels	P	Geoff Zahn
Dec 8, 1980	IF	Chuck Baker	San Diego Padres	OF	Dave Edwards
Dec 12, 1980	P	Byron McLaughlin	Seattle Mariners	OF	Willie Norwood
Dec 19, 1980	OF	Steve Stroughter	Seattle Mariners	P	Mike Bacsik
Dec 19, 1980		No compensation (free agent signing)	New York Mets	3B	Mike Cubbage
Dec 23, 1980		No compensation (free agent signing)	Baltimore Orioles	1B	Jose Morales
March 30, 1981	OF	Mickey Hatcher minor league P Matt Reeves	Los Angeles Dodgers	OF	Ken Landreaux
April 5, 1981		Cash	New York Mets	P	Danny Boitano
Aug 23, 1981	OF	Tim Corcoran	Detroit Tigers	1B	Ron Jackson
Aug 30, 1981	OF	Randy Johnson Minor league SS Ivan Mesa minor league 3B Ronnie Perry and cash	Chicago White Sox	P	Jerry Koosman
Jan 6, 1982	P OF	Bobby Castillo Bobby Mitchell	Los Angeles Dodgers		Minor leaguers P Paul Voigt and C Scotti Madison
April 10, 1982	P P SS	Ron Davis Paul Boris Greg Gagne	New York Yankees	SS	Roy Smalley
May 12, 1982	OF P	Tom Brunansky Mike Walters and $400,000.	California Angels	P 2B	Doug Corbett Rob Wilfong
May 12, 1982	P SS P	John Pacella Larry Milbourne Pete Filson and cash	New York Yankees	C P	Butch Wynegar Roger Erickson
July 3, 1982	OF	Larry Littleton	Cleveland Indians	SS	Larry Milbourne
Nov 1, 1982	P	Len Whitehouse	Texas Rangers	P	John Pacella
Dec 10, 1982	3B	Dave Baker	Toronto Blue Jays	P	Don Cooper
Jan 12, 1983	P	Rick Lysander	Houston Astros	P	Bob Veselic

DATE		ACQUIRED	FROM		IN EXCHANGE FOR
March 25, 1983		Minor league C Stine Poole and cash	Detroit Tigers	C	Sal Butera
March 28, 1983	OF	Tack Wilson	Los Angeles Dodgers		Minor league SS Ivan Mesa
June 21, 1983	OF	Rusty Kuntz	Chicago White Sox		Minor league IF Mike Sodders
Dec 7, 1983	P P	Mike Smithson John Butcher	Texas Rangers	OF	Gary Ward minor league C Sam Sorce
Dec 8, 1983	P	Larry Pashnick	Detroit Tigers	OF	Rusty Kuntz

New York Yankees

The Best Trades

1. Acquired Babe Ruth from the Boston Red Sox for $125,000 and a $300,000 loan, January 3, 1920.
2. Acquired Red Ruffing from the Boston Red Sox for Cedric Durst and $50,000, May 6, 1930.
3. Acquired Sparky Lyle from the Boston Red Sox for Danny Cater, March 22, 1972.
4. Acquired Roger Maris, Joe DeMaestri, and Kent Hadley from the Kansas City Athletics for Hank Bauer, Norm Siebern, and Don Larsen, December 11, 1959.
5. Acquired Graig Nettles and Gerry Moses from the Cleveland Indians for John Ellis, Charlie Spikes, Rusty Torres, and Jerry Kenney, November 27, 1972.

The Worst Trades

1. Traded Scott McGregor, Tippy Martinez, Rick Dempsey, Rudy May, and Dave Pagan to the Baltimore Orioles for Ken Holtzman, Doyle Alexander, Ellie Hendricks, Grant Jackson, and Jimmy Freeman, June 15, 1976.
2. Traded Larry Gura to the Kansas City Royals for Fran Healy, May 16, 1976.
3. Traded Willie McGee to the St. Louis Cardinals for Bob Sykes, October 21, 1981.
4. Traded Chris Chambliss, Damaso Garcia, and Paul Mirabella to the Toronto Blue Jays for Rick Cerone, Tom Underwood, and Ted Wilborn, November 1, 1979.
5. Traded Tommy Holmes to the Boston Braves for Buddy Hassett and Gene Moore, February 5, 1942.

Owner: George Steinbrenner

Say what you will about George Steinbrenner — and everybody has — no one can accuse him of putting the bottom line above performance on the field. Steinbrenner's profligate spending has sent salaries skyrocketing but projected the Yankees into pennant contention year after year.

Steinbrenner has not merely spent for free agents; he has spent lavishly and willingly, and not always wisely. He has shown a willingness to cut his losses and admit his mistakes, as he did with free agents Dave Collins, Rawley Eastwick, and Don Gullett. He has made frequent trades to acquire players about to be free agents and players whose salaries, won in arbitration, put them on a level beyond what their owners wanted to pay. Among the players he's acquired in this fashion are Ken Griffey, Roy Smalley, Shane Rawley, Butch Wynegar, John Mayberry, John Montefusco, and Doyle Alexander. And he has signed several of the "super-premium" free agents to important, trend-setting contracts: Catfish Hunter, Reggie Jackson, Goose Gossage, Tommy John, and Dave Winfield all played pivotal roles on pennant-winning Yankee squads.

The charge most often leveled against Steinbrenner is that of trying to buy a pennant — an irrelevant charge, and hardly a new one. Tom Yawkey of the Red Sox was accused of the same thing when he bought Lefty Grove and Jimmie Foxx in the 1930s; Steinbrenner at least has been successful in his pennant-purchasing efforts. His fierce will to win has brought the Yankees from the second division, where they had languished after the collapse of their last dynasty in the early 1960s, to five divisional titles, four pennants, and two world championships.

But the success of the Yankees cannot be traced wholly to their activity in the free-agent market. The framework of their team of the 1970s was constructed in trades; the free agents added the boost that put them over the top. In a four-year stint as club president, Gabe Paul completely restructured the team. He acquired Graig Nettles from Cleveland for John Ellis, Jerry Kenney, Charlie Spikes, and Rusty Torres; Lou Piniella from Kansas City for Lindy McDaniel; Chris Chambliss and Dick Tidrow from Cleveland for Fritz Peterson, Fred Beene, Tom Buskey, and Steve Kline; Oscar Gamble from the Indians for Pat Dobson; Willie Randolph, Dock Ellis, and Ken Brett from Pittsburgh for Doc Medich; and Mickey Rivers and Ed Figueroa from California for Bobby Bonds. It was the most productive series of trades in Paul's long career.

Given all this, and given their willingness to spend, why don't the Yankees win more often? One reason is their reliance on older players. They have consistently traded away young players who could be vital to their future for the single player they feel they need right now. Among the young players traded away by the Yankees in recent years are Scott McGregor, Tippy Martinez, Rick Dempsey, LaMarr Hoyt, Willie McGee, Tim Lollar, and Damaso Garcia. True, the Yanks have picked up some young players of their own in trades, among them pitchers Ron Davis, Dave Righetti, and Ray Fontenot. But too many of their trades have sent talented young players for an older, established player, even though that player plays a position at which the Yanks are overstocked. Moreover, older players are more susceptible to injury; the more players in your lineup who are over thirty, the more likely you are to be hit by an "unlucky" string of injuries. The Yankee teams of the late 1970s were young and strong up the middle, with Munson, Randolph, Dent, and Rivers to go along with outstanding pitching. The current Yankee team is loaded with people to play the corners, but have serious questions up the middle. It will be interesting to see how Steinbrenner addresses these questions in the years to come.

DATE		ACQUIRED	FROM		IN EXCHANGE FOR
March 1903	1B	Dave Fultz	Philadelphia Athletics		Cash
June 10, 1903	SS	Kid Elberfeld	Detroit Tigers	SS IF	Herman Long Ernie Courtney
Dec 1903	P	Long Tom Hughes	Boston Red Sox	P	Jesse Tannehill
Jan 1904	P	Jack Powell	St. Louis Browns	P C	Harry Howell Jack O'Connor

DATE		ACQUIRED	FROM		IN EXCHANGE FOR
Jan 1904	C	Deacon McGuire	Detroit Tigers		Cash
Jan 1904	3B	Champ Osteen	Washington Senators		Cash
Feb 1904	P	Jack Powell	St. Louis Browns		Cash
Feb 1904	1B	John Anderson	St. Louis Browns		Cash
May 8, 1904	OF	Jack Thoney	Washington Senators		Cash
June 18, 1904	OF	Patsy Dougherty	Boston Red Sox	3B	Bob Unglaub
July 13, 1904	P	Al Orth	Washington Senators	P P	Long Tom Hughes Bill Wolfe
July 25, 1904	C	Frank McManus	Detroit Tigers	C	Monte Beville
Sept 1904	P	Ned Garvin	Brooklyn Dodgers		Waiver price
June 3, 1905		Waiver price	Washington Senators	OF-1B	John Anderson
July 13, 1905	C	Mike Powers	Philadelphia Athletics		Cash
Aug 7, 1905		Cash	Philadelphia Athletics	C	Mike Powers
Sept 1, 1905		Cash	St. Louis Browns	P	Jack Powell
Oct 2, 1905		Cash	Philadelphia Athletics	OF	Rube Oldring
April 1906	P	Noodles Hahn	Cincinnati Reds		Waiver price
May 9, 1906		Cash	Chicago White Sox	OF	Ed Hahn
May 11, 1906	OF	Danny Hoffman	Philadelphia Athletics		Cash
June 6, 1906		Cash	Chicago White Sox	OF	Patsy Dougherty
Dec 1906	C	Branch Rickey	St. Louis Browns		Cash
May 16, 1907	P	Earl Moore	Cleveland Indians	P	Walter Clarkson
May 29, 1907	P	Frank Kitson	Washington Senators		Cash
June 29, 1907		Waiver price	Boston Red Sox	C	Deacon McGuire
		(McGuire was named Boston manager.)			
Oct 1907		Waiver price	Philadelphia Phillies	P	Earl Moore
Oct 1907	1B	Jake Stahl	Chicago White Sox		Cash

DATE	ACQUIRED	FROM	IN EXCHANGE FOR
Nov 1907	2B Harry Niles	St. Louis Browns	Cash
Nov 1907	OF Frank Delahanty	Cleveland Indians	Cash
Dec 12, 1907	Cash	Detroit Tigers	C Ira Thomas
Dec 1907	Cash	Boston Red Sox	2B Frank LaPorte
Jan 1908	3B Mike Donovan	Cleveland Indians	Cash
Feb 1908	P Fred Glade OF Charlie Hemphill	St. Louis Browns	2B Jimmy Williams 3B Hobe Ferris OF Danny Hoffman
March 1908	OF Birdie Cree	Philadelphia Athletics	Cash
July 1908	2B Frank LaPorte	Boston Red Sox	1B Jake Stahl 2B Harry Niles P Charlie Rhodes
Jan 1909	Cash	Detroit Tigers	3B George Moriarty
Feb 1909	SS John Knight	Boston Red Sox	Waiver price
March 1909	2B Joe Ward (Ward was returned to Philadelphia on May 20, 1909.)	Philadelphia Phillies	Cash
May 1909	Cash	Cleveland Indians	SS Neal Ball
Aug 1909	Waiver price	Boston Red Sox	P Jack Chesbro
Dec 16, 1909	$5,000.	Washington Senators	SS Kid Elberfeld
Dec 1909	C Lou Criger	St. Louis Browns	P Joe Lake
May 1910	OF Harry Wolter	Boston Red Sox	3B Clyde Engle
May 1910	Cash	Cincinnati Reds	P Slow Joe Doyle
May 1910	Cash	Boston Red Sox	C Red Kleinow
Jan 1911	OF Roy Hartzell	St. Louis Browns	3B Jimmy Austin 2B Frank LaPorte
Dec 1911	C Gabby Street OF Jack Lelivelt	Washington Senators	IF John Knight SS Roxy Roach
Jan 1912	3B Del Paddock	Chicago White Sox	Cash
March 1912	C Gus Fisher	Cleveland Indians	Waiver price
May 1912	Cash	Philadelphia Phillies	OF Cozy Dolan

DATE		ACQUIRED	FROM		IN EXCHANGE FOR
June 26, 1912		Waiver price	Washington Senators	P	Hippo Vaughn
Nov 1912	SS	Claud Derrick	Philadelphia Athletics		Cash
Dec 1912		Cash	Boston Braves	P OF	George Davis Guy Zinn
April 15, 1913	3B	Bill McKechnie	Boston Braves		Waiver price
May 20, 1913	SS	Roger Peckinpaugh	Cleveland Indians	OF OF	Bill Stumpf Jack Lelivelt
June 23, 1913	2B	Rollie Zeider	Chicago White Sox	1B 1B	Babe Borton Hal Chase
July 7, 1913	IF	John Knight	Washington Senators		Cash
Aug 25, 1913	OF	Frank Gilhooley	St. Louis Cardinals		Cash
Sept 23, 1913		Cash	Chicago Cubs	P	George McConnell
Oct 1913		Cash	Cincinnati Reds	OF	Bert Daniels
Jan 1914		Waiver price	Pittsburgh Pirates	P	Dan Costello
May 13, 1914	C	Les Nunamaker	Boston Red Sox		Cash
May 27, 1914		Cash	Boston Red Sox	P	Guy Cooper
June 10, 1914	OF	Tom Daley	Philadelphia Athletics	OF	Jimmy Walsh
June 1914	P	Boardwalk Brown	Philadelphia Athletics		Cash
Aug 1914		Waiver price	Cincinnati Reds	OF	Bill Holden
Jan 7, 1915	IF	Hugh High	Detroit Tigers		Waiver price
Jan 7, 1915	1B	Wally Pipp	Detroit Tigers		Waiver price
Feb 1915	P	George Mogridge	Chicago White Sox		Cash
March 1915	P	Dazzy Vance	Pittsburgh Pirates		Cash
April 18, 1915	P	Ensign Cottrell	Boston Braves		Cash
July 7, 1915	P	Bob Shawkey	Philadelphia Athletics		$18,000.
July 23, 1915	OF	Elmer Miller	St. Louis Cardinals		Cash
July 30, 1915	C	Walt Alexander	St. Louis Browns		Cash
Aug 19, 1915		Waiver price	Pittsburgh Pirates	OF	Ed Barney

DATE		ACQUIRED	FROM		IN EXCHANGE FOR
Dec 23, 1915	P	Nick Cullop	Kansas City Athletics		Cash
Feb 10, 1916	2B	Germany Schaefer	Newark (Federal League)		Cash
Feb 10, 1916	OF	Lee Magee	Brooklyn (Federal League)		Cash
Feb 15, 1916	3B	Frank Baker	Philadelphia Athletics		$37,500.
July 15, 1917	OF	Armando Marsans	St. Louis Browns	OF	Lee Magee
Aug 21, 1917	C	Muddy Ruel	St. Louis Browns		Cash
Jan 22, 1918	P 2B	Eddie Plank Del Pratt and $15,000.	St. Louis Browns	C IF P P 2B	Les Nunamaker Fritz Maisel Nick Cullop Urban Shocker Joe Gedeon
March 8, 1918	1B	George Burns	Detroit Tigers		Cash
March 8, 1918	OF	Ping Bodie	Philadelphia Athletics	1B	George Burns
April 28, 1918	2B	Lee Magee	St. Louis Browns	OF	Tim Hendryx
April 28, 1918	C	Tommy Clarke	Cincinnati Reds	2B	Lee Magee
May 1918	P	Happy Finneran	Detroit Tigers		Cash
June 19, 1918	OF	Ham Hyatt	Boston Braves		Cash
June 20, 1918	P	Hank Robinson	St. Louis Cardinals		Cash
Dec 9, 1918	P	Pete Schneider	Cincinnati Reds		Cash
Dec 18, 1918	P OF P	Ernie Shore Duffy Lewis Dutch Leonard	Boston Red Sox	OF P P C	Frank Gilhooley Slim Love Ray Caldwell Roxy Walters and $15,000.
		(Leonard refused to report to New York, and remained Boston property.)			
Jan 1919	OF	Al Wickland	Boston Braves		Cash
March 6, 1919		Cash	Boston Braves	P	Ray Keating
March 15, 1919		Waiver price	Cincinnati Reds	P	Ray Fisher
May 1919		Cash	Boston Red Sox	OF	Bill Lamar
July 29, 1919	P	Carl Mays	Boston Red Sox	P P	Allan Russell Bob McGraw and $40,000.

DATE		ACQUIRED	FROM		IN EXCHANGE FOR
Jan 3, 1920	OF	Babe Ruth	Boston Red Sox		$125,000 and a $300,000 loan to Boston owner Harry Frazee
Dec 15, 1920	P	Waite Hoyt	Boston Red Sox	C	Muddy Ruel
	P	Harry Harper		2B	Del Pratt
	C	Wally Schang		OF	Sammy Vick
	IF	Mike McNally		P	Hank Thormahlen
Jan 20, 1921	OF	Braggo Roth	Washington Senators	P	Duffy Lewis
				OF	George Mogridge
Dec 20, 1921	SS	Everett Scott	Boston Red Sox	SS	Roger Peckinpaugh
	P	Joe Bush		P	Jack Quinn
	P	Sad Sam Jones		P	Rip Collins
				P	Bill Piercy
Feb 24, 1922		Waiver price	Boston Red Sox	P	Alex Ferguson
March 17, 1922	OF	Whitey Witt	Philadelphia Athletics		Cash
July 23, 1922	3B	Joe Dugan	Boston Red Sox	OF	Chick Fewster
	OF	Elmer Smith		OF	Elmer Miller
				SS	Johnny Mitchell
				P	Lefty O'Doul and $50,000.
Jan 3, 1923	P	George Pipgras	Boston Red Sox	C	Al DeVormer and cash
	OF	Harvey Hendrick			
Jan 30, 1923	P	Herb Pennock	Boston Red Sox	OF	Camp Skinner
				IF	Norm McMillan
				P	George Murray and $50,000.
May 31, 1923	SS	Ernie Johnson	Chicago White Sox		Waiver price
Dec 11, 1923		Cash	Cincinnati Reds	P	Carl Mays
Dec 10, 1924	3B	Howard Shanks	Boston Red Sox	3B	Mike McNally
Dec 12, 1924	C	Steve O'Neill	Boston Red Sox		Waiver price
Dec 17, 1924	P	Urban Shocker	St. Louis Browns	P	Joe Bush
				P	Milt Gaston
				P	Joe Giard
Feb 1925		Cash	Washington Senators	IF	Mike McNally
May 5, 1925	OF	Bobby Veach	Boston Red Sox	P	Ray Francis and $9,000.
	P	Alex Ferguson			
June 17, 1925		Cash	Washington Senators	SS	Everett Scott
Aug 17, 1925		Waiver price	Washington Senators	OF	Bobby Veach
Aug 19, 1925		Cash	Washington Senators	P	Alex Ferguson
Jan 20, 1926	OF	Spencer Adams	Washington Senators		Cash

DATE		ACQUIRED	FROM		IN EXCHANGE FOR
Feb 1, 1926		$7,500.	Cincinnati Reds	1B	Wally Pipp
Feb 6, 1926	P	George Mogridge and cash	St. Louis Browns	C	Wally Schang
June 15, 1926	OF	Roy Carlyle	Boston Red Sox		Waiver price
June 1926		Waiver price	Boston Braves	P	George Mogridge
July 22, 1926	C	Hank Severeid	Washington Senators		Waiver price
Aug 27, 1926	P	Dutch Ruether	Washington Senators	P OF	Garland Braxton Nick Cullop
		(New York sent Braxton and Cullop to Washington on October 19, 1926.)			
Jan 13, 1927	C 2B	Johnny Grabowski Ray Morehart	Chicago White Sox	2B	Aaron Ward
Feb 8, 1927	OF P	Cedric Durst Joe Giard	St. Louis Browns	P	Sad Sam Jones
Aug 23, 1928	P	Tom Zachary	Washington Senators		Waiver price
Dec 13, 1928		$7,500.	Boston Braves	C	Pat Collins
Dec 29, 1928		Waiver price	Boston Braves	3B	Joe Dugan
June 18, 1929		Cash	Washington Senators	P	Myles Thomas
June 19, 1929		Cash	Philadelphia Athletics	1B	George Burns
Sept 17, 1929		Cash	Boston Braves	3B	Gene Robertson
Oct 16, 1929		Waiver price	Cincinnati Reds	OF	Bob Meusel
Jan 29, 1930	OF	Ken Williams	Boston Red Sox		Waiver price
Feb 2, 1930		Waiver price	Cincinnati Reds	SS	Leo Durocher
May 6, 1930	P	Red Ruffing	Boston Red Sox	OF	Cedric Durst and $50,000.
May 12, 1930		Waiver price	Boston Braves	P	Tom Zachary
May 30, 1930	P SS OF	Ownie Carroll Yats Wuestling Harry Rice	Detroit Tigers	P SS	Waite Hoyt Mark Koenig
July 20, 1930	P	Ken Holloway	Cleveland Indians		Cash
Sept 13, 1930		Cash	Cincinnati Reds	P	Ownie Carroll
Dec 10, 1930	C	Cy Perkins	Philadelphia Athletics		Cash
Jan 13, 1931		Waiver price	Washington Senators	OF	Harry Rice
Jan 1932		Waiver price	St. Louis Cardinals	SS	Jimmy Reese

DATE		ACQUIRED	FROM		IN EXCHANGE FOR
May 1, 1932	P	Wilcy Moore	Boston Red Sox	P	Gordon Rhodes
June 5, 1932	P	Danny MacFayden	Boston Red Sox	P P	Ivy Andrews Hank Johnson and $50,000.
Dec 1932		Cash	St. Louis Browns	P	Ed Wells
May 12, 1933		$100,000.	Boston Red Sox	3B P	Bill Werber George Pipgras
May 15, 1934	IF	Freddie Muller and $20,000.	Boston Red Sox	SS	Lyn Lary
May 26, 1934	P	Burleigh Grimes	Pittsburgh Pirates		Cash
May 30, 1934		Waiver price	Brooklyn Dodgers	P	Harry Smythe
Nov 13, 1934		Cash	Cincinnati Reds	P	Danny MacFayden
Dec 19, 1934		Cash	Cincinnati Reds	OF	Sammy Byrd
March 26, 1935	P	Pat Malone	St. Louis Cardinals		$15,000.
July 15, 1935		Cash	St. Louis Browns	P	Russ Van Atta
Aug 6, 1935	SS	Blondy Ryan	Philadelphia Phillies		Cash
Dec 11, 1935	P P	Monte Pearson Steve Sundra	Cleveland Indians	P	Johnny Allen
Jan 17, 1936	P OF	Bump Hadley Roy Johnson	Washington Senators	P OF	Jimmie DeShong Jesse Hill
Jan 1936		Cash	Brooklyn Dodgers	1B	Buddy Hassett
May 4, 1936		Waiver price	Chicago White Sox	OF	Dixie Walker
June 14, 1936	OF	Jake Powell	Washington Senators	OF	Ben Chapman
Feb 17, 1937	1B	Babe Dahlgren	Boston Red Sox		Cash
June 1937		Waiver price	Boston Braves	OF	Roy Johnson
Aug 14, 1937	P	Ivy Andrews	Cleveland Indians		$7,500.
Feb 15, 1938	SS	Bill Knickerbocker	St. Louis Browns	2B	Don Heffner and $10,000.
April 15, 1938		Cash	Brooklyn Dodgers	OF	Ernie Koy
Oct 26, 1938	P OF	Oral Hildebrand Buster Mills	St. Louis Browns	C OF	Joe Glenn Myril Hoag
Nov 1938		Waiver price	Cleveland Indians	OF	Johnny Broaca
Jan 24, 1939		$25,000.	Chicago Cubs	OF	Jim Gleeson

DATE		ACQUIRED	FROM		IN EXCHANGE FOR
June 13, 1939	2B	Roy Hughes and cash	St. Louis Browns	OF	Joe Gallagher
June 20, 1939	P	Jimmie DeShong	Washington Senators		Waiver price
July 13, 1939	P	Al Hollingsworth	Philadelphia Phillies	2B	Roy Hughes
Aug 12, 1939		Cash	Brooklyn Dodgers	P	Al Hollingsworth
Jan 4, 1940	P	Lee Grissom	Cincinnati Reds	P	Joe Beggs
May 15, 1940		Waiver price	Brooklyn Dodgers	P	Lee Grissom
Dec 30, 1940	3B	Don Lang and $20,000.	Cincinnati Reds	P	Monte Pearson
Dec 31, 1940	C	Ken Silvestri	Chicago White Sox	SS	Bill Knickerbocker
Jan 2, 1941		Cash	New York Giants	P	Bump Hadley
Feb 25, 1941		Cash	Boston Braves	1B	Babe Dahlgren
March 27, 1941		Cash	Washington Senators	P	Steve Sundra
Feb 5, 1942	1B OF	Buddy Hassett Gene Moore	Boston Braves	OF	Tommy Holmes
Feb 24, 1942		Cash	Brooklyn Dodgers	OF	Gene Moore
April 4, 1942		Cash	Boston Braves	OF	Frenchy Bordagaray
July 16, 1942	P	Jim Turner	Cincinnati Reds	OF	Frankie Kelleher
Aug 31, 1942	OF	Roy Cullenbine	Washington Senators		Waiver price
Sept 25, 1942	3B	Hank Majeski	Boston Braves		Cash
Dec 17, 1942	OF 2B	Roy Weatherly Oscar Grimes	Cleveland Indians	OF C	Roy Cullenbine Buddy Rosar
Jan 22, 1943	1B	Nick Etten	Philadelphia Phillies	C P	Tom Padden Al Gerheauser and $10,000.
Jan 25, 1943		Cash	Washington Senators	P	Lefty Gomez
Jan 29, 1943	P	Bill Zuber and cash	Washington Senators	2B P	Gerry Priddy Milo Candini
July 6, 1944		Cash	Philadelphia Athletics	OF	Larry Rosenthal
Dec 15, 1944	P	Jake Wade	Chicago White Sox	P	Johnny Johnson
July 27, 1945		$97,000.	Chicago Cubs	P	Hank Borowy
March 25, 1946		Cash	Philadelphia Phillies	C	Rollie Hemsley

DATE		ACQUIRED	FROM		IN EXCHANGE FOR
May 1946		Waiver price	Philadelphia Phillies	P	Charley Stanceu
June 14, 1946		Cash	Philadelphia Athletics	3B	Hank Majeski
June 18, 1946		Cash	Boston Red Sox	P	Bill Zuber
June 20, 1946	OF	Hal Peck	Philadelphia Athletics		Cash
Oct 19, 1946	P	Allie Reynolds	Cleveland Indians	2B 3B	Joe Gordon Eddie Bockman
Oct 21, 1946	P	Cookie Cuccurullo	Pittsburgh Pirates	P	Ernie Bonham
Dec 20, 1946	C 2B	Sherm Lollar Ray Mack	Cleveland Indians	OF P P	Hal Peck Al Gettel Gene Bearden
March 1, 1947	IF	Johnny Lucadello	St. Louis Browns		Waiver price
June 25, 1947	2B	Lonny Frey	Chicago Cubs		Cash
July 11, 1947	P	Bobo Newsom	Washington Senators		Waiver price
July 11, 1947		Cash	Pittsburgh Pirates	P	Mel Queen
Aug 4, 1947		Cash	Pittsburgh Pirates	P	Al Lyons
Oct 10, 1947	P	Red Embree	Cleveland Indians	OF	Allie Clark
Feb 24, 1948	P	Ed Lopat	Chicago White Sox	C P P	Aaron Robinson Fred Bradley Bill Wight
April 12, 1948		Cash	Cleveland Indians	P	Butch Wensloff
May 13, 1948	OF	Leon Culberson and $15,000.	Washington Senators	OF	Bud Stewart
July 28, 1948		Cash	Chicago White Sox	P	Randy Gumpert
Aug 9, 1948		Cash	St. Louis Browns	P	Karl Drews
Dec 13, 1948	P C	Fred Sanford Roy Partee	St. Louis Browns	C P P	Sherm Lollar Red Embree Dick Starr and $100,000.
Dec 14, 1948	OF	Jim Delsing	Chicago White Sox	1B	Steve Souchock
Jan 17, 1949		Cash	Chicago White Sox	P	Bill Bevens
		(Bevens was returned to New York Yankees on March 28, 1949.)			
Aug 6, 1949		Cash	Pittsburgh Pirates	1B	Jack Phillips
Aug 22, 1949	1B	Johnny Mize	New York Giants		$40,000.

DATE		ACQUIRED	FROM		IN EXCHANGE FOR
Dec 17, 1949	OF	Dick Wakefield	Detroit Tigers	1B	Dick Kryhoski
June 15, 1950	P	Tom Ferrick	St. Louis Browns	OF	Jim Delsing
	OF	Joe Ostrowski		P	Don Johnson
	3B	Leo Thomas		P	Duane Pillette
	P	Sid Schacht		2B	Snuffy Stirnweiss and $50,000.
June 27, 1950		$10,000.	Chicago White Sox	C	Gus Niarhos
Sept 5, 1950	1B	Johnny Hopp	Pittsburgh Pirates		Cash
May 14, 1951	1B	Don Bollweg and $15,000.	St. Louis Cardinals	3B	Billy Johnson
June 15, 1951	P	Stubby Overmire	St. Louis Browns	P	Tommy Byrne and $25,000.
June 15, 1951	P	Bob Kuzava	Washington Senators	P	Fred Sanford
				P	Tom Ferrick
				P	Bob Porterfield
July 31, 1951	P	Bobby Hogue	St. Louis Browns	OF	Cliff Mapes
	3B	Kermit Wahl			
	SS	Ollie Tucker			
	P	Lou Sleater			
Aug 30, 1951	P	Johnny Sain	Boston Braves	P	Lew Burdette and $50,000.
Nov 23, 1951	P	Jim McDonald	St. Louis Browns	C	Clint Courtney
April 7, 1952		Cash	St. Louis Browns	P	Dave Madison
May 3, 1952	OF	Irv Noren	Washington Senators	OF	Jackie Jensen
	SS	Tom Upton		P	Spec Shea
				2B	Jerry Snyder
				OF	Archie Wilson
May 13, 1952		Waiver price	St. Louis Browns	P	Stubby Overmire
Aug 1, 1952	P	Johnny Schmitz	Brooklyn Dodgers		Waiver price
Aug 4, 1952		Waiver price	St. Louis Browns	P	Bobby Hogue
Aug 22, 1952	P	Ray Scarborough	Boston Red Sox		Cash
Aug 28, 1952	P	Ewell Blackwell	Cincinnati Reds	OF	Jim Greengrass
				P	Johnny Schmitz
				P	Ernie Nevel
				OF	Bob Marquis and $35,000.
Feb 17, 1953	P	Johnny Schmitz	Cincinnati Reds		Cash
April 27, 1953		Cash	Philadelphia Athletics	3B	Loren Babe
May 13, 1953		Waiver price	Washington Senators	P	Johnny Schmitz
June 12, 1953	SS	Willie Miranda	St. Louis Browns		Cash

DATE		ACQUIRED	FROM		IN EXCHANGE FOR
Dec 16, 1953	P	Harry Byrd	Philadelphia Athletics	1B	Don Bollweg
	1B	Eddie Robinson		P	John Gray
	1B	Tom Hamilton		C	Jim Robertson
	OF	Carmen Mauro		3B	Jim Finigan
	3B	Loren Babe		1B	Vic Power
				OF	Bill Renna
Feb 23, 1954		$85,000.	St. Louis Cardinals	P	Vic Raschi
April 11, 1954	OF	Enos Slaughter	St. Louis Cardinals	OF	Bill Virdon
				P	Mel Wright
					minor league OF Emil Tellinger
May 11, 1954		Waiver price	Baltimore Orioles	IF	Jim Brideweser
July 4, 1954	P	Marlin Stuart	Baltimore Orioles		Waiver price
Aug 7, 1954		Waiver price	Baltimore Orioles	P	Bob Kuzava
Aug 22, 1954	P	Jim Konstanty	Philadelphia Phillies		Cash
Nov 18, 1954	P	Bob Turley	Baltimore Orioles	P	Harry Byrd
	P	Don Larsen		P	Jim McDonald
	SS	Billy Hunter		C	Hal Smith
				C	Gus Triandos
				OF	Gene Woodling
				SS	Willie Miranda
		(First part of 18-player trade completed on December 1, 1954.)			
Dec 1, 1954	P	Mike Blyzka	Baltimore Orioles	P	Bill Miller
	C	Darrell Johnson		3B	Kal Segrist
	OF	Jim Fridley		2B	Don Leppert
	1B	Dick Kryhoski			minor league OF Ted Del Guercio and a player to be named later
		(Second part of 18-player trade begun on November 18, 1954.)			
March 30, 1955		$50,000.	Kansas City Athletics	1B	Dick Kryhoski
				P	Ewell Blackwell
				P	Tom Gorman
April 28, 1955		Cash	Kansas City Athletics	P	Lou Sleater
May 11, 1955	P	Sonny Dixon and cash	Kansas City Athletics	P	Johnny Sain
				OF	Enos Slaughter
May 11, 1955		Waiver price	Baltimore Orioles	P	Art Schallock
July 30, 1955		Waiver price	Baltimore Orioles	P	Ed Lopat
Sept 11, 1955	P	Gerry Staley	Cincinnati Reds		Waiver price
Feb 8, 1956	P	Mickey McDermott	Washington Senators	C	Lou Berberet
	SS	Bobby Kline		P	Bob Wiesler
				2B	Herb Plews
				OF	Whitey Herzog
				OF	Dick Tettelbach

DATE		ACQUIRED	FROM		IN EXCHANGE FOR
May 28, 1956		Waiver price	Chicago White Sox	P	Gerry Staley
June 14, 1956	P OF	Moe Burtschy Bill Renna and cash	Kansas City Athletics	OF 1B	Lou Skizas Eddie Robinson
Aug 22, 1956	OF	Ted Wilson	New York Giants		Waiver price
Aug 25, 1956	OF	Enos Slaughter	Kansas City Athletics		Waiver price
Oct 16, 1956		Cash	Kansas City Athletics	OF	Bob Cerv
Dec 11, 1956		Cash	Chicago Cubs	C	Charlie Silvera
Feb 19, 1957	P P P 1B 2B 3B	Art Ditmar Bobby Shantz Jack McMahan Wayne Belardi Curt Roberts Clete Boyer	Kansas City Athletics	SS P P P 2B OF	Billy Hunter Rip Coleman Tom Morgan Mickey McDermott Milt Graff Irv Noren
		(New York received Roberts on April 4, and Boyer on June 4, 1957.)			
April 5, 1957		Continuation of Billy Hunter trade of February 19, 1957.	Kansas City Athletics	P	Jack Urban
June 15, 1957	P OF OF	Ryne Duren Jim Pisoni Harry Simpson	Kansas City Athletics	2B P OF	Billy Martin Ralph Terry Woodie Held
Sept 1, 1957	P	Sal Maglie	Brooklyn Dodgers		Waiver price
Sept 10, 1957	OF	Bobby Del Greco	Chicago Cubs		Cash
March 20, 1958		Cash	Philadelphia Phillies	1B	Joe Collins
		(Collins refuesed to report and retired.)			
May 14, 1958		Cash	Washington Senators	P	Al Cicotte
June 15, 1958	P P	Duke Maas Virgil Trucks	Kansas City Athletics	P OF	Bob Grim Harry Simpson
Aug 22, 1958	P	Murry Dickson	Kansas City Athletics	OF	Zeke Bella and cash
April 8, 1959	P	Jack Urban	Kansas City Athletics	P	Mark Freeman
		(Freeman was returned to the Yankees on May 8, 1959.)			
April 12, 1959	IF OF	Mike Baxes Bob Martyn	Kansas City Athletics	OF SS	Russ Snyder Tommy Carroll
May 9, 1959		Cash	Kansas City Athletics	P	Murry Dickson
May 26, 1959	OF P	Hector Lopez Ralph Terry	Kansas City Athletics	P P 2B	Johnny Kucks Tom Sturdivant Jerry Lumpe
July 26, 1959	P	Gary Blaylock	St. Louis Cardinals		Waiver price

DATE		ACQUIRED	FROM		IN EXCHANGE FOR
Sept 12, 1959		Waiver price	Milwaukee Braves	OF	Enos Slaughter
Dec 11, 1959	OF SS 1B	Roger Maris Joe DeMaestri Kent Hadley	Kansas City Athletics	OF P OF	Hank Bauer Don Larsen Norm Siebern
April 5, 1960	P	Fred Kipp	Los Angeles Dodgers	OF	Gordie Windhorn minor league 1B Dick Sanders
May 19, 1960	OF	Bob Cerv	Kansas City Athletics	3B	Andy Carey
May 19, 1960	P	Art Ceccarelli	Chicago Cubs	P	Mark Freeman
Aug 22, 1960	1B	Dale Long	San Francisco Giants		Cash
Dec 16, 1960	P	Danny McDevitt	Los Angeles Dodgers		Cash
May 8, 1961	P OF	Tex Clevenger Bob Cerv	Los Angeles Angels	OF P P	Lee Thomas Ryne Duren Johnny James
July 26, 1961	1B	Bob Hale	Cleveland Indians		Cash
June 12, 1962	OF	Tommy Umphlett and cash	Boston Red Sox	2B	Billy Gardner
July 11, 1962	1B	Dale Long	Washington Senators	OF	Don Lock
Sept 7, 1962	P	Hal Brown	Baltimore Orioles		Cash
Oct 29, 1962		Cash	Los Angeles Angels	P	Bob Turley
Nov 26, 1962	P	Stan Williams	Los Angeles Dodgers	1B	Bill Skowron
April 21, 1963	1B	Harry Bright	Cincinnati Reds		Cash
April 21, 1963		Cash	Houston Astros	P	Hal Brown
April 21, 1963	P	Steve Hamilton	Washington Senators	P	Jim Coates
Nov 27, 1963		Cash	Washington Senators	P	Marshall Bridges
June 12, 1964		Cash	Los Angeles Angels	P	Bob Meyer
Sept 5, 1964	P	Pedro Ramos	Cleveland Indians	P P	Ralph Terry Buddy Daley and $75,000.
March 30, 1965		Cash	Cleveland Indians	P	Stan Williams
May 3, 1965	C	Doc Edwards	Kansas City Athletics	C P	Johnny Blanchard Rollie Sheldon
May 10, 1965	1B	Ray Barker	Cleveland Indians	2B	Pedro Gonzalez

DATE		ACQUIRED	FROM		IN EXCHANGE FOR
Nov 29, 1965	SS	Ruben Amaro	Philadelphia Phillies	2B	Phil Linz
Dec 10, 1965	P	Bob Friend	Pittsburgh Pirates	P	Pete Mikkelsen and cash
Jan 14, 1966	OF	Lu Clinton	Cleveland Indians	C	Doc Edwards
May 3, 1966	P	Al Closter	Washington Senators		Cash
May 11, 1966	SS	Dick Schofield	San Francisco Giants		Cash
June 10, 1966	P C	Fred Talbot Billy Bryan	Kansas City Athletics	P OF P	Gil Blanco Roger Repoz Bill Stafford
June 15, 1966		Cash	New York Mets	P	Bob Friend
Sept 10, 1966	P	Thad Tillotson and cash	Los Angeles Dodgers	SS	Dick Schofield
Nov 29, 1966	OF P	Bill Robinson Chi Chi Olivo	Atlanta Braves	3B	Clete Boyer
Dec 8, 1966	3B	Charley Smith	St. Louis Cardinals	OF	Roger Maris
Dec 14, 1966	P	Joe Verbanic and cash	Philadelphia Phillies	P	Pedro Ramos
Dec 20, 1966	SS	Dick Howser	Cleveland Indians		Minor league P Gil Downs
April 3, 1967	3B	John Kennedy	Los Angeles Dodgers	P OF	Jack Cullen John Miller and $25,000.
May 1, 1967	P	Jack Kralick	Cleveland Indians		Cash
June 29, 1967		Cash	New York Mets	P	Hal Reniff
July 5, 1967	P	Steve Barber	Baltimore Orioles	1B	Ray Barker minor league IFs Chet Trail and Joe Brady and cash
Aug 3, 1967	P P	Ron Klimkowski Pete Magrini	Boston Red Sox	C	Elston Howard
Aug 8, 1967	C	Bob Tillman	Boston Red Sox		Cash
Sept 18, 1967	2B	Len Boehmer	Cincinnati Reds	P	Bill Henry
Nov 30, 1967	SS	Gene Michael	Los Angeles Dodgers		Cash
Dec 7, 1967	3B	Bobby Cox	Atlanta Braves	C P	Bob Tillman Dale Roberts
May 18, 1968	P	John Wyatt	Boston Red Sox		Cash
June 14, 1968		Cash	Seattle Pilots	1B	Mike Hegan

DATE		ACQUIRED	FROM		IN EXCHANGE FOR
June 15, 1968		Cash	Detroit Tigers	P	John Wyatt
July 12, 1968	P	Lindy McDaniel	San Francisco Giants	P	Bill Monbouquette
Sept 30, 1968	P	Jim Rooker	Detroit Tigers		Cash
Oct 21, 1968		Cash	Seattle Pilots	P	Jim Bouton
Nov 13, 1968		Cash	Seattle Pilots	3B	John Kennedy
Dec 4, 1968	OF	Dick Simpson	Houston Astros	P	Dooley Womack
Dec 4, 1968	P	Mike Kekich	Los Angeles Dodgers	OF	Andy Kosco
Dec 6, 1968	IF	Nate Oliver	San Francisco Giants	3B	Charley Smith
April 14, 1969	OF	Jimmie Hall	Cleveland Indians		Cash
April 19, 1969	IF	Lee Elia	Chicago Cubs	IF	Nate Oliver
May 19, 1969	OF	Jose Vidal	Seattle Pilots	OF	Dick Simpson
May 20, 1969	P	Jack Aker	Seattle Pilots	P	Fred Talbot
June 10, 1969	P	Ken Johnson	Atlanta Braves		Cash
June 14, 1969	OF	Ron Woods	Detroit Tigers	OF	Tom Tresh
July 26, 1969		Cash	California Angels	OF	Billy Cowan
Aug 11, 1969		Cash	Chicago Cubs	P	Ken Johnson
Sept 11, 1969		Minor league P Terry Bongiovanni and cash	Chicago Cubs	OF	Jimmie Hall
Dec 4, 1969	1B-OF	Curt Blefary	Houston Astros	1B	Joe Pepitone
Dec 5, 1969	1B C	Danny Cater Ossie Chavarria	Oakland Athletics	P C	Al Downing Frank Fernandez
Dec 18, 1969	OF	Pete Ward	Chicago White Sox	P	Mickey Scott and cash
Feb 28, 1970	SS	Ron Hansen	Chicago White Sox		Cash
May 15, 1970	P	Gary Waslewski	Montreal Expos	1B	Dave McDonald
July 20, 1970	P	Mike McCormick	San Francisco Giants	P	John Cumberland
Sept 9, 1970		Cash	Chicago White Sox	P	Steve Hamilton
April 9, 1971	OF	Felipe Alou	Oakland Athletics	P P	Ron Klimkowski Rob Gardner

DATE		ACQUIRED	FROM		IN EXCHANGE FOR
May 26, 1971	P	Rob Gardner	Oakland Athletics	1B	Curt Blefary
May 28, 1971	P	Jim Hardin	Baltimore Orioles	P	Bill Burbach
June 7, 1971	OF	Danny Walton	Milwaukee Brewers	1B OF	Frank Tepedino Bobby Mitchell
Oct 13, 1971	P	Rich Hinton	Chicago White Sox	OF	Jim Lyttle
Dec 2, 1971	2B	Bernie Allen	Texas Rangers	P	Gary Jones minor league P Terry Lee
Dec 2, 1971	2B	Rich McKinney	Chicago White Sox	P	Stan Bahnsen
Jan 20, 1972	OF	Johnny Callison	Chicago Cubs	P	Jack Aker
Feb 2, 1972	SS	Hal Lanier	San Francisco Giants		Cash
March 22, 1972	P	Sparky Lyle	Boston Red Sox	OF	Danny Cater
April 28, 1972	P	Jim Roland	Oakland Athletics		Cash
June 6, 1972	P	Wade Blasingame	Houston Astros		Cash
Aug 30, 1972	P	Casey Cox	Texas Rangers	P	Jim Roland
Sept 6, 1972		Cash	Texas Rangers	P	Rich Hinton
Sept 16, 1972	P	Steve Blateric	Cincinnati Reds		Cash
Oct 27, 1972	C	Rick Dempsey	Minnesota Twins	OF	Danny Walton
Nov 24, 1972	OF	Matty Alou	Oakland Athletics	P OF	Rob Gardner Rich McKinney
Nov 27, 1972	3B C	Graig Nettles Gerry Moses	Cleveland Indians	C IF OF OF	John Ellis Jerry Kenney Charlie Spikes Rusty Torres
April 5, 1973	IF	Tommy Matchick	Baltimore Orioles	SS	Frank Baker
April 17, 1973	3B	Jim Hart	San Francisco Giants		Cash
June 7, 1973	P	Pat Dobson	Atlanta Braves	1B OF P P	Frank Tepedino Wayne Nordhagen Al Closter Dave Cheadle
June 7, 1973	P	Sam McDowell	San Francisco Giants		Cash
June 12, 1973	P	Lowell Palmer	Cleveland Indians	P	Mike Kekich
Aug 7, 1973	P	Wayne Granger	St. Louis Cardinals	P	Ken Crosby and cash

DATE		ACQUIRED	FROM		IN EXCHANGE FOR
Aug 13, 1973		Cash	Montreal Expos	2B	Bernie Allen
Aug 18, 1973	1B	Mike Hegan	Oakland Athletics		Cash
Sept 6, 1973		Cash	Montreal Expos	1B-OF	Felipe Alou
Sept 6, 1973		Cash	St. Louis Cardinals	OF	Matty Alou
Sept 24, 1973	C	Duke Sims	Detroit Tigers		Cash
Dec 6, 1973	SS	Jim Mason	Texas Rangers		Cash
Dec 7, 1973	UT	Bill Sudakis	Texas Rangers		Cash
Dec 7, 1973	OF P	Lou Piniella Ken Wright	Kansas City Royals	P	Lindy McDaniel
March 19, 1974	P OF P	Rick Sawyer Walt Williams Ed Farmer (Part of three-team trade involving Detroit, New York Yankees, and Cleveland.)	Detroit Tigers	C	Gerry Moses
March 21, 1974		Cash	Philadelphia Phillies	P	Ed Farmer
March 23, 1974	OF	Elliott Maddox	Texas Rangers		Cash
April 27, 1974	1B P P	Chris Chambliss Dick Tidrow Cecil Upshaw	Cleveland Indians	P P P P	Fritz Peterson Steve Kline Fred Beene Tom Buskey
May 3, 1974	P	Mike Wallace	Philadelphia Phillies	P	Ken Wright
May 4, 1974	P	Dick Woodson	Minnesota Twins	P	Mike Pazik
May 5, 1974	IF	Fernando Gonzalez	Kansas City Royals		Cash
May 8, 1974	P	Larry Gura and cash	Texas Rangers	C	Duke Sims
May 13, 1974		Cash	Milwaukee Brewers	1B	Mike Hegan
May 31, 1974		Cash	San Diego Padres	2B	Horace Clarke
May 31, 1974		Cash	San Diego Padres	P	Lowell Palmer
June 15, 1974	P	Rudy May	California Angels		Cash
July 8, 1974	2B	Sandy Alomar	California Angels		Cash
Sept 9, 1974	OF	Alex Johnson	Texas Rangers		Cash
Oct 22, 1974	OF	Bobby Bonds	San Francisco Giants	OF	Bobby Murcer
Dec 1, 1974	UT	Bob Oliver	Baltimore Orioles		Cash
Dec 5, 1974	SS	Eddie Leon	Chicago White Sox	P	Cecil Upshaw

DATE		ACQUIRED	FROM		IN EXCHANGE FOR
Dec 31, 1974	P	Catfish Hunter	Oakland Athletics		No compensation (free agent signing)
April 1, 1975	C	Ed Herrmann	Chicago White Sox		Minor leaguers Ken Bennett Terry Quinn Fred Anyzeski John Narron and cash
June 13, 1975		Cash	St. Louis Cardinals	P	Mike Wallace
June 13, 1975	SS	Ed Brinkman	Texas Rangers		Cash
June 20, 1975	OF	Rich Coggins	Montreal Expos		Cash
Nov 22, 1975	OF	Oscar Gamble	Cleveland Indians	P	Pat Dobson
Dec 11, 1975	OF P	Mickey Rivers Ed Figueroa	California Angels	OF	Bobby Bonds
Dec 11, 1975	2B P P	Willie Randolph Ken Brett Dock Ellis	Pittsburgh Pirates	P	Doc Medich
Jan 8, 1976	P	Jim York	Houston Astros		Cash
Feb 20, 1976		Cash	California Angels	C	Ed Herrmann
May 16, 1976	C	Fran Healy	Kansas City Royals	P	Larry Gura
May 18, 1976	OF	Carlos May	Chicago White Sox	P OF	Ken Brett Rich Coggins
June 15, 1976	P P P C P	Ken Holtzman Doyle Alexander Grant Jackson Ellie Hendricks Jimmy Freeman	Baltimore Orioles	P P P P C	Rudy May Tippy Martinez Dave Pagan Scott McGregor Rick Dempsey
July 10, 1976	OF	Gene Locklear	San Diego Padres	P	Rick Sawyer
Nov 18, 1976	P	Don Gullett	Cincinnati Reds		No compensation (free agent signing)
Nov 23, 1976		No compensation (free agent signing)	Texas Rangers	P	Doyle Alexander
Nov 29, 1976	OF	Reggie Jackson	Baltimore Orioles		No compensation (free agent signing)
Nov 29, 1976	OF	Jimmy Wynn	Atlanta Braves		Cash
Jan 20, 1977	OF	Paul Blair	Baltimore Orioles	OF OF-1B	Elliott Maddox Rick Bladt
Feb 17, 1977	IF IF	Greg Pryor Brian Doyle and cash	Texas Rangers	IF	Sandy Alomar
March 14, 1977	SS	Marty Perez	San Francisco Giants	OF	Terry Whitfield
March 26, 1977	SS	Sergio Ferrer	Philadelphia Phillies	OF	Kerry Dineen

DATE	ACQUIRED	FROM	IN EXCHANGE FOR
April 5, 1977	SS Bucky Dent	Chicago White Sox	OF Oscar Gamble P LaMarr Hoyt minor league P Bob Polinsky and $200,000.
April 27, 1977	P Mike Torrez	Oakland Athletics	P Dock Ellis IF Marty Perez OF Larry Murray
June 15, 1977	OF Cliff Johnson	Houston Astros	P Randy Niemann SS Mike Fischlin OF Dave Bergman
	(Houston received Bergman on November 23.)		
Aug 2, 1977	P Stan Thomas	Seattle Mariners	Cash
Sept 15, 1977	1B Dave Kingman	California Angels	Cash
Sept 16, 1977	Cash	California Angels	OF Carlos May
Nov 17, 1977	No compensation (free agent signing)	Chicago White Sox	OF Ron Blomberg
Nov 23, 1977	No compensation (free agent signing)	Boston Red Sox	P Mike Torrez
Nov 23, 1977	P Goose Gossage	Pittsburgh Pirates	No compensation (free agent signing)
Nov 30, 1977	No compensation (free agent signing)	Chicago Cubs	OF Dave Kingman
Nov 30, 1977	OF Elliott Maddox	Baltimore Orioles	No compensation (free agent signing)
Dec 7, 1977	P Andy Messersmith	Atlanta Braves	Cash
Dec 9, 1977	3B Roy Staiger	New York Mets	SS Sergio Ferrer
Dec 12, 1977	1B Jim Spencer OF Cirilio Cruz minor league P Bob Polinsky	Chicago White Sox	P Stan Thomas minor league P Ed Ricks and cash
Dec 12, 1977	P Rawley Eastwick	St. Louis Cardinals	No compensation (free agent signing)
June 10, 1978	P Ron Davis	Chicago Cubs	P Ken Holtzman
June 10, 1978	OF Jay Johnstone OF Bobby Brown	Philadelphia Phillies	P Rawley Eastwick
June 15, 1978	OF Gary Thomasson	Oakland Athletics	OF Del Alston 3B Mickey Klutts and $50,000.
Aug 2, 1978	P Paul Lindblad	Texas Rangers	Cash

DATE	ACQUIRED	FROM	IN EXCHANGE FOR
Nov 10, 1978	P Dave Righetti OF Juan Beniquez P Mike Griffin P Paul Mirabella minor league P Greg Jamieson	Texas Rangers	SS Domingo Ramos C Mike Heath P Sparky Lyle P Larry McCall P Dave Rajsich and cash
Nov 13, 1978	P Luis Tiant	Boston Red Sox	No compensation (free agent signing)
Nov 21, 1978	P Tommy John	Los Angeles Dodgers	No compensation (free agent signing)
Feb 3, 1979	C Bruce Robinson	Oakland Athletics	$400,000.
Feb 15, 1979	C Brad Gulden	Los Angeles Dodgers	OF Gary Thomasson
May 11, 1979	P Jim Kaat	Philadelphia Phillies	Cash
May 23, 1979	P Ray Burris	Chicago Cubs	P Dick Tidrow
June 15, 1979	P Don Hood	Cleveland Indians	C Cliff Johnson
June 15, 1979	P Dave Wehrmeister	San Diego Padres	OF Jay Johnstone
June 26, 1979	OF Bobby Murcer	Chicago Cubs	Minor league P Pete Semall
Aug 1, 1979	OF Oscar Gamble P Ray Fontenot P Gene Nelson minor league 3B Amos Lewis	Texas Rangers	OF Mickey Rivers minor league Ps Bob Polinsky Neil Merschi and Mark Softy
Aug 2, 1979	3B Lenny Randle	Pittsburgh Pirates	Cash
Aug 20, 1979	Cash	New York Mets	P Ray Burris
Nov 1, 1979	OF Ruppert Jones P Jim Lewis	Seattle Mariners	P Jim Beattie P Rick Anderson OF Juan Beniquez C Jerry Narron
Nov 1, 1979	P Tom Underwood C Rick Cerone OF Ted Wilborn	Toronto Blue Jays	1B Chris Chambliss 2B Damaso Garcia P Paul Mirabella
Nov 8, 1979	1B Bob Watson	Boston Red Sox	No compensation (free agent signing)
Nov 8, 1979	P Rudy May	Montreal Expos	No compensation (free agent signing)
Nov 14, 1979	3B Eric Soderholm	Texas Rangers	Minor league 3B Amos Lewis minor league P Ricky Burdette and cash
Dec 4, 1979	No compensation (free agent signing)	Los Angeles Dodgers	OF Jay Johnstone
April 1, 1980	1B Marshall Brant	New York Mets	Cash

DATE		ACQUIRED	FROM		IN EXCHANGE FOR
April 30, 1980		Cash	St. Louis Cardinals	P	Jim Kaat
July 28, 1980		Cash	Texas Rangers	P	Ed Figueroa
Aug 4, 1980	3B	Aurelio Rodriguez	San Diego Padres		Cash
Aug 14, 1980	P	Gaylord Perry	Texas Rangers	P	Ken Clay minor league OF Marvin Thompson
Oct 24, 1980	3B	Tucker Ashford and cash	Texas Rangers	1B	Roger Holt
Nov 3, 1980	P	Mike Morgan	Oakland Athletics	SS 2B	Fred Stanley Brian Doyle
Nov 18, 1980	IF	Larry Milbourne	Seattle Mariners	C	Brad Gulden and $150,000.
Dec 15, 1980	OF	Dave Winfield	San Diego Padres		No compensation (free agent signing)
Jan 12, 1981		No compensation (free agent signing)	Atlanta Braves	P	Gaylord Perry
Feb 16, 1981		Cash	St. Louis Cardinals	C	Rafael Santana
April 1, 1981	OF P	Jerry Mumphrey John Pacella	San Diego Padres	OF OF P P	Ruppert Jones Joe Lefebvre Tim Lollar Chris Welsh
April 27, 1981	C	Barry Foote	Chicago Cubs	P	Tom Filer and cash
May 20, 1981	1B OF	Dave Revering Mike Patterson minor league P Chuck Dougherty	Oakland Athletics	1B P	Jim Spencer Tom Underwood
June 7, 1981	P	George Frazier	St. Louis Cardinals		Cash
June 12, 1981	P P	Rick Reuschel Jay Howell	Chicago Cubs	P P	Doug Bird Mike Griffin and $400,000.
Aug 19, 1981		Player to be named later (Yankees received Bill Caudill, April 1, 1982, and Jay Howell, August 20, 1982.)	Chicago Cubs	3B	Pat Tabler
Oct 21, 1981	P	Bob Sykes	St. Louis Cardinals	OF	Willie McGee
Nov 4, 1981	OF	Ken Griffey	Cincinnati Reds		Minor league Ps Bryan Ryder and Freddie Tolliver
Nov 17, 1981		Minor league C Mike Lebo	Toronto Blue Jays	3B	Aurelio Rodriguez
Dec 23, 1981	OF	Dave Collins	Cincinnati Reds		No compensation (free agent signing)
Jan 22, 1982		No compensation (free agent signing)	California Angels	OF	Reggie Jackson
Feb 22, 1982	3B	Barry Evans	San Diego Padres		Cash

DATE		ACQUIRED	FROM		IN EXCHANGE FOR
March 24, 1982	3B	Butch Hobson	California Angels	P	Bill Castro
March 24, 1982		Minor league P Scott Behan	Kansas City Royals	1B	Dennis Werth
March 30, 1982	P	Doyle Alexander	San Francisco Giants	P OF	Andy McGaffigan Ted Wilborn
April 1, 1982	P	Bill Caudill	Chicago Cubs		Continuation of Pat Tabler trade of August 18, 1981.
April 1, 1982	P	Shane Rawley	Seattle Mariners	P P OF	Bill Caudill Gene Nelson Bobby Brown
April 5, 1982	C	Bobby Ramos	Montreal Expos	C	Brad Gulden
April 10, 1982	SS	Roy Smalley	Minnesota Twins	P P SS	Ron Davis Paul Boris Greg Gagne
April 23, 1982		Minor league P Scott Patterson	Atlanta Braves	1B	Bob Watson
May 5, 1982	1B	John Mayberry	Toronto Blue Jays	1B	Dave Revering minor league 3B Jeff Reynolds
May 12, 1982	C P	Butch Wynegar Roger Erickson	Minnesota Twins	P SS P	John Pacella Larry Milbourne Pete Filson and cash
Aug 2, 1982	P	Jay Howell	Chicago Cubs		Completes Pat Tabler trade of August 18, 1981.
Aug 8, 1982	1B-OF	Lee Mazzilli	Texas Rangers	SS	Bucky Dent
Aug 23, 1982	2B	Pedro Hernandez	Toronto Blue Jays		Cash
Aug 31, 1982	P	Dennis Rasmussen	California Angels	P	Tommy John
Oct 26, 1982	C	Brad Gulden	Montreal Expos		Cash
Oct 27, 1982		Cash	Toronto Blue Jays	3B	Tucker Ashford
		(Ashford was returned to the Yankees on April 5, 1983.)			
Nov 3, 1982		Cash	Montreal Expos	C	Bobby Ramos
Dec 9, 1982	OF	Steve Kemp	Chicago White Sox		No compensation (free agent signing)
Dec 15, 1982	P	Bob Shirley	Cincinnati Reds		No compensation (free agent signing)
Dec 22, 1982		Four minor leaguers: P John holland P Tim Burke 1B Jose Rivera OF Don Aubin	Pittsburgh Pirates	1B-OF	Lee Mazzilli

DATE		ACQUIRED	FROM		IN EXCHANGE FOR
April 18, 1983		Minor leaguers P Steve Ray and IF Felix Perdomo	New York Mets	3B	Tucker Ashford
June 15, 1983	P	Matt Keough	Oakland Athletics	P 1B	Ben Callahan Marshall Brant and cash
July 16, 1983	2B	Larry Milbourne	Philadelphia Phillies		Cash
Aug 10, 1983	OF	Omar Moreno	Houston Astros	OF	Jerry Mumphrey
Aug 26, 1983	P	John Montefusco	San Diego Padres	P 2B	Dennis Rasmussen Eduardo Rodriguez and $200,000.
Dec 7, 1983	P	Mike Armstrong minor league C Duane Dewey	Kansas City Royals	1B P	Steve Balboni Roger Erickson
Dec 7, 1983	SS	Tim Foli	California Angels	P	Curt Kaufman and cash
Dec 8, 1983	C	Mike O'Berry	California Angels		No compensation (free agent signing)
Dec 19, 1983	P	Curt Brown	California Angels		Minor league P Mike Browning
Dec 20, 1983	OF	Pat Rooney	Montreal Expos		Minor league P Tim Burke
Jan 6, 1984	P	Phil Niekro	Atlanta Braves		No compensation (free agent signing)
Jan 12, 1984		No compensation (free agent signing)	San Diego Padres	P	Goose Gossage
Feb 4, 1984	3B	Toby Harrah and a player to be named later	Cleveland Indians	P OF	Danny Boitano Otis Nixon
Feb 14, 1984		Minor league Ps Eric Parent and Scott Nielsen	Seattle Mariners	2B	Larry Milbourne
March 30, 1984	P	Dennis Rasmussen and a player to be named later	San Diego Padres	3B	Graig Nettles
April 1, 1984		Cash	Cleveland Indians	C	Juan Espino

Oakland A's

The Best Trades

1. Acquired Ken Holtzman from the Chicago Cubs for Rick Monday, November 29, 1971.
2. Acquired Bill Caudill and Darren Akenfelds from the Seattle Mariners for Bob Kearney and Dave Beard, November 21, 1983.
3. Acquired Tony Armas, Rick Langford, Doug Bair, Dave Giusti, Mitchell Page, and Doc Medich from the Pittsburgh Pirates for Phil Garner, Tommy Helms, and Chris Batton, March 15, 1977.

4. Acquired Billy North from the Chicago Cubs for Bob Locker, November 21, 1972.
5. Acquired Davey Lopes from the Los Angeles Dodgers for Lance Hudson, February 8, 1982.

The Worst Trades

1. Traded Chet Lemon and Dave Hamilton to the Chicago White Sox for Stan Bahnsen and Skip Pitlock, June 15, 1975.
2. Traded George Hendrick and Dave Duncan to the Cleveland Indians for Ray Fosse and Jack Heidemann, March 4, 1973.
3. Traded Manny Trillo, Darold Knowles, and Bob Locker to the Chicago Cubs for Billy Williams, October 23, 1974.
4. Traded Dan Ford and Denny Myers to the Minnesota Twins for Pat Bourque, October 23, 1974.
5. Traded Don Stanhouse and Jim Panther to the Texas Rangers for Denny McLain, March 4, 1972.

Owner: Charles O. Finley

Almost from the moment Charlie Finley came into Kansas City as the new owner of the K.C. A's he was regarded as a menace by the American League's more conventional owners. His wild publicity stunts including his mascot mule named Charlie O, his well-publicized feuds, and his loud contract disputes served to strengthen that unfraternal attitude. But Finley did much more than merely generate turbulence; a man ahead of his time, he proposed many innovations that enhanced baseball's popularity and gate appeal.

It was Finley who proposed playing World Series games at night to increase television audiences and revenues. It was he who pushed for the adoption of the designated hitter rule to bring more attack to the game. And it was he who brightened the ballpark with boldly colored uniforms that broke baseball out of its white and grey rut. And, not at all incidentally, he built one of the most colorful teams since St. Louis's Gashouse Gang, and won three straight World Series.

Finley took a last place team and in ten years built it into a powerhouse. An insurance salesman by trade, Finley brought to baseball a keen, inquisitive mind and a willingness to work long hours. His lack of a baseball background did not faze him at all; he shrewdly solicited the opinions of experienced baseball men in subtle, probing conversations, and then acted on their suggestions after filtering them through his own sharp judgment.

With the A's in last place (and still in Kansas City) when the baseball draft began in 1965, Finley took advantage of early round selections to grab Rick Monday and Sal Bando from Arizona State. A year later he signed Reggie Jackson from the same school. Other prospects he picked up included Catfish Hunter, Vida Blue, Rollie Fingers, Blue Moon Odom, Gene Tenace, and Claudell Washington. These players would form the nucleus of the Oakland championship teams.

An innovative promoter, Finley found odd ways of calling attention to himself and to his team. It was Finley who gave Catfish Hunter his nickname, and baseball folklore can thank him for that; no matter how talented a pitcher he might be, "Jim Hunter" would not have attracted as much attention. Finley's "Mustache Day" promotion gave his team its distinctive look, and provided the inspiration for Rollie Fingers's trademark handlebar. But Finley had a destructive streak as well, and in a most unusual fashion, he himself paved the way for his own team's destruction.

It began in 1967 when, in a fit of pique over Ken Harrelson's criticism of him, Finley gave Harrelson his unconditional release, making him the first true free agent. Harrelson signed on with the Boston Red Sox, who were desperate for a power-hitting outfielder to replace their injured star, Tony Conigliaro. After Vida Blue's phenomenal rookie season, he and Finley engaged in a bitter contract dispute, with Finley vowing to break Blue, and Blue threatening to leave baseball. Blue eventually signed, but never became the overpowering star he seemed certain to be. During the 1973 World Series, Finley pressured second baseman Mike Andrews, who had committed two costly errors in the twelfth inning of the second game, to sign a statement claiming injury that would allow Finley to drop him from the squad and put in a replacement. And at the end of the 1974 season, Catfish Hunter claimed that Finley had failed to make payments on an insurance policy guaranteed under his contract, and Hunter was declared a free agent. With freedom beckoning all of Finley's dissatisfied and underpaid stars, Charlie O. read the handwriting on the wall and tried to sell off his players. He dealt Vida Blue to the Yankees for one and a half million dollars, and Joe Rudi and Rollie Fingers to Boston for a million each. But commissioner Bowie Kuhn voided the sales as not being in the best interests of baseball, and Finley was forced to watch helplessly as the players he had developed left for far greener pastures.

Finley's ballclub was perfect for its time — after the institution of the draft, but before free agency. His methods would not have worked ten years earlier, and his club fell with a thud once the free agent exodus was underway. Finley sold the club before the 1981 season, but not before he added one more bizarre chapter to his life in the game. In November 1976, he "traded" his manager, Chuck Tanner, to the Pittsburgh Pirates for catcher Manny Sanguillen and $100,000. And a year later he let the Pirates have Sanguillen back — for another $50,000.

DATE		ACQUIRED	FROM		IN EXCHANGE FOR
Dec 3, 1967	C	Jim Pagliaroni	Pittsburgh Pirates		Cash
July 31, 1968		Cash	Boston Red Sox	OF	Floyd Robinson
Feb 24, 1969	P	Jim Roland	Minnesota Twins		Cash
May 7, 1969	OF	Jose Tartabull	Boston Red Sox		Cash
May 27, 1969		Cash	Seattle Pilots	C	Jim Pagliaroni
June 3, 1969	OF	Federico Velazquez	Seattle Pilots		Cash
June 14, 1969	C	Larry Haney	Seattle Pilots	2B	John Donaldson
July 12, 1969	IF	Bob Johnson	St. Louis Cardinals	OF	Joe Nossek
Aug 22, 1969	OF	Tito Francona	Atlanta Braves		Cash
Aug 29, 1969	P	Fred Talbot	Seattle Pilots	P IF	Bob Meyer Pete Koegel
Sept 21, 1969	P	Juan Pizarro	Cleveland Indians		Cash
Dec 3, 1969	OF	Felipe Alou	Atlanta Braves	P	Jim Nash
Dec 5, 1969	P C	Al Downing Frank Fernandez	New York Yankees	1B C	Danny Cater Ossie Chavarria
Dec 5, 1969	P	Mudcat Grant	St. Louis Cardinals		Cash
Dec 7, 1969	P SS	Diego Segui Ray Oyler	Seattle Pilots	IF P	Ted Kubiak George Lauzerique

DATE		ACQUIRED	FROM		IN EXCHANGE FOR
Jan 15, 1970	1B IF	Don Mincher Ron Clark	Milwaukee Brewers	OF P C P	Mike Hershberger Lew Krausse Phil Roof Ken Sanders
March 24, 1970	IF	Roberto Pena	San Diego Padres	1B	Ramon Webster
April 17, 1970		Cash	California Angels	SS	Ray Oyler
May 16, 1970		Cash	California Angels	OF	Tommie Reynolds
May 18, 1970	2B	John Donaldson	Milwaukee Brewers	IF	Roberto Pena
May 26, 1970		Cash	San Diego Padres	P	Roberto Rodriguez
June 11, 1970	OF	Steve Hovley	Milwaukee Brewers	P OF	Al Downing Tito Francona
June 15, 1970	P	Bob Locker	Milwaukee Brewers		Cash
June 22, 1970	OF	Tommy Davis	Houston Astros		Cash
Sept 14, 1970	OF	Angel Mangual	Pittsburgh Pirates	P	Mudcat Grant
		(Oakland received Mangual on October 20.)			
Sept 16, 1970		Cash	Chicago Cubs	OF	Tommy Davis
Oct 20, 1970		Cash	Cincinnati Reds	P	Ed Sprague
April 9, 1971	P P	Ron Klimkowski Rob Gardner	New York Yankees	OF	Felipe Alou
April 24, 1971	SS	Larry Brown	Cleveland Indians		Cash
May 8, 1971	1B P	Mike Epstein Darold Knowles	Washington Senators	C 1B P	Frank Fernandez Don Mincher Paul Lindblad and cash
May 22, 1971	P	Daryl Patterson	Detroit Tigers	2B	John Donaldson
May 26, 1971	1B	Curt Blefary	New York Yankees	P	Rob Gardner
June 14, 1971	1B	Mike Hegan	Milwaukee Brewers		Cash
June 17, 1971		Cash	Chicago Cubs	1B	Ramon Webster
June 23, 1971		Cash	Washington Senators	C	Frank Fernandez
June 25, 1971		Cash	St. Louis Cardinals	P	Daryl Patterson
		(Patterson was returned to Oakland on October 21, 1971.)			
Aug 10, 1971	P	Mudcat Grant	Pittsburgh Pirates		Cash
Aug 14, 1971		Cash	Atlanta Braves	IF	Tony LaRussa

DATE		ACQUIRED	FROM		IN EXCHANGE FOR
Aug 31, 1971	OF	Adrian Garrett	Chicago Cubs	C OF	Frank Fernandez Bill McNulty
Nov 29, 1971	P	Ken Holtzman	Chicago Cubs	OF	Rick Monday
March 4, 1972	P	Denny McLain	Texas Rangers	P P	Don Stanhouse Jim Panther
April 28, 1972		Cash	New York Yankees	P	Jim Roland
May 9, 1972	P	Mike Kilkenny	Detroit Tigers	1B	Reggie Sanders
May 15, 1972	P	Don Shaw	St. Louis Cardinals	IF	Dwain Anderson
May 17, 1972	OF	Ollie Brown	San Diego Padres	OF P	Curt Blefary Mike Kilkenny minor league OF Greg Schubert
May 18, 1972	IF	Marty Martinez	St. Louis Cardinals	OF	Brant Alyea
June 7, 1972		Cash	St. Louis Cardinals	P	Diego Segui
June 20, 1972	OF	Bill Voss	Milwaukee Brewers	OF	Ron Clark
June 28, 1972	OF	Art Shamsky	Chicago Cubs		Cash
June 29, 1972		Cash	Milwaukee Brewers	OF	Ollie Brown
June 29, 1972	1B	Orlando Cepeda	Atlanta Braves	P	Denny McLain
July 20, 1972	1B SS	Don Mincher Ted Kubiak	Texas Rangers	IF IF P	Marty Martinez Vic Harris Steve Lawson
Aug 27, 1972	OF	Matty Alou	St. Louis Cardinals	OF	Bill Voss minor league P Steve Easton
Aug 30, 1972	SS	Dal Maxvill	St. Louis Cardinals		Minor leaguers IF Joe Lindsey and C Gene Dusen
Sept 6, 1972	C	Larry Haney	San Diego Padres		Cash
Oct 30, 1972	P	Paul Lindblad	Texas Rangers	OF OF	Bill McNulty Brant Alyea
Nov 21, 1972	OF	Billy North	Chicago Cubs	P	Bob Locker
Nov 24, 1972	P OF	Rob Gardner Rich McKinney	New York Yankees	OF	Matty Alou
Nov 30, 1972	P	Horacio Pina	Texas Rangers	1B	Mike Epstein
Feb 14, 1973	OF	Billy Conigliaro	Milwaukee Brewers		Cash
March 24, 1973	C SS	Ray Fosse Jack Heidemann	Cleveland Indians	OF C	George Hendrick Dave Duncan

DATE		ACQUIRED	FROM		IN EXCHANGE FOR
May 2, 1973	1B	Deron Johnson	Philadelphia Phillies		Minor league UT Jack Bastable
May 4, 1973		Cash	Pittsburgh Pirates	C	Jerry McNertney
May 31, 1973		Cash	Milwaukee Brewers	P	Rob Gardner
		(Deal was cancelled and Gardner was returned to Oakland.)			
July 7, 1973		Cash	Pittsburgh Pirates	SS	Dal Maxvill
July 31, 1973	OF	Jesus Alou	Houston Astros		Cash
Aug 1, 1973	OF	Vic Davalillo	Pittsburgh Pirates		Cash
Aug 18, 1973		Cash	New York Yankees	1B	Mike Hegan
Aug 29, 1973	1B	Pat Bourque	Chicago Cubs	1B	Gonzalo Marquez
Sept 1, 1973		Cash	St. Louis Cardinals	P C	Lew Krausse Larry Haney
Sept 11, 1973	OF	Rico Carty	Chicago Cubs		Cash
Sept 18, 1973		Cash	Montreal Expos	OF	Jose Morales
Nov 3, 1973	P	Bob Locker	Chicago Cubs	P	Horacio Pina
Jan 9, 1974		Cash	Philadelphia Phillies	OF	Jay Johnstone
March 25, 1974		Cash	Cleveland Indians	IF	Jack Heidemann
March 26, 1974	C	Larry Haney	St. Louis Cardinals		Cash
June 24, 1974	P	Bill Parsons and cash	Milwaukee Brewers	1B	Deron Johnson
Aug 19, 1974	1B-OF	Jim Holt	Minnesota Twins	1B	Pat Bourque
Oct 23, 1974	OF	Billy Williams	Chicago Cubs	P P 2B	Darold Knowles Bob Locker Manny Trillo
Oct 23, 1974	1B	Pat Bourque	Minnesota Twins	OF	Dan Ford minor league P Denny Myers
Dec 2, 1974		Cash	St. Louis Cardinals	P	Bill Parsons
Dec 31, 1974		No compensation (free agent signing)	New York Yankees	P	Catfish Hunter
March 26, 1975	OF	Don Hopkins	Montreal Expos		Cash
April 6, 1975	P	Jim Todd	Chicago Cubs	OF	Champ Summers and cash
April 28, 1975	OF	Matt Alexander	Chicago Cubs		Minor league P Howell Copeland

DATE		ACQUIRED	FROM		IN EXCHANGE FOR
May 16, 1975	P	Sonny Siebert	San Diego Padres	IF	Ted Kubiak
May 18, 1975	IF	Teddy Martinez	St. Louis Cardinals	 P	Minor league P Steve Staniland Mike Barlow
May 20, 1975	P P	Dick Bosman Jim Perry	Cleveland Indians	P	Blue Moon Odom and cash
June 15, 1975	P P	Stan Bahnsen Skip Pitlock	Chicago White Sox	P OF	Dave Hamilton Chet Lemon
Aug 13, 1975	OF	Tommy Harper	California Angels		Cash
Aug 31, 1975	UT	Cesar Tovar	Texas Rangers		Cash
Oct 28, 1975	SS	Larry Lintz	St. Louis Cardinals	OF	Charlie Chant
Dec 9, 1975		Cash	Cleveland Indians	C	Ray Fosse
April 2, 1976	OF P P	Don Baylor Mike Torrez Paul Mitchell	Baltimore Orioles	OF P	Reggie Jackson Ken Holtzman minor leaguer Bill Van Bommell
April 19, 1976	C	Tim Hosley	Chicago Cubs		Cash
Aug 30, 1976	1B	Willie McCovey	San Diego Padres		Cash
Sept 14, 1976	1B	Ron Fairly	St. Louis Cardinals		Cash
Nov 5, 1976	C	Manny Sanguillen and $100,000.	Pittsburgh Pirates	MGR	Chuck Tanner
Nov 5, 1976	2B	Tommy Helms	Pittsburgh Pirates		Cash
Nov 16, 1976		No compensation (free agent signing)	California Angels	OF	Don Baylor
Nov 17, 1976		No compensation (free agent signing)	California Angels	OF	Joe Rudi
Nov 17, 1976		No compensation (free agent signing)	Texas Rangers	SS	Bert Campaneris
Nov 19, 1976		No compensation (free agent signing)	Milwaukee Brewers	3B	Sal Bando
Dec 6, 1976		Cash	Milwaukee Brewers	C	Larry Haney
Dec 14, 1976		No compensation (free agent signing)	San Diego Padres	P	Rollie Fingers
Dec 14, 1976		No compensation (free agent signing)	San Diego Padres	C	Gene Tenace
Feb 19, 1977		$400,000.	Texas Rangers	P	Paul Lindblad
Feb 24, 1977		Minor league IF Mike Weathers and cash	Toronto Blue Jays	1B	Ron Fairly
Feb 25, 1977		Cash	Milwaukee Brewers	3B	Ken McMullen

DATE		ACQUIRED	FROM		IN EXCHANGE FOR
March 15, 1977	P P P P OF OF	Dave Giusti Doc Medich Doug Bair Rick Langford Tony Armas Mitchell Page	Pittsburgh Pirates	2B 3B P	Phil Garner Tommy Helms Chris Batton
March 15, 1977	IF	Jerry Tabb	Chicago Cubs		Cash
March 15, 1977	P	Joe Coleman	Chicago Cubs	P	Jim Todd
March 15, 1977	1B	Richie Allen	Philadelphia Phillies		No compensation (free agent signing)
March 25, 1977		Cash	St. Louis Cardinals	IF	Tom Sandt
March 26, 1977	P IF	Jim Umbarger Rodney Scott and cash	Texas Rangers	OF	Claudell Washington
March 29, 1977	P	Pablo Torrealba	Atlanta Braves		Cash
April 27, 1977	P IF OF	Dock Ellis Marty Perez Larry Murray	New York Yankees	P	Mike Torrez
May 22, 1977	1B	Mike Jorgensen	Montreal Expos	P	Stan Bahnsen
June 15, 1977	OF	Willie Crawford	Houston Astros	OF	Dennis Walling and cash
June 15, 1977		Cash	Texas Rangers	P	Dock Ellis
Aug 4, 1977		Cash	Seattle Mariners	P	Paul Mitchell
Aug 5, 1977	P	Dave Giusti	Chicago Cubs		Cash
Aug 12, 1977	P	Steve Dunning	St. Louis Cardinals	P	Randy Scarbery
Aug 25, 1977		Cash	Texas Rangers	P	Jim Umbarger
Sept 13, 1977		Cash	Seattle Mariners	P	Doc Medich
Feb 23, 1978		No compensation (free agent signing)	Texas Rangers	1B	Mike Jorgensen
Feb 25, 1978	1B	Dave Revering and cash	Cincinnati Reds	P	Doug Bair
March 15, 1978	C OF P P P P SS	Gary Alexander Gary Thomasson Dave Heaverlo Alan Wirth John Henry Johnson Phil Huffman Mario Guerrero and $300,000.	San Francisco Giants	P	Vida Blue
March 25, 1978	2B	Steve Staggs	Toronto Blue Jays	OF	Sheldon Mallory

DATE		ACQUIRED	FROM		IN EXCHANGE FOR
March 29, 1978	P	Pete Broberg	Chicago Cubs	2B	Rodney Scott and cash
March 30, 1978	P C	Steve Renko Jim Essian	Chicago White Sox	P	Pablo Torrealba
April 1, 1978	3B	Mike Adams	Chicago Cubs		Cash
April 4, 1978	OF P 2B	Miguel Dilone Elias Sosa Mike Edwards	Pittsburgh Pirates	C	Manny Sanguillen
May 17, 1978	OF	Glenn Burke	Los Angeles Dodgers	OF	Billy North
May 22, 1978		Cash	Toronto Blue Jays	P	Joe Coleman
June 15, 1978	OF 3B	Del Alston Mickey Klutts and $50,000.	New York Yankees	OF	Gary Thomasson
June 15, 1978	OF	Joe Wallis	Cleveland Indians	C	Gary Alexander
Aug 15, 1978	DH	Rico Carty	Toronto Blue Jays	DH P	Willie Horton Phil Huffman
Oct 3, 1978		Cash	Toronto Blue Jays	DH	Rico Carty
Jan 9, 1979		No compensation (free agent signing)	Montreal Expos	P	Elias Sosa
Jan 20, 1979		No compensation (free agent signing)	Boston Red Sox	P	Steve Renko
Feb 3, 1979		$400,000.	New York Yankees	C	Bruce Robinson
June 15, 1979	3B C	Dave Chalk Mike Heath and cash	Texas Rangers	P	John Henry Johnson
July 4, 1979		Cash	Chicago Cubs	OF	Miguel Dilone
April 9, 1980		Cash	Seattle Mariners	P	Dave Heaverlo
July 25, 1980	1B	Orlando Gonzalez	Philadelphia Phillies		Cash
Nov 3, 1980	SS 2B	Fred Stanley Brian Doyle	New York Yankees	P	Mike Morgan
Nov 20, 1980		No compensation (free agent signing)	Chicago White Sox	C	Jim Essian
Dec 8, 1980		Cash	Seattle Mariners	SS	Mario Guerrero
Dec 11, 1980	C-1B IF	Cliff Johnson Keith Drumright	Chicago Cubs		Minor league P Mike King
Feb 10, 1981	IF	Jimmy Sexton	Houston Astros	P	Rick Lysander
March 27, 1981	 3B SS	Minor league P Eric Mustard Kevin Bell Tony Phillips	San Diego Padres	P	Bob Lacey minor league P Ray Moretti

DATE		ACQUIRED	FROM		IN EXCHANGE FOR
April 6, 1981	P	Bob Owchinko	Pittsburgh Pirates	P	Ernie Camacho and cash
May 20, 1981	1B P	Jim Spencer Tom Underwood	New York Yankees	1B OF	Dave Revering Mike Patterson minor league P Chuck Dougherty
June 10, 1981	OF	Rick Bosetti	Toronto Blue Jays		Cash
Dec 4, 1981	1B	Joe Rudi	Boston Red Sox		No compensation (free agent signing)
Dec 9, 1981	1B	Dan Meyer	Seattle Mariners	P	Rich Bordi
Dec 9, 1981	OF	Rusty McNealy minor league P Tim Hallgren	Seattle Mariners	P	Roy Thomas
Feb 8, 1982	2B	Davey Lopes	Los Angeles Dodgers		Minor league 2B Lance Hudson
Feb 24, 1982		Minor league P Allen Edwards	Baltimore Orioles	P	Craig Minetto
March 1, 1982	OF	Darrell Brown minor league Ps Mark Fellows and Jack Smith	Detroit Tigers	3B C	Jeff Cox Scott Meyer
April 7, 1982	OF	Jeff Burroughs	Seattle Mariners		No compensation (free agent signing)
May 14, 1982	P	Mike Warren minor league 1B John Evans	Milwaukee Brewers	SS	Rob Picciolo
Nov 15, 1982	P	Tom Burgmeier	Boston Red Sox		No compensation (free agent signing)
Nov 15, 1982	OF	Al Woods	Toronto Blue Jays	DH	Cliff Johnson
Dec 6, 1982	3B OF	Carney Lansford Garry Hancock minor league P Jerry King	Boston Red Sox	OF C	Tony Armas Jeff Newman
Jan 17, 1983		Cash	Boston Red Sox	P	Brian Kingman
Jan 18, 1983	SS	Bill Almon	Chicago White Sox		No compensation (free agent signing)
June 15, 1983	P 1B	Ben Callahan Marshall Brant and cash	New York Yankees	P	Matt Keough
Sept 2, 1983		Minor league Ps Tom Dozier and Jim Strichek	St. Louis Cardinals	P	Steve Baker
Nov 21, 1983	P	Bill Caudill minor league P Darren Akerfelds	Seattle Mariners	P C	Dave Beard Bob Kearney
Dec 6, 1983	C	Jim Essian	Cleveland Indians	SS	Luis Quinones
Dec 7, 1983	P	Ray Burris	Montreal Expos	OF	Rusty McNealy and cash

DATE		ACQUIRED	FROM		IN EXCHANGE FOR
Dec 8, 1983	P	Tim Stoddard	Baltimore Orioles	3B	Wayne Gross
Dec 28, 1983	2B	Joe Morgan	Philadelphia Phillies		No compensation (free agent signing)
Jan 23, 1984	P	Lary Sorensen	Cleveland Indians		No compensation (free agent signing)
Feb 6, 1984		Free agent signing	Baltimore Orioles	P	Tom Underwood
		(Oakland selected P Tim Belcher of New York Yankees from the compensation pool.)			
March 26, 1984		Minor leaguers P Stan Kyles and OF Stan Boderick	Chicago Cubs	P	Tim Stoddard

Philadelphia Athletics

The Best Trades

1. Acquired George Blaeholder from the St. Louis Browns for Ed Coleman and Sugar Cain, May 21, 1935.

The Worst Trades

1. Traded Joe Jackson to the Cleveland Indians for Bris Lord, July 25, 1910.
2. Sold away the following players: Eddie Collins to the Chicago White Sox; Lefty Grove, Rube Walberg and Max Bishop to the Boston Red Sox; Jimmie Foxx to the Boston Red Sox; Mickey Cochrane to the Detroit Tigers.
3. Traded George Kell to the Detroit Tigers for Barney McCosky, May 18, 1946.
4. Traded Nellie Fox to the Chicago White Sox for Joe Tipton, October 19, 1949.
5. Traded Charlie Jamieson, Larry Gardner, and Elmer Myers to the Cleveland Indians for Braggo Roth, March 1, 1919.

Owner: Connie Mack

Only one baseball club was under the domination and management of a single individual for a half century. Under Cornelius McGillicuddy, known to all as Connie Mack, the Philadelphia club built remarkable dynasties that ran roughshod over the opposition in the American League, and then plunged into the depths of the AL cellar when their stars were sold off.

When the A's were good, they were unbeatable. Their two greatest exhibits are the 1910–14 and 1929–31 clubs. Between them these two groupings won seven of Mr. Mack's nine pennants and all five of his World Series. The list of great players discovered by Mack would make a respectable Hall of Fame by itself: Rube Waddell, Eddie Plank, Chief Bender, Eddie Collins, Home Run Baker, Lefty Grove, Al Simmons, Mickey Cochrane, and Jimmie Foxx all played for him, as did such only slightly less stellar men as Jack Coombs, Stuffy McInnis, Wally Schang, Jimmy Dykes, Rube Oldring, Amos Strunk, Bing Miller, George Earnshaw, and Mule Haas.

Not one of these men came to the A's from another major league club. The first Philadelphia dynasty was built largely from players signed by Mack with no previous experience in organized ball. Many came out of college: Eddie Plank from Gettysburg College, Chief Bender from the Carlyle Indian School, Eddie Collins from Columbia University, Jack Barry from Holy Cross, and Jack Coombs from Colby College. With Baker, McInnis, and the others filling in around this nucleus, the A's won World Series in 1910, 1911, and 1913 before falling to the Boston Braves in four straight in the 1914 classic.

Disturbed by the humiliation of losing the Series in four games, and unwilling to pay the higher salaries being dictated by the rival Federal League which had lured Plank and Bender, Mack dismantled his championship squad before the first snowfall. Collins was the first to go, followed rapidly by Coombs, Barry, Herb Pennock, and Bob Shawkey. The A's finished last in 1915, losing an astounding fifty-six more games than the year before. Mack vowed he would rebuild, and he was eventually able to, but it took him a dozen years of lurking in or near the cellar, kept out of it only by a similarly disadvantaged Red Sox squad.

During those lean years, Mack found his next group of stars in the independent minor leagues. Grove, Simmons, Cochrane, Foxx, and Max Bishop were all purchased from minor league squads. By the late 1920s the A's were ready to win again, but were held back by the mighty Yankees. The instant the Yanks faltered the A's were ready, and they rolled to three straight pennants by an average margin of thirteen games.

By the time the Yanks recovered to win the 1932 pennant, the Depression had set in, and Mack was saddled with the biggest payroll in the game. Mack conferred with his co-owners Tom and John Shibe, and decided once again to cash in their players. Simmons, Haas and Dykes went to the White Sox for $150,000. After the A's slipped to third in 1933, Cochrane went to Detroit for $100,000, while Grove, Bishop, and Rube Walberg brought another $125,000 from Boston. Foxx followed those three a year later for $150,000. The transactions did bring the A's some players — Johnny Pasek, Rabbit Warstler, Rob Kline, Gordon Rhodes — who were just enough to fulfill the team's obligation to field nine men at a time. From 1934 until the move to Kansas City twenty years later, the once-proud Athletics finished as high as fourth place just twice.

DATE		ACQUIRED	FROM		IN EXCHANGE FOR
April 23, 1901	P	Bock Baker	Cleveland Indians		Cash
April 1901	SS	Harry Lockhead	Detroit Tigers		Cash
April 1901	C	Farmer Steelman	Brooklyn Dodgers		Cash
May 1901	SS	Joe Dolan	Philadelphia Phillies		Cash
June 1901	C	Tom Leahy	Milwaukee Brewers	OF	Phil Geier
July 1901		Cash	Chicago White Sox	P	Wiley Piatt
July 1901	P	Snake Wiltse	Pittsburgh Pirates		Cash
April 1902	P	Fred Mitchell	Boston Red Sox		Cash
May 16, 1902		Cash	Cleveland Indians	OF	Elmer Flick
June 1902	C 2B	Ossee Schreckengost Frank Bonner	Cleveland Indians	P	Bill Bernhard
June 1902	P	Bert Husting	Boston Red Sox		Cash
June 1902		Cash	Cleveland Indians	2B	Nap Lajoie

DATE		ACQUIRED	FROM		IN EXCHANGE FOR
July 1902		Cash	Baltimore Orioles	P	Snake Wiltse
Feb 1903	3B	Ollie Pickering	Cleveland Indians		Cash
March 1903		Cash	New York Yankees	1B	Dave Fultz
Aug 31, 1904		Cash	Washington Senators	2B	Jim Mullin
Jan 1905		Cash	Washington Senators	3B	Lave Cross
July 13, 1905		Cash	New York Yankees	C	Mike Powers
Aug 7, 1905	C	Mike Powers	New York Yankees		Cash
Oct 2, 1905	OF	Rube Oldring	New York Yankees		Cash
May 11, 1906		Cash	New York Yankees	OF	Danny Hoffman
June 1906		Waiver price	New York Giants	SS	Jack Hannifan
June 7, 1907	3B	Jimmy Collins	Boston Red Sox	3B	Jack Knight
Oct 1907		Cash	St. Louis Browns	P	Rube Waddell
March 1908		Cash	New York Yankees	OF	Birdie Cree
May 1908		Cash	Chicago White Sox	C	Ossee Schreckengost
July 1908	C	Bert Blue	St. Louis Browns	C	Syd Smith
Aug 1908		Cash	Boston Braves	OF	Herbie Moran
Dec 8, 1908	C	Ira Thomas	Detroit Tigers		Cash
May 1909	OF	Bob Ganley	Washington Senators		Cash
May 1910	C	Pat Donahue	Boston Red Sox		Cash
May 1910		Cash	Cleveland Indians	3B	Morrie Rath
July 25, 1910	OF	Bris Lord	Cleveland Indians	OF	Joe Jackson
Sept 1910		Cash	Cleveland Indians	C	Pat Donahue
May 1911		Cash	St. Louis Browns	OF	Happy Hogan
Aug 20, 1911		Cash	Cleveland Indians	C	Steve O'Neill
Dec 1911		Cash	Cleveland Indians	C	Paddy Livingston

DATE		ACQUIRED	FROM		IN EXCHANGE FOR
May 1912	P	Jim Crabb	Chicago White Sox		Cash
July 1912		Cash	Cleveland Indians	P	Harry Krause
Nov 1912		Cash	New York Yankees	SS	Claud Derrick
Dec 1912		Cash	Boston Braves	OF	Bris Lord
Aug 24, 1913	SS	Doc Lavan	St. Louis Browns		Cash
Jan 1914		Waiver price	Pittsburgh Pirates	P	Pat Bohen
Feb 5, 1914		Cash	St. Louis Browns	SS	Doc Lavan
June 10, 1914	OF	Jimmy Walsh	New York Yankees	OF	Tom Daley
June 1914		Cash	New York Yankees	P	Boardwalk Brown
Dec 8, 1914		$50,000.	Chicago White Sox	2B	Eddie Collins
Jan 1915	2B	Nap Lajoie	Cleveland Indians		Waiver price
Jan 1915		Cash	Chicago White Sox	C	Jack Lapp
June 13, 1915		Waiver price	Boston Red Sox	P	Herb Pennock
July 2, 1915		$8,000.	Boston Red Sox	SS	Jack Barry
July 7, 1915		$18,000.	New York Yankees	P	Bob Shawkey
July 15, 1915		$13,500.	Chicago White Sox	OF	Eddie Murphy
Dec 1915		Cash	Cincinnati Reds	SS	Larry Kopf
Feb 15, 1916		$37,500.	New York Yankees	3B	Frank Baker
Sept 2, 1916	C	Ray Haley	Boston Red Sox	OF	Jimmy Walsh
Jan 1917	P	Rube Schauer	New York Giants		Waiver price
Feb 3, 1917		Cash	Washington Senators	2B	Sam Crane
July 17, 1917	OF	Charlie Jamieson	Washington Senators		Waiver price
Dec 14, 1917	P OF C	Vean Gregg Merlin Kopp Pinch Thomas and $60,000.	Boston Red Sox	OF P C	Amos Strunk Joe Bush Wally Schang
Jan 10, 1918	3B OF C	Larry Gardner Tilly Walker Hick Cady	Boston Red Sox	1B	Stuffy McInnis

DATE		ACQUIRED	FROM		IN EXCHANGE FOR
March 8, 1918	1B	George Burns	New York Yankees	OF	Ping Bodie
April 1918	P	Scott Perry	Boston Braves		Cash
May 25, 1918	OF	Merito Acosta	Washington Senators		Cash
Jan 1919	3B	Fred Thomas	Boston Red Sox		Cash
Jan 1919	SS	Terry Turner	Cleveland Indians		Waiver price
March 1, 1919	OF	Braggo Roth	Cleveland Indians	3B P OF	Larry Gardner Elmer Myers Charlie Jamieson
April 1919	2B	Snooks Dowd	Detroit Tigers		Cash
April 1919	P	Tom Rogers	St. Louis Browns		Cash
June 27, 1919	OF SS	Amos Strunk Jack Barry (Barry refused to report, and retired.)	Boston Red Sox	OF OF	Braggo Roth Red Shannon
June 1919		Cash	Washington Senators	2B	Roy Grover
Aug 1919		Cash	Chicago White Sox	P	Wynn Noyes
May 29, 1920		Cash	Cleveland Indians	OF	George Burns
July 23, 1920		Waiver price	Chicago White Sox	OF	Amos Strunk
July 1920	IF	Red Shannon	Washington Senators	OF	Fred Thomas
June 2, 1921		Waiver price	Cleveland Indians	P	Dave Keefe
Dec 1921	C	Frank Bruggy	Philadelphia Phillies		Cash
Jan 10, 1922	P OF	Jose Acosta Bing Miller (Part of three-team trade involving Boston, Philadelphia, and Washington.)	Washington Senators	3B	Joe Dugan
Feb 4, 1922		Cash	Chicago White Sox	P	Jose Acosta
Feb 16, 1922	1B	Doc Johnston	Cleveland Indians		Cash
March 17, 1922		Cash	New York Yankees	OF	Whitey Witt
March 1922	2B	Ralph Young	Detroit Tigers		Waiver price
July 1922		Cash	Detroit Tigers	P	Roy Moore
Feb 8, 1923	OF	Bevo LeBourveau	Philadelphia Phillies		Cash

DATE		ACQUIRED	FROM		IN EXCHANGE FOR
April 1923	P	Rube Walberg	New York Giants		Waiver price
Jan 1924		Cash	Washington Senators	OF	Wid Matthews
April 30, 1924	OF	Amos Strunk	Chicago White Sox		Waiver price
June 19, 1924		Cash	Washington Senators	P	Curly Ogden
July 1, 1925		Cash	Boston Braves	IF	Doc Gautreau
July 10, 1925	P	Jack Quinn	Boston Red Sox		Waiver price
Dec 12, 1925	2B	Bill Wambsganss	Boston Red Sox		$4,000.
June 15, 1926	OF	Baby Doll Jacobson	St. Louis Browns	OF	Bing Miller
June 15, 1926	OF P	Tom Jenkins Howard Ehmke	Boston Red Sox	P P OF	Fred Heimach Slim Harriss Baby Doll Jacobson
Nov 1926		Cash	Boston Red Sox	OF	Frank Welch
Aug 5, 1927	OF	Baby Doll Jacobson	Cleveland Indians		Waiver price
Dec 2, 1927		Cash	St. Louis Browns	SS	Chick Galloway
Dec 13, 1927	OF	Bing Miller	St. Louis Browns	P	Sam Gray
Jan 5, 1929	OF	Homer Summa	Cleveland Indians		Cash
June 7, 1929		Waiver price	Cleveland Indians	1B	Joe Hauser
June 19, 1929	1B	George Burns	New York Yankees		Cash
Dec 11, 1929	C	Wally Schang	St. Louis Browns	3B	Sammy Hale
Dec 1929		Cash	Boston Red Sox	OF	Tom Oliver
Dec 10, 1930		Cash	New York Yankees	C	Cy Perkins
Jan 1931	C	Johnnie Heving	Boston Red Sox		Waiver price
Feb 3, 1931	1B	Phil Todt	Boston Red Sox		Cash
June 30, 1931	P	Waite Hoyt	Detroit Tigers		Cash
June 6, 1932		Cash	Cleveland Indians	SS	Joe Boley
Sept 28, 1932		$100,000.	Chicago White Sox	OF 2B OF	Al Simmons Jimmy Dykes Mule Haas
May 28, 1933		Cash	St. Louis Browns	P	Hank McDonald

DATE		ACQUIRED	FROM		IN EXCHANGE FOR
Dec 12, 1933	P SS	Bob Kline Rabbit Warstler and $125,000.	Boston Red Sox	P P 2B	Lefty Grove Rube Walberg Max Bishop
Dec 12, 1933	C	Johnny Pasek and $100,000.	Detroit Tigers	C	Mickey Cochrane
Dec 12, 1933	C	Charlie Berry and $20,000.	Chicago White Sox	P C	George Earnshaw Johnny Pasek
Dec 1933		Cash	Cincinnati Reds	P	Tony Freitas
Dec 1933		Cash	Boston Braves	P	Dick Barrett
May 1934		Cash	Chicago White Sox	C	Ed Madjeski
June 23, 1934		Cash	Washington Senators	P	Bob Kline
June 30, 1934		Cash	Boston Red Sox	P	Joe Cascarella
May 1, 1935		$50,000.	Boston Red Sox	OF 2B	Bing Miller Dib Williams
May 21, 1935	P	George Blaeholder	St. Louis Browns	OF P	Ed Coleman Sugar Cain
May 25, 1935	C	Paul Richards	New York Giants		Cash
Dec 10, 1935	P	Gordon Rhodes minor league C George Savino and $150,000.	Boston Red Sox	1B P	Jimmie Foxx Johnny Marcum
Jan 4, 1936	P 2B	Hank Johnson Al Niemiec and $75,000.	Boston Red Sox	OF SS	Doc Cramer Eric McNair
Jan 27, 1936		Waiver price	Cleveland Indians	P	George Blaeholder
Jan 29, 1936		Waiver price	St. Louis Browns	P	Roy Mahaffey
July 1, 1936		Waiver price	Washington Senators	P	Bill Dietrich
July 6, 1936		Waiver price	Boston Braves	SS	Rabbit Warstler
Dec 9, 1936	3B	Bill Werber	Boston Red Sox	3B	Pinky Higgins
July 13, 1937	OF	Jesse Hill	Washington Senators		Cash
Jan 1938		Cash	Detroit Tigers	P	Al Benton
March 1938		Cash	New York Giants	2B	Bill Cissell
May 4, 1938		Waiver price	Washington Senators	P	Harry Kelley
March 16, 1939		Cash	Cincinnati Reds	3B	Bill Werber
April 27, 1939		Waiver price	Chicago White Sox	P	Eddie Smith

DATE		ACQUIRED	FROM		IN EXCHANGE FOR
May 1, 1939		Waiver price	Washington Senators	P	Bud Thomas
May 8, 1939		Cash	Boston Red Sox	OF	Lou Finney
Sept 12, 1939		Waiver price	Detroit Tigers	P	Cotton Pippen
Dec 9, 1939	2B P	Benny McCoy Slick Coffman	Detroit Tigers	OF	Wally Moses
		(Commissioner Landis ruled that Detroit had kept McCoy covered up in the minors and declared him a free agent, cancelling the deal. McCoy then signed with Philadelphia for a $10,000 bonus.)			
Feb 23, 1940		Waiver price	Detroit Tigers	P	Lynn Nelson
April 30, 1940		Cash	Chicago White Sox	P	Buck Ross
Nov 16, 1940		Waiver price	St. Louis Browns	P	George Caster
Dec 16, 1940	P	Jack Knott	Chicago White Sox	2B	Dario Lodigiani
March 21, 1941		Cash	Philadelphia Phillies	3B	Bill Nagel
April 30, 1941	P	Bump Hadley	New York Giants		Cash
June 30, 1941		Cash	Boston Red Sox	P	Nels Potter
Aug 9, 1941		Waiver price	Cleveland Indians	OF	Chubby Dean
Sept 22, 1941		Waiver price	Cleveland Indians	P	Tom Ferrick
Dec 9, 1941	OF P	Mike Kreevich Jack Hallett	Chicago White Sox	OF	Wally Moses
April 3, 1942	SS	Bill Knickerbocker	Chicago White Sox		Waiver price
June 1, 1942	P C	Bob Harris Bob Swift	St. Louis Browns	C	Frankie Hayes
July 25, 1942	SS	Eric McNair	Detroit Tigers		Cash
March 21, 1943	OF	Jimmy Esmond and cash	Washington Senators	OF	Bob Johnson
June 14, 1943	2B	Don Heffner	St. Louis Browns		Cash
Oct 11, 1943	OF	Rip Radcliff	Detroit Tigers	2B C	Don Heffner Bob Swift
Dec 13, 1943	P	Bobo Newsom	Washington Senators	P	Roger Wolff
Feb 17, 1944	C	Frankie Hayes	St. Louis Browns	P	Sam Zoldak and minor league OF Barney Lutz
May 7, 1944	OF	Ford Garrison	Boston Red Sox	C	Hal Wagner
July 6, 1944	OF	Larry Rosenthal	New York Yankees		Cash

DATE		ACQUIRED	FROM		IN EXCHANGE FOR
Aug 13, 1944	OF	Charlie Metro	Detroit Tigers		Cash
Aug 19, 1944		Cash	Cincinnati Reds	OF	Jo-Jo White
May 29, 1945	C	Buddy Rosar	Cleveland Indians	C	Frankie Hayes
Oct 2, 1945		Cash	Cleveland Indians	P	Don Black
Oct 16, 1945	1B	George McQuinn	St. Louis Browns	1B	Dick Siebert
May 18, 1946	OF	Barney McCosky	Detroit Tigers	3B	George Kell
May 1946		Cash	Cleveland Indians	P	Joe Berry
June 14, 1946	3B	Hank Majeski	New York Yankees		Cash
June 20, 1946		Cash	New York Yankees	OF	Hal Peck
Dec 2, 1946	C	Mike Guerra	Washington Senators		Cash
Dec 13, 1946		Cash	Chicago White Sox	SS	Jack Wallaesa
Feb 14, 1947		Waiver price	Washington Senators	P	Lum Harris
Feb 14, 1947	OF	George Binks	Washington Senators	P	Lou Knerr
April 9, 1947	OF	Chet Laabs	St. Louis Browns		Cash
April 3, 1948		Cash	Cleveland Indians	P	Russ Christopher
May 15, 1948	P	Nels Potter	St. Louis Browns		Cash
June 4, 1948	OF	Ray Coleman	St. Louis Browns	OF	George Binks and $20,000.
Nov 15, 1948	OF	Taffy Wright	Chicago White Sox		Cash
Dec 16, 1948		Waiver price	St. Louis Browns	P	Bob Savage
Sept 14, 1949	3B	Frankie Gustine	Chicago Cubs		Waiver price
Oct 8, 1949	3B	Billy Hitchcock	Boston Red Sox	C	Buddy Rosar
Oct 19, 1949	C	Joe Tipton	Chicago White Sox	2B	Nellie Fox
Dec 13, 1949	3B OF	Bob Dillinger Paul Lehner	St. Louis Browns	OF 3B	Ray Coleman Frankie Gustine minor league OF Ray Ippolito and $100,000.
Dec 14, 1949	P	Eddie Klieman	Chicago White Sox	3B	Hank Majeski

DATE		ACQUIRED	FROM		IN EXCHANGE FOR
July 20, 1950		$35,000.	Pittsburgh Pirates	2B	Bob Dillinger
Dec 13, 1950		Cash	Boston Red Sox	C	Mike Guerra
April 30, 1951	P C OF	Sam Zoldak Ray Murray Minnie Minoso	Cleveland Indians	P	Lou Brissie
		(Part of three-team trade involving Cleveland, Philadelphia A's, and Chicago White Sox.)			
April 30, 1951	OF OF	Gus Zernial Dave Philley	Chicago White Sox	OF OF	Paul Lehner Minnie Minoso
		(Part of three-team trade involving Chicago White Sox, Philadelphia A's, and Cleveland.)			
May 10, 1951	OF 2B	Allie Clark Lou Klein	Cleveland Indians	OF	Sam Chapman
June 4, 1951	3B	Hank Majeski	Chicago White Sox	SS	Kermit Wahl
May 3, 1952	3B	Hal Bevan	Boston Red Sox		Waiver price
May 19, 1952	2B	Sherry Robertson	Washington Senators		Waiver price
June 10, 1952		Cash	Cleveland Indians	3B	Hank Majeski
June 23, 1952		Waiver price	Cleveland Indians	C	Joe Tipton
Aug 5, 1952	2B	Cass Michaels	St. Louis Browns		Waiver price
Dec 19, 1952	P	Dick Rozek minor league 2B Bob Wilson	Cleveland Indians	P	Bob Hooper
Jan 27, 1953	SS 1B 1B	Joe DeMaestri Eddie Robinson Ed McGhee	Chicago White Sox	1B	Ferris Fain minor league 2B Bob Wilson
Jan 29, 1953	3B	Don Kolloway	Detroit Tigers	3B	Billy Hitchcock
April 27, 1953	3B	Loren Babe	New York Yankees		Cash
May 12, 1953		Waiver price	Chicago White Sox	OF	Allie Clark
June 30, 1953		Waiver price	Washington Senators	OF	Kite Thomas
June 30, 1953	OF	Carmen Mauro	Washington Senators		Waiver price
Dec 8, 1953		Cash	Chicago White Sox	2B	Cass Michaels
Dec 16, 1953	1B P C 3B 1B OF	Don Bollweg John Gray Jim Robertson Jim Finigan Vic Power Bill Renna	New York Yankees	P 1B 1B OF 3B	Harry Byrd Eddie Robinson Tom Hamilton Carmen Mauro Loren Babe

DATE		ACQUIRED	FROM		IN EXCHANGE FOR
Dec 17, 1953	P P	Frank Fanovich Bob Cain	Baltimore Orioles	P	Joe Coleman
Feb 19, 1954	P P	Bill Upton Lee Wheat	Cleveland Indians	OF	Dave Philley
March 28, 1954		$25,000.	Baltimore Orioles	C	Ray Murray
May 7, 1954		Cash	St. Louis Cardinals	P	Carl Scheib
June 11, 1954	P P OF	Sonny Dixon Al Sima Bill Wilson and $20,000.	Chicago White Sox	1B P	Ed McGhee Morrie Martin

St. Louis Browns

The Best Trades

1. Acquired George Stone from the Boston Red Sox for Jesse Burkett, January 16, 1905.
2. Acquired General Crowder from the Washington Senators for Tom Zachary, July 7, 1927.
3. Acquired Heinie Manush and Lu Blue from the Detroit Tigers for Chick Galloway, Elam Vangilder, and Harry Rice, December 2, 1927.
4. Acquired Urban Shocker, Nick Cullop, Les Nunamaker, Fritz Maisel, and Joe Gedeon from the New York Yankees for Eddie Plank, Del Pratt, and $15,000, January 22, 1918.
5. Acquired Sherm Lollar, Red Embree, Dick Starr, and $100,000 from the New York Yankees for Fred Sanford and Roy Partee, December 13, 1948.

The Worst Trades

1. Traded Virgil Trucks and Bob Elliott to the Chicago White Sox for Darrell Johnson, Lou Kretlow, and $75,000, June 13, 1953.
2. Traded Rick Ferrell to the Washington Senators for Gene Moore and cash, March 1, 1944.
3. Traded Heinie Manush and General Crowder to the Washington Senators for Goose Goslin, June 13, 1930.
4. Traded Harlond Clift and Johnny Niggeling to the Washington Senators for Ellis Clary, Ox Miller, and cash, August 18, 1943.
5. Traded George Blaeholder to the Philadelphia Athletics for Ed Coleman and Sugar Cain, May 21, 1935.

Trader: Bill DeWitt

In 1954, Bill DeWitt was hired by the Yankees as an assistant to general manager George Weiss. Many suspected that Weiss hired DeWitt to keep him from landing somewhere else and taking him again. DeWitt had already skewered Weiss once, when he sent pitcher Fred Sanford to New York for $100,000, pitchers Red Embree and Dick Starr, and catcher Sherm Lollar. While Lollar went on to a distinguished career with the White Sox, it was definitely the money that was paramount in DeWitt's mind.

The Browns of the '40s and early '50s were a club on the brink of bankruptcy. Every deal had to be made with that fact in mind. Over a four-year period, the Browns made twenty major player deals with rival American League clubs, and in every trade DeWitt came away with money. Some of the players dealt away had good years elsewhere, particularly the Boston contingent of Vern Stephens, Ellis Kinder, and Jack Kramer. But by and large, the players dealt away didn't fare nearly as well in other uniforms as they did in Brownie flannel, and many of the throw-ins they received performed well enough to be worth some pocket money themselves.

DeWitt's principal customer was Tom Yawkey. The Red Sox made the biggest contribution with their purchase of Stephens and Kramer for seven players and $310,000. Two of the players St. Louis received, Joe Ostrowski and Roy Partee, were subsequently included in deals with the Yankees that netted the Browns an additional $150,000.

While this revolving door kept the Browns alive, it also ensured that they would never be able to get out of the depths of the league. When DeWitt sold his holdings in the Browns to Bill Veeck in 1951, Veeck quickly determined that there was no way for St. Louis to support two teams. His strategy was aimed at driving the Cardinals out of town, a task he realized was impossible once the Busch family purchased the team. After one more season in St. Louis, the club was moved to Baltimore, bringing major league baseball back to that city after a fifty-year absence. DeWitt purchased the Cincinnati Reds in 1961, and was immediately rewarded with a pennant. He later repaid the fans with his worst blunder, the Frank Robinson trade.

DATE		ACQUIRED	FROM		IN EXCHANGE FOR
Feb 1902	C	Joe Sugden	Chicago White Sox		Cash
May 30, 1902	OF	Charlie Hemphill	Cleveland Indians		Player to be named later
		(Cleveland received P Red Donahue in June, 1903.)			
Sept 1902	P	Charlie Shields	Baltimore Orioles		Cash
Dec 1902	P	Ed Siever	Detroit Tigers		Cash
June 1903		Completes Charlie Hemphill trade of May, 1902.	Cleveland Indians	P	Red Donahue
July 1903	OF	Joe Martin	Washington Senators	2B	Barry McCormick
July 1903	P	Clarence Wright	Brooklyn Dodgers	P	Bill Reidy
July 1903	P	LeRoy Evans	Brooklyn Dodgers		Cash
Jan 1904	P C	Harry Howell Jack O'Connor	New York Yankees	P	Jack Powell
Feb 1904		Cash	New York Yankees	P	Jack Powell
Feb 1904		Cash	New York Yankees	1B	John Anderson
June 16, 1904	OF	Frank Huelsman	Detroit Tigers		Cash
July 14, 1904	SS	Charlie Moran	Washington Senators	3B OF	Hunter Hill Frank Huelsman
		(Huelsmann went to Washington on loan.)			
Jan 16, 1905	OF	George Stone	Boston Red Sox	OF OF	Jesse Burkett Frank Huelsman

DATE		ACQUIRED	FROM		IN EXCHANGE FOR
Feb 1905	C	Branch Rickey	Chicago White Sox	C	Frank Roth
March 1905		Cash	Philadelphia Phillies	C	Mike Kahoe
Sept 1, 1905	P	Jack Powell	New York Yankees		Cash
Dec 1905	P	Beany Jacobson	Washington Senators	P	Willie Sudhoff
Dec 1906	C	Fritz Buelow	Cleveland Indians	2B	Pete O'Brien
Dec 1906		Cash	New York Yankees	C	Branch Rickey
June 11, 1907		$2,000.	Washington Senators	2B	Jim Delahanty
June 22, 1907	P	Bill Dinneen	Boston Red Sox	P	Beany Jacobson and $1,000.
Aug 1, 1907		Cash	Boston Red Sox	P	Cy Morgan
Sept 1907	2B	Jim Delahanty	Cincinnati Reds		Cash
Oct 5, 1907	OF	Charlie Jones	Washington Senators	OF	Ollie Pickering
Oct 1907	2B	Hobe Ferris	Boston Red Sox		Cash
Oct 1907	P	Rube Waddell	Philadelphia Athletics		Cash
Nov 1907		Cash	New York Yankees	2B	Harry Niles
Feb 1908	2B 3B OF	Jimmy Williams Hobe Ferris Danny Hoffman	New York Yankees	P OF	Fred Glade Charlie Hemphill
July 1908	C	Syd Smith	Philadelphia Athletics	C	Bert Blue
Dec 12, 1908	C	Lou Criger	Boston Red Sox	C	Tubby Spencer
Aug 20, 1909	1B	Claude Rossman	Detroit Tigers	1B	Tom Jones
Dec 1909	P	Joe Lake	New York Yankees	C	Lou Criger
Jan 1910	1B	Bill Abstein	Pittsburgh Pirates		Cash
April 1910	P	Bob Spade	Cincinnati Reds		Cash
Sept 1910	P	Fred Linke	Cleveland Indians		Cash
Oct 1910	C	Nig Clarke	Cleveland Indians	1B	Art Griggs
Jan 1911	3B 2B	Jimmy Austin Frank LaPorte	New York Yankees	OF	Roy Hartzell

DATE		ACQUIRED	FROM		IN EXCHANGE FOR
April 1911	OF	Paul Meloan	Chicago White Sox		Cash
April 1911		Cash	St. Louis Cardinals	P	Joe Willis
May 1911		Cash	Boston Red Sox	1B	Hap Myers
May 1911	OF	Happy Hogan	Philadelphia Athletics		Cash
June 1911	P	Walter Moser	Boston Red Sox		Cash
Dec 1911	1B	George Stovall	Cleveland Indians	P	Lefty George
Jan 1912		Waiver price	Cincinnati Reds	P	John Frill
May 1912		Cash	Detroit Tigers	P	Joe Lake
June 1912		Cash	Washington Senators	P	Barney Pelty
July 1912		Cash	Washington Senators	2B	Frank LaPorte
Aug 1912		Cash	Philadelphia Phillies	P	Red Nelson
Oct 1912	OF	Tilly Walker	Washington Senators		Cash
Nov 1912		Cash	Brooklyn Dodgers	P	Elmer Brown
March 1913	SS	Rivington Bisland	Pittsburgh Pirates		Waiver price
Aug 24, 1913		Cash	Philadelphia Athletics	SS	Doc Lavan
Feb 5, 1914	SS	Doc Lavan	Philadelphia Athletics		Cash
July 14, 1914	2B	Ivan Howard	Detroit Tigers		Waiver price
July 30, 1915		Cash	New York Yankees	C	Walt Alexander
Aug 18, 1915	OF	Baby Doll Jacobson	Detroit Tigers	P P	Bill James Grover Lowdermilk
Dec 1915		Cash	Boston Red Sox	C	Sam Agnew
Jan 1916		Cash	Cleveland Indians	2B	Ivan Howard
Feb 10, 1916	1B C P 3B P C OF OF P OF SS	Babe Borton Harry Chapman Doc Crandall Charlie Deal Bob Groom Grover Hartley Armando Marsans Ward Miller Eddie Plank Johnny Tobin Ernie Johnson	St. Louis (Federal League)		Cash

DATE		ACQUIRED	FROM		IN EXCHANGE FOR
April 8, 1916		Cash	Boston Red Sox	OF	Tilly Walker
May 30, 1916		Cash	Detroit Tigers	P	Earl Hamilton
June 2, 1916		Cash	Chicago Cubs	3B	Charlie Deal
June 22, 1916	P	Earl Hamilton	Detroit Tigers		Waiver price
May 1917		Waiver price	St. Louis Cardinals	2B	Gene Paulette
July 14, 1917	P	Speed Martin	Chicago White Sox		Cash
July 15, 1917	OF	Lee Magee	New York Yankees	OF	Armando Marsans
Aug 21, 1917		Cash	New York Yankees	C	Muddy Ruel
Oct 1917	P	Grover Lowdermilk	Cleveland Indians		Waiver price
Dec 15, 1917	P	Bert Gallia and $15,000.	Washington Senators	OF IF	Burt Shotton Doc Lavan
Unknown		Cash	Pittsburgh Pirates	P	Earl Hamilton
Jan 22, 1918	C IF P P 2B	Les Nunamaker Fritz Maisel Nick Cullop Urban Shocker Joe Gedeon	New York Yankees	P 2B	Eddie Plank Del Pratt and $15,000.
Feb 15, 1918		Waiver price	Cleveland Indians	P	Bob Groom
April 28, 1918	OF	Tim Hendryx	New York Yankees	2B	Lee Magee
March 1919	C	Josh Billings	Cleveland Indians	C	Les Nunamaker
April 1919		Cash	Philadelphia Athletics	P	Tom Rogers
May 1919		Cash	Chicago White Sox	P	Grover Lowdermilk
Jan 1920		Cash	Boston Red Sox	OF	Tim Hendryx
April 1920		Cash	Philadelphia Phillies	P	Bert Gallia
Jan 1921		Waiver price	Boston Red Sox	P	Allen Sothoron
May 31, 1921	3B	Frank Ellerbe	Washington Senators	OF	Earl Smith
May 1921	P	Joe Bennett	Chicago White Sox		Cash
Dec 14, 1921	OF	Chick Shorten	Detroit Tigers		Waiver price
Aug 15, 1922	3B	Eddie Foster	Boston Red Sox		Waiver price

DATE		ACQUIRED	FROM		IN EXCHANGE FOR
May 12, 1923		Cash	Chicago White Sox	P	Sloppy Thurston
May 1923	1B	Dutch Schliebner	Brooklyn Dodgers		Cash
Dec 1923	2B	Norm McMillan	Boston Red Sox	3B	Homer Ezzell
Jan 1924	OF	Joe Evans	Washington Senators		Cash
June 3, 1924		Cash	Cleveland Indians	3B	Frank Ellerbe
Dec 17, 1924	P P P	Joe Bush Milt Gaston Joe Giard	New York Yankees	P	Urban Shocker
June 8, 1925	P C	George Mogridge Pinky Hargrave	Washington Senators	C	Hank Severeid
Dec 31, 1925	P	Charlie Robertson	Chicago White Sox		Waiver price
Feb 6, 1926	C	Wally Schang	New York Yankees	P	George Mogridge and cash
Feb 1926	P P	Tom Zachary Win Ballou	Washington Senators	P OF	Joe Bush Jack Tobin
June 15, 1926	OF	Bing Miller	Philadelphia Athletics	OF	Baby Doll Jacobson
Jan 15, 1927	P IF 2B IF	Lefty Stewart Frank O'Rourke Billy Mullen Otto Miller	Detroit Tigers	2B IF C	Marty McManus Bobby LaMotte Pinky Hargrave
Feb 8, 1927	P	Sad Sam Jones	New York Yankees	OF P	Cedric Durst Joe Giard
July 7, 1927	P	General Crowder	Washington Senators	P	Tom Zachary
Oct 19, 1927	P OF	Dick Coffman Earl McNeely	Washington Senators	P P	Milt Gaston Sad Sam Jones
Dec 2, 1927	SS	Chick Galloway	Philadelphia Athletics		Cash
Dec 2, 1927	OF 1B	Heinie Manush Lu Blue	Detroit Tigers	SS P OF	Chick Galloway Elam Vangilder Harry Rice
Dec 13, 1927	P	Sam Gray	Philadelphia Athletics	OF	Bing Miller
Dec 14, 1927		$25,000.	Washington Senators	1B	George Sisler
Dec 15, 1927		$10,000.	Boston Red Sox	OF	Ken Williams
April 25, 1928	P	Hal Wiltse	Boston Red Sox	SS	Wally Gerber
May 10, 1928	OF	Frank Wilson	Cleveland Indians		Cash
June 26, 1929	P	Paul Hopkins	Washington Senators		Cash
Dec 11, 1929	3B	Sammy Hale	Philadelphia Athletics	C	Wally Schang

DATE		ACQUIRED	FROM		IN EXCHANGE FOR
June 13, 1930	OF	Goose Goslin	Washington Senators	P OF	General Crowder Heinie Manush
July 21, 1930	OF	Alex Metzler	Chicago White Sox		Cash
April 3, 1931		$15,000.	Chicago White Sox	1B	Lu Blue
July 13, 1931	P	Garland Braxton	Chicago White Sox		Waiver price
April 27, 1932	OF P	Bruce Campbell Bump Hadley	Chicago White Sox	SS	Red Kress
June 9, 1932	P	Carl Fischer	Washington Senators	P	Dick Coffman
Sept 9, 1932		Cash	Chicago White Sox	P	Chad Kimsey
Dec 13, 1932	P	Dick Coffman	Washington Senators	P	Carl Fischer
Dec 14, 1932	OF OF P	Sammy West Carl Reynolds Lloyd Brown and $20,000.	Washington Senators	OF OF P	Goose Goslin Fred Schulte Lefty Stewart
Dec 1932	C	Muddy Ruel	Detroit Tigers		Waiver price
Dec 1932	P	Ed Wells	New York Yankees		Cash
May 9, 1933	C	Merv Shea and cash	Boston Red Sox	C P	Rick Ferrell Lloyd Brown
May 28, 1933	P	Hank McDonald	Philadelphia Athletics		Cash
Aug 3, 1933	C	Rollie Hemsley	Cincinnati Reds		Waiver price
Sept 1, 1933		Waiver price	Cincinnati Reds	C	Jack Crouch
Dec 11, 1933		Cash	Chicago White Sox	C	Merv Shea
Dec 14, 1933	P OF	Ivy Andrews Smead Jolley and cash	Boston Red Sox	OF	Carl Reynolds
Dec 1933	P	Bill McAfee	Washington Senators		Cash
May 15, 1934		Waiver price	Chicago Cubs	P	Jim Weaver
Nov 20, 1934	3B P	Johnny Burnett Bob Weiland and cash	Cleveland Indians	OF	Bruce Campbell
Jan 22, 1935	C	Luke Sewell	Washington Senators	P	Bump Hadley
Jan 22, 1935		Cash	Chicago White Sox	C	Luke Sewell
May 21, 1935	OF P	Ed Coleman Sugar Cain	Philadelphia Athletics	P	George Blaeholder
May 21, 1935	OF	Moose Solters and cash	Boston Red Sox	2B	Oscar Melillo

DATE		ACQUIRED	FROM		IN EXCHANGE FOR
May 21, 1935		$40,000.	Washington Senators	P	Bobo Newsom
June 22, 1935	P	Ron Hansen	Philadelphia Phillies		Cash
June 29, 1935	SS	Lyn Lary	Washington Senators	SS	Alan Strange
July 15, 1935	P	Russ Van Atta	New York Yankees		Cash
Sept 20, 1935		Cash	Chicago White Sox	C	Frank Grube
Sept 24, 1935		Cash	New York Giants	P	Dick Coffman
Jan 29, 1936	P	Roy Mahaffey	Philadelphia Athletics		Waiver price
Jan 1936	P	Tommy Thomas	Philadelphia Phillies		Cash
March 21, 1936	1B	Jim Bottomley	Cincinnati Reds	2B	Johnny Burnett
April 30, 1936	P	Chief Hogsett	Detroit Tigers	1B	Jack Burns
May 5, 1936	P	Les Tietje	Chicago White Sox	P	Sugar Cain
July 1936		Cash	Boston Red Sox	P	Mike Meola
Dec 2, 1936	OF	Ethan Allen	Chicago Cubs		Cash
Jan 17, 1937	SS OF P	Bill Knickerbocker Joe Vosmik Oral Hildebrand	Cleveland Indians	P SS OF	Ivy Andrews Lyn Lary Moose Solters
Oct 2, 1937	P SS OF	Bobo Newsom Red Kress Buster Mills	Boston Red Sox	OF	Joe Vosmik
Dec 1, 1937	P	Ed Linke	Washington Senators	P	Chief Hogsett
Dec 8, 1937	C	Earl Grace	Philadelphia Phillies	OF	Cap Clark
Jan 1938	P	Jim Weaver	Pittsburgh Pirates		Cash
Feb 10, 1938	P 2B C	Ed Cole Roy Hughes Billy Sullivan	Cleveland Indians	C	Rollie Hemsley
Feb 15, 1938	2B	Don Heffner and $10,000.	New York Yankees	SS	Bill Knickerbocker
March 24, 1938		Cash	Washington Senators	C	Tony Giuliani
April 25, 1938		Cash	Cincinnati Reds	P	Jim Weaver
May 1938		Waiver price	Brooklyn Dodgers	P	Vito Tamulis
June 11, 1938	P	Billy Cox	Chicago White Sox	P	Jack Knott

DATE		ACQUIRED	FROM		IN EXCHANGE FOR
June 15, 1938	OF	Mel Almada	Washington Senators	OF	Sammy West
Oct 26, 1938	C	Joe Glenn	New York Yankees	P	Oral Hildebrand
	OF	Myril Hoag		OF	Buster Mills
April 27, 1939	OF	Tommy Thompson	Chicago White Sox		Cash
May 13, 1939	P	Vern Kennedy	Detroit Tigers	OF	Beau Bell
	P	Bob Harris		P	Bobo Newsom
	P	George Gill		SS	Red Kress
	P	Roxie Lawson		P	Jim Walkup
	OF	Chet Laabs			
	3B	Mark Christman			
June 2, 1939	P	John Whitehead	Chicago White Sox	P	Johnny Marcum
June 13, 1939	OF	Joe Gallagher	New York Yankees	2B	Roy Hughes and cash
June 15, 1939		$25,000.	Brooklyn Dodgers	OF	Mel Almada
Aug 2, 1939	OF	Moose Solters	Cleveland Indians		Waiver price
Sept 1939	P	Jake Wade	Boston Red Sox		Cash
Dec 8, 1939	OF	Rip Radcliff	Chicago White Sox	OF	Moose Solters
Jan 4, 1940	P	Johnny Niggeling	Cincinnati Reds		Waiver price
Jan 30, 1940	P	Slick Coffman	Detroit Tigers	C	Billy Sullivan
Feb 8, 1940	P	Eldon Auker	Boston Red Sox		Cash
April 30, 1940		Cash	Chicago White Sox	OF	Myril Hoag
May 15, 1940	C	Rick Ferrell	Washington Senators	P	Vern Kennedy
May 27, 1940	OF	Roy Cullenbine	Brooklyn Dodgers	OF	Joe Gallagher
Nov 16, 1940	P	George Caster	Philadelphia Athletics		Waiver price
Nov 20, 1940	P	Denny Galehouse	Boston Red Sox		Cash
Dec 3, 1940	P	Fritz Ostermueller	Boston Red Sox		Cash
Dec 24, 1940	P	Johnny Allen	Cleveland Indians		$20,000.
Feb 5, 1941		Cash	Brooklyn Dodgers	P	Lefty Mills
May 5, 1941		$25,000.	Detroit Tigers	OF	Rip Radcliff
Aug 4, 1941	P	Archie McKain	Detroit Tigers		Cash

DATE		ACQUIRED	FROM		IN EXCHANGE FOR
May 13, 1942	1B	Babe Dahlgren	Chicago Cubs		Cash
		(Ten-day conditional sale; Dahlgren was returned to the Cubs on May 19, 1940.)			
June 1, 1942	C	Frankie Hayes	Philadelphia Athletics	P C	Bob Harris Bob Swift
June 7, 1942	OF P	Mike Chartak Steve Sundra	Washington Senators	OF P	Roy Cullenbine Bill Trotter
Feb 1, 1943		Cash	Washington Senators	P	Paul Dean
June 14, 1943		Cash	Philadelphia Athletics	2B	Don Heffner
July 15, 1943	P	Bobo Newsom	Brooklyn Dodgers	P P	Fritz Ostermueller Archie McKain
Aug 18, 1943	SS P	Ellis Clary Ox Miller and cash	Washington Senators	3B P	Harlond Clift Johnny Niggeling
Aug 27, 1943	P	Al Milnar	Cleveland Indians		Cash
Aug 31, 1943		Cash	Washington Senators	P	Bobo Newsom
Feb 17, 1944	P	Sam Zoldak and minor league OF Barney Lutz	Philadelphia Athletics	C	Frankie Hayes
March 1, 1944	C OF	Tony Giuliani Gene Moore and cash	Washington Senators	C	Rick Ferrell
		(Giuliani announced his retirement, and St. Louis received Moore to complete the trade.)			
July 31, 1944	C	Tom Turner	Chicago White Sox		Cash
Dec 30, 1944		Cash	Chicago White Sox	3B	Floyd Baker
July 27, 1945	OF	Lou Finney	Boston Red Sox		Cash
Aug 8, 1945		Waiver price	Detroit Tigers	P	George Caster
Oct 16, 1945	1B	Dick Siebert	Philadelphia Athletics	1B	George McQuinn
April 23, 1946	1B	Babe Dahlgren	Pittsburgh Pirates		Cash
June 6, 1946		Waiver price	Chicago White Sox	P	Al Hollingsworth
June 15, 1946	OF	Jeff Heath	Washington Senators	OF P	Joe Grace Al LaMacchia
June 24, 1946	P	Tom Ferrick	Cleveland Indians		Cash
Dec 7, 1946	2B	Rusty Peters	Cleveland Indians		Cash
Dec 16, 1946	C	Frank Mancuso	Washington Senators	C	Jake Early
Jan 14, 1947		Cash	Washington Senators	P	Tom Ferrick

DATE	ACQUIRED	FROM	IN EXCHANGE FOR
Feb 8, 1947	3B Billy Hitchcock	Washington Senators	Cash
March 1, 1947	Waiver price	New York Yankees	IF Johnny Lucadello
April 9, 1947	Cash	Philadelphia Athletics	OF Chet Laabs
April 9, 1947	Cash	Washington Senators	3B Mark Christman
June 20, 1947	Cash	Boston Red Sox	P Denny Galehouse
Nov 17, 1947	C Roy Partee P Jim Wilson P Al Widmar OF Eddie Pellagrini OF Pete Layden P Joe Ostrowski and $310,000.	Boston Red Sox	SS Vern Stephens P Jack Kramer
Nov 18, 1947	SS Sam Dente P Clem Dreisewerd 1B Bill Sommers and $65,000.	Boston Red Sox	P Ellis Kinder 3B Billy Hitchcock
Nov 20, 1947	OF Dick Kokos P Bryan Stephens OF Joe Frazier and $25,000.	Cleveland Indians	P Bob Muncrief OF Walt Judnich
Nov 22, 1947	2B Gerry Priddy	Washington Senators	2B Johnny Berardino
	(Berardino announced his retirement to go into movies. Commissioner Chandler cancelled the trade. Berardino then unretired.)		
Dec 4, 1947	Cash	Boston Braves	OF Jeff Heath
Dec 8, 1947	2B Gerry Priddy	Washington Senators	$25,000.
Dec 9, 1947	OF-1B Catfish Metkovich and $50,000.	Cleveland Indians	2B Johnny Berardino
	(Metkovich was returned to Cleveland because of a broken finger and the St. Louis Browns received another $15,000 to complete the trade.)		
March 26, 1948	Cash	Washington Senators	C Jake Early
May 15, 1948	Cash	Philadelphia Athletics	P Nels Potter
June 4, 1948	OF George Binks and $20,000.	Philadelphia Athletics	OF Ray Coleman
June 15, 1948	P Bill Kennedy and $100,000.	Cleveland Indians	P Sam Zoldak
June 28, 1948	OF Don Lund	Brooklyn Dodgers	Waiver price
Aug 9, 1948	P Karl Drews	New York Yankees	Cash
Oct 4, 1948	P Tom Ferrick SS John Sullivan and $25,000.	Washington Senators	SS Sam Dente

DATE	ACQUIRED	FROM	IN EXCHANGE FOR
Dec 13, 1948	C Sherm Lollar P Red Embree P Dick Starr and $100,000.	New York Yankees	P Fred Sanford C Roy Partee
Dec 16, 1948	P Bob Savage	Philadelphia Athletics	Waiver price
Jan 20, 1949	$15,000.	Detroit Tigers	OF Don Lund
May 8, 1949	OF Stan Spence and cash	Boston Red Sox	OF Al Zarilla
Dec 1, 1949	P Stubby Overmire	Detroit Tigers	Waiver price
Dec 13, 1949	OF Ray Coleman 3B Frankie Gustine minor league OF Ray Ippolito and $100,000.	Philadelphia Athletics	3B Bob Dillinger OF Paul Lehner
Dec 14, 1949	P Lou Kretlow and $100,000.	Detroit Tigers	2B Gerry Priddy
May 9, 1950	P Harry Dorish	Boston Red Sox	Cash
June 15, 1950	OF Jim Delsing P Don Johnson P Duane Pillette 2B Snuffy Stirnweiss and $50,000.	New York Yankees	P Tom Ferrick OF Joe Ostrowski 3B Leo Thomas P Sid Schacht
July 1, 1950	P Jack Bruner	Chicago White Sox	Cash
July 5, 1950	Waiver price	Chicago White Sox	P Lou Kretlow
April 1, 1951	2B Freddie Marsh	Cleveland Indians	2B Snuffy Stirnweiss SS Merrill Combs and $35,000.
May 13, 1951	Waiver price	Boston Braves	P Sid Schacht
May 14, 1951	P Bobby Hogue	Boston Braves	Waiver price
May 17, 1951	C Matt Batts P Jim Suchecki P Jim McDonald and $100,000.	Boston Red Sox	C Les Moss
May 29, 1951	P Bob Mahoney	Chicago White Sox	Waiver price
May 29, 1951	$12,500.	Washington Senators	P Don Johnson
June 1, 1951	1B Dale Long	Pittsburgh Pirates	Waiver price
June 4, 1951	OF Paul Lehner SS Kermit Wahl and cash	Chicago White Sox	OF Don Lenhardt
June 12, 1951	Waiver price	Washington Senators	C Clyde Kluttz

DATE		ACQUIRED	FROM		IN EXCHANGE FOR
June 15, 1951	P	Tommy Byrne and $25,000.	New York Yankees	P	Stubby Overmire
July 16, 1951	OF	Jack Maguire	Pittsburgh Pirates		Waiver price
July 16, 1951	IF	Bill Jennings	New York Giants		Waiver price
July 19, 1951		Waiver price	Cleveland Indians	OF	Paul Lehner
July 30, 1951	P	Fred Sanford	Washington Senators	P	Dick Starr
July 31, 1951		Waiver price	Chicago White Sox	OF	Ray Coleman
July 31, 1951	OF	Cliff Mapes	New York Yankees	P 3B SS P	Bobby Hogue Kermit Wahl Ollie Tucker Lou Sleater
Sept 1, 1951	OF	Earl Rapp	New York Giants		Waiver price
Sept 12, 1951	2B	Mike Goliat	Pittsburgh Pirates		Waiver price
Nov 23, 1951	C	Clint Courtney	New York Yankees	P	Jim McDonald
Nov 27, 1951	SS P C 1B OF	Joe DeMaestri Dick Littlefield Gus Niarhos Gordon Goldsberry Jim Rivera	Chicago White Sox	P C SS	Al Widmar Sherm Lollar Tom Upton
Nov 28, 1951	C OF	Les Moss Tom Wright	Boston Red Sox	OF C	Ken Wood Gus Niarhos
Feb 14, 1952	P P 1B	Gene Bearden Bob Cain Dick Kryhoski	Detroit Tigers	P 1B OF	Dick Littlefield Ben Taylor Cliff Mapes
March 4, 1952		Cash	Pittsburgh Pirates	P	Jim Suchecki
March 13, 1952		Cash	Chicago White Sox	P	Bill Kennedy
April 7, 1952	P	Dave Madison	New York Yankees		Cash
May 12, 1952	2B	Cass Michaels	Washington Senators	P SS	Lou Sleater Freddie Marsh
May 13, 1952	P	Stubby Overmire	New York Yankees		Waiver price
June 10, 1952	SS	Freddie Marsh	Washington Senators	OF	Earl Rapp
June 15, 1952	SS OF	Willie Miranda Al Zarilla	Chicago White Sox	OF 3B	Tom Wright Leo Thomas
June 16, 1952	P	Ken Holcombe	Chicago White Sox		Cash
June 28, 1952		Waiver price	Chicago White Sox	SS	Willie Miranda

DATE		ACQUIRED	FROM		IN EXCHANGE FOR
June 30, 1952		Waiver price	Boston Red Sox	OF	George Schmees
July 28, 1952	C	J W Porter	Chicago White Sox	OF	Jim Rivera
	OF	Ray Coleman		C	Darrell Johnson
Aug 4, 1952	P	Bobby Hogue	New York Yankees		Waiver price
Aug 5, 1952		Waiver price	Philadelphia Athletics	2B	Cass Michaels
Aug 14, 1952	P	Dick Littlefield	Detroit Tigers	OF	Jim Delsing
	P	Marlin Stuart		P	Ned Garver
	OF	Don Lenhardt		P	Dave Madison
	OF	Vic Wertz		P	Bill Black
Aug 27, 1952		Waiver price	Chicago White Sox	P	Hal Hudson
Aug 31, 1952		Cash	Boston Red Sox	OF	Al Zarilla
Oct 1, 1952	P	Bob Habenicht	St. Louis Cardinals		Waiver price
Oct 1, 1952	1B	Ed Mickelson	St. Louis Cardinals		Waiver price
Oct 14, 1952	SS	Billy Hunter	Brooklyn Dodgers	P	Bob Mahoney
				SS	Stan Rojek
				OF	Ray Coleman and $90,000.
Oct 16, 1952	SS	Willie Miranda	Chicago White Sox	SS	Joe DeMaestri
	OF	Hank Edwards		P	Tommy Byrne
Oct 27, 1952	SS	Neil Berry	Detroit Tigers	OF	Rufus Crawford
	OF	Cliff Mapes and $25,000.			
Dec 4, 1952	P	Virgil Trucks	Detroit Tigers	SS	Owen Friend
	P	Hal White		OF	Bob Nieman
	OF	Johnny Groth		C	J W Porter
Jan 20, 1953	SS	Dixie Upright and $25,000.	Chicago White Sox	SS	Freddie Marsh
March 7, 1953		Cash	Chicago White Sox	P	Earl Harrist
March 18, 1953		Waiver price	Chicago White Sox	P	Gene Bearden
April 7, 1953		Cash	Detroit Tigers	3B	George Freese
June 2, 1953		Waiver price	St. Louis Cardinals	P	Hal White
June 12, 1953		Cash	New York Yankees	SS	Willie Miranda
June 13, 1953	C	Darrell Johnson	Chicago White Sox	P	Virgil Trucks
	P	Lou Kretlow and $75,000.		OF	Bob Elliott
July 20, 1953	SS	Vern Stephens	Chicago White Sox		Waiver price
Sept 1, 1953		Waiver price	Chicago White Sox	SS	Neil Berry

DATE		ACQUIRED	FROM		IN EXCHANGE FOR
Sept 8, 1953	SS	Johnny Lipon	Boston Red Sox		Cash

Seattle Pilots

DATE		ACQUIRED	FROM		IN EXCHANGE FOR
June 14, 1968	1B	Mike Hegan	New York Yankees		Cash
Oct 21, 1968	P	Jim Bouton	New York Yankees		Cash
Nov 13, 1968	3B	John Kennedy	New York Yankees		Cash
March 31, 1969	P IF	Gene Brabender Gordon Lund	Baltimore Orioles	IF	Chico Salmon
April 1, 1969	OF P	Steve Whitaker John Gelnar	Kansas City Royals	OF	Lou Piniella
April 30, 1969	P P	John O'Donoghue Tom Fisher and minor league P Lloyd Fourroux	Baltimore Orioles	P IF	Gerry Schoen Mike Ferraro
May 19, 1969	OF	Dick Simpson	New York Yankees	OF	Jose Vidal
May 20, 1969	P	Fred Talbot	New York Yankees	P	Jack Aker
May 27, 1969	C	Jim Pagliaroni	Oakland Athletics		Cash
June 3, 1969		Cash	Oakland Athletics	OF	Federico Velazquez
June 8, 1969	P	Bob Locker	Chicago White Sox	P	Gary Bell
June 14, 1969	2B	John Donaldson	Oakland Athletics	C	Larry Haney
June 23, 1969	P	Garry Roggenburk	Boston Red Sox		Cash
July 8, 1969		Cash	Minnesota Twins	P	Darrell Brandon
July 31, 1969	P	George Brunet	California Angels		Cash
Aug 24, 1969	P P	Dooley Womack Roric Harrison	Houston Astros	P	Jim Bouton
Aug 29, 1969	P IF	Bob Meyer Pete Koegel	Oakland Athletics	P	Fred Talbot
Aug 30, 1969	OF OF	Danny Walton Sandy Valdespino	Houston Astros	OF	Tommy Davis
Sept 13, 1969		Cash	Montreal Expos	IF	Marv Staehle
Nov 21, 1969	P	Wayne Twitchell	Houston Astros		Cash

DATE		ACQUIRED	FROM		IN EXCHANGE FOR
Dec 4, 1969	P	Dave Baldwin	Washington Senators	P	George Brunet
Dec 7, 1969	IF P	Ted Kubiak George Lauzerique	Oakland Athletics	P SS	Diego Segui Ray Oyler
Dec 12, 1969	P	Bobby Bolin	San Francisco Giants	OF OF	Steve Whitaker Dick Simpson

Seattle Mariners

The Best Trades

1. Acquired Rick Honeycutt from the Pittsburgh Pirates for Dave Pagan, July 27, 1977.
2. Acquired Floyd Bannister from the Houston Astros for Craig Reynolds, December 8, 1978.
3. Acquired Jim Beattie, Rick Anderson, Juan Beniquez, and Jerry Narron from the New York Yankees for Ruppert Jones and Jim Lewis, November 1, 1979.
4. Acquired Pat Putnam from the Texas Rangers for Ron Musselman, December 21, 1982.
5. Acquired Steve Henderson from the Chicago Cubs for Rich Bordi, December 9, 1982.

The Worst Trades

1. Traded Rick Honeycutt, Larry Cox, Mario Mendoza, Willie Horton, and Leon Roberts to the Texas Rangers for Brian Allard, Ken Clay, Steve Finch, Jerry Gleaton, Richie Zisk, and Rick Auerbach, December 12, 1980.
2. Traded Bill Caudill and Darren Akerfelds to the Oakland A's for Bob Kearney and Dave Beard, November 21, 1983.

One Good Trade Does *Not* Deserve Another

The trouble with the Seattle Mariners is that they don't know how to quit when they're ahead. True, not too many good things have happened to the Mariners since they've joined the league, but nonetheless they have managed to make life more difficult for themselves with their trading record.

The original Mariners were a typical expansion team: a loose collection of undertalented castoffs. For some reason, several of these expendables proved attractive to teams around the major leagues, and brought some surprisingly worthwhile returns. But instead of using them as a foundation on which to build, the Mariners used the players as trade bait for a new round of deals, and undid most of the good work they had accomplished. Had they been satisfied with their first series of moves, their lineup could have read like this: first base, Bruce Bochte; second base, Julio Cruz; shortstop, Todd Cruz; third base, Lenny Randle; outfielders, Juan Beniquez, Leon Roberts, and Jeff Burroughs; catcher, Jim Essian; pitchers, Floyd Bannister, Shane Rawley, Rick Honeycutt, Bill Caudill, and Odell Jones. Not exactly a pennant contender, but a much better team than the one they're fielding today. With the exception of the Cruzes, all were obtained in trades with other clubs, and all except Bannister and Bochte, who left as free agents, were traded away.

The Mariners' most recent flurry of trades came before the 1984 season. They swapped Bryan Clark to Toronto for Barry Bonnell, Tony Bernazard to Cleveland for Jack Perconte and Gorman Thomas, and Bill Caudill to Oakland for Dave Beard and Bob Kearney. They were much criticized for the Caudill trade, the belief being that had they waited until free agents Goose Gossage and Kent Tekulve signed they would have been able to get much more in exchange for Caudill. It will be interesting to see if these new Mariners will be allowed to drop anchor for a while in Seattle, or if they too will soon be shipped off to new ports of call.

DATE		ACQUIRED	FROM		IN EXCHANGE FOR
Oct 15, 1976	P	Jim Minshall	Pittsburgh Pirates		Cash
Dec 7, 1976	IF IF	Craig Reynolds Jimmy Sexton	Pittsburgh Pirates	P	Grant Jackson
Jan 12, 1977	C	Skip Jutze	Houston Astros		Minor league P Alan Griffin and cash
March 30, 1977	IF	Larry Milbourne	Houston Astros	P	Roy Thomas
April 20, 1977	P	Jim Todd	Chicago Cubs	P	Pete Broberg
May 2, 1977		Cash	Minnesota Twins	P	Dave Johnson
May 28, 1977	P	Tom House	Boston Red Sox		Cash
July 27, 1977	P	Rick Honeycutt	Pittsburgh Pirates	P	Dave Pagan
Aug 2, 1977		Cash	New York Yankees	P	Stan Thomas
Aug 4, 1977	P	Paul Mitchell	Oakland Athletics		Cash
Sept 8, 1977	C	Kevin Pasley	Los Angeles Dodgers		Cash
Sept 9, 1977	C	Ray Fosse	Cleveland Indians	P	Bill Laxton and cash
Sept 13, 1977	P	Doc Medich	Oakland Athletics		Cash
Sept 14, 1977	OF	John Hale	Toronto Blue Jays		Cash
Sept 26, 1977		Cash	New York Mets	P	Doc Medich
Oct 25, 1977		Minor league P Steve Hamrick	Chicago Cubs	C	Larry Cox
Dec 5, 1977	OF	Leon Roberts	Houston Astros	IF	Jimmy Sexton
Dec 7, 1977	P	Mike Parrott	Baltimore Orioles	OF P	Carlos Lopez Tommy Moore
Dec 9, 1977	P	Shane Rawley	Cincinnati Reds	OF-1B	Dave Collins
Dec 20, 1977	1B	Bruce Bochte	Cleveland Indians		No compensation (free agent signing)
March 23, 1978	P	Santo Alcala	Montreal Expos		Cash
		(Alcala was returned to Montreal before the start of the 1979 season.)			
June 1, 1978	P	Jim Colborn	Kansas City Royals	OF	Steve Braun

DATE		ACQUIRED	FROM		IN EXCHANGE FOR
June 26, 1978	OF	Mike Potter	St. Louis Cardinals	IF	Jose Baez
Dec 5, 1978	P P SS	Odell Jones Rafael Vasquez Mario Mendoza	Pittsburgh Pirates	P P SS	Enrique Romo Rick Jones Tommy McMillan
Dec 6, 1978	OF	Bobby Thompson	Texas Rangers		Cash
Dec 8, 1978	P	Floyd Bannister	Houston Astros	SS	Craig Reynolds
Jan 27, 1979	DH	Willie Horton	Detroit Tigers		No compensation (free agent signing)
Feb 23, 1979	P	Mike Davey	Atlanta Braves		Cash
March 20, 1979	C	Larry Cox	Chicago Cubs	OF	Luis Delgado
March 29, 1979	C	Terry Bulling	Minnesota Twins		Cash
June 7, 1979	P	Randy Stein	Milwaukee Brewers	P	Paul Mitchell
June 7, 1979	P	Rob Dressler	St. Louis Cardinals		Cash
July 6, 1979	P	Rich Hinton	Chicago White Sox	3B	Juan Bernhardt
Aug 19, 1979	P	Wayne Twitchell	New York Mets		Cash
Aug 29, 1979	SS	Jim Anderson	California Angels	P	John Montague
Nov 1, 1979	P P OF C	Jim Beattie Rick Anderson Juan Beniquez Jerry Narron	New York Yankees	OF P	Ruppert Jones Jim Lewis
Nov 9, 1979	P	Dan O'Brien	St. Louis Cardinals		Cash
Dec 6, 1979	3B	Ted Cox	Cleveland Indians	P P	Rafael Vasquez Bud Anderson and minor league P Bob Pietburgo
March 8, 1980	3B	Lenny Randle	New York Mets		No compensation (free agent signing)
April 1, 1980	P	Larry Andersen and cash	Pittsburgh Pirates	P	Odell Jones
April 2, 1980		Cash	Chicago Cubs	3B	Lenny Randle
April 9, 1980	P	Dave Heaverlo	Oakland Athletics		Cash
April 24, 1980	P	Dave Roberts	Pittsburgh Pirates		Cash
June 20, 1980	C	Marc Hill	San Francisco Giants		Cash
Nov 18, 1980	C	Brad Gulden and $150,000.	New York Yankees	IF	Larry Milbourne

DATE		ACQUIRED	FROM		IN EXCHANGE FOR
Dec 8, 1980	SS	Mario Guerrero	Oakland Athletics		Cash
Dec 12, 1980	OF	Richie Zisk	Texas Rangers	P	Rick Honeycutt
	IF	Rick Auerbach		SS	Mario Mendoza
	P	Ken Clay		C	Larry Cox
	P	Jerry Gleaton		OF	Leon Roberts
	P	Brian Allard		DH	Willie Horton
	P	Steve Finch			
Dec 12, 1980	OF	Willie Norwood	Minnesota Twins	P	Byron McLaughlin
Dec 19, 1980	P	Mike Bacsik	Minnesota Twins	OF	Steve Stroughter
Dec 29, 1980		No compensation (free agent signing)	California Angels	OF	Juan Beniquez
Dec 29, 1980		No compensation (free agent signing)	Texas Rangers	2B	Bill Stein
March 7, 1981	OF	Jeff Burroughs	Atlanta Braves	P	Carlos Diaz
March 26, 1981	1B	Wayne Cage	Cleveland Indians	OF	Rodney Craig
April 8, 1981	P	Dick Drago	Boston Red Sox	P	Manny Sarmiento
Oct 23, 1981	3B	Manny Castillo	Kansas City Royals	P	Bud Black
Dec 9, 1981	P	Rich Bordi	Oakland Athletics	1B	Dan Meyer
Dec 9, 1981	P	Roy Thomas	Oakland Athletics	OF	Rusty McNealy minor league P Tim Hallgren
Dec 11, 1981	SS	Todd Cruz	Chicago White Sox	OF	Tom Paciorek
	C	Jim Essian			
	OF	Rod Allen			
March 5, 1982	OF	Thad Bosley	Milwaukee Brewers	P	Mike Parrott
March 28, 1982	OF	Al Cowens	Detroit Tigers		Cash
April 1, 1982	P	Bill Caudill	New York Yankees	P	Shane Rawley
	P	Gene Nelson			
	OF	Bobby Brown			
April 7, 1982		No compensation (free agent signing)	Oakland Athletics	OF	Jeff Burroughs
April 9, 1982		Cash	Pittsburgh Pirates	OF	Reggie Walton
May 21, 1982	C	Rick Sweet	New York Mets		Cash
Aug 6, 1982	1B	Dave Revering	Toronto Blue Jays		No compensation (free agent signing)
Dec 9, 1982	OF	Steve Henderson	Chicago Cubs	P	Rich Bordi
Dec 13, 1982		No compensation (free agent signing)	Chicago White Sox	P	Floyd Bannister

DATE	ACQUIRED	FROM	IN EXCHANGE FOR
Dec 21, 1982	1B Pat Putnam	Texas Rangers	P Ron Musselman
Jan 21, 1983	Cash	Cleveland Indians	C Jim Essian
March 31, 1983	1B Ken Phelps	Montreal Expos	Cash
June 15, 1983	2B Tony Bernazard	Chicago White Sox	2B Julio Cruz
June 30, 1983	Cash	Baltimore Orioles	SS-3B Todd Cruz
July 29, 1983	Cash	Philadelphia Phillies	P Larry Andersen
Aug 23, 1983	$100,000.	Detroit Tigers	P Glenn Abbott
Nov 21, 1983	P Dave Beard C Bob Kearney	Oakland Athletics	P Bill Caudill minor league P Darren Akerfelds
Dec 7, 1983	OF Gorman Thomas 2B Jack Perconte	Cleveland Indians	2B Tony Bernazard
Dec 8, 1983	OF Barry Bonnell	Toronto Blue Jays	P Bryan Clark
Jan 15, 1984	Minor league P John Semprini	New York Mets	1B Jim Maler
Feb 14, 1984	2B Larry Milbourne	New York Yankees	Minor league Ps Eric Parent and Scott Nielsen

Texas Rangers

The Best Trades

1. Acquired Gaylord Perry, Joe Carroll, and Tucker Ashford from the San Diego Padres for Willie Montanez, February 18, 1980.
2. Acquired Buddy Bell from the Cleveland Indians for Toby Harrah, December 8, 1978.
3. Acquired Ferguson Jenkins from the Boston Red Sox for John Poloni and cash, December 14, 1977.
4. Acquired Jim Bibby from the St. Louis Cardinals for Mike Nagy and John Wockenfuss, June 6, 1973.
5. Acquired Rusty Staub from the Montreal Expos for LaRue Washington and Chris Smith, March 31, 1980.

The Worst Trades

1. Traded Dave Righetti, Paul Mirabella, Mike Griffin, Greg Jamieson, and Juan Beniquez to the New York Yankees for Sparky Lyle, Domingo Ramos, Mike Heath, Larry McCall, Dave Rajsich, and cash, November 10, 1978.
2. Traded Walt Terrell and Ron Darling to the New York Mets for Lee Mazzilli, April 1, 1982.

3. Traded Roy Smalley, Bill Singer, Mike Cubbage, Jim Gideon, and $250,000 to the Minnesota Twins for Bert Blyleven and Danny Thompson, June 1, 1976.

4. Traded Doyle Alexander, Larvell Blanks, and $50,000 to the Atlanta Braves for Adrian Devine and Pepe Frias, December 6, 1979.

5. Traded Mike Smithson and John Butcher to the Minnesota Twins for Gary Ward and Jim Sorce, December 7, 1983.

Trades: The Revolving Door

History would have you believe that the Texas Rangers always got their man. But the baseball fans in the Dallas–Fort Worth area know that more often than not, the modern-day Rangers have first gotten, then lost their man.

The Rangers' trading record got off to a great start when then-owner Bob Short acquired pitchers Jim Bibby and Ferguson Jenkins within five months of each other. Bibby, picked up from St. Louis for pitcher Steve Nagy and catcher John Wockenfuss in June 1973, won nine games in his first half-season with Texas, one of them a no-hitter. He won 19 for them in '74. Jenkins won 25 for Texas that same season as the surprising Rangers chased Oakland to the wire in the AL West. Officially, the trade is listed as Bill Madlock and Vic Harris for Jenkins, but Short had also sent the Cubs Rico Carty and Mike Paul with the understanding that Jenkins would be available at the end of the season.

Short departed the scene at the end of the '74 season, selling his interest to a group headed by Brad Corbett. Corbett's two general managers were Dan O'Brien and Eddie Robinson, who between them pulled off a long series of dreadful trades, each one worse than the one before. First, he traded shortstop Roy Smalley, third baseman Mike Cubbage, pitchers Bill Singer and Jim Gideon, and $250,000 to Minnesota for Bert Blyleven. Next, twenty-year-old Dave Righetti was sent to the Yankees along with Juan Beniquez and three other pitchers for Sparky Lyle and four players of no distinction. They then traded Mike Hargrove, Kurt Bevacqua, and Bill Fahey for Oscar Gamble, Dave Roberts, and cash; this deal doesn't look so bad, but less than a season later they dealt Gamble to the Yankees along with Ray Fontenot and Gene Nelson for Mickey Rivers and three minor leaguers. Gaylord Perry went to San Diego for Dave Tomlin and cash, and in the least explicable deal, Walt Terrell and Ron Darling were traded to the Mets for Lee Mazzilli. In addition, Eddie Robinson traded Al Oliver to Montreal for Dave Hostetler and Larry Parrish, less than he probably could have gotten for him, because he was misinformed as to the interleague trading deadline, and took the best offer on his desk at the time. An outstanding young pitching staff had been dealt away for next to nothing, and the rebuilding process continued year after year. It was almost unfortunate for the fans that the team never completely fell apart; at least then management might have gotten away from the notion that it just needed one more player to win a pennant.

DATE		ACQUIRED	FROM		IN EXCHANGE FOR
Nov 3, 1971	SS	Ted Kubiak	St. Louis Cardinals	P	Joe Grzenda
Dec 2, 1971	C	Hal King	Atlanta Braves	C	Paul Casanova
Dec 2, 1971	P	Gary Jones minor league P Terry Lee	New York Yankees	2B	Bernie Allen

DATE	ACQUIRED	FROM	IN EXCHANGE FOR
Dec 2, 1971	OF Roy Foster C Ken Suarez P Mike Paul P Rich Hand	Cleveland Indians	OF Del Unser P Denny Riddleberger P Gary Jones minor league P Terry Lee
March 4, 1972	P Don Stanhouse P Jim Panther	Oakland Athletics	P Denny McLain
April 3, 1972	OF Ted Ford	Cleveland Indians	OF Roy Foster 1B Tom McCraw
May 30, 1972	3B Dalton Jones	Detroit Tigers	P Norm McRae
July 20, 1972	IF Marty Martinez IF Vic Harris P Steve Lawson	Oakland Athletics	1B Don Mincher SS Ted Kubiak
Aug 30, 1972	P Jim Roland	New York Yankees	P Casey Cox
Aug 31, 1972	Cash	Detroit Tigers	1B Frank Howard
Sept 6, 1972	P Rich Hinton	New York Yankees	Cash
Oct 27, 1972	OF Rico Carty	Atlanta Braves	P Jim Panther
Oct 30, 1972	OF Bill McNulty OF Brant Alyea	Oakland Athletics	P Paul Lindblad
Nov 30, 1972	1B Mike Epstein	Oakland Athletics	P Horacio Pina
Nov 30, 1972	P Vince Colbert	Cleveland Indians	IF Tom Ragland
Feb 1, 1973	P Charles Hudson	St. Louis Cardinals	P Mike Thompson
March 8, 1973	OF Alex Johnson	Cleveland Indians	P Rich Hinton P Vince Colbert
March 28, 1973	3B Bill Sudakis	New York Mets	OF Bill McNulty
March 31, 1973	P Mike Nagy	St. Louis Cardinals	P Mike Thompson
May 4, 1973	P Sonny Siebert	Boston Red Sox	Cash
May 10, 1973	P Steve Dunning	Cleveland Indians	P Dick Bosman OF Ted Ford
May 20, 1973	1B Jim Spencer P Lloyd Allen	California Angels	1B Mike Epstein P Rich Hand C Rick Stelmaszek
June 6, 1973	P Jim Bibby	St. Louis Cardinals	P Mike Nagy C John Wockenfuss
July 11, 1973	3B Jim Fregosi	New York Mets	Cash
July 16, 1973	P Don Durham	St. Louis Cardinals	P Jim Kremmel
Aug 13, 1973	Cash	Chicago Cubs	OF Rico Carty

DATE		ACQUIRED	FROM		IN EXCHANGE FOR
Aug 31, 1973	P	Larry Gura	Chicago Cubs	P	Mike Paul
Oct 25, 1973	P	Ferguson Jenkins	Chicago Cubs	3B 2B	Bill Madlock Vic Harris
Oct 26, 1973	OF	Cirilio Cruz and cash	St. Louis Cardinals	P	Sonny Siebert
Dec 6, 1973	OF-1B	Terry Crowley	Baltimore Orioles		Cash
Dec 6, 1973		Cash	New York Yankees	SS	Jim Mason
Dec 7, 1973		Cash	New York Yankees	UT	Bill Sudakis
Dec 7, 1973	OF	Cesar Tovar	Philadelphia Phillies		Cash
Dec 20, 1973	P	Pat Jarvis	Montreal Expos	1B	Larry Biittner
Feb 12, 1974	SS	Leo Cardenas	Cleveland Indians	C	Ken Suarez
March 19, 1974		Cash	Cincinnati Reds	OF-1B	Terry Crowley
March 23, 1974		Cash	New York Yankees	OF	Elliott Maddox
March 23, 1974	P	Steve Hargan	Cleveland Indians	P	Bill Gogolewski
May 8, 1974	C	Duke Sims	New York Yankees	P	Larry Gura and cash
July 1, 1974	P	Bob Johnson	Cleveland Indians		Cash
July 1, 1974		Cash	Chicago White Sox	P	Lloyd Allen
Aug 12, 1974		Cash	St. Louis Cardinals	C	Dick Billings
Sept 9, 1974	P	Bill Hands	Minnesota Twins		Cash
Sept 9, 1974		Cash	New York Yankees	OF	Alex Johnson
Dec 5, 1974	P	Clyde Wright	Milwaukee Brewers	P	Pete Broberg
Dec 5, 1974	OF	Willie Davis	Montreal Expos	P SS	Don Stanhouse Pete Mackanin
Feb 25, 1975	P	Stan Perzanowski	Chicago White Sox	P	Steve Dunning
June 4, 1975	SS P	Ed Brinkman Tommy Moore	St. Louis Cardinals	OF	Willie Davis
June 13, 1975	P	Gaylord Perry	Cleveland Indians	P P P	Jim Bibby Jackie Brown Rick Waits and $100,000.
June 13, 1975		Cash	New York Yankees	SS	Ed Brinkman
Aug 31, 1975		Cash	Oakland Athletics	UT	Cesar Tovar

DATE		ACQUIRED	FROM		IN EXCHANGE FOR
Nov 12, 1975	P	Nellie Briles	Kansas City Royals	2B	Dave Nelson
Nov 17, 1975	OF P P	Juan Beniquez Steve Barr Craig Skok	Boston Red Sox	P	Ferguson Jenkins
Dec 9, 1975	C	John Ellis	Cleveland Indians	P C	Stan Thomas Ron Pruitt
Dec 10, 1975	P	Bill Singer	California Angels	1B	Jim Spencer and $100,000.
Dec 12, 1975	OF	Gene Clines	New York Mets	OF	Joe Lovitto
Feb 24, 1976	P	George Stone	New York Mets	P	Bill Hands
May 28, 1976	P	Fritz Peterson	Cleveland Indians	P	Stan Perzanowski and cash
June 1, 1976	P SS	Bert Blyleven Danny Thompson	Minnesota Twins	P SS 3B P	Bill Singer Roy Smalley Mike Cubbage Jim Gideon and $250,000.
June 15, 1976	OF	Joe LaHoud	California Angels		Cash
Oct 22, 1976	P	Mike Wallace	St. Louis Cardinals	P	Johnny Sutton
Nov 8, 1976	P	Mike Thompson	Cincinnati Reds		Minor league P Art DeFilippis
Nov 17, 1976	SS	Bert Campaneris	Oakland Athletics		No compensation (free agent signing)
Nov 23, 1976	P	Doyle Alexander	New York Yankees		No compensation (free agent signing)
Dec 9, 1976	OF OF P P P	Ken Henderson Dave May Carl Morton Roger Moret Adrian Devine and $250,000.	Atlanta Braves	OF	Jeff Burroughs
Feb 5, 1977	P	Darold Knowles	Chicago Cubs	OF	Gene Clines and cash
Feb 17, 1977	IF	Sandy Alomar	New York Yankees	IF IF	Greg Pryor Brian Doyle and cash
Feb 19, 1977	P	Paul Lindblad	Oakland Athletics		$400,000.
March 15, 1977	IF	Rodney Scott	Montreal Expos	P	Jeff Terpko
March 26, 1977	OF	Claudell Washington	Oakland Athletics	P IF	Jim Umbarger Rodney Scott and cash
April 12, 1977	OF	Willie Horton	Detroit Tigers	P	Steve Foucault
April 26, 1977	SS	Rick Auerbach and cash	New York Mets	IF	Lenny Randle

DATE		ACQUIRED	FROM		IN EXCHANGE FOR
April 30, 1977	P	Mike Marshall	Atlanta Braves		Cash
May 9, 1977	P SS	Steve Hargan Jim Mason and $200,000.	Toronto Blue Jays	3B	Roy Howell
June 15, 1977	1B	Ed Kirkpatrick	Pittsburgh Pirates	1B	Jim Fregosi
June 15, 1977		Cash	Atlanta Braves	P	Steve Hargan
June 15, 1977	P	Dock Ellis	Oakland Athletics		Cash
June 15, 1977		Cash	Cincinnati Reds	SS	Rick Auerbach
Aug 20, 1977	OF	Gorman Thomas	Milwaukee Brewers	1B	Ed Kirkpatrick
Aug 25, 1977	P	Jim Umbarger	Oakland Athletics		Cash
Sept 19, 1977		Cash	Baltimore Orioles	P	Nellie Briles
Nov 9, 1977	OF	Richie Zisk	Chicago White Sox		No compensation (free agent signing)
Nov 10, 1977		Cash	Montreal Expos	P	Darold Knowles
Nov 11, 1977	P	Doc Medich	New York Mets		No compensation (free agent signing)
Nov 28, 1977		No compensation (free agent signing)	Chicago White Sox	SS	Greg Pryor
Dec 8, 1977	1B	Willie Montanez	Atlanta Braves	P P OF	Adrian Devine Tommy Boggs Eddie Miller
		(Part of four-team trade involving Texas, Atlanta, Pittsburgh, and New York Mets.)			
Dec 8, 1977	P 1B	Jon Matlack John Milner	New York Mets	1B OF OF	Willie Montanez Ken Henderson Tom Grieve
		(Part of four-team trade involving Texas, New York Mets, Pittsburgh, and Atlanta.)			
Dec 8, 1977	OF	Al Oliver	Pittsburgh Pirates	P OF	Bert Blyleven John Milner
		(Part of four-team trade involving Texas, New York Mets, Pittsburgh, and Atlanta.)			
Dec 14, 1977	P	Ferguson Jenkins	Boston Red Sox	P	John Poloni and cash
Jan 25, 1978	P	Dave Tomlin and $125,000.	San Diego Padres	P	Gaylord Perry
Feb 8, 1978		Cash	Milwaukee Brewers	OF	Gorman Thomas
Feb 23, 1978	1B	Mike Jorgensen	Oakland Athletics		No compensation (free agent signing)
Feb 28, 1978	P OF	Tom Buskey John Lowenstein	Cleveland Indians	OF P	Willie Horton David Clyde
March 28, 1978		Cash	Cincinnati Reds	P	Dave Tomlin

DATE		ACQUIRED	FROM		IN EXCHANGE FOR
April 18, 1978	P	Reggie Cleveland	Boston Red Sox		Cash
May 16, 1978	OF	Bobby Bonds	Chicago White Sox	OF OF	Claudell Washington Rusty Torres
May 17, 1978		Cash	Milwaukee Brewers	OF	Dave May
Aug 2, 1978		Cash	New York Yankees	P	Paul Lindblad
Aug 31, 1978	OF	John Grubb	Cleveland Indians	P	Bobby Cuellar minor league OF Dave Rivera
Oct 3, 1978	P IF	Jim Kern Larvell Blanks	Cleveland Indians	OF P	Bobby Bonds Len Barker
Oct 25, 1978	OF C	Oscar Gamble Dave Roberts and $300,000.	San Diego Padres	1B 3B C	Mike Hargrove Kurt Bevacqua Bill Fahey
Nov 10, 1978	SS C P P P	Domingo Ramos Mike Heath Sparky Lyle Larry McCall Dave Rajsich and cash	New York Yankees	P OF P P	Dave Righetti Juan Beniquez Mike Griffin Paul Mirabella minor league P Greg Jamieson
Nov 27, 1978		Cash	Baltimore Orioles	OF	John Lowenstein
Dec 6, 1978		Cash	Seattle Mariners	OF	Bobby Thompson
Dec 8, 1978	3B	Buddy Bell	Cleveland Indians	3B	Toby Harrah
Dec 8, 1978	OF	Mike Hart	Montreal Expos	SS	Jim Mason
Dec 13, 1978	P	Mac Scarce	Minnesota Twins	P	Mike Bacsik
Dec 15, 1978	P 1B	Ed Farmer Gary Holle and cash	Milwaukee Brewers	P	Reggie Cleveland
May 4, 1979	3B	Dave Chalk	California Angels	SS	Bert Campaneris
June 15, 1979	P P	Bob Myrick Mike Bruhert	New York Mets	P	Dock Ellis
June 15, 1979	P	John Henry Johnson	Oakland Athletics	3B C	Dave Chalk Mike Heath and cash
June 15, 1979	3B	Eric Soderholm	Chicago White Sox	P 1B	Ed Farmer Gary Holle
Aug 1, 1979	OF	Mickey Rivers minor league Ps Bob Polinsky Neil Merschi and Mark Softy	New York Yankees	OF P P	Oscar Gamble Ray Fontenot Gene Nelson minor league 3B Amos Lewis
Aug 12, 1979	1B	Willie Montanez	New York Mets	P 1B	Ed Lynch Mike Jorgensen
Nov 5, 1979		Cash	Toronto Blue Jays	SS	Domingo Ramos

DATE		ACQUIRED	FROM		IN EXCHANGE FOR
Nov 14, 1979		Minor league 3B Amos Lewis minor league P Ricky Burdette and cash	New York Yankees	3B	Eric Soderholm
Dec 6, 1979	P SS	Adrian Devine Pepe Frias	Atlanta Braves	P SS	Doyle Alexander Larvell Blanks and $50,000.
Jan 4, 1980	P OF	David Clyde Jim Norris	Cleveland Indians	P 1B	Larry McCall Gary Gray minor league 3B-OF Mike Bucci
Feb 15, 1980	P 3B	Gaylord Perry Tucker Ashford minor league P Joe Carroll	San Diego Padres	1B	Willie Montanez
March 31, 1980	1B	Rusty Staub	Montreal Expos	SS 3B	LaRue Washington Chris Smith
July 11, 1980	P	Charlie Hough	Los Angeles Dodgers		Cash
July 28, 1980	P	Ed Figueroa	New York Yankees		Cash
Aug 14, 1980	P	Ken Clay minor league OF Marvin Thompson	New York Yankees	P	Gaylord Perry
Sept 13, 1980	P	Kevin Saucier	Philadelphia Phillies	P	Sparky Lyle
Sept 13, 1980	SS	Pepe Frias	Los Angeles Dodgers	P	Dennis Lewallyn
Oct 24, 1980	1B	Roger Holt	New York Yankees	3B	Tucker Ashford and cash
Dec 10, 1980	SS	Mark Wagner	Detroit Tigers	P	Kevin Saucier
Dec 12, 1980	P SS C OF DH	Rick Honeycutt Mario Mendoza Larry Cox Leon Roberts Willie Horton	Seattle Mariners	OF IF P P P P	Richie Zisk Rick Auerbach Ken Clay Jerry Gleaton Brian Allard Steve Finch
Dec 16, 1980		No compensation (free agent signing)	New York Mets	1B	Rusty Staub
Dec 29, 1980	2B	Bill Stein	Seattle Mariners		No compensation (free agent signing)
June 4, 1981		Cash	Chicago Cubs	OF	Bobby Bonds
Aug 12, 1981	OF	Tom Poquette	Boston Red Sox		Cash
Aug 25, 1981		Cash	Cleveland Indians	P	Dennis Lewallyn
Sept 8, 1981	P	Bob Lacey	Cleveland Indians		Cash
Oct 20, 1981	IF	Ramon Aviles	Philadelphia Phillies	P	Dave Rajsich

DATE		ACQUIRED	FROM		IN EXCHANGE FOR
Dec 8, 1981		No compensation (free agent signing)	Chicago Cubs	P	Ferguson Jenkins
Dec 11, 1981	2B P	Doug Flynn Danny Boitano	New York Mets	P	Jim Kern
Jan 6, 1982	P	Frank Tanana	Boston Red Sox		No compensation (free agent signing)
Jan 15, 1982	1B	Lamar Johnson	Chicago White Sox		No compensation (free agent signing)
Jan 15, 1982		No compensation (free agent signing)	Kansas City Royals	OF	Tom Poquette
Feb 19, 1982	P	Steve Luebber	Baltimore Orioles	OF	Rick Lisi
March 26, 1982	P	Paul Mirabella minor league P Paul Semall and cash	Chicago Cubs	2B	Bump Wills
March 31, 1982	3B-OF 1B	Larry Parrish Dave Hostetler	Montreal Expos	1B	Al Oliver
April 1, 1982	OF	Lee Mazzilli	New York Mets	P P	Ron Darling Walt Terrell
April 9, 1982	P	Mike Smithson	Boston Red Sox	P	John Henry Johnson
May 17, 1982	1B	Randy Bass	San Diego Padres		Cash
July 15, 1982		Cash	Toronto Blue Jays	OF	Leon Roberts
Aug 2, 1982		Cash	Montreal Expos	2B	Doug Flynn
Aug 8, 1982	SS	Bucky Dent	New York Yankees	1B-OF	Lee Mazzilli
Aug 11, 1982		Cash	Milwaukee Brewers	P	Doc Medich
Nov 1, 1982	P	John Pacella	Minnesota Twins	P	Len Whitehouse
Dec 21, 1982	P	Ron Musselman	Seattle Mariners	1B	Pat Putnam
Jan 27, 1983	SS	Vance McHenry	Toronto Blue Jays	P	Bob Babcock
March 24, 1983	P	Dave Tobik	Detroit Tigers	P	John Grubb
Aug 19, 1983	P P	Dave Stewart Ricky Wright and $200,000.	Los Angeles Dodgers	P	Rick Honeycutt
Dec 7, 1983	OF	Gary Ward minor league C Sam Sorce	Minnesota Twins	P P	Mike Smithson John Butcher
Dec 8, 1983	C	Ned Yost minor league P Dan Scarpetta	Milwaukee Brewers	C	Jim Sundberg
Feb 7, 1984	P	Jim Bibby	Pittsburgh Pirates		No compensation (free agent signing)

Toronto Blue Jays

The Best Trades

1. Acquired Alfredo Griffin and Phil Lansford from the Cleveland Indians for Victor Cruz, December 5, 1978.
2. Acquired Rick Cerone and John Lowenstein from the Cleveland Indians for Rico Carty, December 6, 1976.
3. Acquired Damaso Garcia, Chris Chambliss, and Paul Mirabella from the New York Yankees for Rick Cerone, Tom Underwood, and Ted Wilborn, November 1, 1979.
4. Acquired Cliff Johnson from the Oakland A's for Al Woods, November 15, 1982.
5. Acquired Rance Mulliniks from the Kansas City Royals for Phil Huffman, March 25, 1982.

The Worst Trades

1. Traded Chris Chambliss and Luis Gomez to the Atlanta Braves for Barry Bonnell, Pat Rockett, and Joey McLaughlin, December 5, 1979.
2. Traded John Lowenstein to the Cleveland Indians for Hector Torres, March 29, 1977.
3. Traded Alan Ashby to the Houston Astros for Mark Lemongello, Joe Cannon, and Pedro Hernandez, November 27, 1978.

Trader: Pat Gillick

The head of baseball operations for the Toronto Blue Jays may look young and innocent, but rival general managers are advised to count their fingers and rings after shaking his hand. Pat Gillick has revamped the expansion Jays into a solid contender by mixing young home-grown talent with useful players picked up in trades.

Of the current Blue Jays squad, only the big three of the pitching staff and outfielders Lloyd Moseby and Jesse Barfield originated in the Toronto farm system. The entire infield and catching staff, as well as the bullpen, were picked up from other teams in one way or other.

First baseman Willie Upshaw, their leading run producer in 1983, was drafted out of the New York Yankees system, as was Garth Iorg, the right-handed hitting half of their third base platoon. Rance Mulliniks, the other half of the platoon, was acquired from Kansas City in a trade for Phil Huffman. The double play combination of Alfredo Griffin and Damaso Garcia came in separate trades; Griffin from Cleveland for Victor Cruz, Garcia with Chris Chambliss from the Yankees for Rick Cerone and Tom Underwood. Outfielder Dave Collins was gratefully unloaded on the Jays by the Yankees, and George Bell was another minor league draftee.

Ernie Whitt, their lefty-hitting catcher, is a holdover from the expansion draft, when the Jays plucked him from Boston. Martinez came to Toronto from Milwaukee in a deal for outfielder Ed Kubski. The 1983 designated hitting pair of Cliff Johnson and Jorge Orta also came in trades, Johnson from Oakland for Al Woods, Orta from the Mets for Steve Senteney. Orta's place in the platoon was taken by Willie Aikens in '84; the two were traded for each other even-up during the winter. The ace of the bullpen, Dennis Lamp, was signed as a free agent. Long relief help is provided by Roy Lee Jackson, ex-Met, and former Oriole, Ranger, Brave, Giant, and Yankee Doyle Alexander has moved smartly into the starting rotation.

This trading record has been all the more remarkable given the relatively short time the Jays have had to develop any tradable talent of their own. Should the Jays battle the established clubs of the American League East to the wire this year, much of the credit should go to Gillick for his role in buying time and finding talent.

DATE		ACQUIRED	FROM		IN EXCHANGE FOR
Oct 21, 1976	C	Phil Roof	Chicago White Sox	P	Larry Anderson
Nov 5, 1976	C 1B	Alan Ashby Doug Howard	Cleveland Indians	P	Al Fitzmorris
Dec 6, 1976	OF C	John Lowenstein Rick Cerone	Cleveland Indians	OF	Rico Carty
Feb 16, 1977	P	Jerry Johnson	San Diego Padres	UT	Dave Roberts
Feb 24, 1977	1B	Ron Fairly	Oakland Athletics		Minor league IF Mike Weathers and cash
March 21, 1977	P	Ken Reynolds	San Diego Padres		Cash
March 29, 1977	SS	Hector Torres	Cleveland Indians	OF	John Lowenstein
May 9, 1977	3B	Roy Howell	Texas Rangers	P SS	Steve Hargan Jim Mason and $200,000.
June 8, 1977	3B	Doug Rader	San Diego Padres		Cash
July 27, 1977	P	Tom Murphy	Boston Red Sox		Cash
Aug 30, 1977	SS	Tim Nordbrook	Chicago White Sox		Cash
Sept 2, 1977	OF	John Hale	Los Angeles Dodgers		Cash
Sept 14, 1977		Cash	Seattle Mariners	OF	John Hale
Oct 31, 1977	P	Joe Henderson	Cincinnati Reds		Cash
Dec 6, 1977	P P	Tom Underwood Victor Cruz	St. Louis Cardinals	P OF	Pete Vuckovich John Scott
Dec 8, 1977	1B	Tom Hutton	Philadelphia Phillies		Cash
Dec 8, 1977	C 1B	Dale Kelly Butch Alberts	California Angels	1B	Ron Fairly
Feb 23, 1978	P	Steve Grilli	Detroit Tigers		Cash
March 15, 1978	OF	Rick Bosetti	St. Louis Cardinals		Cash
March 25, 1978	OF	Sheldon Mallory	Oakland Athletics	2B	Steve Staggs
March 27, 1978	P	Larry Demery	Pittsburgh Pirates		Cash
March 29, 1978	P	Mike Stanton	Houston Astros		Cash
April 4, 1978	1B	John Mayberry	Kansas City Royals		Cash
April 11, 1978	P	Don Kirkwood	Chicago White Sox		Cash
April 13, 1978	P	Balor Moore	California Angels		Cash

DATE		ACQUIRED	FROM		IN EXCHANGE FOR
April 29, 1978	SS	Tim Johnson	Milwaukee Brewers	IF	Tim Nordbrook
May 22, 1978	P	Joe Coleman	Oakland Athletics		Cash
July 20, 1978		Cash	Montreal Expos	1B	Tom Hutton
Aug 15, 1978	DH P	Willie Horton Phil Huffman	Oakland Athletics	DH	Rico Carty
Sept 12, 1978	P	Mark Wiley	San Diego Padres		Minor league OF Andy Dyes
Oct 3, 1978	DH	Rico Carty	Oakland Athletics		Cash
Nov 3, 1978	P	Dave Freisleben	Cleveland Indians	OF	Sheldon Mallory
Nov 27, 1978	OF SS P	Joe Cannon Pedro Hernandez Mark Lemongello	Houston Astros	C	Alan Ashby
Dec 4, 1978		Minor league P Don Pisker	Houston Astros	OF	Gary Woods
Dec 5, 1978	SS	Alfredo Griffin minor league 3B Phil Lansford	Cleveland Indians	P	Victor Cruz
March 25, 1979	OF	Bobby Brown	New York Mets		Cash
June 6, 1979	P	Dyar Miller	California Angels		Cash
July 25, 1979	1B	Craig Kusick	Minnesota Twins		Cash
July 30, 1979	1B	Tony Solaita	Montreal Expos	P	Dyar Miller
Nov 1, 1979	1B 2B P	Chris Chambliss Damaso Garcia Paul Mirabella	New York Yankees	P C OF	Tom Underwood Rick Cerone Ted Wilborn
Nov 5, 1979	SS	Domingo Ramos	Texas Rangers		Cash
Dec 5, 1979	OF SS P	Barry Bonnell Pat Rockett Joey McLaughlin	Atlanta Braves	1B SS	Chris Chambliss Luis Gomez
April 7, 1980		Cash	Chicago Cubs	P	Mark Lemongello
June 3, 1980	P	Ken Schrom	California Angels	P	Dave Lemanczyk
Sept 11, 1980		Cash	Pittsburgh Pirates	P	Jesse Jefferson
Dec 12, 1980	P	Roy Lee Jackson	New York Mets	UT	Bob Bailor
Dec 23, 1980		No compensation (free agent signing)	Milwaukee Brewers	3B	Roy Howell
Jan 15, 1981	3B	Ken Macha	Montreal Expos		Cash
April 6, 1981	P	Mark Bomback	New York Mets	P	Charlie Puleo and cash

DATE		ACQUIRED	FROM		IN EXCHANGE FOR
May 10, 1981	C	Buck Martinez	Milwaukee Brewers	OF	Gil Kubski
June 10, 1981		Cash	Oakland Athletics	OF	Rick Bosetti
Aug 8, 1981	P	Juan Berenguer	Kansas City Royals		Cash
Nov 17, 1981	3B	Aurelio Rodriguez	New York Yankees		Minor league C Mike Lebo
Dec 28, 1981	P	Dave Geisel	Chicago Cubs	P	Paul Mirabella
March 25, 1982	SS	Rance Mulliniks	Kansas City Royals	P	Phil Huffman
April 2, 1982	OF	Wayne Nordhagen	Chicago White Sox	3B	Aurelio Rodriguez
May 5, 1982	1B	Dave Revering minor league 3B Jeff Reynolds	New York Yankees	1B	John Mayberry
June 15, 1982	OF	Dick Davis	Philadelphia Phillies	OF	Wayne Nordhagen
July 15, 1982	OF	Leon Roberts	Texas Rangers		Cash
Aug 6, 1982		No compensation (free agent signing)	Seattle Mariners	1B	Dave Revering
Aug 23, 1982		Cash	New York Yankees	2B	Pedro Hernandez
Oct 27, 1982	3B	Tucker Ashford	New York Yankees		Cash
		(Ashford was returned to the Yankees on April 5, 1983.)			
Nov 15, 1982	DH	Cliff Johnson	Oakland Athletics	OF	Al Woods
Dec 10, 1982		No compensation (free agent signing)	Chicago Cubs	OF	Wayne Nordhagen
Dec 10, 1982	P	Don Cooper	Minnesota Twins	3B	Dave Baker
Jan 18, 1983		Cash	St. Louis Cardinals	P	Jerry Garvin
Jan 27, 1983	P	Bob Babcock	Texas Rangers	SS	Vance McHenry
Feb 4, 1983	OF	Jorge Orta	New York Mets	P	Steve Senteney
Feb 5, 1983		Minor league 1B Cecil Fielder	Kansas City Royals	OF	Leon Roberts
Feb 25, 1983	P	Randy Moffitt	Houston Astros		No compensation (free agent signing)
Dec 8, 1983	P	Bryan Clark	Seattle Mariners	OF	Barry Bonnell
Dec 20, 1983	1B	Willie Aikens	Kansas City Royals	OF	Jorge Orta
Jan 10, 1984	P	Dennis Lamp	Chicago White Sox		Free agent signing
		Chicago selected Tom Seaver of the New York Mets from the compensation pool.			

Washington Senators

The Best Trades

1. Acquired Buddy Myer from the Boston Red Sox for Milt Gaston, Hod Lisenbee, Elliott Bigelow, Bobby Reeves, and Grant Gillis, December 15, 1928.
2. Acquired Stan Coveleski from the Cleveland Indians for Byron Speece and Carr Smith, December 12, 1924.
3. Acquired Rick Ferrell from the St. Louis Browns for Gene Moore and cash, March 1, 1944.
4. Acquired Heinie Manush and General Crowder from the St. Louis Browns for Goose Goslin, June 13, 1930.
5. Acquired Harlond Clift and Johnny Niggeling from the St. Louis Browns for Ellis Clary, Ox Miller, and cash, August 18, 1943.

The Worst Trades

1. Traded Jackie Jensen to the Boston Red Sox for Mickey McDermott and Tommy Umphlett, December 9, 1953.
2. Traded Goose Goslin to the Detroit Tigers for John Stone, December 20, 1932.
3. Traded General Crowder to the St. Louis Browns for Tom Zachary, July 7, 1927.
4. Traded Earl Webb to the Boston Red Sox for Bill Barrett, April 30, 1930.
5. Traded Al Orth to the New York Yankees for Bill Wolfe and Long Tom Hughes, January 23, 1904.

Owner: Clark Griffith

One of the game's immortals, Clark Griffith spent sixty-eight years, all but four of them in the majors, contributing to the building of the game of baseball. He was one of the great pitchers of pre-1900 ball, but his greatest accomplishments came off the field. A co-founder of the American League, Griffith came to Washington as manager and part-owner of the Senators in 1912.

When Griffith came to the club, they were the poorest franchise in the league, despite the presence of Walter Johnson. In eleven seasons, Washington had yet to finish in the first division. Gradually, Griffith rebuilt the team, trading off virtually the entire roster except Johnson and fleet outfielder Clyde Milan, replacing his forgettables with such stars as Sam Rice, Goose Goslin, Bucky Harris, Joe Judge, Roger Peckinpaugh, Ossie Bluege, Tom Zachary, Fred Marberry, and George Mogridge. Under Griffith's direction the Senators won pennants in '24, '25, and '33.

Griffith's sole income came from baseball; this was as much a disadvantage to him then as it is today to his nephew Cal. It was difficult for him to compete with the wealthier owners, but he kept the franchise going for forty years through shrewd manipulations and astute trades; they didn't call him "The Old Fox" for nothing. He specialized in picking up unwanted players and getting excellent production out of them. In the winter of 1924, he acquired veteran pitcher Stan Coveleski from Cleveland for a couple of third-string arms. The Indians thought Coveleski was washed up, but he won 20 for the Senators in '25 as they won their second straight pennant.

In 1928, Griffith traded Buddy Myer to Boston for shortstop Topper Rigney. He quickly realized he had made a mistake, and gave up five players to get Myer back the following season. Myer replaced Bucky Harris at second and teamed with Peckinpaugh, obtained in an earlier deal with Boston, to form the best double-play combination in the game. Griffith had no hesitation about reacquiring players he had traded away; at one time or other he dealt away Myer, Goose Goslin, Alvin Crowder, Sam West, Bobo Newsom, Firpo Marberry, Rick Ferrell, Bucky Harris, Tom Zachary, George Case, and Mickey Vernon and brought them all back to Washington.

There was one club Griffith would never deal with, and that was the Yankees. He had a deep and abiding hatred for them, perhaps because they had dropped him as manager before he moved on to Washington, perhaps because he resented Jake Ruppert's money while he himself was always operating on a shoestring. It was at Griffith's urging that the league put through a rule forbidding pennant winners from making trades; the rule, blatantly aimed at curbing the Yankees' runaway success, lasted just one year.

Always recognized as the premier trader in the game, Griffith climaxed his long record in player swaps when, at the end of the 1934 season, he sold his son-in-law, shortstop and manager Joe Cronin, to the Boston Red Sox for $225,000. The Senators had purchased Cronin from Kansas City of the American Association for $7,500 during the 1928 season. Cronin quickly developed into the best shortstop in the league, and in his first year as player-manager led the Senators to the AL pennant. A broken wrist kept Cronin out of the lineup for much of '34, and the Senators skidded to seventh. Cronin took advantage of the time off to marry Griffith's adopted daughter, Mildred Robertson.

During the '34 World Series, Tom Yawkey visited Griffith and told him, "Clark, I want to buy Joe Cronin. I will give you a check for $225,000 for him."

"Not a chance," replied Griffith. But a couple of weeks later, Griffith received a phone call from Yawkey.

"My offer still stands," Yawkey said. "Two hundred and twenty-five thousand dollars. How about it? Do we have a deal?"

"No," barked Griffith. "I'm not selling, and Tom, please don't call me again."

But Yawkey wouldn't give up. After another week, Yawkey was on the phone again. "I want Cronin as my manager," he said. "I can do more for your son-in-law than you can, Clark. I'll be in New York tomorrow. Please meet me there."

Griffith thought about Yawkey's words. It was true that Yawkey, a millionaire, could do things for Joe and Mildred that Griffith would never be able to do. Also, the Washington club had lost a lot of money in 1934, and Griffith owed the banks $124,000. He decided that he had no choice but to let Cronin go, but not before he gained some extra concessions out of Yawkey. He insisted on receiving a shortstop in return, and accepted Lyn Lary. He also got Yawkey to pay Cronin a then-handsome salary of $30,000.

It was the first and only time in his career that Clark Griffith sold away a top-notch star.

DATE	ACQUIRED		FROM	IN EXCHANGE FOR	
May 1901		Cash	Baltimore Orioles	1B	Tim Jordan
May 1901		Cash	Cleveland Indians	OF	Jack O'Brien
Sept 1901		Cash	Chicago White Sox	OF	Pop Foster
Sept 1902	C	Lew Drill	Baltimore Orioles		Cash
Feb 1903	OF	Ducky Holmes	Detroit Tigers		Cash
June 1903	P	Davey Dunkle	Chicago White Sox	OF	Ducky Holmes
June 1903	C	Malachi Kittredge	Boston Braves		Cash

DATE		ACQUIRED	FROM		IN EXCHANGE FOR
July 1903	2B	Barry McCormick	St. Louis Browns	OF	Joe Martin
Jan 16, 1904	OF	George Stone	Boston Red Sox		Cash
Jan 16, 1904	1B	Jake Stahl	Boston Red Sox		Cash
Jan 1904		Cash	New York Yankees	3B	Champ Osteen
May 8, 1904		Cash	New York Yankees	OF	Jack Thoney
July 4, 1904	OF	Bill O'Neill	Boston Red Sox	OF	Kip Selbach
July 13, 1904	P P	Long Tom Hughes Bill Wolfe	New York Yankees	P	Al Orth
July 14, 1904	3B OF	Hunter Hill Frank Huelsman (Huelsmann went to Washington on loan.)	St. Louis Browns	SS	Charlie Moran
Aug 10, 1904		$7,500.	Detroit Tigers	3B C	Bill Coughlin Lew Drill
Aug 31, 1904	2B	Jim Mullin	Philadelphia Athletics		Cash
Jan 16, 1905		Cash	Boston Red Sox	OF	George Stone
Jan 16, 1905	OF	Frank Huelsman (St. Louis reclaimed Huelsmann, who was with Washington on loan, and traded him to Boston. Boston then sent him to Washington as payment for George Stone.)	Boston Red Sox		See note
Jan 1905	3B	Lave Cross	Philadelphia Athletics		Cash
March 1905	OF	Harry Cassady	Pittsburgh Pirates		Waiver price
June 3, 1905	OF-1B	John Anderson	New York Yankees		Waiver price
July 6, 1905	1B	Piano Legs Hickman	Detroit Tigers		Cash
Dec 1905	P	Frank Kitson	Detroit Tigers		Cash
Dec 1905	P	Willie Sudhoff	St. Louis Browns	P	Beany Jacobson
Jan 1906		Cash	Cleveland Indians	P	Jack Townsend
Feb 1906	C	Howard Wakefield	Cleveland Indians		Cash
Aug 13, 1906	C	John Warner	Detroit Tigers		Cash
Aug 15, 1906		Cash	Cleveland Indians	C	Malachi Kittredge
Feb 1907		Cash	Cleveland Indians	C	Howard Wakefield
Feb 1907	OF	Bob Ganley	Pittsburgh Pirates		Cash

DATE	ACQUIRED	FROM	IN EXCHANGE FOR
March 1907	Cash	Chicago White Sox	1B Jake Stahl
	(Stahl refused to report and was sold by Chicago to the New York Yankees.)		
May 29, 1907	Cash	New York Yankees	P Frank Kitson
June 11, 1907	2B Jim Delahanty	St. Louis Browns	$2,000.
June 26, 1907	OF Otis Clymer	Pittsburgh Pirates	Cash
June 27, 1907	C Mike Kahoe	Chicago Cubs	Cash
Aug 1, 1907	Cash	Chicago White Sox	1B Piano Legs Hickman
Aug 11, 1907	2B Pete O'Brien C Howard Wakefield	Cleveland Indians	2B Rabbit Nill
Aug 11, 1907	P Frank Oberlin	Boston Red Sox	Cash
Oct 5, 1907	OF Ollie Pickering	St. Louis Browns	OF Charlie Jones
Jan 1908	Cash	Chicago White Sox	1B John Anderson
July 1908	P Jesse Tannehill 1B Bob Unglaub	Boston Red Sox	P Casey Patten
Aug 1908	Cash	Cleveland Indians	P Cy Falkenberg 2B Dave Altizer
Aug 1908	1B Jiggs Donahue	Chicago White Sox	Cash
May 16, 1909	P Nick Altrock OF Gavvy Cravath 1B Jiggs Donahue	Chicago White Sox	P Bill Burns
May 21, 1909	OF George Browne	Chicago Cubs	Waiver price
May 1909	Cash	Philadelphia Athletics	OF Bob Ganley
Aug 13, 1909	2B Germany Schaefer C Red Killefer	Detroit Tigers	2B Jim Delahanty
Sept 1909	OF Doc Gessler	Boston Red Sox	P Charlie Smith
Sept 1909	OF Jimmy Sebring	Brooklyn Dodgers	Cash
Dec 16, 1909	SS Kid Elberfeld	New York Yankees	$5,000.
April 1910	C Heinie Beckendorf	Detroit Tigers	Cash
May 1910	Cash	Chicago White Sox	OF George Browne
Dec 1911	IF John Knight SS Roxy Roach	New York Yankees	C Gabby Street OF Jack Lelivelt
Jan 1912	C Rip Williams	Boston Red Sox	Waiver price
Feb 1912	1B John Flynn	Pittsburgh Pirates	Waiver price

DATE		ACQUIRED	FROM		IN EXCHANGE FOR
June 26, 1912	P	Hippo Vaughn	New York Yankees		Waiver price
June 1912	P	Barney Pelty	St. Louis Browns		Cash
July 1912	2B	Frank LaPorte	St. Louis Browns		Cash
Oct 1912		Cash	St. Louis Browns	OF	Tilly Walker
April 10, 1913		Cash	Boston Braves	OF	Joe Connolly
May 17, 1913	P	George Mullin	Detroit Tigers		Waiver price
July 7, 1913		Cash	New York Yankees	IF	John Knight
July 20, 1914	OF	Mike Mitchell	Pittsburgh Pirates		Waiver price
Feb 10, 1916	OF	Mike Menosky	Pittsburgh (Federal League)		Cash
Feb 15, 1916		$7,500.	Cleveland Indians	1B	Chick Gandil
Aug 18, 1916	OF 3B	Elmer Smith Joe Leonard	Cleveland Indians	P OF	Joe Boehling Danny Moeller
Feb 3, 1917	2B	Sam Crane	Philadelphia Athletics		Cash
June 13, 1917		$4,000.	Cleveland Indians	OF	Elmer Smith
July 17, 1917		Waiver price	Philadelphia Athletics	OF	Charlie Jamieson
Dec 15, 1917	OF IF	Burt Shotton Doc Lavan	St. Louis Browns	P	Bert Gallia and $15,000.
Dec 1917		Cash	Boston Braves	C	John Henry
Dec 1917	OF	Wildfire Schulte	Philadelphia Phillies		Cash
May 25, 1918		Cash	Philadelphia Athletics	OF	Merito Acosta
June 1918		Cash	Cleveland Indians	P	Ad Brennan
Jan 17, 1919	IF	Hal Janvrin and cash	Boston Red Sox	C P	Eddie Ainsmith George Dumont
Jan 1919	C	Sam Agnew	Boston Red Sox		Cash
Jan 1919		Cash	St. Louis Cardinals	SS	Doc Lavan
Feb 1, 1919		Waiver price	St. Louis Cardinals	OF	Burt Shotton
June 1919	2B	Roy Grover	Philadelphia Athletics		Cash

DATE		ACQUIRED	FROM		IN EXCHANGE FOR
July 5, 1919	P	Eric Erickson	Detroit Tigers	P	Doc Ayers
Sept 10, 1919		Waiver price	St. Louis Cardinals	2B	Hal Janvrin
Oct 1919	P	Frank Miller	Pittsburgh Pirates		Cash
Jan 20, 1920	OF SS	Braggo Roth Red Shannon	Boston Red Sox	OF P 3B	Mike Menosky Harry Harper Eddie Foster
Jan 1920	SS	Frank O'Rourke	Brooklyn Dodgers		Cash
July 1920	OF	Fred Thomas	Philadelphia Athletics	IF	Red Shannon
Jan 20, 1921	P OF	Duffy Lewis George Mogridge	New York Yankees	OF	Braggo Roth
May 31, 1921	OF	Earl Smith	St. Louis Browns	3B	Frank Ellerbe
July 1921		Cash	Pittsburgh Pirates	C	Tony Brottem
Aug 20, 1921	SS	Donie Bush	Detroit Tigers		Waiver price
Jan 10, 1922	3B	Joe Dugan	Philadelphia Athletics	P OF	Jose Acosta Bing Miller
		(Part of three-team trade involving Boston, Philadelphia, and Washington.)			
Jan 10, 1922	SS	Roger Peckinpaugh	Boston Red Sox	3B OF	Joe Dugan Frank O'Rourke
		(Part of three-team trade involving Boston, Philadelphia, and Washington.)			
May 1922		Cash	Chicago White Sox	P	Henry Courtney
Nov 24, 1922	SS	Chick Gagnon	Detroit Tigers	P	Ray Francis
Jan 8, 1923	OF	Joe Evans	Cleveland Indians	IF	Frank Brower
Feb 10, 1923	C P	Muddy Ruel Allan Russell	Boston Red Sox	C IF OF	Val Picinich Howard Shanks Ed Goebel
May 26, 1923	OF	Nemo Leibold	Boston Red Sox		Waiver price
Dec 1923	OF	Bert Griffith	Brooklyn Dodgers	P	Bonnie Hollingsworth
Jan 1924		Cash	St. Louis Browns	OF	Joe Evans
Jan 1924	OF	Wid Matthews	Philadelphia Athletics		Cash
June 19, 1924	P	Curly Ogden	Philadelphia Athletics		Cash
Sept 10, 1924		Cash	Boston Red Sox	P	Ted Wingfield
Oct 1924	OF	Pat Duncan	Cincinnati Reds		Waiver price
Dec 11, 1924	3B	Mike McNally	Boston Red Sox	3B	Doc Prothro

DATE		ACQUIRED	FROM		IN EXCHANGE FOR
Dec 12, 1924	P	Stan Coveleski	Cleveland Indians	P OF	Byron Speece Carr Smith
Dec 17, 1924	P	Dutch Ruether	Brooklyn Dodgers		Cash
Feb 1925	IF	Mike McNally	New York Yankees		Cash
April 26, 1925	1B	Joe Harris	Boston Red Sox	P OF	Paul Zahniser Roy Carlyle
June 8, 1925	C	Hank Severeid	St. Louis Browns	P C	George Mogridge Pinky Hargrave
June 17, 1925	SS	Everett Scott	New York Yankees		Cash
Aug 17, 1925	OF	Bobby Veach	New York Yankees		Waiver price
Aug 19, 1925	P	Alex Ferguson	New York Yankees		Cash
Jan 20, 1926		Cash	New York Yankees	OF	Spencer Adams
Feb 1926	P OF	Joe Bush Jack Tobin	St. Louis Browns	P P	Tom Zachary Win Ballou
July 1, 1926		Cash	Pittsburgh Pirates	P	Joe Bush
July 22, 1926		Waiver price	New York Yankees	C	Hank Severeid
July 31, 1926		Cash	Boston Red Sox	OF	Jack Tobin
Aug 27, 1926	P OF	Garland Braxton Nick Cullop	New York Yankees	P	Dutch Ruether
		(New York sent Braxton and Cullop to Washington on October 19, 1926.)			
Oct 1926		Cash	Philadelphia Phillies	P	Alex Ferguson
Dec 1926	C	Mickey O'Neil	Brooklyn Dodgers		Cash
Jan 15, 1927	P P	Sloppy Thurston Leo Mangum	Chicago White Sox	SS	Roger Peckinpaugh
Feb 4, 1927		Waiver price	Pittsburgh Pirates	1B	Joe Harris
May 2, 1927	SS	Topper Rigney	Boston Red Sox	3B	Buddy Myer
May 25, 1927		Cash	New York Giants	C	Mickey O'Neil
July 7, 1927	P	Tom Zachary	St. Louis Browns	P	General Crowder
Oct 19, 1927	P P	Milt Gaston Sad Sam Jones	St. Louis Browns	P OF	Dick Coffman Earl McNeely
Dec 14, 1927	1B	George Sisler	St. Louis Browns		$25,000.
May 27, 1928		$7,500.	Boston Braves	1B	George Sisler
Aug 23, 1928		Waiver price	New York Yankees	P	Tom Zachary

DATE		ACQUIRED	FROM		IN EXCHANGE FOR
Dec 15, 1928	3B	Buddy Myer	Boston Red Sox	P	Milt Gaston
				P	Hod Lisenbee
				2B	Bobby Reeves
				3B	Grant Gillis
				OF	Elliott Bigelow
Dec 19, 1928	SS	Jack Warner	Detroit Tigers	2B	Bucky Harris
		(Harris was named Detroit manager.)			
June 18, 1929	P	Myles Thomas	New York Yankees		Cash
June 26, 1929		Cash	St. Louis Browns	P	Paul Hopkins
July 12, 1929		Waiver price	Pittsburgh Pirates	OF	Ira Flagstead
April 4, 1930	OF	Earl Webb	Cincinnati Reds		Waiver price
April 30, 1930	OF	Bill Barrett	Boston Red Sox	OF	Earl Webb
June 13, 1930	1B	Dave Harris	Chicago White Sox	OF	Red Barnes
June 13, 1930	P	General Crowder	St. Louis Browns	OF	Goose Goslin
	OF	Heinie Manush			
June 16, 1930	1B	Art Shires	Chicago White Sox	P	Garland Braxton
				C	Bennie Tate
Sept 10, 1930	C	Pinky Hargrave	Detroit Tigers		Cash
Dec 15, 1930		Cash	Boston Red Sox	C	Muddy Ruel
Jan 13, 1931	OF	Harry Rice	New York Yankees		Waiver price
Nov 1931		Waiver price	Chicago White Sox	P	Sad Sam Jones
Dec 4, 1931	OF	Carl Reynolds	Chicago White Sox	2B	Jackie Hayes
	2B	John Kerr		P	Bump Hadley
				P	Sad Sam Jones
Dec 1931		Waiver price	Boston Braves	C	Pinky Hargrave
June 9, 1932	P	Dick Coffman	St. Louis Browns	P	Carl Fischer
June 11, 1932	P	Tommy Thomas	Chicago White Sox		Cash
Dec 13, 1932	P	Carl Fischer	St. Louis Browns	P	Dick Coffman
Dec 14, 1932	OF	Goose Goslin	St. Louis Browns	OF	Sammy West
	OF	Fred Schulte		OF	Carl Reynolds
	P	Lefty Stewart		P	Lloyd Brown and $20,000.
Dec 14, 1932	P	Earl Whitehill	Detroit Tigers	P	Firpo Marberry
				P	Carl Fischer
Dec 15, 1932	P	Jack Russell	Cleveland Indians	1B	Harley Boss
	OF	Bruce Connatser			

DATE		ACQUIRED	FROM		IN EXCHANGE FOR
Jan 7, 1933	C	Luke Sewell	Cleveland Indians	C	Roy Spencer
Dec 20, 1933	OF	John Stone	Detroit Tigers	OF	Goose Goslin
Dec 1933		Cash	St. Louis Browns	P	Bill McAfee
May 9, 1934	SS	Red Kress	Chicago White Sox	SS	Bob Boken
June 23, 1934	P	Bob Kline	Philadelphia Athletics		Cash
Aug 4, 1934		Waiver price	Detroit Tigers	P	General Crowder
Oct 26, 1934	SS	Lyn Lary and $225,000.	Boston Red Sox	SS	Joe Cronin
Dec 1934		Cash	Cleveland Indians	C	Eddie Phillips
Jan 22, 1935	P	Bump Hadley	St. Louis Browns	C	Luke Sewell
May 14, 1935	P	Belve Bean	Cleveland Indians	P	Lefty Stewart
May 20, 1935		Waiver price	Philadelphia Phillies	P	Tommy Thomas
May 21, 1935	P	Bobo Newsom	St. Louis Browns		$40,000.
June 29, 1935	SS	Alan Strange	St. Louis Browns	SS	Lyn Lary
Dec 17, 1935	OF OF	Carl Reynolds Roy Johnson	Boston Red Sox	OF	Heinie Manush
Dec 1935	C	Shanty Hogan	Boston Braves		Cash
Jan 17, 1936	P OF	Jimmie DeShong Jesse Hill	New York Yankees	P OF	Bump Hadley Roy Johnson
Jan 30, 1936		Waiver price	Pittsburgh Pirates	OF	Fred Schulte
June 13, 1936	P	Joe Cascarella	Boston Red Sox	P	Jack Russell
June 14, 1936	OF	Ben Chapman	New York Yankees	OF	Jake Powell
July 1, 1936	P	Bill Dietrich	Philadelphia Athletics		Waiver price
July 20, 1936		Waiver price	Chicago White Sox	P	Bill Dietrich
Dec 10, 1936	P	Jack Salveson	Cleveland Indians	P	Earl Whitehill
		(Part of three-team trade involving Chicago, Cleveland, and Washington.)			
April 4, 1937	OF	Al Simmons	Detroit Tigers		$15,000.
May 1937	P	Carl Fischer	Cleveland Indians		Cash

DATE		ACQUIRED	FROM		IN EXCHANGE FOR
June 10, 1937		Waiver price	Detroit Tigers	C	Cliff Bolton
June 11, 1937	P C OF	Wes Ferrell Rick Ferrell Mel Almada	Boston Red Sox	OF P	Ben Chapman Bobo Newsom
July 3, 1937		Cash	Cincinnati Reds	P	Joe Cascarella
July 13, 1937		Cash	Philadelphia Athletics	OF	Jesse Hill
Dec 1, 1937	P	Chief Hogsett	St. Louis Browns	P	Ed Linke
March 18, 1938	1B	Zeke Bonura	Chicago White Sox	1B	Joe Kuhel
March 24, 1938	C	Tony Giuliani	St. Louis Browns		Cash
May 4, 1938	P	Harry Kelley	Philadelphia Athletics		Waiver price
June 15, 1938	OF	Sammy West	St. Louis Browns	OF	Mel Almada
Dec 11, 1938	IF P	Jim Carlin Tom Baker and $20,000.	New York Giants	1B	Zeke Bonura
Dec 29, 1938		Cash	Boston Braves	OF	Al Simmons
Feb 1939		Cash	Boston Red Sox	P	Monte Weaver
May 1, 1939	P	Bud Thomas	Philadelphia Athletics		Waiver price
May 18, 1939		Waiver price	Detroit Tigers	P	Bud Thomas
June 20, 1939		Waiver price	New York Yankees	P	Jimmie DeShong
Dec 8, 1939	OF	Gee Walker	Chicago White Sox	OF P	Taffy Wright Pete Appleton
April 21, 1940	P	Bill Zuber	Cleveland Indians		Cash
April 26, 1940	1B	Zeke Bonura	New York Giants		$20,000.
April 1940		Cash	Pittsburgh Pirates	IF	Ed Leip
May 15, 1940	P	Vern Kennedy	St. Louis Browns	C	Rick Ferrell
May 25, 1940		Cash	Brooklyn Dodgers	1B	Jimmy Wasdell
July 22, 1940		Cash	Chicago Cubs	1B	Zeke Bonura
Aug 30, 1940		Waiver price	Boston Red Sox	3B	Charley Gelbert
Dec 12, 1940	OF	Doc Cramer	Boston Red Sox	OF	Gee Walker
Dec 24, 1940	OF	Ben Chapman	Cleveland Indians	P	Joe Krakauskas

DATE		ACQUIRED	FROM		IN EXCHANGE FOR
Jan 4, 1941		Cash	Chicago White Sox	P	Joe Haynes
March 27, 1941	P	Steve Sundra	New York Yankees		Cash
Dec 11, 1941		Cash	Cleveland Indians	P	Vern Kennedy
Dec 12, 1941	2B OF	Frank Croucher Bruce Campbell	Detroit Tigers	2B OF	Jimmy Bloodworth Doc Cramer
Dec 13, 1941	OF P	Stan Spence Jack Wilson	Boston Red Sox	P OF	Ken Chase Johnny Welaj
March 31, 1942	P	Bobo Newsom	Detroit Tigers		$40,000.
June 7, 1942	OF P	Roy Cullenbine Bill Trotter	St. Louis Browns	OF P	Mike Chartak Steve Sundra
July 17, 1942	SS	Eric McNair (McNair refused to report.)	Detroit Tigers	P	Jack Wilson
Aug 30, 1942		$25,000.	Brooklyn Dodgers	P	Bobo Newsom
Aug 31, 1942		Waiver price	New York Yankees	OF	Roy Cullenbine
Aug 31, 1942	OF	Gene Moore	Brooklyn Dodgers		Cash
Jan 25, 1943	P	Lefty Gomez	New York Yankees		Cash
Jan 29, 1943	2B P	Gerry Priddy Milo Candini	New York Yankees	P	Bill Zuber and cash
Feb 1, 1943	P	Paul Dean	St. Louis Browns		Cash
March 21, 1943	OF	Bob Johnson	Philadelphia Athletics	OF	Jimmy Esmond and cash
May 20, 1943	3B	Alex Kampouris	Brooklyn Dodgers		Cash
Aug 18, 1943	3B P	Harlond Clift Johnny Niggeling	St. Louis Browns	SS P	Ellis Clary Ox Miller and cash
Aug 31, 1943	P	Bobo Newsom	St. Louis Browns		Cash
Nov 24, 1943	1B	Joe Kuhel	Chicago White Sox		Cash
Dec 4, 1943		Cash	Boston Red Sox	OF	Bob Johnson
Dec 13, 1943	P	Roger Wolff	Philadelphia Athletics	P	Bobo Newsom
March 1, 1944	C	Rick Ferrell	St. Louis Browns	C OF	Tony Giuliani Gene Moore and cash
		(Giuliani announced his retirement, and St. Louis received Moore to complete the trade.)			
Dec 14, 1945	OF	Jeff Heath	Cleveland Indians	OF	George Case
Jan 2, 1946		Cash	Chicago White Sox	P SS	Alex Carrasquel Fred Vaughn

DATE	ACQUIRED	FROM	IN EXCHANGE FOR
May 16, 1946	IF Billy Hitchcock	Detroit Tigers	Cash
June 15, 1946	OF Joe Grace P Al LaMacchia	St. Louis Browns	OF Jeff Heath
Dec 2, 1946	Cash	Philadelphia Athletics	C Mike Guerra
Dec 9, 1946	Cash	Philadelphia Phillies	P Dutch Leonard
Dec 16, 1946	C Jake Early	St. Louis Browns	C Frank Mancuso
Jan 14, 1947	P Tom Ferrick	St. Louis Browns	Cash
Feb 8, 1947	Cash	St. Louis Browns	3B Billy Hitchcock
Feb 14, 1947	P Lum Harris	Philadelphia Athletics	Waiver price
Feb 14, 1947	P Lou Knerr	Philadelphia Athletics	OF George Binks
March 4, 1947	OF George Case	Cleveland Indians	P Roger Wolff
April 9, 1947	3B Mark Christman	St. Louis Browns	Cash
May 14, 1947	OF Tom McBride	Boston Red Sox	Cash
July 11, 1947	Waiver price	New York Yankees	P Bobo Newsom
Nov 22, 1947	2B Johnny Berardino	St. Louis Browns	2B Gerry Priddy
	(Berardino announced his retirement to go into movies. Commissioner Chandler cancelled the trade. Berardino then unretired.)		
Dec 8, 1947	$25,000.	St. Louis Browns	2B Gerry Priddy
Dec 10, 1947	OF Leon Culberson 3B Al Kozar	Boston Red Sox	OF Stan Spence
Dec 1947	Cash	Pittsburgh Pirates	OF Joe Grace
March 26, 1948	C Jake Early	St. Louis Browns	Cash
May 13, 1948	OF Bud Stewart	New York Yankees	OF Leon Culberson and $15,000.
June 9, 1948	P Earl Harrist	Chicago White Sox	P Marino Pieretti
Oct 4, 1948	SS Sam Dente	St. Louis Browns	P Tom Ferrick SS John Sullivan and $25,000.
Dec 14, 1948	P Joe Haynes P Eddie Klieman 1B Eddie Robinson	Cleveland Indians	1B Mickey Vernon P Early Wynn
April 15, 1949	C Ralph Weigel	Chicago White Sox	Cash
June 13, 1949	OF Sam Mele P Mickey Harris	Boston Red Sox	P Walt Masterson

DATE		ACQUIRED	FROM		IN EXCHANGE FOR
July 12, 1949	P	Al Gettel	Chicago White Sox		Cash
July 21, 1949		Cash	Chicago White Sox	P	Mickey Haefner
Feb 15, 1950		Waiver price	Detroit Tigers	P	Paul Calvert
May 8, 1950	OF SS	Tommy O'Brien Merrill Combs	Boston Red Sox	OF	Clyde Vollmer
May 31, 1950	P 2B OF	Bob Kuzava Cass Michaels John Ostrowski	Chicago White Sox	2B P 1B	Al Kozar Ray Scarborough Eddie Robinson
June 14, 1950	1B	Mickey Vernon	Cleveland Indians	P	Dick Weik
Aug 2, 1950	P	Gene Bearden	Cleveland Indians		Waiver price
Dec 11, 1950	OF	Mike McCormick	Chicago White Sox	OF	Bud Stewart
Feb 5, 1951		Waiver price	Boston Red Sox	C	Al Evans
April 26, 1951		Waiver price	Detroit Tigers	P	Gene Bearden
May 29, 1951	P	Don Johnson	St. Louis Browns		$12,500.
June 12, 1951	C	Clyde Kluttz	St. Louis Browns		Waiver price
June 15, 1951	P P P	Fred Sanford Tom Ferrick Bob Porterfield	New York Yankees	P	Bob Kuzava
July 30, 1951	P	Dick Starr	St. Louis Browns	P	Fred Sanford
Sept 19, 1951	OF	Dino Restelli	Pittsburgh Pirates		Waiver price
Oct 24, 1951	3B	Floyd Baker	Chicago White Sox	SS	Willie Miranda
Nov 27, 1951	SS	Tom Upton	Chicago White Sox	SS	Sam Dente
April 22, 1952		Waiver price	Cleveland Indians	P	Mickey Harris
May 3, 1952	OF 2B	Jim Busby Mel Hoderlein	Chicago White Sox	OF	Sam Mele
May 3, 1952	OF P 2B OF	Jackie Jensen Spec Shea Jerry Snyder Archie Wilson	New York Yankees	OF SS	Irv Noren Tom Upton
May 12, 1952	P SS	Lou Sleater Freddie Marsh	St. Louis Browns	2B	Cass Michaels
May 19, 1952		Waiver price	Philadelphia Athletics	2B	Sherry Robertson
June 9, 1952	OF	Ken Wood	Boston Red Sox	OF	Archie Wilson

DATE		ACQUIRED	FROM		IN EXCHANGE FOR
June 10, 1952	OF	Earl Rapp	St. Louis Browns	SS	Freddie Marsh
June 10, 1952	P P	Randy Gumpert Walt Masterson	Boston Red Sox	P	Sid Hudson
Sept 23, 1952	3B	Wayne Terwilliger	Brooklyn Dodgers		Waiver price
Dec 10, 1952	P	Chuck Stobbs	Chicago White Sox	P	Mike Fornieles
April 22, 1953	OF	Clyde Vollmer	Boston Red Sox		Cash
May 12, 1953		Cash	Boston Red Sox	3B	Floyd Baker
May 12, 1953		Cash	Chicago White Sox	P	Sandy Consuegra
May 13, 1953	C	Ed Fitz Gerald	Pittsburgh Pirates		Cash
May 13, 1953	P	Johnny Schmitz	New York Yankees		Waiver price
May 26, 1953	OF	Carmen Mauro	Brooklyn Dodgers		Waiver price
June 11, 1953	P	Tommy Byrne	Chicago White Sox		Cash
June 30, 1953		Waiver price	Philadelphia Athletics	OF	Carmen Mauro
June 30, 1953	OF	Kite Thomas	Philadelphia Athletics		Waiver price
Dec 9, 1953	P OF	Mickey McDermott Tommy Umphlett	Boston Red Sox	OF	Jackie Jensen
Jan 20, 1954	C	Joe Tipton	Cleveland Indians	C	Mickey Grasso
Feb 18, 1954	OF	Roy Sievers	Baltimore Orioles	OF	Gil Coan
May 12, 1954	OF	Jim Lemon	Cleveland Indians		Cash
May 27, 1954	OF	Tom Wright	Chicago White Sox		Waiver price
June 11, 1954	P	Gus Keriazakos	Chicago White Sox	P	Sonny Dixon
June 14, 1954	3B	Johnny Pesky	Detroit Tigers	3B	Mel Hoderlein
June 7, 1955	P C OF	Bob Chakales Clint Courtney Johnny Groth	Chicago White Sox	OF	Jim Busby
Nov 8, 1955	OF P P OF	Karl Olson Dick Brodowski Tex Clevenger Neil Chrisley and minor league P Al Curtis	Boston Red Sox	P P 1B OF	Bob Porterfield Johnny Schmitz Mickey Vernon Tommy Umphlett

DATE		ACQUIRED	FROM		IN EXCHANGE FOR
Feb 8, 1956	C P 2B OF OF	Lou Berberet Bob Wiesler Herb Plews Whitey Herzog Dick Tettelbach	New York Yankees	P SS	Mickey McDermott Bobby Kline
April 16, 1956		Cash	Kansas City Athletics	OF	Johnny Groth
May 11, 1956		Waiver price	Detroit Tigers	P	Walt Masterson
April 29, 1957	2B P OF	Milt Bolling Russ Kemmerer Faye Throneberry	Boston Red Sox	P P	Dean Stone Bob Chakales
April 30, 1957		Cash	Boston Red Sox	OF	Karl Olson
May 15, 1957	OF	Bob Usher	Cleveland Indians		Cash
May 20, 1957	SS	Rocky Bridges	Cincinnati Reds		Waiver price
June 12, 1957	OF	Art Schult	Cincinnati Reds		Cash
Jan 23, 1958	OF OF	Albie Pearson Norm Zauchin	Boston Red Sox	2B	Pete Runnels
Feb 25, 1958		Minor league P Pete Mesa	Cleveland Indians	2B	Milt Bolling
May 1, 1958	2B	Ken Aspromonte	Boston Red Sox	C	Lou Berberet
May 14, 1958	P	Al Cicotte	New York Yankees		Cash
May 14, 1958		Cash	Kansas City Athletics	OF	Whitey Herzog
June 23, 1958	P	Vito Valentinetti	Detroit Tigers	P	Al Cicotte
June 24, 1958	P	Jack Spring	Boston Red Sox	P	Bud Byerly
July 9, 1958		Waiver price	St. Louis Cardinals	P	Chuck Stobbs
July 12, 1958	P	Jim Constable	Cleveland Indians		Waiver price
Sept 11, 1958	P	Bill Fischer	Detroit Tigers		Waiver price
Oct 27, 1958	C	J W Porter	Cleveland Indians	IF	Ossie Alvarez
Dec 6, 1958	2B 2B OF	Reno Bertoia Ron Samford Jim Delsing	Detroit Tigers	3B SS OF	Eddie Yost Rocky Bridges Neil Chrisley
April 1, 1959	P	Billy Loes	Baltimore Orioles	P	Vito Valentinetti
		(Trade was cancelled on April 8, 1959, by Commissioner Frick due to Loes's sore arm.)			
May 25, 1959	P C	Hal Woodeshick Hal Naragon	Cleveland Indians	C	Ed Fitz Gerald

DATE		ACQUIRED	FROM		IN EXCHANGE FOR
May 26, 1959	OF	Lenny Green	Baltimore Orioles	OF	Albie Pearson
June 11, 1959	2B P	Billy Consolo Murray Wall	Boston Red Sox	P 2B	Dick Hyde Herb Plews
		(Hyde was returned to Washington and Wall was returned to Boston.)			
July 25, 1959		Waiver price	St. Louis Cardinals	C	J W Porter
April 3, 1960	2B	Billy Gardner	Baltimore Orioles	C 2B	Clint Courtney Ron Samford
April 4, 1960	C 1B	Earl Battey Don Mincher and $150,000.	Chicago White Sox	OF	Roy Sievers
May 15, 1960	OF	Pete Whisenant	Cleveland Indians	2B	Ken Aspromonte
May 18, 1960		Cash	Chicago White Sox	P	Russ Kemmerer
June 13, 1960	P	Ray Moore	Chicago White Sox		Cash
July 22, 1960	P	Tom Morgan	Detroit Tigers	P	Bill Fischer

Washington Senators

The Best Trades

1. Acquired Frank Howard, Pete Richert, Phil Ortega, and Dick Nen from the Los Angeles Dodgers for Claude Osteen, John Kennedy, and $100,000, December 4, 1964.
2. Acquired Claude Osteen from the Cincinnati Reds for Dave Sisler and cash, September 16, 1961.
3. Acquired Mike McCormick from the Baltimore Orioles for Steve Herman and $20,000, April 4, 1965.
4. Acquired Darold Knowles and cash from the Philadelphia Phillies for Don Lock, November 30, 1966.
5. Acquired Dave Stenhouse and Bob Schmidt from the Cincinnati Reds for Johnny Klippstein and Marty Keough, December 15, 1961.

The Worst Trades

1. Traded Joe Coleman, Ed Brinkman, Aurelio Rodriguez, and Jim Hannan to the Detroit Tigers for Denny McLain, Don Wert, Elliott Maddox, and Norm McRae, October 9, 1970.
2. Traded Mike McCormick to the San Francisco Giants for Cap Peterson and Bob Priddy, December 3, 1966.
3. Traded Diego Segui to the Kansas City Athletics for Jim Duckworth, July 30, 1966.
4. Traded Mike Epstein and Darold Knowles to the Oakland A's for Frank Fernandez, Don Mincher, Paul Lindblad, and cash, May 8, 1971.
5. Traded Lou Piniella to the Baltimore Orioles for Buster Narum, March 31, 1964.

The Short Reign of the Second Senators

The brief stewardship of Bob Short as owner of the Washington Senators left an indelible imprint on the baseball fans of the nation's capital. What many wretched teams over a sixty-eight-year span couldn't accomplish, Short did in just three seasons: he not only rid the team of its few good players, but he rid the city of the team once and for all.

If Short had planned from the start to show Washington's long-suffering fans that they were better off without a team, he could not have done a better job. Originally conceived as a replacement for the old Senators, who moved to Minnesota in the '61 expansion (why saddle a new market with a bad club when Washington was so used to having them?), the expansion Senators had begun to show signs of life in 1969, finishing above .500 under new manager Ted Williams. But when the club fell back into the cellar the following year, Short panicked. In one of baseball's all-time worst trades, he sent the left side of his infield and two of his best pitchers to Detroit for faded ace Denny McLain and three journeymen.

The Tigers had been desperately trying to deal McLain, who had won 55 games in '68-'69 but had spent most of 1970 under suspension for bookmaking activities. Short's fascination with the former Cy Young winner led him to give up shortstop Ed Brinkman, third baseman Aurelio Rodriguez, and pitchers Joe Coleman and Jim Hannan. McLain fell hard and fast, losing 22 for the Senators in '71; Coleman won 20 in two of his first three seasons with the Tigers, and Brinkman and Rodriguez anchored the Detroit infield for the next four seasons. McLain was soon banished to Oakland, and the team moved south to Texas before the 1972 season.

DATE		ACQUIRED	FROM		IN EXCHANGE FOR
Dec 16, 1960	P 3B 1B	Bennie Daniels Harry Bright R C Stevens	Pittsburgh Pirates	P	Bobby Shantz
Dec 29, 1960	P	Marty Kutyna and cash	Kansas City Athletics	C	Haywood Sullivan
Jan 3, 1961		Cash	Los Angeles Angels	P	Tom Morgan
Jan 4, 1961		Cash	Los Angeles Angels	IF	Leo Burke
April 7, 1961		Cash	Los Angeles Angels	P	Ray Semproch
June 5, 1961	2B	Chuck Cottier	Detroit Tigers	P	Hal Woodeshick
June 29, 1961	P	Tom Cheney	Pittsburgh Pirates	P	Tom Sturdivant
Sept 16, 1961	P	Claude Osteen	Cincinnati Reds	P	Dave Sisler and cash
Sept 25, 1961	P	Freddie Green	Pittsburgh Pirates		Waiver price
Oct 5, 1961	OF	Jimmy Piersall	Cleveland Indians	P C SS	Dick Donovan Gene Green Jim Mahoney
Oct 14, 1961	P	Joe Schaffernoth	Cleveland Indians		Cash
Oct 14, 1961	P	Dave Tyriver	Cleveland Indians		Cash
Dec 15, 1961	P C	Dave Stenhouse Bob Schmidt	Cincinnati Reds	P OF	Johnny Klippstein Marty Keough

DATE		ACQUIRED	FROM		IN EXCHANGE FOR
Dec 21, 1961		Cash	Pittsburgh Pirates	SS	Coot Veal
April 5, 1962		Cash	Philadelphia Phillies	3B	Billy Klaus
May 3, 1962	P P	Steve Hamilton Don Rudolph	Cleveland Indians	OF	Willie Tasby
June 15, 1962		Cash	New York Mets	OF	Gene Woodling
July 11, 1962	OF	Don Lock	New York Yankees	1B	Dale Long
Nov 24, 1962	1B	Rogelio Alvarez	Cincinnati Reds	3B	Harry Bright
Dec 5, 1962	OF 2B	Barry Shetrone Marv Breeding and minor league P Art Quick	Baltimore Orioles	2B P	Bob Johnson Pete Burnside
Dec 15, 1962	C	Don Leppert	Pittsburgh Pirates		Minor league P Ron Honeycutt and cash
March 18, 1963	P	Ron Kline	Detroit Tigers		Cash
April 2, 1963	OF	Minnie Minoso	St. Louis Cardinals		Cash and minor league player to be named later
April 21, 1963	P	Jim Coates	New York Yankees	P	Steve Hamilton
May 8, 1963	C	Hobie Landrith	Baltimore Orioles		Cash
May 23, 1963	1B	Gil Hodges	New York Mets	OF	Jimmy Piersall
		(Hodges was named Washington manager.)			
May 31, 1963	P	Casey Cox	Cleveland Indians		Waiver price
June 24, 1963	3B	Don Zimmer	Los Angeles Dodgers		Cash
July 1, 1963	2B	Don Blasingame	Cincinnati Reds		Cash
July 20, 1963	P	Ed Roebuck	Los Angeles Dodgers	2B	Marv Breeding
Sept 12, 1963	OF	Ken Hunt	Los Angeles Angels		Cash
Oct 11, 1963	OF	Fred Valentine	Baltimore Orioles		Cash
Oct 14, 1963	C	Mike Brumley	Los Angeles Dodgers		Cash
Nov 27, 1963	P	Marshall Bridges	New York Yankees		Cash
Dec 6, 1963	1B	Bill Skowron	Los Angeles Dodgers		Cash
March 31, 1964	P	Buster Narum	Baltimore Orioles	OF	Lou Piniella

DATE	ACQUIRED	FROM	IN EXCHANGE FOR
April 11, 1964	P Pete Craig	Detroit Tigers	Waiver price
April 21, 1964	Cash	Philadelphia Phillies	P Ed Roebuck
May 9, 1964	P Alan Koch	Detroit Tigers	Cash
July 13, 1964	1B Joe Cunningham P Frank Kreutzer	Chicago White Sox	1B Bill Skowron P Carl Bouldin
July 16, 1964	OF Roy Sievers	Philadelphia Phillies	Cash
Aug 12, 1964	OF Willie Kirkland	Baltimore Orioles	Cash
Oct 15, 1964	C Joe McCabe	Minnesota Twins	C Ken Retzer
Oct 15, 1964	P Nick Willhite	Los Angeles Dodgers	Cash
Nov 30, 1964	C Doug Camilli	Los Angeles Dodgers	Cash
Dec 1, 1964	1B Bob Chance OF Woodie Held	Cleveland Indians	OF Chuck Hinton
Dec 4, 1964	OF Frank Howard P Phil Ortega P Pete Richert 1B Dick Nen	Los Angeles Dodgers	P Claude Osteen SS John Kennedy and $100,000.
April 4, 1965	P Mike McCormick	Baltimore Orioles	Minor league P Steve Herman and $20,000.
April 11, 1965	P Dallas Green	Philadelphia Phillies	Cash
May 11, 1965	Cash	Los Angeles Dodgers	P Nick Willhite
Oct 12, 1965	C John Orsino	Baltimore Orioles	OF Woodie Held
April 2, 1966	P Bob Humphreys	Chicago Cubs	OF Ken Hunt
April 5, 1966	P Al Closter	Cleveland Indians	Cash
April 13, 1966	Cash	Philadelphia Phillies	P Steve Ridzik
April 13, 1966	P Diego Segui	Kansas City Athletics	Cash
May 3, 1966	Cash	New York Yankees	P Al Closter
June 23, 1966	OF Ken Harrelson	Kansas City Athletics	P Jim Duckworth
July 30, 1966	P Jim Duckworth	Kansas City Athletics	P Diego Segui
Nov 30, 1966	P Darold Knowles and cash	Philadelphia Phillies	OF Don Lock
Dec 3, 1966	OF Cap Peterson P Bob Priddy	San Francisco Giants	P Mike McCormick

DATE		ACQUIRED	FROM		IN EXCHANGE FOR
Dec 3, 1966	2B P	Bernie Allen Camilo Pascual	Minnesota Twins	P	Ron Kline
Feb 16, 1967		Cash	California Angels	2B	Chuck Cottier
May 29, 1967	1B P	Mike Epstein Frank Bertaina	Baltimore Orioles	P	Pete Richert
June 9, 1967		Cash	Kansas City Athletics	OF	Ken Harrelson
June 15, 1967	OF	Ed Stroud	Chicago White Sox	OF	Jim King
Nov 27, 1967	P	Bill Denehy and $100,000. (Hodges was named New York manager.)	New York Mets	MGR	Gil Hodges
Feb 13, 1968	P P SS	Dennis Higgins Steve Jones Ron Hansen	Chicago White Sox	2B P P	Tim Cullen Buster Narum Bob Priddy
April 3, 1968		Cash	Chicago Cubs	1B	Dick Nen
June 15, 1968	P	Bruce Howard	Baltimore Orioles	P	Fred Valentine
Aug 2, 1968	2B	Tim Cullen	Chicago White Sox	SS	Ron Hansen
Oct 1, 1968	1B	Dick Nen	Chicago Cubs		Cash
March 31, 1969		Minor league P George Woodson	Cleveland Indians	OF	Cap Peterson
April 4, 1969		Cash	California Angels	P	Phil Ortega
May 17, 1969	P	Jim Shellenback	Pittsburgh Pirates	P	Frank Kreutzer
June 20, 1969	OF	Lee Maye	Cleveland Indians		Cash
July 7, 1969		Cash	Cincinnati Reds	P	Camilo Pascual
July 26, 1969	SS	Zoilo Versalles	Cleveland Indians		Cash
Aug 25, 1969	P	Cisco Carlos	Chicago White Sox		Cash
Sept 1, 1969		Cash	Los Angeles Dodgers	P	Jack Jenkins
Dec 1, 1969	IF	Bob Schroder	San Francisco Giants		Cash
Dec 4, 1969	P	George Brunet	Seattle Pilots	P	Dave Baldwin
Dec 5, 1969	IF P P	Dave Nelson Horacio Pina Ron Law	Cleveland Indians	P P	Dennis Higgins Barry Moore
March 21, 1970	P P	Joe Grzenda Charley Walters	Minnesota Twins	OF	Brant Alyea
April 27, 1970	3B OF	Aurelio Rodriguez Rick Reichardt	California Angels	3B	Ken McMullen

DATE	ACQUIRED	FROM	IN EXCHANGE FOR
May 11, 1970	OF Wayne Comer	Milwaukee Brewers	OF Hank Allen IF Ron Theobald
Aug 31, 1970	P Denny Riddleberger and cash	Pittsburgh Pirates	P George Brunet
Sept 10, 1970	Cash	Chicago White Sox	OF Lee Maye
Oct 9, 1970	P Denny McLain 3B Don Wert P Norm McRae OF Elliott Maddox	Detroit Tigers	P Joe Coleman SS Ed Brinkman 3B Aurelio Rodriguez P Jim Hannan
Oct 23, 1970	OF Richie Scheinblum	Cleveland Indians	Cash
Nov 3, 1970	OF Curt Flood	Philadelphia Phillies	C Greg Goossen P Jeff Terpko 1B Gene Martin
Feb 9, 1971	P Gerry Janeski	Chicago White Sox	OF Rick Reichardt
March 29, 1971	1B Tom McCraw	Chicago White Sox	OF Ed Stroud
May 8, 1971	C Frank Fernandez 1B Don Mincher P Paul Lindblad and cash	Oakland Athletics	1B Mike Epstein P Darold Knowles
June 23, 1971	C Frank Fernandez	Oakland Athletics	Cash

Player Index

Listed below are all the major league players involved in transactions listed in this book. The team listed for each entry is the team to which the player moved on the date indicated.

Hank Aaron
MIL A Nov 2, 1974

Don Aase
CAL A Dec 8, 1977

Ed Abbaticchio
PIT N Dec 1906
BOS N May 1910

Glenn Abbott
DET A Aug 23, 1983

Al Aber
DET A June 15, 1953
KC A Aug 27, 1957

Ted Abernathy
CHI N Apr 14, 1965
ATL N May 28, 1966
CHI N Jan 9, 1969
STL N May 29, 1970
KC A July 1, 1970

Cal Abrams
CIN N June 9, 1952
PIT N Oct 14, 1952
BAL A May 25, 1954
CHI A Oct 18, 1955

Bill Abstein
STL A Jan 1910

Tom Acker
KC A Nov 21, 1959

Fritz Ackley
STL N Nov 24, 1964

Cecilio Acosta
PHI N Mar 17, 1975

Ed Acosta
SD N Aug 10, 1971

Jose Acosta
PHI A Jan 10, 1922
CHI A Feb 4, 1922

Merito Acosta
PHI A May 25, 1918

Jerry Adair
CHI A June 12, 1966
BOS A June 3, 1967

Babe Adams
PIT N Oct 1907

Bert Adams
PHI N Jan 1915

Bob Adams
MIN A Mar 29, 1971

Bobby Adams
CHI A July 26, 1955
BAL A Oct 18, 1955

Buster Adams
PHI N June 1, 1943
STL N May 8, 1945
PHI N Mar 21, 1947

Glenn Adams
MIN A Dec 6, 1976

Herb Adams
CLE A Nov 11, 1950

Mike Adams
OAK A Apr 1, 1978

Sparky Adams
PIT N Nov 28, 1927
STL N Nov 1929
CIN N May 7, 1933

Spencer Adams
NY A Jan 20, 1926

Joe Adcock
MIL N Feb 16, 1953
CLE A Nov 27, 1962
LA A Dec 2, 1963

Bob Addis
CHI N Oct 11, 1951
PIT N June 4, 1953

Dave Adlesh
STL N Oct 11, 1968
ATL N Mar 25, 1969

Tommie Agee
CHI A Jan 20, 1965
NY N Dec 15, 1967
HOU N Nov 27, 1972
STL N Aug 18, 1973
LA N Dec 5, 1973

Sam Agnew
BOS A Dec 1915
WAS A Jan 1919

Hank Aguirre
DET A Feb 18, 1958
LA N Apr 3, 1968

Willie Aikens
KC A Dec 6, 1979
TOR A Dec 20, 1983

Eddie Ainsmith
BOS A Jan 17, 1919
DET A Jan 17, 1919

Jack Aker
NY A May 20, 1969
CHI N Jan 20, 1972
NY N June 14, 1974

Butch Alberts
TOR A Dec 8, 1977

Santo Alcala
MON N May 21, 1977
SEA A Mar 23, 1978

Luis Alcaraz
CHI A Mar 24, 1971

Vic Aldridge
PIT N Oct 27, 1924
NY N Feb 11, 1928
BKN N Dec 9, 1928

Dale Alexander
BOS A June 12, 1932

Doyle Alexander
BAL A Dec 2, 1971
NY A June 15, 1976
TEX A Nov 23, 1976
ATL N Dec 6, 1979
SF N Dec 12, 1980
NY A Mar 30, 1982

Gary Alexander
OAK A Mar 15, 1978
CLE A June 15, 1978
PIT N Dec 9, 1980

Grover Alexander
CHI N Dec 11, 1917
STL N June 22, 1926
PHI N Dec 11, 1929

Matt Alexander
OAK A Apr 28, 1975

Walt Alexander
NY A July 30, 1915

Brian Allard
SEA A Dec 12, 1980

Bernie Allen
WAS A Dec 3, 1966
NY A Dec 2, 1971
MON N Aug 13, 1973

Bob Allen
PIT N Dec 14, 1963

Ethan Allen
NY N May 27, 1930
STL N Oct 10, 1932
PHI N Jan 1934
CHI N May 21, 1936
STL A Dec 2, 1936

Frank Allen
BOS N Feb 10, 1916

Hank Allen
MIL A May 11, 1970
ATL N Dec 2, 1970

Johnny Allen
CLE A Dec 11, 1935
STL A Dec 24, 1940
PHI N Dec 12, 1942
BKN N Apr 22, 1943
NY N July 31, 1943

Lloyd Allen
TEX A May 20, 1973
CHI A July 1, 1974
STL N Aug 1, 1975

Neil Allen
STL N June 15, 1983

Nick Allen
CHI N Feb 10, 1916

Richie Allen
STL N Oct 7, 1969
LA N Oct 5, 1970
CHI A Dec 2, 1971
ATL N Dec 3, 1974
PHI N May 7, 1975
OAK A Mar 15, 1977

Rod Allen
SEA A Dec 11, 1981

Mel Almada
WAS A June 11, 1937
STL A June 15, 1938
BKN N June 15, 1939

Bill Almon
MON N Nov 27, 1979
NY N July 11, 1980
CHI A Feb 4, 1981
OAK A Jan 18, 1983

Sandy Alomar
HOU N Dec 31, 1966
NY N Mar 24, 1967
CHI A Aug 15, 1967
CAL A May 14, 1969
NY A July 8, 1974
TEX A Feb 17, 1977

Felipe Alou
MIL N Dec 3, 1963
OAK A Dec 3, 1969
NY A Apr 9, 1971
MON N Sept 6, 1973
MIL A Dec 7, 1973

Jesus Alou
HOU N Jan 22, 1969
OAK A July 31, 1973

Matty Alou
PIT N Oct 1, 1965
STL N Jan 29, 1971
OAK A Aug 27, 1972
NY A Nov 24, 1972
STL N Sept 6, 1973
SD N Oct 25, 1973

Del Alston
OAK A June 15, 1978

Porfirio Altamirano
CHI N Mar 26, 1984

Dave Altizer
CLE A Aug 1908

George Altman
STL N Oct 17, 1962
NY N Nov 4, 1963
CHI N Jan 15, 1965

Nick Altrock
CHI A Apr 1903
WAS A May 16, 1909

George Alusik
KC A May 7, 1962

Luis Alvarado
CHI A Dec 1, 1970
STL N Apr 27, 1974
CLE A June 1, 1974
STL N Sept 30, 1975
DET A Nov 6, 1976
NY N Feb 25, 1977

Jesus Alvarez
CAL A Mar 31, 1976

Jose Alvarez
HOU N Feb 14, 1984

Ossie Alvarez
CLE A Oct 27, 1958
DET A Nov 20, 1958

Rogelio Alvarez
WAS A Nov 24, 1962

Max Alvis
MIL A Apr 4, 1970

Brant Alyea
MIN A Mar 21, 1970
STL N May 18, 1972
TEX A Oct 30, 1972

Joey Amalfitano
SF N Nov 30, 1962

Ruben Amaro
PHI N Dec 3, 1958
NY A Nov 29, 1965

Red Ames
CIN N May 22, 1913
STL N July 24, 1915
PHI N Sept 5, 1919

Sandy Amoros
DET A May 7, 1960

Larry Andersen
PIT N Dec 21, 1979
SEA A Apr 1, 1980
PHI N July 29, 1983

Bob Anderson
DET A Nov 28, 1962
KC A Nov 18, 1963

Bud Anderson
CLE A Dec 6, 1979

Dwain Anderson
STL N May 15, 1972
SD N June 7, 1973

Fred Anderson
NY N Feb 10, 1916

Harry Anderson
CIN N June 15, 1960

Jim Anderson
SEA A Aug 29, 1979

John Anderson
HOU N May 7, 1962

John Anderson
NY A Feb 1904
WAS A June 3, 1905
CHI A Jan 1908

Larry Anderson
CHI A Oct 21, 1976
CHI N Aug 18, 1977
PHI N Aug 6, 1978

Mike Anderson
STL N Dec 9, 1975

Rick Anderson
SEA A Nov 1, 1979

Sparky Anderson
PHI N Dec 23, 1958

Fred Andrews
NY N Mar 24, 1978

Ivy Andrews
BOS A June 5, 1932
STL A Dec 14, 1933
CLE A Jan 17, 1937
NY A Aug 14, 1937

John Andrews
CAL A Dec 6, 1973

Mike Andrews
CHI A Dec 1, 1970

Nate Andrews
CLE A Sept 25, 1939
BOS N Dec 4, 1942
CIN N Aug 22, 1945

Rob Andrews
HOU N Dec 3, 1974

Joaquin Andujar
HOU N Oct 24, 1975
STL N June 7, 1981

John Antonelli
PHI N May 8, 1945

Johnny Antonelli
NY N Feb 1, 1954
CLE A Dec 3, 1960
MIL N July 4, 1961
NY N Oct 11, 1961

Luis Aparicio
BAL A Jan 14, 1963
CHI A Nov 29, 1967
BOS A Dec 1, 1970

Luis Aponte
CLE A Mar 24, 1984

Pete Appleton
BOS A June 10, 1932
CHI A Dec 8, 1939

Jim Archer
KC A Jan 24, 1961

Jimmy Archer
PIT N Dec 1917
BKN N July 1918
CIN N Sept 1918

Steve Arlin
CLE A June 15, 1974

Tony Armas
OAK A Mar 15, 1977
BOS A Dec 6, 1982

Ed Armbrister
CIN N Nov 29, 1971

Charlie Armbruster
CHI A Sept 1, 1907

Mike Armstrong
KC A Apr 4, 1982
NY A Dec 7, 1983

Morrie Arnovich
CIN N June 15, 1940
NY N Dec 10, 1940

Jerry Arrigo
CIN N Dec 4, 1964
NY N May 20, 1966
CIN N Aug 16, 1966
CHI A Dec 15, 1969

Fernando Arroyo
MIN A Dec 5, 1979

Luis Arroyo
PIT N May 5, 1956

Rudy Arroyo
LA N Oct 26, 1972

Richie Ashburn
CHI N Jan 11, 1960

Alan Ashby
TOR A Nov 5, 1976
HOU N Nov 27, 1978

Tucker Ashford
TEX A Feb 15, 1980
NY A Oct 24, 1980
TOR A Oct 27, 1982
NY N Apr 18, 1983
KC A Apr 1, 1984

Bob Aspromonte
ATL N Dec 4, 1968
NY N Dec 1, 1970

Ken Aspromonte
WAS A May 1, 1958
CLE A May 15, 1960
MIL N June 24, 1962
CHI N Dec 3, 1962

Bill Atkinson
CHI A Dec 12, 1979

Toby Atwell
PIT N June 4, 1953

Rick Auerbach
LA N Oct 27, 1973
NY N Feb 7, 1977
TEX A Apr 26, 1977
CIN N June 15, 1977
SEA A Dec 12, 1980

Eldon Auker
BOS A Dec 15, 1938
STL A Feb 8, 1940

Jimmy Austin
STL A Jan 1911
CHI N June 1911

Chick Autry
BOS N May 1909

Martin Autry
CHI A Feb 28, 1929

Earl Averill
DET A June 14, 1939
CHI N Jan 23, 1959
CHI A Aug 13, 1960
PHI N Dec 11, 1962

Bobby Avila
BAL A Dec 2, 1958
BOS A May 21, 1959
MIL N July 21, 1959

Ramon Aviles
PHI N Apr 5, 1978
TEX A Oct 20, 1981

Benny Ayala
STL N Mar 30, 1977

Doc Ayers
DET A July 5, 1919

Joe Azcue
CLE A May 25, 1963
BOS A Apr 19, 1969
CAL A June 15, 1969
MIL A July 28, 1972

Charlie Babb
NY N Dec 12, 1903

Bob Babcock
TOR A Jan 27, 1983

Loren Babe
PHI A Apr 27, 1953
NY A Dec 16, 1953

Johnny Babich
BOS N Feb 6, 1936
CIN N Aug 10, 1938

Mike Bacsik
MIN A Dec 13, 1978
SEA A Dec 19, 1980

Fred Baczewski
CIN N June 12, 1953

Jose Baez
STL N June 26, 1978

Jim Bagby
PIT N Nov 5, 1922

Jim Bagby
CLE A Dec 12, 1940
BOS A Dec 12, 1946
PIT N Feb 10, 1947

Stan Bahnsen
CHI A Dec 2, 1971
OAK A June 15, 1975
MON N May 22, 1977

Bob Bailey
LA N Dec 1, 1966
MON N Oct 21, 1968
CIN N Dec 12, 1975
BOS A Sept 19, 1977

Ed Bailey
SF N Apr 27, 1961
MIL N Dec 3, 1963
SF N Feb 1, 1965
CHI N May 29, 1965
CAL A Feb 15, 1966

Gene Bailey
BOS A May 1920

Sweetbreads Bailey
BKN N May 1921

Bob Bailor
NY N Dec 12, 1980
LA N Dec 8, 1983

Doug Bair
OAK A Mar 15, 1977
CIN N Feb 25, 1978
STL N Sept 19, 1981
DET A June 22, 1983

Doug Baird
STL N June 14, 1917
PHI N Jan 21, 1919
STL N July 14, 1919
BKN N Aug 1919
NY N May 1920

Bill Baker
PIT N May 12, 1941

Bock Baker
PHI A Apr 23, 1901

Chuck Baker
MIN A Dec 8, 1980

Dave Baker
MIN A Dec 10, 1982

Dusty Baker
LA N Nov 17, 1975

Floyd Baker
CHI A Dec 30, 1944
WAS A Oct 24, 1951
BOS A May 12, 1953
PHI N July 18, 1954

Frank Baker
CAL A Oct 5, 1971

Frank Baker
BAL A Apr 5, 1973

Frank Baker
NY A Feb 15, 1916

Gene Baker
PIT N May 1, 1957

Howard Baker
NY N July 1915

Jack Baker
CLE A Dec 9, 1977

Kirtly Baker
BOS N Jan 10, 1900

Steve Baker
STL N Sept 2, 1983

Tom Baker
NY N June 11, 1937
WAS A Dec 11, 1938

John Balaz
BOS A Mar 3, 1976

Steve Balboni
KC A Dec 7, 1983

Jack Baldschun
BAL A Dec 6, 1965
CIN N Dec 9, 1965

Bobby Baldwin
NY N Dec 12, 1975

Dave Baldwin
SEA A Dec 4, 1969

Reggie Baldwin
NY N Feb 20, 1980

Lee Bales
HOU N Oct 13, 1966

Neal Ball
CLE A May 1909
BOS A May 1912

Jay Baller
CLE A Dec 9, 1982

Win Ballou
STL A Feb 1926

Dave Bancroft
NY N June 8, 1920
BOS N Nov 12, 1923

Sal Bando
MIL A Nov 19, 1976

Ed Bane
KC A Jan 15, 1980

Dick Baney
BAL A June 15, 1970

George Banks
CLE A June 15, 1964

Alan Bannister
CHI A Dec 10, 1975
CLE A June 13, 1980
HOU N Mar 25, 1984

Floyd Bannister
SEA A Dec 8, 1978
CHI A Dec 13, 1982

Walter Barbare
PIT N Jan 1919
BOS N Feb 23, 1921

Jap Barbeau
STL N Aug 19, 1909

Steve Barber
NY A July 5, 1967
MIL A Oct 22, 1973

Turner Barber
BKN N Jan 2, 1923

George Barclay
BOS N Sept 11, 1904

Ray Bare
DET A Apr 4, 1975

Len Barker
CLE A Oct 3, 1978
ATL N Aug 28, 1983

Ray Barker
CLE A Nov 16, 1961
NY A May 10, 1965
BAL A July 5, 1967

Mike Barlow
STL N May 18, 1975
HOU N Sept 30, 1975
CAL A June 6, 1976

Frank Barnes
CHI A May 19, 1960
PHI N Dec 15, 1961

Jesse Barnes
NY N Jan 8, 1918
BOS N June 7, 1923
BKN N Oct 7, 1925

Red Barnes
CHI A June 13, 1930

Rich Barnes
CLE A Aug 25, 1983

Virgil Barnes
BOS N June 15, 1928

Ed Barney
PIT N Aug 19, 1915

Jim Barr
CAL A Dec 3, 1978

Steve Barr
TEX A Nov 17, 1975

Cuno Barragan
LA N Dec 13, 1963

German Barranca
CIN N Jan 21, 1981
DET A Sept 7, 1982

Bill Barrett
BOS A May 23, 1929
WAS A Apr 30, 1930

Bob Barrett
BKN N May 10, 1925

Dick Barrett
BOS N Dec 1933
PHI N July 1943

Jimmy Barrett
CIN N Feb 1906

Johnny Barrett
BOS N June 12, 1946

Red Barrett
STL N May 23, 1945
BOS N Dec 9, 1946

Jack Barry
BOS A July 2, 1915
PHI A June 27, 1919

Shad Barry
BOS N Jan 10, 1900
PHI N June 1901
CHI N July 20, 1904
CIN N May 20, 1905
STL N July 25, 1906
NY N July 1908

Dick Bartell
PHI N Nov 6, 1930
NY N Nov 1, 1934
CHI N Dec 6, 1938
DET A Dec 6, 1939

Bob Barton
SD N Dec 5, 1969
CIN N June 11, 1972

Eddie Basinski
PIT N Dec 5, 1946

Kevin Bass
HOU N Aug 30, 1982

Randy Bass
SD N Aug 11, 1980
TEX A May 17, 1982

John Bateman
PHI N June 14, 1972

Johnny Bates
PHI N July 16, 1909
CIN N Feb 1911
CHI N Aug 1914

Earl Battey
WAS A Apr 4, 1960

Chris Batton
PIT N Mar 15, 1977

Matt Batts
STL A May 17, 1951
CHI A May 29, 1954
BAL A Dec 6, 1954

Hank Bauer
KC A Dec 11, 1959

Frank Baumann
CHI A Nov 3, 1959
CHI N Dec 1, 1964

Ross Baumgarten
PIT N Mar 21, 1982

Frankie Baumholtz
CHI N June 15, 1949
PHI N Dec 9, 1955

Ed Bauta
STL N May 28, 1960
NY N Aug 5, 1963

Mike Baxes
NY A Apr 12, 1959

Don Baylor
OAK A Apr 2, 1976
CAL A Nov 16, 1976

Bill Bayne
BOS A Dec 1928

Bob Beall
ATL N Dec 4, 1973

Belve Bean
WAS A May 14, 1935

Dave Beard
SEA A Nov 21, 1983

Gene Bearden
CLE A Dec 20, 1946
WAS A Aug 2, 1950
DET A Apr 26, 1951
STL A Feb 14, 1952
CHI A Mar 18, 1953

Gary Beare
PHI N Mar 28, 1979

Jim Beattie
SEA A Nov 1, 1979

Jim Beauchamp
HOU N Feb 17, 1964
MIL N May 13, 1965
CIN N Oct 10, 1967
STL N June 13, 1970
NY N Oct 18, 1971

Ginger Beaumont
BOS N Dec 1906
CHI N Feb 1910

Johnny Beazley
BOS N Apr 18, 1947

Clyde Beck
CIN N Jan 1931

Fred Beck
CIN N Mar 1911
PHI N July 15, 1911

Heinie Beckendorf
WAS A Apr 1910

Beals Becker
BOS N June 1908
NY N Dec 1909
PHI N June 5, 1913

Heinz Becker
CLE A May 1946

Glenn Beckert
SD N Nov 7, 1973

Jake Beckley
STL N Feb 1904

Joe Beckwith
KC A Dec 7, 1983

Fred Beebe
STL N July 1, 1906
CIN N Feb 1910
PHI N Feb 1911

Fred Beene
SD N Dec 1, 1970
CLE A Apr 27, 1974

Joe Beggs
CIN N Jan 4, 1940
NY N June 7, 1947

Rick Behenna
CLE A Aug 28, 1983

Mel Behney
BOS A Mar 27, 1973

Hank Behrman
PIT N May 3, 1947
BKN N June 14, 1947

Ollie Bejma
CLE A Jan 10, 1940

Mark Belanger
LA N Dec 11, 1981

Wayne Belardi
DET A June 9, 1954
KC A Dec 5, 1956
NY A Feb 19, 1957

Bo Belinsky
PHI N Dec 3, 1964

Beau Bell
DET A May 13, 1939
CLE A Jan 20, 1940

Buddy Bell
TEX A Dec 8, 1978

Gary Bell
BOS A June 4, 1967
CHI A June 8, 1969

Gus Bell
CIN N Oct 14, 1952

Kevin Bell
OAK A Mar 27, 1981

Les Bell
BOS N Mar 25, 1928
CHI N Oct 29, 1929

Zeke Bella
KC A Aug 22, 1958

Bob Belloir
ATL N June 7, 1975

Chief Bender
PHI N Feb 10, 1916

Ray Benge
BKN N Dec 15, 1932
BOS N Dec 12, 1935
PHI N Aug 4, 1936

Juan Beniquez
TEX A Nov 17, 1975
NY A Nov 10, 1978
SEA A Nov 1, 1979
CAL A Dec 29, 1980

Dennis Bennett
BOS A Nov 29, 1964
NY N June 24, 1967

Joe Bennett
STL A May 1921

Jack Bentley
PHI N Dec 30, 1925
NY N Sept 15, 1926

Al Benton
DET A Jan 1938
CLE A Apr 20, 1949

Butch Benton
CHI N Apr 6, 1981

Larry Benton
NY N June 12, 1927
CIN N May 21, 1930

Rube Benton
NY N Aug 19, 1915
CIN N July 30, 1922

Johnny Berardino
WAS A Nov 22, 1947
CLE A Dec 9, 1947
PIT N Aug 18, 1952

Lou Berberet
WAS A Feb 8, 1956
BOS A May 1, 1958
DET A Dec 2, 1958

Juan Berenguer
KC A Mar 31, 1981
TOR A Aug 8, 1981

Moe Berg
CHI A Aug 1925
CLE A Apr 2, 1931

Bill Bergen
BKN N Feb 1904

Boze Berger
CHI A Apr 1937
BOS A Dec 21, 1938
BKN N Dec 26, 1939

Wally Berger
NY N June 15, 1937
CIN N June 6, 1938

Dave Bergman
HOU N June 15, 1977
SF N Apr 20, 1981
PHI N Mar 24, 1984
DET A Mar 24, 1984

Dwight Bernard
MIL A Oct 26, 1979

Tony Bernazard
CHI A Dec 12, 1980
SEA A June 15, 1983
CLE A Dec 7, 1983

Bill Bernhard
CLE A June 1902

Juan Bernhardt
CHI A July 6, 1979

Ray Berres
BOS N June 14, 1940
NY N Mar 1942

Charlie Berry
CHI A Apr 29, 1932
PHI A Dec 12, 1933

Joe Berry
CLE A May 1946

Ken Berry
CAL A Nov 30, 1970
MIL A Oct 22, 1973

Neil Berry
STL A Oct 27, 1952
CHI A Sept 1, 1953
BAL A Feb 5, 1954

Frank Bertaina
WAS A May 29, 1967
STL N Aug 14, 1970

Dick Bertell
SF N May 29, 1965

Reno Bertoia
WAS A Dec 6, 1958
KC A June 1, 1961
DET A Aug 2, 1961

Bob Bescher
NY N Dec 12, 1913
STL N Apr 8, 1915

Kurt Bevacqua
CLE A May 8, 1971
KC A Nov 2, 1972
PIT N Dec 4, 1973
KC A July 8, 1974
MIL A Mar 6, 1975
SD N Oct 25, 1978
PIT N Aug 5, 1980

Hal Bevan
PHI A May 3, 1952

Bill Bevens
CHI A Jan 17, 1949

Monte Beville
DET A July 25, 1904

Jim Bibby
STL N Oct 18, 1971
TEX A June 6, 1973
CLE A June 13, 1975
PIT N Mar 15, 1978
TEX A Feb 7, 1984

Vern Bickford
BAL A Feb 10, 1954

Elliott Bigelow
BOS A Dec 15, 1928

Larry Biittner
MON N Dec 20, 1973
CHI N May 17, 1976
CIN N Jan 8, 1981

Steve Bilko
CHI N Apr 30, 1954
LA N June 15, 1958

Jack Billingham
HOU N Jan 22, 1969
CIN N Nov 29, 1971
DET A Mar 6, 1978
BOS A May 12, 1980

Dick Billings
STL N Aug 12, 1974

Josh Billings
STL A Mar 1919

George Binks
PHI A Feb 14, 1947
STL A June 4, 1948

Doug Bird
PHI N Apr 3, 1979
CHI N June 12, 1981
BOS A Dec 10, 1982

Ralph Birkofer
BKN N Dec 4, 1936

Babe Birrer
BAL A Apr 5, 1956

John Bischoff
BOS A July 11, 1925

Max Bishop
BOS A Dec 12, 1933

Rivington Bisland
STL A Mar 1913

Hi Bithorn
PIT N Jan 25, 1947
CHI A Mar 22, 1947

George Bjorkman
HOU N Mar 16, 1983

Bill Black
DET A Aug 14, 1952

Bud Black
KC A Oct 23, 1981

Don Black
CLE A Oct 2, 1945

Joe Black
CIN N June 9, 1955

Earl Blackburn
CIN N June 1912
CHI N Jan 1917

Lena Blackburne
BOS N Feb 1919
PHI N May 1919

Ewell Blackwell
NY A Aug 28, 1952
KC A Mar 30, 1955

Tim Blackwell
PHI N Apr 19, 1976
MON N June 15, 1977
MON N Jan 14, 1982

Rick Bladt
BAL A Jan 20, 1977

George Blaeholder
PHI A May 21, 1935
CLE A Jan 27, 1936

Dennis Blair
BAL A July 14, 1977

Paul Blair
NY A Jan 20, 1977

Sheriff Blake
PHI N July 27, 1931

Johnny Blanchard
KC A May 3, 1965
MIL N Sept 9, 1965

Gil Blanco
KC A June 10, 1966

Ossie Blanco
CHI N Nov 30, 1970

Larvell Blanks
CHI A Dec 12, 1975
CLE A Dec 12, 1975
TEX A Oct 3, 1978
ATL N Dec 6, 1979

Don Blasingame
SF N Dec 15, 1959
CIN N Apr 27, 1961
WAS A July 1, 1963

Wade Blasingame
HOU N June 15, 1967
NY A June 6, 1972

Steve Blateric
NY A Sept 16, 1972

Johnny Blatnik
STL N Apr 27, 1950
STL N Apr 27, 1951

Gary Blaylock
NY A July 26, 1959

Curt Blefary
HOU N Dec 4, 1968
NY A Dec 4, 1969
OAK A May 26, 1971
SD N May 17, 1972

Ron Blomberg
CHI A Nov 17, 1977

Jimmy Bloodworth
DET A Dec 12, 1941
PIT N Dec 12, 1946
PHI N May 10, 1950

Bert Blue
PHI A July 1908

Lu Blue
STL A Dec 2, 1927
CHI A Apr 3, 1931

Vida Blue
SF N Mar 15, 1978
KC A Mar 30, 1982

Otto Bluege
PHI N Dec 20, 1933

Jim Bluejacket
CIN N Feb 10, 1916

Bert Blyleven
TEX A June 1, 1976
PIT N Dec 8, 1977
CLE A Dec 9, 1980

Mike Blyzka
NY A Dec 1, 1954

Randy Bobb
NY N Mar 29, 1970

John Boccabella
SF N Apr 1, 1974

Bruce Bochte
CLE A May 11, 1977
SEA A Dec 20, 1977

Bruce Bochy
NY N Feb 11, 1981

Eddie Bockman
CLE A Oct 19, 1946
PIT N Jan 16, 1948

Ping Bodie
NY A Mar 8, 1918

Tony Boeckel
BOS N June 12, 1919

Joe Boehling
CLE A Aug 18, 1916

Len Boehmer
NY A Sept 18, 1967

Tommy Boggs
ATL N Dec 8, 1977

Pat Bohen
PIT N Jan 1914

Sammy Bohne
BKN N June 15, 1926

Danny Boitano
MIL A Mar 28, 1979
NY N Apr 5, 1981
TEX A Dec 11, 1981
CLE A Feb 4, 1984

Bob Boken
CHI A May 9, 1934

Joe Boley
CLE A June 6, 1932

Jim Bolger
CHI N Oct 1, 1954
CLE A Jan 23, 1959
CIN N June 6, 1959
HOU N Nov 30, 1962

Bobby Bolin
SEA A Dec 12, 1969
BOS A Sept 10, 1970

Frank Bolling
MIL N Dec 7, 1960

Milt Bolling
WAS A Apr 29, 1957
CLE A Feb 25, 1958
DET A Mar 27, 1958

Don Bollweg
NY A May 14, 1951
PHI A Dec 16, 1953

Cliff Bolton
DET A June 10, 1937

Mark Bomback
NY N Oct 26, 1979
TOR A Apr 6, 1981

Bobby Bonds
NY A Oct 22, 1974
CAL A Dec 11, 1975
CHI A Dec 5, 1977
TEX A May 16, 1978
CLE A Oct 3, 1978
STL N Dec 7, 1979
CHI N June 4, 1981

Bill Bonham
CIN N Oct 31, 1977

Ernie Bonham
PIT N Oct 21, 1946

Juan Bonilla
SD N Apr 1, 1981

Barry Bonnell
ATL N May 7, 1975
TOR A Dec 5, 1979
SEA A Dec 8, 1983

Frank Bonner
PHI A June 1902

Zeke Bonura
WAS A Mar 18, 1938
NY N Dec 11, 1938
WAS A Apr 26, 1940
CHI N July 22, 1940

Al Bool
BOS N Jan 1931

Bob Boone
CAL A Dec 6, 1981

Dan Boone
HOU N June 8, 1982

Danny Boone
BOS A Jan 7, 1924

Ray Boone
DET A June 15, 1953
CHI A June 15, 1958
KC A May 2, 1959
MIL N Aug 20, 1959
BOS A May 17, 1960

Pedro Borbon
CIN N Nov 25, 1969
SF N June 28, 1979

Frenchy Bordagaray
STL N Dec 3, 1936
CIN N Dec 8, 1938
BOS N Apr 4, 1942

Rich Bordi
SEA A Dec 9, 1981
CHI N Dec 9, 1982

Paul Boris
MIN A Apr 10, 1982

Bob Borkowski
CIN N Oct 4, 1951
BKN N June 9, 1955

Tom Borland
HOU N Mar 24, 1962

Steve Boros
CHI N Nov 28, 1962

Hank Borowy
CHI N July 27, 1945
PHI N Dec 14, 1948
PIT N June 12, 1950
DET A Aug 3, 1950

Babe Borton
CHI A June 23, 1913
STL A Feb 10, 1916

Don Bosch
NY N Dec 6, 1966
MON N Oct 16, 1968

Rick Bosetti
STL N June 15, 1977
TOR A Mar 15, 1978
OAK A June 10, 1981

Thad Bosley
CHI A Dec 5, 1977
MIL A Apr 1, 1981
SEA A Mar 5, 1982
CHI N July 16, 1983

Dick Bosman
CLE A May 10, 1973
OAK A May 20, 1975

Harley Boss
CLE A Dec 15, 1932

Lyman Bostock
CAL A Nov 21, 1976

Ken Boswell
HOU N Oct 29, 1974

Dick Botelho
CHI N Feb 23, 1979
CHI N Mar 30, 1984

Jim Bottomley
CIN N Dec 17, 1932
STL A Mar 21, 1936

Ed Bouchee
CHI N May 13, 1960

Carl Bouldin
CHI A July 13, 1964

Chris Bourjos
BAL A Apr 1, 1981

Pat Bourque
OAK A Aug 29, 1973
MIN A Aug 19, 1974
OAK A Oct 23, 1974

Jim Bouton
SEA A Oct 21, 1968
HOU N Aug 24, 1969

Larry Bowa
CHI N Jan 27, 1982

Frank Bowerman
NY N Feb 1900
BOS N Oct 7, 1907

Bob Bowman
NY N Dec 5, 1940
CHI N Dec 4, 1941

Ernie Bowman
MIL N Dec 3, 1963

Joe Bowman
PHI N Dec 13, 1934
PIT N Apr 16, 1937

Roger Bowman
PIT N May 12, 1953

Ted Bowsfield
CLE A June 13, 1960
KC A Nov 30, 1962

Bob Boyd
KC A Jan 24, 1961
MIL N June 10, 1961

Clete Boyer
NY A Feb 19, 1957
ATL N Nov 29, 1966

Ken Boyer
NY N Oct 20, 1965
CHI A July 22, 1967

Dorian Boyland
SF N Dec 11, 1981

Gene Brabender
SEA A Mar 31, 1969
CAL A Jan 28, 1971

Gib Brack
PHI N July 11, 1938

Buddy Bradford
CLE A June 15, 1970
CIN N May 8, 1971
STL N June 30, 1975
CHI A Dec 12, 1975

Fred Bradley
CHI A Feb 24, 1948

Mark Bradley
NY N Mar 29, 1983

Tom Bradley
CHI A Nov 30, 1970
SF N Nov 28, 1972

Charlie Brady
PIT N Oct 1906

Bobby Bragan
BKN N Mar 24, 1943

Dave Brain
PIT N July 4, 1905
BOS N Dec 15, 1905
CIN N Feb 1908
NY N July 1908

Ralph Branca
DET A July 10, 1953

Harvey Branch
STL N Sept 1, 1962

Darrell Brandon
BOS A Sept 14, 1965
MIN A July 8, 1969

Ed Brandt
BKN N Dec 12, 1935
PIT N Dec 4, 1936

Jackie Brandt
NY N June 14, 1956
BAL A Nov 30, 1959
PHI N Dec 6, 1965
HOU N June 3, 1967

Kitty Bransfield
PHI N Dec 20, 1904
CHI N Aug 9, 1911

Marshall Brant
NY A Apr 1, 1980
OAK A June 15, 1983

Steve Braun
KC A June 1, 1978

Angel Bravo
CIN N Dec 15, 1969
SD N May 13, 1971

Garland Braxton
WAS A Aug 27, 1926
CHI A June 16, 1930
STL A July 13, 1931

Danny Breeden
SD N Dec 3, 1968
CIN N June 30, 1969
CHI N Nov 30, 1970
STL N Nov 18, 1974

Hal Breeden
CHI N Nov 30, 1970
MON N Apr 7, 1972

Marv Breeding
WAS A Dec 5, 1962
LA N July 20, 1963

Fred Breining
SF N June 28, 1979
MON N Feb 27, 1984

Ad Brennan
PHI N Jan 20, 1910
CLE A June 1918

Tom Brennan
CHI A Jan 21, 1984

Roger Bresnahan
STL N Dec 12, 1908
CHI N June 8, 1913

Rube Bressler
BKN N Mar 13, 1928
STL N June 28, 1932

Ed Bressoud
BOS A Nov 26, 1961
NY N Nov 30, 1965
STL N Apr 1, 1967

Ken Brett
MIL A Oct 11, 1971
PHI N Oct 31, 1972
PIT N Oct 18, 1973
NY A Dec 11, 1975
CHI A May 18, 1976
CAL A June 15, 1977

Jim Brewer
LA N Dec 13, 1963
CAL A July 15, 1975

Fred Brickell
PHI N Aug 7, 1930

Jim Brideweser
BAL A May 11, 1954
CHI A Dec 6, 1954
DET A May 15, 1956
NY N Feb 8, 1957
BAL A Feb 8, 1957
STL N Oct 14, 1958

Marshall Bridges
CIN N Aug 2, 1960
WAS A Nov 27, 1963

Rocky Bridges
CIN N Feb 16, 1953
MIL N Feb 16, 1953
WAS A May 20, 1957
DET A Dec 6, 1958
CLE A July 26, 1960
STL N Sept 2, 1960

Al Bridwell
BOS N Mar 1906
NY N Oct 7, 1907
BOS N July 22, 1911
CHI N Nov 1912

Buttons Briggs
BKN N Dec 30, 1905

Dan Briggs
SD N Mar 30, 1979
MON N Nov 27, 1979
CHI N Mar 16, 1982

John Briggs
MIL A Apr 22, 1971
MIN A June 14, 1975

Johnny Briggs
CLE A Jan 23, 1959
KC A July 30, 1960

Harry Bright
WAS A Dec 16, 1960
CIN N Nov 24, 1962
NY A Apr 21, 1963

Nellie Briles
PIT N Jan 29, 1971
KC A Dec 4, 1973
TEX A Nov 12, 1975
BAL A Sept 19, 1977

Chuck Brinkman
PIT N July 11, 1974

Ed Brinkman
DET A Oct 9, 1970
STL N Nov 18, 1974
SD N Nov 18, 1974
TEX A June 4, 1975
NY A June 13, 1975

Lou Brissie
CLE A Apr 30, 1951

Jim Britton
MON N Dec 2, 1969

Johnny Broaca
CLE A Nov 1938

Pete Broberg
MIL A Dec 5, 1974
CHI N Apr 20, 1977
OAK A Mar 29, 1978

Lou Brock
STL N June 15, 1964

Dick Brodowski
WAS A Nov 8, 1955

Ernie Broglio
STL N Oct 8, 1958
CHI N June 15, 1964

Jack Brohamer
CHI A Dec 12, 1975
CLE A June 20, 1980

Jim Brosnan
STL N May 20, 1958
CIN N June 8, 1959
CHI A May 5, 1963

Tony Brottem
PIT N July 1921

Frank Brower
CLE A Jan 8, 1923

Boardwalk Brown
NY A June 1914

Bobby Brown
NY A June 10, 1978
TOR A Mar 25, 1979
SEA A Apr 1, 1982

Buster Brown
BOS N July 16, 1909

Charlie Brown
PHI N June 10, 1907

Clint Brown
CHI A Apr 11, 1936
CLE A Feb 7, 1941

Curt Brown
NY A Dec 19, 1983

Darrell Brown
OAK A Mar 1, 1982

Dick Brown
CHI A Dec 6, 1959
MIL N Nov 28, 1960
DET A Dec 7, 1960
BAL A Nov 26, 1962

Eddie Brown
BOS N Oct 7, 1925

Elmer Brown
BKN N Nov 1912

Hal Brown
BOS A Feb 9, 1953
NY A Sept 7, 1962
HOU N Apr 21, 1963

Jackie Brown
CLE A June 13, 1975
MON N Dec 10, 1976

Jimmy Brown
PIT N Jan 5, 1946

Jumbo Brown
NY N June 1937

Larry Brown
OAK A Apr 24, 1971

Leon Brown
STL N Dec 9, 1976

Lloyd Brown
STL A Dec 14, 1932
BOS A May 9, 1933
CLE A Oct 12, 1933

Mace Brown
BKN N Apr 22, 1941
BOS A Dec 10, 1941

Ollie Brown
OAK A May 17, 1972
MIL A June 29, 1972
CAL A Oct 22, 1973
HOU N Mar 28, 1974
PHI N June 24, 1974

Scott Brown
KC A Dec 11, 1981

Three Finger Brown
CHI N Dec 12, 1903
CHI N Feb 10, 1916

Tommy Brown
PHI N June 8, 1951
CHI N June 15, 1952

Byron Browne
HOU N May 4, 1968
PHI N Oct 7, 1969

Earl Browne
PHI N Apr 16, 1937

George Browne
NY N July 1902
BOS N Oct 7, 1907
CHI N Sept 1908
WAS A May 21, 1909
CHI A May 1910

Cal Browning
LA A Jan 26, 1961

Bob Bruce
HOU N Dec 1, 1961
ATL N Dec 31, 1966

Frank Bruggy
PHI A Dec 1921

Mike Bruhert
TEX A June 15, 1979

Mike Brumley
WAS A Oct 14, 1963

Tom Brunansky
MIN A May 12, 1982

Jack Bruner
STL A July 1, 1950

George Brunet
MIL N May 11, 1960
BAL A July 14, 1963
HOU N May 12, 1964
LA A Aug 18, 1964
SEA A July 31, 1969
WAS A Dec 4, 1969
PIT N Aug 31, 1970
STL N Jan 29, 1971

Warren Brusstar
CHI A Aug 30, 1982
CHI N Jan 25, 1983

Bill Bruton
DET A Dec 7, 1960

Billy Bryan
NY A June 10, 1966

Don Bryant
SF N Apr 3, 1967

Ron Bryant
STL N May 9, 1975

Steve Brye
MIL A Mar 21, 1977

Johnny Bucha
BKN N June 9, 1954

Jerry Buchek
NY N Apr 1, 1967
PHI N Apr 3, 1969

Jim Bucher
STL N Oct 4, 1937

Garland Buckeye
NY N July 7, 1928

Bill Buckner
CHI N Jan 11, 1977

Don Buddin
SF N Nov 26, 1961
DET A July 20, 1962

Fritz Buelow
CLE A Aug 7, 1904
STL A Dec 1906

Don Buford
BAL A Nov 29, 1967

Bob Buhl
CHI N Apr 30, 1962
PHI N Apr 21, 1966

Terry Bulling
SEA A Mar 29, 1979

Jim Bunning
PHI N Dec 4, 1963
PIT N Dec 15, 1967
LA N Aug 15, 1969

Bill Burbach
BAL A May 28, 1971

Al Burch
BKN N July 5, 1907

Bob Burda
SF N Feb 11, 1965
MIL A June 9, 1970
STL N Feb 2, 1971
BOS A Mar 20, 1972

Lew Burdette
BOS N Aug 30, 1951
STL N June 15, 1963
CHI N June 2, 1964
PHI N May 30, 1965

Smoky Burgess
CIN N Oct 4, 1951
PHI N Dec 10, 1951
CIN N Apr 30, 1955
PIT N Jan 30, 1959
CHI A Sept 12, 1964

Tom Burgmeier
MIN A Oct 24, 1973
OAK A Nov 15, 1982

Sandy Burk
STL N Apr 1912

Glenn Burke
OAK A May 17, 1978

Jimmy Burke
CHI A July 1901
PIT N Sept 1901
STL N Jan 1903

Leo Burke
LA A Jan 4, 1961
STL N Mar 25, 1963
CHI N June 24, 1963

Jesse Burkett
BOS A Jan 16, 1905

Ken Burkhart
CIN N Nov 8, 1948

Rick Burleson
CAL A Dec 10, 1980

Johnny Burnett
STL A Nov 20, 1934
CIN N Mar 21, 1936

Bill Burns
CHI A May 16, 1909
CIN N Apr 1910
PHI N July 15, 1911

George Burns
NY A Mar 8, 1918
PHI A Mar 8, 1918
CLE A May 29, 1920
BOS A Dec 24, 1921
CLE A Jan 7, 1924
PHI A June 19, 1929

George Burns
CIN N Dec 6, 1921
PHI N Apr 2, 1925

Jack Burns
DET A Apr 30, 1936

Pete Burnside
DET A Oct 5, 1958
BAL A Dec 5, 1962

Sheldon Burnside
CIN N May 25, 1979

Larry Burright
NY N Nov 30, 1962

Ray Burris
NY A May 23, 1979
NY N Aug 20, 1979
MON N Feb 18, 1981
OAK A Dec 7, 1983

Jeff Burroughs
ATL N Dec 9, 1976
SEA A Mar 7, 1981
OAK A Apr 7, 1982

Ellis Burton
LA A Jan 26, 1961
CLE A Apr 2, 1963

Jim Burton
NY N Mar 29, 1978

Moe Burtschy
NY A June 14, 1956

Jim Busby
WAS A May 3, 1952
CHI A June 7, 1955
CLE A Oct 25, 1955
BAL A June 13, 1957
BOS A Dec 15, 1958

Donie Bush
WAS A Aug 20, 1921

Guy Bush
PIT N Nov 22, 1934
STL N Feb 2, 1938

Joe Bush
BOS A Dec 14, 1917
NY A Dec 20, 1921
STL A Dec 17, 1924
WAS A Feb 1926
PIT N July 1, 1926
NY N June 28, 1927

Mike Buskey
PHI N Dec 10, 1975
HOU N Sept 11, 1978

Tom Buskey
CLE A Apr 27, 1974
TEX A Feb 28, 1978

Ray Busse
STL N Nov 28, 1972
HOU N June 8, 1973

John Butcher
MIN A Dec 7, 1983

Max Butcher
PHI N Aug 8, 1938
PIT N July 28, 1939

Sal Butera
DET A Mar 25, 1983

Art Butler
PIT N Jan 1912
STL N Dec 12, 1913

Bill Butler
CLE A July 11, 1972

Brett Butler
CLE A Aug 28, 1983

Johnny Butler
CHI N Dec 1927

John Buzhardt
PHI N Jan 11, 1960
CHI A Nov 28, 1961
BAL A Aug 21, 1967
HOU N Sept 23, 1967

Bud Byerly
BKN N June 15, 1952
BOS A June 24, 1958

Harry Byrd
NY A Dec 16, 1953
BAL A Nov 18, 1954
CHI A June 15, 1955
DET A May 15, 1956

Sammy Byrd
CIN N Dec 19, 1934

Bobby Byrne
PIT N Aug 19, 1909
PHI N Aug 20, 1913
CHI A Sept 1917

Tommy Byrne
STL A June 15, 1951
CHI A Oct 16, 1952
WAS A June 11, 1953

Enos Cabell
HOU N Dec 3, 1974
SF N Dec 8, 1980
DET A Mar 4, 1982
HOU N Feb 14, 1984

Craig Cacek
CAL A Dec 17, 1981

Leon Cadore
CHI A July 6, 1923

Hick Cady
PHI A Jan 10, 1918

Wayne Cage
SEA A Mar 26, 1981

Bob Cain
STL A Feb 14, 1952
PHI A Dec 17, 1953

Sugar Cain
STL A May 21, 1935
CHI A May 5, 1936

Sammy Calderone
MIL N Feb 1, 1954

Mike Caldwell
SF N Oct 25, 1973
STL N Oct 20, 1976
CIN N Mar 29, 1977
MIL A June 15, 1977

Ray Caldwell
BOS A Dec 18, 1918

Ben Callahan
OAK A June 15, 1983

Johnny Callison
PHI N Dec 9, 1959
CHI N Nov 17, 1969
NY A Jan 20, 1972

Paul Calvert
DET A Feb 15, 1950

Ernie Camacho
PIT N Apr 6, 1981
CHI A Mar 21, 1982
CLE A June 6, 1983

Hank Camelli
BOS N Sept 30, 1946

Dolf Camilli
PHI N June 11, 1934
BKN N Mar 6, 1938
NY N July 31, 1943

Doug Camilli
WAS A Nov 30, 1964

Howie Camnitz
PHI N Aug 20, 1913

Bert Campaneris
TEX A Nov 17, 1976
CAL A May 4, 1979

Jim Campanis
KC A Dec 5, 1968
PIT N Dec 2, 1970

Bill Campbell
BOS A Nov 6, 1976
CHI N Dec 8, 1981
PHI N Mar 26, 1984

Bruce Campbell
STL A Apr 27, 1932
CLE A Nov 20, 1934
DET A Jan 20, 1940
WAS A Dec 12, 1941

Dave Campbell
MON N Mar 31, 1979

Dave Campbell
SD N Dec 4, 1969
STL N June 7, 1973
HOU N Aug 18, 1973

Jim Campbell
CIN N Oct 9, 1963

Jim Campbell
BOS A Oct 21, 1970

Ron Campbell
PIT N Jan 15, 1969

Vin Campbell
PIT N Jan 1910
BOS N Feb 1912

Card Camper
CLE A May 28, 1976

Sal Campisi
MIN A Oct 20, 1970

Milo Candini
WAS A Jan 29, 1943

Chris Cannizzaro
DET A Dec 19, 1966
PIT N Nov 29, 1967
SD N Mar 28, 1969
CHI N May 19, 1971
LA N Dec 17, 1971

Joe Cannon
TOR A Nov 27, 1978

Ben Cantwell
BOS N June 15, 1928
NY N Jan 27, 1937
BKN N Aug 9, 1937

Doug Capilla
CIN N June 15, 1977
CHI N May 3, 1979
SF N Dec 7, 1981

George Cappuzzello
CIN N Mar 6, 1978

Buzz Capra
ATL N Mar 26, 1974

Ralph Capron
PHI N Jan 1913

Bernie Carbo
STL N May 19, 1972
BOS A Oct 26, 1973
MIL A June 3, 1976
BOS A Dec 6, 1976
CLE A June 15, 1978
STL N Mar 10, 1979

Jose Cardenal
LA A Nov 21, 1964
CLE A Nov 29, 1967
STL N Nov 21, 1969
MIL A July 29, 1971
CHI N Dec 3, 1971
PHI N Oct 25, 1977
NY N Aug 2, 1979

Leo Cardenas
MIN A Nov 21, 1968
CAL A Nov 30, 1971
CLE A Apr 2, 1973
TEX A Feb 12, 1974

Don Cardwell
CHI N May 13, 1960
STL N Oct 17, 1962
PIT N Nov 19, 1962
NY N Dec 6, 1966
ATL N July 12, 1970

Rod Carew
CAL A Feb 3, 1979

Andy Carey
KC A May 19, 1960
CHI A June 10, 1961
PHI N Dec 15, 1961
LA N Mar 24, 1962

Max Carey
BKN N Aug 13, 1926

Tex Carleton
CHI N Nov 21, 1934

Jim Carlin
WAS A Dec 11, 1938

Cisco Carlos
WAS A Aug 25, 1969

Hal Carlson
CHI N June 7, 1927

Steve Carlton
PHI N Feb 25, 1972

Roy Carlyle
BOS A Apr 26, 1925
NY A June 15, 1926

Duke Carmel
NY N July 29, 1963

Eddie Carnett
CLE A Dec 12, 1944

Charlie Carr
CLE A Aug 7, 1904
CIN N Feb 1906

Alex Carrasquel
CHI A Jan 2, 1946

Chico Carrasquel
CLE A Oct 25, 1955
KC A June 12, 1958
BAL A Oct 2, 1958

Cam Carreon
CLE A Jan 20, 1965

Don Carrithers
MON N Apr 1, 1974
MIN A Apr 6, 1977

Clay Carroll
CIN N June 11, 1968
CHI A Dec 12, 1975
STL N Mar 23, 1977
CHI A Aug 31, 1977

Ownie Carroll
NY A May 30, 1930
CIN N Sept 13, 1930
STL N Dec 17, 1932
BKN N Feb 1933

Tom Carroll
PIT N Nov 6, 1976

Tommy Carroll
KC A Apr 12, 1959

Rico Carty
TEX A Oct 27, 1972
CHI N Aug 13, 1973
OAK A Sept 11, 1973
CLE A Dec 6, 1976
OAK A Aug 15, 1978
TOR A Oct 3, 1978

Jerry Casale
DET A June 7, 1961

Paul Casanova
ATL N Dec 2, 1971

Joe Cascarella
BOS A June 30, 1934
WAS A June 13, 1936
CIN N July 3, 1937

George Case
CLE A Dec 14, 1945
WAS A Mar 4, 1947

Doc Casey
BKN N Dec 30, 1905

Dave Cash
PHI N Oct 18, 1973
MON N Nov 17, 1976
SD N Nov 27, 1979

Norm Cash
CLE A Dec 6, 1959
DET A Apr 12, 1960

Harry Cassady
WAS A Mar 1905

George Caster
STL A Nov 16, 1940
DET A Aug 8, 1945

Pete Castiglione
STL N June 14, 1953

Bobby Castillo
MIN A Jan 6, 1982

Manny Castillo
SEA A Oct 23, 1981

Foster Castleman
BAL A Mar 24, 1958

Bill Castro
CAL A Mar 24, 1982

Danny Cater
CHI A Dec 1, 1964
KC A May 27, 1966
NY A Dec 5, 1969
BOS A Mar 22, 1972
STL N Mar 29, 1975

Ted Cather
BOS N June 1914

Bill Caudill
CIN N Mar 28, 1977
CHI N Oct 31, 1977
NY A Apr 1, 1982
SEA A Apr 1, 1982
OAK A Nov 21, 1983

Red Causey
BOS N Aug 15, 1919
NY N July 1, 1921

Wayne Causey
KC A Jan 24, 1961
CHI A May 27, 1966
CAL A July 20, 1968
ATL N July 29, 1968

Art Ceccarelli
BAL A Oct 11, 1956
STL N Oct 14, 1958
NY A May 19, 1960

Cesar Cedeno
CIN N Dec 18, 1981

Orlando Cepeda
STL N May 8, 1966
ATL N Mar 17, 1969
OAK A June 29, 1972

Rick Cerone
TOR A Dec 6, 1976
NY A Nov 1, 1979

Bob Cerv
KC A Oct 16, 1956
NY A May 19, 1960
NY A May 8, 1961

Ron Cey
CHI N Jan 20, 1983

Elio Chacon
STL N Dec 7, 1964

Leon Chagnon
NY N Dec 1934

Bob Chakales
BAL A June 1, 1954
CHI A Dec 6, 1954
WAS A June 7, 1955
BOS A Apr 29, 1957

Dave Chalk
TEX A May 4, 1979
OAK A June 15, 1979

Craig Chamberlain
SF N Mar 30, 1982

Icebox Chamberlain
PIT N Jan 1900

Cliff Chambers
PIT N Dec 8, 1948
STL N June 15, 1951

Chris Chambliss
NY A Apr 27, 1974
TOR A Nov 1, 1979
ATL N Dec 5, 1979

Billy Champion
MIL A Oct 31, 1972

Mike Champion
CLE A Mar 30, 1979

Bob Chance
WAS A Dec 1, 1964

Dean Chance
MIN A Dec 2, 1966
CLE A Dec 10, 1969
NY N Sept 18, 1970
DET A Mar 30, 1971

Darrell Chaney
ATL N Dec 12, 1975

Charlie Chant
STL N Oct 28, 1975

Ben Chapman
WAS A June 14, 1936
BOS A June 11, 1937
CLE A Dec 15, 1938
WAS A Dec 24, 1940
PHI N June 15, 1945

Harry Chapman
CIN N Dec 15, 1912
STL A Feb 10, 1916

Sam Chapman
CLE A May 10, 1951

Larry Chappell
CLE A Aug 21, 1915
BOS N May 1916

Bill Chappelle
CIN N May 1909

Chappy Charles
CIN N Aug 22, 1909

Ed Charles
NY N May 10, 1967

Mike Chartak
STL A June 7, 1942

Hal Chase
CHI A June 23, 1913
NY N Feb 2, 1919

Ken Chase
BOS A Dec 13, 1941

Ossie Chavarria
NY A Dec 5, 1969

Dave Cheadle
ATL N June 7, 1973

Charlie Chech
BOS A Feb 18, 1909

Larry Cheney
BKN N Aug 1915
BOS N June 1919
PHI N Aug 1919

Tom Cheney
PIT N Dec 21, 1959
WAS A June 29, 1961

Jack Chesbro
BOS A Aug 1909

Cupid Childs
CHI N Jan 1900

Rich Chiles
NY N Nov 27, 1972

Lou Chiozza
NY N Dec 8, 1936

Bob Chipman
CHI N June 6, 1944
BOS N Apr 18, 1950

Tom Chism
MIN A Dec 7, 1979

Harry Chiti
DET A July 26, 1960
CLE A Nov 16, 1961
NY N Apr 26, 1962

Nels Chittum
BOS A Mar 15, 1959
LA N May 6, 1960

Bob Chlupsa
SD N June 20, 1972

Don Choate
SF N Mar 25, 1959

Mike Chris
SF N Dec 9, 1981
CHI N Sept 30, 1983

Neil Chrisley
WAS A Nov 8, 1955
DET A Dec 6, 1958
MIL N Dec 7, 1960
NY N Oct 16, 1961

Bob Christian
CHI A Sept 30, 1968

Mark Christman
STL A May 13, 1939
WAS A Apr 9, 1947

Steve Christmas
CHI A Nov 21, 1983

Joe Christopher
BOS A Nov 30, 1965
DET A June 14, 1966

Russ Christopher
CLE A Apr 3, 1948

Bubba Church
CIN N May 23, 1952
CHI N June 12, 1953

Chuck Churn
CLE A Mar 26, 1958

Al Cicotte
WAS A May 14, 1958
DET A June 23, 1958
CLE A Nov 20, 1958
STL N Jan 26, 1961
HOU N Oct 13, 1961

Eddie Cicotte
CHI A July 22, 1912

Pete Cimino
CAL A Dec 2, 1966

Gino Cimoli
STL N Dec 4, 1958
PIT N Dec 21, 1959

Galen Cisco
NY N Sept 7, 1962

Bill Cissell
CLE A Apr 24, 1932
BOS A Oct 12, 1933
NY N Mar 1938

Doug Clarey
NY N Mar 30, 1977

Allie Clark
CLE A Oct 10, 1947
PHI A May 10, 1951
CHI A May 12, 1953

Bobby Clark
MIL A Dec 20, 1983

Bryan Clark
TOR A Dec 8, 1983

Cap Clark
PHI N Dec 8, 1937

Danny Clark
BOS A Oct 30, 1922

Jim Clark
KC A July 10, 1972

Rickey Clark
PHI N Jan 29, 1973

Ron Clark
OAK A Jan 15, 1970
MIL A June 20, 1972
CAL A July 28, 1972

Watty Clark
NY N June 16, 1933

Fred Clarke
PIT N Jan 1900

Horace Clarke
SD N May 31, 1974

Nig Clarke
DET A Aug 1, 1905
CLE A Aug 11, 1905
STL A Oct 1910
PIT N Nov 1919

Tommy Clarke
NY A Apr 28, 1918

Bill Clarkson
BOS N June 15, 1928

Walter Clarkson
CLE A May 16, 1907

Ellis Clary
STL A Aug 18, 1943

Dain Clay
PHI N June 1, 1943

Ken Clay
TEX A Aug 14, 1980
SEA A Dec 12, 1980

Mark Clear
BOS A Dec 10, 1980

Clem Clemens
CHI N Feb 10, 1916

Doug Clemens
CHI N June 15, 1964
PHI N Jan 10, 1966

Jack Clements
BOS N Jan 1900

Lance Clemons
HOU N Dec 2, 1971
STL N Apr 15, 1972
BOS A Jan 24, 1973

Donn Clendenon
HOU N Jan 22, 1969
NY N June 15, 1969

Reggie Cleveland
BOS A Dec 7, 1973
TEX A Apr 18, 1978
MIL A Dec 15, 1978

Tex Clevenger
WAS A Nov 8, 1955
NY A May 8, 1961

Harlond Clift
WAS A Aug 18, 1943

Ty Cline
MIL N Nov 27, 1962
SF N May 31, 1967
CIN N June 15, 1970

Gene Clines
NY N Oct 22, 1974
TEX A Dec 12, 1975
CHI N Feb 5, 1977

Billy Clingman
CHI N Jan 1900

Lu Clinton
LA A June 4, 1964
CLE A Sept 9, 1965
NY A Jan 14, 1966

Tony Cloninger
CIN N June 11, 1968
STL N Mar 24, 1972

Al Closter
WAS A Apr 5, 1966
NY A May 3, 1966
ATL N June 7, 1973

David Clyde
CLE A Feb 28, 1978
TEX A Jan 4, 1980

Otis Clymer
WAS A June 26, 1907
BOS N July 1913

Andy Coakley
CHI N Sept 1908

Gil Coan
BAL A Feb 18, 1954
CHI A July 17, 1955
NY N Aug 26, 1955

Jim Coates
WAS A Apr 21, 1963

Mickey Cochrane
DET A Dec 12, 1933

Jack Coffey
BOS A July 1918

Dick Coffman
STL A Oct 19, 1927
WAS A June 9, 1932
STL A Dec 13, 1932
NY N Sept 24, 1935

Slick Coffman
PHI A Dec 9, 1939
STL A Jan 30, 1940

Frank Coggins
CLE A Apr 4, 1970

Rich Coggins
MON N Dec 4, 1974
NY A June 20, 1975
CHI A May 18, 1976
PHI N July 14, 1976

Jimmie Coker
BAL A Nov 21, 1962
SF N Dec 15, 1962
STL N Oct 1, 1963
MIL N Apr 9, 1964

Rocky Colavito
DET A Apr 17, 1960
KC A Nov 18, 1963
CHI A Jan 20, 1965
CLE A Jan 20, 1965
CHI A July 29, 1967
LA N Mar 26, 1968

Nate Colbert
DET A Nov 18, 1974
MON N June 15, 1975

Vince Colbert
TEX A Nov 30, 1972
CLE A Mar 8, 1973

Jim Colborn
MIL A Dec 3, 1971
KC A Dec 6, 1976
SEA A June 1, 1978

Bert Cole
CLE A July 1925

Dave Cole
CHI N Mar 20, 1954
PHI N Mar 19, 1955

Dick Cole
PIT N Junc 15, 1951
MIL N Apr 3, 1957

Ed Cole
STL A Feb 10, 1938

King Cole
PIT N June 22, 1912

Ed Coleman
STL A May 21, 1935

Joe Coleman
DET A Oct 9, 1970
CHI N June 8, 1976
OAK A Mar 15, 1977
TOR A May 22, 1978

Joe Coleman
BAL A Dec 17, 1953

Ray Coleman
PHI A June 4, 1948
STL A Dec 13, 1949
CHI A July 31, 1951
STL A July 28, 1952
BKN N Oct 14, 1952

Rip Coleman
KC A Feb 19, 1957
BAL A Sept 6, 1959

Chris Coletta
CAL A Aug 15, 1972
CAL A Aug 14, 1973

Bill Collins
CHI N June 10, 1911

Dave Collins
CIN N Dec 9, 1977
NY A Dec 23, 1981

Don Collins
CLE A Feb 15, 1980

Eddie Collins
CHI A Dec 8, 1914

Jimmy Collins
PHI A June 7, 1907

Joe Collins
PHI N Mar 20, 1958

Kevin Collins
MON N June 15, 1969
CLE A June 15, 1973

Pat Collins
BOS N Dec 13, 1928

Phil Collins
STL N May 18, 1934

Rip Collins
BOS A Dec 20, 1921
DET A Oct 30, 1922

Ripper Collins
CHI N Oct 8, 1936

Shano Collins
BOS A Mar 4, 1921

Zip Collins
BOS N Sept 3, 1915

Jackie Collum
CIN N May 23, 1953
STL N Jan 31, 1956
CHI N Dec 11, 1956
CHI N May 23, 1957
CLE A Aug 20, 1962

Bob Coluccio
CHI A May 8, 1975
STL N June 8, 1978
NY N Oct 2, 1978

Merrill Combs
WAS A May 8, 1950
CLE A Apr 1, 1951

Wayne Comer
WAS A May 11, 1970

Adam Comorosky
CIN N Oct 17, 1933

Pete Compton
PIT N June 1916

Bunk Congalton
BOS A May 20, 1907

Billy Conigliaro
MIL A Oct 11, 1971
OAK A Feb 14, 1973

Tony Conigliaro
CAL A Oct 11, 1970

Gene Conley
PHI N Mar 31, 1959
BOS A Dec 15, 1960

Bruce Connatser
WAS A Dec 15, 1932

Joe Connolly
BOS N Apr 10, 1913

Joe Connolly
BOS A Jan 7, 1924

Joc Connor
CLE A June 1901

Bill Connors
NY N Aug 20, 1967

Chuck Connors
CHI N Oct 10, 1950

Billy Consolo
WAS A June 11, 1959
MIL N June 1, 1961
LA A May 8, 1962
KC A June 26, 1962

Jim Constable
CLE A June 7, 1958
WAS A July 12, 1958

Sandy Consuegra
CHI A May 12, 1953
BAL A May 14, 1956
NY N May 14, 1957

Jack Conway
NY N Jan 16, 1948

Cliff Cook
NY N May 7, 1962

Dusty Cooke
STL N Dec 8, 1938

Duff Cooley
PIT N Feb 1900
BOS N May 1901
DET A Oct 1904
DET A Dec 1905

Danny Coombs
SD N Oct 22, 1969

Jimmy Cooney
CHI N Dec 11, 1925
PHI N June 7, 1927
STL N Dec 13, 1927
BOS N Dec 18, 1927

Johnny Cooney
STL N Oct 4, 1937

Cecil Cooper
MIL A Dec 6, 1976

Claude Cooper
PHI N Feb 10, 1916

Don Cooper
TOR A Dec 10, 1982

Guy Cooper
BOS A May 27, 1914

Mort Cooper
BOS N May 23, 1945
NY N June 13, 1947

Walker Cooper
NY N Jan 5, 1946
CIN N June 13, 1949
BOS N May 10, 1950
CHI N May 19, 1954

Wilbur Cooper
CHI N Oct 27, 1924
DET A June 7, 1926

Doug Corbett
CAL A May 12, 1982

Claude Corbitt
CIN N Mar 18, 1946

Tim Corcoran
MIN A Aug 23, 1981

Mardie Cornejo
DET A Mar 13, 1979

Pat Corrales
STL N Oct 27, 1965
CIN N Feb 8, 1968
SD N June 11, 1972

Vic Correll
ATL N Mar 26, 1974

Red Corriden
CIN N Nov 16, 1912
CHI N Dec 15, 1912

Frank Corridon
PHI N July 20, 1904
STL N Feb 1910

Pete Coscarart
PIT N Dec 12, 1941

Dan Costello
PIT N Jan 1914

Dick Cotter
CHI N Oct 1911

Chuck Cottier
DET A Dec 7, 1960
WAS A June 5, 1961
CAL A Feb 16, 1967

Ensign Cottrell
CHI N Jan 1912
NY A Apr 18, 1915

Johnny Couch
PHI N Aug 2, 1923

Bill Coughlin
DET A Aug 10, 1904

Marlan Coughtry
KC A May 12, 1962
CLE A July 2, 1962

Tom Coulter
NY N Oct 18, 1971

Fritz Coumbe
CLE A Aug 20, 1914

Clint Courtney
STL A Nov 23, 1951
CHI A Dec 6, 1954
WAS A June 7, 1955
BAL A Apr 3, 1960

Ernie Courtney
DET A June 10, 1903

Henry Courtney
CHI A May 1922

Harry Coveleski
CIN N Jan 20, 1910

Stan Coveleski
WAS A Dec 12, 1924

Wes Covington
CHI A May 10, 1961
KC A June 10, 1961
PHI N July 2, 1961
CHI N Jan 10, 1966

Billy Cowan
NY N Jan 15, 1965
CHI N Apr 28, 1966
CAL A July 26, 1969

Al Cowens
CAL A Dec 6, 1979
DET A May 27, 1980
SEA A Mar 28, 1982

Billy Cox
STL A June 11, 1938
BKN N Dec 8, 1947
BAL A Dec 13, 1954
CLE A June 15, 1955

Bobby Cox
NY A Dec 7, 1967

Casey Cox
WAS A May 31, 1963
NY A Aug 30, 1972

Glenn Cox
KC A Sept 12, 1955

Jeff Cox
DET A Mar 1, 1982

Larry Cox
MIN A Oct 24, 1975
CHI N Oct 25, 1977
SEA A Mar 20, 1979
TEX A Dec 12, 1980

Ted Cox
SEA A Dec 6, 1979

Jim Crabb
PHI A May 1912

Estel Crabtree
STL N Dec 17, 1932

Pete Craig
WAS A Apr 11, 1964

Rodney Craig
CLE A Mar 26, 1981

Roger Craig
STL N Nov 4, 1963
CIN N Dec 14, 1964

Doc Cramer
BOS A Jan 4, 1936
WAS A Dec 12, 1940
DET A Dec 12, 1941

Del Crandall
SF N Dec 3, 1963
PIT N Feb 11, 1965

Doc Crandall
STL N July 1913
NY N July 1913
STL A Feb 10, 1916

Sam Crane
WAS A Feb 3, 1917
BKN N Jan 24, 1922

Gavvy Cravath
CHI A Aug 1908
WAS A May 16, 1909

Glenn Crawford
PHI N May 8, 1945

Jim Crawford
DET A Dec 6, 1975

Pat Crawford
CIN N May 27, 1930

Rufus Crawford
DET A Oct 27, 1952

Willie Crawford
STL N Mar 2, 1976
SF N Oct 20, 1976
OAK A June 15, 1977

Birdie Cree
NY A Mar 1908

Lou Criger
STL A Dec 12, 1908
NY A Dec 1909

Jack Crimian
CIN N Dec 2, 1953
DET A Dec 5, 1956

Leo Cristante
DET A Dec 6, 1954

Hughie Critz
NY N May 21, 1930

Fred Crolius
PIT N Feb 1902

Ray Crone
NY N June 15, 1957

Joe Cronin
BOS A Oct 26, 1934

John Cronin
NY N Dec 12, 1903

Ed Crosby
CIN N July 27, 1973
STL N Mar 29, 1974
CLE A June 1, 1974

Ken Crosby
STL N Aug 7, 1973

Jeff Cross
CHI N May 2, 1948

Lave Cross
BKN N May 1900
WAS A Jan 1905

Bill Crouch
PHI N Nov 11, 1940

Jack Crouch
CIN N Sept 1, 1933

Frank Croucher
WAS A Dec 12, 1941

General Crowder
STL A July 7, 1927
WAS A June 13, 1930
DET A Aug 4, 1934

George Crowe
CIN N Apr 9, 1956
STL N Oct 3, 1958

Terry Crowley
TEX A Dec 6, 1973
CIN N Mar 19, 1974
ATL N Apr 7, 1976

Walt Cruise
BOS N May 1919

Cirilio Cruz
TEX A Oct 26, 1973
NY A Dec 12, 1977

Hector Cruz
CHI N Dec 8, 1977
SF N June 15, 1978
CIN N June 28, 1979
CHI N Dec 12, 1980

Henry Cruz
CHI A Sept 2, 1977

Jose Cruz
HOU N Oct 24, 1974

Julio Cruz
CHI A June 15, 1983

Todd Cruz
KC A Apr 3, 1979
CAL A Dec 6, 1979
CHI A June 12, 1980
SEA A Dec 11, 1981
BAL A June 30, 1983

Victor Cruz
TOR A Dec 6, 1977
CLE A Dec 5, 1978
PIT N Dec 9, 1980

Mike Cubbage
MIN A June 1, 1976
NY N Dec 19, 1980

Tony Cuccinello
BKN N Mar 14, 1932
BOS N Dec 12, 1935
NY N June 15, 1940

Cookie Cuccurullo
NY A Oct 21, 1946

Bobby Cuellar
CLE A Aug 31, 1978

Mike Cuellar
HOU N June 15, 1965
BAL A Dec 4, 1968

Leon Culberson
WAS A Dec 10, 1947
NY A May 13, 1948

Jack Cullen
LA N Apr 3, 1967

Tim Cullen
CHI A Feb 13, 1968
WAS A Aug 2, 1968

Roy Cullenbine
STL A May 27, 1940
WAS A June 7, 1942
NY A Aug 31, 1942
CLE A Dec 17, 1942
DET A Apr 27, 1945

Dick Culler
CHI N Mar 1, 1948

Nick Cullop
WAS A Aug 27, 1926
STL N Dec 2, 1931

Nick Cullop
NY A Dec 23, 1915
STL A Jan 22, 1918

Wil Culmer
CLE A Sept 12, 1982

Ray Culp
CHI N Dec 7, 1966
BOS A Nov 30, 1967

George Culver
CIN N Nov 21, 1967
STL N Nov 5, 1969
HOU N June 13, 1970
LA N Mar 26, 1973
PHI N Aug 10, 1973

John Cumberland
SF N July 20, 1970
STL N June 16, 1972
MIN A Nov 29, 1972

Jack Cummings
BOS N July 14, 1929

Bert Cunningham
CHI N Jan 1900

Bill Cunningham
BOS N Nov 12, 1923

Bruce Cunningham
BOS N Nov 7, 1928

Joe Cunningham
CHI A Nov 27, 1961
WAS A July 13, 1964

Nig Cuppy
BOS N Jan 1900

Clarence Currie
STL N Aug 1902
CHI N July 1903

Tony Curry
CLE A Mar 20, 1962
HOU N July 19, 1966

Cliff Curtis
CHI N June 10, 1911
PHI N Aug 1911
BKN N May 1912

Jack Curtis
MIL N Apr 30, 1962
CLE A Nov 27, 1962

John Curtis
STL N Dec 7, 1973
SF N Oct 20, 1976
SD N Nov 26, 1979
CAL A Aug 31, 1982

Jack Cusick
BOS N Oct 11, 1951

George Cutshaw
PIT N Jan 9, 1918
DET A Dec 29, 1921

Kiki Cuyler
CHI N Nov 28, 1927

Mike Cvengros
CHI N Dec 1927

John D'Acquisto
STL N Oct 20, 1976
SD N May 17, 1977
MON N Aug 11, 1980
CAL A Nov 3, 1980

Paul Dade
SD N June 14, 1979

Bill Dahlen
BKN N Dec 12, 1903
BOS N Oct 7, 1907

Babe Dahlgren
NY A Feb 17, 1937
BOS N Feb 25, 1941
CHI N June 15, 1941
STL A May 13, 1942
BKN N May 19, 1942
PHI N Mar 9, 1943
PIT N Dec 30, 1943
STL A Apr 23, 1946

Bill Dailey
MIN A Apr 8, 1963

Bruce Dal Canton
KC A Dec 2, 1970
ATL N June 30, 1975

Buddy Daley
CHI A Apr 1, 1958
KC A Apr 17, 1958
CLE A Sept 5, 1964

Pete Daley
KC A Dec 3, 1959

Tom Daley
NY A June 10, 1914

Clay Dalrymple
BAL A Jan 20, 1969

Jack Dalton
DET A Feb 10, 1916

Tom Daly
CLE A Dec 1915

Tom Daly
CIN N June 1903

Bennie Daniels
WAS A Dec 16, 1960

Bert Daniels
CIN N Oct 1913

Pat Darcy
CIN N Feb 18, 1974
STL N Mar 29, 1977

Alvin Dark
NY N Dec 14, 1949
STL N June 14, 1956
CHI N May 20, 1958
PHI N Jan 11, 1960
MIL N June 23, 1960
SF N Oct 31, 1960

Ron Darling
NY N Apr 1, 1982

Bobby Darwin
MIN A Oct 22, 1971
MIL A June 14, 1975
BOS A June 3, 1976
CHI N May 28, 1977

Jake Daubert
CIN N Feb 1, 1919

Vic Davalillo
CAL A June 15, 1968
STL N May 30, 1969
PIT N Jan 29, 1971
OAK A Aug 1, 1973

Jerry Davanon
STL N May 22, 1969
BAL A Nov 30, 1970
CAL A June 10, 1972
STL N Nov 23, 1976

Mike Davey
SEA A Feb 23, 1979

Ted Davidson
ATL N June 11, 1968

Bill Davis
SD N Oct 21, 1968
STL N May 22, 1969

Brock Davis
MIL A Dec 3, 1971
CLE A Feb 25, 1975

Curt Davis
CHI N May 21, 1936
STL N Apr 16, 1938
BKN N June 12, 1940

Dick Davis
PHI N Mar 1, 1981
TOR A June 15, 1982

Dixie Davis
STL N Jan 21, 1919

George Davis
BOS N Dec 1912

Jacke Davis
LA A Dec 11, 1962
SF N Mar 29, 1963
STL N July 29, 1963

Jim Davis
STL N Dec 11, 1956
NY N June 4, 1957

Kiddo Davis
NY N Dec 12, 1932
STL N Feb 1934
PHI N June 15, 1934
NY N Dec 13, 1934
CIN N Aug 4, 1937

Lefty Davis
PIT N May 1901

Mark Davis
SF N Dec 14, 1982

Peaches Davis
PHI N Aug 19, 1939

Ron Davis
STL N June 15, 1968
SD N Dec 3, 1968
PIT N Mar 28, 1969

Ron Davis
NY A June 10, 1978
MIN A Apr 10, 1982

Spud Davis
PHI N May 11, 1928
STL N Nov 15, 1933
CIN N Dec 2, 1936
PHI N June 13, 1938
PIT N Oct 27, 1939

Tommy Davis
NY N Nov 29, 1966
CHI A Dec 15, 1967
HOU N Aug 30, 1969
OAK A June 22, 1970
CHI N Sept 16, 1970
BAL A Aug 18, 1972
KC A Sept 20, 1976

Willie Davis
MON N Dec 5, 1973
TEX A Dec 5, 1974
STL N June 4, 1975
SD N Oct 20, 1975

Bill Dawley
HOU N Mar 31, 1983

Boots Day
CHI N Dec 4, 1969
MON N May 12, 1970

Charlie Deal
BOS N June 1913
STL A Feb 10, 1916
CHI N June 2, 1916

Chubby Dean
CLE A Aug 9, 1941

Dizzy Dean
CHI N Apr 16, 1938

Paul Dean
STL N May 14, 1940
WAS A Feb 1, 1943

Tommy Dean
SD N Apr 17, 1969

Wayland Dean
PHI N Dec 30, 1925
CHI N June 14, 1927

Denny DeBarr
CHI N June 26, 1978

Art Decatur
PHI N May 1, 1925

Doug DeCinces
CAL A Jan 28, 1982

Joe Decker
MIN A Nov 30, 1972

Marty Decker
SD N Aug 31, 1983

Charlie Dees
SF N Mar 29, 1963

Tony DeFate
DET A Sept 1917

Ivan DeJesus
CHI N Jan 11, 1977
PHI N Jan 27, 1982

Frank Delahanty
NY A Nov 1907

Jim Delahanty
NY N Feb 1902
CIN N Mar 1906
WAS A June 11, 1907
STL A Sept 1907
DET A Aug 13, 1909

Mike de la Hoz
MIL N Apr 1, 1964

Luis DeLeon
SD N Dec 10, 1981

Luis Delgado
CHI N Mar 20, 1979

Bobby Del Greco
STL N May 17, 1956
CHI N Apr 20, 1957
NY A Sept 10, 1957
KC A July 2, 1961

Eddie Delker
PHI N May 30, 1932
STL N Nov 15, 1933

Garton Del Savio
PHI N Apr 2, 1943

Jim Delsing
NY A Dec 14, 1948
STL A June 15, 1950
DET A Aug 14, 1952
CHI A May 15, 1956
WAS A Dec 6, 1958

Joe DeMaestri
STL A Nov 27, 1951
CHI A Oct 16, 1952
PHI A Jan 27, 1953
NY A Dec 11, 1959

Al Demaree
PHI N Jan 1915
CHI N Apr 2, 1917
NY N Aug 15, 1917
BOS N Feb 1919

Frank Demaree
NY N Dec 6, 1938
BOS N July 21, 1941
STL N Jan 1943

Larry Demery
TOR A Mar 27, 1978

Don Demeter
PHI N May 4, 1961
DET A Dec 4, 1963
BOS A June 14, 1966
CLE A June 4, 1967

Steve Demeter
CLE A Apr 12, 1960

Ray Demmitt
CHI A Apr 1914

Gene DeMontreville
BKN N Jan 1900
BOS N Feb 1901

Rick Dempsey
NY A Oct 27, 1972
BAL A June 15, 1976

Bill Denehy
WAS A Nov 27, 1967
DET A Mar 30, 1971

Don Dennis
CHI A Dec 14, 1966

John Denny
CLE A Dec 7, 1979
PHI N Sept 12, 1982

Bucky Dent
NY A Apr 5, 1977
TEX A Aug 8, 1982

Sam Dente
STL A Nov 18, 1947
WAS A Oct 4, 1948
CHI A Nov 27, 1951

Bob Dernier
CHI N Mar 26, 1984

Claud Derrick
NY A Nov 1912
CHI N July 20, 1914

Paul Derringer
CIN N May 7, 1933
CHI N Jan 27, 1943

Gene Desautels
CLE A Dec 12, 1940

Jimmie DeShong
WAS A Jan 17, 1936
NY A June 20, 1939

Bob Detherage
STL N June 15, 1976
MON N Nov 23, 1976

Tom Dettore
CHI N Apr 1, 1974

Adrian Devine
TEX A Dec 9, 1976
ATL N Dec 8, 1977
TEX A Dec 6, 1979

Art Devlin
BOS N Dec 1911

Josh Devore
CIN N May 22, 1913
PHI N June 5, 1913
BOS N June 1914

Al DeVormer
BOS A Jan 3, 1923

Charlie Dexter
CHI N Jan 1900
BOS N July 1902

Bo Diaz
PHI N Nov 20, 1981

Carlos Diaz
ATL N Mar 7, 1981
NY N Sept 10, 1982
LA N Dec 8, 1983

Mike Diaz
PHI N Mar 26, 1984

Leo Dickerman
STL N June 13, 1924

Johnny Dickshot
BOS N Dec 16, 1938

Jim Dickson
CIN N Jan 20, 1964

Murry Dickson
PIT N Jan 29, 1949
PHI N Jan 13, 1954
STL N May 11, 1956
NY A Aug 22, 1958
KC A May 9, 1959

Bob Didier
DET A May 14, 1973
BOS A Mar 26, 1974

Chuck Diering
NY N Dec 11, 1951

Larry Dierker
STL N Nov 23, 1976

Bill Dietrich
WAS A July 1, 1936
CHI A July 20, 1936

Dick Dietz
LA N Apr 14, 1972
ATL N Mar 27, 1973

Dutch Dietz
PIT N Aug 1940
PHI N June 15, 1943

Don Dillard
MIL N Nov 27, 1962

Steve Dillard
DET A Jan 30, 1978
CHI N Mar 20, 1979

Pickles Dillhoefer
PHI N Dec 11, 1917
STL N Jan 21, 1919

Bob Dillinger
PHI A Dec 13, 1949
PIT N July 20, 1950
CHI A May 16, 1951

Bill Dillman
STL N Dec 5, 1969

Pop Dillon
DET A Jan 1901

Miguel Dilone
OAK A Apr 4, 1978
CHI N July 4, 1979
CLE A May 7, 1980
CHI A Aug 25, 1983
PIT N Sept 7, 1983
MON N Jan 19, 1984

Vince DiMaggio
CIN N Aug 10, 1938
PIT N May 8, 1940
PHI N Mar 31, 1945
NY N May 1, 1946

Kerry Dineen
PHI N Mar 26, 1977

Bill Dinneen
BOS N Jan 10, 1900
STL A June 22, 1907

Frank DiPino
HOU N Aug 30, 1982

Art Ditmar
NY A Feb 19, 1957

Jack Dittmer
DET A Feb 12, 1957

Sonny Dixon
CHI A June 11, 1954
PHI A June 11, 1954
NY A May 11, 1955

Bill Doak
BKN N June 13, 1924

Dan Dobbek
CIN N Jan 30, 1962

John Dobbs
CHI N July 1902
BKN N May 1903

Joe Dobson
BOS A Dec 12, 1940
CHI A Dec 10, 1950

Pat Dobson
SD N Dec 4, 1969
BAL A Dec 1, 1970
ATL N Dec 30, 1972
NY A June 7, 1973
CLE A Nov 22, 1975

Larry Doby
CHI A Oct 25, 1955
BAL A Dec 3, 1957
CLE A Apr 1, 1958
DET A Mar 21, 1959
CHI A May 13, 1959

John Dodge
CIN N June 5, 1913

Ed Doheny
PIT N June 1901

Cozy Dolan
PHI N May 1912
PIT N Aug 20, 1913
STL N Dec 12, 1913

Cozy Dolan
BKN N June 1901
CIN N May 1903
BOS N June 6, 1905

Joe Dolan
PHI A May 1901

Jiggs Donahue
WAS A Aug 1908
WAS A May 16, 1909

Pat Donahue
PHI A May 1910
CLE A Sept 1910

Red Donahue
CLE A June 1903
DET A Feb 1906

John Donaldson
SEA A June 14, 1969
OAK A May 18, 1970
DET A May 22, 1971

Mike Donlin
NY N July 3, 1904
BOS N Aug 1, 1911
PIT N Feb 1912
PHI N Dec 1912

Blix Donnelly
PHI N July 6, 1946
BOS N Apr 16, 1951

Jim Donohue
LA N June 15, 1960
LA A June 7, 1961
MIN A May 29, 1962

Pete Donohue
NY N May 27, 1930

Dick Donovan
CLE A Oct 5, 1961

Mike Donovan
NY A Jan 1908

Patsy Donovan
STL N Jan 1900

Red Dooin
CIN N Nov 1914
NY N July 6, 1915

Mickey Doolan
CHI N Feb 10, 1916
NY N Aug 28, 1916

Tom Doran
DET A May 18, 1905

Harry Dorish
STL A May 9, 1950
BAL A June 6, 1955
BOS A June 25, 1956

Gus Dorner
BOS N May 13, 1906

Jim Dorsey
BOS A Jan 23, 1981

Jack Doscher
BKN N June 1903

Rich Dotson
CHI A Dec 5, 1977

Dutch Dotterer
KC A Oct 15, 1960

Patsy Dougherty
NY A June 18, 1904
CHI A June 6, 1906

Phil Douglas
BKN N June 13, 1915
CHI N Sept 8, 1915
NY N July 25, 1919

Whammy Douglas
CIN N Jan 30, 1959

Taylor Douthit
CIN N June 15, 1931
CHI N Apr 29, 1933

Snooks Dowd
PHI A Apr 1919

Dave Dowling
CLE A May 1901
CHI N May 11, 1965
STL N Apr 22, 1968

Tom Downey
CHI N Aug 1912

Al Downing
OAK A Dec 5, 1969
MIL A June 11, 1970
LA N Feb 10, 1971

Brian Downing
CAL A Dec 5, 1977

Red Downs
CHI N May 1912

Brian Doyle
NY A Feb 17, 1977
OAK A Nov 3, 1980

Carl Doyle
STL N June 12, 1940

Conny Doyle
PIT N Jan 1900

Denny Doyle
CAL A Aug 14, 1973
BOS A June 14, 1975

Jack Doyle
CHI N Feb 1901
NY N Feb 1902
BKN N Jan 30, 1903
PHI N Apr 30, 1904

Larry Doyle
CHI N Aug 28, 1916
BOS N Jan 4, 1918
NY N Jan 8, 1918

Paul Doyle
CAL A Nov 27, 1969
SD N Aug 25, 1970

Slow Joe Doyle
CIN N May 1910

Moe Drabowsky
MIL N Mar 31, 1961
KC A Aug 13, 1962
BAL A June 15, 1970
STL N Nov 30, 1970

Dick Drago
BOS A Oct 24, 1973
CAL A Mar 3, 1976
BAL A June 13, 1977
SEA A Apr 8, 1981

Solly Drake
PHI N June 9, 1959

Clem Dreisewerd
STL A Nov 18, 1947

Rob Dressler
STL N July 18, 1978
SEA A June 7, 1979

Karl Drews
STL A Aug 9, 1948
CIN N June 15, 1954

Lew Drill
WAS A Sept 1902
DET A Aug 10, 1904

Walt Dropo
DET A June 3, 1952
CHI A Dec 6, 1954
CIN N June 24, 1958
BAL A June 23, 1959

Carl Druhot
STL N July 25, 1906

Keith Drumright
KC A Apr 27, 1979
OAK A Dec 11, 1980

Monk Dubiel
CHI N Dec 14, 1948
BOS N Dec 20, 1952

Jim Duckworth
KC A June 23, 1966
WAS A July 30, 1966

Clise Dudley
PHI N Oct 14, 1930

Jim Duffalo
CIN N May 4, 1965

Frank Duffy
SF N May 29, 1971
CLE A Nov 29, 1971
BOS A Mar 24, 1978

Joe Dugan
BOS A Jan 10, 1922
WAS A Jan 10, 1922
NY A July 23, 1922
BOS N Dec 29, 1928

Gus Dugas
NY N Dec 12, 1932
PHI N Dec 12, 1932

Oscar Dugey
PHI N Feb 14, 1915

Bill Duggleby
PIT N July 15, 1907

Tom Dukes
HOU N Oct 13, 1966
BAL A Dec 1, 1970

George Dumont
BOS A Jan 17, 1919

Dave Duncan
CLE A Mar 24, 1973
BAL A Feb 25, 1975
CHI A Nov 18, 1976

Pat Duncan
WAS A Oct 1924

Taylor Duncan
BAL A Dec 30, 1972
STL N Sept 7, 1977

Davey Dunkle
WAS A June 1903

Jack Dunn
PHI N June 1900

Steve Dunning
TEX A May 10, 1973
CHI A Feb 25, 1975
CAL A Dec 11, 1975
STL N Nov 6, 1976
OAK A Aug 12, 1977

Kid Durbin
PIT N May 1909

Ryne Duren
KC A Oct 11, 1956
NY A June 15, 1957
LA A May 8, 1961
PHI N Mar 14, 1963
CIN N May 13, 1964

Don Durham
TEX A July 16, 1973

Ed Durham
CHI A Dec 15, 1932

Leon Durham
CHI N Dec 9, 1980

Leo Durocher
CIN N Feb 2, 1930
STL N May 7, 1933
BKN N Oct 4, 1937

Cedric Durst
NY A Feb 8, 1927
BOS A May 6, 1930

Erv Dusak
PIT N May 17, 1951

Jim Dwyer
MON N July 25, 1975
NY N July 21, 1976
CHI N Dec 8, 1976
SF N Oct 25, 1977
BOS A Mar 15, 1979
BAL A Dec 23, 1980

Jerry Dybzinski
CHI A Apr 1, 1983

Jim Dyck
CLE A Apr 17, 1954
BAL A July 16, 1955
CIN N May 11, 1956

Duffy Dyer
PIT N Oct 22, 1974
DET A Mar 15, 1980

Jimmy Dykes
CHI A Sept 28, 1932
CLE A Aug 10, 1960

Arnie Earley
MIL N Dec 15, 1965

Jake Early
WAS A Dec 16, 1946
WAS A Mar 26, 1948

George Earnshaw
CHI A Dec 12, 1933
BKN N May 16, 1934
STL N July 1936

Mike Easler
STL N Sept 30, 1975
CAL A Sept 3, 1976
PIT N Apr 4, 1977
BOS A Oct 27, 1978
PIT N Mar 15, 1979
BOS A Dec 6, 1983

Mal Eason
BOS N Apr 1902

Jamie Easterly
MON N Oct 19, 1979
MIL A Sept 22, 1980
CLE A June 6, 1983

Ted Easterly
CHI A Jan 1912

Rawley Eastwick
STL N June 15, 1977
NY A Dec 12, 1977
PHI N June 10, 1978

Craig Eaton
CAL A Dec 6, 1979

Eddie Eayrs
BKN N July 1921

Don Eddy
SD N July 9, 1972

Joe Edelen
CIN N Sept 19, 1981

Mike Eden
ATL N June 13, 1976

Butch Edge
PIT N Mar 21, 1982

Bill Edgerton
CLE A Feb 15, 1965
KC A Apr 9, 1965

Bruce Edwards
CHI N June 15, 1951

Dave Edwards
SD N Dec 8, 1980

Doc Edwards
KC A May 25, 1963
NY A May 3, 1965
CLE A Jan 14, 1966
HOU N Jan 4, 1967

Hank Edwards
BKN N Oct 10, 1950
CIN N July 21, 1951
CHI A Sept 1, 1952
STL A Oct 16, 1952

Jim Joe Edwards
CHI A July 1925

Johnny Edwards
STL N Feb 8, 1968
HOU N Oct 11, 1968

Mike Edwards
OAK A Apr 4, 1978

Ben Egan
CLE A Aug 20, 1914

Dick Egan
CIN N Dec 1913
BKN N Apr 1914
BOS N May 1, 1915

Dick Egan
LA N May 27, 1966

Tom Egan
CHI A Nov 30, 1970

Howard Ehmke
DET A Feb 10, 1916
BOS A Oct 30, 1922
PHI A June 15, 1926

Rube Ehrhardt
CIN N Apr 18, 1929

Juan Eichelberger
CLE A Nov 18, 1982

Dave Eilers
NY N Aug 18, 1965

Harry Eisenstat
CLE A June 14, 1939

Kid Elberfeld
NY A June 10, 1903
WAS A Dec 16, 1909

Lee Elia
NY A Apr 19, 1969

Frank Ellerbe
STL A May 31, 1921
CLE A June 3, 1924

Bruce Ellingsen
CLE A Apr 3, 1974

Larry Elliot
KC A May 10, 1967

Bob Elliott
BOS N Sept 30, 1946
NY N Apr 8, 1952
CHI A June 13, 1953

Claude Elliott
NY N Aug 1904

Jumbo Elliott
PHI N Oct 14, 1930
BOS N May 26, 1934

Dock Ellis
NY A Dec 11, 1975
OAK A Apr 27, 1977
TEX A June 15, 1977
NY N June 15, 1979
PIT N Sept 21, 1979

Jim Ellis
LA N Apr 23, 1968
MIL A Oct 20, 1970

John Ellis
CLE A Nov 27, 1972
TEX A Dec 9, 1975

Sammy Ellis
CAL A Nov 29, 1967
CHI A Jan 20, 1969
CLE A June 13, 1969

Dick Ellsworth
PHI N Dec 7, 1966
BOS A Dec 15, 1967
CLE A Apr 19, 1969
MIL A Aug 7, 1970

Don Elston
BKN N Dec 9, 1955
BKN N May 23, 1957

Red Embree
NY A Oct 10, 1947
STL A Dec 13, 1948

Clyde Engle
BOS A May 1910
CLE A Feb 10, 1916

Dave Engle
MIN A Feb 3, 1979

Gil English
BOS N June 1937
CIN N Aug 10, 1938

Woody English
BKN N Dec 5, 1936
CIN N July 8, 1938

Del Ennis
STL N Nov 19, 1956
CIN N Oct 3, 1958
CHI A May 1, 1959

Johnny Enzmann
PHI N Dec 1919

Mike Epstein
WAS A May 29, 1967
OAK A May 8, 1971
TEX A Nov 30, 1972
CAL A May 20, 1973

Eddie Erautt
STL N May 23, 1953

Eric Erickson
WAS A July 5, 1919

Paul Erickson
PHI N May 20, 1948
NY N July 1, 1948
PIT N July 30, 1948

Roger Erickson
NY A May 12, 1982
KC A Dec 7, 1983

Tex Erwin
CIN N June 1914

Jimmy Esmond
PHI A Mar 21, 1943

Juan Espino
SF N Dec 11, 1981
CLE A Apr 1, 1984

Nino Espinosa
PHI N Mar 27, 1979

Cecil Espy
LA N Mar 30, 1982

Chuck Essegian
STL N Dec 3, 1958
LA N June 15, 1959
CLE A May 3, 1961
KC A Feb 27, 1963

Jim Essian
ATL N May 7, 1975
CHI A May 15, 1975
OAK A Mar 30, 1978
CHI A Nov 20, 1980
SEA A Dec 11, 1981
CLE A Jan 21, 1983
OAK A Dec 6, 1983

Francisco Estrada
CAL A Dec 10, 1971
BAL A June 12, 1972
CHI N Oct 27, 1972

Andy Etchebarren
CAL A June 15, 1975
MIL A Dec 15, 1977

Bobby Etheridge
SD N Dec 5, 1969

Nick Etten
NY A Jan 22, 1943

Al Evans
BOS A Feb 5, 1951

Barry Evans
NY A Feb 22, 1982

Darrell Evans
SF N June 13, 1976
DET A Dec 19, 1983

Joe Evans
WAS A Jan 8, 1923
STL A Jan 1924

LeRoy Evans
BKN N July 1902
STL A July 1903

Leon Everitt
SD N Apr 17, 1969

Hoot Evers
BOS A June 3, 1952
NY N May 18, 1954
DET A July 29, 1954
BAL A Jan 3, 1955
CLE A July 13, 1955
BAL A May 13, 1956

Johnny Evers
BOS N Feb 1914
PHI N July 12, 1917

Bob Ewing
PHI N Jan 1910

Homer Ezzell
BOS A Dec 1923
DET A Dec 9, 1925

Roy Face
DET A Aug 31, 1968

Bill Fahey
SD N Oct 25, 1978
DET A Mar 24, 1981

Ferris Fain
CHI A Jan 27, 1953
DET A Dec 6, 1954

Ron Fairly
MON N June 11, 1969
STL N Dec 6, 1974
OAK A Sept 14, 1976
TOR A Feb 24, 1977
CAL A Dec 8, 1977

Pete Falcone
STL N Dec 8, 1975
NY N Dec 5, 1978
ATL N Jan 25, 1983

Bibb Falk
CLE A Feb 28, 1929

Cy Falkenberg
CLE A Aug 1908

Frank Fanovich
PHI A Dec 17, 1953

Carmen Fanzone
CHI N Dec 3, 1970

Bob Farley
DET A June 25, 1962

Ed Farmer
DET A June 15, 1973
NY A Mar 19, 1974
PHI N Mar 21, 1974
TEX A Dec 15, 1978
CHI A June 15, 1979
PHI N Jan 28, 1982

Dick Farrell
LA N May 4, 1961
PHI N May 8, 1967

Doc Farrell
BOS N June 12, 1927
NY N June 14, 1929
STL N Apr 10, 1930
CHI N June 29, 1930

Bill Faul
CHI N Mar 27, 1965

Ernie Fazio
KC A June 4, 1965

Gus Felix
BKN N Oct 7, 1925

Bobby Fenwick
STL N Nov 28, 1972
SD N Nov 7, 1973

Alex Ferguson
BOS A Feb 24, 1922
NY A May 5, 1925
WAS A Aug 19, 1925
PHI N Oct 1926
BKN N May 14, 1929

George Ferguson
BOS N Oct 7, 1907

Joe Ferguson
STL N June 15, 1976
MON N Nov 23, 1976
LA N July 1, 1978

Chico Fernandez
PHI N Apr 5, 1957
DET A Dec 5, 1959
MIL N May 8, 1963
NY N May 8, 1963
CHI A Apr 23, 1964

Frank Fernandez
OAK A Dec 5, 1969
WAS A May 8, 1971
WAS A June 23, 1971
CHI N Aug 31, 1971

Sid Fernandez
NY N Dec 8, 1983

Al Ferrara
CIN N May 13, 1971

Don Ferrarese
BAL A Dec 6, 1954
CLE A Apr 1, 1958
CHI A Dec 6, 1959
STL N Apr 28, 1962

Mike Ferraro
BAL A Apr 30, 1969
MIN A Mar 27, 1973

Rick Ferrell
BOS A May 9, 1933
WAS A June 11, 1937
STL A May 15, 1940
WAS A Mar 1, 1944

Wes Ferrell
BOS A May 25, 1934
WAS A June 11, 1937

Sergio Ferrer
PHI N Oct 24, 1975
NY A Mar 26, 1977
NY N Dec 9, 1977

Tom Ferrick
CLE A Sept 22, 1941
STL A June 24, 1946
WAS A Jan 14, 1947
STL A Oct 4, 1948
NY A June 15, 1950
WAS A June 15, 1951

Hobe Ferris
STL A Oct 1907
STL A Feb 1908

Lou Fette
BKN N July 1940

Chick Fewster
BOS A July 23, 1922
CLE A Jan 7, 1924
BKN N Jan 1926

Neil Fiala
CIN N Sept 19, 1981

Dan Fife
MIN A Mar 27, 1973

Ed Figueroa
NY A Dec 11, 1975
TEX A July 28, 1980

Jesus Figueroa
SF N Dec 12, 1980

Tom Filer
CHI N Apr 27, 1981

Pete Filson
MIN A May 12, 1982

Jack Fimple
LA N Dec 9, 1981

Steve Finch
SEA A Dec 12, 1980

Rollie Fingers
SD N Dec 14, 1976
STL N Dec 8, 1980
MIL A Dec 12, 1980

Jim Finigan
PHI A Dec 16, 1953
DET A Dec 5, 1956
SF N Jan 28, 1958
BAL A Oct 14, 1958

Mickey Finn
PHI N Dec 15, 1932

Happy Finneran
NY A May 1918

Lou Finney
BOS A May 8, 1939
STL A July 27, 1945

Mike Fiore
BOS A May 28, 1970
STL N Mar 20, 1972
SD N June 20, 1972

Steve Fireovid
PHI N Aug 31, 1983

Bill Fischer
CHI N Feb 10, 1916
PIT N July 29, 1916

Bill Fischer
DET A June 15, 1958
WAS A Sept 11, 1958
DET A July 22, 1960
KC A Aug 2, 1961

Carl Fischer
STL A June 9, 1932
WAS A Dec 13, 1932
DET A Dec 14, 1932
CHI A May 17, 1934
WAS A May 1937

Hank Fischer
CIN N June 15, 1966
BOS A Aug 15, 1966

Mike Fischlin
HOU N June 15, 1977
CLE A Apr 3, 1981

Bob Fisher
CIN N Jan 1916

Chauncey Fisher
STL N May 1901

Eddie Fisher
CHI A Nov 30, 1961
BAL A June 12, 1966
CLE A Nov 28, 1967
CAL A Oct 8, 1968
CHI A Aug 17, 1972
STL N Aug 29, 1973

Gus Fisher
NY A Mar 1912

Jack Fisher
SF N Dec 15, 1962
NY N Oct 10, 1963
CHI A Dec 15, 1967
CIN N Dec 5, 1968
CAL A Jan 14, 1970

Ray Fisher
CIN N Mar 15, 1919

Showboat Fisher
STL N Apr 10, 1930

Tom Fisher
SEA A Apr 30, 1969

Carlton Fisk
CHI A Mar 9, 1981

Ed Fitz Gerald
WAS A May 13, 1953
CLE A May 25, 1959

Al Fitzmorris
CLE A Nov 5, 1976

Freddie Fitzsimmons
BKN N June 11, 1937

Max Flack
CHI N Feb 10, 1916
STL N May 30, 1922

Ira Flagstead
BOS A Apr 20, 1923
PIT N July 12, 1929

Patsy Flaherty
PIT N Jan 1900
BOS N Dec 1906

John Flannery
CHI A June 15, 1977

Les Fleming
PIT N Dec 4, 1947

Art Fletcher
PHI N June 8, 1920

Elbie Fletcher
PIT N June 15, 1939
CLE A Dec 4, 1947

Scott Fletcher
CHI A Jan 25, 1983

Elmer Flick
CLE A May 16, 1902

John Flinn
MIL A Dec 6, 1979

Curt Flood
STL N Dec 5, 1957
PHI N Oct 7, 1969
WAS A Nov 3, 1970

Gil Flores
NY N July 28, 1978

Ben Flowers
STL N Sept 8, 1955
PHI N May 11, 1956
KC A Oct 15, 1956

Jake Flowers
BKN N Feb 28, 1927
STL N June 15, 1931
BKN N Feb 1933

Bobby Floyd
KC A June 15, 1970

Doug Flynn
NY N June 15, 1977
TEX A Dec 11, 1981
MON N Aug 2, 1982

John Flynn
WAS A Feb 1912

Lee Fohl
CIN N Oct 1903

Hank Foiles
CLE A May 3, 1953
PIT N May 15, 1956
KC A Dec 15, 1959
PIT N June 1, 1960
CLE A June 2, 1960
DET A July 26, 1960
CIN N Apr 20, 1962

Tim Foli
MON N Apr 5, 1972
SF N Apr 27, 1977
NY N Dec 7, 1977
PIT N Apr 19, 1979
CAL A Dec 11, 1981
NY A Dec 7, 1983

Rich Folkers
STL N Oct 18, 1971
SD N Nov 18, 1974
MIL A Mar 23, 1977
DET A Dec 9, 1977

Dee Fondy
CHI N Oct 10, 1950
PIT N May 1, 1957
CIN N Dec 28, 1957

Lew Fonseca
PHI N Mar 30, 1925
CHI A May 17, 1931

Ray Fontenot
NY A Aug 1, 1979

Jim Foor
PIT N Nov 30, 1972
KC A Mar 28, 1974

Barry Foote
PHI N June 15, 1977
CHI N Feb 23, 1979
NY A Apr 27, 1981

Dan Ford
MIN A Oct 23, 1974
CAL A Dec 4, 1978
BAL A Jan 28, 1982

Hod Ford
PHI N Dec 15, 1923
BKN N May 16, 1925
STL N Jan 26, 1932

Ted Ford
TEX A Apr 3, 1972
CLE A May 10, 1973

Mike Fornieles
CHI A Dec 10, 1952
BAL A May 21, 1956
BOS A June 14, 1957
MIN A June 14, 1963

Ken Forsch
CAL A Apr 1, 1981

Terry Forster
PIT N Dec 10, 1976
LA N Nov 22, 1977
ATL N Dec 10, 1982

Larry Foss
NY N Sept 6, 1962
MIL N May 8, 1963

Ray Fosse
OAK A Mar 24, 1973
CLE A Dec 9, 1975
SEA A Sept 9, 1977

Alan Foster
CLE A Dec 11, 1970
CAL A Oct 5, 1971
STL N Apr 5, 1973
SD N Nov 18, 1974

Eddie Foster
BOS A Jan 20, 1920
STL A Aug 15, 1922

George Foster
CIN N May 29, 1971
NY N Feb 10, 1982

Len Foster
BOS A Mar 29, 1978

Pop Foster
CHI A Sept 1901

Roy Foster
CLE A Apr 4, 1970
TEX A Dec 2, 1971
CLE A Apr 3, 1972

Rube Foster
CIN N Apr 1918

Bob Fothergill
CHI A July 18, 1930
BOS A Dec 15, 1932

Steve Foucault
DET A Apr 12, 1977
KC A Aug 16, 1978

Jack Fournier
CHI A May 8, 1912
BKN N Feb 15, 1923
BOS N Nov 5, 1926

Howie Fox
PHI N Dec 10, 1951

Nellie Fox
CHI A Oct 19, 1949
HOU N Dec 10, 1963

Pete Fox
BOS A Dec 12, 1940

Terry Fox
DET A Dec 7, 1960
PHI N May 10, 1966

Bill Foxen
CHI N July 1910

Jimmie Foxx
BOS A Dec 10, 1935
CHI N June 1, 1942

Joe Foy
NY N Dec 3, 1969

Paul Foytack
LA A June 15, 1963

Ken Frailing
CHI N Dec 11, 1973

Ray Francis
DET A Nov 24, 1922
BOS A May 5, 1925

Julio Franco
CLE A Dec 9, 1982

Tito Francona
CHI A Dec 3, 1957
DET A June 15, 1958
CLE A Mar 21, 1959
STL N Dec 15, 1964
PHI N Apr 10, 1967
ATL N June 12, 1967
OAK A Aug 22, 1969
MIL A June 11, 1970

Fred Frankhouse
BOS N June 16, 1930
BKN N Feb 6, 1936
BKN N Feb 3, 1939

Herman Franks
BKN N Feb 6, 1940

Chick Fraser
BOS N Dec 20, 1904
CIN N Mar 1906
CIN N Oct 1906

George Frazier
STL N Dec 8, 1977
NY A June 7, 1981

Joe Frazier
STL A Nov 20, 1947
CIN N May 16, 1956

Vic Frazier
DET A June 2, 1933

Roger Freed
PHI N Dec 16, 1970
CLE A Nov 30, 1972

Hersh Freeman
CIN N May 10, 1955
CHI N May 8, 1958

Jimmy Freeman
BAL A Apr 17, 1975
NY A June 15, 1976

Mark Freeman
KC A Apr 8, 1959
CHI N May 19, 1960

Gene Freese
STL N June 15, 1958
PHI N Sept 29, 1958
CHI A Dec 9, 1959
CIN N Dec 15, 1960
PIT N Nov 26, 1963
CHI A Aug 25, 1965
HOU N July 20, 1966

George Freese
DET A Apr 7, 1953
PIT N June 4, 1953

Jim Fregosi
NY N Dec 10, 1971
TEX A July 11, 1973
PIT N June 15, 1977

Howard Freigau
CHI N May 23, 1925
BKN N Dec 1927
BOS N June 23, 1928

Dave Freisleben
CLE A June 22, 1978
TOR A Nov 3, 1978

Tony Freitas
CIN N Dec 1933

Charlie French
CHI A May 1910

Larry French
CHI N Nov 22, 1934
BKN N Aug 20, 1941

Benny Frey
STL N Apr 11, 1932
CIN N May 10, 1932

Lonny Frey
CHI N Dec 5, 1936
CIN N Feb 4, 1938
CHI N Apr 16, 1947
NY A June 25, 1947

Pepe Frias
ATL N Mar 31, 1979
TEX A Dec 6, 1979
TEX A Sept 13, 1980

Barney Friberg
PHI N June 15, 1925
BOS A Jan 7, 1932
BOS A Jan 7, 1933

Jim Fridley
NY A Dec 1, 1954

Bob Friend
NY A Dec 10, 1965
NY N June 15, 1966

Owen Friend
DET A Dec 4, 1952
CLE A June 15, 1953

John Frill
CIN N Jan 1912

Charlie Frisbee
NY N Feb 17, 1900

Frankie Frisch
STL N Dec 20, 1926

Danny Frisella
ATL N Nov 2, 1972
SD N Nov 8, 1974
STL N Apr 8, 1976
MIL A June 7, 1976

Sam Frock
BOS N June 1, 1910

Art Fromme
CIN N Dec 12, 1908
NY N May 22, 1913

Dave Frost
CAL A Dec 5, 1977
KC A Feb 20, 1982

Woodie Fryman
PHI N Dec 15, 1967
DET A Aug 2, 1972
MON N Dec 4, 1974
CIN N Dec 16, 1976
CHI N Oct 31, 1977
MON N June 9, 1978

Tito Fuentes
SD N Dec 6, 1974
DET A Feb 23, 1977
MON N Jan 30, 1978

Chick Fullis
PHI N Dec 12, 1932
STL N June 15, 1934

Dave Fultz
NY A Mar 1903

Frank Funk
MIL N Nov 27, 1962

Fred Fussell
PIT N Dec 1927

Frank Gabler
BOS N June 15, 1937
CHI A May 2, 1938

Len Gabrielson
CHI N June 3, 1964
SF N May 29, 1965
CAL A Dec 14, 1966
LA N May 10, 1967

Phil Gagliano
CHI N May 29, 1970
BOS A Dec 3, 1970
CIN N Mar 27, 1973

Greg Gagne
MIN A Apr 10, 1982

Chick Gagnon
WAS A Nov 24, 1922

Joe Gaines
BAL A Dec 15, 1962
HOU N June 15, 1964

Del Gainor
BOS A June 2, 1911
BOS A June 2, 1914

Augie Galan
CIN N Dec 4, 1946

Rich Gale
SF N Dec 11, 1981
CIN N Jan 5, 1983

Denny Galehouse
BOS A Dec 15, 1938
STL A Nov 20, 1940
BOS A June 20, 1947

Alan Gallagher
CAL A Apr 14, 1973

Bob Gallagher
NY N Oct 29, 1974

Joe Gallagher
STL A June 13, 1939
BKN N May 27, 1940

Bert Gallia
STL A Dec 15, 1917
PHI N Apr 1920

Chick Galloway
DET A Dec 2, 1927
STL A Dec 2, 1927

Oscar Gamble
PHI N Nov 17, 1969
CLE A Nov 30, 1972
NY A Nov 22, 1975
CHI A Apr 5, 1977
SD N Nov 29, 1977
TEX A Oct 25, 1978
NY A Aug 1, 1979

Chick Gandil
CLE A Feb 15, 1916
CHI A Feb 25, 1917

Bob Ganley
WAS A Feb 1907
PHI A May 1909

John Ganzel
NY N Feb 1901

Joe Garagiola
PIT N June 15, 1951
CHI N June 4, 1953
NY N Sept 8, 1954

Gene Garber
KC A Oct 25, 1972
ATL N June 15, 1978

Damaso Garcia
TOR A Nov 1, 1979

Kiko Garcia
HOU N Apr 1, 1981

Pedro Garcia
DET A June 10, 1976

Billy Gardner
BAL A Apr 21, 1956
WAS A Apr 3, 1960
BOS A June 12, 1962

Larry Gardner
PHI A Jan 10, 1918
CLE A Mar 1, 1919

Rob Gardner
CHI N June 12, 1967
CLE A Mar 30, 1968
OAK A Apr 9, 1971
NY A May 26, 1971
OAK A Nov 24, 1972
MIL A May 31, 1973

Wayne Garland
CLE A Nov 19, 1976

Mike Garman
STL N Dec 7, 1973
CHI N Oct 28, 1975
LA N Jan 11, 1977
MON N May 20, 1978

Debs Garms
PIT N Mar 3, 1940

Phil Garner
PIT N Mar 15, 1977
HOU N Aug 31, 1981

Ralph Garr
CHI A Dec 12, 1975
CAL A Sept 20, 1979

Adrian Garrett
MIL N May 8, 1964
OAK A Aug 31, 1971
CAL A July 31, 1975

Greg Garrett
CIN N Dec 15, 1970

Wayne Garrett
MON N July 21, 1976
STL N July 21, 1978

Gil Garrido
ATL N May 16, 1966
PHI N Dec 4, 1973

Ford Garrison
PHI A May 7, 1944

Ned Garver
DET A Aug 14, 1952
KC A Dec 5, 1956

Steve Garvey
SD N Dec 21, 1982

Jerry Garvin
STL N Jan 18, 1983

Ned Garvin
NY A Sept 1904

Rod Gaspar
SD N Sept 1, 1970

Clarence Gaston
ATL N Nov 8, 1974
PIT N Sept 22, 1978

Milt Gaston
STL A Dec 17, 1924
WAS A Oct 19, 1927
BOS A Dec 15, 1928
CHI A Dec 2, 1931

Doc Gautreau
BOS N July 1, 1925

Dinty Gearin
BOS N June 5, 1924

Joe Gedeon
STL A Jan 22, 1918

Johnny Gee
NY N June 12, 1944

Gary Geiger
BOS A Dec 2, 1958

Dave Geisel
TOR A Dec 28, 1981

Vern Geishert
CIN N Nov 25, 1969
SF N May 29, 1971

Charley Gelbert
CIN N Dec 2, 1936
DET A July 9, 1937
BOS A Aug 30, 1940

John Gelnar
KC A Oct 18, 1968
SEA A Apr 1, 1969
DET A May 11, 1971

Joe Genewich
NY N June 15, 1928

Jim Gentile
KC A Nov 27, 1963
HOU N June 4, 1965
CLE A July 19, 1966

Gary Gentry
ATL N Nov 2, 1972

Lefty George
CLE A Dec 1911

Jug Gerard
HOU N Mar 28, 1963

Wally Gerber
BOS A Apr 25, 1928

Al Gerheauser
PHI N Jan 22, 1943
PIT N Mar 31, 1945
BKN N Dec 5, 1946

John Gerlach
CLE A Jan 10, 1940

Dick Gernert
CHI N Nov 21, 1959
DET A Aug 31, 1960

Cesar Geronimo
CIN N Nov 29, 1971
KC A Jan 21, 1981

Doc Gessler
CHI N May 8, 1906
WAS A Sept 1909

Al Gettel
CLE A Dec 20, 1946
CHI A June 2, 1948
WAS A July 12, 1949

Gus Getz
PIT N June 1918

Joe Giard
STL A Dec 17, 1924
NY A Feb 8, 1927

Joe Gibbon
SF N Oct 1, 1965
PIT N June 10, 1969

George Gibson
NY N Aug 5, 1916
NY N Jan 1917

Russ Gibson
SF N Apr 4, 1970

Jim Gideon
MIN A June 1, 1976

Paul Giel
PIT N Apr 13, 1959
KC A June 1, 1961

Bob Giggie
KC A May 11, 1960

Charlie Gilbert
CHI N May 6, 1941
PHI N June 15, 1946

Wally Gilbert
CIN N Mar 14, 1932

Bill Gilbreth
CAL A Sept 6, 1972

Frank Gilhooley
NY A Aug 25, 1913
BOS A Dec 18, 1918

George Gill
STL A May 13, 1939

Grant Gillis
BOS A Dec 15, 1928

Hal Gilson
HOU N June 15, 1968

Joe Ginsberg
CLE A June 15, 1953
BAL A Aug 17, 1956

Al Gionfriddo
BKN N May 3, 1947

Tony Giuliani
WAS A Mar 24, 1938
STL A Mar 1, 1944

Dave Giusti
STL N Oct 11, 1968
STL N Dec 3, 1968
PIT N Oct 21, 1969
OAK A Mar 15, 1977
OAK A Aug 5, 1977

Fred Gladding
HOU N Aug 17, 1967

Fred Glade
NY A Feb 1908

Tommy Glaviano
PHI N Sept 30, 1952

Whitey Glazner
PHI N May 22, 1923

Jerry Gleaton
SEA A Dec 12, 1980

Jim Gleeson
CHI N Jan 24, 1939
CIN N Dec 4, 1940

Joe Glenn
STL A Oct 26, 1938

John Glenn
STL N June 15, 1960

Al Glossop
BOS N June 15, 1940
BKN N Mar 9, 1943
CHI N Sept 28, 1943

Ed Glynn
NY N Mar 13, 1979
CLE A Apr 6, 1981

Danny Godby
BOS A Mar 29, 1975

Ed Goebel
BOS A Feb 10, 1923

Chuck Goggin
ATL N May 24, 1973
BOS A Mar 26, 1974

Bill Gogolewski
CLE A Mar 23, 1974

Jim Golden
LA N Dec 23, 1958
CHI A Dec 10, 1963

Gordon Goldsberry
STL A Nov 27, 1951

Mike Goliat
STL A Sept 12, 1951

Dave Goltz
LA N Nov 15, 1979

Lefty Gomez
WAS A Jan 25, 1943

Luis Gomez
ATL N Dec 5, 1979

Ruben Gomez
PHI N Dec 3, 1958
MIN A Aug 20, 1962

Jesse Gonder
NY N July 1, 1963
MIL N July 21, 1965

Fernando Gonzalez
KC A Dec 4, 1973
NY A May 5, 1974
SD N June 5, 1978

Julio Gonzalez
HOU N Dec 8, 1976

Mike Gonzalez
STL N Apr 8, 1915
NY N May 1919
CIN N Dec 6, 1921
STL N Apr 27, 1924
CHI N May 23, 1925

Orlando Gonzalez
OAK A July 25, 1980

Pedro Gonzalez
CLE A May 10, 1965

Tony Gonzalez
PHI N June 15, 1960
ATL N June 12, 1969
CAL A Aug 31, 1970

Johnny Gooch
BKN N June 8, 1928
CIN N Apr 18, 1929

Wilbur Good
CHI N June 10, 1911
PHI N Feb 3, 1916

Billy Goodman
BAL A June 14, 1957
CHI A Dec 3, 1957

Ival Goodman
CIN N Nov 3, 1934
CHI N Nov 14, 1942

Ed Goodson
ATL N June 11, 1975
LA N Nov 17, 1975

Danny Goodwin
MIN A Dec 4, 1978

Greg Goossen
PHI N Nov 3, 1970

Glen Gorbous
PHI N Apr 30, 1955
STL N May 10, 1957

Joe Gordon
CLE A Oct 19, 1946
DET A Aug 10, 1960

Sid Gordon
BOS N Dec 14, 1949
PIT N Dec 26, 1953
NY N May 23, 1955

Tom Gorman
KC A Mar 30, 1955

Tom Gorman
NY N Aug 4, 1982

Hank Gornicki
CHI N Sept 2, 1941
PIT N Dec 1, 1941

John Goryl
LA N Apr 8, 1960

Jim Gosger
KC A June 13, 1966
SF N Dec 12, 1969
MON N Apr 20, 1970

Goose Goslin
STL A June 13, 1930
WAS A Dec 14, 1932
DET A Dec 20, 1933

Howie Goss
HOU N Apr 4, 1963

Goose Gossage
PIT N Dec 10, 1976
NY A Nov 23, 1977
SD N Jan 12, 1984

Julio Gotay
PIT N Nov 19, 1962

Hank Gowdy
BOS N July 22, 1911
NY N June 7, 1923

Billy Grabarkewitz
CAL A Nov 28, 1972
PHI N Aug 14, 1973
CHI N July 10, 1974

Johnny Grabowski
NY A Jan 13, 1927

Earl Grace
PIT N June 13, 1931
PHI N Nov 21, 1935
STL A Dec 8, 1937

Joe Grace
WAS A June 15, 1946
PIT N Dec 1947

Milt Graff
KC A Feb 19, 1957

Dan Graham
BAL A Dec 7, 1979

Jack Graham
NY N May 1946

Peaches Graham
PHI N Oct 1911

Wayne Graham
PHI N Aug 7, 1964
PHI N Feb 22, 1966

Alex Grammas
STL N Dec 2, 1953
CIN N May 16, 1956
STL N Oct 3, 1958
CHI N June 5, 1962

Wayne Granger
CIN N Oct 11, 1968
MIN A Dec 3, 1971
STL N Nov 29, 1972
NY A Aug 7, 1973

Eddie Grant
CIN N Feb 1911
NY N May 22, 1913
NY N June 1913

Jimmy Grant
CLE A Aug 11, 1943

Mudcat Grant
MIN A June 15, 1964
LA N Nov 28, 1967
STL N June 3, 1969
OAK A Dec 5, 1969
PIT N Sept 14, 1970
OAK A Aug 10, 1971

George Grantham
PIT N Oct 27, 1924
CIN N Feb 4, 1932
NY N Nov 15, 1933

Mickey Grasso
CLE A Jan 20, 1954

Dick Gray
STL N June 15, 1959
PIT N May 28, 1960

Gary Gray
CLE A Jan 4, 1980

John Gray
PHI A Dec 16, 1953

Sam Gray
STL A Dec 13, 1927

Ted Gray
CHI A Dec 6, 1954

Dallas Green
WAS A Apr 11, 1965

David Green
STL N Dec 12, 1980

Freddie Green
WAS A Sept 25, 1961

Gene Green
BAL A Dec 2, 1959
CLE A Oct 5, 1961
CIN N Aug 1, 1963

Lenny Green
WAS A May 26, 1959
LA A June 11, 1964
BAL A Sept 5, 1964

Pumpsie Green
NY N Dec 11, 1962

Hank Greenberg
PIT N Jan 18, 1947

Al Greene
STL N June 2, 1980

Kent Greenfield
BOS N June 12, 1927
BKN N July 4, 1929

Jim Greengrass
CIN N Aug 28, 1952
PHI N Apr 30, 1955

Hal Gregg
PIT N Dec 8, 1947

Vean Gregg
BOS A Aug 20, 1914
PHI A Dec 14, 1917

Bill Greif
SD N Dec 3, 1971
STL N May 19, 1976
MON N Nov 6, 1976

Bobby Grich
CAL A Nov 24, 1976

Tom Grieve
NY N Dec 8, 1977
STL N Dec 5, 1978

Ken Griffey
NY A Nov 4, 1981

Alfredo Griffin
TOR A Dec 5, 1978

Doug Griffin
BOS A Oct 11, 1970

Hank Griffin
BOS N June 1911

Mike Griffin
NY A Nov 10, 1978
CHI N June 12, 1981
MON N Mar 16, 1982
SD N June 8, 1982

Tom Griffin
SD N Aug 3, 1976
PIT N Dec 11, 1981

Bert Griffith
WAS A Dec 1923

Derrell Griffith
NY N Nov 29, 1966
HOU N Mar 24, 1967

Tommy Griffith
BKN N Feb 1, 1919
CHI N May 10, 1925

Art Griggs
CLE A Oct 1910

Guido Grilli
KC A June 13, 1966

Steve Grilli
TOR A Feb 23, 1978

Bob Grim
KC A June 15, 1958
CLE A Apr 5, 1960
CIN N May 18, 1960
STL N July 29, 1960

Burleigh Grimes
BKN N Jan 9, 1918
NY N Jan 9, 1927
PIT N Feb 11, 1928
BOS N Apr 9, 1930
STL N June 16, 1930
CHI N Dec 1931
STL N Aug 4, 1933
PIT N May 1934
NY A May 26, 1934

Oscar Grimes
NY A Dec 17, 1942

Charlie Grimm
CHI N Oct 27, 1924

Ross Grimsley
BAL A Dec 4, 1973
MON N Dec 21, 1977
CLE A July 11, 1980

Lee Grissom
NY A Jan 4, 1940
BKN N May 15, 1940
PHI N May 6, 1941

Marv Grissom
BOS A Feb 9, 1953
NY N July 1, 1953
STL N Oct 8, 1958

Dick Groat
STL N Nov 19, 1962
PHI N Oct 27, 1965
SF N June 22, 1967

Connie Grob
HOU N Nov 30, 1962

Heinie Groh
CIN N May 22, 1913
NY N Dec 6, 1921

Steve Gromek
DET A June 15, 1953

Bob Groom
STL A Feb 10, 1916
CLE A Feb 15, 1918

Don Gross
PIT N Dec 9, 1957

Greg Gross
CHI N Dec 8, 1976
PHI N Feb 23, 1979

Wayne Gross
BAL A Dec 8, 1983

Jerry Grote
NY N Oct 19, 1965
KC A Feb 5, 1981

Ernie Groth
CHI A Oct 2, 1948

Johnny Groth
STL A Dec 4, 1952
CHI A Feb 5, 1954
WAS A June 7, 1955
KC A Apr 16, 1956
DET A Aug 1, 1957

Lefty Grove
BOS A Dec 12, 1933

Roy Grover
WAS A June 1919

John Grubb
CLE A Dec 8, 1976
TEX A Aug 31, 1978
DET A Mar 24, 1983

Frank Grube
CHI A Sept 20, 1935

Joe Grzenda
NY N Aug 14, 1967
MIN A Nov 29, 1967
WAS A Mar 21, 1970
STL N Nov 3, 1971

Mike Guerra
PHI A Dec 2, 1946
BOS A Dec 13, 1950

Mario Guerrero
STL N Apr 4, 1975
CAL A May 29, 1976
OAK A Mar 15, 1978
SEA A Dec 8, 1980

Pedro Guerrero
LA N Apr 3, 1974

Skip Guinn
HOU N Jan 22, 1969

Brad Gulden
NY A Feb 15, 1979
SEA A Nov 18, 1980
MON N Apr 5, 1982
NY A Oct 26, 1982

Don Gullett
NY A Nov 18, 1976

Harry Gumbert
STL N May 14, 1940
CIN N June 15, 1944
PIT N July 27, 1949

Randy Gumpert
CHI A July 28, 1948
BOS A Nov 13, 1951
WAS A June 10, 1952

Larry Gura
TEX A Aug 31, 1973
NY A May 8, 1974
KC A May 16, 1976

Frankie Gustine
CHI N Dec 8, 1948
PHI A Sept 14, 1949
STL A Dec 13, 1949

Cesar Gutierrez
DET A Sept 2, 1969
MON N Mar 24, 1972

Don Gutteridge
PIT N Mar 26, 1948

Bert Haas
STL N June 12, 1940
PHI N Dec 11, 1947

Eddie Haas
MIL N Dec 5, 1957

Mule Haas
CHI A Sept 28, 1932

Bob Habenicht
STL A Oct 1, 1952

Rich Hacker
MON N Mar 31, 1971

Warren Hacker
CIN N Nov 13, 1956
PHI N June 26, 1957

Harvey Haddix
PHI N May 11, 1956
CIN N Dec 16, 1957
PIT N Jan 30, 1959
BAL A Dec 14, 1963

Bump Hadley
CHI A Dec 4, 1931
STL A Apr 27, 1932
WAS A Jan 22, 1935
NY A Jan 17, 1936
NY N Jan 2, 1941
PHI A Apr 30, 1941

Kent Hadley
KC A Nov 20, 1957
NY A Dec 11, 1959

Mickey Haefner
CHI A July 21, 1949
BOS N Aug 8, 1950

Bud Hafey
PHI N Aug 5, 1939

Chick Hafey
CIN N Apr 11, 1932

Casey Hageman
BKN N June 1914
CHI N June 1914

Joe Hague
CIN N May 19, 1972

Don Hahn
NY N Mar 31, 1971
PHI N Dec 3, 1974
SD N June 24, 1975

Ed Hahn
CHI A May 9, 1906

Noodles Hahn
NY A Apr 1906

Hal Haid
BOS N Jan 1931

Jerry Hairston
PIT N June 13, 1977

Bob Hale
NY A July 26, 1961

John Hale
TOR A Sept 2, 1977
SEA A Sept 14, 1977

Odell Hale
BOS A Dec 12, 1940
NY N June 19, 1941

Sammy Hale
STL A Dec 11, 1929

Ray Haley
PHI A Sept 2, 1916

Ed Halicki
CAL A June 20, 1980

Bob Hall
BKN N Apr 1905

Dick Hall
KC A Dec 15, 1959
PHI N Dec 15, 1966

Jimmie Hall
CAL A Dec 2, 1966
CLE A June 15, 1968
NY A Apr 14, 1969
CHI N Sept 11, 1969
ATL N June 29, 1970

Tom Hall
CIN N Dec 3, 1971
NY N Apr 15, 1975
KC A May 7, 1976

Bill Hallahan
CIN N May 31, 1936

Tom Haller
LA N Feb 13, 1968
DET A Dec 2, 1971
PHI N Oct 25, 1972

Jack Hallett
PHI A Dec 9, 1941

Dave Hamilton
CHI A June 15, 1975
STL N Aug 31, 1977
PIT N May 28, 1978

Earl Hamilton
DET A May 30, 1916
STL A June 22, 1916
PIT N Unknown
PHI N Dec 1923

Jack Hamilton
DET A Dec 4, 1963
NY N Oct 14, 1965
CAL A June 10, 1967
CLE A Oct 8, 1968
CHI A June 13, 1969

Steve Hamilton
WAS A May 3, 1962
NY A Apr 21, 1963
CHI A Sept 9, 1970
SF N Mar 23, 1971

Tom Hamilton
NY A Dec 16, 1953

Ken Hamlin
KC A Dec 15, 1959

Luke Hamlin
PIT N Dec 12, 1941

Pete Hamm
CHI A Feb 5, 1972

Atlee Hammaker
SF N Mar 30, 1982

Jack Hammond
PIT N Apr 1922

Steve Hammond
KC A Apr 28, 1982

Granny Hamner
CLE A May 16, 1959

Ike Hampton
CAL A Mar 22, 1975

Garry Hancock
BOS A Dec 9, 1977
OAK A Dec 6, 1982

Rich Hand
TEX A Dec 2, 1971
CAL A May 20, 1973

Bill Hands
CHI N Dec 2, 1965
MIN A Nov 30, 1972
TEX A Sept 9, 1974
NY N Feb 24, 1976

Harry Hanebrink
PHI N Mar 31, 1959

Fred Haney
BOS A Dec 9, 1925
CHI N July 12, 1927

Larry Haney
OAK A June 14, 1969
OAK A Sept 6, 1972
STL N Sept 1, 1973
OAK A Mar 26, 1974
MIL A Dec 6, 1976

Gerry Hannahs
LA N May 20, 1978

Jim Hannan
DET A Oct 9, 1970
MIL A May 11, 1971

Jack Hannifan
NY N June 1906
BOS N Apr 1908

Andy Hansen
PIT N Jan 13, 1954

Ron Hansen
STL A June 22, 1935
CHI A Jan 14, 1963
WAS A Feb 13, 1968
CHI A Aug 2, 1968
NY A Feb 28, 1970

Jim Hardin
NY A May 28, 1971

Carroll Hardy
BOS A June 13, 1960
HOU N Dec 10, 1962

Larry Hardy
HOU N Dec 11, 1975

Steve Hargan
TEX A Mar 23, 1974
TEX A May 9, 1977
ATL N June 15, 1977

Alan Hargesheimer
CHI N Oct 15, 1982
KC A Mar 30, 1984

Pinky Hargrave
STL A June 8, 1925
DET A Jan 15, 1927
WAS A Sept 10, 1930
BOS N Dec 1931

Charlie Hargreaves
PIT N June 8, 1928

Mike Hargrove
SD N Oct 25, 1978
CLE A June 14, 1979

Tim Harkness
BKN N Apr 5, 1957
NY N Nov 30, 1962

Dick Harley
CIN N Apr 1900

Larry Harlow
CAL A June 5, 1979

Bob Harmon
PIT N Dec 12, 1913

Chuck Harmon
STL N May 16, 1956
PHI N May 10, 1957

Brian Harper
PIT N Dec 11, 1981

George Harper
PHI N May 30, 1924
NY N Jan 9, 1927
STL N May 1, 1928
BOS N Dec 8, 1928

Harry Harper
BOS A Jan 20, 1920
NY A Dec 15, 1920

Jack Harper
STL N Jan 1900
CHI N Oct 1906

Tommy Harper
CLE A Nov 21, 1967
BOS A Oct 11, 1971
CAL A Dec 2, 1974
OAK A Aug 13, 1975

Toby Harrah
CLE A Dec 8, 1978
NY A Feb 4, 1984

Billy Harrell
STL N Feb 2, 1959

Ray Harrell
CHI N Dec 8, 1938
PHI N May 29, 1939
PIT N Jan 22, 1940

Bill Harrelson
CIN N Jan 14, 1970

Bud Harrelson
PHI N Mar 24, 1978
PHI N May 25, 1979

Ken Harrelson
WAS A June 23, 1966
KC A June 9, 1967
CLE A Apr 19, 1969

Bill Harrington
DET A Dec 5, 1956

Bob Harris
STL A May 13, 1939
PHI A June 1, 1942

Bucky Harris
DET A Dec 19, 1928

Buddy Harris
NY N Nov 27, 1972

Dave Harris
WAS A June 13, 1930

Gail Harris
DET A Jan 28, 1958
LA N May 7, 1960

Greg Harris
CIN N Feb 10, 1982
MON N Sept 27, 1983

Joe Harris
BOS A Dec 24, 1921
WAS A Apr 26, 1925
PIT N Feb 4, 1927
BKN N June 8, 1928

John Harris
CIN N Jan 10, 1983

Lum Harris
WAS A Feb 14, 1947

Mickey Harris
WAS A June 13, 1949
CLE A Apr 22, 1952

Vic Harris
TEX A July 20, 1972
CHI N Oct 25, 1973
STL N Dec 22, 1975
SF N Oct 20, 1976

Chuck Harrison
ATL N Oct 8, 1967
KC A Oct 17, 1968

Roric Harrison
SEA A Aug 24, 1969
BAL A Apr 5, 1971
ATL N Dec 30, 1972
CLE A June 7, 1975
STL N Apr 7, 1976

Slim Harriss
BOS A June 15, 1926

Earl Harrist
WAS A June 9, 1948
CHI A Mar 7, 1953
DET A May 23, 1953

Jack Harshman
BAL A Dec 3, 1957
CLE A July 30, 1959

Jim Hart
NY A Apr 17, 1973

Mike Hart
TEX A Dec 8, 1978

Chuck Hartenstein
PIT N Jan 15, 1969
STL N June 22, 1970

Grover Hartley
CIN N Dec 12, 1913
STL A Feb 10, 1916
CLE A Dec 1927

Bob Hartman
CLE A June 24, 1962

Topsy Hartsel
CHI N Apr 1901

Roy Hartsfield
BKN N Jan 17, 1953

Paul Hartzell
MIN A Feb 3, 1979

Roy Hartzell
NY A Jan 1911

Erwin Harvey
CLE A May 1901

Mickey Haslin
BOS N Jan 29, 1936
BOS N May 1936
NY N Dec 4, 1936

Buddy Hassett
BKN N Jan 1936
BOS N Dec 13, 1938
NY A Feb 5, 1942

Andy Hassler
KC A July 5, 1976
BOS A July 24, 1978
NY N June 15, 1979
PIT N Nov 19, 1979
CAL A June 10, 1980

Mickey Hatcher
MIN A Mar 30, 1981

Fred Hatfield
DET A June 3, 1952
CHI A May 15, 1956
CLE A Dec 4, 1957
CIN N Apr 23, 1958

Joe Hatten
CHI N June 15, 1951

Grady Hatton
CHI A Apr 18, 1954
BOS A May 23, 1954
STL N May 11, 1956
BAL A Aug 1, 1956

Phil Haugstad
CIN N May 25, 1952

Joe Hauser
CLE A June 7, 1929

Tom Hausman
NY N Nov 21, 1977
ATL N Sept 10, 1982

Brad Havens
MIN A Feb 3, 1979

Wynn Hawkins
NY N Nov 27, 1962

Pink Hawley
NY N Feb 27, 1900

Hal Haydel
CHI N Mar 28, 1963

Frankie Hayes
STL A June 1, 1942
PHI A Feb 17, 1944
CLE A May 29, 1945
CHI A June 1946

Jackie Hayes
CHI A Dec 4, 1931

Von Hayes
PHI N Dec 9, 1982

Joe Haynes
CHI A Jan 4, 1941
CLE A Nov 22, 1948
WAS A Dec 14, 1948

Ray Hayworth
BKN N Sept 14, 1938
NY N Aug 23, 1939

Bob Hazle
MIL N Apr 9, 1956
DET A May 24, 1958

Fran Healy
KC A Apr 2, 1973
NY A May 16, 1976

Jim Hearn
NY N May 1950
PHI N Oct 11, 1956

Bill Heath
CHI A Oct 15, 1964
HOU N Dec 1, 1965

Jeff Heath
WAS A Dec 14, 1945
STL A June 15, 1946
BOS N Dec 4, 1947

Mickey Heath
BKN N May 7, 1931

Mike Heath
TEX A Nov 10, 1978
OAK A June 15, 1979

Cliff Heathcote
CHI N May 30, 1922
CIN N Apr 1, 1931
PHI N June 25, 1932

Dave Heaverlo
OAK A Mar 15, 1978
SEA A Apr 9, 1980

Richie Hebner
PHI N Dec 15, 1976
NY N Mar 27, 1979
DET A Oct 31, 1979
PIT N Aug 16, 1982
CHI N Jan 5, 1984

Mike Hechinger
BKN N May 1913

Mike Hedlund
CLE A Nov 2, 1972

Danny Heep
NY N Dec 10, 1982

Don Heffner
STL A Feb 15, 1938
PHI A June 14, 1943
DET A Oct 11, 1943

Jim Hegan
DET A Feb 18, 1958
PHI N July 27, 1958
SF N June 14, 1959

Mike Hegan
SEA A June 14, 1968
OAK A June 14, 1971
NY A Aug 18, 1973
MIL A May 13, 1974

Jack Heidemann
OAK A Mar 24, 1973
CLE A Mar 25, 1974
STL N June 1, 1974
NY N Dec 11, 1974
MIL A June 22, 1976

Harry Heilmann
CIN N Oct 14, 1929

Fred Heimach
BOS A June 15, 1926

Ken Heintzelman
PHI N May 9, 1947

Tom Heintzelman
SF N Oct 14, 1974

Bob Heise
SF N Dec 12, 1969
MIL A June 1, 1971
STL N Dec 8, 1973
CAL A July 31, 1974
BOS A Dec 2, 1974
KC A Dec 6, 1976

Woodie Held
KC A June 15, 1957
CLE A June 15, 1958
WAS A Dec 1, 1964
BAL A Oct 12, 1965
CAL A June 15, 1967
CHI A July 20, 1968

Tommy Helms
HOU N Nov 29, 1971
PIT N Dec 12, 1975
OAK A Nov 5, 1976
PIT N Mar 15, 1977

Russ Heman
BAL A Dec 3, 1957
CLE A Dec 2, 1958
LA A June 5, 1961

Charlie Hemphill
STL A May 30, 1902
NY A Feb 1908

Rollie Hemsley
CHI N June 13, 1931
CIN N Nov 30, 1932
STL A Aug 3, 1933
CLE A Feb 10, 1938
CIN N Dec 4, 1941
PHI N Mar 25, 1946

Solly Hemus
PHI N May 14, 1956
STL N Sept 29, 1958

Joe Henderson
TOR A Oct 31, 1977

Ken Henderson
CHI A Nov 28, 1972
ATL N Dec 12, 1975
TEX A Dec 9, 1976
NY N Dec 8, 1977
CIN N May 19, 1978
CHI N June 28, 1979

Steve Henderson
NY N June 15, 1977
CHI N Feb 28, 1981
SEA A Dec 9, 1982

Bob Hendley
SF N Dec 3, 1963
CHI N May 29, 1965
NY N June 12, 1967

George Hendrick
CLE A Mar 24, 1973
SD N Dec 8, 1976
STL N May 26, 1978

Harvey Hendrick
NY A Jan 3, 1923
CIN N May 7, 1931
STL N Apr 11, 1932
CIN N June 5, 1932
PHI N Nov 21, 1933

Ellie Hendricks
CHI N Aug 18, 1972
BAL A Oct 27, 1972
NY A June 15, 1976

Jack Hendricks
CHI N July 1902

Claude Hendrix
CHI N Feb 10, 1916

Tim Hendryx
STL A Apr 28, 1918
BOS A Jan 1920

Gail Henley
PIT N Oct 14, 1952

Butch Henline
PHI N July 25, 1921
BKN N Jan 9, 1927
NY N Jan 9, 1927
STL N May 7, 1933

Phil Hennigan
NY N Nov 27, 1972

Bill Henry
CIN N Sept 18, 1967

Bill Henry
CIN N Dec 6, 1959
SF N May 4, 1965
PIT N June 27, 1968

Dutch Henry
CHI A Sept 27, 1929

John Henry
BOS N Dec 1917

Roy Henshaw
BKN N Dec 5, 1936
STL N Oct 4, 1937

Ron Herbel
SD N Dec 5, 1969
NY N Sept 1, 1970
ATL N Dec 1, 1970

Ray Herbert
KC A May 11, 1955
CHI A June 10, 1961
PHI N Dec 1, 1964

Babe Herman
BOS A Oct 30, 1922
CIN N Mar 14, 1932
CHI N Nov 30, 1932
PIT N Nov 22, 1934
CIN N June 21, 1935
DET A Apr 1, 1937

Billy Herman
BKN N May 6, 1941
BOS N June 15, 1946
PIT N Sept 30, 1946

Gene Hermanski
CHI N June 15, 1951
PIT N June 4, 1953

Enzo Hernandez
BAL A Dec 4, 1968
SD N Dec 1, 1970

Jackie Hernandez
MIN A Dec 2, 1966
PIT N Dec 2, 1970
PHI N Jan 31, 1974

Keith Hernandez
NY N June 15, 1983

Leo Hernandez
BAL A Apr 28, 1982

Pedro Hernandez
TOR A Nov 27, 1978
NY A Aug 23, 1982

Ramon Hernandez
CHI N Sept 8, 1976
BOS A May 28, 1977

Willie Hernandez
PHI N May 22, 1983
DET A Mar 24, 1984

Larry Herndon
SF N May 9, 1975
DET A Dec 9, 1981

Jose Herrera
DET A May 11, 1971

Pancho Herrera
PIT N Nov 28, 1963

Art Herring
BKN N Dec 1933
PIT N Oct 19, 1946

Ed Herrmann
NY A Apr 1, 1975
CAL A Feb 20, 1976
HOU N June 6, 1976
MON N June 9, 1978

John Herrnstein
CHI N Apr 21, 1966
ATL N May 29, 1966

Mike Hershberger
KC A Jan 20, 1965
MIL A Jan 15, 1970

Buck Herzog
BOS N Dec 1909
NY N July 22, 1911
CIN N Dec 12, 1913
NY N July 20, 1916
BOS N Jan 8, 1918
CIII N Aug 1919

Whitey Herzog
WAS A Feb 8, 1956
KC A May 14, 1958
BAL A Jan 24, 1961
DET A Nov 26, 1962

Ed Heusser
BKN N Dec 4, 1946

Joe Heving
BOS A Aug 1938
CLE A Feb 3, 1941

Johnnie Heving
PHI A Jan 1931

Jack Hiatt
SF N Nov 21, 1964
MON N Apr 6, 1970
CHI N May 12, 1970
HOU N Dec 1, 1970
CAL A July 29, 1972

Dave Hickman
BKN N Feb 10, 1916

Jess Hickman
KC A June 4, 1965

Jim Hickman
LA N Nov 29, 1966
CHI N Apr 23, 1968
STL N Mar 23, 1974

Piano Legs Hickman
NY N Feb 17, 1900
CLE A May 30, 1902
DET A Aug 7, 1904
WAS A July 6, 1905
CHI A Aug 1, 1907
CLE A Nov 1907

Jim Hicks
STL N Oct 13, 1967
CAL A May 30, 1969

Kirby Higbe
PHI N May 29, 1939
BKN N Nov 11, 1940
PIT N May 3, 1947
NY N June 6, 1949

Dennis Higgins
WAS A Feb 13, 1968
CLE A Dec 5, 1969
STL N July 15, 1971
SD N Sept 1, 1972

Pinky Higgins
BOS A Dec 9, 1936
DET A Dec 15, 1938
BOS A May 19, 1946

Andy High
BOS N July 25, 1925
STL N Mar 25, 1928
CIN N Dec 2, 1931

Hugh High
NY A Jan 7, 1915

Oral Hildebrand
STL A Jan 17, 1937
NY A Oct 26, 1938

Tom Hilgendorf
CLE A July 10, 1972
PHI N Mar 6, 1975

Carmen Hill
STL N Aug 28, 1929

Herman Hill
STL N Oct 20, 1970

Hunter Hill
WAS A July 14, 1904

Jesse Hill
WAS A Jan 17, 1936
PHI A July 13, 1937

Marc Hill
SF N Oct 14, 1974
SEA A June 20, 1980
CHI A Feb 12, 1981

Chuck Hiller
NY N May 12, 1965
PHI N July 11, 1967

Frank Hiller
CIN N Jan 3, 1952

Dave Hillman
BOS A Nov 21, 1959

Chuck Hinton
CLE A Dec 1, 1964
CAL A Nov 29, 1967
CLE A Apr 4, 1969

Rich Hinton
NY A Oct 13, 1971
TEX A Sept 6, 1972
CLE A Mar 8, 1973
CIN N Dec 12, 1975
SEA A July 6, 1979

Larry Hisle
LA N Oct 21, 1971
STL N Oct 26, 1972
MIN A Nov 29, 1972
MIL A Nov 17, 1977

Billy Hitchcock
WAS A May 16, 1946
STL A Feb 8, 1947
BOS A Nov 18, 1947
PHI A Oct 8, 1949
DET A Jan 29, 1953

Myril Hoag
STL A Oct 26, 1938
CHI A Apr 30, 1940
CLE A June 27, 1944

Don Hoak
CHI N Dec 9, 1955
CIN N Nov 13, 1956
PIT N Jan 30, 1959
PHI N Nov 28, 1963

Glen Hobbie
STL N June 2, 1964

Dick Hoblitzell
BOS A July 16, 1914

Butch Hobson
CAL A Dec 10, 1980
NY A Mar 24, 1982

Oris Hockett
CHI A Dec 12, 1944

Johnny Hodapp
CHI A Apr 24, 1932
BOS A Dec 15, 1932

Mel Hoderlein
CHI A Nov 13, 1951
WAS A May 3, 1952
DET A June 14, 1954

Gil Hodges
WAS A May 23, 1963
NY N Nov 27, 1967

Billy Hoeft
BOS A May 2, 1959
SF N Dec 15, 1962
MIL N Dec 3, 1963

Joe Hoerner
PHI N Oct 7, 1969
ATL N June 15, 1972
KC A July 18, 1973

Bill Hoffer
CLE A Jan 1901

Stew Hofferth
BKN N June 15, 1946

Danny Hoffman
NY A May 11, 1906
STL A Feb 1908

John Hoffman
ATL N Oct 13, 1966

Solly Hofman
CHI N Jan 1904
PIT N June 22, 1912

Happy Hogan
STL A May 1911

Shanty Hogan
NY N Jan 10, 1928
BOS N Dec 29, 1932
WAS A Dec 1935

Chief Hogsett
PHI N Nov 21, 1933
STL A Apr 30, 1936
WAS A Dec 1, 1937

Bobby Hogue
STL A May 14, 1951
NY A July 31, 1951
STL A Aug 4, 1952

Ken Holcombe
STL A June 16, 1952

Bill Holden
CIN N Aug 1914

Fred Holdsworth
BAL A May 29, 1975
MON N July 14, 1977

Walter Holke
BOS N Feb 1919
CIN N July 9, 1925

Al Holland
SF N June 28, 1979
PHI N Dec 14, 1982

Gary Holle
TEX A Dec 15, 1978
CHI A June 15, 1979
PHI N Oct 30, 1981

Ed Holley
PIT N June 10, 1934

Carl Holling
BOS A Oct 30, 1922

Al Hollingsworth
PHI N June 13, 1938
NY A July 13, 1939
BKN N Aug 12, 1939
CHI A June 6, 1946

Bonnie Hollingsworth
BKN N Dec 1923

Ken Holloway
CLE A Dec 11, 1928
NY A July 20, 1930

Jeff Holly
DET A Dec 5, 1979

Billy Holm
BOS A Dec 1944

Ducky Holmes
WAS A Feb 1903
CHI A June 1903

Tommy Holmes
BOS N Feb 5, 1942

Jim Holt
OAK A Aug 19, 1974

Roger Holt
TEX A Oct 24, 1980

Ken Holtzman
OAK A Nov 29, 1971
BAL A Apr 2, 1976
NY A June 15, 1976
CHI N June 10, 1978

Rick Honeycutt
SEA A July 27, 1977
TEX A Dec 12, 1980
LA N Aug 19, 1983

Don Hood
CLE A Feb 25, 1975
NY A June 15, 1979

Wally Hood
PIT N July 1920

Jay Hook
MIL N May 8, 1964

Bob Hooper
CLE A Dec 19, 1952
CIN N Apr 13, 1955

Harry Hooper
CHI A Mar 4, 1921

Burt Hooton
LA N May 2, 1975

Don Hopkins
OAK A Mar 26, 1975

Gail Hopkins
KC A Oct 13, 1970
LA N July 11, 1974

Marty Hopkins
CHI A June 27, 1934

Paul Hopkins
STL A June 26, 1929

Johnny Hopp
BOS N Feb 5, 1945
BOS N Feb 5, 1946
PIT N Nov 18, 1947
BKN N May 18, 1949
NY A Sept 5, 1950

Rogers Hornsby
NY N Dec 20, 1926
BOS N Jan 10, 1928
CHI N Nov 7, 1928

Tony Horton
CLE A June 4, 1967

Willie Horton
TEX A Apr 12, 1977
CLE A Feb 28, 1978
TOR A Aug 15, 1978
SEA A Jan 27, 1979
TEX A Dec 12, 1980

Tim Hosley
OAK A Apr 19, 1976

Gene Host
KC A Dec 5, 1956

Dave Hostetler
TEX A Mar 31, 1982

Charlie Hough
TEX A July 11, 1980

Frank House
KC A Nov 20, 1957
CIN N Nov 21, 1959

Tom House
BOS A Dec 12, 1975
SEA A May 28, 1977

Art Houtteman
CLE A June 15, 1953
BAL A May 20, 1957

Steve Hovley
OAK A June 11, 1970

Bruce Howard
BAL A Nov 29, 1967
WAS A June 15, 1968

Del Howard
PIT N Dec 20, 1904
BOS N Dec 15, 1905
CHI N June 24, 1907

Doug Howard
STL N July 31, 1974
CLE A Sept 30, 1975
TOR A Nov 5, 1976

Elston Howard
BOS A Aug 3, 1967

Frank Howard
WAS A Dec 4, 1964
DET A Aug 31, 1972

Ivan Howard
STL A July 14, 1914
CLE A Jan 1916

Larry Howard
ATL N May 22, 1973

Art Howe
HOU N Dec 12, 1975
STL N Feb 22, 1984

Dixie Howell
PIT N May 3, 1947

Harry Howell
BKN N Jan 1900
STL A Jan 1904

Jay Howell
CHI N Oct 17, 1980
NY A June 12, 1981
NY A Aug 2, 1982

Roy Howell
TOR A May 9, 1977
MIL A Dec 23, 1980

Bill Howerton
PIT N June 15, 1951
NY N May 7, 1952

Dick Howser
CLE A May 25, 1963
NY A Dec 20, 1966

LaMarr Hoyt
CHI A Apr 5, 1977

Waite Hoyt
NY A Dec 15, 1920
DET A May 30, 1930
PHI A June 30, 1931
PIT N Nov 1932

Al Hrabosky
KC A Dec 8, 1977
ATL N Nov 20, 1979

Walt Hriniak
SD N June 12, 1969

Bill Hubbell
PHI N June 8, 1920
BKN N May 1, 1925

Charles Hudson
STL N Oct 18, 1971
TEX A Feb 1, 1973

Hal Hudson
CHI A Aug 27, 1952

Johnny Hudson
CHI N May 6, 1941

Sid Hudson
BOS A June 10, 1952

Frank Huelsman
DET A May 30, 1904
STL A June 16, 1904
WAS A July 14, 1904
BOS A Jan 16, 1905
WAS A Jan 16, 1905

Phil Huffman
OAK A Mar 15, 1978
TOR A Aug 15, 1978
KC A Mar 25, 1982

Miller Huggins
STL N Feb 1910

Jim Hughes
CHI N May 15, 1956

Long Tom Hughes
BOS A July 1902
NY A Dec 1903
WAS A July 13, 1904

Roy Hughes
STL A Feb 10, 1938
NY A June 13, 1939
PHI N July 13, 1939
PHI N Jan 21, 1946

Terry Hughes
BOS A Dec 7, 1973

Tommy Hughes
CIN N Dec 11, 1947

Jim Hughey
STL N Jan 1900

Emil Huhn
CIN N Feb 10, 1916

Rudy Hulswitt
STL N Dec 1908

Terry Humphrey
DET A Dec 4, 1974
HOU N Dec 6, 1975
CAL A June 6, 1976

Bob Humphreys
STL N Mar 25, 1963
CHI N Apr 10, 1965
WAS A Apr 2, 1966

Bert Humphries
CIN N July 15, 1911
CHI N Dec 15, 1912
PHI N Aug 8, 1915

John Humphries
CHI A Feb 7, 1941

Randy Hundley
CHI N Dec 2, 1965
MIN A Dec 6, 1973
CHI N Apr 13, 1976

Bill Hunnefield
CLE A Nov 1930
BOS N May 28, 1931
NY N June 30, 1931

Ken Hunt
WAS A Sept 12, 1963
CHI N Apr 2, 1966

Ron Hunt
LA N Nov 29, 1966
SF N Feb 13, 1968
MON N Dec 30, 1970
STL N Sept 5, 1974

Billy Hunter
STL A Oct 14, 1952
NY A Nov 18, 1954
KC A Feb 19, 1957
CLE A June 12, 1958

Buddy Hunter
KC A Dec 10, 1973

Catfish Hunter
NY A Dec 31, 1974

Herb Hunter
CHI N Aug 28, 1916

Steve Huntz
SD N Apr 2, 1970
SF N Dec 4, 1970
CHI A Mar 23, 1971
LA N Dec 2, 1971

Walter Huntzinger
CHI N June 21, 1926

Clint Hurdle
CIN N Dec 11, 1981

Don Hurst
CHI N June 11, 1934

Bert Husting
PHI A June 1902

Johnny Hutchings
BOS N June 12, 1941

Ira Hutchinson
BKN N Dec 13, 1938
STL N June 13, 1940

Jim Hutto
PHI N Apr 3, 1969
BAL A Dec 16, 1970

Tom Hutton
PHI N Oct 21, 1971
TOR A Dec 8, 1977
MON N July 20, 1978

Ham Hyatt
STL N Feb 28, 1915
NY A June 19, 1918

Dick Hyde
BOS A June 11, 1959

Scotty Ingerton
BOS N Jan 1911

Dane Iorg
STL N June 15, 1977

Hooks Iott
PIT N Apr 9, 1952

Charlie Irwin
BKN N July 2, 1901

Tommy Irwin
BOS A Dec 15, 1938

Mike Ivie
SF N Feb 28, 1978
HOU N Apr 20, 1981

Ray Jablonski
CIN N Dec 8, 1954
CHI N Nov 13, 1956
NY N Apr 16, 1957
STL N Mar 25, 1959
KC A Aug 20, 1959

Fred Jacklitsch
BKN N Feb 1903

Al Jackson
STL N Oct 20, 1965
NY N July 16, 1967
CIN N June 13, 1969

Grant Jackson
BAL A Dec 16, 1970
NY A June 15, 1976
PIT N Dec 7, 1976
MON N Sept 1, 1981
KC A Jan 14, 1982

Joe Jackson
CLE A July 25, 1910
CHI A Aug 21, 1915

Larry Jackson
CHI N Oct 17, 1962
PHI N Apr 21, 1966

Lou Jackson
CIN N Dec 6, 1959

Mike Jackson
PHI N Sept 6, 1969
STL N Sept 13, 1971

Randy Jackson
BKN N Dec 9, 1955
CLE A Aug 4, 1958
CHI N May 4, 1959

Reggie Jackson
BAL A Apr 2, 1976
NY A Nov 29, 1976
CAL A Jan 22, 1982

Ron Jackson
BOS A Nov 3, 1959
MIL N May 17, 1960

Ron Jackson
MIN A Dec 4, 1978
DET A Aug 23, 1981
CAL A Apr 20, 1982

Roy Lee Jackson
TOR A Dec 12, 1980

Sonny Jackson
ATL N Oct 8, 1967

Elmer Jacobs
PIT N Dec 1915
PHI N July 1, 1918
STL N July 14, 1919

Spook Jacobs
PIT N June 23, 1956

Baby Doll Jacobson
STL A Aug 18, 1915
BOS A June 15, 1926
PHI A June 15, 1926
CLE A June 12, 1927
PHI A Aug 5, 1927

Beany Jacobson
STL A Dec 1905
BOS A June 22, 1907

Merwin Jacobson
CHI N Aug 28, 1916

Brook Jacoby
CLE A Aug 28, 1983

Pat Jacquez
CHI A Nov 30, 1970
STL N Nov 28, 1972

Art Jahn
PHI N May 29, 1928

Bill James
DET A Aug 18, 1915
BOS A Aug 1919
CHI A Aug 1919

Bob James
MON N May 4, 1983

Charlie James
CIN N Dec 14, 1964

Johnny James
LA A May 8, 1961

Skip James
MIL A Mar 27, 1979

Charlie Jamieson
PHI A July 17, 1917
CLE A Mar 1, 1919

Gerry Janeski
CHI A Dec 13, 1969
WAS A Feb 9, 1971

Hal Janvrin
WAS A Jan 17, 1919
STL N Sept 10, 1919
BKN N June 18, 1921

Pat Jarvis
MON N Feb 28, 1973
TEX A Dec 20, 1973

Ray Jarvis
CAL A Oct 11, 1970

Larry Jaster
ATL N Dec 2, 1969

Julian Javier
STL N May 28, 1960
CIN N Mar 24, 1972

Joey Jay
CIN N Dec 15, 1960
ATL N June 15, 1966

Hal Jeffcoat
CIN N Nov 28, 1955
STL N June 8, 1959

Jesse Jefferson
CHI A June 15, 1975
PIT N Sept 11, 1980

Irv Jeffries
PHI N Dec 20, 1933

Ferguson Jenkins
CHI N Apr 21, 1966
TEX A Oct 25, 1973
BOS A Nov 17, 1975
TEX A Dec 14, 1977
CHI N Dec 8, 1981

Jack Jenkins
LA N Sept 1, 1969

Tom Jenkins
PHI A June 15, 1926

Bill Jennings
STL A July 16, 1951

Hughie Jennings
PHI N Feb 1901

Jackie Jensen
WAS A May 3, 1952
BOS A Dec 9, 1953

Garry Jestadt
SD N May 19, 1971

John Jeter
SD N Aug 10, 1971
CHI A Oct 28, 1972

Sam Jethroe
PIT N Dec 26, 1953

Manny Jimenez
CHI N Jan 15, 1969

Tommy John
CHI A Jan 20, 1965
LA N Dec 2, 1971
NY A Nov 21, 1978
CAL A Aug 31, 1982

Adam Johnson
CLE A Aug 20, 1914

Alex Johnson
STL N Oct 27, 1965
CIN N Jan 11, 1968
CAL A Nov 25, 1969
CLE A Oct 5, 1971
TEX A Mar 8, 1973
NY A Sept 9, 1974

Ben Johnson
CHI N Nov 10, 1957

Bill Johnson
CHI N May 22, 1983

Billy Johnson
STL N May 14, 1951

Bob Johnson
KC A Dec 3, 1969
PIT N Dec 2, 1970
CLE A Dec 7, 1973
TEX A July 1, 1974

Bob Johnson
WAS A Mar 21, 1943
BOS A Dec 4, 1943

Bob Johnson
BAL A Dec 5, 1962
NY N May 10, 1967
CIN N Nov 8, 1967
ATL N June 11, 1968
STL N Mar 25, 1969
OAK A July 12, 1969

Cliff Johnson
NY A June 15, 1977
CLE A June 15, 1979
CHI N June 23, 1980
OAK A Dec 11, 1980
TOR A Nov 15, 1982

Connie Johnson
BAL A May 21, 1956

Darrell Johnson
CHI A July 28, 1952
STL A June 13, 1953
NY A Dec 1, 1954
CIN N Aug 14, 1961

Dave Johnson
MIN A May 2, 1977

Davy Johnson
ATL N Dec 30, 1972
CHI N Aug 6, 1978

Deron Johnson
ATL N Oct 10, 1967
PHI N Dec 3, 1968
OAK A May 2, 1973
MIL A June 24, 1974
BOS A Sept 7, 1974
BOS A Sept 22, 1975

Don Johnson
STL A June 15, 1950
WAS A May 29, 1951
BAL A Dec 6, 1954

Ernie Johnson
STL A Feb 10, 1916
NY A May 31, 1923

Hank Johnson
BOS A June 5, 1932
PHI A Jan 4, 1936

Jerry Johnson
STL N Oct 7, 1969
SF N May 19, 1970
CLE A Mar 6, 1973
HOU N Nov 3, 1973
TOR A Feb 16, 1977

John Henry Johnson
OAK A Mar 15, 1978
TEX A June 15, 1979
BOS A Apr 9, 1982

Johnny Johnson
CHI A Dec 15, 1944

Ken Johnson
PHI N Apr 27, 1950
PHI N Apr 27, 1951
DET A Mar 21, 1952

Ken Johnson
CIN N July 21, 1961
MIL N May 13, 1965
NY A June 10, 1969
CHI N Aug 11, 1969

Lamar Johnson
TEX A Jan 15, 1982

Lou Johnson
LA A Apr 1, 1961
DET A May 8, 1963
LA N Apr 9, 1964
CHI N Nov 30, 1967
CLE A June 28, 1968
CAL A Apr 4, 1969

Mike Johnson
SD N June 12, 1973

Randy Johnson
MIN A Aug 30, 1981

Roy Johnson
BOS A June 12, 1932
WAS A Dec 17, 1935
NY A Jan 17, 1936
BOS N June 1937

Si Johnson
STL N Aug 6, 1936
BOS N Apr 24, 1946

Stan Johnson
KC A June 10, 1961

Syl Johnson
CIN N Jan 11, 1934
PHI N May 8, 1934

Tim Johnson
MIL A Apr 24, 1973
TOR A Apr 29, 1978

Vic Johnson
CLE A Dec 12, 1946

Wallace Johnson
SF N May 25, 1983

Doc Johnston
PIT N Feb 1915
PHI A Feb 16, 1922

Jimmy Johnston
BOS N Oct 7, 1925
NY N Oct 7, 1926

Jay Johnstone
CHI A Nov 30, 1970
PHI N Jan 9, 1974
NY A June 10, 1978
SD N June 15, 1979
LA N Dec 4, 1979

Stan Jok
CHI A May 10, 1954

Smead Jolley
BOS A Apr 29, 1932
STL A Dec 14, 1933

Dave Jolly
NY N Oct 15, 1957

Charlie Jones
STL A Oct 5, 1907

Clarence Jones
CIN N Jan 9, 1969

Dalton Jones
DET A Dec 13, 1969
TEX A May 30, 1972

Davy Jones
CHI A Dec 1912

Gary Jones
CLE A Dec 2, 1971
TEX A Dec 2, 1971

Gordon Jones
NY N June 14, 1956
NY N Oct 1, 1956
BAL A Nov 30, 1959

Jake Jones
BOS A June 14, 1947

Johnny Jones
BOS N Aug 15, 1919

Mack Jones
CIN N Oct 10, 1967

Odell Jones
SEA A Dec 5, 1978
PIT N Apr 1, 1980

Percy Jones
BOS N Nov 7, 1928
PIT N Apr 9, 1930

Randy Jones
NY N Dec 15, 1980

Rick Jones
PIT N Dec 5, 1978

Ruppert Jones
NY A Nov 1, 1979
SD N Apr 1, 1981

Sad Sam Jones
BOS A Apr 12, 1916
NY A Dec 20, 1921
STL A Feb 8, 1927
WAS A Oct 19, 1927
CHI A Nov 1931
CHI A Dec 4, 1931

Sam Jones
CHI N Nov 16, 1954
STL N Dec 11, 1956
SF N Mar 25, 1959
DET A Dec 1, 1961

Sheldon Jones
BOS N Apr 8, 1952
CHI N Dec 20, 1952

Sherman Jones
CIN N Apr 27, 1961

Steve Jones
WAS A Feb 13, 1968

Tim Jones
MON N Mar 29, 1978

Tom Jones
DET A Aug 20, 1909

Willie Jones
CLE A June 6, 1959
CIN N July 1, 1959

Bubber Jonnard
STL N Dec 13, 1927

Eddie Joost
BOS N Dec 4, 1942
STL N Feb 5, 1945

Buck Jordan
CIN N May 12, 1937
PHI N June 10, 1938

Niles Jordan
CIN N Dec 10, 1951

Tom Jordan
CLE A June 1946

Mike Jorgensen
MON N Apr 5, 1972
OAK A May 22, 1977
TEX A Feb 23, 1978
NY N Aug 12, 1979
ATL N June 15, 1983

Duane Josephson
BOS A Mar 31, 1971

Von Joshua
SF N Jan 29, 1975
MIL A June 2, 1976
SD N Dec 3, 1979

Mike Joyce
NY N Mar 31, 1964

Oscar Judd
PHI N May 31, 1945

Ralph Judd
STL N May 15, 1930

Walt Judnich
CLE A Nov 20, 1947
PIT N Feb 9, 1949

Howie Judson
CIN N Sept 1, 1952

Bill Jurges
NY N Dec 6, 1938

Al Jurisich
PHI N Feb 5, 1946

Skip Jutze
HOU N Nov 28, 1972
SEA A Jan 12, 1977

Jim Kaat
CHI A Aug 15, 1973
PHI N Dec 10, 1975
NY A May 11, 1979
STL N Apr 30, 1980

Mike Kahoe
CHI N Apr 1901
PHI N Mar 1905
WAS A June 27, 1907

Al Kaiser
BOS N June 10, 1911

Don Kaiser
MIL N Dec 5, 1957
DET A Oct 15, 1959

Willie Kamm
CLE A May 17, 1931

Alex Kampouris
NY N June 6, 1938
WAS A May 20, 1943

John Kane
CHI N Oct 1908

Erv Kantlehner
PHI N Sept 2, 1916

Ed Karger
STL N June 3, 1906
CIN N Dec 12, 1908
BOS A June 1909

Andy Karl
BOS N May 27, 1947

Eddie Kasko
CIN N Oct 3, 1958
HOU N Jan 20, 1964
BOS A Apr 3, 1966

Ray Katt
STL N June 14, 1956
CHI N Dec 11, 1956
NY N Apr 16, 1957
STL N Apr 2, 1958

Benny Kauff
NY N Dec 23, 1915

Curt Kaufman
CAL A Dec 7, 1983

Tony Kaufmann
PHI N June 7, 1927
STL N Sept 10, 1927

Marty Kavanagh
CLE A May 1916
STL N June 1918
DET A Aug 1918

Eddie Kazak
CIN N May 13, 1952

Ted Kazanski
MIL N Mar 31, 1959

Steve Kealey
CHI A Mar 15, 1971
CIN N Aug 29, 1973

Bob Kearney
SEA A Nov 21, 1983

Ray Keating
BOS N Mar 6, 1919

Dave Keefe
CLE A June 2, 1921

Vic Keen
STL N Dec 11, 1925

Rickey Keeton
HOU N Oct 23, 1981

Bill Keister
STL N Feb 11, 1900

Mike Kekich
NY A Dec 4, 1968
CLE A June 12, 1973

George Kell
DET A May 18, 1946
BOS A June 3, 1952
CHI A May 23, 1954
BAL A May 21, 1956

Frankie Kelleher
CIN N July 16, 1942

John Kelleher
BOS N Jan 1924

Mick Kelleher
HOU N Oct 23, 1973
STL N Dec 13, 1974
CHI N Dec 22, 1975
DET A Apr 1, 1981
CAL A Apr 21, 1982

Frank Kellert
BKN N Mar 17, 1955
CHI N Oct 11, 1955

Harry Kelley
WAS A May 4, 1938

Alex Kellner
CIN N June 23, 1958
STL N Oct 3, 1958

Win Kellum
STL N Feb 1905

Bill Kelly
PIT N Jan 1911

Bob Kelly
CIN N June 12, 1953
CLE A Apr 23, 1958

Dale Kelly
TOR A Dec 8, 1977

George Kelly
PIT N July 25, 1917
NY N Aug 4, 1917
CIN N Feb 9, 1927

Joe Kelly
BOS N Jan 1917

Mike Kelly
PIT N Jan 1900

Pat Kelly
CHI A Oct 13, 1970
BAL A Nov 18, 1976
CLE A Dec 29, 1980

Van Kelly
SD N June 12, 1969

Bill Kelso
CIN N Nov 29, 1967
BAL A Mar 18, 1969

Russ Kemmerer
WAS A Apr 29, 1957
CHI A May 18, 1960
HOU N June 22, 1962

Steve Kemp
CHI A Nov 27, 1981
NY A Dec 9, 1982

Fred Kendall
CLE A Dec 8, 1976

Bill Kennedy
STL A June 15, 1948
CHI A Mar 13, 1952
BOS A Feb 9, 1953

Bob Kennedy
CLE A June 2, 1948
BAL A Apr 17, 1954
CHI A May 30, 1955
DET A May 15, 1956
BKN N May 20, 1957

Brickyard Kennedy
PIT N Jan 1903

Jim Kennedy
MIN A Oct 20, 1970

John Kennedy
LA N Dec 4, 1964
NY A Apr 3, 1967
SEA A Nov 13, 1968
BOS A June 26, 1970

Junior Kennedy
CIN N Dec 4, 1973
CHI N Oct 23, 1981

Terry Kennedy
SD N Dec 8, 1980

Vern Kennedy
DET A Dec 2, 1937
STL A May 13, 1939
WAS A May 15, 1940
CLE A Dec 11, 1941
PHI N July 28, 1944

Jerry Kenney
CLE A Nov 27, 1972

Joe Keough
CHI A Feb 1, 1973

Marty Keough
CLE A June 13, 1960
CIN N Dec 15, 1961
ATL N Apr 4, 1966
CHI N May 29, 1966

Matt Keough
NY A June 15, 1983

Gus Keriazakos
WAS A June 11, 1954

Bill Kerksieck
BOS N June 15, 1939

Jim Kern
TEX A Oct 3, 1978
NY N Dec 11, 1981
CIN N Feb 10, 1982
CHI A Aug 23, 1982

George Kernek
CHI A Oct 13, 1967

Buddy Kerr
BOS N Dec 14, 1949

John Kerr
WAS A Dec 4, 1931

Joe Kerrigan
BAL A Dec 7, 1977

Don Kessinger
STL N Oct 28, 1975
CHI A Aug 20, 1977

Leo Kiely
CLE A Jan 8, 1960
KC A Apr 5, 1960

Pete Kilduff
CHI N Aug 15, 1917
BKN N June 2, 1919

Mike Kilkenny
OAK A May 9, 1972
SD N May 17, 1972
CLE A June 11, 1972

Bill Killefer
CHI N Dec 11, 1917

Red Killefer
WAS A Aug 13, 1909
NY N July 20, 1916

Frank Killen
CHI N Unknown

Ed Killian
DET A Jan 1904

Newt Kimball
STL N Apr 15, 1940
PHI N May 20, 1943

Bruce Kimm
CAL A Aug 17, 1972
CHI N Aug 30, 1979

Chad Kimsey
CHI A Sept 9, 1932

Jerry Kindall
CLE A June 11, 1964

Ellis Kinder
BOS A Nov 18, 1947
STL N Dec 4, 1955
CHI A July 11, 1956

Ralph Kiner
CHI N June 4, 1953
CLE A Nov 16, 1954

Charlie King
MIL N Feb 12, 1957
CHI N Nov 10, 1957
STL N May 19, 1959

Clyde King
CIN N Oct 10, 1952

Hal King
TEX A Dec 2, 1971

Jim King
STL N Apr 20, 1957
SF N Apr 2, 1958
CHI A June 15, 1967
CLE A July 29, 1967

Lee King
PHI N July 1, 1921
PHI N July 1921

Lee King
NY N Jan 1919

Brian Kingman
BOS A Jan 17, 1983

Dave Kingman
NY N Feb 28, 1975
SD N June 15, 1977
CAL A Sept 6, 1977
NY A Sept 15, 1977
CHI N Nov 30, 1977
NY N Feb 28, 1981

Dennis Kinney
SD N June 14, 1978
DET A Dec 12, 1980

Fred Kipp
NY A Apr 5, 1960

Clay Kirby
CIN N Nov 9, 1973
MON N Dec 12, 1975

Willie Kirkland
CLE A Dec 3, 1960
BAL A Dec 4, 1963
WAS A Aug 12, 1964

Ed Kirkpatrick
KC A Dec 12, 1968
PIT N Dec 4, 1973
TEX A June 15, 1977
MIL A Aug 20, 1977

Don Kirkwood
CHI A June 15, 1977
TOR A Apr 11, 1978

Bruce Kison
CAL A Nov 16, 1979

Frank Kitson
BKN N Jan 1900
WAS A Dec 1905
NY A May 29, 1907

Malachi Kittredge
WAS A June 1903
CLE A Aug 15, 1906

Billy Klaus
NY N Feb 1, 1954
BOS A Dec 14, 1954
BAL A Dec 15, 1958
PHI N Apr 5, 1962

Bobby Klaus
NY N July 19, 1964
PHI N Feb 22, 1966
PIT N Mar 28, 1969

Chuck Klein
CHI N Nov 21, 1933
PHI N May 21, 1936

Lou Klein
CIN N Dec 14, 1949
PHI A May 10, 1951

Ted Kleinhans
PHI N Nov 21, 1933
CIN N May 8, 1934

Red Kleinow
BOS A May 1910
PHI N June 1911

Ed Klepfer
CLE A Aug 21, 1915

Eddie Klieman
WAS A Dec 14, 1948
PHI A Dec 14, 1949

Ron Klimkowski
NY A Aug 3, 1967
OAK A Apr 9, 1971

Bob Kline
PHI A Dec 12, 1933
WAS A June 23, 1934

Bobby Kline
NY A Feb 8, 1956

Ron Kline
STL N Dec 21, 1959
LA A Apr 10, 1961
DET A Aug 10, 1961
WAS A Mar 18, 1963
MIN A Dec 3, 1966
PIT N Dec 2, 1967
SF N June 10, 1969
BOS A July 5, 1969

Steve Kline
CLE A Apr 27, 1974

Johnny Kling
BOS N June 10, 1911
CIN N Feb 1913

Johnny Klippstein
CIN N Oct 1, 1954
LA N June 15, 1958
CLE A Apr 11, 1960
CIN N Dec 15, 1961
PHI N Mar 25, 1963
MIN A June 29, 1964

Ted Kluszewski
PIT N Dec 28, 1957
CHI A Aug 25, 1959

Mickey Klutts
OAK A June 15, 1978

Clyde Kluttz
NY N June 16, 1945
PHI N May 1, 1946
STL N May 2, 1946
PIT N Dec 26, 1946
WAS A June 12, 1951

Otto Knabe
PIT N Feb 10, 1916
CHI N July 29, 1916

Chris Knapp
CAL A Dec 5, 1977

Lou Knerr
WAS A Feb 14, 1947

Elmer Knetzer
BOS N Feb 10, 1916
CIN N Apr 1916

Alan Knicely
CIN N Mar 31, 1983

Bill Knickerbocker
STL A Jan 17, 1937
NY A Feb 15, 1938
CHI A Dec 31, 1940
PHI A Apr 3, 1942

Jack Knight
BOS A June 7, 1907

John Knight
NY A Feb 1909
WAS A Dec 1911
NY A July 7, 1913

Ray Knight
HOU N Dec 18, 1981

Pete Knisely
CHI N Dec 15, 1912

Bobby Knoop
CHI A May 14, 1969
KC A Mar 24, 1971

Fritz Knothe
PHI N June 17, 1933

Jack Knott
CHI A June 11, 1938
PHI A Dec 16, 1940

Darold Knowles
PHI N Dec 6, 1965
WAS A Nov 30, 1966
OAK A May 8, 1971
CHI N Oct 23, 1974
TEX A Feb 5, 1977
MON N Nov 10, 1977

Kevin Kobel
KC A June 17, 1980

Alan Koch
WAS A May 9, 1964

Pete Koegel
SEA A Aug 29, 1969
PHI N Apr 22, 1971

Mark Koenig
DET A May 30, 1930
CIN N Dec 20, 1933
NY N Dec 14, 1934

Elmer Koestner
CIN N Aug 1914

Dick Kokos
STL A Nov 20, 1947

Gary Kolb
MIL N Apr 9, 1964
NY N July 21, 1965
PIT N Dec 6, 1966

Don Kolloway
DET A May 7, 1949
PHI A Jan 29, 1953

Ed Konetchy
PIT N Dec 12, 1913
BOS N Feb 10, 1916
BKN N Apr 14, 1919
PHI N July 4, 1921

Jim Konstanty
BOS N Apr 18, 1946
NY A Aug 22, 1954

Cal Koonce
NY N Aug 2, 1967
BOS A June 8, 1970

Jerry Koosman
MIN A Dec 8, 1978
CHI A Aug 30, 1981
PHI N Dec 5, 1983

Larry Kopf
CIN N Dec 1915
CIN N Feb 18, 1922

Merlin Kopp
PHI A Dec 14, 1917

Joe Koppe
PHI N Mar 31, 1959
LA N May 4, 1961

Andy Kosco
LA N Dec 4, 1968
MIL A Feb 10, 1971
CAL A Jan 26, 1972
BOS A Aug 15, 1972
CIN N Mar 27, 1973

Dave Koslo
BAL A Apr 8, 1954

Frank Kostro
DET A June 15, 1963
MIN A June 11, 1964

Lou Koupal
PHI N July 24, 1929

Fabian Kowalik
PHI N May 21, 1936
BOS N Aug 4, 1936

Ernie Koy
BKN N Apr 15, 1938
STL N June 12, 1940
CIN N May 14, 1941
PHI N May 2, 1942

Al Kozar
WAS A Dec 10, 1947
CHI A May 31, 1950

Joe Krakauskas
CLE A Dec 24, 1940

Jack Kralick
CLE A May 2, 1963
NY A May 1, 1967

Jack Kramer
BOS A Nov 17, 1947
NY N Mar 26, 1950

Tex Kraus
PHI N Mar 24, 1943

Harry Krause
CLE A July 1912

Lew Krausse
MIL A Jan 15, 1970
STL N Sept 1, 1973

Lew Krausse
BOS A Oct 11, 1971

Ken Kravec
CHI N Mar 28, 1981

Danny Kravitz
KC A June 1, 1960
CIN N Oct 15, 1960

Mike Kreevich
PHI A Dec 9, 1941

Jim Kremmel
STL N July 16, 1973
CHI A Oct 26, 1973
CHI N Dec 11, 1973

Wayne Krenchicki
CIN N Feb 9, 1982
DET A June 30, 1983
CIN N Nov 21, 1983

Charlie Kress
CHI A June 8, 1949
BKN N June 9, 1954

Red Kress
CHI A Apr 27, 1932
WAS A May 9, 1934
STL A Oct 2, 1937
DET A May 13, 1939

Lou Kretlow
STL A Dec 14, 1949
CHI A July 5, 1950
STL A June 13, 1953

Rick Kreuger
CLE A Mar 24, 1978

Frank Kreutzer
WAS A July 13, 1964
PIT N May 17, 1969

Gary Kroll
MIN A Aug 7, 1964
HOU N Jan 6, 1966
CLE A July 20, 1967

John Kroner
CLE A Dec 1936

Rocky Krsnich
CIN N Dec 10, 1953

Art Krueger
BOS N Sept 1910

Ernie Krueger
BKN N May 1917
CIN N Feb 17, 1922

Otto Krueger
STL N Jan 1900
PIT N Jan 1903
PHI N Dec 20, 1904
PHI N Jan 1905

Mike Krukow
SF N Dec 14, 1982

Dick Kryhoski
DET A Dec 17, 1949
STL A Feb 14, 1952
NY A Dec 1, 1954
KC A Mar 30, 1955

Ted Kubiak
SEA A Dec 7, 1969
STL N July 29, 1971
TEX A Nov 3, 1971
OAK A July 20, 1972
SD N May 16, 1975

Jack Kubiszyn
STL N Dec 15, 1962

Gil Kubski
MIL A May 10, 1981

Jack Kucek
PHI N Apr 13, 1979

Johnny Kucks
KC A May 26, 1959
BAL A Oct 11, 1961
STL N Dec 1, 1961

Harvey Kuenn
CLE A Apr 17, 1960
SF N Dec 3, 1960
CHI N May 29, 1965
PHI N Apr 23, 1966

Joe Kuhel
CHI A Mar 18, 1938
WAS A Nov 24, 1943

Duane Kuiper
SF N Nov 14, 1981

Rusty Kuntz
MIN A June 21, 1983
DET A Dec 8, 1983

Craig Kusick
TOR A July 25, 1979

Art Kusnyer
MIL A Oct 22, 1973

Marty Kutyna
CIN N Dec 5, 1957
WAS A Dec 29, 1960

Bob Kuzava
CHI A Oct 2, 1948
WAS A May 31, 1950
NY A June 15, 1951
BAL A Aug 7, 1954
PHI N May 23, 1955

Chet Laabs
STL A May 13, 1939
PHI A Apr 9, 1947

Clem Labine
DET A June 15, 1960

Bob Lacey
SD N Mar 27, 1981
CLE A Apr 1, 1981
TEX A Sept 8, 1981

Candy LaChance
BOS A May 30, 1902

Pete LaCock
KC A Dec 8, 1976

Frank LaCorte
HOU N May 25, 1979
CAL A Dec 8, 1983

Mike LaCoss
HOU N Apr 6, 1982

Lee Lacy
ATL N Nov 17, 1975
LA N June 23, 1976
PIT N Jan 18, 1979

Pete Ladd
HOU N June 13, 1979
MIL A Oct 23, 1981

Lerrin LaGrow
STL N Apr 2, 1976
CHI A Mar 23, 1977
LA N May 11, 1979

Joe LaHoud
MIL A Oct 11, 1971
CAL A Oct 22, 1973
TEX A June 15, 1976

Jeff Lahti
STL N Apr 1, 1982

Nap Lajoie
CLE A June 1902
PHI A Jan 1915

Eddie Lake
DET A Jan 3, 1946

Joe Lake
STL A Dec 1909
DET A May 1912

Steve Lake
CHI N Apr 1, 1983

Al Lakeman
PHI N June 14, 1947

Jack Lamabe
BOS A Nov 20, 1962
HOU N Sept 14, 1965
CHI A Dec 1, 1965
NY N Apr 26, 1967
STL N July 16, 1967
CHI N Apr 22, 1968
MON N June 11, 1969

Al LaMacchia
WAS A June 15, 1946

Bill Lamar
BOS A May 1919
BKN N Mar 1920

Wayne LaMaster
BKN N Aug 8, 1938

Ray Lamb
CLE A Dec 11, 1970

Gene Lamont
DET A May 14, 1973

Bobby LaMotte
DET A Jan 15, 1927

Dennis Lamp
CHI A Mar 28, 1981
TOR A Jan 10, 1984

Gary Lance
SD N June 5, 1978

Rick Lancellotti
SD N Aug 5, 1980
MON N Oct 7, 1982

Rafael Landestoy
HOU N July 1, 1978
CIN N June 8, 1981
LA N May 9, 1983

Jim Landis
KC A Jan 20, 1965
CLE A Oct 1, 1965
HOU N Jan 4, 1967
DET A June 29, 1967

Ken Landreaux
MIN A Feb 3, 1979
LA N Mar 30, 1981

Larry Landreth
LA N May 20, 1978

Hobie Landrith
CHI N Nov 28, 1955
STL N Dec 11, 1956
SF N Oct 8, 1958
BAL A May 9, 1962
WAS A May 8, 1963

Don Landrum
CHI N June 5, 1962
SF N Dec 2, 1965

Tito Landrum
BAL A June 15, 1983
STL N Mar 25, 1984

Don Lang
NY A Dec 30, 1940

Rick Langford
OAK A Mar 15, 1977

Hal Lanier
NY A Feb 2, 1972

Max Lanier
NY N Dec 11, 1951

Johnny Lanning
PIT N Dec 6, 1939

Carney Lansford
BOS A Dec 10, 1980
OAK A Dec 6, 1982

Paul LaPalme
STL N Jan 11, 1955
CIN N May 1, 1956
CHI A June 22, 1956

Dave LaPoint
STL N Dec 12, 1980

Ralph LaPointe
STL N Apr 7, 1948

Frank LaPorte
BOS A Dec 1907
NY A July 1908
STL A Jan 1911
WAS A July 1912

Jack Lapp
CHI A Jan 1915

Norm Larker
MIL N Nov 30, 1962
SF N Aug 8, 1963

Dave LaRoche
MIN A Nov 30, 1971
CHI N Nov 30, 1972
CLE A Feb 25, 1975
CAL A May 11, 1977

Don Larsen
NY A Nov 18, 1954
KC A Dec 11, 1959
CHI A June 10, 1961
SF N Nov 30, 1961
HOU N May 20, 1964
BAL A Apr 24, 1965

Dan Larson
HOU N Aug 15, 1974

Tony LaRussa
ATL N Aug 14, 1971
CHI N Oct 20, 1972

Frank Lary
NY N May 30, 1964
MIL N Aug 8, 1964
NY N Mar 20, 1965
CHI A July 8, 1965

Lyn Lary
BOS A May 15, 1934
WAS A Oct 26, 1934
STL A June 29, 1935
CLE A Jan 17, 1937
BKN N May 3, 1939
STL N Aug 14, 1939

Fred Lasher
CLE A May 22, 1970

Tacks Latimer
PIT N Jan 1900

Barry Latman
CLE A Apr 18, 1960
LA A Dec 2, 1963
HOU N Dec 15, 1965

Charlie Lau
MIL N Oct 15, 1959
KC A July 1, 1963
BAL A June 15, 1964
ATL N May 31, 1967

George Lauzerique
SEA A Dec 7, 1969
STL N Oct 20, 1970

Cookie Lavagetto
BKN N Dec 4, 1936

Doc Lavan
PHI A Aug 24, 1913
STL A Feb 5, 1914
WAS A Dec 15, 1917
STL N Jan 1919

Jimmy Lavender
PHI N Apr 2, 1917

Ron Law
WAS A Dec 5, 1969

Rudy Law
CHI A Mar 30, 1982

Vance Law
CHI A Mar 21, 1982

Brooks Lawrence
CIN N Jan 31, 1956

Roxie Lawson
STL A May 13, 1939

Steve Lawson
TEX A July 20, 1972

Bill Laxton
PHI N Dec 15, 1967
DET A Dec 12, 1975
CLE A Sept 9, 1977
SD N June 22, 1978

Pete Layden
STL A Nov 17, 1947

Freddy Leach
NY N Oct 29, 1928
BOS N Mar 19, 1932

Tommy Leach
PIT N Jan 1900
CHI N June 22, 1912

Tom Leahy
PHI A June 1901

Fred Lear
NY N Feb 1920

Bevo LeBourveau
PHI A Feb 8, 1923

Bill Lee
PHI N Aug 5, 1943
BOS N July 14, 1945

Bill Lee
MON N Dec 7, 1978

Bob Lee
LA N Dec 15, 1966
CIN N May 31, 1967

Cliff Lee
PHI N May 1921
CIN N June 20, 1924

Don Lee
MIL N Oct 15, 1959
LA A May 29, 1962
HOU N July 6, 1965

Hal Lee
PHI N Oct 14, 1930
BOS N June 17, 1933

Leron Lee
SD N June 11, 1971
CLE A Mar 28, 1974

Mark Lee
PIT N Aug 5, 1980

Thornton Lee
CHI A Dec 10, 1936

Joe Lefebvre
SD N Apr 1, 1981
PHI N May 2, 1983

Craig Lefferts
SD N Dec 7, 1983

Ron LeFlore
MON N Dec 7, 1979
CHI A Dec 6, 1980

Lou Legett
BOS N Nov 7, 1928

Ken Lehman
BAL A June 4, 1957
PHI N Oct 2, 1958
CLE A Mar 20, 1962

Paul Lehner
PHI A Dec 13, 1949
CHI A Apr 30, 1951
STL A June 4, 1951
CLE A July 19, 1951
BOS A June 25, 1952

Hank Leiber
CHI N Dec 6, 1938
NY N Dec 4, 1941

Nemo Leibold
CHI A July 7, 1915
BOS A Mar 4, 1921
WAS A May 26, 1923

Lefty Leifield
CHI N May 1911
CHI N June 22, 1912

Ed Leip
PIT N Apr 1940

Dummy Leitner
CHI A May 1902

Frank Leja
LA A Mar 30, 1962

Jack Lelivelt
NY A Dec 1911
CLE A May 20, 1913

Dave Lemanczyk
CAL A June 3, 1980

Denny Lemaster
HOU N Oct 8, 1967
MON N Oct 14, 1971

Dick LeMay
HOU N Nov 30, 1962
CHI N Mar 28, 1963

Chet Lemon
CHI A June 15, 1975
DET A Nov 27, 1981

Jim Lemon
WAS A May 12, 1954
PHI N May 4, 1963
CHI A June 28, 1963

Dave Lemonds
CHI A Nov 30, 1970

Mark Lemongello
HOU N Dec 6, 1975
TOR A Nov 27, 1978
CHI N Apr 7, 1980

Don Lenhardt
CHI A June 4, 1951
BOS A Nov 13, 1951
DET A June 3, 1952
STL A Aug 14, 1952
BOS A Feb 12, 1954

Bob Lennon
CHI N Apr 16, 1957

Jim Lentine
DET A June 2, 1980
HOU N Apr 3, 1981

Eddie Leon
CHI A Oct 19, 1972
NY A Dec 5, 1974

Dutch Leonard
PHI N Dec 9, 1946
CHI N Dec 14, 1948

Dutch Leonard
NY A Dec 18, 1918
DET A Jan 1919

Jeff Leonard
HOU N July 1, 1978
SF N Apr 20, 1981

Joe Leonard
WAS A Aug 18, 1916

Ted Lepcio
DET A May 2, 1959
PHI N Dec 5, 1959
CHI A Apr 3, 1961

Don Leppert
BAL A Dec 1, 1954

Don Leppert
WAS A Dec 15, 1962

Randy Lerch
MIL A Mar 1, 1981
MON N Aug 14, 1982

Barry Lersch
ATL N Dec 3, 1973
STL N Sept 14, 1974

Don Leshnock
PHI N Oct 25, 1972

Sam Leslie
BKN N June 16, 1933
NY N Feb 20, 1936

Dennis Lewallyn
MIN A Nov 23, 1977
LA N Sept 13, 1980
CLE A Aug 25, 1981

Duffy Lewis
NY A Dec 18, 1918
WAS A Jan 20, 1921

Jim Lewis
NY A Nov 1, 1979

Johnny Lewis
NY N Dec 7, 1964

Sixto Lezcano
STL N Dec 12, 1980
SD N Dec 10, 1981
PHI N Aug 31, 1983

Francisco Libran
SD N Apr 25, 1969

Don Liddle
NY N Feb 1, 1954
STL N June 14, 1956

Fred Liese
BOS N Feb 1910

Gene Lillard
STL N Dec 27, 1939

Bob Lillis
STL N May 30, 1961

Vive Lindaman
BOS N Dec 15, 1905

Paul Lindblad
WAS A May 8, 1971
OAK A Oct 30, 1972
TEX A Feb 19, 1977
NY A Aug 2, 1978

Johnny Lindell
PHI N Aug 31, 1953

Freddie Lindstrom
PIT N Dec 12, 1932
CHI N Nov 22, 1934

Ed Linke
STL A Dec 1, 1937

Fred Linke
STL A Sept 1910

Larry Lintz
STL N July 25, 1975
OAK A Oct 28, 1975

Phil Linz
PHI N Nov 29, 1965
NY N July 11, 1967

Frank Linzy
STL N May 19, 1970
MIL A Mar 26, 1972
PHI N Nov 7, 1973

Johnny Lipon
BOS A June 3, 1952
STL A Sept 8, 1953
CHI A Feb 5, 1954
CIN N Apr 18, 1954

Joe Lis
MIN A Nov 30, 1972
CLE A June 5, 1974

Hod Lisenbee
BOS A Dec 15, 1928

Rick Lisi
BAL A Feb 19, 1982

Mark Littell
STL N Dec 8, 1977

Dick Littlefield
CHI A Dec 10, 1950
STL A Nov 27, 1951
DET A Feb 14, 1952
STL A Aug 14, 1952
PIT N May 25, 1954
STL N May 17, 1956
NY N June 14, 1956
BKN N Dec 13, 1956
CHI N Apr 16, 1957
MIL N Mar 30, 1958

John Littlefield
SD N Dec 8, 1980

Larry Littleton
CLE A Dec 21, 1979
MIN A July 3, 1982

Danny Litwhiler
STL N June 1, 1943
BOS N June 9, 1946
CIN N May 11, 1948

Mickey Livingston
PHI N Nov 11, 1940
CHI N Aug 5, 1943
NY N July 7, 1947

Paddy Livingston
CLE A Dec 1911

Hans Lobert
CIN N Mar 1906
PHI N Feb 1911
NY N Jan 1915

Don Lock
WAS A July 11, 1962
PHI N Nov 30, 1966
BOS A May 5, 1969

Larry Locke
STL N Apr 7, 1962
PHI N Apr 28, 1962
LA A Oct 15, 1964
CIN N July 28, 1965
CAL A June 3, 1966

Bob Locker
SEA A June 8, 1969
OAK A June 15, 1970
CHI N Nov 21, 1972
OAK A Nov 3, 1973
CHI N Oct 23, 1974

Harry Lockhead
PHI A Apr 1901

Gene Locklear
SD N June 12, 1973
NY A July 10, 1976

Whitey Lockman
STL N June 14, 1956
NY N Feb 26, 1957
BAL A Feb 14, 1959
CIN N June 23, 1959

Skip Lockwood
CAL A Oct 22, 1973
NY N Dec 3, 1974
BOS A Nov 27, 1979

Dario Lodigiani
CHI A Dec 16, 1940

Billy Loes
BAL A May 14, 1956
WAS A Apr 1, 1959
SF N Nov 30, 1959
NY N Oct 16, 1961

Lucky Lohrke
PHI N Dec 13, 1951
PIT N Jan 13, 1954

Bill Lohrman
STL N Dec 11, 1941
NY N May 5, 1942
BKN N July 31, 1943

Mickey Lolich
NY N Dec 12, 1975

Sherm Lollar
NY A Dec 20, 1946
STL A Dec 13, 1948
CHI A Nov 27, 1951

Tim Lollar
SD N Apr 1, 1981

Ernie Lombardi
CIN N Mar 14, 1932
BOS N Feb 7, 1942
NY N Apr 27, 1943

Vic Lombardi
PIT N Dec 8, 1947

Jim Lonborg
MIL A Oct 11, 1971
PHI N Oct 31, 1972

Dale Long
STL A June 1, 1951
CHI N May 1, 1957
SF N Apr 5, 1960
NY A Aug 22, 1960
NY A July 11, 1962

Herman Long
DET A June 10, 1903

Jeoff Long
CHI A July 7, 1964

Joe Lonnett
MIL N June 13, 1958

Ed Lopat
NY A Feb 24, 1948
BAL A July 30, 1955

Stan Lopata
MIL N Mar 31, 1959

Davey Lopes
OAK A Feb 8, 1982

Al Lopez
BOS N Dec 12, 1935
PIT N June 14, 1940
CLE A Dec 7, 1946

Aurelio Lopez
DET A Dec 4, 1978

Carlos Lopez
BAL A Dec 7, 1977

Hector Lopez
NY A May 26, 1959

Marcelino Lopez
LA A Sept 9, 1964
BAL A June 15, 1967
MIL A Apr 5, 1971
CLE A Mar 29, 1972

Bris Lord
PHI A July 25, 1910
BOS N Dec 1912

Harry Lord
CHI A Aug 9, 1910

Baldy Louden
CIN N Dec 23, 1915

Slim Love
BOS A Dec 18, 1918
DET A Jan 17, 1919

Jay Loviglio
CHI A Apr 1, 1981
CHI N Nov 29, 1982

Joe Lovitto
NY N Dec 12, 1975

Grover Lowdermilk
CIN N Dec 15, 1912
DET A Aug 18, 1915
CLE A Aug 1916
STL A Oct 1917
CHI A May 1919

Bobby Lowe
CHI N July 1902
PIT N Apr 20, 1904
DET A Apr 30, 1904

John Lowenstein
TOR A Dec 6, 1976
CLE A Mar 29, 1977
TEX A Feb 28, 1978
BAL A Nov 27, 1978

Turk Lown
CIN N May 8, 1958
CHI A June 23, 1958

Peanuts Lowrey
CIN N June 15, 1949
STL N Sept 7, 1950

Johnny Lucadello
NY A Mar 1, 1947

Gary Lucas
MON N Dec 7, 1983

Red Lucas
PIT N Oct 17, 1933

Fred Luderus
PHI N July 1910

Steve Luebber
TEX A Feb 19, 1982

Dick Luebke
CIN N Dec 15, 1962

Mike Lum
CIN N Dec 12, 1975
ATL N Feb 15, 1978

Jerry Lumpe
KC A May 26, 1959
DET A Nov 18, 1963

Don Lund
STL A June 28, 1948
DET A Jan 20, 1949

Gordon Lund
BAL A Nov 28, 1967
SEA A Mar 31, 1969

Tony Lupien
PHI N Apr 13, 1944
DET A Jan 26, 1949

Al Luplow
NY N Nov 29, 1965

Dolf Luque
BKN N Feb 1930

Billy Lush
CLE A Jan 1904

Johnny Lush
STL N June 10, 1907

Greg Luzinski
CHI A Mar 30, 1981

Sparky Lyle
NY A Mar 22, 1972
TEX A Nov 10, 1978
PHI N Sept 13, 1980
CHI A Aug 21, 1982

Ed Lynch
NY N Aug 12, 1979

Jerry Lynch
PIT N May 23, 1963

Fred Lynn
CAL A Jan 23, 1981

Red Lynn
NY N May 9, 1939

Al Lyons
PIT N Aug 4, 1947
BOS N Nov 18, 1947

Rick Lysander
HOU N Feb 10, 1981
MIN A Jan 12, 1983

Jim Lyttle
CHI A Oct 13, 1971
KC A Feb 1, 1973
MON N July 10, 1973
MON N July 18, 1975

Duke Maas
KC A Nov 20, 1957
NY A June 15, 1958

Bob Mabe
CIN N Oct 3, 1958

Danny MacFayden
NY A June 5, 1932
CIN N Nov 13, 1934
BOS N June 15, 1935
PIT N Dec 8, 1939

Ken Macha
TOR A Jan 15, 1981

Dave Machemer
BOS A Mar 3, 1976

Ray Mack
NY A Dec 20, 1946

Pete Mackanin
MON N Dec 5, 1974
PHI N Sept 5, 1978
MIN A Dec 7, 1979

Ken MacKenzie
NY N Oct 11, 1961
STL N Aug 5, 1963
SF N Oct 1, 1963

Mike Madden
HOU N Aug 30, 1982

Tom Madden
PHI N May 1911

Elliott Maddox
WAS A Oct 9, 1970
NY A Mar 23, 1974
BAL A Jan 20, 1977
NY A Nov 30, 1977

Garry Maddox
PHI N May 4, 1975

Dave Madison
STL A Apr 7, 1952
DET A Aug 14, 1952

Ed Madjeski
CHI A May 1934

Bill Madlock
CHI N Oct 25, 1973
SF N Feb 11, 1977
PIT N June 28, 1979

Bill Magee
NY N May 1901
PHI N May 1902

Lee Magee
NY A Feb 10, 1916
STL A July 15, 1917
CIN N Apr 28, 1918
NY A Apr 28, 1918
CHI N June 2, 1919
BKN N July 1919

Sherry Magee
BOS N Feb 14, 1915
CIN N Aug 1, 1917

Sal Maglie
CLE A July 31, 1955
BKN N May 15, 1956
NY A Sept 1, 1957
STL N June 14, 1958

Pete Magrini
NY A Aug 3, 1967

Freddie Maguire
BOS N Nov 7, 1928

Jack Maguire
PIT N June 5, 1951
STL A July 16, 1951

Art Mahaffey
STL N Oct 27, 1965
NY N Apr 1, 1967

Roy Mahaffey
STL A Jan 29, 1936

Mickey Mahler
CAL A Apr 1, 1981

Bob Mahoney
STL A May 29, 1951
BKN N Oct 14, 1952

Jim Mahoney
CLE A Oct 5, 1961
CHI A July 20, 1966

Fritz Maisel
STL A Jan 22, 1918

Hank Majeski
NY A Sept 25, 1942
PHI A June 14, 1946
CHI A Dec 14, 1949
PHI A June 4, 1951
CLE A June 10, 1952
BAL A June 27, 1955

Jim Maler
NY N Jan 15, 1984

Sheldon Mallory
CHI N Dec 8, 1976
NY N Dec 8, 1976
TOR A Mar 25, 1978
CLE A Nov 3, 1978

Bob Malloy
PIT N Apr 28, 1947

Harry Malmberg
DET A Apr 7, 1955

Pat Malone
STL N Oct 26, 1934
NY A Mar 26, 1935

Billy Maloney
BKN N Dec 30, 1905

Jim Maloney
CAL A Dec 15, 1970

Al Mamaux
BKN N Jan 9, 1918

Frank Mancuso
STL A Dec 16, 1946

Gus Mancuso
NY N Oct 10, 1932
CHI N Dec 6, 1938
BKN N Dec 8, 1939
STL N Dec 4, 1940
NY N May 5, 1942

Jim Mangan
NY N Mar 5, 1956

Angel Mangual
OAK A Sept 14, 1970

Pepe Mangual
NY N July 21, 1976

Leo Mangum
WAS A Jan 15, 1927

Phil Mankowski
NY N Oct 31, 1979

Les Mann
CHI N Feb 10, 1916
BOS N Aug 1919
STL N Nov 9, 1920
NY N July 18, 1927

Rick Manning
MIL A June 6, 1983

Felix Mantilla
BOS A Dec 11, 1962
HOU N Apr 3, 1966

Jerry Manuel
MON N Mar 15, 1980
SD N May 22, 1982
MON N June 8, 1982

Heinie Manush
STL A Dec 2, 1927
WAS A June 13, 1930
BOS A Dec 17, 1935
PIT N May 1938

Dick Manville
PIT N Dec 3, 1952

Cliff Mapes
STL A July 31, 1951
DET A Feb 14, 1952
STL A Oct 27, 1952

Georges Maranda
CLE A Aug 20, 1962

Rabbit Maranville
PIT N Feb 23, 1921
CHI N Oct 27, 1924
BKN N Nov 9, 1925
BOS N Dec 8, 1928

Firpo Marberry
DET A Dec 14, 1932

Johnny Marcum
BOS A Dec 10, 1935
CHI A June 2, 1939

Juan Marichal
BOS A Dec 7, 1973

Roger Maris
KC A June 15, 1958
NY A Dec 11, 1959
STL N Dec 8, 1966

Dick Marlowe
CHI A Sept 17, 1956

Rube Marquard
BKN N Aug 31, 1915
CIN N Dec 15, 1920
BOS N Feb 18, 1922

Gonzalo Marquez
CHI N Aug 29, 1973

Luis Marquez
PIT N June 14, 1954

Bob Marquis
CIN N Aug 28, 1952

Bill Marriott
BKN N Apr 1926

Armando Marsans
STL A Feb 10, 1916
NY A July 15, 1917

Freddie Marsh
STL A Apr 1, 1951
WAS A May 12, 1952
STL A June 10, 1952
CHI A Jan 20, 1953
BAL A Dec 6, 1954

Dave Marshall
NY N Dec 12, 1969
SD N Nov 30, 1972

Doc Marshall
NY N May 1904
BOS N Aug 7, 1904
STL N July 13, 1906
CHI N June 1908
BKN N Nov 1908

Jim Marshall
BAL A Dec 3, 1957
CHI N Aug 23, 1958
BOS A Nov 21, 1959
CLE A Mar 16, 1960
SF N Mar 29, 1960
NY N Oct 13, 1961
PIT N May 7, 1962

Mike Marshall
LA N Dec 5, 1973
ATL N June 23, 1976
TEX A Apr 30, 1977

Willard Marshall
BOS N Dec 14, 1949
CIN N June 4, 1952
CHI A Dec 10, 1953

Billy Martin
KC A June 15, 1957
DET A Nov 20, 1957
CLE A Nov 20, 1958
MIL N Dec 3, 1960
MIN A June 1, 1961

Gene Martin
PHI N Nov 3, 1970

J. C. Martin
NY N July 22, 1967
CHI N Mar 29, 1970

Jack Martin
PHI N June 1914

Jerry Martin
CHI N Feb 23, 1979
SF N Dec 12, 1980
KC A Dec 11, 1981

Joe Martin
STL A July 1903

John Martin
STL N June 2, 1980
DET A Aug 4, 1983

Morrie Martin
CHI A June 11, 1954
BAL A July 13, 1956
CLE A July 2, 1958

Renie Martin
SF N Mar 30, 1982

Speed Martin
STL A July 14, 1917

Stu Martin
PIT N Dec 2, 1940

Buck Martinez
KC A Dec 16, 1968
STL N Dec 8, 1977
MIL A Dec 8, 1977
TOR A May 10, 1981

Carmelo Martinez
SD N Dec 7, 1983

Marty Martinez
HOU N Dec 4, 1968
STL N Nov 3, 1971
OAK A May 18, 1972
TEX A July 20, 1972

Silvio Martinez
CHI A Dec 10, 1976
STL N Aug 31, 1977
CLE A Nov 20, 1981

Teddy Martinez
STL N Dec 11, 1974
OAK A May 18, 1975

Tippy Martinez
BAL A June 15, 1976

Tony Martinez
NY N Apr 1, 1967

Joe Marty
PHI N May 29, 1939

Bob Martyn
NY A Apr 12, 1959

Randy Martz
CHI A Jan 25, 1983

Clyde Mashore
MON N June 15, 1970

Phil Masi
PIT N June 15, 1949
CHI A Feb 2, 1950

Don Mason
SD N Dec 4, 1970

Jim Mason
NY A Dec 6, 1973
TEX A May 9, 1977
MON N Dec 8, 1978

Walt Masterson
BOS A June 13, 1949
WAS A June 10, 1952
DET A May 11, 1956

Tommy Matchick
BOS A Dec 13, 1969
KC A May 28, 1970
MIL A May 11, 1971
NY A Apr 5, 1973

Eddie Mathews
HOU N Dec 31, 1966
DET A Aug 17, 1967

Nelson Mathews
KC A Dec 15, 1963

Christy Mathewson
NY N Dec 15, 1900
CIN N July 20, 1916

John Matias
CHI A Nov 29, 1967
KC A Oct 13, 1970

Jon Matlack
TEX A Dec 8, 1977

Gary Matthews
ATL N Nov 17, 1976
PHI N Mar 25, 1981
CHI N Mar 26, 1984

Wid Matthews
WAS A Jan 1924

Bobby Mattick
CIN N Dec 4, 1940

Gene Mauch
PIT N May 3, 1947
BKN N Dec 8, 1947
CHI N June 17, 1948
BOS N Dec 14, 1949
STL N Mar 26, 1952

Al Maul
PHI N Feb 1900

Carmen Mauro
WAS A May 26, 1953
PHI A June 30, 1953
NY A Dec 16, 1953

Dal Maxvill
OAK A Aug 30, 1972
PIT N July 7, 1973

Charlie Maxwell
BAL A Nov 24, 1954
DET A May 11, 1955
CHI A June 25, 1962

Carlos May
NY A May 18, 1976
CAL A Sept 16, 1977

Dave May
MIL A June 15, 1970
ATL N Nov 2, 1974
TEX A Dec 9, 1976
MIL A May 17, 1978
PIT N Sept 13, 1978

Jakie May
CHI N Oct 14, 1930

Jerry May
KC A Dec 2, 1970
NY N May 14, 1973

Lee May
HOU N Nov 29, 1971
BAL A Dec 3, 1974

Milt May
HOU N Oct 31, 1973
DET A Dec 6, 1975
CHI A May 27, 1979
SF N Nov 1, 1979
PIT N Aug 19, 1983

Rudy May
PHI N Oct 15, 1964
LA A Dec 3, 1964
NY A June 15, 1974
BAL A June 15, 1976
MON N Dec 7, 1977
NY A Nov 8, 1979

John Mayberry
KC A Dec 2, 1971
TOR A Apr 4, 1978
NY A May 5, 1982

Lee Maye
HOU N May 13, 1965
CLE A Jan 4, 1967
WAS A June 20, 1969
CHI A Sept 10, 1970
KC A Dec 9, 1980

Ed Mayer
CHI N Apr 20, 1957

Erskine Mayer
PIT N July 1, 1918
CHI A Aug 1919

Eddie Mayo
BOS N Dec 4, 1936

Carl Mays
NY A July 29, 1919
CIN N Dec 11, 1923

Willie Mays
NY N May 11, 1972

Lee Mazzilli
TEX A Apr 1, 1982
NY A Aug 8, 1982
PIT N Dec 22, 1982

Bill McAfee
BOS N Oct 14, 1930
STL A Dec 1933

Jim McAnany
CHI N Apr 1, 1961

Jim McAndrew
SD N Dec 20, 1973

Ike McAuley
STL N May 24, 1917

Dick McAuliffe
BOS A Oct 23, 1973

Al McBean
LA N Apr 17, 1969

Algie McBride
NY N May 30, 1901

Bake McBride
PHI N June 15, 1977
CLE A Feb 16, 1982

George McBride
STL N July 4, 1905

Tom McBride
WAS A May 14, 1947

Bill McCabe
BKN N May 1920

Joe McCabe
WAS A Oct 15, 1964

Larry McCall
CAL A Sept 16, 1974
TEX A Nov 10, 1978
CLE A Jan 4, 1980

Roger McCardell
BAL A Nov 30, 1959

Alex McCarthy
CHI N July 1915
PIT N July 1916

Jack McCarthy
CHI N Feb 10, 1900
BKN N Dec 30, 1905

Johnny McCarthy
NY N Jan 1936
STL N Dec 11, 1941

Tom McCarthy
PIT N Jan 1908
BOS N June 1908

Lew McCarty
NY N Aug 20, 1916
STL N Aug 1920

Tim McCarver
PHI N Oct 7, 1969
MON N June 14, 1972
STL N Nov 6, 1972
BOS A Sept 1, 1974

Joe McClain
NY N June 14, 1958

Bob McClure
MIL A Dec 6, 1976

Amby McConnell
CHI A Aug 9, 1910

George McConnell
CHI N Sept 23, 1913
CHI N Feb 10, 1916

Billy McCool
STL N Apr 2, 1970

Barry McCormick
WAS A July 1903

Mike McCormick
BAL A Dec 15, 1962
WAS A Apr 4, 1965
SF N Dec 3, 1966
NY A July 20, 1970

Mike McCormick
BOS N June 3, 1946
BKN N Dec 15, 1948
WAS A Dec 11, 1950

Moose McCormick
NY N July 1903
PIT N Aug 9, 1904
PHI N Dec 20, 1904
NY N May 1908

Barney McCosky
PHI A May 18, 1946
CLE A July 21, 1951

Willie McCovey
SD N Oct 25, 1973
OAK A Aug 30, 1976
SF N Jan 6, 1977

Benny McCoy
PHI A Dec 9, 1939

Tom McCraw
WAS A Mar 29, 1971
CLE A Apr 3, 1972
CAL A Apr 2, 1973
CLE A July 17, 1974

Tom McCreery
BKN N May 1901
BOS N June 1903

Clyde McCullough
PIT N Dec 8, 1948
CHI N Dec 3, 1952

Harry McCurdy
PHI N Dec 11, 1929
CIN N Nov 1933

Lindy McDaniel
CHI N Oct 17, 1962
SF N Dec 2, 1965
NY A July 12, 1968
KC A Dec 7, 1973

Mickey McDermott
WAS A Dec 9, 1953
NY A Feb 8, 1956
KC A Feb 19, 1957
DET A Nov 20, 1957
KC A July 21, 1961

Danny McDevitt
NY A Dec 16, 1960
KC A Apr 10, 1962

Dave McDonald
MON N May 15, 1970
SF N Dec 30, 1970

Hank McDonald
STL A May 28, 1933

Jim McDonald
STL A May 17, 1951
NY A Nov 23, 1951
BAL A Nov 18, 1954

Tex McDonald
BOS N June 1913

Sam McDowell
SF N Nov 29, 1971
NY A June 7, 1973

Will McEnaney
MON N Dec 16, 1976
PIT N Mar 29, 1978

Leon McFadden
STL N June 13, 1970

Chappie McFarland
PIT N June 3, 1906
BKN N Aug 1, 1906

Orlando McFarlane
CAL A Apr 10, 1967

Andy McGaffigan
SF N Mar 30, 1982
MON N Feb 27, 1984

Dan McGann
STL N Jan 17, 1900
BOS N Oct 7, 1907

Bill McGee
NY N May 14, 1940

Willie McGee
STL N Oct 21, 1981

Ed McGhee
PHI A Jan 27, 1953
CHI A June 11, 1954

Randy McGilberry
NY N June 17, 1980

Dan McGinn
CHI N Apr 7, 1972

Joe McGinnity
BKN N Jan 1900

Lynn McGlothen
STL N Dec 7, 1973
SF N Dec 10, 1976
CHI N June 15, 1978
CHI A Aug 15, 1981

Jim McGlothlin
CIN N Nov 25, 1969
CHI A Aug 29, 1973

Bob McGraw
BOS A July 29, 1919
STL N Feb 28, 1927
PHI N Dec 1927
STL N Dec 11, 1929

John McGraw
STL N Feb 11, 1900

Tug McGraw
PHI N Dec 3, 1974

Scott McGregor
BAL A June 15, 1976

Deacon McGuire
NY A Jan 1904
BOS A June 29, 1907
CLE A Aug 1908

Marty McHale
CLE A May 1916

Vance McHenry
TEX A Jan 27, 1983

Stuffy McInnis
BOS A Jan 10, 1918
CLE A Dec 24, 1921
BOS N Jan 1923

Joe McIntosh
HOU N Dec 11, 1975

Matty McIntyre
CHI A Jan 1911

Archie McKain
DET A Dec 15, 1938
STL A Aug 4, 1941
BKN N July 15, 1943

Bill McKechnie
BOS N Dec 1912
NY A Apr 15, 1913
NY N Dec 23, 1915
CIN N July 20, 1916
PIT N Mar 1918

Rich McKinney
NY A Dec 2, 1971
OAK A Nov 24, 1972

Jim McKnight
CHI N June 15, 1960
MIL N Dec 3, 1962

Denny McLain
DET A Apr 8, 1963
WAS A Oct 9, 1970
OAK A Mar 4, 1972
ATL N June 29, 1972

Bo McLaughlin
ATL N May 25, 1979

Byron McLaughlin
MIN A Dec 12, 1980

Joey McLaughlin
TOR A Dec 5, 1979

Warren McLaughlin
PHI N Mar 1903

Larry McLean
STL N Dec 12, 1903
NY N July 1913

Cal McLish
PIT N May 3, 1947
CHI N Dec 8, 1948
CHI A Dec 15, 1960
PHI N Dec 15, 1961

Jack McMahan
KC A June 23, 1956
NY A Feb 19, 1957

Don McMahon
HOU N May 9, 1962
CLE A Sept 30, 1963
BOS A June 2, 1966
CHI A June 3, 1967
DET A July 21, 1968
SF N Aug 9, 1969

Frank McManus
NY A July 25, 1904

Jim McManus
KC A Nov 20, 1957

Marty McManus
DET A Jan 15, 1927
BOS A Aug 31, 1931

Norm McMillan
BOS A Jan 30, 1923
STL A Dec 1923

Roy McMillan
MIL N Dec 15, 1960
NY N May 8, 1964

Tommy McMillan
PIT N Dec 5, 1978

Tommy McMillan
CIN N May 1910

Ken McMullen
CAL A Apr 27, 1970
LA N Nov 28, 1972
MIL A Feb 25, 1977

Eric McNair
BOS A Jan 4, 1936
CHI A Dec 21, 1938
DET A Dec 18, 1940
WAS A July 17, 1942
PHI A July 25, 1942

Dave McNally
MON N Dec 4, 1974

Mike McNally
NY A Dec 15, 1920
BOS A Dec 10, 1924
WAS A Dec 11, 1924
WAS A Feb 1925

Tim McNamara
NY N Apr 17, 1925

Rusty McNealy
OAK A Dec 9, 1981
MON N Dec 7, 1983

Earl McNeely
STL A Oct 19, 1927

Jerry McNertney
STL N Oct 20, 1970
PIT N May 4, 1973

Bill McNulty
CHI N Aug 31, 1971
TEX A Oct 30, 1972
NY N Mar 28, 1973

George McQuillan
CIN N Feb 1911
PHI N Feb 14, 1915

Hugh McQuillan
NY N July 30, 1922
BOS N June 12, 1927

George McQuinn
PHI A Oct 16, 1945

Hal McRae
KC A Nov 30, 1972

Norm McRae
WAS A Oct 9, 1970
DET A May 30, 1972
PIT N Nov 30, 1972

Doug McWeeny
CIN N Feb 1930

Larry McWilliams
PIT N June 30, 1982

Lee Meadows
PHI N July 14, 1919
PIT N May 22, 1923

Doc Medich
PIT N Dec 11, 1975
OAK A Mar 15, 1977
SEA A Sept 13, 1977
NY N Sept 26, 1977
TEX A Nov 11, 1977
MIL A Aug 11, 1982

Joe Medwick
BKN N June 12, 1940
NY N July 6, 1943
BOS N June 16, 1945

Jouett Meekin
PIT N Jan 1900

Roman Mejias
BOS A Nov 26, 1962

Sam Mejias
STL N June 7, 1976
MON N Nov 6, 1976
CHI N Dec 14, 1978
CIN N July 4, 1979

Sam Mele
WAS A June 13, 1949
CHI A May 3, 1952
BAL A Feb 5, 1954
BOS A July 29, 1954
CIN N June 23, 1955

Luis Melendez
SD N May 19, 1976

Oscar Melillo
BOS A May 21, 1935

Paul Meloan
STL A Apr 1911

Bill Melton
CAL A Dec 11, 1975
CLE A Dec 3, 1976

Rube Melton
BKN N Dec 12, 1942

Mario Mendoza
SEA A Dec 5, 1978
TEX A Dec 12, 1980

Denis Menke
HOU N Oct 8, 1967
CIN N Nov 29, 1971
HOU N Feb 18, 1974

Mike Menosky
WAS A Feb 10, 1916
BOS A Jan 20, 1920

Mike Meola
BOS A July 1936

Rudi Meoli
SD N Sept 17, 1975
CIN N Apr 5, 1976

Win Mercer
NY N Feb 9, 1900

Spike Merena
DET A Sept 24, 1934

Fred Merkle
BKN N Aug 20, 1916
CHI N Aug 16, 1917

Lloyd Merriman
CHI A Feb 10, 1955

Jim Merritt
CIN N Nov 21, 1968

Lloyd Merritt
LA N June 15, 1959

Sam Mertes
STL N July 13, 1906

Steve Mesner
STL N Dec 27, 1939
BKN N Feb 1, 1943

Andy Messersmith
LA N Nov 28, 1972
ATL N Apr 10, 1976
NY A Dec 7, 1977

Catfish Metkovich
CLE A Apr 2, 1947
STL A Dec 9, 1947
CHI N June 4, 1953
MIL N Dec 7, 1953

Charlie Metro
PHI A Aug 13, 1944

Clarence Metzger
SD N Dec 6, 1974
STL N May 17, 1977
NY N Apr 5, 1978
PHI N July 4, 1978

Roger Metzger
HOU N Oct 12, 1970
SF N June 15, 1978

Alex Metzler
STL A July 21, 1930

Bob Meusel
CIN N Oct 16, 1929

Irish Meusel
NY N July 25, 1921

Bob Meyer
LA A June 12, 1964
KC A July 29, 1964
SEA A Aug 29, 1969

Dan Meyer
OAK A Dec 9, 1981

Dutch Meyer
CLE A Apr 27, 1945

Russ Meyer
PHI N Oct 11, 1948
BKN N Feb 16, 1953
MIL N Feb 16, 1953
CHI N Dec 9, 1955
CIN N Sept 1, 1956
BOS A Apr 13, 1957

Scott Meyer
DET A Mar 1, 1982

Chief Meyers
BKN N Feb 10, 1916
BOS N Aug 16, 1917

Gene Michael
LA N Dec 1, 1966
NY A Nov 30, 1967

Cass Michaels
WAS A May 31, 1950
STL A May 12, 1952
PHI A Aug 5, 1952
CHI A Dec 8, 1953

Ed Mickelson
STL A Oct 1, 1952

Pete Mikkelsen
PIT N Dec 10, 1965
CHI N Aug 4, 1967
STL N Apr 22, 1968
LA N Oct 21, 1968

Eddie Miksis
CHI N June 15, 1951
STL N Dec 11, 1956
BAL A Sept 19, 1957

Larry Milbourne
SEA A Mar 30, 1977
NY A Nov 18, 1980
MIN A May 12, 1982
CLE A July 3, 1982
PHI N Dec 9, 1982
NY A July 16, 1983
SEA A Feb 14, 1984

Johnny Miljus
CLE A July 10, 1928

Felix Millan
NY N Nov 2, 1972

Bill Miller
BAL A Dec 1, 1954

Bing Miller
PHI A Jan 10, 1922
STL A June 15, 1926
PHI A Dec 13, 1927
BOS A May 1, 1935

Bob Miller
NY N May 7, 1962

Bob Miller
LA N Nov 30, 1962
MIN A Nov 28, 1967
CLE A Dec 10, 1969
CHI A June 15, 1970
CHI A Sept 1, 1970
PIT N Aug 10, 1971
SD N June 22, 1973
NY N Sept 23, 1973

Bruce Miller
CAL A Aug 17, 1972
SF N Apr 14, 1973

Doc Miller
BOS N Apr 1910
PHI N July 1, 1912
CIN N Dec 1913

Dots Miller
STL N Dec 12, 1913
PHI N Jan 1920

Dusty Miller
STL N Unknown

Dyar Miller
CAL A June 13, 1977
TOR A June 6, 1979
MON N July 30, 1979

Eddie Miller
ATL N Dec 8, 1977
DET A Mar 23, 1982

Eddie Miller
BOS N Aug 10, 1938
CIN N Dec 4, 1942
PHI N Feb 7, 1948
STL N May 3, 1950

Elmer Miller
NY A July 23, 1915
BOS A July 23, 1922

Frank Miller
WAS A Oct 1919

John Miller
LA N Apr 3, 1967

John Miller
NY N May 10, 1967

Larry Miller
NY N Oct 15, 1964

Norm Miller
ATL N Apr 22, 1973

Otto Miller
STL A Jan 15, 1927

Ox Miller
STL A Aug 18, 1943

Randy Miller
MON N Dec 7, 1977

Rick Miller
CAL A Dec 21, 1977
BOS A Dec 10, 1980

Roscoe Miller
PIT N Feb 1904

Stu Miller
PHI N May 11, 1956
NY N Oct 11, 1956
BAL A Dec 15, 1962
ATL N Apr 1, 1968

Ward Miller
CIN N May 1909
STL A Feb 10, 1916

Buster Mills
STL A Oct 2, 1937
NY A Oct 26, 1938

Lefty Mills
BKN N Feb 5, 1941

Al Milnar
STL A Aug 27, 1943

John Milner
PIT N Dec 8, 1977
TEX A Dec 8, 1977
MON N Aug 20, 1981

Don Mincher
WAS A Apr 4, 1960
CAL A Dec 2, 1966
OAK A Jan 15, 1970
WAS A May 8, 1971
OAK A July 20, 1972

Craig Minetto
BAL A Feb 24, 1982
HOU N Dec 21, 1983

Paul Minner
CHI N Oct 14, 1949

Minnie Minoso
CHI A Apr 30, 1951
PHI A Apr 30, 1951
CLE A Dec 4, 1957
CHI A Dec 6, 1959
STL N Nov 27, 1961
WAS A Apr 2, 1963

Jim Minshall
SEA A Oct 15, 1976

Greg Minton
SF N Apr 2, 1973

Paul Mirabella
NY A Nov 10, 1978
TOR A Nov 1, 1979
CHI N Dec 28, 1981
TEX A Mar 26, 1982

Willie Miranda
CHI A Oct 24, 1951
STL A June 15, 1952
CHI A June 28, 1952
STL A Oct 16, 1952
NY A June 12, 1953
BAL A Nov 18, 1954

Bobby Mitchell
MIN A Jan 6, 1982

Bobby Mitchell
MIL A June 7, 1971

Clarence Mitchell
BKN N Feb 1918
PHI N Feb 11, 1923
NY N May 15, 1930

Dale Mitchell
BKN N July 29, 1956

Fred Mitchell
PHI A Apr 1902
BKN N Aug 18, 1904

Johnny Mitchell
BOS A July 23, 1922
BKN N Nov 1923

Mike Mitchell
CHI N Dec 15, 1912
PIT N July 29, 1913
WAS A July 20, 1914

Paul Mitchell
OAK A Apr 2, 1976
SEA A Aug 4, 1977
MIL A June 7, 1979

Roy Mitchell
CIN N Apr 1918

Willie Mitchell
DET A June 20, 1916

George Mitterwald
CHI N Dec 6, 1973

Johnny Mize
CIN N Dec 13, 1934
NY N Dec 11, 1941
NY A Aug 22, 1949

Vinegar Bend Mizell
PIT N May 28, 1960
NY N May 7, 1962

Danny Moeller
CLE A Aug 18, 1916

Randy Moffitt
TOR A Feb 25, 1983

Herb Moford
BOS A Dec 2, 1958

George Mogridge
NY A Feb 1915
WAS A Jan 20, 1921
STL A June 8, 1925
NY A Feb 6, 1926
BOS N June 1926

Johnny Mokan
PHI N July 14, 1922
STL N Dec 13, 1927

Bob Molinaro
CHI A Sept 22, 1977
BAL A Aug 30, 1979
CHI A Oct 3, 1979
CHI N Aug 15, 1981
PHI N Sept 1, 1982

Fritz Mollwitz
CIN N July 20, 1914
CHI N July 22, 1916
PIT N Feb 4, 1917
STL N Aug 1919

Bill Monbouquette
DET A Oct 4, 1965
SF N July 12, 1968
HOU N Dec 21, 1968

Rick Monday
CHI N Nov 29, 1971
LA N Jan 11, 1977

Don Money
PHI N Dec 15, 1967
MIL A Oct 31, 1972

Sid Monge
CLE A May 11, 1977
PHI N Feb 16, 1982
SD N May 2, 1983

John Monroe
PHI N June 1921

John Montague
PHI N Sept 2, 1975
CAL A Aug 29, 1979

Willie Montanez
PHI N Apr 8, 1970
SF N May 4, 1975
ATL N June 13, 1976
NY N Dec 8, 1977
TEX A Dec 8, 1977
TEX A Aug 12, 1979
SD N Feb 15, 1980
MON N Aug 31, 1980
PIT N Aug 20, 1981

Aurelio Monteagudo
HOU N May 17, 1966
CIN N Sept 27, 1966
CAL A Aug 14, 1973

John Montefusco
ATL N Dec 12, 1980
SD N Apr 6, 1982
NY A Aug 26, 1983

Manny Montejo
HOU N Dec 1, 1961

Wally Moon
LA N Dec 4, 1958

Jim Mooney
STL N Oct 10, 1932

Balor Moore
TOR A Apr 13, 1978

Barry Moore
CLE A Dec 5, 1969
CHI A June 15, 1970

Cy Moore
PHI N Dec 15, 1932

Donnie Moore
STL N Oct 17, 1979
MIL A Sept 3, 1981
ATL N Feb 1, 1982

Earl Moore
NY A May 16, 1907
PHI N Oct 1907
CHI N July 1913

Eddie Moore
BOS N July 20, 1926

Euel Moore
NY N Aug 2, 1935

Gene Moore
BOS N Feb 6, 1936
BKN N Dec 13, 1938
BOS N Feb 3, 1939
BOS N May 29, 1940
NY A Feb 5, 1942
BKN N Feb 24, 1942
WAS A Aug 31, 1942
STL A Mar 1, 1944

Jim Moore
CLE A Apr 24, 1932

Johnny Moore
CIN N Nov 30, 1932
PHI N May 8, 1934

Kelvin Moore
MIL A Feb 19, 1984

Randy Moore
BKN N Dec 12, 1935
STL N July 1937

Ray Moore
CHI A Dec 3, 1957
WAS A June 13, 1960

Roy Moore
DET A July 1922

Tommy Moore
STL N Oct 13, 1974
TEX A June 4, 1975
BAL A Dec 7, 1977

Wilcy Moore
NY A May 1, 1932

Jerry Morales
CHI N Nov 7, 1973
STL N Dec 8, 1977
DET A Dec 4, 1978
NY N Oct 31, 1979

Jose Morales
MON N Sept 18, 1973
MIN A Mar 29, 1978
BAL A Dec 23, 1980
LA N Apr 28, 1982

Rich Morales
SD N May 26, 1973

Al Moran
NY N Dec 11, 1962

Billy Moran
LA A June 11, 1964
MIN A June 11, 1964

Charlie Moran
STL A July 14, 1904

Herbie Moran
BOS N Aug 1908
BOS N Jan 1914
CIN N Apr 1914

Pat Moran
CHI N Feb 1906

Ray Morehart
NY A Jan 13, 1927

Seth Morehead
CHI N May 12, 1959
MIL N Mar 31, 1961

Jose Moreno
NY N Mar 27, 1979
SD N Dec 15, 1980

Omar Moreno
HOU N Dec 10, 1982
NY A Aug 10, 1983

Roger Moret
ATL N Dec 12, 1975
TEX A Dec 9, 1976

Bobby Morgan
PHI N Mar 28, 1954
STL N May 14, 1956
PHI N Nov 19, 1956
CHI N May 13, 1957

Chet Morgan
BOS A Dec 15, 1938

Cy Morgan
BOS A Aug 1, 1907

Eddie Morgan
PHI N Mar 6, 1938

Joe Morgan
CIN N Nov 29, 1971
PHI N Dec 14, 1982
OAK A Dec 28, 1983

Joe Morgan
PHI N June 23, 1960
CLE A Aug 9, 1960
STL N May 10, 1961

Mike Morgan
NY A Nov 3, 1980

Tom Morgan
KC A Feb 19, 1957
DET A Nov 20, 1957
WAS A July 22, 1960
LA A Jan 3, 1961

George Moriarty
DET A Jan 1909

Dan Morogiello
STL N Feb 1, 1982

John Morris
BAL A Dec 15, 1966

Jim Morrison
CHI A Apr 13, 1979
PIT N June 14, 1982

Bubba Morton
MIL N May 4, 1963
CAL A June 15, 1965

Carl Morton
ATL N Feb 28, 1973
TEX A Dec 9, 1976

Walt Moryn
CHI N Dec 9, 1955
STL N June 15, 1960
PIT N June 15, 1961

Earl Moseley
CIN N Dec 23, 1915

Walter Moser
STL A June 1911

Gerry Moses
CAL A Oct 11, 1970
CLE A Oct 5, 1971
NY A Nov 27, 1972
DET A Mar 19, 1974
NY N Jan 30, 1975
SD N Apr 28, 1975
CHI A July 18, 1975

Wally Moses
DET A Dec 9, 1939
CHI A Dec 9, 1941
BOS A July 23, 1946

Paul Moskau
BAL A Feb 9, 1982
PIT N Apr 3, 1982

Les Moss
BOS A May 17, 1951
STL A Nov 28, 1951
CHI A June 6, 1955

Ray Moss
BOS N May 28, 1931

Don Mossi
DET A Nov 20, 1958
CHI A Mar 18, 1964

Manny Mota
HOU N Nov 30, 1962
PIT N Apr 4, 1963
LA N June 11, 1969

Curt Motton
MIL A Dec 9, 1971

Mike Mowrey
CIN N Oct 1908
STL N Aug 22, 1909
PIT N Dec 12, 1913
BKN N Feb 10, 1916

Don Mueller
CHI A Mar 21, 1958

Heinie Mueller
NY N June 14, 1926

Ray Mueller
PIT N Dec 16, 1938
NY N June 13, 1949
PIT N May 17, 1950

Billy Muffett
SF N Oct 8, 1958

Hugh Mulcahy
PIT N Jan 1947

Greg Mulleavy
BOS A Dec 15, 1932

Billy Mullen
STL A Jan 15, 1927

Freddie Muller
NY A May 15, 1934

George Mullin
WAS A May 17, 1913

Jim Mullin
WAS A Aug 31, 1904

Rance Mulliniks
KC A Dec 6, 1979
TOR A Mar 25, 1982

Fran Mullins
CIN N Nov 21, 1983

Jerry Mumphrey
CLE A Dec 7, 1979
SD N Feb 15, 1980
NY A Apr 1, 1981
HOU N Aug 10, 1983

Bob Muncrief
CLE A Nov 20, 1947
PIT N Nov 20, 1948
CHI N June 6, 1949

George Munger
PIT N May 3, 1952

Scott Munninghoff
CLE A Nov 20, 1981

Steve Mura
CHI A Jan 26, 1983

Bobby Murcer
SF N Oct 22, 1974
CHI N Feb 11, 1977
NY A June 26, 1979

Danny Murphy
HOU N Mar 28, 1963
CHI A Dec 10, 1963
BOS A Mar 31, 1971

Eddie Murphy
CHI A July 15, 1915

Frank Murphy
NY N July 1901

Tom Murphy
KC A May 5, 1972
STL N May 8, 1973
MIL A Dec 8, 1973
BOS A June 3, 1976
TOR A July 27, 1977

Dale Murray
CIN N Dec 16, 1976
NY N May 19, 1978
MON N Aug 30, 1979
NY A Dec 9, 1982

George Murray
BOS A Jan 30, 1923

Larry Murray
OAK A Apr 27, 1977

Ray Murray
PHI A Apr 30, 1951
BAL A Mar 28, 1954

Red Murray
NY N Dec 12, 1908

Ivan Murrell
ATL N Apr 1, 1974

Danny Murtaugh
PIT N Nov 18, 1947

Tony Muser
CHI A Mar 31, 1971
BAL A June 15, 1975

Ron Musselman
TEX A Dec 21, 1982

Buddy Myer
BOS A May 2, 1927
WAS A Dec 15, 1928

Billy Myers
CIN N Dec 14, 1934
CHI N Dec 4, 1940

Elmer Myers
CLE A Mar 1, 1919
BOS A June 1920

Hap Myers
BOS A May 1911

Hy Myers
STL N Feb 15, 1923
CIN N Apr 22, 1925
STL N May 4, 1925

Bob Myrick
TEX A June 15, 1979

Bill Nagel
PHI N Mar 21, 1941

Rusty Nagelson
DET A May 22, 1970

Judge Nagle
BOS A July 1911

Mike Nagy
STL N Jan 24, 1973
TEX A Mar 31, 1973
STL N June 6, 1973

Sam Nahem
STL N June 12, 1940

Bill Nahorodny
CHI A Sept 8, 1977
ATL N Dec 3, 1979

Danny Napoleon
STL N Apr 1, 1967

Hal Naragon
WAS A May 25, 1959

Ray Narleski
DET A Nov 20, 1958

Jerry Narron
SEA A Nov 1, 1979

Buster Narum
WAS A Mar 31, 1964
CHI A Feb 13, 1968

Cotton Nash
CHI A May 6, 1967

Jim Nash
ATL N Dec 3, 1969
PHI N June 15, 1972

Phil Nastu
CHI N Dec 12, 1980

Julio Navarro
DET A Apr 28, 1964
BOS A June 14, 1966

Earl Naylor
STL N June 1, 1943

Charlie Neal
NY N Dec 15, 1961
CIN N July 1, 1963

Greasy Neale
PHI N Nov 22, 1920
CIN N June 2, 1921

Tom Needham
NY N Oct 7, 1907
CHI N Dec 1908

Cal Neeman
PHI N May 13, 1960

Ron Negray
BKN N Apr 5, 1957

Art Nehf
NY N Aug 15, 1919
CIN N May 11, 1926
CHI N Sept 4, 1927

Gary Neibauer
PHI N June 15, 1972

Bernie Neis
BOS N Feb 4, 1925
CHI A June 15, 1927

Dave Nelson
WAS A Dec 5, 1969
KC A Nov 12, 1975

Gene Nelson
NY A Aug 1, 1979
SEA A Apr 1, 1982

Lynn Nelson
DET A Feb 23, 1940

Red Nelson
PHI N Aug 1912
CIN N June 5, 1913

Rocky Nelson
PIT N May 17, 1951
CHI A Sept 20, 1951
STL N July 30, 1956

Roger Nelson
BAL A Nov 29, 1967
CIN N Nov 30, 1972
CHI A Oct 25, 1974

Dick Nen
WAS A Dec 4, 1964
CHI N Apr 3, 1968
WAS A Oct 1, 1968

Graig Nettles
CLE A Dec 10, 1969
NY A Nov 27, 1972
SD N Mar 30, 1984

Morris Nettles
CHI A Dec 11, 1975

Dan Neumeier
HOU N Oct 23, 1973

Ernie Nevel
CIN N Aug 28, 1952
BKN N June 9, 1954

Don Newcombe
CIN N June 15, 1958
CLE A July 29, 1960

Jeff Newman
BOS A Dec 6, 1982

Ray Newman
DET A Dec 6, 1973

Bobo Newsom
WAS A May 21, 1935
BOS A June 11, 1937
STL A Oct 2, 1937
DET A May 13, 1939
WAS A Mar 31, 1942
BKN N Aug 30, 1942
STL A July 15, 1943
WAS A Aug 31, 1943
PHI A Dec 13, 1943
NY A July 11, 1947

Skeeter Newsome
PHI N Dec 12, 1945

Doc Newton
BKN N July 1901

Gus Niarhos
CHI A June 27, 1950
STL A Nov 27, 1951
BOS A Nov 28, 1951

Kid Nichols
PHI N July 16, 1905

Bill Nicholson
PHI N Oct 4, 1948

Dave Nicholson
CHI A Jan 14, 1963
HOU N Dec 1, 1965
ATL N Dec 31, 1966

Fred Nicholson
PIT N July 1919
BOS N Feb 23, 1921

Steve Nicosia
SF N Aug 19, 1983

Al Niehaus
PIT N Oct 27, 1924
CIN N May 20, 1925

Bert Niehoff
PHI N Nov 1914
STL N Apr 4, 1918
NY N May 18, 1918

Joe Niekro
SD N Apr 25, 1969
DET A Dec 4, 1969
ATL N Aug 7, 1973
HOU N Apr 6, 1975

Phil Niekro
NY A Jan 6, 1984

Bob Nieman
DET A Dec 4, 1952
CHI A Dec 6, 1954
BAL A May 21, 1956
STL N Dec 2, 1959
CLE A May 10, 1961
SF N Apr 29, 1962

Randy Niemann
HOU N June 15, 1977
PIT N Aug 31, 1981
CHI A Sept 7, 1983

Al Niemiec
PHI A Jan 4, 1936

Johnny Niggeling
STL A Jan 4, 1940
WAS A Aug 18, 1943

Harry Niles
NY A Nov 1907
BOS A July 1908
CLE A May 1910

Rabbit Nill
CLE A Aug 11, 1907

Ron Nischwitz
CLE A Nov 27, 1962

Otis Nixon
CLE A Feb 4, 1984

Russ Nixon
BOS A Mar 16, 1960
BOS A June 13, 1960
MIN A Apr 6, 1966

Gary Nolan
CAL A June 15, 1977

Joe Nolan
BAL A Mar 26, 1982

Pete Noonan
STL N July 1, 1906

Jerry Nops
BKN N Jan 1900

Tim Nordbrook
CAL A Sept 9, 1976
TOR A Aug 30, 1977
MIL A Apr 29, 1978

Wayne Nordhagen
ATL N June 7, 1973
STL N May 28, 1975
CHI A July 14, 1976
TOR A Apr 2, 1982
PHI N June 15, 1982
PIT N June 15, 1982
CHI N Dec 10, 1982

Irv Noren
NY A May 3, 1952
KC A Feb 19, 1957
STL N Aug 31, 1957
CHI N May 19, 1959

Dan Norman
NY N June 15, 1977
MON N May 29, 1981

Fred Norman
CHI N Dec 15, 1963
STL N Sept 28, 1970
SD N June 11, 1971
CIN N June 12, 1973

Jim Norris
TEX A Jan 4, 1980

Billy North
OAK A Nov 21, 1972
LA N May 17, 1978

Lou North
BOS N June 17, 1924

Hub Northen
BKN N Apr 1911

Ron Northey
STL N May 3, 1947
CIN N Dec 14, 1949
CHI N June 7, 1950

Jim Northrup
MON N Aug 7, 1974
BAL A Sept 16, 1974

Willie Norwood
SEA A Dec 12, 1980

Joe Nossek
KC A May 11, 1966
STL N July 12, 1969

Don Nottebart
HOU N Nov 30, 1962
CHI N Apr 27, 1969

Wynn Noyes
CHI A Aug 1919

Les Nunamaker
NY A May 13, 1914
STL A Jan 22, 1918
CLE A Mar 1919

Howie Nunn
NY N Dec 21, 1961

Rich Nye
STL N Dec 4, 1969
MON N May 15, 1970

Jerry Nyman
SD N Mar 30, 1970

Nyls Nyman
STL N Aug 31, 1977

Rebel Oakes
STL N Feb 1910

Johnny Oates
ATL N Dec 30, 1972
PHI N May 7, 1975
LA N Dec 20, 1976

Frank Oberlin
WAS A Aug 11, 1907

Mike O'Berry
CHI N Aug 17, 1979
CIN N Oct 17, 1980
CAL A Jan 10, 1983
NY A Dec 8, 1983

Bob O'Brien
BAL A Dec 2, 1971

Buck O'Brien
CHI A July 1913

Dan O'Brien
SEA A Nov 9, 1979

Jack O'Brien
CLE A May 1901

Johnny O'Brien
STL N June 15, 1958
MIL N Mar 31, 1959

Pete O'Brien
CLE A Dec 1906
WAS A Aug 11, 1907

Syd O'Brien
CHI A Dec 13, 1969
CAL A Nov 30, 1970
MIL A July 28, 1972

Tom O'Brien
PIT N Feb 1900

Tommy O'Brien
WAS A May 8, 1950

Danny O'Connell
MIL N Dec 26, 1953
NY N June 15, 1957

Jack O'Connor
PIT N May 10, 1900
STL A Jan 1904

Ken O'Dea
CHI N Oct 26, 1934
NY N Dec 6, 1938
STL N Dec 11, 1941
BOS N July 8, 1946

Billy O'Dell
SF N Nov 30, 1959
MIL N Feb 1, 1965
PIT N June 15, 1966

Blue Moon Odom
CLE A May 20, 1975
ATL N June 7, 1975
CHI A June 15, 1976

John O'Donoghue
CLE A Apr 6, 1966
BAL A Nov 28, 1967
SEA A Apr 30, 1969
MON N June 15, 1970

Lefty O'Doul
BOS A July 23, 1922
PHI N Oct 29, 1928
BKN N Oct 14, 1930
NY N June 16, 1933

Joe Oeschger
NY N May 27, 1919
BOS N Aug 15, 1919
NY N Nov 12, 1923
PHI N July 1, 1924
BKN N Apr 20, 1925

Bob O'Farrell
STL N May 23, 1925
NY N May 1, 1928
STL N Oct 10, 1932
CIN N Jan 11, 1934

Rowland Office
MON N Dec 4, 1979

Curly Ogden
WAS A June 19, 1924

Jack Ogden
STL N May 7, 1933

Ben Oglivie
DET A Oct 23, 1973
MIL A Dec 9, 1977

Hal O'Hagan
NY N July 1902

Bob Oldis
PHI N Oct 13, 1961

Rube Oldring
PHI A Oct 2, 1905

Al Oliver
TEX A Dec 8, 1977
MON N Mar 31, 1982
SF N Feb 27, 1984

Bob Oliver
MIN A Dec 2, 1967
CAL A May 5, 1972
BAL A Sept 11, 1974
NY A Dec 1, 1974

Dave Oliver
MON N July 11, 1980

Gene Oliver
MIL N June 15, 1963
PHI N June 6, 1967
BOS A Dec 15, 1967
CHI N June 27, 1968

Nate Oliver
SF N Feb 13, 1968
NY A Dec 6, 1968
CHI N Apr 19, 1969

Tom Oliver
BOS A Dec 1929

Chi Chi Olivo
NY A Nov 29, 1966

Diomedes Olivo
STL N Nov 19, 1962

Luis Olmo
BOS N Dec 24, 1949

Alan Olmsted
SD N Dec 8, 1980

Ivy Olson
CIN N Dec 14, 1914
BKN N Aug 1915

Karl Olson
WAS A Nov 8, 1955
BOS A Apr 30, 1957
DET A Apr 30, 1957

Mickey O'Neil
BOS N Aug 15, 1919
BKN N Oct 7, 1925
WAS A Dec 1926
NY N May 25, 1927

Bill O'Neill
WAS A July 4, 1904

Jack O'Neill
CHI N Dec 12, 1903
BOS N Jan 1906

Steve O'Neill
CLE A Aug 20, 1911
BOS A Jan 7, 1924
NY A Dec 12, 1924

Steve Ontiveros
CHI N Feb 11, 1977

Joe Orengo
NY N Nov 25, 1940
BKN N July 31, 1943
CHI A Dec 12, 1944

Don O'Riley
CHI A Oct 13, 1970

Jesse Orosco
NY N Dec 8, 1978

Frank O'Rourke
WAS A Jan 1920
BOS A Jan 10, 1922
DET A Oct 24, 1922
STL A Jan 15, 1927

John Orsino
BAL A Dec 15, 1962
WAS A Oct 12, 1965

Jorge Orta
CLE A Dec 19, 1979
LA N Dec 9, 1981
NY N Dec 28, 1982
TOR A Feb 4, 1983
KC A Dec 20, 1983

Phil Ortega
WAS A Dec 4, 1964
CAL A Apr 4, 1969

Frank Ortenzio
CHI A Feb 15, 1978

Al Orth
NY A July 13, 1904

Jose Ortiz
CHI N Nov 30, 1970

Junior Ortiz
NY N June 14, 1983

Roberto Ortiz
BKN N Mar 8, 1943

Bob Osborn
PIT N Jan 1931

Danny Osborn
ATL N Dec 12, 1975

Pat Osborn
MIL A Oct 22, 1974

Tiny Osborne
BKN N May 16, 1924

Dan Osinski
LA A Nov 30, 1962
LA A July 23, 1963
MIL N Oct 14, 1964
BOS A Dec 15, 1965

Champ Osteen
NY A Jan 1904

Claude Osteen
WAS A Sept 16, 1961
LA N Dec 4, 1964
HOU N Dec 6, 1973
STL N Aug 15, 1974

Darrell Osteen
KC A Oct 20, 1967

Fritz Ostermueller
STL A Dec 3, 1940
BKN N July 15, 1943

Joe Ostrowski
STL A Nov 17, 1947
NY A June 15, 1950

John Ostrowski
WAS A May 31, 1950

Amos Otis
KC A Dec 3, 1969
PIT N Dec 19, 1983

Denny O'Toole
STL N Oct 26, 1973

Jim O'Toole
CHI A Dec 15, 1966

Marty O'Toole
NY N Aug 14, 1914

Ed Ott
CAL A Apr 1, 1981

Jimmy Outlaw
BOS N Dec 13, 1938
BKN N Dec 13, 1938

Orval Overall
CHI N June 2, 1906

Stubby Overmire
STL A Dec 1, 1949
NY A June 15, 1951
STL A May 13, 1952

Bob Owchinko
CLE A Feb 15, 1980
PIT N Dec 9, 1980
OAK A Apr 6, 1981
CIN N Nov 12, 1983

Marv Owen
CHI A Dec 2, 1937
BOS A Dec 8, 1939

Mickey Owen
BKN N Dec 4, 1940

Jim Owens
CIN N Nov 27, 1962

Rick Ownbey
STL N June 15, 1983

Ray Oyler
OAK A Dec 7, 1969
CAL A Apr 17, 1970

John Pacella
SD N Dec 15, 1980
NY A Apr 1, 1981
MIN A May 12, 1982
TEX A Nov 1, 1982

Tom Paciorek
ATL N Nov 17, 1975
CHI A Dec 11, 1981

Gene Packard
CHI N Feb 10, 1916
STL N Apr 1917
PHI N Jan 21, 1919

Tom Padden
STL N Oct 1937
PHI N Jan 22, 1943

Del Paddock
NY A Jan 1912

Don Padgett
BKN N Dec 10, 1941
BOS N June 12, 1946
PHI N May 27, 1947

Ernie Padgett
CLE A Feb 1926

Dennis Paepke
KC A Dec 12, 1968

Andy Pafko
BKN N June 15, 1951
MIL N Jan 17, 1953

Dave Pagan
BAL A June 15, 1976
PIT N July 27, 1977

Jose Pagan
PIT N May 22, 1965

Mitchell Page
OAK A Mar 15, 1977

Karl Pagel
CLE A June 23, 1980

Jim Pagliaroni
PIT N Nov 20, 1962
OAK A Dec 3, 1967
SEA A May 27, 1969

Phil Paine
STL N Apr 19, 1958
LA N Dec 4, 1958

Erv Palica
BAL A Mar 17, 1955

Lowell Palmer
CLE A Sept 18, 1972
NY A June 12, 1973
SD N May 31, 1974

Stan Palys
CIN N Apr 30, 1955
DET A Apr 3, 1958

Jim Panther
TEX A Mar 4, 1972
ATL N Oct 27, 1972

Stan Papi
STL N June 8, 1973
BOS A Dec 7, 1978
PHI N Mar 30, 1980
DET A May 29, 1980

Frank Papish
CLE A Oct 2, 1948
PIT N Dec 14, 1949

Milt Pappas
CIN N Dec 9, 1965
ATL N June 11, 1968
CHI N June 23, 1970

Freddy Parent
CHI A Apr 1908

Kelly Paris
CIN N Mar 31, 1983
CHI A Nov 28, 1983

Dave Parker
CIN N Dec 7, 1983

Harry Parker
NY N Oct 18, 1971
STL N Aug 4, 1975
CLE A Apr 7, 1976

Roy Parmelee
STL N Dec 9, 1935
CHI N Oct 8, 1936

Sam Parrilla
BAL A Dec 16, 1970

Larry Parrish
TEX A Mar 31, 1982

Mike Parrott
SEA A Dec 7, 1977
MIL A Mar 5, 1982

Bill Parsons
OAK A June 24, 1974
STL N Dec 2, 1974
CHI A June 30, 1975

Tom Parsons
HOU N Oct 19, 1965

Roy Partee
STL A Nov 17, 1947
NY A Dec 13, 1948

Camilo Pascual
WAS A Dec 3, 1966
CIN N July 7, 1969
SD N May 22, 1971

Johnny Pasek
CHI A Dec 12, 1933
PHI A Dec 12, 1933

Larry Pashnick
MIN A Dec 8, 1983

Dode Paskert
PHI N Feb 1911
CHI N Dec 26, 1917
CIN N Dec 1920

Kevin Pasley
SEA A Sept 8, 1977

Claude Passeau
PHI N Nov 21, 1935
CHI N May 29, 1939

Freddie Patek
KC A Dec 2, 1970
CAL A Dec 5, 1979

Casey Patten
BOS A July 1908

Daryl Patterson
OAK A May 22, 1971
STL N June 25, 1971

Mike Patterson
NY A May 20, 1981

Reggie Patterson
CHI N Dec 10, 1982

Marty Pattin
BOS A Oct 11, 1971
KC A Oct 24, 1973

Mike Paul
TEX A Dec 2, 1971
CHI N Aug 31, 1973

Gene Paulette
STL N May 1917
PHI N July 14, 1919

Don Pavletich
CHI A Dec 5, 1968
BOS A Dec 13, 1969
MIL A Oct 11, 1971

Mike Pazik
MIN A May 4, 1974

Johnny Peacock
PHI N June 11, 1944
BKN N June 15, 1945

Albie Pearson
WAS A Jan 23, 1958
BAL A May 26, 1959

Monte Pearson
NY A Dec 11, 1935
CIN N Dec 30, 1940

Charlie Pechous
CHI N Feb 10, 1916

Hal Peck
CHI N May 15, 1943
NY A June 20, 1946
CLE A Dec 20, 1946

Roger Peckinpaugh
NY A May 20, 1913
BOS A Dec 20, 1921
WAS A Jan 10, 1922
CHI A Jan 15, 1927

Homer Peel
PHI N May 11, 1928
STL N Dec 11, 1929

Heinie Peitz
PIT N Dec 1905

Eddie Pellagrini
STL A Nov 17, 1947
CIN N Dec 10, 1951
PIT N Apr 17, 1953

Barney Pelty
WAS A June 1912

Brock Pemberton
STL N Dec 9, 1976

Orlando Pena
DET A June 23, 1965
CLE A May 6, 1967
STL N June 15, 1973

Roberto Pena
CHI N Dec 9, 1964
OAK A Mar 24, 1970
MIL A May 18, 1970

Jim Pendleton
MIL N Feb 16, 1953
PIT N Apr 3, 1957
CIN N Jan 30, 1959

Herb Pennock
BOS A June 13, 1915
NY A Jan 30, 1923

Gene Pentz
HOU N Dec 6, 1975

Joe Pepitone
HOU N Dec 4, 1969
CHI N July 29, 1970
ATL N May 19, 1973

Don Pepper
MON N Mar 25, 1969

Jack Perconte
CLE A Dec 9, 1981
SEA A Dec 7, 1983

Hub Perdue
STL N June 1914

Marty Perez
ATL N Oct 21, 1970
SF N June 13, 1976
NY A Mar 14, 1977
OAK A Apr 27, 1977

Pascual Perez
ATL N June 30, 1982

Tony Perez
MON N Dec 16, 1976
BOS A Nov 20, 1979
CIN N Dec 6, 1983

Broderick Perkins
CLE A Nov 18, 1982

Cy Perkins
NY A Dec 10, 1930

Harry Perkowski
CHI N Oct 1, 1954

Ron Perranoski
LA N Apr 8, 1960
MIN A Nov 28, 1967
DET A July 30, 1971

Pol Perritt
NY N Feb 18, 1915
DET A June 1921

Gaylord Perry
CLE A Nov 29, 1971
TEX A June 13, 1975
SD N Jan 25, 1978
TEX A Feb 15, 1980
NY A Aug 14, 1980
ATL N Jan 12, 1981

Jim Perry
MIN A May 2, 1963
DET A Mar 27, 1973
CLE A Mar 19, 1974
OAK A May 20, 1975

Scott Perry
CIN N Apr 26, 1917
BOS N May 28, 1917
PHI A Apr 1918

Stan Perzanowski
TEX A Feb 25, 1975
CLE A May 28, 1976
CAL A Dec 3, 1976

Johnny Pesky
DET A June 3, 1952
WAS A June 14, 1954

Gary Peters
BOS A Dec 13, 1969

Ray Peters
PHI N Apr 22, 1971

Rusty Peters
STL A Dec 7, 1946

Cap Peterson
WAS A Dec 3, 1966
CLE A Mar 31, 1969

Fritz Peterson
CLE A Apr 27, 1974
TEX A May 28, 1976

Kent Peterson
PHI N May 23, 1952

Joe Pettini
SF N June 13, 1979

Jesse Petty
PIT N Dec 11, 1928
CHI N Aug 24, 1930

Pretzels Pezzullo
PHI N Nov 1, 1934

Big Jeff Pfeffer
BOS N Jan 1906
BOS N Jan 1911

Jeff Pfeffer
STL N June 18, 1921
PIT N July 11, 1924

Bobby Pfeil
STL N Apr 10, 1965
MIL A Feb 8, 1972
BOS A Mar 20, 1972

Art Phelan
CHI N Dec 15, 1912

Babe Phelps
BKN N Dec 31, 1934
PIT N Dec 12, 1941
PHI N Dec 30, 1943

Ed Phelps
CIN N Dec 1905
PIT N May 20, 1906

Ken Phelps
MON N Jan 14, 1982
SEA A Mar 31, 1983

Dave Philley
PHI A Apr 30, 1951
CLE A Feb 19, 1954
BAL A July 2, 1955
CHI A May 21, 1956
DET A June 14, 1957
PHI N Dec 11, 1957
SF N May 12, 1960
BAL A Sept 1, 1960
BOS A Mar 24, 1962

Deacon Phillippe
PIT N Jan 1900

Adolfo Phillips
CHI N Apr 21, 1966
MON N June 11, 1969

Bubba Phillips
CHI A Nov 30, 1955
CLE A Dec 6, 1959
DET A Nov 27, 1962

Eddie Phillips
PIT N Jan 1931
CLE A Dec 1934

Jack Phillips
PIT N Aug 6, 1949
DET A Dec 6, 1954
BOS A Apr 30, 1957

Mike Phillips
NY N May 3, 1975
STL N June 15, 1977
SD N Dec 8, 1980
MON N May 10, 1981

Taylor Phillips
CHI N Dec 5, 1957
PHI N May 12, 1959
CHI A Dec 15, 1961

Tony Phillips
SD N Aug 31, 1980
OAK A Mar 27, 1981

Tom Phoebus
SD N Dec 1, 1970
CHI N Apr 20, 1972
ATL N Oct 20, 1972

Wiley Piatt
CHI A July 1901

Rob Picciolo
MIL A May 14, 1982
CAL A Feb 6, 1984

Ron Piche
LA A Oct 14, 1964
CHI N Apr 22, 1968

Val Picinich
BOS A Feb 10, 1923
CIN N Feb 10, 1926
BKN N Apr 18, 1929
PIT N June 23, 1933

Charlie Pick
BOS N Aug 1919

Ollie Pickering
PHI A Feb 1903
WAS A Oct 5, 1907

Billy Pierce
CHI A Nov 10, 1948
SF N Nov 30, 1961

Jack Pierce
DET A Mar 29, 1975

Bill Piercy
BOS A Dec 20, 1921

Marino Pieretti
CHI A June 9, 1948
CLE A Apr 16, 1950

Jimmy Piersall
CLE A Dec 2, 1958
WAS A Oct 5, 1961
NY N May 23, 1963

Tony Piet
CIN N Oct 17, 1933
CHI A June 4, 1935
DET A Dec 2, 1937

Joe Pignatano
KC A Jan 31, 1961
NY N July 13, 1962

Al Pilarcik
BAL A Oct 11, 1956
KC A Jan 24, 1961
CHI A June 10, 1961

Duane Pillette
STL A June 15, 1950

Horacio Pina
WAS A Dec 5, 1969
OAK A Nov 30, 1972
CHI N Nov 3, 1973
CAL A July 28, 1974

Babe Pinelli
DET A Dec 1919

Lou Piniella
BAL A Mar 31, 1964
KC A Apr 1, 1969
NY A Dec 7, 1973

Vada Pinson
STL N Oct 11, 1968
CLE A Nov 21, 1969
CAL A Oct 5, 1971
KC A Feb 23, 1974

George Pipgras
NY A Jan 3, 1923
BOS A May 12, 1933

Wally Pipp
NY A Jan 7, 1915
CIN N Feb 1, 1926

Cotton Pippen
DET A Sept 12, 1939

Jim Pisoni
KC A Oct 11, 1956
NY A June 15, 1957

Skip Pitlock
OAK A June 15, 1975

Togie Pittinger
PHI N Dec 20, 1904

Joe Pittman
SD N June 8, 1982
SF N Dec 6, 1983

Juan Pizarro
CIN N Dec 15, 1960
CHI A Dec 15, 1960
PIT N Oct 12, 1966
BOS A June 27, 1968
CLE A Apr 19, 1969
OAK A Sept 21, 1969
CHI N July 9, 1970

Eddie Plank
STL A Feb 10, 1916
NY A Jan 22, 1918

Herb Plews
WAS A Feb 8, 1956
BOS A June 11, 1959

Bill Plummer
CIN N Jan 9, 1969

Ray Poat
PIT N June 6, 1949

Bud Podbielan
CIN N June 15, 1952

Johnny Podgajny
PIT N June 15, 1943

Johnny Podres
DET A May 10, 1966

John Poff
MIL A Sept 1, 1980
CHI A Apr 1, 1981

Boots Poffenberger
BKN N Jan 1939

Tom Poholsky
CHI N Dec 11, 1956
NY N Dec 10, 1957

Aaron Pointer
CHI N May 4, 1968

Hugh Poland
BOS N Apr 27, 1943
CIN N June 14, 1947

Howie Pollet
PIT N June 15, 1951
CHI N June 4, 1953
PIT N Apr 16, 1956

John Poloni
BOS A Dec 14, 1977

Elmer Ponder
CHI N July 1, 1921

Ed Poole
CIN N Apr 1902
BKN N Feb 1904

Dave Pope
BAL A June 15, 1955
CLE A May 13, 1956

Paul Popovich
LA N Nov 30, 1967
MON N June 11, 1969
CHI N June 11, 1969
PIT N Apr 1, 1974

Tom Poquette
BOS A June 13, 1979
TEX A Aug 12, 1981
KC A Jan 15, 1982

Darrell Porter
KC A Dec 6, 1976
STL N Dec 13, 1980

Dick Porter
BOS A May 25, 1934

J W Porter
STL A July 28, 1952
DET A Dec 4, 1952
CLE A Feb 18, 1958
WAS A Oct 27, 1958
STL N July 25, 1959

Bob Porterfield
WAS A June 15, 1951
BOS A Nov 8, 1955
PIT N May 7, 1958

Arnie Portocarrero
CLE A Apr 17, 1958

Bill Posedel
BOS N Mar 31, 1939

Wally Post
PHI N Dec 16, 1957
CIN N June 15, 1960
MIN A May 16, 1963

Dykes Potter
CHI N Feb 10, 1916

Mike Potter
SEA A June 26, 1978

Nels Potter
BOS A June 30, 1941
PHI A May 15, 1948

Boog Powell
CLE A Feb 25, 1975

Jack Powell
NY A Jan 1904
NY A Feb 1904
STL A Sept 1, 1905

Jake Powell
NY A June 14, 1936

Paul Powell
LA N Oct 22, 1971

Ray Powell
PHI N Dec 15, 1923

Ted Power
CIN N Oct 15, 1982

Vic Power
PHI A Dec 16, 1953
CLE A June 15, 1958
MIN A Apr 2, 1962
LA A June 11, 1964
PHI N Sept 9, 1964
LA A Nov 30, 1964

Johnny Powers
CIN N Jan 30, 1959
BAL A Dec 15, 1959
CLE A May 12, 1960
PIT N June 2, 1960

Mike Powers
NY A July 13, 1905
PHI A Aug 7, 1905

Willie Prall
CHI N Mar 19, 1974

Johnny Pramesa
CHI N Oct 4, 1951

Del Pratt
NY A Jan 22, 1918
BOS A Dec 15, 1920
DET A Oct 30, 1922

Mike Prendergast
PHI N Dec 11, 1917

Tot Pressnell
STL N Nov 19, 1940
CIN N Dec 16, 1940
CHI N Feb 4, 1941

Jim Price
DET A Apr 7, 1967

Bob Priddy
SF N Feb 11, 1965
WAS A Dec 3, 1966
CHI A Feb 13, 1968
CAL A May 14, 1969
ATL N Sept 9, 1969

Gerry Priddy
WAS A Jan 29, 1943
STL A Nov 22, 1947
STL A Dec 8, 1947
DET A Dec 14, 1949

Mike Proly
PHI N Apr 1, 1981

Doc Prothro
BOS A Dec 11, 1924

Ron Pruitt
CLE A Dec 9, 1975
CHI A June 13, 1980

Greg Pryor
NY A Feb 17, 1977
CHI A Nov 28, 1977
KC A Mar 24, 1982

Charlie Puleo
NY N Apr 6, 1981
CIN N Dec 16, 1982

Bob Purkey
CIN N Dec 9, 1957
STL N Dec 14, 1964
PIT N Apr 7, 1966

Billy Purtell
BOS A Aug 9, 1910

Ed Putman
DET A Mar 20, 1979

Pat Putnam
SEA A Dec 21, 1982

Ewald Pyle
NY N June 16, 1945

Frankie Pytlak
BOS A Dec 12, 1940

Jim Qualls
MON N Apr 22, 1970

Tom Qualters
CHI A Apr 30, 1958

Mel Queen
CAL A Oct 24, 1969

Mel Queen
PIT N July 11, 1947

Jack Quinn
BOS A Dec 20, 1921
PHI A July 10, 1925

Joe Quinn
STL N Jan 1900
CIN N May 1900

Luis Quinones
CLE A Dec 6, 1983

Jamie Quirk
MIL A Dec 6, 1976
KC A Aug 3, 1978
STL N Jan 28, 1983

Marv Rackley
PIT N May 18, 1949

Dick Radatz
CLE A June 2, 1966
CHI N Apr 25, 1967
MON N June 15, 1969

Rip Radcliff
STL A Dec 8, 1939
DET A May 5, 1941
PHI A Oct 11, 1943

Dave Rader
STL N Oct 20, 1976
CHI N Dec 8, 1977
PHI N Feb 23, 1979
BOS A Mar 30, 1980

Doug Rader
SD N Dec 11, 1975
TOR A June 8, 1977

Ken Raffensberger
CHI N Dec 27, 1939
CIN N June 14, 1947

Pat Ragan
CHI N May 20, 1909
BOS N May 1, 1915
NY N May 1919
CHI A Sept 1919

Tom Ragland
CLE A Nov 30, 1972

Chuck Rainey
CHI N Dec 10, 1982

Dave Rajsich
TEX A Nov 10, 1978
PHI N Oct 20, 1981

Gary Rajsich
NY N Apr 3, 1981

Ed Rakow
KC A Mar 30, 1961
DET A Nov 18, 1963

Bob Ramazzotti
CHI N May 16, 1949

Allan Ramirez
SD N Dec 7, 1983

Milt Ramirez
HOU N Nov 28, 1972

Bobby Ramos
NY A Apr 5, 1982
MON N Nov 3, 1982

Domingo Ramos
TEX A Nov 10, 1978
TOR A Nov 5, 1979

Pedro Ramos
CLE A Apr 2, 1962
NY A Sept 5, 1964
PHI N Dec 14, 1966

Willie Ramsdell
CIN N May 10, 1950
CHI N Jan 3, 1952

Newt Randall
BOS N June 24, 1907

Lenny Randle
NY N Apr 26, 1977
PIT N June 28, 1979
NY A Aug 2, 1979
SEA A Mar 8, 1980
CHI N Apr 2, 1980

Willie Randolph
NY A Dec 11, 1975

Merritt Ranew
CHI N Mar 28, 1963
MIL N June 3, 1964

Earl Rapp
STL A Sept 1, 1951
WAS A June 10, 1952

Goldie Rapp
PHI N July 1, 1921

Vern Rapp
CHI A May 7, 1949

Bill Rariden
NY N Dec 23, 1915
CIN N Feb 2, 1919

Vic Raschi
STL N Feb 23, 1954

Dennis Rasmussen
NY A Aug 31, 1982
SD N Aug 26, 1983
NY A Mar 30, 1984

Eric Rasmussen
SD N May 26, 1978
KC A Aug 2, 1983

Morrie Rath
CLE A May 1910

Gene Ratliff
ATL N Oct 13, 1966

Paul Ratliff
MIL A July 8, 1971
CAL A July 28, 1972

Steve Ratzer
NY N Dec 11, 1981

Bob Rauch
CLE A Nov 27, 1972

Bob Raudman
CLE A Apr 25, 1967

Lance Rautzhan
MIL A May 11, 1979
KC A Oct 24, 1979

Shane Rawley
CIN N May 21, 1977
SEA A Dec 9, 1977
NY A Apr 1, 1982

Johnny Rawlings
PHI N June 1920
NY N July 1, 1921
PHI N May 11, 1923
PIT N May 22, 1923

Jim Ray
DET A Nov 3, 1973
PIT N Dec 6, 1974

Johnny Ray
PIT N Aug 31, 1981

Curt Raydon
PIT N Dec 26, 1953

Floyd Rayford
BAL A June 5, 1979
STL N June 15, 1983
BAL A Mar 30, 1984

Bugs Raymond
NY N Dec 12, 1908

Claude Raymond
HOU N Oct 10, 1963
ATL N June 15, 1967
MON N Aug 19, 1969

Barry Raziano
CAL A Feb 23, 1974

Jeff Reardon
MON N May 29, 1981

Frank Reberger
SF N Dec 5, 1969

Howie Reed
LA N Mar 30, 1961
CAL A May 27, 1966
MON N Apr 3, 1969

Jerry Reed
CLE A Sept 12, 1982

Ron Reed
STL N May 28, 1975
PHI N Dec 9, 1975
CHI A Dec 5, 1983

Jimmy Reese
STL N Jan 1932

Rich Reese
DET A Nov 30, 1972

Bobby Reeves
BOS A Dec 15, 1928

Bill Regan
PIT N Jan 1931

Phil Regan
LA N Dec 15, 1965
CHI N Apr 23, 1968
CHI A June 2, 1972

Wally Rehg
BOS A Jan 1913
CIN N Feb 1919

Rick Reichardt
WAS A Apr 27, 1970
CHI A Feb 9, 1971

Bill Reidy
BKN N July 1903

Bobby Reis
BOS N Dec 12, 1935

Tommy Reis
BOS N May 23, 1938
CIN N Aug 10, 1938

Pete Reiser
BOS N Dec 15, 1948

Heinie Reitz
PHI N Feb 1900

Ken Reitz
SF N Dec 8, 1975
STL N Dec 10, 1976
CHI N Dec 9, 1980

Jerry Remy
BOS A Dec 8, 1977

Hal Reniff
NY N June 29, 1967

Steve Renko
MON N June 15, 1969
CHI N May 17, 1976
CHI A Aug 18, 1977
OAK A Mar 30, 1978
BOS A Jan 20, 1979
CAL A Jan 23, 1981
KC A Feb 9, 1983

Bill Renna
PHI A Dec 16, 1953
NY A June 14, 1956

Tony Rensa
PHI N June 1930

Andy Replogle
MIL A Apr 4, 1978

Roger Repoz
KC A June 10, 1966
CAL A June 15, 1967
BAL A June 10, 1972

Rip Repulski
PHI N Nov 19, 1956
LA N Dec 23, 1958
BOS A May 6, 1960

Dino Restelli
WAS A Sept 19, 1951

Merv Rettenmund
CIN N Dec 4, 1973
SD N Apr 5, 1976

Ken Retzer
MIN A Oct 15, 1964
CLE A Jan 4, 1967

Ed Reulbach
BKN N Aug 14, 1913
BOS N Apr 12, 1916

Paul Reuschel
CLE A June 26, 1978

Rick Reuschel
NY A June 12, 1981

Jerry Reuss
HOU N Apr 15, 1972
PIT N Oct 31, 1973
LA N Apr 7, 1979

Dave Revering
OAK A Feb 25, 1978
NY A May 20, 1981
TOR A May 5, 1982
SEA A Aug 6, 1982

Allie Reynolds
NY A Oct 19, 1946

Archie Reynolds
CAL A July 9, 1970

Bob Reynolds
STL N June 15, 1971
MIL A July 29, 1971
BAL A Dec 9, 1971
DET A May 29, 1975
CLE A Aug 26, 1975

Carl Reynolds
WAS A Dec 4, 1931
STL A Dec 14, 1932
BOS A Dec 14, 1933
WAS A Dec 17, 1935

Craig Reynolds
SEA A Dec 7, 1976
HOU N Dec 8, 1978

Ken Reynolds
MIN A Nov 30, 1972
MIL A Mar 27, 1973
SD N Apr 8, 1976
TOR A Mar 21, 1977

Tommie Reynolds
CAL A May 16, 1970
MIL A Jan 26, 1972

Bobby Rhawn
PIT N June 6, 1949

Flint Rhem
PHI N May 30, 1932
STL N Feb 11, 1934
BOS A June 23, 1934

Bob Rhoads
STL N Apr 1903

Rick Rhoden
PIT N Apr 7, 1979

Charlie Rhodes
STL N May 1908
BOS A July 1908

Gordon Rhodes
BOS A May 1, 1932
PHI A Dec 10, 1935

Hal Rhyne
CHI A Dec 15, 1932

Dennis Ribant
NY N Aug 8, 1964
PIT N Dec 6, 1966
DET A Nov 28, 1967
CHI A July 21, 1968

Frank Riccelli
STL N Oct 25, 1977
HOU N June 8, 1978

Del Rice
MIL N June 3, 1955
BAL A Sept 7, 1960

Hal Rice
PIT N June 14, 1953
CHI N June 14, 1954

Harry Rice
DET A Dec 2, 1927
NY A May 30, 1930
WAS A Jan 13, 1931

Lee Richard
STL N Dec 12, 1975

Gene Richards
SF N Mar 31, 1984

Paul Richards
NY N Dec 1932
PHI A May 25, 1935

Gordie Richardson
NY N Dec 7, 1964

Lance Richbourg
PHI N July 1, 1921
CHI N Dec 17, 1931
CIN N Nov 30, 1932

Pete Richert
WAS A Dec 4, 1964
BAL A May 29, 1967
LA N Dec 2, 1971
STL N Dec 5, 1973
PHI N June 21, 1974

Lew Richie
BOS N July 16, 1909
CHI N Apr 1910

Marv Rickert
CIN N Oct 8, 1947
BOS N May 11, 1948
PIT N Dec 14, 1949
CHI A May 29, 1950

Dave Ricketts
PIT N Oct 21, 1969

Branch Rickey
STL A Feb 1905
NY A Dec 1906

Fred Rico
STL N June 13, 1970
MIN A Sept 1, 1971

Harry Riconda
PIT N Dec 11, 1928

Elmer Riddle
PIT N Dec 10, 1947

Johnny Riddle
CIN N Aug 10, 1938

Denny Riddleberger
WAS A Aug 31, 1970
CLE A Dec 2, 1971

Steve Ridzik
CIN N Apr 30, 1955
PHI N Apr 13, 1966

Joe Riggert
STL N June 1914

Lew Riggs
CIN N Nov 3, 1934
BKN N Dec 9, 1940

Dave Righetti
NY A Nov 10, 1978

Topper Rigney
BOS A Apr 7, 1926
WAS A May 2, 1927

Jimmy Ring
PHI N Nov 22, 1920
NY N Dec 30, 1925
STL N Dec 20, 1926
PHI N Dec 13, 1927

Juan Rios
KC A Mar 25, 1969
MIL A Sept 15, 1970

Allen Ripley
SF N Apr 6, 1980
CHI N Dec 7, 1981

Charlie Ripple
PIT N Aug 18, 1952

Jimmy Ripple
BKN N Aug 23, 1939
CIN N Aug 23, 1940

Claude Ritchey
PIT N Jan 1900
BOS N Dec 1906

Jay Ritchie
MIL N Dec 15, 1965
CIN N Oct 10, 1967

Jim Rittwage
SF N Dec 2, 1965

Jim Rivera
STL A Nov 27, 1951
CHI A July 28, 1952

Mickey Rivers
NY A Dec 11, 1975
TEX A Aug 1, 1979

Eppa Rixey
CIN N Nov 22, 1920

Johnny Rizzo
CIN N May 8, 1940
PHI N June 15, 1940
BKN N Dec 10, 1941

Mel Roach
CHI N May 9, 1961
PHI N Mar 20, 1962

Roxy Roach
WAS A Dec 1911

Mike Roarke
DET A Oct 15, 1959

Curt Roberts
NY A Feb 19, 1957

Dale Roberts
ATL N Dec 7, 1967

Dave Roberts
HOU N Dec 3, 1971
DET A Dec 6, 1975
CHI N July 30, 1977
PIT N June 28, 1979
SEA A Apr 24, 1980

Dave Roberts
BAL A Sept 12, 1966

Dave Roberts
SD N Feb 16, 1977
TEX A Oct 25, 1978
PHI N Mar 28, 1982

Leon Roberts
HOU N Dec 6, 1975
SEA A Dec 5, 1977
TEX A Dec 12, 1980
TOR A July 15, 1982
KC A Feb 5, 1983

Robin Roberts
BAL A Oct 16, 1961

Charlie Robertson
STL A Dec 31, 1925

Daryl Robertson
CHI N Mar 31, 1961
STL N June 5, 1962

Dave Robertson
CHI N July 25, 1919
PIT N July 1, 1921
NY N Dec 1921

Gene Robertson
BOS N Sept 17, 1929

Jerry Robertson
DET A Dec 3, 1969
NY N Mar 30, 1971

Jim Robertson
PHI A Dec 16, 1953

Sherry Robertson
PHI A May 19, 1952

Aaron Robinson
CHI A Feb 24, 1948
DET A Nov 10, 1948
BOS A Aug 6, 1951

Bill Robinson
NY A Nov 29, 1966
PIT N Apr 5, 1975
PHI N June 15, 1982

Bruce Robinson
NY A Feb 3, 1979

Craig Robinson
ATL N Dec 3, 1973
SF N June 11, 1975
ATL N June 13, 1976

Dewey Robinson
PHI N Oct 30, 1981

Earl Robinson
BAL A Dec 15, 1960

Eddie Robinson
WAS A Dec 14, 1948
CHI A May 31, 1950
PHI A Jan 27, 1953
NY A Dec 16, 1953
KC A June 14, 1956
DET A Dec 5, 1956

Floyd Robinson
CIN N Dec 15, 1966
KC A Oct 20, 1967
BOS A July 31, 1968

Frank Robinson
BAL A Dec 9, 1965
LA N Dec 2, 1971
CAL A Nov 28, 1972
CLE A Sept 12, 1974

Hank Robinson
STL N Dec 12, 1913
NY A June 20, 1918

Humberto Robinson
CLE A Apr 11, 1959
PHI N May 16, 1959

Jackie Robinson
NY N Dec 13, 1956

Wilbert Robinson
STL N Feb 11, 1900

Rafael Robles
STL N June 20, 1972

Sergio Robles
BAL A Dec 2, 1971

Mickey Rocco
CHI N May 1946

Pat Rockett
TOR A Dec 5, 1979

Andre Rodgers
MIL N Oct 31, 1960
CHI N Mar 31, 1961
PIT N Dec 9, 1964

Bill Rodgers
BOS A May 1915
CIN N June 1915

Aurelio Rodriguez
WAS A Apr 27, 1970
DET A Oct 9, 1970
SD N Dec 7, 1979
NY A Aug 4, 1980
TOR A Nov 17, 1981
CHI A Apr 2, 1982
BAL A Feb 7, 1983

Ed Rodriguez
KC A Feb 26, 1979

Eduardo Rodriguez
SD N Aug 26, 1983

Elly Rodriguez
MIL A Feb 2, 1971
CAL A Oct 22, 1973
LA N Mar 31, 1976

Freddy Rodriguez
CHI N Dec 10, 1957

Roberto Rodriguez
SD N May 26, 1970
CHI N June 23, 1970

Preacher Roe
BKN N Dec 8, 1947
BAL A Dec 13, 1954

Ed Roebuck
WAS A July 20, 1963
PHI N Apr 21, 1964

Gary Roenicke
BAL A Dec 7, 1977

Wally Roettger
NY N Apr 10, 1930
CIN N Oct 29, 1930
STL N June 15, 1931
CIN N Dec 1931
PIT N Oct 17, 1933

Billy Rogell
CHI N Dec 6, 1939

Tom Rogers
PHI A Apr 1919

Garry Roggenburk
BOS A Sept 7, 1966
SEA A June 23, 1969

Saul Rogovin
CIN N Dec 10, 1953

Billy Rohr
DET A May 22, 1970

Cookie Rojas
PHI N Nov 27, 1962
STL N Oct 7, 1969
KC A June 13, 1970

Stan Rojek
PIT N Nov 14, 1947
STL N May 17, 1951
BKN N Oct 14, 1952

Jim Roland
OAK A Feb 24, 1969
NY A Apr 28, 1972
TEX A Aug 30, 1972

Johnny Romano
CLE A Dec 6, 1959
CHI A Jan 20, 1965
STL N Dec 14, 1966

Enrique Romo
PIT N Dec 5, 1978

Vicente Romo
BOS A Apr 19, 1969
CHI A Mar 31, 1971
SD N Oct 28, 1972

Gene Roof
MON N Sept 16, 1983

Phil Roof
LA A Oct 14, 1964
CLE A June 15, 1965
KC A Oct 1, 1965
MIL A Jan 15, 1970
MIN A July 8, 1971
TOR A Oct 21, 1976

Jim Rooker
NY A Sept 30, 1968
PIT N Oct 25, 1972

Pat Rooney
NY A Dec 20, 1983

Jorge Roque
MON N Nov 6, 1972

Buddy Rosar
CLE A Dec 17, 1942
PHI A May 29, 1945
BOS A Oct 8, 1949

Don Rose
CAL A Dec 10, 1971

Pete Rose
PHI N Dec 5, 1978
MON N Jan 20, 1984

Johnny Roseboro
MIN A Nov 28, 1967

Dave Rosello
CLE A Dec 5, 1977

Goody Rosen
NY N Apr 27, 1946

Larry Rosenthal
CLE A May 29, 1941
PHI A July 6, 1944

Buck Ross
CHI A Apr 30, 1940

Don Ross
BKN N Sept 14, 1938
CLE A Apr 27, 1945

Gary Ross
SD N Apr 25, 1969
CAL A Sept 17, 1975

Joe Rossi
PIT N Oct 14, 1952

Claude Rossman
DET A Dec 1906
STL A Aug 20, 1909

Braggo Roth
CLE A Aug 21, 1915
PHI A Mar 1, 1919
BOS A June 27, 1919
WAS A Jan 20, 1920
NY A Jan 20, 1921

Frank Roth
CHI A Feb 1905

Jack Rothrock
CHI A Apr 30, 1932

Edd Roush
NY N Dec 23, 1915
CIN N July 20, 1916
NY N Feb 9, 1927

Jack Rowan
PHI N Feb 1911
CHI N Aug 1911

Ken Rowe
BAL A Sept 10, 1964

Schoolboy Rowe
BKN N Apr 30, 1942
PHI N Mar 24, 1943

Bama Rowell
BKN N Mar 6, 1948
PHI N Apr 15, 1948

Luther Roy
BKN N July 24, 1929

Jerry Royster
ATL N Nov 17, 1975

Dick Rozek
PHI A Dec 19, 1952

Vic Roznovsky
BAL A Mar 30, 1966

John Ruberto
SD N May 22, 1969

Jorge Rubio
CIN N Nov 29, 1967

Art Ruble
CIN N May 8, 1934

Dave Rucker
STL N June 22, 1983

Joe Rudi
KC A Oct 1, 1965
CAL A Nov 17, 1976
BOS A Jan 23, 1981
OAK A Dec 4, 1981

Don Rudolph
CIN N May 1, 1959
WAS A May 3, 1962

Ken Rudolph
SF N Mar 19, 1974
STL N Oct 14, 1974
BAL A July 27, 1977

Muddy Ruel
NY A Aug 21, 1917
BOS A Dec 15, 1920
WAS A Feb 10, 1923
BOS A Dec 15, 1930
DET A Aug 31, 1931
STL A Dec 1932

Dutch Ruether
CIN N July 17, 1917
BKN N Dec 15, 1920
WAS A Dec 17, 1924
NY A Aug 27, 1926

Rudy Rufer
BKN N June 9, 1952

Red Ruffing
NY A May 6, 1930

Chico Ruiz
CAL A Nov 25, 1969

Pete Runnels
BOS A Jan 23, 1958
HOU N Nov 26, 1962

Bob Rush
MIL N Dec 5, 1957
CHI A June 11, 1960

Amos Rusie
CIN N Dec 15, 1900

Allan Russell
BOS A July 29, 1919
WAS A Feb 10, 1923

Jack Russell
CLE A June 10, 1932
WAS A Dec 15, 1932
BOS A June 13, 1936

Jim Russell
BOS N Nov 18, 1947
BKN N Dec 24, 1949

Babe Ruth
NY A Jan 3, 1920

Dick Ruthven
CHI A Dec 10, 1975
ATL N Dec 12, 1975
PHI N June 15, 1978
CHI N May 22, 1983

Blondy Ryan
PHI N Nov 1, 1934
NY A Aug 6, 1935

Connie Ryan
BOS N Apr 27, 1943
CIN N May 10, 1950
PHI N Dec 10, 1951
CHI A Aug 25, 1953
CIN N Dec 10, 1953

Jack Ryan
BOS A Feb 18, 1909

Mike Ryan
PHI N Dec 15, 1967
PIT N Jan 31, 1974

Nolan Ryan
CAL A Dec 10, 1971
HOU N Nov 19, 1979

Rosy Ryan
BOS N Apr 17, 1925

Gary Ryerson
CAL A Oct 22, 1973

Ray Sadecki
SF N May 8, 1966
NY N Dec 12, 1969
STL N Oct 13, 1974
ATL N May 28, 1975
KC A June 30, 1975

Bob Sadowski
MIL N June 15, 1963
BOS A Dec 15, 1965

Bob Sadowski
CHI A Dec 15, 1961

Jim Sadowski
CIN N Nov 6, 1976

Tom Saffell
KC A Sept 14, 1955
BKN N Apr 16, 1956

Johnny Sain
NY A Aug 30, 1951
KC A May 11, 1955

Ebba St. Claire
NY N Feb 1, 1954

Lenn Sakata
BAL A Dec 6, 1979

Luis Salazar
SD N Aug 5, 1980

Bill Salkeld
BOS N Nov 18, 1947
CHI A Sept 26, 1949

Slim Sallee
NY N July 23, 1916
CIN N Mar 8, 1919
NY N Sept 5, 1920

Chico Salmon
CLE A Apr 1, 1964
BAL A Mar 31, 1969

Jack Salveson
PIT N Dec 11, 1934
CHI A June 16, 1935
CLE A Dec 10, 1936
WAS A Dec 10, 1936

Manny Salvo
BOS N June 15, 1940
PHI N May 12, 1943

Ron Samford
DET A Apr 8, 1955
WAS A Dec 6, 1958
BAL A Apr 3, 1960

Amado Samuel
NY N Oct 15, 1963

Alejandro Sanchez
SF N Mar 24, 1984

Luis Sanchez
CIN N Oct 24, 1975

Heinie Sand
STL N Dec 13, 1928

Ryne Sandberg
CHI N Jan 27, 1982

Ken Sanders
KC A June 13, 1966
MIL A Jan 15, 1970
PHI N Oct 31, 1972
MIN A Nov 30, 1972
CLE A Aug 3, 1973
NY N Mar 22, 1975
KC A Sept 17, 1976

Ray Sanders
BOS N Apr 15, 1946
BKN N Mar 6, 1948
BOS N Apr 19, 1948

Reggie Sanders
DET A May 9, 1972
ATL N Mar 29, 1975

Scott Sanderson
SD N Dec 7, 1983
CHI N Dec 7, 1983

Mike Sandlock
PHI N Dec 19, 1953

Charlie Sands
DET A Apr 2, 1973

Tom Sandt
STL N Mar 25, 1977

Fred Sanford
NY A Dec 13, 1948
WAS A June 15, 1951
STL A June 30, 1951

Jack Sanford
SF N Dec 3, 1958
CAL A Aug 18, 1965
KC A June 15, 1967

Manny Sanguillen
OAK A Nov 5, 1976
PIT N Apr 4, 1978
CLE A Dec 9, 1980

Rafael Santana
STL N Feb 16, 1981

Jose Santiago
KC A May 16, 1956

Ron Santo
CHI A Dec 11, 1973

Al Santorini
STL N June 11, 1971
ATL N May 8, 1973

Manny Sarmiento
BOS A Apr 8, 1981
PIT N Oct 23, 1981

Bill Sarni
NY N June 14, 1956

Tom Satriano
BOS A June 15, 1969

Kevin Saucier
TEX A Sept 13, 1980
DET A Dec 10, 1980

Ed Sauer
PIT N June 15, 1949
BOS N June 15, 1949
BKN N Dec 24, 1949

Hank Sauer
CHI N June 15, 1949
STL N Mar 30, 1956

Bob Savage
STL A Dec 16, 1948

Ted Savage
PIT N Nov 28, 1963
CHI N May 14, 1967
LA N Apr 23, 1968
CIN N Mar 30, 1969
MIL A Apr 5, 1970
KC A May 11, 1971

Bob Saverine
HOU N Apr 24, 1965

Carl Sawatski
CHI A Nov 30, 1953
PHI N June 13, 1958
STL N Dec 4, 1959

Rick Sawyer
DET A Mar 19, 1974
NY A Mar 19, 1974
SD N July 10, 1976
MON N Sept 29, 1977

Bill Sayles
BKN N July 31, 1943

Doc Scanlan
BKN N Aug 1, 1904

Pat Scanlon
STL N Nov 6, 1976
SD N May 17, 1977

Randy Scarbery
STL N Aug 12, 1977
CAL A June 12, 1980

Ray Scarborough
CHI A May 31, 1950
BOS A Dec 10, 1950
NY A Aug 22, 1952

Mac Scarce
NY N Dec 3, 1974
CIN N Apr 15, 1975
TEX A Dec 13, 1978

Les Scarsella
BOS N Dec 6, 1939

Paul Schaal
CAL A Apr 30, 1974

Sid Schacht
NY A June 15, 1950
BOS N May 13, 1951

Germany Schaefer
WAS A Aug 13, 1909
NY A Feb 10, 1916

Mark Schaeffer
SD N Dec 3, 1971

Jimmie Schaffer
CHI N Oct 17, 1962
CHI A Dec 1, 1964
NY N July 8, 1965
PHI N Feb 22, 1966
LA N Mar 30, 1969

Joe Schaffernoth
CLE A July 7, 1961
WAS A Oct 14, 1961

Art Schallock
BAL A May 11, 1955

Bobby Schang
NY N June 1915

Wally Schang
BOS A Dec 14, 1917
NY A Dec 15, 1920
STL A Feb 6, 1926
PHI A Dec 11, 1929

George Scharein
PHI N Dec 8, 1936

Jeff Schattinger
CHI A Mar 24, 1982

Dan Schatzeder
DET A Dec 7, 1979
SF N Dec 9, 1981
MON N June 15, 1982

Rube Schauer
PHI A Jan 1917

Bob Scheffing
CIN N June 7, 1950
STL N Aug 1, 1951

Carl Scheib
STL N May 7, 1954

Richie Scheinblum
WAS A Oct 23, 1970
CIN N Nov 30, 1972
CAL A June 15, 1973
KC A Apr 30, 1974
STL N Aug 5, 1974

Hank Schenz
BKN N May 16, 1949
PIT N Nov 4, 1949
NY N July 10, 1951

Fred Scherman
HOU N Nov 3, 1973
MON N June 8, 1975

Chuck Schilling
MIN A Apr 6, 1966

Admiral Schlei
STL N Dec 12, 1908
NY N Dec 12, 1908

Rudy Schlesinger
PHI N May 5, 1969

Jay Schleuter
BAL A Dec 3, 1974

Dutch Schliebner
STL A May 1923

Ray Schmandt
STL N Feb 15, 1923

George Schmees
BOS A June 30, 1952

Bob Schmidt
CIN N Apr 27, 1961
WAS A Dec 15, 1961

Freddy Schmidt
PHI N May 3, 1947

Johnny Schmitz
BKN N June 15, 1951
NY A Aug 1, 1952
CIN N Aug 28, 1952
NY A Feb 17, 1953
WAS A May 13, 1953
BOS A Nov 8, 1955
BAL A May 14, 1956

Dave Schneck
PHI N Dec 3, 1974
CHI N Feb 16, 1977

Dan Schneider
HOU N Oct 13, 1966

Jeff Schneider
CAL A Jan 28, 1982

Pete Schneider
NY A Dec 9, 1918

Gerry Schoen
BAL A Apr 30, 1969

Red Schoendienst
NY N June 14, 1956
MIL N June 15, 1957

Dick Schofield
PIT N June 15, 1958
SF N May 22, 1965
NY A May 11, 1966
LA N Sept 10, 1966
BOS A Dec 2, 1968
STL N Oct 21, 1970
MIL A July 29, 1971

Gene Schott
BKN N May 5, 1939

Ossee Schreckengost
CLE A Oct 1901
PHI A June 1902
CHI A May 1908

Pop Schriver
STL N Unknown

Bob Schroder
WAS A Dec 1, 1969

Ken Schrom
TOR A June 3, 1980

Ron Schueler
PHI N Dec 3, 1973
MIN A Mar 31, 1977

Dave Schuler
CAL A May 11, 1977

Wes Schulmerich
BOS N Oct 14, 1930
PHI N June 17, 1933
CIN N May 8, 1934

Art Schult
WAS A June 12, 1957

Fred Schulte
WAS A Dec 14, 1932
PIT N Jan 30, 1936

Johnny Schulte
PHI N Dec 13, 1927
CHI N Feb 1929

Wildfire Schulte
PIT N July 29, 1916
PHI N June 14, 1917
WAS A Dec 1917

Barney Schultz
STL N June 24, 1963

Bob Schultz
PIT N June 1, 1953
DET A Dec 29, 1954

Buddy Schultz
STL N Feb 28, 1977

Howie Schultz
PHI N May 10, 1947

Joe Schultz
CHI N Aug 1915
PIT N Jan 1916
PHI N June 6, 1924
CIN N June 23, 1925

Al Schulz
CIN N Feb 10, 1916

Ferdie Schupp
STL N July 1919
BKN N June 18, 1921
CHI A Dec 1921

Bill Schuster
BOS N June 15, 1939

Don Schwall
PIT N Nov 20, 1962
ATL N June 15, 1966

Herb Score
CHI A Apr 18, 1960

Dick Scott
CHI N Dec 13, 1963

Everett Scott
NY A Dec 20, 1921
WAS A June 17, 1925
CIN N July 6, 1926

George Scott
MIL A Oct 11, 1971
BOS A Dec 6, 1976
KC A June 13, 1979

Jack Scott
CIN N Feb 18, 1922
PHI N Jan 9, 1927

John Scott
STL N Dec 6, 1977
CHI A Oct 23, 1978

Mickey Scott
CHI A Dec 18, 1969
MON N May 22, 1973
CAL A Sept 11, 1974

Mike Scott
HOU N Dec 10, 1982

Pete Scott
PIT N Nov 28, 1927

Rodney Scott
MON N Dec 12, 1975
TEX A Mar 15, 1977
OAK A Mar 26, 1977
CHI N Mar 29, 1978
MON N Dec 14, 1978

Tony Scott
STL N Nov 6, 1976
HOU N June 7, 1981

Kim Seaman
STL N Dec 5, 1978
SD N Dec 8, 1980
MON N May 22, 1982

Ray Searage
CLE A Jan 8, 1982
SD N Dec 15, 1982

Tom Seaton
CHI N Feb 10, 1916

Tom Seaver
CIN N June 15, 1977
NY N Dec 16, 1982
CHI A Jan 20, 1984

Jimmy Sebring
CIN N Aug 11, 1904
WAS A Sept 1909

Don Secrist
CHI A Dec 5, 1968

Bob Seeds
CHI A Apr 24, 1932
BOS A Dec 15, 1932
CLE A May 25, 1934
DET A Dec 1934

Pat Seerey
CHI A June 2, 1948

Herman Segelke
SF N Oct 15, 1982

Kal Segrist
BAL A Dec 1, 1954

Diego Segui
WAS A Apr 13, 1966
KC A July 30, 1966
OAK A Dec 7, 1969
STL N June 7, 1972
BOS A Dec 7, 1973

Socks Seibold
BOS N Nov 7, 1928

Kip Selbach
NY N Feb 29, 1900
BOS A July 4, 1904

Dick Selma
CHI N Apr 25, 1969
PHI N Nov 17, 1969
MIL A July 29, 1974

Andy Seminick
CIN N Dec 10, 1951
PHI N Apr 30, 1955

Ray Semproch
DET A Dec 5, 1959
LA N June 15, 1960
LA A Apr 7, 1961

Sonny Senerchia
CIN N Jan 31, 1956

Steve Senteney
NY N Feb 4, 1983
PIT N June 14, 1983

Bill Serena
CHI A Sept 30, 1954

Walter Sessi
BKN N Jan 30, 1947

Hank Severeid
WAS A June 8, 1925
NY A July 22, 1926

Al Severinsen
SD N Dec 1, 1970
NY N Nov 30, 1972

Luke Sewell
WAS A Jan 7, 1933
CHI A Jan 22, 1935
STL A Jan 22, 1935
BKN N Dec 19, 1938

Jimmy Sexton
SEA A Dec 7, 1976
HOU N Dec 5, 1977
OAK A Feb 10, 1981

Gordon Seyfried
DET A Nov 27, 1962

Cy Seymour
NY N July 14, 1906

Art Shamsky
NY N Nov 8, 1967
STL N Oct 18, 1971
OAK A June 28, 1972

Howard Shanks
BOS A Feb 10, 1923
NY A Dec 10, 1924

Red Shannon
BOS A June 27, 1919
WAS A Jan 20, 1920
PHI A July 1920

Spike Shannon
NY N July 13, 1906
PIT N July 1908

Bobby Shantz
NY A Feb 19, 1957
PIT N Dec 16, 1960
STL N May 7, 1962
CHI N June 15, 1964
PHI N Aug 15, 1964

Dick Sharon
DET A Nov 30, 1972
SD N Nov 18, 1974
STL N Oct 20, 1975
BOS A Mar 3, 1976

Bill Sharp
MIL A May 8, 1975

Bud Sharpe
PIT N Sept 1910

Joe Shaute
CIN N Dec 1933

Al Shaw
CHI A Jan 1908

Bob Shaw
CHI A June 15, 1958
KC A June 10, 1961
SF N Dec 3, 1963
NY N June 10, 1966
CHI N July 24, 1967

Don Shaw
OAK A May 15, 1972

Bob Shawkey
NY A July 7, 1915

Merv Shea
STL A May 9, 1933
CHI A Dec 11, 1933

Spec Shea
WAS A May 3, 1952

Steve Shea
MON N Apr 3, 1969

Dave Shean
BOS N July 16, 1909
CHI N Jan 1911
BOS N Oct 1911
BOS A Apr 1918

Jimmy Sheckard
BKN N Jan 1900
CHI N Dec 30, 1905
STL N Apr 1913
CIN N July 1913

Tom Sheehan
PIT N May 20, 1925

Tommy Sheehan
BKN N Jan 1908

Rollie Sheldon
KC A May 3, 1965
BOS A June 13, 1966

Jim Shellenback
WAS A May 17, 1969

Bill Sherdel
BOS N June 16, 1930
STL N May 18, 1932

Larry Sherry
DET A Apr 9, 1964
HOU N June 29, 1967

Norm Sherry
NY N Oct 11, 1962

Barry Shetrone
WAS A Dec 5, 1962

Charlie Shields
STL A Sept 1902

Art Shires
WAS A June 16, 1930

Bob Shirley
STL N Dec 8, 1980
CIN N Apr 1, 1982
NY A Dec 15, 1982

Urban Shocker
STL A Jan 22, 1918
NY A Dec 17, 1924

Costen Shockley
LA A Dec 3, 1964

Milt Shoffner
CIN N Aug 19, 1939

Ernie Shore
NY A Dec 18, 1918

Bill Short
BOS A Aug 15, 1966
PIT N Oct 17, 1966
NY N Nov 29, 1967

Chick Shorten
DET A Jan 17, 1919
STL A Dec 14, 1921

Burt Shotton
WAS A Dec 15, 1917
STL N Feb 1, 1919

Clyde Shoun
STL N Apr 16, 1938
CIN N May 6, 1942
BOS N June 7, 1947
CHI A May 11, 1949

Harry Shuman
PHI N July 27, 1944

Eddie Sicking
PHI N May 27, 1919
CIN N July 1920

Norm Siebern
KC A Dec 11, 1959
BAL A Nov 27, 1963
CAL A Dec 2, 1965
SF N Dec 14, 1966
BOS A July 16, 1967

Dick Siebert
STL A Oct 16, 1945

Paul Siebert
NY N June 15, 1977
STL N Oct 2, 1978

Sonny Siebert
BOS A Apr 19, 1969
TEX A May 4, 1973
STL N Oct 26, 1973
SD N Nov 18, 1974
OAK A May 16, 1975

Ed Siever
STL A Dec 1902

Roy Sievers
WAS A Feb 18, 1954
CHI A Apr 4, 1960
PHI N Nov 28, 1961
WAS A July 16, 1964

Frank Sigafoos
CHI A June 22, 1929

Charlie Silvera
CHI N Dec 11, 1956

Ken Silvestri
NY A Dec 31, 1940

Al Sima
PHI A June 11, 1954

Al Simmons
CHI A Sept 28, 1932
DET A Dec 10, 1935
WAS A Apr 4, 1937
BOS N Dec 29, 1938
CIN N Aug 31, 1939

Curt Simmons
CHI N June 22, 1966
CAL A Aug 2, 1967

Ted Simmons
MIL A Dec 12, 1980

Dick Simpson
BAL A Dec 2, 1965
CIN N Dec 9, 1965
STL N Jan 11, 1968
HOU N June 15, 1968
NY A Dec 4, 1968
SEA A May 19, 1969
SF N Dec 12, 1969

Harry Simpson
KC A May 11, 1955
NY A June 15, 1957
KC A June 15, 1958
CHI A May 2, 1959
PIT N Aug 25, 1959

Steve Simpson
NY N Dec 20, 1973

Wayne Simpson
KC A Nov 30, 1972
PIT N Mar 28, 1974
PHI N Apr 5, 1975
CAL A Apr 8, 1976

Duke Sims
LA N Dec 11, 1970
NY A Sept 24, 1973
TEX A May 8, 1974

Bill Singer
CAL A Nov 28, 1972
TEX A Dec 10, 1975
MIN A June 1, 1976

Elmer Singleton
PIT N Sept 30, 1946
CHI N Nov 13, 1956

Ken Singleton
MON N Apr 5, 1972
BAL A Dec 4, 1974

John Sipin
SD N May 22, 1969

Tommie Sisk
SD N Mar 28, 1969
CHI A Mar 30, 1970

Dave Sisler
DET A May 2, 1959
CIN N Sept 16, 1961

Dick Sisler
PHI N Apr 7, 1948
CIN N Dec 10, 1951
STL N May 13, 1952

George Sisler
WAS A Dec 14, 1927
BOS N May 27, 1928

Ted Sizemore
STL N Oct 5, 1970
LA N Mar 2, 1976
PHI N Dec 20, 1976
CHI N Feb 23, 1979
BOS A Aug 17, 1979

Dave Skaggs
CAL A May 13, 1980

Roe Skidmore
CHI A Nov 30, 1970
STL N July 27, 1973

Bob Skinner
CIN N May 23, 1963
STL N June 13, 1964

Camp Skinner
BOS A Jan 30, 1923

Joel Skinner
CHI A Feb 2, 1982

Lou Skizas
KC A June 14, 1956
DET A Nov 20, 1957
CIN N May 1, 1959

Craig Skok
TEX A Nov 17, 1975

Bill Skowron
LA N Nov 26, 1962
WAS A Dec 6, 1963
CHI A July 13, 1964
CAL A May 6, 1967

Pat Skrable
BOS A Oct 11, 1971

Gordon Slade
STL N Feb 1933
CIN N Dec 1933

Jimmy Slagle
PHI N Jan 1900
BOS N June 1901

Jim Slaton
DET A Dec 9, 1977
MIL A Nov 29, 1978
CAL A Dec 20, 1983

Jack Slattery
CHI A Apr 1903

Enos Slaughter
NY A Apr 11, 1954
KC A May 11, 1955
NY A Aug 25, 1956
MIL N Sept 12, 1959

Lou Sleater
NY A July 31, 1951
WAS A May 12, 1952
KC A Apr 28, 1955
BAL A June 2, 1958

Jim Small
KC A Nov 20, 1957

Roy Smalley
MIL N Mar 20, 1954
PHI N Apr 30, 1955

Roy Smalley
MIN A June 1, 1976
NY A Apr 10, 1982

Al Smith
STL N Dec 20, 1937
PHI N Dec 29, 1937

Al Smith
CHI A Dec 4, 1957
BAL A Jan 14, 1963
CLE A Dec 4, 1963

Bob Smith
CHI N Oct 14, 1930
CIN N Nov 30, 1932
BOS N Aug 2, 1933

Bob Smith
PIT N May 14, 1957
DET A June 13, 1959

Bobby Gene Smith
PHI N Dec 4, 1959
CHI N Apr 26, 1962
STL N June 5, 1962

Broadway Aleck Smith
BKN N Jan 1900

Bryn Smith
MON N Dec 7, 1977

Carr Smith
CLE A Dec 12, 1924

Charley Smith
PHI N May 4, 1961
CHI A Nov 28, 1961
NY N Apr 23, 1964
STL N Oct 20, 1965
NY A Dec 8, 1966
SF N Dec 6, 1968
CHI N Mar 28, 1969

Charlie Smith
BOS A Sept 1909
CHI N Apr 1911

Chris Smith
MON N Mar 31, 1980
SF N Feb 2, 1983

Dick Smith
NY N Oct 11, 1962
LA N Oct 15, 1964

Earl Smith
WAS A May 31, 1921

Earl Smith
BOS N June 7, 1923
PIT N July 6, 1924
STL N July 10, 1928

Eddie Smith
CHI A Apr 27, 1939

Elmer Smith
NY N Aug 8, 1900
PIT N Jan 1901
BOS N May 1901

Elmer Smith
WAS A Aug 18, 1916
CLE A June 13, 1917
BOS A Dec 24, 1921
NY A July 23, 1922

Frank Smith
BOS A Aug 9, 1910
CIN N May 11, 1911

Frank Smith
STL N Dec 8, 1954
CIN N Apr 10, 1956

George Smith
NY N June 20, 1918
BKN N July 15, 1918
NY N Oct 1918
PHI N May 27, 1919
BKN N Feb 11, 1923

George Smith
BOS A Oct 4, 1965

Hal Smith
BAL A Nov 18, 1954
KC A Aug 17, 1956
PIT N Dec 15, 1959

Harry Smith
BOS N Jan 1908

Heinie Smith
NY N June 1901

Jack Smith
BOS N Apr 19, 1926

Jimmy Smith
PIT N Feb 10, 1916
NY N Jan 1917
BOS N Oct 1918
NY N Feb 1919
CIN N Feb 1919
PHI N June 28, 1921

Lonnie Smith
STL N Nov 20, 1981
CLE A Nov 20, 1981

Milt Smith
STL N May 1, 1956

Nate Smith
BAL A Sept 10, 1962

Paul Smith
CHI N May 6, 1958

Red Smith
BOS N July 1914

Reggie Smith
STL N Oct 26, 1973
LA N June 15, 1976
SF N Apr 5, 1982

Riverboat Smith
CHI N Mar 9, 1959
CLE A May 4, 1959

Sherry Smith
CLE A Sept 18, 1922

Syd Smith
STL A July 1908

Tommy Smith
KC A Dec 16, 1968

Willie Smith
LA A Apr 28, 1964
CHI N June 28, 1968
CIN N Nov 30, 1970

Mike Smithson
TEX A Apr 9, 1982
MIN A Dec 7, 1983

Homer Smoot
CIN N July 25, 1906

Harry Smythe
BKN N May 30, 1934

Duke Snider
NY N Apr 1, 1963
SF N Apr 14, 1964

Fred Snodgrass
BOS N Aug 1915

Frank Snyder
NY N July 1919

Gene Snyder
LA N Dec 23, 1958

Jerry Snyder
WAS A May 3, 1952

Russ Snyder
KC A Apr 12, 1959
BAL A Jan 24, 1961
CHI A Nov 29, 1967
CLE A June 13, 1968
MIL A Apr 4, 1970

Eric Soderholm
CHI A Nov 26, 1976
TEX A June 15, 1979
NY A Nov 14, 1979

Tony Solaita
CAL A July 14, 1976
MON N Dec 5, 1978
TOR A July 30, 1979

Eddie Solomon
CHI N May 2, 1975
PIT N Mar 28, 1980
CHI A June 14, 1982

Moose Solters
STL A May 21, 1935
CLE A Jan 17, 1937
STL A Aug 2, 1939
CHI A Dec 8, 1939

Bill Sommers
STL A Nov 18, 1947

Don Songer
NY N May 9, 1927

Lary Sorensen
STL N Dec 12, 1980
CLE A Nov 20, 1981
OAK A Jan 23, 1984

Elias Sosa
STL N Oct 14, 1974
ATL N May 28, 1975
LA N June 23, 1976
PIT N Jan 31, 1978
OAK A Apr 4, 1978
MON N Jan 9, 1979
DET A Mar 30, 1982
SD N Oct 7, 1982

Denny Sothern
PIT N Aug 7, 1930

Allen Sothoron
BOS A Jan 1921
CLE A Apr 1921

Steve Souchock
CHI A Dec 14, 1948

Billy Southworth
BOS N Feb 23, 1921
NY N Nov 12, 1923
STL N June 14, 1926

Bob Spade
STL A Apr 1910

Warren Spahn
NY N Nov 23, 1964

Al Spangler
CAL A July 6, 1965

Tully Sparks
PHI N Feb 1900

Joe Sparma
MON N Dec 3, 1969

Bob Speake
SF N Apr 3, 1958

Tris Speaker
CLE A Apr 12, 1916

Byron Speece
CLE A Dec 12, 1924

Chris Speier
MON N Apr 27, 1977

Stan Spence
WAS A Dec 13, 1941
BOS A Dec 10, 1947
STL A May 8, 1949

Daryl Spencer
STL N Dec 15, 1959
LA N May 30, 1961

Glenn Spencer
NY N Dec 12, 1932
CIN N Nov 15, 1933
STL N Jan 11, 1934

Jim Spencer
TEX A May 20, 1973
CAL A Dec 10, 1975
CHI A Dec 11, 1975
NY A Dec 12, 1977
OAK A May 20, 1981

Roy Spencer
CLE A Jan 7, 1933

Tom Spencer
CHI A Nov 6, 1976

Tubby Spencer
BOS A Dec 12, 1908

Rob Sperring
SF N Feb 11, 1977

Ed Spiezio
SD N Dec 3, 1968
CHI A July 9, 1972

Charlie Spikes
CLE A Nov 27, 1972
DET A Dec 9, 1977

Dan Spillner
CLE A June 14, 1978

Harry Spilman
HOU N June 8, 1981

Scipio Spinks
STL N Apr 15, 1972
CHI N Mar 23, 1974

Al Spohrer
BOS N June 15, 1928

Ed Sprague
CIN N Oct 20, 1970
STL N July 27, 1973
MIL A Sept 4, 1973

George Spriggs
NY N Mar 15, 1971

Jack Spring
WAS A June 24, 1958
CHI N May 15, 1964
STL N June 15, 1964

Bobby Sprowl
HOU N June 13, 1979
BAL A Dec 21, 1983

Eddie Stack
BKN N Dec 1911
CHI N Aug 14, 1913

Marv Staehle
CLE A July 29, 1967
MON N Sept 13, 1969

Bill Stafford
KC A June 10, 1966
CIN N Aug 15, 1966

Steve Staggs
OAK A Mar 25, 1978

Jake Stahl
WAS A Jan 16, 1904
CHI A Mar 1907
NY A Oct 1907
BOS A July 1908

Larry Stahl
NY N Oct 14, 1966
CIN N Nov 30, 1972

Roy Staiger
NY A Dec 9, 1977

Tuck Stainback
STL N Apr 16, 1938
PHI N June 1938
BKN N July 11, 1938

Gerry Staley
CIN N Dec 8, 1954
NY A Sept 11, 1955
CHI A May 28, 1956
KC A June 10, 1961
DET A Aug 2, 1961

Tracy Stallard
NY N Dec 11, 1962
STL N Dec 7, 1964

Virgil Stallcup
STL N May 13, 1952

Oscar Stanage
CIN N May 17, 1906

Charley Stanceu
PHI N May 1946

Lee Stange
CLE A June 15, 1964
BOS A June 2, 1966
CHI A June 29, 1970

Don Stanhouse
TEX A Mar 4, 1972
MON N Dec 5, 1974
BAL A Dec 7, 1977
LA N Nov 17, 1979

Eddie Stanky
BKN N June 6, 1944
BOS N Mar 6, 1948
NY N Dec 14, 1949
STL N Dec 11, 1951

Fred Stanley
SD N June 11, 1972
OAK A Nov 3, 1980

Leroy Stanton
CAL A Dec 10, 1971

Mike Stanton
TOR A Mar 29, 1978
STL N Dec 7, 1981
CLE A Feb 8, 1982

Charlie Starr
PHI N July 16, 1909
BOS N Sept 1909

Dick Starr
STL A Dec 13, 1948
WAS A July 30, 1951

Ray Starr
NY N Oct 10, 1932
BOS N June 12, 1933
PIT N May 27, 1944
CHI N June 23, 1945

Jigger Statz
BOS A July 1920

Rusty Staub
MON N Jan 22, 1969
NY N Apr 5, 1972
DET A Dec 12, 1975
MON N July 20, 1979
TEX A Mar 31, 1980
NY N Dec 16, 1980

John Stearns
NY N Dec 3, 1974

Bill Steele
BKN N July 1914

Bob Steele
PIT N June 14, 1917
NY N June 1918

Elmer Steele
PIT N Feb 1910
BKN N Aug 31, 1911

Farmer Steelman
BKN N Jan 1900
PHI A Apr 1901

Bill Steen
DET A June 1915

Dave Stegman
SD N Dec 12, 1980

Bill Stein
TEX A Dec 29, 1980

Justin Stein
CIN N June 10, 1938

Randy Stein
SEA A June 7, 1979

Ray Steineder
PHI N May 25, 1924

Harry Steinfeldt
CHI N Mar 1906
BOS N Mar 1911

Rick Stelmaszek
CAL A May 20, 1973
CHI N July 28, 1974

Casey Stengel
PIT N Jan 9, 1918
PHI N Aug 1919
NY N July 1, 1921
BOS N Nov 12, 1923

Dave Stenhouse
WAS A Dec 15, 1961

Rennie Stennett
SF N Nov 29, 1979

Buzz Stephen
BAL A June 15, 1970

Bryan Stephens
STL A Nov 20, 1947

Gene Stephens
BAL A June 9, 1960
KC A June 8, 1961

Vern Stephens
BOS A Nov 17, 1947
CHI A Feb 9, 1953
STL A July 20, 1953

Earl Stephenson
MIL A Dec 3, 1971
PHI N Oct 31, 1972

Johnny Stephenson
CHI N June 12, 1967

Ed Stevens
PIT N Nov 14, 1947

R C Stevens
WAS A Dec 16, 1960

Bud Stewart
WAS A May 13, 1948
CHI A Dec 11, 1950

Dave Stewart
TEX A Aug 19, 1983

Jimmy Stewart
CHI A May 22, 1967
HOU N Nov 29, 1971

Lefty Stewart
STL A Jan 15, 1927
WAS A Dec 14, 1932
CLE A May 14, 1935

Stuffy Stewart
PHI N Jan 21, 1919

Dick Stigman
MIN A Apr 2, 1962
BOS A Apr 6, 1966
CIN N Aug 15, 1966

Royle Stillman
BAL A Dec 2, 1971

Craig Stimac
CLE A Jan 27, 1982

Bob Stinson
STL N Oct 5, 1970
HOU N Nov 3, 1971
MON N Mar 28, 1973
KC A Mar 31, 1975

Snuffy Stirnweiss
STL A June 15, 1950
CLE A Apr 1, 1951

Chuck Stobbs
CHI A Nov 13, 1951
WAS A Dec 10, 1952
STL N July 9, 1958

Milt Stock
PHI N Jan 1915
STL N Jan 21, 1919
BKN N Apr 27, 1924

Wes Stock
KC A June 15, 1964

Tim Stoddard
OAK A Dec 8, 1983
CHI N Mar 26, 1984

Dean Stone
BOS A Apr 29, 1957
STL N Mar 15, 1959
CHI A June 22, 1962

George Stone
NY N Nov 2, 1972
TEX A Feb 24, 1976

George Stone
WAS A Jan 16, 1904
BOS A Jan 16, 1905
STL A Jan 16, 1905

John Stone
WAS A Dec 20, 1933

Ron Stone
PHI N Jan 20, 1969

Steve Stone
CHI A Nov 28, 1972
CHI N Dec 11, 1973
CHI A Nov 24, 1976
BAL A Nov 29, 1978

Bill Stoneman
CAL A Apr 4, 1974

Alan Storke
STL N Aug 19, 1909
CIN N Feb 1910

Allyn Stout
CIN N May 7, 1933
NY N Dec 14, 1934

George Stovall
STL A Dec 1911

Jesse Stovall
DET A Jan 1904

Mike Strahler
CAL A Nov 28, 1972
MIL A Dec 6, 1973

Joe Strain
CHI N Dec 12, 1980

Bob Strampe
SD N Nov 18, 1974

Sammy Strang
NY N Feb 1901
BKN N Mar 1903
NY N Feb 1905

Alan Strange
WAS A June 29, 1935

Gabby Street
BOS N June 6, 1905
CIN N July 30, 1905
NY A Dec 1911

George Strickland
CLE A Aug 18, 1952

Jake Striker
CHI A Dec 6, 1959

Nick Strincevich
PIT N May 7, 1940
PHI N May 15, 1948

Joe Stripp
BKN N Mar 14, 1932
STL N Oct 4, 1937
BOS N Aug 1, 1938

John Strohmayer
NY N July 16, 1973

Brent Strom
CLE A Nov 27, 1972
SD N June 15, 1974

Ed Stroud
WAS A June 15, 1967
CHI A Mar 29, 1971

Steve Stroughter
MIN A Dec 19, 1980

Amos Strunk
BOS A Dec 14, 1917
PHI A June 27, 1919
CHI A July 23, 1920
PHI A Apr 30, 1924

Dick Stuart
BOS A Nov 20, 1962
PHI N Nov 29, 1964
NY N Feb 22, 1966

Marlin Stuart
STL A Aug 14, 1952
NY A July 4, 1954

Bill Stumpf
CLE A May 20, 1913

Tom Sturdivant
KC A May 26, 1959
BOS A Dec 3, 1959
PIT N June 29, 1961
DET A May 4, 1963
KC A May 23, 1963

Bobby Sturgeon
BOS N Mar 1, 1948

Ken Suarez
TEX A Dec 2, 1971
CLE A Feb 12, 1974
CAL A Sept 12, 1974

Jim Suchecki
STL A May 17, 1951
PIT N Mar 4, 1952
CHI A May 5, 1952

Bill Sudakis
NY N Mar 27, 1972
TEX A Mar 28, 1973
NY A Dec 7, 1973
CAL A Dec 3, 1974

Willie Sudhoff
WAS A Dec 1905

Joe Sugden
STL A Feb 1902

Gus Suhr
PHI N July 28, 1939

Clyde Sukeforth
BKN N Mar 14, 1932

Billy Sullivan
STL A Feb 10, 1938
DET A Jan 30, 1940
BKN N Mar 13, 1942

Billy Sullivan
CLE A Jan 29, 1936

Denny Sullivan
CLE A Sept 1908

Frank Sullivan
PHI N Dec 15, 1960

Haywood Sullivan
KC A Dec 29, 1960

Joe Sullivan
PIT N June 20, 1941

John Sullivan
CHI N Sept 1921

John Sullivan
STL A Oct 4, 1948

Homer Summa
PHI A Jan 5, 1929

Champ Summers
CHI N Apr 6, 1975
CIN N Feb 16, 1977
DET A May 25, 1979
SF N Mar 4, 1982
SD N Dec 6, 1983

Jim Sundberg
MIL A Dec 8, 1983

Steve Sundra
NY A Dec 11, 1935
WAS A Mar 27, 1941
STL A June 7, 1942

Max Surkont
BOS N Apr 15, 1946
PIT N Dec 26, 1953
STL N May 5, 1956

George Susce
DET A May 12, 1958

Rick Sutcliffe
CLE A Dec 9, 1981

Gary Sutherland
MIL A June 10, 1976

Bruce Sutter
STL N Dec 9, 1980

Jack Sutthoff
PHI N July 20, 1904

Don Sutton
HOU N Dec 4, 1980
MIL A Aug 30, 1982

Johnny Sutton
STL N Oct 22, 1976

Bill Sweeney
BOS N June 24, 1907
CHI N Feb 1914

Rick Sweet
SEA A May 21, 1982

Les Sweetland
CHI N Oct 13, 1930

Bill Swift
BOS N Dec 8, 1939

Bob Swift
PHI A June 1, 1942
DET A Oct 11, 1943

Steve Swisher
CHI N Dec 11, 1973
STL N Dec 8, 1977
SD N Dec 8, 1980

Ron Swoboda
MON N Mar 31, 1971

Bob Sykes
STL N Dec 4, 1978
NY A Oct 21, 1981

Jerry Tabb
OAK A Mar 15, 1977

Pat Tabler
CHI N Aug 19, 1981
CHI A Jan 25, 1983
CLE A Apr 1, 1983

Jim Tabor
PHI N Jan 22, 1946

Doug Taitt
CHI A May 23, 1929

Fred Talbot
KC A Jan 20, 1965
NY A June 10, 1966
SEA A May 20, 1969
OAK A Aug 29, 1969

John Tamargo
SF N July 18, 1978
MON N June 13, 1979

Vito Tamulis
BKN N May 1938
PHI N Nov 11, 1940
BKN N May 6, 1941

Frank Tanana
BOS A Jan 23, 1981
TEX A Jan 6, 1982

Jesse Tannehill
BOS A Dec 1903
WAS A July 1908

Chuck Tanner
CHI N June 8, 1957
BOS A Mar 9, 1959
PIT N Nov 5, 1976

Ted Tappe
CHI N Oct 1, 1954

Jose Tartabull
BOS A June 13, 1966
OAK A May 7, 1969

Willie Tasby
BOS A June 9, 1960
CLE A May 3, 1962

Bennie Tate
CHI A June 16, 1930
BOS A Apr 29, 1932

Jarvis Tatum
BOS A Oct 11, 1970

Ken Tatum
BOS A Oct 11, 1970
STL N Oct 26, 1973
CHI A Apr 27, 1974

Tommy Tatum
CIN N May 13, 1947

Jackie Tavener
CLE A Dec 11, 1928

Frank Taveras
NY N Apr 19, 1979
MON N Dec 11, 1981

Ben Taylor
DET A Feb 14, 1952

Carl Taylor
STL N Oct 21, 1969
MIL A Oct 20, 1970
KC A Feb 2, 1971
PIT N Sept 3, 1971

Chuck Taylor
HOU N Feb 17, 1964
STL N June 15, 1965
NY N Oct 18, 1971
MIL A Sept 13, 1972

Danny Taylor
BKN N May 7, 1932

Hawk Taylor
NY N Dec 2, 1963
CAL A July 24, 1967

Jack Taylor
STL N Dec 12, 1903
CHI N July 1, 1906

Joe Taylor
STL N Dec 5, 1957
BAL A July 25, 1958

Ron Taylor
STL N Dec 15, 1962
HOU N June 15, 1965
NY N Feb 10, 1967
MON N Oct 20, 1971

Sammy Taylor
CHI N Dec 5, 1957
NY N Apr 26, 1962
CIN N July 1, 1963
CLE A Aug 1, 1963

Tony Taylor
PHI N May 13, 1960
DET A June 12, 1971

Zack Taylor
BOS N Oct 7, 1925
NY N June 12, 1927
BOS N Feb 1928
CHI N July 6, 1929

Bud Teachout
STL N Dec 1931

Birdie Tebbetts
BOS A May 20, 1947

Tom Tellmann
MIL A Oct 15, 1982

Johnny Temple
BAL A Nov 16, 1961
HOU N Aug 11, 1962

Garry Templeton
SD N Dec 10, 1981

Gene Tenace
SD N Dec 14, 1976
STL N Dec 8, 1980
PIT N Dec 1, 1982

Fred Tenney
NY N Oct 7, 1907

Frank Tepedino
MIL A June 7, 1971
ATL N June 7, 1973

Greg Terlecky
CHI A Dec 12, 1975

Jeff Terpko
PHI N Nov 3, 1970
MON N Mar 15, 1977

Walt Terrell
NY N Apr 1, 1982

Ralph Terry
KC A June 15, 1957
NY A May 26, 1959
CLE A Sept 5, 1964
KC A Apr 6, 1966
NY N Aug 6, 1966

Zeb Terry
CHI N Jan 1920

Wayne Terwilliger
BKN N June 15, 1951
WAS A Sept 23, 1952

Dick Tettelbach
WAS A Feb 8, 1956

Moe Thacker
STL N Oct 17, 1962

Ron Theobald
MIL A May 11, 1970

Tommy Thevenow
PHI N Dec 13, 1928
PIT N Nov 6, 1930
CIN N Dec 12, 1935
BOS N Jan 6, 1937

Henry Thielman
BKN N Jan 1903

Jake Thielman
BOS A Aug 1908

Bud Thomas
WAS A May 1, 1939
DET A May 18, 1939

Derrel Thomas
SD N Dec 3, 1971
SF N Dec 6, 1974
SD N Feb 28, 1978
LA N Nov 14, 1978
MON N Feb 7, 1984

Frank Thomas
CIN N Jan 30, 1959
CHI N Dec 6, 1959
MIL N May 9, 1961
NY N Nov 28, 1961
PHI N Aug 7, 1964
MIL N Apr 4, 1965
HOU N July 10, 1965

Fred Thomas
BOS A Apr 12, 1916
PHI A Jan 1919
WAS A July 1920

George Thomas
LA A June 26, 1961
DET A June 15, 1963
BOS A Oct 4, 1965

Gorman Thomas
TEX A Aug 20, 1977
MIL A Feb 8, 1978
CLE A June 6, 1983
SEA A Dec 7, 1983

Herb Thomas
NY N June 12, 1927

Ira Thomas
DET A Dec 12, 1907
PHI A Dec 8, 1908

Kite Thomas
WAS A June 30, 1953

Lee Thomas
LA A May 8, 1961
BOS A June 4, 1964
MIL N Dec 15, 1965
CHI N May 28, 1966
HOU N Feb 9, 1968

Leo Thomas
NY A June 15, 1950
CHI A June 15, 1952

Myles Thomas
WAS A June 18, 1929

Pinch Thomas
PHI A Dec 14, 1917
CLE A June 1, 1918

Roy Thomas
PIT N Apr 1908
BOS N Feb 1909

Roy Thomas
CHI A Dec 10, 1975
HOU N Mar 30, 1977
STL N June 23, 1978
SEA A Dec 9, 1981

Stan Thomas
CLE A Dec 9, 1975
NY A Aug 2, 1977
CHI A Dec 12, 1977

Tommy Thomas
WAS A June 11, 1932
PHI N May 20, 1935
STL A Jan 1936

Valmy Thomas
PHI N Dec 3, 1958

Gary Thomasson
OAK A Mar 15, 1978
NY A June 15, 1978
LA N Feb 15, 1979

Bobby Thompson
SEA A Dec 6, 1978

Danny Thompson
TEX A June 1, 1976

Fresco Thompson
PHI N Jan 9, 1927
BKN N Oct 14, 1930

Jason Thompson
CAL A May 27, 1980
PIT N Apr 1, 1981

Mike Thompson
STL N Feb 1, 1973
STL N Mar 31, 1973
ATL N Sept 10, 1974
CIN N Apr 7, 1976
TEX A Nov 8, 1976

Tim Thompson
KC A Apr 16, 1956
DET A Nov 20, 1957

Tommy Thompson
STL A Apr 27, 1939

Bobby Thomson
MIL N Feb 1, 1954
NY N June 15, 1957
CHI N Apr 3, 1958

Dickie Thon
HOU N Apr 1, 1981

Jack Thoney
NY A May 8, 1904

Hank Thormahlen
BOS A Dec 15, 1920

Paul Thormodsgard
PHI N Dec 7, 1979

Andre Thornton
ATL N June 15, 1972
CHI N May 19, 1973
MON N May 17, 1976
CLE A Dec 10, 1976

Jim Thorpe
CIN N Apr 24, 1917
BOS N May 1919

Faye Throneberry
WAS A Apr 29, 1957

Marv Throneberry
BAL A June 8, 1961
NY N May 9, 1962

George Throop
HOU N Apr 27, 1979

Sloppy Thurston
CHI A May 12, 1923
WAS A Jan 15, 1927

Luis Tiant
MIN A Dec 10, 1969
NY A Nov 13, 1978

Dick Tidrow
NY A Apr 27, 1974
CHI N May 23, 1979
CHI A Jan 25, 1983
NY N Jan 27, 1984

Bobby Tiefenauer
DET A Sept 8, 1955
CHI A Nov 30, 1961
CHI N Mar 30, 1968

Cotton Tierney
PHI N May 22, 1923
BOS N Dec 15, 1923
BKN N Feb 4, 1925

Les Tietje
STL A May 5, 1936

Bob Tillman
NY A Aug 8, 1967
ATL N Dec 7, 1967
MIL A Dec 2, 1970

Thad Tillotson
NY A Sept 10, 1966

Tom Timmerman
CLE A June 15, 1973

Joe Tinker
CIN N Dec 15, 1912
BKN N Dec 1913
CHI N Feb 10, 1916

Bud Tinning
STL N Nov 21, 1934

Joe Tipton
CHI A Nov 22, 1948
PHI A Oct 19, 1949
CLE A June 23, 1952
WAS A Jan 20, 1954

John Titus
BOS N July 1, 1912

Dave Tobik
TEX A Mar 24, 1983

Jack Tobin
WAS A Feb 1926
BOS A July 31, 1926

Jim Tobin
BOS N Dec 6, 1939
DET A Aug 1945

Johnny Tobin
STL A Feb 10, 1916

Al Todd
PIT N Nov 21, 1935
BOS N Dec 16, 1938
BKN N Mar 31, 1939
CHI N Dec 8, 1939

Jackson Todd
PHI N Mar 27, 1978

Jim Todd
OAK A Apr 6, 1975
CHI N Mar 15, 1977
SEA A Apr 20, 1977

Phil Todt
PHI A Feb 3, 1931

Bobby Tolan
CIN N Oct 11, 1968
SD N Nov 9, 1973

Dick Tomanek
KC A June 15, 1958

Dave Tomlin
SD N Nov 9, 1973
TEX A Jan 25, 1978
CIN N Mar 28, 1978
MON N Sept 8, 1982
PIT N Aug 2, 1983

Ron Tompkins
CIN N Oct 20, 1967
KC A Oct 21, 1969

Fred Toney
CIN N Feb 22, 1915
NY N July 25, 1918
STL N Oct 1922

Jeff Torborg
CAL A Mar 13, 1971
STL N Dec 6, 1973

Earl Torgeson
PHI N Feb 16, 1953
DET A June 15, 1955
CHI A June 14, 1957

Joe Torre
STL N Mar 17, 1969
NY N Oct 13, 1974

Pablo Torrealba
OAK A Mar 29, 1977
CHI A Mar 30, 1978

Angel Torres
MON N Nov 6, 1976
CIN N May 21, 1977

Hector Torres
HOU N Aug 7, 1967
CHI N Oct 12, 1970
MON N Apr 7, 1972
HOU N Apr 4, 1973
CHI A Oct 23, 1973
CLE A Dec 8, 1976
TOR A Mar 29, 1977

Rusty Torres
CLE A Nov 27, 1972
CAL A Sept 12, 1974
CHI A May 16, 1978

Mike Torrez
MON N June 15, 1971
BAL A Dec 4, 1974
OAK A Apr 2, 1976
NY A Apr 27, 1977
BOS A Nov 23, 1977
NY N Jan 14, 1983

Lou Tost
PIT N Mar 25, 1947

Paul Toth
CHI N Sept 1, 1962
STL N June 15, 1964

Cesar Tovar
MIN A Dec 4, 1964
PHI N Nov 30, 1972
TEX A Dec 7, 1973
OAK A Aug 31, 1975

Jack Townsend
CLE A Jan 1906

Dick Tracewski
DET A Dec 15, 1965

Jim Tracy
HOU N Dec 9, 1981

Walt Tragesser
PHI N May 1919

Bill Travers
CAL A Jan 26, 1981

Mike Tresh
CHI A Dec 2, 1937
CLE A Jan 12, 1949

Tom Tresh
DET A June 14, 1969

Alex Trevino
CIN N Feb 10, 1982

Gus Triandos
BAL A Nov 18, 1954
DET A Nov 26, 1962
PHI N Dec 4, 1963
HOU N June 14, 1965

Manny Trillo
CHI N Oct 23, 1974
PHI N Feb 23, 1979
CLE A Dec 9, 1982
MON N Aug 17, 1983
SF N Dec 21, 1983

Ken Trinkle
PHI N Dec 14, 1948

Coaker Triplett
PHI N June 1, 1943

Hal Trosky
CHI A Nov 6, 1943

Bill Trotter
WAS A June 7, 1942

Dizzy Trout
BOS A June 3, 1952

Steve Trout
CHI N Jan 25, 1983

Bob Trowbridge
KC A Oct 12, 1959

Virgil Trucks
STL A Dec 4, 1952
CHI A June 13, 1953
DET A Nov 30, 1955
KC A Dec 5, 1956
NY A June 15, 1958

John Tsitouris
KC A Nov 20, 1957

Ollie Tucker
NY A July 31, 1951

Thurman Tucker
CLE A Jan 27, 1948

John Tudor
PIT N Dec 6, 1983

Bob Tufts
KC A Mar 30, 1982

Bob Turley
NY A Nov 18, 1954
LA A Oct 29, 1962

Jerry Turner
CHI A Sept 9, 1981
DET A Jan 30, 1982

Jim Turner
CIN N Dec 6, 1939
NY A July 16, 1942

Terry Turner
PHI A Jan 1919

Tom Turner
STL A July 31, 1944

Bill Tuttle
KC A Nov 20, 1957
MIN A June 1, 1961

Wayne Twitchell
SEA A Nov 21, 1969
MON N June 15, 1977
SEA A Aug 19, 1979

Lefty Tyler
CHI N Jan 4, 1918

Dave Tyriver
WAS A Oct 14, 1961

Mike Tyson
CHI N Oct 17, 1979

Bob Uecker
STL N Apr 9, 1964
PHI N Oct 27, 1965
ATL N June 6, 1967

Ted Uhlaender
CLE A Dec 10, 1969
CIN N Dec 6, 1971

George Uhle
DET A Dec 11, 1928
NY N Apr 21, 1933

Arnie Umbach
HOU N Dec 31, 1966

Jim Umbarger
OAK A Mar 26, 1977
TEX A Aug 25, 1977

Tommy Umphlett
WAS A Dec 9, 1953
BOS A Nov 8, 1955
NY A June 12, 1962

Pat Underwood
CIN N June 30, 1983

Tom Underwood
STL N June 15, 1977
TOR A Dec 6, 1977
NY A Nov 1, 1979
OAK A May 20, 1981
BAL A Feb 6, 1984

Bob Unglaub
BOS A June 18, 1904
WAS A July 1908

Del Unser
CLE A Dec 2, 1971
PHI N Nov 30, 1972
NY N Dec 3, 1974
MON N July 21, 1976

Dixie Upright
STL A Jan 20, 1953

Cecil Upshaw
HOU N Apr 22, 1973
CLE A Nov 3, 1973
NY A Apr 27, 1974
CHI A Dec 5, 1974

Bill Upton
PHI A Feb 19, 1954

Tom Upton
CHI A Nov 27, 1951
WAS A Nov 27, 1951
NY A May 3, 1952

Jack Urban
KC A Apr 5, 1957
NY A Apr 8, 1959

John Urrea
SD N Dec 8, 1980

Bob Usher
CHI N Oct 4, 1951
WAS A May 15, 1957

Tex Vache
DET A Dec 9, 1925

Mike Vail
NY N Dec 11, 1974
CLE A Mar 26, 1978
CHI N June 15, 1978
CIN N Dec 12, 1980
SF N Jan 5, 1983
MON N May 25, 1983

Sandy Valdespino
SEA A Aug 30, 1969

Bobby Valentine
CAL A Nov 28, 1972
SD N Sept 17, 1975
NY N June 15, 1977

Corky Valentine
MIL N Apr 9, 1956

Ellis Valentine
NY N May 29, 1981
CAL A Jan 24, 1983

Fred Valentine
WAS A Oct 11, 1963
BAL A June 15, 1968

Vito Valentinetti
CHI N May 23, 1957
CLE A Aug 24, 1957
DET A Mar 27, 1958
WAS A June 23, 1958
BAL A Apr 1, 1959

Benny Valenzuela
SF N Oct 8, 1958

Elmer Valo
BKN N Apr 5, 1957

Russ Van Atta
STL A July 15, 1935

Deacon Van Buren
PHI N Apr 30, 1904

Dazzy Vance
NY A Mar 1915
STL N Feb 1933
CIN N June 25, 1934

Elam Vangilder
DET A Dec 2, 1927

Pete Varney
ATL N June 15, 1976

Rafael Vasquez
SEA A Dec 5, 1978
CLE A Dec 6, 1979
PIT N Dec 9, 1980

Arky Vaughan
BKN N Dec 12, 1941

Fred Vaughn
CHI A Jan 2, 1946

Hippo Vaughn
WAS A June 26, 1912

Bobby Veach
BOS A Mar 12, 1924
NY A May 5, 1925
WAS A Aug 17, 1925

Coot Veal
PIT N Dec 21, 1961

Bob Veale
BOS A Sept 2, 1972

Federico Velazquez
OAK A June 3, 1969

Max Venable
MON N Feb 27, 1984

Emil Verban
PHI N May 2, 1946
CHI N Aug 3, 1948

Joe Verbanic
NY A Dec 14, 1966

Johnny Vergez
PHI N Nov 1, 1934
STL N July 1936

John Verhoeven
CHI A June 15, 1977

Mickey Vernon
CLE A Dec 14, 1948
WAS A June 14, 1950
BOS A Nov 8, 1955
CLE A Jan 29, 1958
MIL N Apr 11, 1959

Zoilo Versalles
LA N Nov 28, 1967
CLE A Oct 21, 1968
WAS A July 26, 1969

Tom Veryzer
CLE A Dec 9, 1977
NY N Jan 8, 1982
CHI N Apr 2, 1983

Bob Veselic
HOU N Jan 12, 1983

Sammy Vick
BOS A Dec 15, 1920

Jose Vidal
NY A May 19, 1969

Rube Vinson
CHI A Feb 1906

Bill Virdon
STL N Apr 11, 1954
PIT N May 17, 1956

Ozzie Virgil
DET A Jan 28, 1958
KC A Aug 2, 1961
SF N Oct 1, 1965

Ossie Vitt
BOS A Jan 17, 1919

Bill Voiselle
BOS N June 13, 1947
CHI N Dec 14, 1949

Clyde Vollmer
BOS A May 8, 1950
WAS A Apr 22, 1953

Joe Vosmik
STL A Jan 17, 1937
BOS A Oct 2, 1937
BKN N Feb 12, 1940

Bill Voss
CAL A Jan 20, 1969
MIL A Jan 28, 1971
OAK A June 20, 1972
STL N Aug 27, 1972
CIN N Nov 28, 1972

Pete Vuckovich
STL N Dec 6, 1977
MIL A Dec 12, 1980

George Vukovich
CLE A Dec 9, 1982

John Vukovich
MIL A Oct 31, 1972
CIN N Oct 22, 1974

Rube Waddell
PIT N Jan 1900
CHI N May 1901
STL A Oct 1907

Ben Wade
STL N Aug 8, 1954
PIT N Jan 11, 1955

Gale Wade
CHI N Nov 16, 1954

Jake Wade
BOS A Dec 15, 1938
STL A Sept 1939
NY A Dec 15, 1944

Bill Wagner
BOS N Oct 1917

Gary Wagner
BOS A Sept 6, 1969

Hal Wagner
BOS A May 7, 1944
DET A May 20, 1947
PHI N Sept 13, 1948

Honus Wagner
PIT N Jan 1900

Leon Wagner
STL N Dec 15, 1959
LA A Jan 26, 1961
CLE A Dec 2, 1963
CHI A June 13, 1968
CIN N Dec 5, 1968

Mark Wagner
TEX A Dec 10, 1980

Kermit Wahl
CHI A June 4, 1951
STL A June 4, 1951
NY A July 31, 1951

Eddie Waitkus
PHI N Dec 14, 1948
BAL A Mar 16, 1954

Rick Waits
CLE A June 13, 1975
MIL A June 6, 1983

Bill Wakefield
NY N Nov 4, 1963

Dick Wakefield
NY A Dec 17, 1949

Howard Wakefield
WAS A Feb 1906
CLE A Feb 1907
WAS A Aug 11, 1907

Rube Walberg
PHI A Apr 1923
BOS A Dec 12, 1933

Bob Walk
ATL N Mar 25, 1981

Bill Walker
STL N Oct 10, 1932
CIN N Aug 6, 1936

Curt Walker
PHI N July 25, 1921
CIN N May 30, 1924

Dixie Walker
CHI A May 4, 1936
DET A Dec 2, 1937
BKN N July 24, 1939
PIT N Dec 8, 1947

Gee Walker
CHI A Dec 2, 1937
WAS A Dec 8, 1939
BOS A Dec 12, 1940
CLE A Dec 12, 1940
CIN N Mar 26, 1942

Harry Walker
PHI N May 3, 1947
CHI N Oct 4, 1948
CIN N June 15, 1949
STL N Dec 14, 1949

Jerry Walker
CLE A Feb 27, 1963

Luke Walker
DET A Dec 5, 1973

Rube Walker
BKN N June 15, 1951

Tilly Walker
STL A Oct 1912
BOS A Apr 8, 1916
PHI A Jan 10, 1918

Tom Walker
DET A Dec 4, 1974
STL N Feb 3, 1976
CAL A July 13, 1977

Jim Walkup
DET A May 13, 1939

Joe Wall
BKN N July 1902

Murray Wall
WAS A June 11, 1959

Don Wallace
NY N July 24, 1967

Mike Wallace
NY A May 3, 1974
STL N June 13, 1975
TEX A Oct 22, 1976

Jack Wallaesa
CHI A Dec 13, 1946

Ty Waller
CHI N Dec 9, 1980
CHI A Dec 10, 1982

Dennis Walling
HOU N June 15, 1977

Joe Wallis
CLE A June 15, 1978
OAK A June 15, 1978

Lee Walls
CHI N May 1, 1957
CIN N Dec 6, 1959
PHI N June 15, 1960
LA N Dec 15, 1961

Jimmy Walsh
PHI A June 10, 1914
BOS A Sept 2, 1916

Bucky Walters
PHI N June 14, 1934
CIN N June 13, 1938

Charley Walters
WAS A Mar 21, 1970

Fred Walters
PIT N Dec 26, 1953

Ken Walters
PHI N Dec 5, 1959

Mike Walters
MIN A May 12, 1982

Roxy Walters
BOS A Dec 18, 1918
CLE A Jan 7, 1924

Danny Walton
SEA A Aug 30, 1969
NY A June 7, 1971
MIN A Oct 27, 1972

Reggie Walton
PIT N Apr 9, 1982

Bill Wambsganss
BOS A Jan 7, 1924
PHI A Dec 12, 1925

Lloyd Waner
BOS N May 7, 1940
CIN N June 12, 1941
BKN N Mar 9, 1943

Aaron Ward
CHI A Jan 13, 1927
CLE A Mar 4, 1928

Chuck Ward
BKN N Jan 9, 1918

Dick Ward
STL N Nov 21, 1934

Gary Ward
TEX A Dec 7, 1983

Joe Ward
NY A Mar 1909

Pete Ward
CHI A Jan 14, 1963
NY A Dec 18, 1969

Preston Ward
CHI N Oct 14, 1949
PIT N June 4, 1953
CLE A May 15, 1956
KC A June 15, 1958

Lon Warneke
STL N Oct 8, 1936
CHI N July 8, 1942

Jack Warner
WAS A Dec 19, 1928
PHI N Dec 15, 1932

Jackie Warner
KC A June 15, 1967

John Warner
STL N Jan 1905
DET A Aug 10, 1905
WAS A Aug 13, 1906

Bennie Warren
PIT N Sept 9, 1942
CHI N Nov 17, 1942
NY N Apr 4, 1946

Mike Warren
OAK A May 14, 1982

Rabbit Warstler
PHI A Dec 12, 1933
BOS N July 6, 1936
CHI N July 24, 1940

Dan Warthen
PHI N June 15, 1977

Carl Warwick
STL N May 30, 1961
HOU N May 7, 1962
STL N Feb 17, 1964
BAL A July 24, 1965
CHI N Mar 30, 1966

Jimmy Wasdell
BKN N May 25, 1940
PIT N Dec 12, 1941
PHI N Apr 30, 1943

George Washburn
PHI N Apr 16, 1943
BKN N Apr 22, 1943

Ray Washburn
CIN N Nov 5, 1969

Claudell Washington
TEX A Mar 26, 1977
CHI A May 16, 1978
NY N June 7, 1980
ATL N Nov 17, 1980

LaRue Washington
MON N Mar 31, 1980

Gary Waslewski
STL N Dec 2, 1968
MON N June 3, 1969
NY A May 15, 1970

Steve Waterbury
PHI N June 15, 1977

George Watkins
NY N Feb 1934
PHI N Nov 1, 1934
BKN N May 1936

Bob Watson
BOS A June 13, 1979
NY A Nov 8, 1979
ATL N Apr 23, 1982

Milt Watson
PHI N Apr 4, 1918

Mule Watson
PIT N Aug 28, 1920
BOS N June 30, 1921
NY N June 7, 1923

Eddie Watt
PHI N Dec 7, 1973

Cliff Watwood
BOS A Apr 29, 1932

Roy Weatherly
NY A Dec 17, 1942

Art Weaver
PIT N June 1903

Floyd Weaver
MIL A June 30, 1971

Jim Weaver
HOU N Jan 4, 1967
CAL A Aug 7, 1967

Jim Weaver
CHI N May 15, 1934
PIT N Nov 22, 1934
STL A Jan 1938
CIN N Apr 25, 1938

Monte Weaver
BOS A Feb 1939

Orlie Weaver
BOS N June 10, 1911

Roger Weaver
ATL N Mar 23, 1982

Earl Webb
WAS A Apr 4, 1930
BOS A Apr 30, 1930
DET A June 12, 1932
CHI A May 14, 1933

Hank Webb
LA N Feb 7, 1977

Red Webb
BOS N Dec 14, 1949

Skeeter Webb
CHI A Jan 10, 1940
DET A Dec 12, 1944

Ramon Webster
SD N Mar 24, 1970
CHI N June 17, 1971

Ray Webster
BOS A Jan 8, 1960

Johnny Weekly
BAL A June 15, 1964
NY N Jan 6, 1966

Herm Wehmeier
PHI N June 12, 1954
STL N May 11, 1956
DET A May 13, 1958

Dave Wehrmeister
NY A June 15, 1979

Ralph Weigel
CHI A Jan 27, 1948
WAS A Apr 15, 1949

Dick Weik
CLE A June 14, 1950
DET A June 15, 1953

Bob Weiland
BOS A Dec 2, 1931
CLE A May 25, 1934
STL A Nov 20, 1934

Jake Weimer
CIN N Mar 1906

Phil Weintraub
STL N Dec 9, 1935

Al Weis
NY N Dec 15, 1967

Johnny Welaj
BOS A Dec 13, 1941

Frank Welch
BOS A Nov 1926

Johnny Welch
PIT N July 1936

Brad Wellman
SF N Mar 30, 1982

Ed Wells
STL A Dec 1932

Chris Welsh
SD N Apr 1, 1981
MON N May 4, 1983

Jimmy Welsh
NY N Jan 10, 1928
BOS N June 14, 1929
CHI N Oct 14, 1930

Butch Wensloff
CLE A Apr 12, 1948

Stan Wentzel
PIT N Sept 30, 1946

Fred Wenz
PHI N Nov 25, 1969

Bill Werber
BOS A May 12, 1933
PHI A Dec 9, 1936
CIN N Mar 16, 1939
NY N Dec 9, 1941

Johnny Werhas
CAL A May 10, 1967

Bill Werle
STL N May 3, 1952

Don Werner
CHI N Mar 30, 1984

Don Wert
WAS A Oct 9, 1970

Dennis Werth
KC A Mar 24, 1982

Vic Wertz
STL A Aug 14, 1952
CLE A June 1, 1954
BOS A Dec 2, 1958
DET A Sept 8, 1961

Max West
CIN N Apr 18, 1946

Sammy West
STL A Dec 14, 1932
WAS A June 15, 1938

Wally Westlake
STL N June 15, 1951
CIN N May 13, 1952
CLE A Aug 7, 1952
BAL A June 15, 1955

Gus Weyhing
STL N Jan 17, 1900
BKN N July 1900

Lee Wheat
PHI A Feb 19, 1954
BKN N Apr 16, 1956

Mack Wheat
PHI N Oct 1919

Pete Whisenant
STL N June 3, 1955
CHI N Mar 30, 1956
CIN N Nov 13, 1956
CLE A Apr 29, 1960
WAS A May 15, 1960

Steve Whitaker
SEA A Apr 1, 1969
SF N Dec 12, 1969

Bill White
STL N Mar 25, 1959
PHI N Oct 27, 1965
STL N Apr 3, 1969

Charlie White
MIL N Feb 10, 1954

Ernie White
BOS N May 14, 1946

Hal White
STL A Dec 4, 1952
STL N June 2, 1953

Jerry White
CHI N June 9, 1978
MON N Dec 14, 1978

Jo-Jo White
CIN N Aug 19, 1944

Kirby White
PIT N June 1, 1910

Larry White
LA N Dec 9, 1981

Sammy White
CLE A Mar 16, 1960
MIL N June 15, 1961

Burgess Whitehead
NY N Dec 9, 1935

John Whitehead
STL A June 2, 1939

Earl Whitehill
WAS A Dec 14, 1932
CLE A Dec 10, 1936

Len Whitehouse
MIN A Nov 1, 1982

Fred Whitfield
CLE A Dec 15, 1962
CIN N Nov 21, 1967

Terry Whitfield
SF N Mar 14, 1977

Dick Whitman
PHI N Sept 14, 1949
BKN N June 8, 1951

Pinky Whitney
BOS N June 17, 1933
PHI N Jan 29, 1936

Ed Whitson
SF N June 28, 1979
CLE A Nov 14, 1981
SD N Nov 18, 1982

Possum Whitted
BOS N June 1914
PHI N Feb 14, 1915
PIT N Aug 1919
BKN N Mar 14, 1922

Bob Wicker
CHI N Apr 1903
CIN N June 2, 1906

Floyd Wicker
SF N June 1, 1971

Dave Wickersham
DET A Nov 18, 1963
PIT N Nov 28, 1967
KC A Oct 21, 1968
ATL N Oct 21, 1969

Al Wickland
NY A Jan 1919

Al Widmar
STL A Nov 17, 1947
CHI A Nov 27, 1951

Ted Wieand
CIN N Dec 5, 1957

Tom Wieghaus
HOU N Feb 24, 1984

Bob Wiesler
WAS A Feb 8, 1956

Whitey Wietelmann
PIT N Sept 30, 1946

Bill Wight
CHI A Feb 24, 1948
BOS A Dec 10, 1950
DET A June 3, 1952
CLE A June 15, 1953
CIN N Dec 4, 1957

Del Wilber
BOS A May 12, 1952
NY N Dec 14, 1954

Ted Wilborn
NY A Nov 1, 1979
SF N Mar 30, 1982

Milt Wilcox
CLE A Dec 6, 1971
CHI A Feb 25, 1975

Randy Wiles
STL N Aug 23, 1977
HOU N Dec 9, 1977

Mark Wiley
TOR A Sept 12, 1978

Rob Wilfong
CAL A May 12, 1982

Hoyt Wilhelm
STL N Feb 26, 1957
CLE A Sept 21, 1957
BAL A Aug 23, 1958
CHI A Jan 14, 1963
CAL A Dec 12, 1968
ATL N Sept 8, 1969
CHI N Sept 21, 1970
ATL N Nov 30, 1970

Jim Wilhelm
CLE A Feb 15, 1980

Kaiser Wilhelm
BOS N Jan 1904

Joe Wilhoit
PIT N July 29, 1917
NY N Aug 5, 1917

Ted Wilks
PIT N June 15, 1951
CLE A Aug 18, 1952

Carl Willey
NY N Mar 23, 1963

Nick Willhite
WAS A Oct 15, 1964
LA N May 11, 1965
CAL A Dec 15, 1966
NY N June 10, 1967

Bernie Williams
SD N Oct 25, 1973

Billy Williams
OAK A Oct 23, 1974

Charlie Williams
SF N May 11, 1972

Cy Williams
PHI N Dec 26, 1917

Dallas Williams
CIN N Mar 26, 1982
DET A Mar 30, 1984

Dib Williams
BOS A May 1, 1935

Dick Williams
BAL A June 25, 1956
CLE A June 13, 1957
CHI A Apr 1, 1958
KC A Oct 2, 1958
HOU N Oct 12, 1962
BOS A Dec 10, 1962

Earl Williams
BAL A Dec 30, 1972
ATL N Apr 17, 1975
MON N July 24, 1976

Jimmy Williams
STL A Feb 1908

Ken Williams
BOS A Dec 15, 1927
NY A Jan 29, 1930

Otto Williams
CHI N July 1903

Pop Williams
PHI N Apr 1903
BOS N June 1903

Rip Williams
WAS A Jan 1912

Stan Williams
NY A Nov 26, 1962
CLE A Mar 30, 1965
MIN A Dec 10, 1969
STL N Sept 1, 1971

Walt Williams
CHI A Dec 14, 1966
CLE A Oct 19, 1972
DET A Mar 19, 1974
NY A Mar 19, 1974

Jim Willis
CIN N Oct 1, 1954

Joe Willis
STL N Apr 1911

Ron Willis
HOU N Aug 8, 1969

Vic Willis
PIT N Dec 15, 1905
STL N Jan 1910

Claude Willoughby
PIT N Nov 6, 1930

Jim Willoughby
STL N Oct 14, 1974
BOS A Apr 4, 1975
CHI A Apr 5, 1978
STL N Oct 23, 1978

Bump Wills
CHI N Mar 26, 1982

Maury Wills
PIT N Dec 1, 1966
LA N June 11, 1969

Ted Wills
CIN N May 8, 1962

Terry Wilshusen
CIN N June 15, 1973

Archie Wilson
WAS A May 3, 1952
BOS A June 9, 1952

Art Wilson
PIT N Feb 10, 1916
CHI N July 29, 1916
BOS N Jan 4, 1918

Bill Wilson
PHI A June 11, 1954

Bill Wilson
MIL A Nov 7, 1973

Earl Wilson
DET A June 14, 1966
SD N July 15, 1970

Frank Wilson
STL A May 10, 1928

Glenn Wilson
PHI N Mar 24, 1984

Grady Wilson
PIT N Apr 5, 1948

Hack Wilson
STL N Dec 1931
BKN N Jan 23, 1932

Jack Wilson
WAS A Dec 13, 1941
DET A July 17, 1942

Jim Wilson
STL A Nov 17, 1947
BAL A Apr 13, 1955
CHI A May 21, 1956

Jimmie Wilson
STL N May 11, 1928
PHI N Nov 15, 1933

Owen Wilson
STL N Dec 12, 1913

Red Wilson
DET A May 29, 1954
CLE A July 26, 1960

Tack Wilson
MIN A Mar 28, 1983

Ted Wilson
NY N May 8, 1952
NY A Aug 22, 1956

Hal Wiltse
STL A Apr 25, 1928

Snake Wiltse
PHI A July 1901

Gordie Windhorn
LA N Apr 5, 1960
LA A May 12, 1962
KC A July 23, 1963

Dave Winfield
NY A Dec 15, 1980

Jim Winford
BKN N Mar 1939

Ted Wingfield
BOS A Sept 10, 1924

Ivy Wingo
CIN N Apr 8, 1915

Lave Winham
PIT N Feb 1903

Tom Winsett
BKN N Dec 3, 1936

George Winter
DET A Jan 1908

Jesse Winters
PHI N July 25, 1921

Alan Wirth
OAK A Mar 15, 1978

Casey Wise
MIL N Nov 10, 1957
DET A Oct 15, 1959

Rick Wise
STL N Feb 25, 1972
BOS A Oct 26, 1973
SD N Nov 19, 1979

George Witt
LA A Oct 10, 1961

Whitey Witt
NY A Mar 17, 1922

John Wockenfuss
STL N June 6, 1973
PHI N Mar 24, 1984

Jim Wohlford
MIL A Dec 6, 1976
SF N Nov 29, 1979
MON N Feb 2, 1983

Pete Wojey
CLE A Mar 27, 1958

Wally Wolf
CIN N Jan 20, 1964

Bill Wolfe
WAS A July 13, 1904

Harry Wolfe
PIT N Aug 1917

Roger Wolff
WAS A Dec 13, 1943
CLE A Mar 4, 1947
PIT N June 14, 1947

Harry Wolter
PIT N June 17, 1907
STL N July 4, 1907
NY A May 1910

Harry Wolverton
PHI N Apr 28, 1900
BOS N Dec 20, 1904

Dooley Womack
HOU N Dec 4, 1968
SEA A Aug 24, 1969

Jake Wood
CIN N June 23, 1967

Joe Wood
CLE A Feb 24, 1917

Ken Wood
BOS A Nov 28, 1951
WAS A June 9, 1952

Roy Wood
CLE A Jan 1914

Wilbur Wood
CHI A Oct 12, 1966

Hal Woodeshick
CLE A Feb 18, 1958
WAS A May 25, 1959
DET A June 5, 1961
STL N June 15, 1965

Gene Woodling
PIT N Dec 7, 1946
BAL A Nov 18, 1954
CLE A June 15, 1955
CHI A Apr 1, 1958
NY N June 15, 1962

Al Woods
OAK A Nov 15, 1982

Gary Woods
HOU N Dec 4, 1978
CHI N Dec 9, 1981

Jim Woods
PHI N Jan 11, 1960

Ron Woods
NY A June 14, 1969

Walt Woods
PIT N Jan 1900

Dick Woodson
MIN A May 4, 1974

Frank Woodward
STL N July 14, 1919

Woody Woodward
CIN N June 11, 1968

Chuck Workman
PIT N June 12, 1946

Ralph Works
CIN N Aug 1912

Rich Wortham
MON N Dec 12, 1980

Al Worthington
BOS A Mar 29, 1960

Red Worthington
STL N Sept 11, 1934

Clarence Wright
STL A July 1903

Clyde Wright
MIL A Oct 22, 1973
TEX A Dec 5, 1974

Glenn Wright
BKN N Dec 11, 1928

Ken Wright
NY A Dec 7, 1973
PHI N May 3, 1974

Mel Wright
STL N Apr 11, 1954

Ricky Wright
TEX A Aug 19, 1983

Taffy Wright
CHI A Dec 8, 1939
PHI A Nov 15, 1948

Tom Wright
STL A Nov 28, 1951
CHI A June 15, 1952
WAS A May 27, 1954

Russ Wrightstone
NY N May 29, 1928

Yats Wuestling
NY A May 30, 1930

John Wyatt
BOS A June 13, 1966
NY A May 18, 1968
DET A June 15, 1968

Whit Wyatt
CHI A June 2, 1933
PHI N Mar 28, 1945

Butch Wynegar
NY A May 12, 1982

Early Wynn
CLE A Dec 14, 1948
CHI A Dec 4, 1957

Jimmy Wynn
LA N Dec 6, 1973
ATL N Nov 17, 1975
NY A Nov 29, 1976

Billy Wynne
CHI A Dec 15, 1967
CAL A Nov 30, 1970

Marvell Wynne
NY N Mar 31, 1981
PIT N June 14, 1983

Johnny Wyrostek
BOS N Feb 5, 1946
CIN N Feb 7, 1948
PHI N May 23, 1952

Hugh Yancy
CIN N Nov 6, 1976

Al Yates
BOS A June 24, 1967

Steve Yerkes
CHI N Feb 10, 1916

Earl Yingling
CIN N Apr 1914

Jim York
HOU N Dec 2, 1971
NY A Jan 8, 1976

Rudy York
BOS A Jan 3, 1946
CHI A June 14, 1947

Eddie Yost
DET A Dec 6, 1958

Ned Yost
TEX A Dec 8, 1983

Babe Young
CIN N June 7, 1947
STL N Nov 8, 1948

Bobby Young
CLE A June 27, 1955

Cy Young
CLE A Feb 18, 1909
BOS N July 1911

Dick Young
BKN N Mar 28, 1954

Don Young
STL N May 14, 1967
CHI N Aug 1, 1967

Harley Young
BOS N June 1908

Irv Young
PIT N June 1908

Pep Young
CIN N Dec 9, 1940

Ralph Young
PHI A Mar 1922

Joel Youngblood
STL N Mar 28, 1977
NY N June 15, 1977
MON N Aug 4, 1982
SF N Feb 7, 1983

Sal Yvars
STL N June 15, 1953

Chris Zachary
STL N July 1, 1970
PIT N Apr 2, 1973

Tom Zachary
STL A Feb 1926
WAS A July 7, 1927
NY A Aug 23, 1928
BOS N May 12, 1930
BKN N June 12, 1934

Elmer Zacher
STL N May 1910

Pat Zachry
NY N June 15, 1977
LA N Dec 28, 1982

Geoff Zahn
CHI N May 2, 1975
CAL A Dec 2, 1980

Paul Zahniser
BOS A Apr 26, 1925

Dom Zanni
CHI A Nov 30, 1961
CIN N May 5, 1963

Al Zarilla
BOS A May 8, 1949
CHI A Dec 10, 1950
STL A June 15, 1952
BOS A Aug 31, 1952

Norm Zauchin
WAS A Jan 23, 1958

Joe Zdeb
CHI A Jan 15, 1980

Rollie Zeider
NY A June 23, 1913
CHI N Feb 10, 1916

Bill Zepp
DET A Mar 29, 1971

Gus Zernial
PHI A Apr 30, 1951
DET A Nov 20, 1957

Chief Zimmer
PIT N Jan 1900
PHI N Jan 1903

Don Zimmer
CHI N Apr 8, 1960
CIN N May 7, 1962
LA N Jan 24, 1963
WAS A June 24, 1963

Heinie Zimmerman
NY N Aug 28, 1916

Jerry Zimmerman
MIN A Jan 30, 1962

Guy Zinn
BOS N Dec 1912

Richie Zisk
CHI A Dec 10, 1976
TEX A Nov 9, 1977
SEA A Dec 12, 1980

Billy Zitzmann
CIN N June 1919

Sam Zoldak
STL A Feb 17, 1944
CLE A June 15, 1948
PHI A Apr 30, 1951

Bill Zuber
WAS A Apr 21, 1940
NY A Jan 29, 1943
BOS A June 18, 1946

George Zuverink
BAL A July 8, 1955